HISTORY OF BIBLICAL ISRAEL

CULTURE AND HISTORY OF
THE ANCIENT NEAR EAST

EDITED BY

B. HALPERN, M. H. E. WEIPPERT

TH. P.J. VAN DEN HOUT, I. WINTER

VOLUME 7

HISTORY
OF
BIBLICAL ISRAEL

Major Problems and Minor Issues

BY

ABRAHAM MALAMAT

BRILL
LEIDEN · BOSTON · KÖLN
2001

This book is printed on acid-free paper.

Library of Congress Cataloging-in-Publication Data

Malamat, Abraham.
   History of Biblical Israel : major problems and minor issues / by Abraham Malamat.
    p. cm.—(Culture and history of the ancient Near East ; v. 7)
   Includes bibliographical references (p.) and index.
   ISBN 9004120092 (alk. paper)
   1. Palestine—History—To 70 A.D. 2. Bible. O.T.—History of contemporary events.
3. Jews—History—953-586 B.C. 4. Jews—History—586 B.C.-70 A.D. I. Title.
II. Series

DS121 .M33   2001
933—dc21
                                          00-069780
                                              CIP

Die Deutsche Bibliothek – CIP-Einheitsaufnahme

Malāmāt, Avrāhām:
History of biblical Israel : major problems and minor issues / by Abraham Malamat. –
Leiden ; Boston ; Köln : Brill, 2001
   (Culture and history of the ancient Near East ; Vol. 7)
   ISBN 90-04-12009-2

ISSN   1566-2055
ISBN   90 04 12009 2

To

Dana   Iddo

Roʻi   Hadas

CONTENTS

PART THREE

THE RISE OF THE DAVIDIC DYNASTY

PART FOUR

TWILIGHT OF JUDAH AND THE DESTRUCTION OF THE FIRST TEMPLE

PART FIVE

HISTORICAL EPISODES IN THE FORMER PROPHETS AND IN THE PROPHETICAL BOOKS

EXCURSUS

PREFACE

This Book contains twenty six papers, long and short, spanning a period of half a century, from the early fifties until the present (two articles are published here for the first time). The papers on the history of Biblical Israel have been divided into five sections, from the emergence of Israel unto the time of Jeremiah and the destruction of the First Temple. There are also three Excursus on semi-historical topics, not on historical periods *par excellence*. The articles *per se* were updated only in a limited manner, but at the end of the Book *Addenda* are supplied to each chapter, written in the year 2000, with recent bibliographical apparatus.

In the first part, "The Dawn of Israel", the author emphasizes his views on the authenticity of the Biblical record, leaning towards a "maximalist" approach rather than a "minimalist" one. Here also the importance of the Mari documents for the early history of Israel is stressed, ending with a comparative study between the Biblical and African genealogies. In "Forming a Nation" (part two) the major problem consists of the Exodus and Conquest of Canaan. It is followed by the Period of the Judges and the peculiar nature of their leadership. In part three "The Kingdom of David and Solomon" is analysed especially from a political point of view, followed by a treatment of the Organs of Statecraft in the Israelite Monarchy. Part four is dedicated to the "Twilight of Judah", beginning with Kings Amon and Josiah until the destruction of Jerusalem. Part five is a collection of shorter papers on historical episodes contained in the Former and Latter Prophetical Books.

Thus the Book represents the major phases of the history of Biblical Israel. The arrangement of the chapters within the Book lends a smoother reading of the continuity of the historical record in the Bible. The volume is of an inter- as well as multi-disciplinary nature. Many of the papers are based upon archaeological evidence and even, to a greater extent, the papers are set against the background of ancient Near Eastern research. In addition they relate to modern sciences, such as present Military thought, Sociology and Politology.

Under the title of each chapter the source of the original publication has been indicated.

We express our thanks to the many journals as well as to the publishers of books (several of them not widely available) for granting
me permission to use the materials in the present Volume.

The author owes sincere thanks to Brill Academic Publisher, who
in addition to my earlier book (Mari and the Bible, 1998) undertook the publication of this collection, and in particular to Ms. Patricia
Radder and to Mr. Jan Fehrmann, who took care of the production
of this book. My thanks go also to Mrs. R. Nikolsky and U. Gabbay,
who assisted me in preparing the indexes.

Jerusalem
December 2000

ABBREVIATIONS

AAA	*Annals of Archaeology and Anthropology*
AASOR	*The Annual of the American Schools of Oriental Research*
ABD	*Anchor Bible Dictionary, 1992*
AES	*Archives Européennes de Sociology*
AfO	*Archiv für Orientforschung*
AHw	W. von Soden, *Akkadisches Handwörterbuch*
AION	*Annali Istituto Orientali di Napoli*
AJA	*American Journal of Archaeology*
AJSL	*American Journal of Semitic Languages and Literatures*
AnBi	*Anchor Bible*
ANET	*Ancient Near Eastern Texts Relating to the Old Testament, ed. J. Pritchard, 1950, 3rd ed. 1969*
AnSt	*Anatolian Studies*
AoF	*Altorientalische Forschungen*
ARA	D.D. Luckenbill, *Ancient Records of Assyria and Babylonia*
ARM(T)	*Archives Royales de Mari*
ARI	W.F. Albright: *Archaeology and the Religion of Israel, 1946*
ArOr	*Archiv Orientalni*
ATD	*Das Alte Testament Deutsch*
BA	*Biblical Archaeologist*
BAR	*Biblical Archaeology Review*
BASOR	*Bulletin of the American Schools of Oriental Research*
BJPES	*Bulletin of the Jewish Palestine Exploration Society*
BK(AT)	*Biblischer Kommentar AT*
CAD	*Chicago Assyrian Dictionary*
CAH	*The Cambridge Ancient History*
CBQ	*Catholic Biblical Quarterly*
CCK	*D.J. Wiseman Chronicles of Chaldean Kings*
EAEHL	*Encyclopedia of Archaeological Excavations in the Holy Land, 1975, 2nd ed. 1993*
HTR	*Havard Theological Review*
HUCA	*Hebrew Union College Annual*
ICC	*International Critical Commentary*
IEJ	*Israel Exploration Journal*
JANES	*The Journal of the Ancient Near Eastern Society*

JAOS	*Journal of the American Oriental Society*
JARCE	*Journal of the American Research Center in Egypt*
JBL	*Journal of Biblical Literature*
JCS	*Journal of Cuneiform Studies*
JEA	*Journal of Egyptian Archaeology*
JESHO	*Journal of the Economic and Social History of the Orient*
JNES	*Journal of Near Eastern Studies*
JPOS	*Journal of the Palestine Oriental Society*
JQuR	*Jewish Quarterly Review*
JSOT	*Journal of the Study of the Old Testament*
JSOT.SS	*Journal of the Study of the Old Testament, Suppl. Series*
JSS	*Journal of Semitic Studies*
JThS	*Journal of Theological Studies*
KAI	H. Donner – W. Röllig, *Kanaanäische und aramäische Inschriften*, 2nd ed. 1966
KBo	*Keilschrifttexte aus Boghazköi*
KHC	*Kurzer Handcommentar zum AT*
KUB	*Keilschrift Urkunden aus Boghazköi*
LA	*Lexikon der Ägyptologie*
MDAIK	*Mitteilungen des Deutschen Archaeologischen Institut Kairo*
MDOG	*Mitteilungen der Deutschen Orientgesellschaft*
MGWJ	*Monatsschrift der Geschichte und Wissenschaft des Judentums*
MT	*Masoretic Text*
MVAG	*Mitteilungen der Vorderasiatisch—Agyptischen Gesellschaft*
OA	*Oriens Antiquus*
OLP	*Orientalia Lovaniensia Periodica*
OLZ	*Orientalistische Literaturzeitung*
OTL	*Old Testament Library*
OTS	*Outestamentische Studien*
PEFQS	*Palestine Exploration Fund, Quarterly Statement*
PEQ	*Palestine Exploration Quarterly*
PJb	*Palästina Jahrbuch*
RA	*Revue d'Assyriology*
RB	*Revue Biblique*
RHA	*Revue Hittite et Asianique*
SAK	*Studien der Altägyptischen Kultur*
ThLZ	*Theologische Literaturzeitung*
ThWAT	*Theologisches Wörterbuch zum Alten Testament*
ThWNT	*Theologisches Wörterbuch zum Neuen Testament*
ThZ	*Theologische Zeitschrift*

VT	*Vetus Testamentum*
SVT	*Vetus Testamentum Supplement*
WBC	*Word Biblical Commentary*
WHJP	*World History of the Jewish People*
WO	*Welt des Orients*
ZA	*Zeitschrift der Assyriologie*
ZAS	*Zeitschrift für Agyptische Sprache*
ZAW	*Zeitschrift für die Alttestamentliche Wissenschaft*
BZAW	*Beihefte ZAW*
ZDMG	*Zeitschrift der Deutschen Morgenländischen Gesellschaft*
ZDPV	*Zeitschrift des Deutschen Palästinavereins*

PART ONE

THE DAWN OF ISRAEL

1

THE PROTO-HISTORY OF ISRAEL: A STUDY
IN METHOD*

Proto-History Versus History

In considering the study of the proto-history of Israel in all its complexity—as against the study of the historical period of biblical Israel—let us begin by defining this "proto-history" and its chronological boundaries.[1] "Proto-history" must be differentiated from both "pre-history" and "history." Despite its popularity among students of the Bible, the term "the pre-history of Israel" should be avoided, since by definition it implies a time prior to Israel's existence. "Proto-history," on the other hand, describes the span of time during which an embryonic Israel took shape, the span culminating in its emergence as an ethnic/territorial entity in Canaan. In conventional terms this would encompass the so-called Patriarchal Age, the descent to Egypt, the Exodus from the "house of bondage," the subsequent wanderings in the wilderness (including the events at Mount Sinai), the eventual conquest of the land of Canaan, and finally the settlement of the Israelite tribes.

It should be pointed out that this "standard" sequence, and indeed the very division into these particular stages, may be nothing more than a reflection of the Bible's own highly schematic division of the Israelite past: the Five Books of Moses, the Book of Joshua, and (to some extent) the Book of Judges. Thus the conventional stages listed above are in fact problematic as conceptualizations of historical reality. This applies to the very first stage of Israelite proto-history, the "Patriarchal Age," an expression presupposing a specific, well-defined period in time. This avoidable term ignores the possibility that the

---

* This article was originally published in: *Essays D.N. Freedman*, Eisenbrauns Philadelphia, 1983, 303–313.
[1] This is an English version of part of the introductory chapter to a forthcoming collection of Hebrew essays by the author. The archeological aspects of the subject treated, though of relevance in themselves, fall outside the scope of our discussion of historiography.

"Age" may be an artificial construct telescoping a prolonged historical process (see below). An even more radical approach contends that the Patriarchs are pure fable and thus have no particular time of their own at all (e.g., Mazar 1969; Thompson 1974, 1978, 1979; Van Seters 1975).

Questions of chronology and content naturally obscure the upper limits of Israelite proto-history, but the lower limit—the line dividing it from "history"—is more accessible. A given scholar's placement of this dividing line generally hinges on just where he sees real historiography beginning to appear in the flow of biblical narrative—a matter subject to argument. Two contradictory views have recently been advanced in this regard.

W.W. Hallo, for one, sees a more or less credible and coherent record beginning with the opening chapter of Exodus (1:8), and so he fixes the beginning of the historical period in the time of the Israelites' oppression in Egypt, when an "awareness of a 'group identity' ... first dawned on" them (Hallo 1980: 16ff.). Hallo's view seems to coincide with that of the biblical historiographer, who in Exod. 1:9 first uses the expression "the People of the Children of Israel" (ʿam bĕnê Yiśrāʾēl). Prior to that, in the introductory verses of Exodus and in all of Genesis, the common term is "Children of Israel" (bĕnê Yiśrāʾēl)—limited in meaning to the actual offspring of the Patriarch Jacob (i.e., Israel) as individuals. (Of course, here one has to exclude general statements or anachronisms, such as Gen. 32:33: "That is why the children of Israel to this day do not eat the thigh muscle that is on the socket of the hip . . ."; 34:7: ". . . an outrage in Israel . . ."; 36:31: ". . . before any king reigned over the children of Israel"; 48:20: ". . . by you shall Israel invoke blessings . . ."; or, for that matter, 49:7: ". . . scatter them in Israel"; 16,28: . . . "at one with the tribes of Israel," "All these were the tribes of Israel. . . .") On the other hand, the shorter term "People of Israel" (ʿam Yiśrāʾēl) first occurs in the Book of Samuel (2 Sam. 18:7; 19:41; but cf. Josh. 8:33, though the usage there is awkward).[2] Significantly, this parallels the occurrence of the geographical descriptions, "land of the Children of Israel"

---

[2] This issue is, of course, more complex and calls for further elucidation. Note that already in the "early" books, the following expressions are found: ʿădat/qĕhal Yiśrāʾēl, "Congregation/Assembly of Israel" (Exod. 12:3; Josh. 8:35); bēt Yiśrāʾēl, "House of Israel" (Exod. 16:31; 40:38); and, above all, the name "Israel" itself, referring to the nation or to a group of tribes (especially in the Book of Judges; and see Danell 1946).

(*ereṣ běnê Yiśrā'ēl*), first appearing in Josh. 11:22, and "Land of Israel" (*ereṣ Yiśrā'ēl*), the shorter term again making its first appearance only in the Book of Samuel (1 Sam. 13:19). Thus what emerges from the textual evidence is a progression of terms: first "Children of Israel," then "People of the Children of Israel," and finally "People of Israel." These are likely to reflect critical junctures in the formation of the People of Israel or, in any event, stages in the developing consciousness of a national identity. The last term, "People of Israel," is clearly more national and political in character than the designation "People of the Children of Israel" (which still smacks of tribalism), and its first use coincides with the beginning of the period of the monarchy. The same applies to the geographical term "Land of Israel."[3]

The second view, recently adopted by J.A. Soggin, fixes the starting point of the historical era in the early monarchy—when there arose conditions conducive to true historiography, in the time of David and Solomon (Soggin 1978). But, as Hallo has shown, Soggin's reasoning leads to a kind of circular argument: "History begins where historiography begins, and historiography begins . . . where history is said to have its datum point" (Hallo 1980: 9–10).

The truth probably lies somewhere between these two views. As noted, I see the transition from Israelite proto-history as occurring when the Israelite tribes crystallized within Canaan, becoming the dominant, sovereign force there. Thus, the dividing line between proto-history and history proper would fall at the time when the migratory movements of the Israelites had effectively come to a close, the tribes having consolidated what were to be their hereditary holdings for hundreds of years to come. This situation[4] emerged apparently in the first half of or around the middle of the 12th century B.C.E.—in biblical terms, at some point in the period of the Judges—and the tribal territories remained stable "for the duration." It is this historical-territorial zygote which set the stage for the subsequent narrative of events in the Bible.

The biblical record retains only vague recollections and indirect evidence of the primary, dynamic stage in the process of Israelite

---

[3] But note the "early" terms: *gěbûl Yiśrā'ēl*, "Territory of Israel" (Judg. 19:29; 1 Sam. 7:13); *naḥălat Yiśrā'ēl*, "Inheritance of Israel" (Judg. 20:6); *har Yiśrā'ēl*, "hill country of Israel" (Josh. 11:16, 21).

[4] This view basically resembles that of Noth in his various studies (e.g., 1958: 85ff.), though arrived at by an entirely different path. Noth regarded the nation's emergence as a gradual federation of tribes, culminating in an amphictyonic league.

settlement (except for the removal of the tribe of Dan to Laish) (Kallai 1967; Malamat 1970, chap. 9 in this book; 1976a: 60ff.). Though a more advanced stage is described in Judges, the book's schematic structure and arbitrary chronological framework do not reflect the actual unfolding of historical events (Malamat 1976b: especially pp. 152–56, chap. 8 in this book). Therefore, in our quest for this dividing line we must shake free from a characteristic short-coming—sole dependence upon the reliability of biblical historiography. We must take into account additional factors, such as the ongoing formation of Israelite society and the molding of national solidarity—the establishment of inter-tribal and supra-tribal structures, and the narrowing of the gap between tribal and national identity. Moreover, in considering the extra-biblical data, too, we must take into account their particular character, and especially the fact that different methodologies apply to the study of proto-history and of historical periods, respectively. To a great extent this difference stems from the special quality and scope of the data available, both extra-biblical and biblical.

Admittedly, biblical sources are also problematical in regard to the period of the monarchy (Van Seters 1981). Not only are they selective (as is all historiography); they are tendentious and have undergone various stages of editing. Yet for all their shortcomings, the biblical sources for the monarchical period are decidedly more reliable than the stories which describe Israelite proto-history. Moreover, they enable us to trace with some precision the actual, historical-chronological sequence of events, as distinct from the "evidence" of epic depictions of Israel's distant past. Even so, the Bible does not present authentic documents contemporary to events described, as are to be found in quantity for many of the peoples of the Ancient Near East. By contrast, significant contemporaneous evidence directly relating to the history of the Israelite and Judean monarchies is available from outside the Bible: the epigraphic sources from Assyria, Babylonia, and Egypt, as well as numerous Hebrew inscriptions. Two astonishing examples relate to the same period: the Babylonian Chronicle from the reign of Nebuchadnezzar II, mentioning the precise date of the surrender of Jerusalem during Jehoiachin's reign (the second of Adar of the seventh year of the Babylonian king, i.e., 16 March 597 B.C.E.; chap. 17) (Wiseman 1956: 33, 72f.); and, on a different plane, a seal-impression (bulla) reading "Belonging to Berachiahu, son of Neriahu, the scribe"—apparently the biblical figure Baruch, Jeremiah's amanuensis (Avigad 1978).

Alas, such fortunate discoveries are not to be expected in con-junction with Israelite proto-history; both the internal and the exter-nal data simply do not allow for such analysis on the micro-level of history. Explicit, external references to biblical events and personal-ities are utterly lacking for this remote period. Even the pharaohs mentioned in the Joseph and Moses cycles are anonymous. The first king of Egypt mentioned by name in the Bible is Shishak, contem-porary with Solomon. Thus precisely those data which would be of the essence to the historian's craft are lacking: synchronisms and cor-relates which would link the biblical text to events in the broader world.

The earliest extra-biblical use of the collective name "Israel" for an entity clearly within the land of Canaan occurs in the well-known "Israel Stele" of Merneptah (*ca.* 1220 B.C.E.) (see, comprehensively, Engel 1979). The exact nature of this entity is elusive; it may be a pan-Israelite league of twelve tribes, or a more limited group such as the "House of Joseph" (more probable in light of the geograph-ical sequence of toponyms in the stele). Whatever its nature, the fact remains: "Israel" is mentioned in an early historical, historiograph-ical document—heralding the threshold of Israelite history.

Despite the general absence of directly related external sources for the early period of Israel's past, we do have a wealth of indirect sources. These shed circumstantial light on the geographical and ethno-cultural milieu of Israel's formative period. But the asymme-try in the historical documentation—between the extreme paucity of directly related material and the vast body of indirect, external evi-dence, and especially between it and the abundant biblical source material—dictates *a priori* the parameters of historical research and the limits of plausible conclusions. A multitude of unknowns are encountered in comparison to research into later periods. The his-torian must weave a complex but loose fabric from the threads of internal and external sources, and he must risk putting forth much bolder hypotheses than those tolerated for later historical periods. But it is doubtful whether research into the proto-history of Israel will ever exceed the bounds of speculation.

Israel was the only people amongst those of the ancient Near East to preserve a comprehensive national tradition of its origins. That Israel's neighbors did have similar traditions seems to be reflected in several oblique biblical references, such as one in the book of Amos: "True, I brought Israel up from the land of Egypt, but also the Philistines from Caphtor and the Arameans from Kir" (9:7). In Amos' time (mid-8th century B.C.E.), some 400 years after the appearance of the Philistines and the Arameans in their historical domains, traditions were still circulating regarding migrations in their distant pasts: the Philistines from Caphtor (Crete or, more likely, the Aegean world in general), and the Arameans from somewhere called Kir.[5] These two nations seem to have transmitted traditions, over many generations, concerning their removal from their original homes— much as the Patriarchal, Exodus and Conquest narratives were maintained in Israel within a broad, multi-faceted tradition.

The Nature of the Biblical Tradition

The historian studying the origins of Israel is thus obviously not confronted by any lack of biblical source material, but rather by the question of the historical reliability of that material. It need hardly be added that the intention here is not to claim that biblical folktales be taken at face value, nor that historicity is to be conferred upon myriad independent details, many of which no doubt reflect merely literary artifice. Rather, the tradition should be considered in a broader focus, appraising the historicity of its basic elements— what Goethe calls *die grossen Züge*, "the broad sweep of matters," forming the historical picture. In the Patriarchal narratives, for instance, these principal features can be outlined as follows: (a) the Patriarchal migration from Mesopotamia to Canaan; (b) residence as aliens (Hebrew *gērîm*) in their new habitat (and not indigenous to Canaan, *contra* much current scholarly conjecture; e.g., de Geus 1976; Gottwald 1979); (c) maintenance of ties with their erstwhile homeland (e.g., the marriages of Isaac and Jacob); (d) restriction of migratory movements within Canaan to the central hill country and the Negev; (e) existence as semi-nomadic herdsmen, in close relationship with various Canaanite cities (*contra* Gordon 1958; Albright 1961; 1968; 56ff.); (f) practice of monolatry, their god being the patrondeity of the Patriarchal clan (the name Yahweh, and the monotheism attached to it, are an anachronistic legacy from the time of Moses; cf. Exod. 3:6; 6:3).

---

[5] It has been brought to my attention that Professor C.H. Gordon has orally cited this passage in a similar context.

But do such features reveal an accurate reflection of the historical events? When the historian attempts to derive history from the
biblical tradition, he is confronted by several hazards in method (see,
e.g., Smend 1977 and references there; also see Tsevat 1980). One
of these is that all the available direct evidence is self-testimony—
internal evidence, both subjective and ethnocentric. The distant past
is idealized and romanticized, and cut to fit later ideological exi-
gencies (see, e.g., most recently Herion 1981). To use an intriguing
example, some scholars have assumed that Abraham, Father of the
Nation, or alternately, Melchizedek, king and priest, find a simple
prototype in King David, the "earlier" figures initially contrived as
it were, to lend legitimacy to David's kingdom (e.g., Mazar 1969: 74).

These deficiencies are, or course, somewhat offset by the intrinsic value of having a record of a nation's own perception of its past
(Dinur 1968; Harrelson 1977 and cf. for general questions of method
Gadamer 1979). Israel's self-portrait of its singularity is painted on
several levels. (a) Israel's position on the *ethnic* map of the family of
man—its descent from Shem and Eber, basing its specific lineage
on Abraham, Isaac, and Jacob and his twelve sons. An elaborate
genealogy of this sort (based on both vertical and horizontal lines)
has no counterpart in the literature of the ancient Near East (Malamat
1968; chap 4; Wilson 1977). (b) Israel's *religious* distinctiveness, the
divine revelation to the Patriarchs (with the attendant promise of
land and progeny), and the later revelation through Moses of a rev-
olutionary, monotheistic doctrine, having no antecedents in the surrounding world. (c) On the *societal* level, growth from a basic domestic
unit (Hebrew *bêt 'āb*), eventually expanding into clans and tribes,
and culminating in a nation. (d) On the *territorial* plane, an acute
consciousness of a national home—not merely a geographical domain
but sacred soil. (e) *Destiny*, the signal bond between the Chosen People
and the Promised Land.

In this connection a further stumbling block confronting us in the
biblical tradition, from the historical point of view, is the fact that
the received text underwent complex literary reworking for hundreds
of years after the events it relates (see references in Weippert 1973:
415–27; and recently Buss 1979). Only two of the processes affecting biblical historiography and blurring historical reality need be
noted here.

The first process is known in scholarship as "reflection." Rudi-
mentary ancient descriptions were recontemplated in the current

intellectual and theological terms, yielding new appraisals and motivations for past events. Thus, for example, why did the Israelites conquer Canaan? Because—by way of *contemplation*—the land had been promised to the Patriarchs long before. And how was Canaan conquered? By the God of Israel (rather than by the human actors in the drama)—*in contemplation* (Seeligmann 1969–74: 273ff.).

The second process is "telescoping," the compression of a chain of historical events into a simplified, artificial account. Later redactors would, in retrospect, compress a complex of events into a severely curtailed time-span. A signal example is the attribution of the protracted process of the Conquest to a single national hero, Joshua. I would also impute to telescoping the compression of a centuries-long "Patriarchal" experience into a literary précis: the brief, three-generation scheme of Abraham-Isaac-Jacob. The Patriarchal narrative cycles may preserve isolated reminiscences of a dim past, perhaps harking back as far as the West Semitic movements westward from the end of the third millennium B.C.E. on. The literary result thus resembles a closed accordion, and the full extent of the original events can be reconstituted by opening it out accordingly. This is why the sensational Ebla discoveries should not overly unsettle our historical cool: if the material there indeed proves at all relevant to the Patriarchal tradition, the accordion can simply be stretched out to accommodate another few centuries or so.

All these hazards notwithstanding, there is no cause for the degree of skepticism, occasionally extreme, to which scholars often fall prey. The received tradition can indeed be utilized in reconstructing early events, but criteria must first be established by which the historical kernel may be identified and distinguished from later accretions. This task can be accomplished only by careful critique of the biblical texts themselves, and of the relevant extra-biblical sources, and subsequent meaningful comparison of them (similarly Hallo 1980), undertaken in a controlled manner which eschews all superficiality and romanticism (for support of the comparative method in general, see Gelb 1980). In other words, "typological" or "phenomenological" links must be sought out, focussing upon parallel features essentially typical to both the biblical and the extra-biblical sources.

A prime means for such comparison is provided by the large royal archive of the 18th century B.C.E. found at Mari, the unusually broad spectrum of which—probably more than any other extra-biblical source—has put the proto-history of Israel into a new perspective (Malamat 1971, 1989). Some scholars have been inclined to link the Mari evidence directly to the roots of Israel, supposing a primary, genetic relationship between the tribal elements reflected in the Mari texts and the Patriarchs (e.g., Albright 1961, 1973; Parrot 1962). Though we should not altogether discount the possibility of a direct relationship, the external data currently available are certainly inadequate to demonstrate such a tie.

The likelihood is that the milieu of Israel's formative period as described in the Bible is reliable and "authentic"—given the assumptions and qualifications noted above—if the overall historical reality of the first two-thirds of the second millennium B.C.E. tallies with it in various realms. This likelihood increases particularly when extra-biblical circumstances and their biblical counterparts conflict with norms of the later Israelite period, or when these common elements are entirely void of meaning in a first millennium B.C.E. context.

There are several aspects of the Mari material which can serve as points of departure for fertile comparison (for a more expanded description see chap. 2).

CHRONOLOGY. For those who place the Patriarchal period in the first third of the second millennium B.C.E. (e.g., Albright 1961; de Vaux 1978: 257ff.), the Mari archives represent a nearly contemporaneous picture, and thus a "genetic" approach would be suitable for them. But my attitude toward the "Patriarchal Age," clearly stated above, would deprive such a direct comparison of much of its validity, though the Mari material could well lie *within* the span of the "un-telescoped" proto-history of Israel.

GEOGRAPHY. The relevant Mari data is on several levels: the region encompassed by the Mari documents includes "Aram Naharaim," whence, according to the Bible, the Patriarchs came to Canaan. Haran and Nahor, home-towns of the Patriarchs, are frequently mentioned at Mari as focal points of nomadic tribes. The documents also reveal extensive diplomatic and commercial caravan activities, as well as tribal migrations, between the Middle Euphrates region and Canaan—providing a realistic background for the Patriarchal movements, which proceed roughly between the same regions. On a different level, the Mari documents make specific mention of two cities within what later became the Land of Israel—Hazor and Laish (later called Dan). A recently published document even mentions "Canaan" or "Canaanites," though it is not clear whether the use here is ethnic or geographical (Dossin 1973; Rainey 1979: 161).

SOCIETAL ASPECT. The clearest and most extensive picture of tribal society in all the extra-biblical literature of the ancient Near East is revealed in the Mari documents: the various patterns and mechanisms of tribal structure and organization, and a variegated spectrum of settlement (ranging from wholly nomadic to permanently settled) are attested. Significantly, Mari reveals a synchronic cross-section of the various stages of settlement, whereas the Bible provides a diachronic view, with the earliest Israelites progressing through a multi-stage settlement process. These two sources together can produce a "stereoscopic" view of the phenomena. A specific facet common to both sources is the fascinating confrontation between tribal and urban societies, the symbiotic process eventually leading to interdependence. Many and various institutions and rituals can also be clarified, for example, such vestiges of tribal heritage as the covenant-making ritual (Malamat 1971: 18).

ETHNO-LINGUISTIC AFFINITIES. Like the Patriarchs, most of the peoples associated with the Mari documents were of West Semitic stock, as revealed by their personal names and their idiom. Personal names were a sort of ethnic calling-card in antiquity, and such names as Abram, Ishmael, Laban, Leah, and Jacob were current at Mari. The name Jacob is to be found in Akkadian documents from other sites as well, from the 19th to the 17th centuries B.C.E., although always with an additional theophoric element: *Yaḥqub-el, -aḥ, -ʿam,* or the like; the name *Yaʿqob-har* (or *-el*) was even borne by one of the Hyksos rulers of Egypt (Albright 1968: index, s.v. Jacob; Giveon 1981). On another plane, the Babylonian language of the Mari documents displays intrusive West Semitic idioms. The Mari scribes seem occasionally to have found themselves at a loss for the right word or phrase, and would use typical West Semitic expressions. Some of these usages have no Babylonian equivalents, and others are standard Babylonian used in a modified manner. Significantly, some such terms appear in early Biblical Hebrew as well: in the realm of tribal organization, *gōy/gāʾum, ḥeber/ḥibrum* and *ummâ/ummatum*; concepts of settlement, *naḥălâ/niḥlatum* and *nāweh/nawûm* (in the sense of a pastoral encampment cum flock and pasturage; cf. *nĕwēh midbār*); tribal leadership, *šōpeṭ/šāpiṭum*; the cardinal points of the compass, *qedem/ aqdamātum, ʾāḥōr/aḥarātum, yāmîn/*yamīna* and *śĕmōl/*simʾal* (for further examples, see Malamat 1971: 13ff., 1989).

All in all, however, and despite the body and substance of the Mari material, it does not constitute any more than circumstantial evidence: Abrams and Jacobs were indeed doing much the same things at Mari as Abraham and Jacob were doing in the Patriarchal narratives. So, too, with the other extra-biblical sources; it is doubtful that even the material from Ebla will be able to contribute significantly beyond this.

A Note on Method

Given these circumstances, as well as others not treated here, recent scholarship has taken up a broad variety of approaches in grappling with the problems of Israelite proto-history, ranging from the neo-fundamentalistic to the hypercritical (altogether denying validity to the biblical tradition, e.g., Thompson 1974 especially pp. 324–26; still more extreme 1979; 1978; Van Seters 1975; de Geus 1976). The general outline of my own position within this spectrum will emerge more clearly from the following. It has become fashionable to borrow models from such fields as sociology and anthropology (Mendenhall 1962; 1978; Gottwald 1979)—as indeed I do, too (Malamat 1976b see chap. 8)—but these must not be imposed arbitrarily upon Israelite proto-history *per se*. Such misapplications often lead to disqualification of the biblical text, distortion of it, or simply disregard for it. We could all do well to give heed to Wellhausen's dictum, astounding for him: "If it [the Israelite tradition] is at all feasible, it would be utter folly (*Torheit*) to give preference to any other feasibility" (Wellhausen 1899: 347, albeit limited in context; for the general issue of tradition, see now Shils 1981).

Let us regard the biblical account itself as a conceptual model of Israel's genesis. It is as if the Israelites themselves formulated an articulate portrayal of their distant past, much as modern scholarship does. Such a paradigm for a description of Israel's emergence is feasible. This projection embedded within the biblical text has certain clear advantages over modern speculation: being much closer to the actual events—by thousands of years—and being a product of the locale itself, it inherently draws upon a much greater intimacy with the land, its topography, demography, military situation, ecology, and the like.[6]

---

[6] For application to specific episodes, see Malamat 1976a: 40–46 (concerning the Exodus from Egypt) and, in particular, Malamat 1979 (concerning the Conquest of Canaan). Cf. chaps. 5 & 6.

Such a working hypothesis enables us to avoid the extremes which have all too often left their imprint upon modern historiography in our field. By conceding that the biblical tradition could be a reflective, "theorizing" account—rather than strictly factual, "Wie es eigentlich gewesen" (Ranke)—we sidestep the pitfall of neofundamentalism. And by spurning the view of Israel's proto-history as a deliberately fabricated tradition, we keep from being swept into the other, radical—and now more fashionable—extreme. This paves the way, on an operative plane, to a dialectical approach to the biblical text, one which retains the option that the tradition represents an admixture of ancient, reliable, historical components and late, untrustworthy, anachronistic elements.

Bibliography

Albright, W.F.
  1961 Abram the Hebrew. *Bulletin of the American Schools of Oriental Research* 163: 36–54.
  1968 *Yahweh and the Gods of Canaan.* London: Athlone.
  1973 From the Patriarchs to Moses. *Biblical Archaeologist* 36: 5–33.
Avigad, N.
  1978 Baruch the Scribe and Jerahmeel the King's Son. *Israel Exploration Journal* 28: 52–56.
Buss, M.J., ed.
  1979 *Encounter with the Text. Form and History in the Hebrew Bible.* Philadelphia: Fortress. Especially Willis 1979.
Danell, G.A.
  1946 *Studies in the Name Israel in the Old Testament.* Uppsala: Appelbergs.
Dinur, B.Z.
  1968 Jewish History—Its Uniqueness and Continuity. *Journal of World History* 11: 15–29.
Dossin, G.
  1973 Une mention de Cananéens dans une lettre de Mari. *Syria* 50: 277–82.
Engel, H.
  1979 Die Siegesstele des Merenptah. *Biblica* 60: 373–99.
Gadamer, H.G.
  1979 The Problem of Historical Consciousness. Pp. 103–60 in *Interpretive Social Science. A Reader*, ed. P. Rabinow and W.M. Sullivan. Berkeley: University of California Press.
Gelb, I.J.
  1980 Comparative Method in the Study of the Society and Economy of the Ancient Near East. *Rocznik Orientalistyczny* 41: 29–36.
de Geus, C.H.J.
  1976 *The Tribes of Israel.* Assen/Amsterdam: Van Gorcum.
Giveon, R.
  1981 Ya'qob-har. *Göttinger Miszellen* 44: 17–19.

Gordon, C.H.
   1958   Abraham and Merchants of Ura. *Journal of Near Eastern Studies* 17: 28–31.
Gottwald, N.K.
   1979   *The Tribes of Yahweh*. Maryknoll, NY: Orbis.
Hallo, W.W.
   1980   Biblical History in its Near Eastern Setting: The Contextual Approach. Pp. 1–26 in *Scripture in Context. Essays on the Comparative Method*, ed. C.D. Evans, W.W. Hallo, and J.B. White, Pittsburgh: Pickwick.
Harrelson, W.
   1977   Life, Faith and the Emergence of Tradition. Pp. 11–30 in *Tradition and Theology in the Old Testament*, ed. D.A. Knight. Philadelphia: Fortress.
Herion, G.A.
   1981   The Role of Historical Narrative in Biblical Thought: The Tendencies Underlying Old Testament Historiography. *Journal for the Study of the Old Testament* 21: 25–57.
Kallai, Z.
   1967   *The Tribes of Israel*. Jerusalem: Bialik Institute (Hebrew) (English 1986).
Malamat, A.
   1968   King Lists of the Old Babylonian Period and Biblical Genealogies. *Journal of the American Oriental Society* 88: 163–73.
   1970   The Danite Migration and the Pan-Israelite Exodus-Conquest. A Biblical Narrative Pattern. *Biblia* 51: 1–16.
   1971   Mari. *Biblical Archaeologist* 34: 2–22.
   1976a   Origins and the Formative Period. Pp. 3–87 in *A History of the Jewish People*, ed. H.H. Ben-Sasson. Cambridge, MA: Harvard University.
   1976b   Charismatic Leadership in the Book of Judges. Pp. 152–168 in *Magnalia Dei: The Mighty Acts of God. Studies . . . G.E. Wright*, ed. F.M. Cross et al. Garden City, NY: Doubleday.
   1979   Conquest of Canaan: Israelite Conduct of War according to Biblical Tradition. *Revue internationale d'histoire militaire* (Tel Aviv) 42: 25–52.
   1989   Mari and the Early Israelite Experience (London-Oxford).
Mazar, B.
   1969   The Historical Background of the Book of Genesis. *Journal of Near Eastern Studies* 28: 73–83.
Mendenhall, G.
   1962   The Hebrew Conquest of Palestine. *Biblical Archaeologist* 25: 66–87.
   1978   Between Theology and Archaeology. *Journal for the Study of the Old Testament* 7: 28–34.
Noth, M.
   1958   *The History of Israel*. Trans. P. Ackroyd. New York: Harper.
Parrot, A.
   1962   *Abraham et son temps*. Neuchatel: Delachaux & Niestlé.
Rainey, A.F.
   1979   Toponymic Problems. *Tel-Aviv* 6: 158–61.
Seeligmann, A.L.
   1969–74   From Historical Reality to Historiographical Conception in the Bible. *P'raqim* 2: 273–313 (Hebrew).
Shils, E.
   1981   *Tradition*. Chicago: University of Chicago Press.
Smend, R.
   1977   Tradition and History: A Complex Relation. Pp. 49–68 in *Tradition and Theology in the Old Testament*, ed. D.A. Knight. Philadelphia: Fortress.

Soggin, J.A.
 1978 The History of Ancient Israel—A Study in Some Questions of Method. *Eretz-Israel* 14 (H.L. Ginsberg Volume): 44*–51*.
Thompson, L.T.
 1974 *The Historicity of the Patriarchal Narratives: The Quest for the Historical Abraham.* Beihefte zur Zeitschrift für die Alttestamentliche Wissenschaft 133. Berlin: de Gruyter.
 1978 The Background of the Patriarchs: A Reply to W. Dever and M. Clark. *Journal for the Study of the Old Testament* 9: 2–43.
 1979 Conflict Themes in the Jacob Narratives. *Semeia* 15: 5–26.
Tsevat, M.
 1980 Israelite History and the Historical Books of The Old Testament. Pp. 177–87 in M. Tsevat, *The Meaning of the Book of Job and other Biblical Studies.* New York: KTAV.
Van Seters, J.
 1975 *Abraham in History and Tradition.* New Haven: Yale University.
 1981 Histories and Historians of the Ancient Near East: The Israelites. *Orientalia* 50: 137–85.
de Vaux, R.
 1978 *The Early History of Israel.* London; Darton, Longman & Todd.
Weippert, M.
 1973 Fragen des israelitischen Bewusstseins. *Vetus Testamentum* 23: 415–42.
Wellhausen, J.
 1899 *Die Composition des Hexateuch³.* Berlin: Reimer.
Willis, J.T.
 1979 Redaction Criticism and Historical Reconstruction. Pp. 83–89 in Buss 1979.
Wilson, R.R.
 1977 *Genealogy and History in the Biblical World.* New Haven: Yale University Press.
Wiseman, D.J.
 1956 *Chronicles of the Chaldaean Kings (626–556 B.C.) in the British Museum.* London: British Museum.

2

MARI AND EARLY ISRAEL* **

Just over fifty years have passed since Mari, situated on the Middle Euphrates slightly north of the Syrian-Iraqi border, was discovered accidentally, like Ugarit and El-Amarna. Since 1933, the French have exposed significant parts of the site, initially under the direction of the late André Parrot, who conducted twenty-one seasons of excavations, and since 1979 under Jean Margueron. The excavations have yielded a virtual treasure house of archaeological and epigraphical finds, and the results have exceeded all expectations.

Here we shall concentrate on the royal archives discovered in the magnificent palace of the Old Babylonian period, at which time Mari came under West Semitic control. It is this textual material which is of prime relevance to our subject. Of the 20,000 odd tablets unearthed in the palace, dating from the first or the second half of the eighteenth century B.C.E., depending on which chronological system one adopts, only a quarter or so have been published in a score of volumes, the most recent of which is *Archives royales de Mari* (henceforth *ARMT*), vol. XXIII (Paris, 1984). Even this fraction of the documentary material from Mari is sufficient to reveal the enormous potential of the discovery.

After half a century, what have we gained from these Mari texts? How have they contributed to the study of ancient Palestine, the history of early Israel or the earliest stratum of the Hebrew language? In short, how have they benefited biblical research as a whole? For our purposes, in contrast to Ugarit, for example, the main impact of Old Babylonian Mari is felt in the elucidation of Israel's proto-history, placing it in a perspective so far not attained from any other extra-biblical source.

* This article was originally published in: *Biblical Archaeology Today*, Israel Exp. Soc., Jerusalem 1985, 235–243.

** This study was made possible through a grant from the Fund for Basic Research administered by the Israel Academy of Sciences and Humanities, and was carried out during my terms as a fellow of the Institute for Advanced Studies at The Hebrew University of Jerusalem.

Mari, like Palestine, is situated on the fringe of the Syro-Arabian Desert—albeit on an entirely different flank. The city-states of the so-called Fertile Crescent were frequently infiltrated, and the West Semitic groups with whom we are concerned here, often simply called Amorites, were just one more of these intrusive movements. Old Babylonian Mari apparently did share ultimate origins with the early Israelites and many other peoples of the West. Thus, a comparison between early Israel and Mari can, should, and must be made. Indeed, the broad spectrum of the Mari archives—the largest extra-biblical body of material within this West Semitic milieu—actually invites such a comparison.

But first a cautionary word on the comparative method in regard to Mari and the Bible. Valid, meaningful comparisons can yield significant results, and can preclude shallow or extreme conclusions. Lack of discretion on this point has been a pitfall in the past, the outstanding example being the somewhat sensational hullabaloo surrounding the early announcements of the epigraphic finds at Ebla, although these finds are quite remarkable in themselves. I would reject any romanticist or neofundamentalist approach to the Mari documents, such as were adopted by some scholars soon after their discovery. André Parrot, the French excavator of Mari, never really freed himself of this attitude, and this fever was rampant in other lands as well. Such an approach tends to relate Mari *directly* with the Israelite cradle, almost as if there had been an initial, genetic connection between the tribal populations reflected in the Mari documents and the Patriarchs of the Hebrews.

Avoiding any such "genetic" view, the comparative method which I advocate could best be called "typological" or "phenomenological." In other words, efforts should be concentrated on examination of typical phenomena, seeking out common sets of concepts, and elucidating institutions and practices which were more or less parallel at Mari and among the Israelites. This approach can place our comparisons on a firm, constructive basis.

Valid comparison, however, also involves a contrastive approach, and the basic difference underlying Mari and the Bible must not be neglected. This difference—surprisingly ignored in most research—lies in the very nature of the two sources, for, in quality, they are as different as "the raw and the cooked," to use a phrase of Levi-Strauss. The Mari documents are everyday, firsthand material directly reflecting the reality of their matrix. Further, they were intended for limited, internal consumption. In decided contrast, the biblical material—mainly in the genre of folk narrative—has been "processed," that is, edited and re-edited, and in part indeed composed, centuries after the events described. Nonetheless, this latter point would in no way preclude, *a priori*, some erstwhile historical connection with Mari, though there is nothing in the data presently available which would support such an assumption.

We can now embark on a comparative study of Mari and the Bible, based on these assumptions and reservations. Mari at first appears to be remote from the Bible, in terms of time and space. Indeed, the earliest parts of the biblical text can go back little more than the twelfth century B.C.E., so we are faced with a gap of approximately half a millennium between the time Hammurabi sacked the Mari palace and the time when the earliest parts of the Bible, as we have it, were set down. However, it seems that reminiscences in the patriarchal narratives hark back much earlier than the twelfth century. The problem is—how much further back? This, as you are aware, is a major bone of contention among scholars.

Chronological Aspect

The most difficult problem arising from the patriarchal narratives is probably that of chronology. The so-called Patriarchal Age has often been ascribed to the first quarter, or third, of the second millennium B.C.E.—in archaeological terms, the Middle Bronze Age I (as held foremost by Nelson Glueck and W.F. Albright), or the Middle Bronze Age II (as held, *inter alia*, by Père R. de Vaux and E. Speiser). As the Mari documents are regarded by some authorities as more or less "contemporaneous" with Abraham, Isaac and Jacob, scholars could readily be enticed into adopting a "genetic" approach, leading to overevaluation of the extra-biblical evidence for the historicity of the Israelite Patriarchs. Another school of thought has gone to the opposite extreme, contending that the "Patriarchal Age" and the "Patriarchs" are no more than pure fable, a creation of the later biblical authors, and consequently, possessing no particular time of their own.

My own attitude is that the Patriarchs should not be assigned to any specific, well-defined set of dates, in other words, to a "Patriarchal Age." Hence, this oft-used term is of doubtful legitimacy. I am not suggesting the negation of the very essence of the Patriarchs, but I do, with certain other scholars, regard the Genesis narratives as an artificial construct, based on a limited three-generation scheme. This was the product of later biblical historiographers, who used the scheme to formulate what was actually a prolonged historical process. By such tendentious means as what we call "telescoping," the entire complex of Israel's protohistory was compressed into a simplistic and narrow chronological framework. The cycle of patriarchal narratives must originally have spanned hundreds of years, and probably pre-served isolated reminiscences of an even dimmer past, of the early days of the Amorite tribes in Syro-Palestine at the end of the third millennium B.C.E. The literary end product of all this artifice re-sembles, by way of metaphor, an accordion which has been closed; in order to recover the full historical span, one must expand the accordion.

It is precisely this elasticity which should allay our suspicions con-cerning the Ebla discoveries and their historical consequences for the patriarchal narratives. If, indeed, the Ebla material does prove rel-evant to Hebrew origins, then our accordion should simply be extended somewhat further, to accommodate another half millennium or so.

How does all this affect an intelligent, considered comparison with Mari? With all due reservation, the Old Babylonian material at Mari could lie within the "reconstituted" or "untelescoped" purview of the protohistory of Israel, and hence be relevant for comparison with the Bible.

The Ethno-Linguistic Aspect

Viewing the problem from another angle, what can we find to strengthen the chronological basis for comparison? One prominent means is the onomasticon common to Mari and early Israel, a most potent argument in favor of the antiquity of Israel's protohistorical kernel. We shall limit our discussion solely to the members of the patriarchal family, some of whom find their namesakes at Mari. The best documented of these biblical names is *Ya'ᵃqob* (Jacob), the com-mon occurrence of which at Mari can serve as hard evidence for its antiquity. It appears in tens of cuneiform documents in various forms, such as *Yahqub-El*, *Haqbu-El*, *Haqba-ahu* and *(H)aqba/a-Hammû*. The biblical form, as with many other names in the Book of Genesis, is truncated, a sort of nickname lacking its theophoric component, which was apparently El. Significantly, the name Jacob is also found somewhat later among the Semitic rulers of Egypt, the famous Hyksos kings, but there it appears with a different theophoric component.

Other "biblical" names at Mari are: Ishmael in the form *Yasmah-El*; Laban with theophoric elements, as in *El-Laban* or *Ahi-Laban*; and finally, Abram or Abraham in the form of *Abi-Ram*. A recently published Mari text (*ARMT* XXII, No. 328) contains the personal name *Bi-ni-ya-mi-na*, that is, Benjamin. This is the first time that this name appears in its full form in syllabic spelling, leaving no doubt as to its reading, and it is very significant to those initiated into this intricate problem. Admittedly, these names also occur in later periods, a fact which has often been offered as an argument negating an early date, especially by Th.L. Thompson and J. Van Seters. However, we cannot overlook the fact that they are used extensively, particularly in Old Babylonian and Hyksos contexts, and that, with the exception of the name of Abram, they are (especially the name Jacob) much less common in later periods.

Thus our comparison is of twofold significance. On the one hand, it demonstrates the horizon on which the patriarchal names should be evaluated; the majority of these names surely represent early models of personal names among the Israelites. On the other hand, these names are clear indicators of the ethnic affinity of Israel's ancestors, the West Semitic or Amorite stock. Therefore, personal names can often serve, in effect, as ethnic "calling cards," although serious limitations must be taken into account when using this as an isolated criterion.

We certainly have additional criteria of even greater weight for determining the West Semitic character of many of the population groups reflected in the Mari documents, on the one hand, and of the early Israelites, on the other. Foremost at Mari is a linguistic factor. The Mari texts are basically written in a chancery style Babylonian of the Hammurabi period. However, this language is permeated with West Semiticisms in grammar and, more significantly, in vocabulary and idiom. Numerous terms and expressions betray the everyday speech of the scribes, who frequently resorted to typical West Semitic words, or gave specifically West Semitic nuances to standard Akkadian terms.

Many of these very same West Semitic idioms are present in the Hebrew Bible as well, particularly in poetic or exalted language. I could readily cite numerous examples, especially concerning the conceptual world and lifestyle of the West Semites—idioms having no true equivalents in standard Akkadian since their referents are entirely foreign to the Assyro-Babylonian social and ideological milieu.

Since the details are somewhat tedious, we shall mention very few examples, slightly elaborating on one of them later on. Limiting ourselves to West Semitic terms in the realm of tribal society, we find the Mari terms: *ga-yum*, Hebrew *gōy*—originally a tribal unit of perhaps modest extent, already organized into a territorial, administrative framework (there is even mention of a *gāyu Amurru*, that is, an Amorite clan); *ummatum*, Hebrew *ummāh*—another tribal entity derived from the word for "mother," apparently a unit originally attributed to a matriarch, like the Leahite and Rachelite tribes among the Israelites; *hibrum*, Hebrew *ḥeber*—an association of clans, but linked by communal wanderings; *niḥlatum*, Hebrew *naḥᵃlāh*—"patrimony," an inalienable family property; and *šāpiṭum*, Hebrew *šōfēṭ*—conventionally translated "judge" in the Bible, but as we can clearly learn from Mari, the term had a much broader sense—a person not merely dispensing justice, but ruling in general.

The Societal Aspect

All this West Semitic terminology, in one way or another, reflects a thoroughly tribalistic milieu, mainly of nonurban populations, but to some extent also of urban society. This is so at Mari as well as in early Israel, and it is only in these two sources—among all the documentary evidence of the ancient Near East till Islamic times—that tribal society manifests itself in full bloom.

If modern sociology and comparative anthropology are still very much groping about in their treatment of present-day societies, they are confounded all the more so in their attempt to grasp ancient, extinct societies. Despite this serious shortcoming, the variegated patterns and mechanisms of tribal structure and organization are often parallel in our two sources, though in other facets they diverge widely.

In such patrilineal tribal regimes as in the case of Mari and early Israel, the basic social and economic unit is the extended family— the *bēt āb* of biblical Hebrew, and the Akkadian *bit ābim* at Mari. Such units aggregate to form a clan and, subsequently, broader tribal associations. The best documented of the latter at Mari are the more or less sedentarized Haneans and the seminomadic Yaminites. The Yaminites, unattested outside Mari, are seen as a still somewhat unruly and independent group. Their name, literally meaning "sons of the right," that is, southerners, is outwardly identical with the name of the Israelite tribe of Benjamin, a fact which has occasionally been entirely blown out of proportion. For the present, however, I can see no connection between the two entities, beyond the similarity of name.

The process of tribal settlement as revealed at Mari can be seen to range over a broad spectrum of simultaneous stages of sedentarization, from the nomadic to the permanently settled. In the Bible, we see a diachronic view of this gradual process, the progressive stages depicted as if in sequence: entrance of the early Israelites into Canaan, roving about it, taking possession of parts of the land and, finally, settling it as a permanent, sedentary population. However, at Man, we see this variegated process as a synchronous, side by side picture at one single, brief point in time. The stereoscopic picture obtained by viewing these two depictions—the synchronic and the diachronic—yields a depth and perspective otherwise unattainable. Mari provides "raw facts in the field," so to speak, almost like modern fieldwork, while the Bible, with its historical perception, has broken the process down into typified stages.

Throughout the biblical narratives we read of the encounter between tribal society and well-established urban culture, an ambivalent relationship of friction and symbiosis. At Mari too, such a picture is projected, and in this light we are now in a better position to assess the mode by which the Israelites were able to penetrate into urbanized Canaan and succeed in their process of *Landnahme*. In the Israelite—Canaanite encounter, it would seem that, more often than not, friction developed between the two rival social and political systems. A single indicative episode in this context, even if only of symbolic nature, was Jacob's encounter with the town of Shechem after the rape of his daughter, Dinah. Though the inhabitants of the city welcomed him and offered him land and connubial relations, Jacob and his sons, despite the fact that their rejection of the offer entailed a considerable loss of potential economic advantage, preferred to avenge the family honor.

That Israelite tenacity won out is history. This is in contrast to the experience in Mesopotamia, where there seems to have been much more mutual assimilation amongst the rival societies; the Akkadian-

Babylonian culture on the one hand, and the various tribal, West Semitic elements on the other.

In Israel's protohistory we also encounter a symbiotic relationship of mutuality and cultural sharing between tribe and city. This sort of dimorphic society seems to be mirrored by recent archaeological discoveries from the Middle Bronze Age II in Palestine. Most significant in this respect are the various open satellite villages, mainly rather small and short-lived, found adjacent to Middle Bronze Age towns. The biblical traditions concerning the encampments of the Patriarchs alongside Canaanite cities such as Shechem, Bethel (Genesis 12:6,8) and Hebron (Genesis 13:18), fit in well with such an archaeological picture.

In the Mari documents, this mode of life is best illustrated in the concept of the *nawûm*. In standard Akkadian, this word means "desert, steppe, uncultivated field," but in its specialized West Semitic usage, it denotes semifertile pasturage and, by association, encampment there. Such a meaning can also be seen in the biblical Hebrew form of this word, *nāweh*. This word, although it does not appear in the patriarchal narratives, is found, in retrospective use, in poetic passages such as Psalms 79:7 and Jeremiah 10:25, as in the expression *n'weh Ya'ᶜqob*, the "habitation" of Jacob.

Occasionally, a *nawûm* is mentioned as being attached to a city, as is implied by such phrases as "the *nawûm* of Carchemish" or Sippar and its *nawûm*. This is quite reminiscent of the depictions of the Patriarchs dwelling on the outskirts of Canaanite towns, which we have just noted. On the other hand, the outlying *nawûm*s of the Mari texts are reflected in the biblical narrative regarding Jacob's sons (Genesis 37:12ff.), who pastured their flocks as far away from their father's base at Hebron as Shechem and even Dothan.

An interesting series of values emerges from a study of this word, *nawûm/nāweh*, in the Mesopotamian-Syrian-Palestinian sphere. The attitude toward the *nawûm* in the standard urban-orientated Assyrian-Babylonian culture is negative, regarding it as disruptive to civilization. At Mari, in the midst of the mixing bowl of Mesopotamian and West Semitic cultures, the general attitude is practical and sympathetic, accepting the *nawûm* as a fact of life. In the Bible, we see a sort of internal, self view of the *nāweh*, fully identifying with it and its way of life. Indeed, among the Israelites, the *nāweh* even assumed a theological dimension, as can clearly be seen in the best known of all the Psalms, Psalm 23: "The Lord is my shepherd, I shall not want; he makes me lie down in green *nāweh*s," that is, in green pastures!

The Geographical Aspect

Turning now to the geographical side of our subject, we find that the Mari documents are of value on several planes. First and foremost, they encompass the region known in the Bible as Aram-Naharaim, and today called the Jezireh in northeastern Syria. This was the land from which, traditionally, the Patriarchs came to Canaan. In this context, it is most significant that the two cities which were erstwhile habitats of the patriarchal clan—Haran and Nahor—find frequent mention in the Mari letters, specifically as focal points of nomadic tribal activity. Harran, in the Upper Balikh Valley, was a central station in the itinerary of the Hebrews on their way to Canaan. Nahor, on the western arm of the Habur River, east of Haran, is noted as the residence of Laban, a relative of the patriarchal clan, from whose family both Isaac and Jacob took their wives.

No less significant than the appearance of the early patriarchal habitat is the light shed on the dynamic dimension of mobility in the entire region. The comings and goings of the Patriarchs, between Aram-Naharaim and Canaan, are thus now brought into comprehensible perspective. The numerous references in the Mari documents to merchant caravans, official missions and, especially significant, the movements of tribal groups making their way from the Middle Euphrates region to as far away as northern Canaan, provide a much more convincing and reliable backdrop than the simple, almost naive picture reflected in Genesis. The obsolete view of a centrifugal flow from the Arabian Desert into the surrounding areas must now give way to another model. Metaphorically, we can now grasp the major tribal movements as a sort of "alternating current." Such a model exactly fits the descriptions of the patriarchal migrations between Aram-Naharaim and Canaan.

What other points of contact with the "Holy Land" do we find at Mari? Actually, very few. The name Canaan seems to appear in a recently published letter, in the form LÚ *Ki-na-ah-num*[MEŠ], that is, "Canaanites," and it occurs in connection with the term *habbātum*, "marauders," a synonym of *Habiru/'Apiru*. This, then, is the earliest attestation of Canaan, pushing the documentation some three centuries further back than the hitherto known earliest reference to this name. Besides this, Hazor in northern Canaan is mentioned in some ten published Mari texts (including *ARMT*, vol. XXIII), all but one of them from the days of Zimri-Lim, the last ruler of Mari. Hazor, excavated during the 1950s and 1960s by Yigael Yadin, grew to greatness in the Mari period, having an "acropolis" and a lower city totaling 200 acres (700 dunams) in area (about the same size as Qatna and Ebla). What is significant for us is the fact that several cuneiform documents were also found there, raising our hopes that one day a royal archive of this period will be discovered at Hazor.

What did Mari and Hazor seek from one another? Hazor was beyond Mari's normal political sphere of influence, but it was on the very edge of its horizon of commerce. There are several Mari texts which deal in particular with a "strategic" commodity—tin, the metal which was alloyed with copper in a ratio of about one to eight in order to yield bronze. Trade in tin was brisk in this period, and Mari was a major tin emporium. In one Mari document alone, 500 kg of tin are listed, and other smaller quantities are noted as being received from or despatched to several destinations and persons in the West. Besides consignments to the king of Aleppo, quantities were apparently sent to Ugarit, to a Caphtorite there (that is, a merchant from Crete), and to a *ta-ar-ga-ma-an-num*. This is one of the earliest occurrences of this *Kulturwort* which is still used, after almost 4,000 years, in more or less the same meaning, "dragoman." What is of greatest concern to us in this document, is the fact that it includes three consignments of tin for Hazor, totaling over 35 kg, sufficient for the manufacture of some 300 kg of bronze. Furthermore, it is consigned to "Ibni-Adad, King of Hazor," revealing the personal name of the ruler of the city.

In this same tin text, we find mention of perhaps another city in Palestine—Laish, some 30 km north of Hazor. In recent years, Laish has been the object of extensive excavations directed by A. Biran. These excavations have revealed a large city of 200 dunams, encompassed by massive fortifications of the Middle Bronze Age II, that is, the Mari period. It is therefore likely that Mari, especially under Zimri-Lim, might have been responsible for the intensification of bronze manufacture in the Canaanite sphere.

Not long ago, I was privileged to publish a Mari text indicative of the commerce between Mari and Hazor. It seems that one of Zimri-Lim's servants was sent to Hazor, to purchase precious materials for use in the Mari palace. To quote: "This man took away from Hazor silver, gold and precious stones and made off," apparently without paying for them. In retaliation, the Hazor authorities detained a caravan from Mari. Matters were further complicated when the servant from Mari was assaulted and brutally robbed on his way home, at Emar on the Euphrates—claiming that both the goods and the sealed receipt for them had been stolen from him. Zimri-Lim appealed to Yarim-Lim, King of Aleppo, who enjoyed considerable influence throughout Syria, apparently to obtain release of his caravan at Hazor and to recover his property stolen at Emar. We shall never know the outcome of the affair, but it does provide a fascinating glimpse into the trials and tribulations of international trade at that time, especially in the West.

Another important realm which can contribute toward an understanding of the ancient Israelite experience can only briefly be referred to—religious manifestations and ritual practices, such as the covenant-making ceremony, enforcement of the ban as penalty for certain types of transgression, and the more controversial census-taking and ritual expiation. In all of these, certain essential similarities between Mari and Israel are evident. More important is the appearance at Mari of intuitive prophecy, that is, prophetic revelation without resort to mantic or oracular devices and techniques. Despite the considerable ideological hiatus between prophecy at Mari and in the Bible, the early manifestation of intuitive prophecy at Mari should not be belittled. See A. Malamat, Mari and the Bible, Leiden 1998, Part two. We can see in existence there prophetic emissaries among West-Semitic tribes many centuries before the similar, though more mature manifestation among the Israelites. In my opinion, however, the outstanding element in this comparison is twofold. Firstly, the unsolicited nature of the revelations, neither the "prophet" nor the addressee deliberately seeking them, and secondly, the sense of mission borne by the medium. We can now regard this sort of divine revelation as another facet of the pantographic relationship between Mari and early Israel—the parallelism between their ethnically and socially analogous population groups.

Treasure house that it is, Mari cannot for the present serve as anything more than indirect or circumstantial evidence for Israel's protohistory. Mari is not the Patriarchs, but it is of their world and it is closer to them than any other extra-biblical source.

3

PRE-MONARCHICAL SOCIAL INSTITUTIONS
IN ISRAEL IN THE LIGHT OF MARI*

In recent years it has again become fashionable, in some quarters, to discredit the historical reliability of various biblical descriptions of pre-monarchic institutions in Israel. In order to counteract such scepticism we may adduce a number of biblical references to early social and legal practices which point to the existence of legitimate pre-monarchical institutions. Thus, for example, we see evidence of an ancient family law, including inheritance provisions and marriage customs, in other words, a law not royal in authority. We note the recruitment of troops along gentilic lines, from individual settlements, rather than the formation of a national army. In short, it is the life of the family or clan that is dominant here and not the later royal system. An indication of a different sort can be found in the so-called anti-monarchic pericopes within the Bible, several of which no doubt draw their inspiration from pre-monarchical times. Finally—and this will be our major argument—there is the extra-biblical evidence, and in this context the Mari documents are of prime importance.

Old Babylonian Mari apparently shared common origins with the early Israelites as well as with many other West Semitic peoples. Thus, a comparison between early Israel and Mari can and should be made. Indeed, the broad spectrum of the Mari archives—the largest extra-biblical body of material within the West Semitic milieu— actually invites such a comparison.[1] Furthermore, this comparative study reveals an aggregate of similarities which thus cannot simply be regarded as a result of common patterns of human behaviour.

First and foremost in such a comparison is the linguistic factor,

---

* This article was originally published in: *SVT 40*, 1988, 165–176.

[1] On the comparative approach, including similarities as well as contrasts, see my brief remarks in "Mari and Early Israel," *Biblical Archaeology Today. Proceedings of the International Congress on Biblical Archaeology* (Jerusalem, 1985), pp. 235–43; (here chap. 2). On the method in general see I.J. Gelb, "Comparative Method in the Study of the Society and Economy of the Ancient Near East," *Rocznik Orientalistyczny* 41 (1980), pp. 24–36.

that is, the lexical items which are parallel in the corpora of both Mari and the Bible. Significantly, a perusal of such West Semitic terminology has its major impact on the societal level and reflects, in one way or another, a thoroughly tribalistic milieu, mainly of non-urban population. This is so in Mari as well as in early Israel, and it is only through sources associated with these two entities—in all documentary evidence of the ancient Near East until Islamic times— that tribal society is manifested in full bloom.

The terminology is unique to the Akkadian of Mari and to Hebrew, although occasionally it is found in other West Semitic languages as well (in particular, Ugaritic, Aramaic and Arabic), but there are no true cognates in standard Akkadian. At Mari the referents are entirely foreign to the Assyro-Babylonian milieu. The Mari documents contain a set of West Semitic terms denoting tribal units, forms of tribal settlements and tribal leadership, in short: tribal institutions and customs. A comparative study of these terms with their Hebrew cognates not only sheds light on the meaning of individual words but also serves to illuminate the underlying structures and institutions of the societies involved. We employ the concept of institution in a broad sense encompassing *inter alia* various life-styles. Let us first enumerate the Mari-Bible equivalents in the various social realms: tribal units—*gāʾum/gāyum/hibrum/ummatum*—Hebrew *gōy, ḥeber, ʾummāh*; forms of settlement—*nawûm/haṣārum*—*nāweh, ḥāṣēr*; and finally the institution of patrimony—*nihlatum*—Hebrew *naḥᵃlāh*. We shall not deal here with terms for tribal leadership—*šāpiṭum/merhûm*—*šōpēṭ, mērēaʿ*—since they have been the subject of several recent satisfactory discussions.[2]

gāyum/gāʾum—gōy[3]

We shall commence our discussion with the term for the tribal unit *gāyum*, Hebrew *gōy*, which was relatively small in scope. In Mari we witness the occurrence of personal names composed of *gāyum* as well,

[2] See J. Safren, "New Evidence for the Title of the Provincial Governor," *HUCA* 50 (1979), pp. 1–15; idem, "*merhûm* and *merhûtum* in Mari," *Orientalia*, N.S. 51 (1982), pp. 1–29.

[3] See my previous treatments of *gāyum/gōy* in *JAOS* 82 (1962), pp. 143–4, n. 3; 15ᶜ *Rencontre Assyriologique Internationale, Comptes rendus* (Liège, 1967), pp. 133ff.; most recently cf. Ph. Talon in J.M. Durand and J.-R. Kupper (ed.), *Miscellanea Babylonica*

in particular *Bahlu-gāyim* (the leader of a clan notably named Amurru; see below). In addition to Mari, *gāyum* is now also confirmed by a single occurrence in the contemporary texts of Tell Rimah (ancient Karana).[4] It must be determined whether this term, as well as *ḥibrum* and *ummatum*, should be treated as an ethnic gentilic concept or simply as designating a group of individuals not related by blood ties. Perhaps it may even be taken in a territorial sense. All these interpretations are reflected in the various translations advanced by the editors of the Mari texts, while the *CAD* defines *gāyum* in a noncommittal manner as "gang or group (of workmen)." The difficulty in determining the exact meaning of *gāyum* and similar sociological terms at Mari is due to the fluctuations of tribal structure and the loosening of kinship ties in the process of transition towards a sedentary way of life.

The definition of *gāyum* is further complicated by the fact that the tribes, as a result of continuous raids by the kings of Mari, were exposed to the practices of the royal administration. Hence, this expression is already used in the context of territorial and administrative organization. This additional shade of meaning takes its place alongside the original ethnic value, thereby becoming an ethno-geographic but by no means a purely geographic or administrative concept, for the pattern of settlement was, as a rule, the outgrowth of the common wanderings. Thus, the ethnic gentilic connotation as a sort of "clan" is applicable to all the references of the word *gāyum* in the Mari texts, as well as to the term *gōy* in some early biblical sources. Interestingly enough, the *gāyum* thus far occurs only with reference to the federation of the Haneans. There is a lengthy economic list of 258 Hanean recipients of quantities of oil. These are divided into 13 groups, 9 of which carry the designation *gāyum* and the clan name.[5] One *gāyum* is of particular interest since it is called Amurrum and indeed almost all the 35 individual members bear Amorite names, which points to the ethnic homogeneity of the clan. A further occurrence of a *gāyum Amurru* appears in a recently pub-

---

(*Mélanges M. Birot*) (Paris, 1985), pp. 277–84; and G.J. Botterweck, R.E. Clements, *ThWAT* 1 (1973), cols 965–73 (s.v. *gōy*).

[4] See S. Dalley et alii, *The Old Babylonian Tablets from Tell al Rimah* (Hertford, 1976), pp. 220–1 (no. 305:18).

[5] See M. Birot, "Trois textes économiques de Mari," *Revue d'Assyriologie* 47 (1953), pp. 121–30, 161–74; 49 (1955), pp. 15–31.

lished document (*ARM* XXIV 235:8). The term *gāyum* never occurs in connection with the Yaminites. Could the reason lie, as some scholars seem to think, in the different character of the two tribes— the Haneans being more sedentary and already "clannish" while the still nomadic Yaminites lack a mature tribal structure reflecting a distinct clan system?[6]

Like *ummatum* in Mari and *ʿamm* in Hebrew, *gāyum* acquired a military sense (*ARM* VI 28:7–9), since in the earliest stages armies were organized along gentilic lines, both in Old Babylonian times and in ancient Israel. Furthermore, the Hebrew term *gōy* shares a common evolution with *ʾummāh, ḥeber* and *ʿamm*—whereas the primary meanings seem to be identical with the Mari cognates. In time, the four Hebrew terms came to encompass entire peoples or nations. Contrary to their original narrow gentilic sense, they ultimately expanded their scope—that is, they underwent an "anaemic" process so to speak, namely, a loosening of blood ties in the kinship system.

hibrum—ḥeber *and* ummatum—ʾummāh

Recent texts from Mari add little to our previous studies on the tribal units *hibrum*[7] and *ummatum*,[8] and so we shall not deal with them here.

nawûm—nāweh[9]

Now we shall proceed to forms of settlement, focusing on a specific mode of life, best illustrated in the Mari documents by the concept

---

[6] Cf. M.B. Rowton, "Dimorphic Structure and the Parasocial Element," *JNES* 36 (1977), p. 189.

[7] For my previous treatment see *JAOS* 82 (1962), pp. 144ff. See also S. Arbeli in H. Heltzer, *The Suteans* (Naples, 1981), pp. 101–4, who adopts my hypothesis concerning Heber the Kenite as symbolizing a tribal unit (albeit without acknowledgement).

[8] See "*Ummatum* in Old Babylonian Texts and its Ugaritic and Biblical Counterparts," *UF* 11 (1979), pp. 527–36.

[9] My preliminary treatments are *JAOS* 82 (1962), p. 146; 15ᵉ *Renc. Ass. Int.*, pp. 135ff. For further studies on *nāweh/nawûm* see: P. Artzi, *Enc. Bibl.* 5 (1968), cols 71–2; *idem*, in *Ezekiel Enc. World of the Bible* (Revivim Publishing House, 1984), pp.

nawûm. In standard Akkadian, this word means "desert, steppe, uncultivated field," as well as "ruin," and even "savage"; but in its specialized West Semitic usage it denotes semi-fertile pasturage and, by
association, an encampment there. Such a meaning can be seen both
in Mari and in the biblical cognate *nāweh.* It is this latter collective
meaning that yields the concept of a migratory group or, similarly,
transhumance.[10] We present here a possible additional meaning,
namely "frontier country."[11]

The term *nawûm/nāweh*, in Mari encompasses the various biblical
expressions: tent, shepherds (*rō'īm*), livestock (*n°wēh ṣō'n*) and pasturage
(*n°'ōt deše'* and *n°wēh midbār*—the latter does not mean "oasis," as
often rendered, but rather "grazing lands").[12] In short, this term portrays the pastoralist way of life, embracing man, animals and camp-
ing area. The *mawûm* was the very antithesis of the city or village,
the close interaction of which formed the dimorphic structure of the
tribal society at Mari, dwelling partly in urban centres and partly in
the hinterland of the encampments.

In Mari the term appears freaquently in connection with the tribal
organization of the Haneans and the Yaminites; and there is one
mention of a *mawûm* of the Simalites (DUMU.MEŠ-*sim'al*, the
Northerners, in contrast to the DUMU.MEŠ-*yamina*, the Southerners;
ARM II 33:21). In turn we also find the expression *Hana ša nawêm*,
the Haneans of the pasturage or frontier (*ARM* I 6:26–8; 42:5–7),
the as yet nomadic segments of this tribal organization, which was
already predominantly settled. On one occasion 2000 men of this
particular non-sedentary group were to be recruited for a military
expedition (*ARM* I 42:5–11), since the *nawûms* generally served as a

---

176–7 (both Hebrew); H. Ringgren, *ThWAT* 5, fasc. 3/4 (1985), cols 293–7; V.H.
Matthews, *Pastoral Nomadism in the Mari Kingdom* (Cambridge, Mass., 1978), pp. 59–63;
M. Anbar, *Les tribus amorites de Mari* (Freiburg, 1991).

[10] For the various meanings of *nawûm* see previous note and *CAD* N, pp. 241ff.
(s.v. *namû* A); F.R. Kraus, *RA* 70 (1976), pp. 172ff. ("Sommerung, Sommerweidegebiet").

[11] As elaborated by L. Thompson and H. Lamar, *The Frontier in History* (New
Haven, Conn., 1981); see foreword "Comparative Frontier History," pp. 3–13. Cf.
M.L. Chaney in D.N. Freedman and D.F. Graf (ed.), *Palestine in Transition* (Sheffield,
1983), pp. 48ff.

[12] Whereas *midbār* in the Bible often denotes "desert," in certain contexts it cannot but mean "grazing area," such as *midbār* of Gibeon; *midbār* of Dothan; *midbār*
of Beer-Sheba; *midbār* of Tekoa; *midbār* of Ziph; *midbār* of Maon; *midbār* of Jeruel;
midbār of En-Gedi; *midbār* of Kadesh, and finally *midbār* of Judah itself, all of them
pastures adjacent to a village or district.

major source of recruits.[13] We also hear several times that the Suteans, and Yaminites in particular, attacked *nawûm*s of other tribes. On the other hand, a *nawûm* of the Yaminites at Hen (*Hi-en*) was seized by king Yahdunlim, as attested in one of his year formulas.[14] An interesting possibility arises if we consider that the word "Hen" (usually interpreted as Hana; cf. *ARM* XVI/1, p. 15) is not originally a toponym but rather corresponds to the West Semitic term *'ayin*— "spring, water source," perhaps Ras el-Ayin, on one of the tributaries of the Habur.

In the Bible, *nāweh* (like other terms with Mari parallels) appears, as a rule, in exalted, poetic or archaic language. Accordingly, this word is not found in the prosaic portions of the Bible, and is absent most conspicuously from the Patriarchal narratives, although it would best portray the Patriarchs' mode of life.[15] It is found, however, in such passages as Ps. lxxix 7 and Jer. x 25 (cf. Lam. ii 2), in retrospective use, as in the expression *n^ewēh ya^{ca}qōb*, "the habitation of Jacob." Such exalted usage is also found in connection with David, whom God took "from the pasture, from following the sheep" or, we may suggest, the "frontier" (*min-hannāweh*; 2 Sam. vii 8).

At Mari the *nawûm* was an economic, sociological, political and also a para-military factor. Such mobile units of the tribal society were occasionally the concern of official policy, for Mariote flocks, even royal flocks, were entrusted to the *mawûms* for pasturage. Note such expressions as: *nawûm ša abia* ("*nawûm* of my father," *ARM* II 45:10), *nawûm ša bēlia* ("*nawûm* of my lord") and *nawûm ša halṣim* ("*nawûm* of the district").

Occasionally a *nawûm* is mentioned as being attached to a city, as is implied in such phrases as "the *nawûm* of Carchemish" (in a Mari document), "*nawûm* of Larsa," Sippar and its *nawûm* (*Sippar u nawēšu*), and even "the *nawûm* of Babylon" (in Old Babylonian texts apart from Mari). This is reminiscent of the depictions of the Patriarchs

---

[13] See M.B. Rowton, "Dimorphic Structure and the Tribal Elite," *Studi Istituti Anthropos* 28 (1976), p. 243. D. Charpin and J.M. Durand, *Mari: Archives de Recherches Interdisciplinaires* 4 (1985), p. 307, n. 70, now also dissociate this word from Hana but still conceive of it as a true toponym.

[14] See G. Dossin, *Studia Mariana* (Leiden, 1950), p. 52, year formula 6; and cf. H. Klengel, *Zwischen Zelt und Palast* (Leipzig, 1972), p. 55.

[15] See V. Worschech, *Abraham* (Frankfurt, 1983), pp. 50ff., who analyses Abraham's life-style according to the book of Genesis. Cf. N.K. Gottwald, *The Tribes of Yahweh* (Maryknoll, New York, 1979, and London, 1980), pp. 451ff.

as dwelling on the outskirts of Canaanite towns. According to biblical tradition, the encampments of the Patriarchs were alongside
Canaanite cites such as Shechem and Bethel (Gen. xii 6, 8), Hebron
(Gen. xii 18) and Beer-Sheba (Gen. xxvi 25). This conforms well to
the archaelogical picture in Palestine during the Middle Bronze Age
II, conjuring up a dimorphic society and involving "enclosed"
nomadism.[16] Most significant in this respect are the many open settlements, satellite villages—often small and short-lived—which archaeologists have found adjacent to Middle Bronze Age cities. One good
illustration is the Middle Bronze Age II B open settlement at Givat-
Sharet, 1.5 km. from ancient Beth-Shemesh.[17] A later example, alluded
to in the Saul-David narrative, is revealed in the obscure biblical
expression *nwyt* (*K'tib; Q're: nāyōt*), referred to several times in 1 Sam.
xix 18–xx 1 as the dwelling place of a band of prophets. This is
surely not a toponym or a locality in or near Ramah of Benjamin
(as is generally held) but rather the common name *nāweh*, pl. *nā'ōt*:
to put it in Mari terms, *Ramah u nawēšu*.[18]

On the other hand, the relationship between a village base and
an outlying *nawûm*, as seen in a Mari text (*ARM* II 48:8ff.), is reflected
in the biblical narrative of Jacob's sons. They ranged from their base
encampment near Hebron "in the valley of the city" to distant pasturages, as far away as Shechem, and even near Dothan (Gen. xxxvii
12ff.). Here, too, we see a grazing pattern, as at Mari, which evolved
during the spring and summer seasons. This may be inferred from
the biblical reference to the "pit" in the midst of the pasture land
of Dothan (here called the *midbār* of Dothan), into which Joseph was
cast, containing no water; that is to say, it had dried up (Gen. xxxvii
12ff.). In Job we find a similar illustration of what was surely the
typical institution of *nawûm/nāweh*, although as in Genesis the actual
term does not appear in the prose framework. Job himself dwelt at
a base encampment, while his sons ranged over the pasturage with
their oxen, asses, sheep and camels—the same basic pictures as with
Jacob and his sons. In the book of Job (i 14–19), the outlying camp

---

[16] For this concept see Rowton (nn. 6 and 13 and further bibliographical references there).

[17] The site was excavated by C. Epstein and D. Bahat in 1971–2; see preliminary remarks by Bahat, *BAR* 4 (1978), pp. 8ff.

[18] Cf. A. Malamat, *JAOS* 82 (1962), p. 146b; see now P.K. McCarter, *I Samuel*
(Garden City, New York, 1980), p. 328.

is devastated by man and by nature ("God"); the flocks are plundered and stricken, and the servants are killed.

Both in the Bible and at Mari we see that the transient nature of the *nawûm* exposed it to marauders, as was true of the frontier country. At Mari the aggressive, nomadic Suteans preyed upon the "*nawûm* in the land of Qatna" in Middle Syria (*ARM* V 23), and on the *nawûm* of the Yaminites.[19]

In a poetic passage in the body of the book of Job there is an actual usage of the term *nāweh* with reference to a surprise raid (v 3). This is in marked contrast to the reference concerning the security of the divinely-protected fold (*nāweh*) in Job v 24: "You shall know that your tent is safe, and you shall inspect your fold (*nāwᵉkā*) and miss nothing" (*RSV*). The last phrase (*wᵉlōʾ teḥeṭāʾ*), better translated "and shall not be amiss,"[20] finds its idiomatic parallel at Mari, although antithetically (*ARM* III 15:15ff.). When the *nawûm* of the Haneans grazed on the eastern bank of the Euphrates, hostile elements could surprise it and cause "damage" (*ḥiṭṭum*, literally "damage, failing")—cognate with the very Hebrew word *teḥᵉṭāʾ* used above. This is in contrast to the biblical passage where God protects the *nāweh*. The protected encampment may have been referred to as *nᵉwēh ʾētān* (Jer. xlix 19, l 44), i.e. a strong and secure *nāweh*.

An interesting series of values emerges from the study of the word *nawûm/nāweh*, in its Mesopotamian-Syrian-Palestinian context. The attitude toward the *nawûm* in the standard, urban-oriented Assyro-Babylonian culture was negative, regarding it as disruptive to civilization. The Bible, too, refers several times to the *nāweh* as counter-productive, where fertile lands have been devastated, but this negative attitude concerns mainly the *nāweh* of foreign peoples (cf. Isa. xxxiv 13, xxxv 7, xxvii 11; Ezek. xxv 5; Zeph. ii 6, etc.). In general, both the Bible and Mari are positive in their approach to the *mawûm/nāweh*. At Mari, at the confluence of Mesopotamian and West Semitic cultures, the general attitude is practical and sympathetic, taking the *nawûm* as a fact of life. In the Bible we see a sort

---

[19] See G. Dossin, "Bejaminites dans les textes de Mari," *Mélanges Dussaud* II (Paris, 1939), p. 987.

[20] F. Horst, *Hiob* 1² (Neukirchen-Vluyn, 1969), p. 88, points out that *ḥṭʾ* is employed here in an archaic usage, meaning "vermissen"; similarly M.H. Pope, *Job* (Garden City, New York, 1973), p. 46, emphasizes the sense "to miss" rather than the common meaning "to sin."

of internal self-view of the *nāweh*, fully identified with it and its way of life. Perhaps the most idyllic picture of the biblical *nāweh* is found in Ezek. xxxiv 14: "I will feed them on a good pasture (*b^enāweh ṭōb*) and upon the high mountains shall their fold be (*n^ewēhem*); there shall they be in a good fold (*mir^eeh*) and in a fat pasture shall they feed upon the mountain of Israel."[21]

The concept *nāweh* in the Bible is value-laden, and led to such idioms as "a peaceful habitation" (Isa. xxxii 18), "a quiet habitation" (Isa. xxxiii 20), "habitation of righteousness" (Jer. xxxi 23), and "holy abode" (Exod. xv 14). Among the Israelites, the *nāweh* even assumed a theological dimension, as is clearly seen in the best known of all Psalms—Ps. xxiii 1: "The Lord is my shepherd, I shall not want; he makes me lie down in green *nāwehs*—green pastures" (and cf. *n^eʾōt ʾ^elōhīm* in Ps. lxxxiii 13).

Patrimony as a Tribal Institution[22]

A basic facet of West Semitic social institutions—as revealed at Mari and, especially, in the Bible—is reflected in the practice of land transfer not by means of formal sale but exclusively through inheritance. The relevant terminology is identical in both the Mari idiom and Hebrew: the Mari verb *nahālum*, Hebrew *nḥl*, "apportion, assign, inherit," and the nominal derivative *nihlatum*/*naḥ^alāh*, designating the hereditary share, inheritance portion or, simply, the patrimony. These expressions are unknown in other Mesopotamian contexts, but occur in the West Semitic languages. In the Akkadian texts of Ugarit the noun *nahālum* is attested once, but the root appears commonly in the alphabetic texts there (*nḥl*, "heir," *nḥlt*, "inheritance").

At Mari in the context of an actual land transfer, not an inheritance, the purchaser still received the property in the guise of a hereditary portion; that is, the transfer was effected by fictitious

---

[21] On this passage see now B. Willmes, *Die sogennante Hirtenallegorie Ez. 34* (Frankfurt, 1984), passim. The *nawûs* of *hārē m^erōm-yiśrāʾēl* "high mountains of Israel" may actually refer to pasturages on lofty terraced fields; cf. in different contexts L. Stager, *BASOR* 260 (1985), pp. 5ff.

[22] Cf. A. Malamat, *JAOS* 82 (1962), pp. 147ff.; and now E. Lipiński, *ThWAT* 5, 3/4 (1985), cols. 341–60, s.v. *naḥ^alāh*. Recently, however, B. Batto contests the supposed meaning of patrimony at Mari, and suggests the original sense of a royal land grant, *Journal of the Economic and Social History of the Orient* 23 (1980), pp. 225ff.

means. Thus, in one document (*ARM* VIII 11) Yarim-Addu (a palace official) received (*inhil*) a large field from the Awin clan of the Rabbean tribe, and to do so he had to be introduced into the circle of co-heirs within the extended family or clan. He is symbolically adopted as a "brother" of the thirteen sons of Awin. In another document (*ARM* VIII 12), the transfer of land to the same Yarim-Addu is effected without payment, but in two further transactions (*ARM* VIII 13, 14) payment *per se* is made. The remarkable feature here is that even the remuneration is referred to by the verb *nahālum*, and thus was considered a sort of inherited property. Furthermore, this payment was made *ina ṭūbi libbim*, "of his own free will"—a legal formula known from much later times (Neo-Assyrian and Elephantine documents). Hence, such transactions were effected under the guise of reciprocal inheritance, a kind of mutual sharing of patrimonies. These instances are drawn from the corpus of legal documents from Mari (*ARM* VIII). There are further instances at Mari of the actual inheritance procedure, as in the case of a daughter of Zimri-Lim, who complained that her royal parents did not hand over to her (*inhilunini*) a field and a garden; that is, she was provided with no patrimony (*ARM* X 90; 3ff.; and cf. also *ARM* I 91:6').

Significantly, the transfer procedure for hereditary portions is always described by the verb *nahālum* in the *qal* or base stem, although it has also been argued that *inhil*, in the *qal* stem, may have been contracted from a West Semitic causative form **yanhil*.[23] Admittedly, in Hebrew in such transitive contexts, the causative *hiphʿîl* is generally applied, though the *piʿēl* or event the *qal* is occasionally found. The Mari usage of the base stem now shows that there is no justification for emending the *qal* forms of *nhl* in the Bible (Num. xxiv 17, 18; Josh. xix 49) into the *piʿēl*, as has been done when the meaning is certainly transitive.

In Israel the apportioning of land was originally effected by casting lots (*gōrāl*), as is reflected in the biblical description of the allotting of the tribal domains (Josh. xiii 6, xiv 1–2, xviii 10; and see Num. xxvi 52–6, xxxiv 13, xxxvi 2; as well as the idealized picture in Ezek. xlvi 1, xlvii 22, etc.). In any case, these traditions (ascribed

---

[23] Cf. Lipiński, p. 346. See now also the verbal form Gt *ittahlu* for the transfer of property (*ARM* XXV 96: tr. 1). It consists of silver (the royal tax)—a similar use of *nahūlum* to that in *ARM* VIII 13, 14 (see above).

mainly to the late source P) reflect actual, early procedures for distribution of land (cf. esp. Micah ii 5).

Like *naḥªlāh* in Hebrew, the verb at Mari yields a substantive, *ni/ehlatum*, in the sense of hereditary portion, patrimony, but also property or estate *per se*. Thus, in *ARM* I 91:6' the phrase *nihlatam inahhil* should be translated "he will inherit a patrimony." One of the prophetic documents (A 1121, recently joined with A 2731)[24] is illuminating in this respect: *āpilū*-diviners, speaking on behalf of the god Adad of Kallassu (at or near Aleppo), demand from Zimri-Lim a *nihlatum* (1. 15), perhaps best translated here as property, estate.[25] The cultic personnel or temple functionaries seem to have sought control over a specific piece of land (at Alahtum, 1.27, presumably in the border region between Mari and Yamhad). The diviners remind Zimri-Lim that it was Adad who made him king over Mari, and they threaten that, should he not adhere to the god's demand, the god would deprive him of all his possessions. However should Zimri-Lim provide the *nihlatum*, Adad would give him "throne upon throne, palace upon palace, territory upon territory, city upon city" (II. 19–21).

The relationship here is in decided contrast to that of the biblical concept, where it is Yahwe who promises an inheritance to the Patriarchs (Exod. xxxii 13; Ps. cv 8–11; Ezek. xlvii 14; 1 Chron. xvi 15–18) and, later, to the Israelite king (Ps. ii 8, lxxxix 28—where the inheritance comprises the nations of the world and their rulers). Indeed, the land of Canaan (and by metaphor also the people of Israel) is designated by the appellative *naḥªlat yahwe* or *naḥªlat ʾelōhīm* (Deut. iv 20, ix 26, 29; 1 Kgs. viii 51, 53), a theological imagery;[26] and, in contrast, by the more realistic *naḥªlat yiśrāʾēl* (Judg. xx 6) and *naḥªlat yaʿªqōb* (Isa. lviii 14). In the Bible there is at least one distinct occurrence, however, where *naḥªlat yahwe* is confined to a specific domain, just as at Mari: the city of Abel-Beth-Maacah in Upper Galilee is designated *naḥªlat yahwe* (2 Sam. x 19), presumable because of its conquest by David's army and its subsequent incorporation

---

[24] Cf. B. Lafont, *RA* 78 (1984), pp. 7–14.

[25] A. Malamat, "A Mari Prophecy and Nathan's Dynastic Oracle," J.A. Emerton (ed.), *Prophecy. Essays . . . G. Fohrer* (Berlin-New York, 1980), pp. 68–82. A. Malamat, Mari and the Bible, Leiden 1998, chap. 9.

[26] Cf. H.D. Forshey, "The Construct Chain *naḥªlat YHWH/ʾelōhīm*," *BASOR* 220 (1975), pp. 51–3; and now S.E. Loewenstamm, "*nḥlt yhwh*," in S. Japhet (ed.), *Studies in Bible 1986, Scripta Hierosolymitana* 31 (Jerusalem, 1986), pp. 155–92.

within his realm; that is, within the collective *naḥᵃlāh* of God. Similarly, the Song of the Sea refers to the sanctuary on Mount Zion as *har naḥᵃlāṭᵏā* (Exod. xv 17),[27] which might approximate the *nihlatum* for Adad in the Mari document. Despite the supporting statement in Ps. lxxix 1, the *naḥᵃlāh* in the Song of the Sea perhaps refers to the entire land of Canaan, or at least to the western hill-country. This very same motif, of a god possessing his *naḥᵃlāh* on a mountain, appears at Ugarit in the Baal Myth, in the expression *ġr nḥlty*, that is, Baal's patrimony on Mount Zaphon.

In other cases the Mari documents offer an even closer parallel to the biblical concept of the *naḥᵃlāh* (and the Hebrew verb *nḥl*). In both Mari and Israel the patrimony was taken to be an essentially inalienable piece of land, possessed solely by a gentilic unit. Its transfer could thus be effected, as stated above, only within an inheritance framework. This mechanism perpetuated the stability of the patriarchal-tribal organization over the generations. At Mari we see several means devised to evade this restriction (see above), but such evasions are actually significant indicators of the very rule. In the Bible there are strict rules against the transfer of a *naḥᵃlāh* from one clan to another. These, whether explicit or implied, are found in legal passages, narrative and poetry alike. The most explicit expression of the prevention of a patrimony from passing to another tribe can be seen in the case of the daughters of Zelophehad, and in the laws specifically appended to the episode: "The inheritance portion (*naḥᵃlāh*) of the people of Israel shall not be transferred from one tribe to another, for every one of the people of Israel shall cleave to the inheritance portion of the tribe of his fathers" (Num. xxxvi 7; and cf. Num. xxvii 1–11; Josh. xi 3–6). This case refers to a situation where there are only daughters to inherit the patrimony. There are only two exceptions to this rule in the biblical narratives: (1) Rachel and Leah complain "Is there any portion or inheritance (*ḥēleq wᵉnaḥᵃlāh*) left to us in our father's house?" (Gen. xxxi 14), although they have brothers; and (2) the three daughters of Job inherit a *naḥᵃlāh*, alongside their seven brothers (Job xlii 13–15).[28]

---

[27] For reference to a sanctuary on Mt Zion see, e.g. J. Jeremias, in *Probleme biblischer Theologie. G. von Rad zum 70. Geburtstag* (München, 1971), p. 196; Loewenstamm, pp. 166–7.

[28] Lipiński, p. 348.

Further, in the legal corpus proper of the Bible, there is provision for the redemption of all inheritance portions to their original owners in the Jubilee year, terminating all "long-term leases" (Lev. xxv 13, 25–8). This is also found in the inheritance of the future ruler of Israel, in Ezekiel's vision. Whereas the land which he leaves to his sons remains in their permanent possession, "if he makes a gift out of his hereditary portion (*naḥ*ᵃ*lātō*) to one of his servants, it shall be his to the year of liberty (*yōbēl*, jubilee); then it shall revert to the ruler (*nāśîʾ*)" (Ezek. xlvi 17). The tenacity with which individual Israelites actually clung to their ancestral plots, still in monarchic times, is amply demonstrated by the incident of Naboth's vineyard, which was part of his *naḥ*ᵃ*lat ʾābōt* ("the patrimony of his forefathers"; cf. 1 Kgs. xxi).[29]

In the final analysis, the entire concept of the institution of patrimony was a product of the semi-nomadic environment of Mari and of the patriarchal-tribal structure of the Israelites. In the urban society of Mesopotamia, organized on an entirely different pattern, such an institution was hardly able to gain a foothold. There, greater importance was attached to freedom of the individual, especially in the realm of real estate, and a liberal policy evolved regarding purchase and sale of lands, modes diametrically opposed to the ideals implicit in the biblical institution of the patrimony.

---

[29] On Naboth's ancestral patrimony see, e.g., R. Bohlen, *Der Fall Nabot* (Trier, 1980), pp. 320–50.

4

TRIBAL SOCIETIES: BIBLICAL GENEALOGIES
AND AFRICAN LINEAGE SYSTEMS*

Let me start with a personal note, by stating that my training and profession are in the field of the Hebrew Bible, particularly Biblical history and that I am far less at home in African studies. I have, however, made an effort to familiarise myself with numerous studies on various African societies, such as the Nuer of southern Sudan, the Tallensi in Ghana, the Luapula of Northern Rhodesia and the Tiv in Nigeria. Having paid attention to the tribal structure of these and other societies, and specifically their lineage systems, I have become cognizant of the utter relevance and keen insights which may be gleaned from a comparative study of such with the tribal society of ancient Israel and the Biblical genealogical patterns; this in spite of the different historical and sociological contexts, and first and foremost the fact that the African societies were of an entirely illiterate nature, in contrast to ancient Israel. In view of Israel's literacy—since the founding of the Hebrew monarchy around 1000 B.C., or even earlier, in the period of the Judges—I cannot accept the dictum of many anthropologists, such as Mrs Bohannan, who states that "a lineage system can survive only in an illiterate society like the Tiv of northern Nigeria, or possibly in one which avoids committing its constitution to paper."[1] However, I think that Israelite society, where only initially were the genealogies no doubt passed on orally, is a case in decided contrast to this dictum.

I shall now present some of the basic principles and mechanisms of Biblical genealogies with only casual remarks on African analogies. For a conclusive study of the highly intriguing subject must be left to a combined effort with modern social anthropology, true cooperation between the Bible scholar and the Africanologist.

To begin with, I would like to stress the fact that Biblical genealogies represent a unique historiographical genre within the literature

---

* This article was originally published in: *Archives Europ. Sociologie*, XIV (1973), 147–158.
[1] Laura Bohannan, A Genealogical Charter, *Africa*, XXII (1952), p. 314.

of the entire ancient Near East. I have here in mind not the so-called vertical lines of individuals such as the royal or priestly pedigrees, which are common anywhere, but rather the ethnographical tables contained in the Book of Genesis, say, of the Hebrews, Nahorites, Ishmaelites or Edomites; even more so, I would like to refer to the ramified and wide-spread genealogies of the various Israelite tribes, assembled in the first nine chapters of I Chronicles. All these have no equal anywhere else in the ancient Near East, at latest not in the extant sources. Only at the start of the Islamic period, a millennium later than the compilation of the latest of the Biblical genealogies, did Arab chronographers create such broad genealogical tables, embracing more than 6,000 Arabian tribes, divided into northern and southern branches. The selfsame phenomenon, but preserved only in oral tradition, is found in present-day tribal societies, first and foremost in Africa, but also elsewhere.

It is superfluous entering here in detail into the *raison d'être* of the genealogies. Like the African lineages, the Biblical genealogical lists served to determine the rights and duties of the individual, and were of impact on social and political, economic and religious planes. It will suffice to mention their role in inheritance and marriage laws, as well as in incest taboos, in taxation and land distribution, in census taking and military conscription, and in the institution of blood vengeance. A further use of the genealogical lists in ancient Israel can, I think, be found in ancestor worship, as is common in African societies.[2]

We shall concentrate here merely on the structural and schematic aspects of the Biblical genealogies, as well as on the inherent symbolism or message they were meant to convey.

As already hinted at, the uniqueness of Biblical genealogies in ancient time lies in the fact that they are not based solely on vertical constructions, but spread out over a horizontal plane. A good example is the twelve sons or tribes stemming from Jacob. Only such a two-dimensional pattern can form a true family tree. Thus, it reveals what could be called a genealogical panorama, whether of small tribal units or of an entire tribe or people, or even encompassing the population of the world as a whole, as in the famous

---

[2] Cf. A. Malamat, King Lists of the Old Babylonian Period and Biblical Genealogies, *Journal of the American Oriental Society*, LXXXVIII (1968), p. 173 n. 29.

Table of Nations in *Genesis* X—that is, the descendants of Ham, Shem and Japheth the sons of Noah.

In such a ramified network, the Bible frequently accommodates female elements, as well: wives or concubines, mothers and daughters. But such elements figure there solely on the horizontal plane; they have no place in the strictly vertical lineages of a society based on agnatic descent—that is, descent traceable exclusively through males, and which was typical of Israelite society. In anthropological terms, the Israelite kinship system may be defined as *unilineal* and of a distinct *patrilineal* type (the so-called 'Omaha' kinship model), like the Nuer in Sudan or the Tiv in Nigeria—and in contrast to the Tallensi and other matrilineal tribes, well-known throughout Africa. There are hardly any vestiges of matrilineages in the Bible, though some scholars hold otherwise.

Vertical, one-dimensional patterns record only "genealogical depth" and the sequence of generations. Table 2 shows the Babylonian and Assyrian king lists (in the left-hand columns) and the royal lines of Saul and David (on the right). The two-dimensional scheme, in contrast, forms points of segmentation, that is, it encompasses what the anthropologist calls nodal points, and which I prefer to designate as nodal eponyms. From each nodal point stem several descendants who, in turn can act as founding ancestors of peoples, tribes, clans and so forth. This is well-illustrated on Tables 1 and 3.

Table 1 shows that Terah, the last in the immediate line of Shem, serves as an eponym for the lineage of Abraham, Nahor and Haran. Biblical Hebrew uses here the formula *toledot* (*we-elle toledot Terah*, like *toledot* Shem or *toledot* Noah), which should be translated as 'line' or 'lineage'. These three sons again figure as eponyms of entire tribal organizations or peoples. For instance, Nahor, the brother of Abraham, is the founding father of a highly interesting genealogy (see *Genesis* XXII, 20–24). This genealogy embraces twelve sons, like the Israelite and Ishmaelite systems, consisting of two descent groups—eight sons by his wife Milcah, and four sons by his concubine Reumah. The twofold division here is seemingly geographical: the wife's descendants represent tribal and geographical entities in the Patriarchs' ancestral homeland in Mesopotamia, whereas the sons of the concubine represent place-names in northern Canaan. Nahor's genealogy is quite similar to the Israelite model where Jacob (alias Israel) is the founding ancestor of twelve sons (or tribes) who are born of two wives, Leah and Rachel, or their respective handmaidens, Zilpah

Table 1

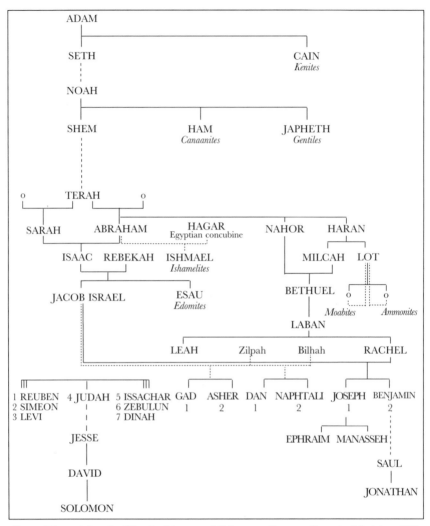

From Edmund Leach, The Legitimacy of Solomon, *European Journal of Sociology*, VII (1966), p. 75, Fig. 1.

Skeleton Genealogy

Notes: (i) Sarah, Abraham's half-sister has the status of wife. Hagar the Egyptian is bond-servant to Sarah and concubine to Abraham.

(ii) Leah and Rachel are full sisters and kin to Jacob through both parents. Zilpah is bond-servant to Leah; Bilhah is bond-servant to Rachel.

(iii) Benjamin is the youngest child of Jacob-Israel. Rachel dies at his birth. He is the only one of the children to be born within the confines of the territory later allocated to his descendants. The name Benjamin means "son of the right hand."

(iv) Esau and Jacob are twins. Esau is the elder but he sells his birth-right to Jacob. In sharp contrast to Jacob, Esau's wives are all Canaanites (*Genesis* XXXVI).

Table 2

Comparative structural table of royal genealogies

	BABYLONIA	ASSYRIA	ISRAEL	
	(Sumuabum)	(Shamshi-Adad)	(David)	(Saul)
Group (a) Genealogical Stock	Ara(m/Ḫarḫar) (I)	Ṭudiya (1)	Shem (1)	
	Madara (2)	Adamu (2)	Arpa//chshad (2)	
	Tu(b)ti(ya) (3)	Yangi (3)	(Kenan) (3)	
	(Y)amuta/Atamu (4)	Sa/i/uḫlamu (4)	Shelah (4)	
	Yamqu (5)	Ḫarḫaru (5)	Eber (5)	
	Suḫ(ḫa)la(m)ma (6)	Mandaru (6)	Peleg (6)	
	Ḫeana (7)	Emṣu (7)	Reu (7)	
	Namz/ṣū (8)	ḪARṣu (8)	Serug (8)	
	Ditānu (9)	Didānu (9)	Nahor (9)	
	Zummabu (10)	Ḫanū (10)	Terah (10)	
	Namḫū (11)	Zu'abu (11)		
		Nuabu (12)		
Group (b) Determinative Line	Amnānu (12)	Abazu (13)	Abraham	
	Yaḫrurum (13)	Bēlū (14)	Isaac	
		Azaraḫ (15)	Jacob	
		Ušpiya (16)		
		Apiašal (17)	Judah ⟋⟍ Benjamin	
Group (c) Table of Ancestors	Ipti-yamūta (14)	Ḫalē (18)	Perez (1)	–
	Buḫazum (15)	Samanu (19)	Hezron (2)	–
	Su-malika (16)	Ḫayanu (20)	Ram (3)	X (a Benjaminite)
	Ašmadu (17)	Ilu-mer (21)	Amminadab (4)	Aphiah
	Abi-yamūta (18)	Yakmesi (22)	Nahshon (5)	Bechorath
	Abi-ditan (19)	Yakmeni (23)	Salma (6)	Zeror
	Ma-am (?) -x-x-x (20)	Yazkur-ēl (24)	Boaz (7)	Abiel
	Su-x-ni (?) -x (21)	Ila-kabkaku (25)	Obed (8)	⟨Ner⟩
	Dad(banaya[?]) (22)	Aminu (26)	Jesse (9)	Kish
	Sumuabum (23)	Shamshi-Adad (27)	David (10)	Saul
Group (d) Historical Line	(Sumula'ēl) (24)	(etc.)	(etc.)	(etc.)
	(Zābium) (25)			
	(Apil-Sīn) (26)			
	(Sīn-muballiṭ) (27)			
	(Ḫammurapi) (28)			
	(etc.)			

From A. Malamat, King Lists of the Old Babylonian Period and Biblical Genealogies, *Journal of the American Oriental Society*, LXXXVIII (1968), p. 172.

Table 3

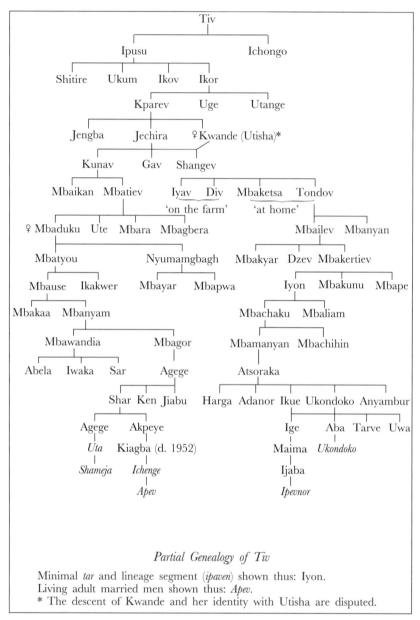

Partial Genealogy of Tiv

Minimal *tar* and lineage segment (*ipaven*) shown thus: Iyon.
Living adult married men shown thus: *Apev*.
* The descent of Kwande and her identity with Utisha are disputed.

Authorized reproduction by permission of the International African Institute, from
L. Bohannan, A Genealogical Charter, *Africa*, XXVI (1952), p. 302, Fig. 1.

and Bilhah (see Table 1). The two major groupings of the so-called "Leah tribes" and "Rachel tribes" can be conceived as sorts of 'moieties' or rather compound or super-moieties—as occur in the organizational pattern of some primitive societies. Each son, in turn, acts as an eponym of one of the twelve tribes of Israel; the tribes encompass broad lineages which are divided (using the terminology of Evans-Pritchard) into maximal, major, minor and minimal lines. Such are clearly found in the tribal genealogies contained in I *Chronicles* II–IX.

Furthermore, these various lineages in time came to correspond with territorial segments designated after them—the tribal and sub-tribal portions of Palestine. This widespread tendency towards tribal splitting or segmentation, as well as its correspondence to territorial entities, finds close parallels in some of the African lineage systems, in particular among the Nuer and the Tiv (see Table 3).

Both in the Bible and in Africa this segmentation, with its wide range of primary and secondary lineages, is the foremost concept in the genealogical positioning of the individual, and in the ascertaining of his kinship relations. To cite one Biblical example, we may refer to the Achan affair in the Book of *Joshua* VII, 17–18: "So Joshua rose early next morning and had Israel come forward by *tribes (shĕvaṭim)*. And the tribe of Judah was indicated. Then he had the *clans (mishpaḥot,* which probably is better translated as 'phratries') of Judah come forward and the clan of Zerah was indicated. Then he had the clan of Zerah come forward by *families* (the Hebrew text reads here *gĕvarim,* 'men', but the intent is surely to *bātē av,* 'households', as can be inferred from the continuation), and Zabdi was indicated. Finally, he had his family (*bayit,* 'household') come forward by individuals (*gĕvarim*) and Achan, the son of Carmi, the son of Zabdi, the son of Zerah, belonging to the tribe of Judah, was indicated." Here we have an illuminating instance of the graduated scheme of tribal division—pinpointing the individual's position within the broad lineal framework.

We shall now turn to some of the possible 'codes' inherent in the schematisation of the Biblical genealogical lists concerning the internal tribal structure, on the one hand, and the inter-tribal relations and groupings (or re-groupings), on the other hand. No doubt, the various schemes project the complex processes involved in the rise and decline of the specific sub-units within the tribal framework—the continual fluctuation of dissolution and eventual unification, the transmigration of one branch to another tribal territory, and the often long-range wanderings from one region to another.

I am unable, here, to penetrate more specifically into the African analogies, but allow me to quote a statement by Evans-Pritchard on the Nuer: "When the brothers [*of certain Nuer lineages*] are spoken about as quarreling, migrating and so forth, it must be understood that the lineages and the local communities of which they form part are being personified and dramatized."[3] Such personifications are equally characteristic of the Biblical genealogies. Not all the intricacies of the Biblical family trees are entirely comprehensible, or can be explained satisfactorily at this stage. However, some key to their interpretation is supplied by the very system adopted by the creators of these lists, who applied ordinary familial concepts and relations, undoubtedly intending to convey a definite symbolism. Thus, I suggest that the actual family (in the narrow sense of the term) was taken as a pattern for formulating the genealogical schemes of the Bible—which therefore can be regarded as large-scale projections of real family relationships.

Hence, it has been suggested, wherever in these lists marriage ties are indicated—that is, where *A* takes *B* to wife—this in fact should be taken to imply the linkage or merger of two tribal units. When a clan or household is presented within the lineage as the eldest son (*bechor* in Hebrew), what was intended is that this unit was considered the oldest or most powerful body within the tribal segment. Daughters, on the other hand, generally represent either clans or, rather, settlements—dependent on and subject to the principal tribal group or urban center: hence, the Biblical expression *'ir u-benoteyha*, "the city and the daughters thereof," that is, its dependent villages.

The merging of a tribe, settling in a new area, with an earlier or indigenous population may be formulated as the marriage of the tribal eponym with one of the local women. Union with a concubine may personify a fusion with a foreign or inferior ethnic element, as in the case of Abraham and Hagar, Sarah's Egyptian handmaid (see Table 1).

Elsewhere, I have tried to demonstrate that, in attributing lineage through a concubine or maidservant, the Bible intends to convey the idea of migration of such clan members from their ancestral home to peripheral regions. I reached this conclusion through anal-

---

[3] E.E. Evans-Pritchard, *The Nuer*[2] (Oxford, Clarendon Press, 1940), p. 242.

ogy with the manner in which actual families would expel the offspring of a concubine, as evidenced in the concrete case of the Biblical judge Jephtah (*Judges* XI, 1–2). (Cf. chap. 7) The same principle was applied to Ishmael, Abraham's son by Hagar, who had also been expelled.

In a more abstract manner, we have the explicit Biblical statement regarding Abraham in *Genesis* XXV, 6: "But to his sons by concubinage he made grants [. . .] as he sent them eastward, away from his son Isaac, to the country of the East." Thus the Midianites, Hagarites, Ishmaelites and Amalekites and some tribes of the Nahorides are all traceable back to maidservants or concubines. This is done, in my opinion, with the implicit intention of conveying the idea that these tribal confederations (which Biblical tradition derived from the patriarchal clan and its habitat), had migrated or were forced to move to outlying regions—in these instances, to the desert fringes.

One may perhaps find here an explanation also for the situation within the Israelite genealogical system in which the four tribes of Dan, Naphtali, Asher and Gad are descendants of Jacob's maidservants Zilpah and Bilhah (see Table 1). All four tribes eventually settled in the northern or eastern periphery of the Israelite settlement framework. And there is indeed evidence for Dan and Asher having departed from the central part of the country to these distant regions.

I am not aware of African parallels for the above examples, but surely there are analogies for the following phenomenon occurring in the Bible—the variation in relative position of a given name within different genealogical contexts. That is, on one occasion *A* may appear as the father of *B*, while in another instance as his son (or even nephew); once *A* is a brother of *B*, and on another occasion he is his son, etc. All these point to shifts in power, and a constant fluidity within the tribal framework.

Another quite common feature in the genealogies is the frequent recurrence of one and the same name, or more significantly a cluster of names (that is, three or four names in association), within two or even three different tribal lineages. This would seemingly point, *inter alia*, to migratory movements of clans or sub-clans from one tribal area to another—or at any rate to a continuous process of inter-tribal regrouping. A case in point is the clan of Beriah, recurring in the genealogy of Ephraim, and of Benjamin—and even of the distant tribe of Asher. Thus, this clan or parts of it became associated in the course of time with several tribes. Moreover, some five clan names in the lineage of remote Asher, in north-western Palestine, are identical with those of clans or districts on the border of Ephraim and Benjamin, in the central sector. We can deduce from this that the families in question, or parts thereof, migrated from central Palestine to the far north, parallel to the well-known migration of the tribe of Dan, as related in the Bible (*Judges* XVIII).

A further phenomenon evident in the tribal genealogies is the intermingling of the newly settled tribes of Israel with the indigenous population of Canaan, and the assimilation or absorption of foreign ethnic elements within the Israelite framework. This can be inferred from the numerous foreign names, whether Canaanite, Horite or otherwise, included in the various tribal lineages—and sometimes even from the explicit inclusion of Canaanite women. Thus, at the very opening of the genealogy of Judah, three of his five immediate progeny are born of a Canaanite wife (I *Chr.* II, 3); one of Simeon's sons is ascribed to a Canaanite mother (*Gen.* XLVI, 10), and two other of his offspring bear names identical to those of Ishmael's sons.

The frequency or paucity of such foreign elements could serve as indicators for exogamic or endogamic leanings of the particular Israelite tribe. Initially, Israel's tribal society seems to have maintained a fundamentally endogamic attitude, the nation's Patriarchs marrying only with near blood relations. However, later developments, accelerated by the process of settlement, gave way to an increasingly exogamic tendency. Thus, by painstaking analysis of the lineage systems of Judah and Simeon, a strong exogamic principle is revealed, while other tribes were stricter in preserving the 'purity' of their stock.

In summary, we may state that the Israelite tribal genealogies are of utmost significance in unravelling what I call the dynamics of the settlement process in Palestine, and for elucidating the involved and complex anatomy of a particular tribal make-up. The same is certainly true for the various African lineage systems and their respective societies.

In this final part of my discussion, allow me to refer briefly to several of the conclusions concerning the nature of Biblical genealogies in a study undertaken by me several years ago and which may be of significance, in one way or another, for the African lineage systems, as well. This study[4] can be consulted for explicit details.

---

[4] Malamat, *op. cit.*, 163–173.

The impetus for it was the discovery by J.J. Finkelstein of the genealogy of the dynasty of Hammurapi, the famous king of Babylon who lived in the XVIIIth century B.C. This royal genealogy, shown in the left-hand column of Table 2, lists some thirty names in an uninterrupted line, which we are now able analytically to divide into several sections. It also throws new light on the upper part of the Assyrian king list (second column from the left), both documents stemming from more or less the same time—the old Babylonian period—and pertaining to parallel West Semitic dynasties.

The following conclusions concerning the Biblical genealogies are now apparent. Firstly, the vertical genealogical compositions in the Bible evidently go back to archetypes which had circulated among West Semitic tribes hundreds of years prior to those of the Bible. Secondly, both the earlier and the later compositions were created in similar techniques of fictitiously linking historical personages—such as Hammurapi, on the one hand, and King David or Saul, on the other hand—to putative ancestors, often of quasi-mythological character, representing *inter alia* tribes and localities. Thirdly, since the uppermost generations of the Babylonian and Assyrian king lists are practically of identical (putative) eponyms, a common genealogical tradition must have been shared by a number of cognate groups. A similar consciousness of common ancestry is displayed within the genealogical accounts in the Book of Genesis, where many of the peoples other than Israel are assigned to the same family tree.

The ego-Israelite attitude is specifically apparent only in the tendency to portray the family tree in Israelite terms; that is, the central cord or "senior lineage" is Israelite, from which the other peoples radiate as secondary branches. If we were to conjure up, say, an Ishmaelite or an Edomite 'Bible', we would encounter essentially the same family tree, but with the "senior lineage" occupied by one of these very peoples, with the Israelites relegated to one of the side branches. All the above-mentioned features (with the exception of the first point) might very well apply to the African lineage systems, as well.

Yet, to arrive at the core of a genealogical composition, it must undergo a structural analysis. Such analysis of the vertical genealogical patterns, as in my aforementioned study, reveals four successive groups, distinct in their historiographical character and functional purpose, from which a most instructive lesson might be derived for the various African lineage models.

a) The first group, called here the "genealogical stock," includes common antecedent generations. This is an apparent artificial composition, personal names, tribal names, toponyms and appellatives, adjoined to obtain a genealogical depth of some ten generations, in imitation of an authentic pedigree account (see group (c)).

b) Then follows what I am inclined to regard as the "determinative line," since it serves to determine the specific affiliation of a people or individual. In the case of the Israelites, it includes the three Patriarchs and the specific tribal eponym (that is, one of the twelve sons of Jacob)—these four generations defining each and every Israelite lineage. This group links the genealogical stock with (c), the "table of ancestors" or actual pedigree of (d), a concrete historical line or personage.

The ideal model of "table of ancestors" (*Ahnentafel*), in Israel as elsewhere in the ancient Near East, and as clearly shown on Table 2, was based on a fixed ten-generation depth. In this connection the archaeological discoveries in Palestine of stelae shrines at Gezer (*ca.* 1600 B.C.) and Hazor (XIVth–XIIIth centuries B.C.) may be of more than minor interest. It has been assumed that one of the functions of such stelae was *pro memoria*, i.e. commemorating the deceased amongst the nobility.[5] Significantly, the stelae at the shrines at both Gezer and Hazor are exactly *ten* in number (at Gezer there is archaeological proof that they have even been erected simultaneously), probably serving as memorial stones and for mortuary rites for ancestors of a single lineage. If so, we have here tangible evidence for our schematic "ancestor tables." A similar genealogical depth is typical for many modern tribal societies throughout the world, such as the Beduin, and in particular in African lineage systems. Thus, Evans-Pritchard reports of the Nuer that "All the main clans have about ten to twelve generations from the present day to the ancestors who gave rise to them."[6] Gluckman refers to a similar situation among other African tribes, such as the Ashanti and Tallensi in West Africa, and the Zulu in South Africa.[7]

Furthermore, in the African lineage models only four to six generations at the bottom represent real ancestors and relationships,

---

[5] Cf. K. Galling, Erwägungen zum Stelenheiligtum von Hazor, *Zeitschrift des deutschen Palästina-Vereins*, LXXV (1959), 1–13, and most recently C.F. Graesser, Standing Stones in Ancient Palestine, *The Biblical Archaeologist*, XXXV (1972), 34–63.

[6] Evans-Pritchard, *op. cit.*, p. 199.

[7] Cf. Max Gluckman, *Politics, Law and Ritual in Tribal Society* (Chicago, 1965), p. 274.

while the six to seven at the top are putative.[8] The same situation held true for Israel, as is evidenced by the initial generations in David's or Saul's ancestor-table, which are artificial, reflecting no more than a graduated intra-tribal division—clan, sub-clan and family (see Table 3).

Moreover, in both African and Biblical lineages, an obvious process of selection and telescoping was at work (sometimes referred by anthropologists as "structural amnesia"), thus depriving them of true chronological value—for the generational depth represented is much too shallow to fill the real historical time-span.[9] In this connection we should emphasize, however, that dominant tribal lineages (e.g. Judah), and royal or aristocratic pedigrees, have normally been transmitted with greater care and are thus deeper than their less important counterparts, where telescoping is more often resorted to. Thus, among the Luapula of Rhodesia, for example, the royal line is preserved to a 9-generation depth, as against the commoner lineages which embrace only 4 to 7 generations.[10] A similar situation is found in Burundi, in Rwanda and elsewhere, as noted by J. Vansina.[11] Finally, we may state that the study of genealogies indicates, moreover, a phenomenon characterizing oral traditions generally, which, in the words of one authority, "have a beginning, the 'remote past' and an end 'the recent past' and episodes which should belong to a middle period between these extremes are pushed either into the 'remote' or the 'recent past' or are forgotten altogether."[12]*

---

[8] See both aforementioned authors, *ibid.*

[9] As for Africa, see in addition to the aforementioned authors recently J.S. Boston, Oral Tradition and the History of Igala, *Journal of African History*, X (1969), 29–43, and concerning the Biblical analogies our remarks in *Journal of the American Oriental Society, op. cit.*, pp. 170 sqq. and note 22 for further bibliography. For the universal phenomenon of sometimes telescoping genealogies and at other times artificially expanding them, see now also D.P. Henige, Oral Tradition and Chronology, *Journal of African History*, XII (1971), 371–389.

[10] Cf. I. Cunnison, History and Genealogies in a Conquest State, *American Anthropologist*, LIX (1957), p. 27.

[11] J. Vansina, *Oral Tradition: a study in historical methodology* (London, 1965), p. 153.

[12] G.I. Jones, Time and Oral Tradition with Special Reference to Eastern Nigeria, *Journal of African History*, VI (1965), p. 160, and for an allusion to Biblical genealogies cf. W.F. Albright, *New Horizons in Biblical Research* (London, 1966), p. II *n.* I. Both studies mentioned in passing now also by R.C. Culley, Oral Tradition and Historicity, *in* J.W. Wevers *and* D.B. Redford (eds), *Studies on the Ancient Palestinian World* (Toronto, 1972), p. 108.

* This paper was first given as a lecture at the Jerusalem Congress on Black Africa and the Bible, 27 April 1972.

PART TWO

FORMING A NATION

5

THE EXODUS: EGYPTIAN ANALOGIES*

At the outset, we briefly discuss the Exodus in the bible and then consider the Egyptian material, which may serve as an analogy to the biblical account and perhaps, in part, even as an indirect proof for the Israelite episode. Before we proceed, however, it should be emphasized that none of the Egyptian sources substantiates the story of the Exodus.

The Exodus[1] figures most prominently in the biblical tradition as one of the foundations of Israelite faith, referred to in retrospect throughout the Bible more often than any other event of Israel's past—in historiography, in prophecy, and in the Psalms. Thus, the historian is faced here, first and foremost, with the dilemma of whether the story is merely the product of later contemplation, mainly of a theological nature, or indeed, an event of any historic credence. As the story is handed down to us in the form of a folktale, it is obviously not necessary to insist upon the historicity of its various elements of folklore and artifice; rather, we should focus on the substantial features, what Goethe called *die grossen Züge*, the broad sweep of affairs. I am referring to such components as the Israelites' sojourn in Egypt, the enslavement there in what the Bible terms בית עבדים (*bēth avādim*), "the house of bondage" (a most extraordinary coinage, which aptly characterizes totalitarian regimes throughout history); the exit and flight from Egypt into the Sinai desert; and finally, the takeover of Canaan. Do any of these components hold a kernel of

---

* This article was originally published in: *Exodus*, eds. E.S. Frerichs and L.H. Lesko, Eisenbrauns, Winona Lake, In., 1997, 15–27.

[1] From the plethora of studies on the biblical Exodus in the Egyptian context, we may cite a few of recent date: H. Cazelles, *Autour de l'Exode* (Paris, 1987), esp. pp. 189–231, and "Peut-on circonsrire un événement Exode?" in *La protohistoire d'Israel*, ed. E.-M. Laperrousaz (Paris, 1990), pp. 29–65; N.M. Sarna, *Exploring Exodus* (New York, 1986); W.H. Stiebing, *Out of the Desert?* (Buffalo, NY, 1989); M. Görg, "Exodus," in *Neues Bibel-Lexikon*, ed. Görg and B. Lang, Lieferung 4 (1990), cols. 631–636; K.A. Kitchen, "Exodus, The," in *Anchor Bible Dictionary*, ed. D.N. Freedman (New York, 1992), vol. 2, pp. 700–708.

historical truth, or are they merely figments of the imagination of later scribes?[2]

True, the absence of any direct extra-biblical evidence, Egyptian or otherwise, need not engender undue skepticism, which, vis-à-vis the biblical tradition, has been occasionally extreme. Rather, the indifference of external sources should merely indicate that the Exodus and the Conquest did not shake the foundations of the political and military scene of the day. These events proved central, however, to Israel's turbulent history.

As for dating the Exodus, we face the problem (known also regarding other facets of Israel's proto-history) of what I term the "telescoping process" of biblical historiography, namely, the compression of a chain of historical events into a simplified and brief account. Later editors would, in retrospect, compress a complex of events into a severely curtailed timespan.[3] We face the alternatives of a relatively brief streamlined exodus, as told in the Bible—a "punctual" event—or a "durative" event, postulating two or more exoduses, or even a steady flow of Israelites coming out of Egypt during a lengthy period, perhaps encompassing hundreds of years. In the latter case, the search for a specific date of the Exodus is a futile undertaking, as a time span ranging from the 15th to 12th centuries B.C.E. may be involved. Yet even so, we may assume a peak period for a stream of Israelites coming out of Egypt—let us call it the Moses movement—whereby we are confronted with the delineation of a definite chronology for the Exodus. Here we have to take into account Egyptian history as well as the history of the "West," (i.e., Anatolia, Syria, and Palestine).

Like many scholars, I used to accept the reign of Ramesses II, more precisely the period subsequent to the famous Battle of Kadesh between Ramesses II and the Hittites in the former's fifth year (now dated around 1273 B.C.E.), as the opportune time for the Exodus. The battle seemed to have been—in contrast to their Egyptian sources—a fiasco for the Egyptians, who were then undergoing a process of temporary decline, especially in Canaan, where the local rulers revolted. Such a situation in the wake of the Battle of Kadesh

---

[2] A. Malamat, "The Proto-History of Israel: A Study in Method," in *The Word of the Lord Shall Go Forth: Essays in Honor of David Noel Freedman*, ed. Carol Meyers and M. O'Connor (Philadelphia, 1983), pp. 303–313; (here chap. 1).

[3] Malamat, "Proto-History," pp. 307f.; cf. above chap. 1.

could well have facilitated, in a broad manner of speaking, an Israelite exodus.

Now, however, I tend to lower the date of a "punctual" exodus—
the climatic stage within a durative event—toward the end of the
XIXth Dynasty (the late 13th century B.C.E. and the early years of
the 12th century). This period saw the breakdown of both the Egyptian
and Hittite empires—in modern terminology, the collapse of the
bipolar political system of the day. The simultaneous decline of the
two provided a rare opportunity for the oppressed, the small peoples and the ethnic minorities from Anatolia to lower Egypt—in
Machiavellian terms, the "occasione." It is in this fluid context that
we may find the true setting that enabled the Israelites to set out
from Egypt for Canaan.

While there is no direct extra-biblical source on the Exodus (or
Conquest) or on the Israelite servitude in Egypt, we do possess several significant *indirect* sources—a sort of circumstantial evidence that
lends greater authority to the biblical account. I shall just mention
some of the more illuminating of these sources, well known in research,
and shall at the end dwell upon two such items. The first is often
referred to in the debate on the Exodus but perhaps not analyzed
comprehensively. The second, a recent discovery, has been hardly
dealth with concerning our issue.

(1) A well-known biblical passage, usually drawn into the discussion of the Exodus (Exodus 1:11), is the building of the store-cities
Pithom and Ramesses by the enslaved Israelites. Despite the alleged
relevancy of this passage, many scholars see here an anachronistic
statement of much later times[4] and find other difficulties, such as
the form of the biblical toponym "Ramesses" instead of the standard Egyptian name of "Pi-Ramesses."

(2) Connected in some way with this passage and serving as probable evidence of the Israelite servitude in Egypt is Papyrus Leiden
348. It is a decree by an official of Ramesses II concerning construction work at his new capital of Pi-Ramesses, declaring, "Distribute

---

[4] See esp. D.B. Redford, "Exodus 1:11," *Vetus Testamentum* 13 (1963), pp. 401–418,
and "An Egyptological Perspective on the Exodus Narrative," in *Egypt, Israel, Sinai*,
ed. A.F. Rainey (Tel Aviv, 1987), pp. 137–161. This author assumes a sixth-cen-
tury B.C.E. (or even later) date; cf. also B.J. Diebner, "Erwägungen zum Thema
'Exodus,'" *Studien zur Altägyptischen Kultur* 11 (1984), pp. 596–630. In contrast, Stiebing
(*Out of the Desert?*) refutes such a late date and on the other hand rejects the extreme
early-15th-century B.C.E. date.

grain rations to the soldiers and to the ʿApiru who transport stones to the great pylon of Ramesses."

(2a) More recently, a similar document was published,[5] an undated ostracon in hieratic script, again referring to the ʿApiru, engaged in construction work at the city of Pi-Ramesses. We can not enter here into the ʿApiru problem and its complex relation with the Habiru and Hebrew. Suffice it to state that we concur with many scholars in assuming that the Hebrews are somehow connected linguistically and ethnically with the ʿApiru. This assumption may rule out the connection often surmised of the Hebrews/Israelites with the Shasu.[6] If so, the Hebrews were engaged in forced labor at the construction of the capital city of Ramesses. The problem, which remains outside the scope of the Egyptian context, is the affiliation between the Israelites and the Hebrews, the latter designating a broader ethnicity. In short, each and every Israelite is a Hebrew and likely an ʿApiru, while not every Hebrew or ʿApiru is necessarily an Israelite. Thus, even here there is no definite proof that Israelites were engaged in the city's building. At best, we have in this case merely circumstantial evidence of a questionable nature. But this remains the utter limit for the historian of the Exodus; he can go no further. Evidence of a more "scientific" caliber is no longer within the reach of historical research.

(3) Everyone here has dealt with the Merneptah Stele of the fifth year of this pharaoh, now to be dated to 1208 B.C.E.[7] The only statement I wish to make in this context is that this stele has little or nothing to do with the Exodus. It merely attests to the actual presence of a group designated "Israel" in Canaan towards the end of the 13th century B.C.E. What tribes this Israelite group included is unknown, yet in view of the geographical sequence in the text, Israel could presumably be found in northern Palestine or in its hinterland.

---

[5] See Cazelles, "The Hebrews," in *Peoples of the Old Testament*, ed. D.J. Wiseman (Oxford, 1973), p. 14.

[6] An identity propagated esp. by R. Giveon in his book *Les bédouins Shosou des documents égyptiens* (Leiden, 1971).

[7] The most recent studies of this document from a historical viewpoint are H. Engel, "Die Siegesstele des Merenptah," *Biblica* 60 (1979), pp. 373–399; L.E. Stager, "Merenptah, Israel and the Sea Peoples," *Eretz-Israel* 18 (1985), 56*–64*; F.J. Yurco, "Merenptah's Canaanite Campaign," *Journal of the American Research Center in Egypt* 23 (1986); J.J. Bimson, "Merenptah's Israel and Recent Theories of Israelite Origins," *Journal for the Study of the Old Testament* 49 (1991), pp. 3–29.

(4) The next possible connection between the biblical tradition and the Egyptian sources is of quite a different nature. Exodus 13:17 states, "When Pharaoh let the people go, God did not lead them by way of the land of the Philistines, although that was near; for God said: 'Lest the people repent when they see war and return to Egypt.'" This passage about the journey of the Israelites through Sinai may be better understood if we take into account the military road that the Egyptians constructed along the coast of northern Sinai, the biblical "way of the Philistines." This route was fortified with a tight network of strongholds by Seti I early in the 13th century B.C.E. and remained under strict control of the Egyptians throughout that century.[8] It might easily have become a trap for the wandering Israelites; hence the command attributed to God. The Bible continues, quoting Pharaoh in Exodus 14:3: "For Pharaoh will say of the people of Israel 'They are entangled in the land [i.e., Sinai]; the wilderness has shut them in.'" reflecting the Egyptian view that because of the fortification line the Israelites were forced to make a detour and venture into the desert.

(5) Particularly significant typologically are the following documents reporting on Egyptian frontier officials stationed on the border zone between Egypt and Sinai (located along the northern section of the present-day Suez Canal). The texts are contained in several of the Papyri Anastasi (purchased as early as 1839) which were originally used as schoolboys' copy books of model letters. Some of them reveal the tight control of the Egyptian authorities over their eastern frontier in the last decades of the 13th century. Each and every group or individual, whether Egyptian or foreign, could neither enter nor leave Egypt without a special permit. I view this situation as an "Iron Curtain," an idiom coined by Winston Churchill in his famous speech in 1946 at Westminster College in Fulton, Missouri. The Iron Curtain functioned in both directions of the passage—entrance and exit. Indeed, without this fortification line entire minority groups, and probably Egyptians as well would have escaped from the delta into Sinai and Palestine. This also sheds light in the persistent pleas to Pharaoh by Moses and Aaron, "Let my people go!"

---

[8] A. Gardiner, "The Ancient Military Road Between Egypt and Palestine," *Journal of Egyptian Archaeology* 6 (1920), pp. 99–116; E.D. Oren, "'Ways of Horus' in North Sinai," in Rainey, *Egypt, Israel, Sinai*, pp. 69–119.

(5a) Thus Papyrus Anastasi III[9] records daily crossings of individuals in either direction in the time of Merneptah.

(5b) Anastasi VI[10] illustrates the passage into Egypt of an entire tribe coming down from Edom during a drought. This report is reminiscent of several patriarchal episodes concerning Abraham and Jacob, who were also said to have descended into Egypt because of a drought.

(6) But most exciting for our purpose is Papyrus Anastasi V,[11] dating to the end of the XIXth Dynasty (the end of the 13th century), which reports the escape of two slaves or servants from the royal residence at Pi-Ramesses, on the western edge of Wadi Tumilat. The fugitives flee into the Sinai wilderness by way of the fortified border. The writer of the letter, a high-ranking Egyptian military commander, had been ordered by the Egyptian authorities to ensure that the runaways were captured and returned to Egypt:

> Another matter, to wit: I was sent forth from the broad-halls of the palace—life, prosperity, health!—in the third month of the third season, day 9, at the time of evening, following after these two slaves. Now when I reached the enclosure-wall of Tjeku on the 3rd month of the third season, day 10, they told [me] they were saying to the south that they had passed by on the 3rd month of the third season, day 10. (xx 1) [Now] when [I] reached the fortress, they told me that the *scout* had come from the desert [saying that] they had passed the walled place north of the Migdol of Seti Mer-ne-Ptah—life, prosperity, health!—Beloved like Seth.

> When my letter reaches you, write to me about all that has happened to [them]. Who found their tracks? Which watch found their tracks? What people are after them? Write to me about all that has happened to them and how many people you send out after them.

> [May your health] be good!

> Anastasi V[12]

---

[9] J.B. Pritchard, ed., *Ancient Near Eastern Texts Relating to the Old Testament*, 3rd ed. (Princeton, 1969), pp. 258f.; R.M. Caminos, *Late-Egyptian Miscellanies* (Oxford, 1954), pp. 69ff.

[10] Pritchard, *Texts*, p. 259; Caminos, *Late-Egyptian Miscellanies*, pp. 293–296; and H. Goedicke, "Papyrus Anastasi VI 51–61," *Studien zur Altägyptischen Kultur* 14 (1987), pp. 83–98.

[11] "The Pursuit of Runaway Slaves," in Pritchard, *Texts*, p. 259; see Caminos, *Late-Egyptian Miscellanies*, pp. 254–258.

[12] Pritchard, *Texts*, p. 259.

We witness here several striking parallels of the Exodus episode—in miniature of course—as opposed to the biblical 600,000 foot soldiers setting out from Egypt (Exodus 12:37). (A note on the figure 600,000:[13] There is no doubt that we have here a typological number. As I have shown elsewhere, the Bible refers quite often to 600 soldiers, or multiples thereof, conveying, to my mind, the idea of the size of a platoon or regiment. The 600,000 are likely comprised of 1,000 platoons, while the number 1,000 is again to be taken as typological [see Deuteronomy 1:11], implying a multitude of soldiers, an expression actually used in the Exodus story [Exodus 1:9,20].)

We can outline four parallel features between Anastasi V and the Exodus episode:

1) The escape of slaves, or semi-slaves, from the area of the city of Ramesses in search of freedom.

2) Egyptian military forces pursue the runaways in order to return them to Egypt.

3) The escape route into Sinai is roughly identical with the biblical report. After leaving Ramesses we find the two Egyptians in Tjeku, most likely biblical Sukkoth (with all due reservation), the second station on the Exodus route (still in Wadi Tumilat). We then hear of the escapees near Migdol (the text has *sgwr* = a fortress in the Canaanite language, like *migdol*) or perhaps north of it. Migdol, well known in the Bible and mentioned as another station in the Exodus route, is beyond the present Suez Canal, north of el-Kantara. In 1920 Alan Gardiner identified the city with Tell el-Her, which was excavated by Eliezer Oren in the 1970s.[14] Significantly, the fleeing Israelites turned north of Migdol and camped between the city and the Mediterranean (Exodus 14:2).

4) The flight took place under the cover of darkness, as one would expect, and as is hinted by the pursuing Egyptian official, who left a short time after the escapees from the capital city, "at the time of evening, following after these two slaves." Similarly, we may remember that the Israelites Exodus started בַּחֲצֹת הַלַּיְלָה, "at midnight" (Exodus 11:4).

---

[13] See Malamat, "The Danite Migration and the Pan-Israelite Exodus-Conquest," *Biblica* 51 (1970), pp. 9f.

[14] For Gardiner, see "Military Road," pp. 107–109; see also Oren, "Migdol: A New Fortress on the Edge of the Eastern Nile Delta," *Bulletin of the American Schools of Oriental Research* 256 (1984), pp. 7–44.

The Elephantine Stele

Finally, we come to a document from Elephantine,[15] published recently
by D. Bidoli, which is a royal stele from the second (?) year of
Pharaoh Sethnakht, founder of the XXth Dynasty. The stele, dating in absolute chronology from the first or second decade of the
12th century B.C.E., has been newly edited by Rosemarie Drenkhahn
in her monograph *Die Elephantine-Stele des Sethnacht* (1980) and more
recently was dealt with by Friedrich Junge. It reflects the final years
of the XIXth Dynasty and the first two years of Sethnakht. For our
purpose, it is important to mention that the political situation in
Egypt at that time was marred by the enigmatic intervention of
Asiatics (*sṯtw*), who were approached and bribed by a faction of
Egyptians, let us call it A, who revolted against another faction, let
us call it B, who remained loyal to Sethnakht. The Egyptians bribed
the Asiatics with silver and gold, as well as copper, "the possession
of Egypt," in order that they assist faction A in their plot. However,
Sethnakht foiled faction A and drove the Asiatics out of Egypt, forcing them to embark upon an exodus of sorts, which led them towards
southern Palestine.

As for the delivery of the precious metals to the Asiatics (which
were eventually recovered by faction B), three Exodus passages may
be of unexpected significance:[16] Exodus 3:21–22, 11:2, and 12:35–36.
They read, according to the Revised Standard Version:

> And when you go you shall not go empty, but each woman shall take
> of her neighbor, and of her who sojourn in her house, objects of sil-
> ver and gold, and clothing . . . thus you shall despoil the Egyptians"
> (Exodus 3:21–22); ". . . that they (the people) ask every man of his
> neighbor (and every woman of her neighbor), objects of silver and of
> gold" (Exodus 11:2); "The people of Israel had also done as Moses
> told them, for they had asked of the Egyptians objects of silver and
> of gold, and clothing. And the Lord had given the people favor in the

---

[15] Published by D. Bidoli in *Mitteilungen des deutschen archäologischen Instituts, Kairo*
28 (1972), pp. 195–200, pl. 49; and investigated by R. Drenkhahn, *Die Elephantine-
Stele des Sethnacht* (Wiesbaden, 1980); cf. A. Spalinger, review of *Elephantine-Stele*, by
Drenkhahn, *Bibliotheca Orientalis* 39 (1982), cols. 272–288. For a revised reading see
F. Junge in *Elephantine* 11 (1988), pp. 55–58.

[16] Some vague allusions to a biblical-Egyptian connection have already been
made; cf. Görg, *Kairos* 20 (1978), pp. 279f. and n. 28; J.C. de Moor, *The Rise of
Yahwism* (Leuven, 1990), pp. 136ff.; M. Dijkstra, *Netherlands Theologisch Tijdschrift* 45
(1991), pp. 1–15.

sight of the Egyptians, so that they let them have what they asked. Thus they despoiled the Egyptians.

Exodus 12:35–6; see also Psalm 105:37

We have here an interesting analog between the Egyptian stele and an awkward tradition within the Exodus story (which, admittedly, does not belong to the "*grossen Züge*"), according to which the Israelites, prior to their impending exodus, receive or appropriate precious objects from the Egyptians (in all three cases here, שאל means to "appropriate," rather than the usual meaning, "to ask" or "to borrow"). This would liken the Israelites to the Asiatics of the Elephantine Stele, both of whom were given the same objects by the Egyptians. Of course, we may simply have here parallel literary motifs. But note also the biblical statement, put into Pharaoh's mouth, which is often overlooked: "Come let us deal shrewdly with them (i.e., the Israelites) . . . and if war befall us, they join our enemies and fight against us and escape from the land" (Exodus 1:10). Here we can witness the trauma that befell the Egyptians because of the Israelites (Elephantine Stele: Asiatics), who could become a potential threat if they chose to join the enemies of Egypt.

In sum, although an Israelite exodus is not mentioned in Egyptian sources, a number of important analogs are apparent, beginning perhaps with the time of the Hyksos. These analogs become more concentrated around 1200 B.C.E. and are suggestive of the biblical event.[17]

Excursus: Irsu and Beya

The sequence and chronology of the last rulers of the XIXth Dynasty is now believed to be as follows: Seti II (1203–1197 B.C.E.), during whose reign several of the Papyri Anastasi were composed, was followed by his son Siptah (1197–1192 B.C.E.), after whose death Queen Tausert (1192–1190 B.C.E.), the widow of Seti II and regent during the reign of Siptah, ascended the throne. Then, in the aftermath

---

[17] For such a dating, based on different reasons, see M.B. Rowton, "The Problem of the Exodus," *Palestine Exploration Quarterly* 85 (1953), pp. 46–60; cf. Görg, "Exodus," col. 635; de Moor, *Rise of Yahwism*, p. 150. See also G.A. Rendsburg, "The Date of the Exodus," *Vetus Testamentum* 42 (1992), pp. 510–527.

of bitter internal struggles, the future Pharaoh Sethnakht (1190–1188 B.C.E.) became the founder of the XXth Dynasty.[18]

It is within this period, especially during the later part, that we should place the Syrian-Palestinian usurpation of Egypt as described in Papyrus Harris 1, which portrays the desolate conditions prior to the reign of Ramesses III. The leader of the Asiatic intruders was someone called Irsu. For our purpose, it does not matter whether we have here a personal name or an Egyptian phrase meaning "he made himself," as held by many Egyptologists. At any rate, the papyrus contains the determinative ʿ*3mw*, designating a Semitic Syrian or a Semitic Palestinian. On the assumption that we have here a personal name, various identifications have been suggested.[19] Some connection with the Asiatics of the Elephantine Stele is not altogether implausible and certainly seems intriguing.

The common contemporary, albeit doubtful, belief identifies Irsu with Beya, a prominent Egyptian official who was active from the reign of Seti II until Tausert, bearing a possibly Semitic name and known in modern parlance as the "king maker." Should this identification prove true, then a recently discovered letter (in Akkadian) sent by Beya to the last ruler of Ugarit may enable us to date the Semitic usurpation of Egypt more precisely, i.e., about 1195–1190 B.C.E.[20] Furthermore, there are now a few scholars who boldly maintain that Beya/Irsu is in fact the biblical Moses,[21] bringing us back to the very subject of our paper. But such an assumption is hardly supported by any documentation, and so it remains highly speculative.

---

[18] Gardiner, *Egypt of the Pharaohs* (Oxford, 1966), pp. 277–280; L.H. Lesko, "A Little More Evidence for the End of the 19th Dynasty," *Journal of the American Reserach Center in Egypt* 5 (1966), pp. 29–32; Drenkhahn, *Elephantine-Stele*.

[19] See my own attempt made more than forty years ago, "Cushan Rishataim and the Decline of the Near East Around 1200 B.C.E.," *Journal of Near Eastern Studies* 13 (1954), pp. 231ff.; see also, from among many studies, J.-M. Kruchten, "La fin de la XIXe Dynastie vue d'après la section 'historique' du Papyrus Harris I," *Annuaire de l'Institut de philologie et d'historie orientales et slaves* 25 (1981), pp. 51–64.

[20] On (Irsu-) Beya, see recently (and there the earlier literature) M. Yon, *In the Crisis Years: The 12th Century B.C.E.*, ed. W.A. Ward and M. Sharp Joukowsky (Dubuque, IA, 1992), pp. 119f.; C. Maderna-Sieben, "Der historische Abschnitt des Papyrus Harris I," *Göttinger Miszellen* 123 (1991), pp. 57–90, esp. 87 (the equation of Irsu-Beya, suggested first, hesistantly, by J. Černý and Gardiner, became here already "sicherlich").

[21] See E.A. Knauf, *Midian* (Wiesbaden, 1988), pp. 135ff.; de Moor, *Rise of Yahwism*, chap. 4.6: Beya-Moses, pp. 136–151.

Addendum

This paper was written for the colloquy "The Exodus" at Brown University in the spring of 1992. The publication of the proceedings was much delayed; in the meantime the paper of J. de Moor, "Egypt, Ugarit and Exodus," in *Ugarit, Religion and Culture*, ed. N. Wyatt et al. (Münster, 1996), pp. 213–247, appeared. The author independently uses much of the material dealt with above and concludes, as we do, that the Exodus, or its dominant phase, took place around 1190 B.C.E. However, he still maintains, I believe unjustifiably, his previous identification of Moses and other biblical figures—A.M.

6

CONQUEST OF CANAAN: ISRAELITE CONDUCT OF WAR ACCORDING TO BIBLICAL TRADITION* **

A major dilemma confronts the student of the Israelite Conquest of Canaan, encountered also in other facets of Israel's protohistory: What degree of historicity can be ascribed to the biblical tradition (more precisely, those traditions as formed in Num. and Deut.) concerning the conquest of Trans-Jordan and (in Josh. and Judg. 1) Cis-Jordan? For this tradition, which crystallized only after generations of complex literary reworking, might be devoid of any actual historical value.

Our problem becomes acute when we realize that the scores of extrabiblical sources on Canaan in the 13th century B.C.E.—the generally conceded period of the Israelite Conquest, or at least of its central phase—make no mention of these events. Nevertheless, this should not lead to an exaggerated skepticism (often met with) as if the entire episode were fabricated. This deficiency can probably be ascribed to the fact that the Israelite Conquest made no ruffle in the international political scene, in any event nothing sufficient to make an impression upon contemporaneous records, especially those of Canaan's overlord—Egypt. This, of course, imposes upon us all the limitations of self-evidence—its subjectivity and the adherent suspicions of idealization and aggrandizement, subservient to political and religious ideologies. Further, the historical trust-worthiness of biblical traditions receded with the lapse of time between events and their literary recording. But this memory gap was not

* This article was originally published in: *Revue Internationale d'Histoire Militaire* 42, 1979, 25–52.

** This article is a somewhat modified and updated version of a paper published in *Encyclopaedia Judaica, Yearbook* 1975/76, 166–182, and in *Proceedings of Symposia*, 1979: "The Archaeology and Chronology of the First Period of the Iron Age (Problems of Early Israelite History)" in honor of the Seventy-Fifth Anniversary of the American Schools of Oriental Research. The author is grateful to the "American Schools" and Professor F.M. Cross, for kind permission to publish it here.

For full references to the works cited below, see *Bibliography*.

acting alone for, more significantly, two other processes were affecting biblical historiography, gradually obscuring the initial reality.

The first operant was "reflection," which subjected the Conquest to contemplation—why and how Canaan fell—and conjured new assessments and motivations, grafting them onto the early events. There thus arose in the biblical sources a historiosophy subordinate to an explicit theological doctrine.[1] Whereas in the relatively raw, early depictions of the Israelite wars, the mortal and the divine are intertwined, the later redactors (the so-called Deuteronomist) have accentuated and brought to the fore the role of the Lord of Israel, submerging human feat. Thus crystallized the ideology of the Holy War, or rather the "Yahwe War," whether of offensive or defensive nature.[2] Such "real" factors as numbers of soldiers or the weaponry involved are of no consequence here, nor is the disparity in strength between Israel and her adversaries (as, for instance, in the Gideon and Deborah episodes).[3] The sacred element increasingly outshines the profane: God fights for his people (Josh. 10:14) and even sends forth before the Israelites the mysterious *zir'ah* (hornet?, terror?)[4] to overwhelm the enemy ("not by your sword and not by your bow"; Josh. 24:12; and cf. Ex. 23:27–28; Deut. 7:20).

The second operant, "telescoping," (see chap. 1) is the compression of a string of events into a unified narrative of a relatively brief time-span. Long, involved campaigns were chronologically foreshortened by late redactors, thereby creating in retrospect a historical account of artificial simplicity.

Thus, there eventually emerged the culminating level of biblical

---

[1] Cf. Seeligmann, *P'raqim* II, 273ff.

[2] The basic study on the Holy War in the Bible is von Rad, *Heilige Krieg*; he restricts this concept to the defensive mode of Israel's wars, as manifest primarily in the Book of Judges. Stolz, *Jahwes und Israels Kriege*, however, justly extends it to the offensive aspect, as in the Book of Joshua. For a recent treatment of this subject, see Jones, *VT* 25 (1975), where a sharp distinction is made between "Holy War"— the biblical redactors' retrospective schematization of early Israelite military experience—and that actual experience, preferably termed "Yahwe War." For a comparative study on divine warfare in Israel and Mesopotamia, cf. Weippert, *ZAW* 84.

[3] Cf. Miller, *Divine Warrior*, 156ff.

[4] Garstang, *Joshua*, 259ff., in a novel interpretation, assumes that the *zir'ah*, "hornet", refers figuratively to the Pharaohs (cf. the hieroglyph *bity*, "King of Lower Egypt"), whose thrusts into Canaan would have paved the way for the Israelite invasion. But the basis for this assumption—his identification of the hieroglyph as a hornet rather than a bee—is precarious.

consciousness, what I would term the "official" or "canonical" tradition of the Conquest. This tradition presents a more or less organic and continuous chain of events, in straightforward narrative: The territory on both sides of the Jordan was occupied in a swift military operation, a sort of *Blitzkrieg*. Initially under Moses and then under Joshua—and with full divine collaboration—all twelve Israelite tribes acted in concert. Canaan was conquered almost in its entirety (redeeming a divine pledge to the Patriarchs). As hinted above, remnants of variant traditions among the biblical sources, occasionally exist contradicting the finalized version just described. Exemplary is the conquest of Cis-Jordan (that is, Western Palestine) according to Judges 1. This source negates the entire depiction of a unified, pan-Israelite conquest upheld by the "official" tradition. Not only does this deviant chapter describe particularistic tribal conquests, but the very direction of conquest is reversed—from the north-central-hill-country towards the Negev in the south. Furthermore, the chapter contradicts the "total conquest" by specifying the alien enclaves which held on in the midst of the domains of the individual tribes, too strong to be dispossessed. Thus, the actual course of events comprising the Conquest was very much more complex than the simplistic, streamlined, pan-Israelite description projected by the "official" tradition.

On the Phenomenology of the Conquest

Having assessed the biblical source material, we may now turn to the task at hand. On this occasion we shall avoid a factual reconstruction of the course of the Conquest, as so often sought by those who presuppose its actual military nature,[5] nor shall we delve into literary criticism of the biblical text, or treat the extra-biblical and archaeological material as such. Our less pretentious scrutiny of the extant Conquest tradition (and partly that of Judges) is solely from the military viewpoint; and our analysis of real historical situations is complemented by schematized, hypothetical projections. Such an approach, it is hoped, will provide a point of departure for reaffirming

---

[5] For recent comprehensive treatments, see e.g., Mazar, *World History of the Jewish People* III, and Yeivin, *Conquest of Canaan*.

the tenability of much of the biblical tradition, and thereby retrieve it from the clutches of current criticism.

We shall presuppose two guiding principles in our working hypothesis:

(1) The biblical evidence is basically no more than an ancient conceptual model depicting the Conquest as if the Israelites themselves (especially in the "official" tradition) sought to form an articulate concept of their inheritance and domination of Canaan (much like the modern conjectures of Bible research). Despite poetic embellishment and distortion, this ancient "theory" had the advantage of being the product of a close and authentic intimacy with the land, its topography, demography and military situation, etc. Thus, it provides an operative basis for

(2) our "typological approach," (see chap. 5) which serves to determine and define the prevalent and underlying phenomena within the traditions of Conquest and Settlement, avoiding the fetters of the continuity of the biblical account. Several of the outstanding phenomena exemplifying the Conquest may be noted at the outset:

(a) It is an elementary basis of Israelite consciousness that Canaan was "inherited" by force, whether an act of man or God. This tenet, a leitmotif running throughout the biblical sources, diametrically contradicts the widespread scholarly assumption (fostered primarily by the Alt-Noth school of thought),[6] which postulates an initially peaceful occupation, largely through transhumance. The biblical thesis, however, finds weighty support in the archaeological evidence, demonstrating that several Canaanite cities (such as Lachish in the south, Bethel in the central sector, and Hazor in the north), which according to the Bible were conquered by the Israelites, were indeed destroyed in the 13th century B.C.E., or, more precisely in the second half of that century.[7] With a few albeit significant exceptions (where the archaeological results indeed remain problematic), there is considerable agreement between the archaeological and biblical evidence,

---

[6] See Alt, *Kleine Schriften* I, and Noth, *Josua*, and in other of his works. This critical school of thought has been opposed strongly by Kaufmann, in *Scripta Hierosolymitana*, 327ff., as well as in his other works cited in the Bibliography. On the various contemporary schools of thought see now J.M. Miller, The Israelite Occupation of Canaan, *Israelite & Judaean History* (ed. by J.H. Hayes & J.M. Miller, 1977), 213–284.

[7] See Albright, *BASOR* 74; in addition, for Bethel, see J.L. Kelso, *The Excavations of Bethel (Annual of the American Schools of Oriental Research* 39), 1968, esp. p. 32; and for Hazor, Y. Yadin, *Hazor (Schweich Lectures* 1970), 1972, esp. pp. 108, 131.

and any denial of this correspondence would appear hypercritical.[8]

(b) Another major feature in the several biblical traditions is that the Israelites leaving Egypt were deflected from forcing direct entry into Canaan by the shortest route, from the south. The road along the northern coast of Sinai, known in the Bible as the "way of the land of the Philistines," was surely blocked to the Israelites, it being the Egyptian military route *par excellence*. The reliefs of Seti I (c. 1300 B.C.E.) depict a series of fortifications protecting this highway, showing that the Egyptians could readily have stemmed any Israelite movement along it. Indeed, these circumstances may be reflected in the Book of Exodus: "When Pharaoh let the people go, God did not lead them by the way of the land of the Philistines, although that was near; for God said, 'Lest the people repent when they see war, and return to Egypt'" (13:17). (chap. 5) On the other hand, the Israelite attempt to penetrate northward through the Negev, farther inland, ended in failure, for Canaanite strongholds such as Hormah (cf. Num. 14:40–45; 21:1; Deut. 1:44), east of Beersheba, effectively protected the southern hill-country. Unable to advance, the Israelites made a broad swing around into Trans-Jordan, crossing the Jordan river to invade Canaan from its eastern flank. Thus, they supplanted an ineffective frontal assault with a strategically indirect approach (for this military means, see below).

(c) The Canaanite populace west of the Jordan had no unified, overall military organization with which to confront the invaders. Furthermore, the absence of political cohesion was matched by the lack of any Canaanite national consciousness. Only twice are Canaanite fronts against the Israelites, albeit limited, in evidence: once in the south, of five allied Canaanite city-states led by the King of Jerusalem (initially only intended to oppose the Gibeonites); and once in the north, an alliance of four Canaanite kings under the leadership of the King of Hazor, which fought at the Waters of Merom. These instances were exceptional (as was Gezer's aid to Lachish; Josh. 10:33), however, and in general the Canaanite cities stood in political and military disunity. Thus, for example, no one came to the aid of Jericho or (apparently) Ai in the hour of peril. This extreme political fragmentation in Canaan is demonstrated by the situation depicted in the Amarna Letters, of the mid-14th century B.C.E., as

---

[8] Cf. now *inter alia* Bright, *History of Israel*,[2] 127ff.

well as in the list of 31 Canaanite kings allegedly defeated by Joshua (Josh. 12:9–24).

(d) Due to the lack of a broad Canaanite territorial defense system, no attempt was made to stop the Israelites from fording the Jordan. The river was a potential impediment for the Israelites, and provided the Canaanites with a fine means of forestalling the invasion.[9] That the Jordan could be utilized for military purposes is no idle assumption, for this was demonstrated more than once by the Israelites themselves during the period of the Judges. The fords of the Jordan were seized to cut off an enemy's line of retreat on three occasions: to prevent the Moabite army from escaping to Trans-Jordan, in the days of Ehud (Judg. 3:28–29); to prevent the Midianites' retreat to the desert, in the days of Gideon (Judg. 7:24–25); and to halt the escape of Ephraimites, in the days of Jephthah (the Shibboleth incident—Judg. 12:5–6).

(e) During the days of the Conquest and the first stages of the Settlement, the Israelites were successful against the Canaanites only in the hill-country and its western slopes. Indeed—and quite contrary to popular notion—an inferior force (such as that of the Israelites) assailing large bodies of defenders in mountainous terrain (such as the Canaanites) holds a relatively military advantage, especially in open battle.[10] Such a mountain mentality in warfare, and the complementary reluctance to engage in lowland fighting was attributed to the Israelites still many generations later: "Their gods are gods of the hills, and so they were stonger than we [the 'Arameans']; but let us fight against them in the plain, and surely we shall be stronger than they" (I Kings 20:23; and cf. the Syrian taunt to the Jews, in I Maccabees 10:70ff.: "Why do you defy us up there in the hills . . . come down to meet us on the plain . . ."). It was in the low-lands (the Jezreel and Beth-Shean valleys, and the coastal plain) that the Israelite invaders were unable to dislodge the dense indigenous population. The biblical historiographer realized the military reason underlying this: "he took possession of the hill-country, but he could not drive out the inhabitants of the plain, because they had chariots of iron" (Judg. 1:19, on the tribe of Judah; Josh. 17:16, on the Joseph tribes; and cf. Judg. 1:34, on the Danites). In other words,

---

[9] On rivers constituting military barriers, see Clausewitz, *War*, 433ff.
[10] See *ibid.*, 417ff.

the Israelite inability to capture the plains was a consequence of the Canaanite chariot, a weapon most effectively employed in flat terrain.

Canaanite-Israelite Disparity

In espousing the principal biblical maxim of a military subjugation of Canaan, as the decisive factor in the Israelite takeover, we are confronted by the cardinal question: How could the semi-nomadic Israelite tribes, emerging from the desert fringes, surmount an adversary of long military experience and possessing a superior technology? How was an unmounted horde able to overthrow an array of strongly fortified cities and well-trained forces, including formidable chariotry? This obvious military disparity was one of the prime motives in weaning many Bible critics away from the traditional view and leading them to hypothesize the peaceful infiltration of Canaan. Granting that such infiltration occurred side-by-side with military campaigns, it hardly can be considered as the initial or principal factor of the Israelite occupation (as is a prevalent view in biblical criticism). History is too littered with analogous instances of ancient states and even empires being overwhelmed by "uncivilized" tribes, two outstanding examples being the Arab conquest of Byzantine Palestine, and the destruction of the Roman Empire by the Germanic tribes. In seeking a rationale for the Israelite Conquest, we must focus upon two prime factors: a relative decline of the Canaanite city-states at this time, and the specific conduct of warfare assumed by the invading Israelites.

The Canaanite city-states, which flowered in the 15th and 14th centuries B.C.E., were frequently the target of Egyptian military attacks. Having endured a prolonged period of colonial rule resulting from these campaigns, they reached a state of deterioration in the 13th century. This deterioration on the eve of and during the Conquest was a factor serving to counterbalance the military deficiencies of the Israelites, and facilitating the relatively rapid overrunning of the country. The insecurity of the countryside is also clearly reflected in the roughly contemporaneous Papyrus Anastasi I (second half of the 13th century B.C.E., and cf. the description in the Song of Deborah, Judg. 5:6: "caravans ceased and travelers kept to the byways"). The Egyptian policy of *divide et impera* intensified the incessant disputes among the Canaanite city-states, as evidenced by the

Amarna Letters (second quarter of the 14th century B.C.E.), which also inform us that the actual numbers of warriors kept by the Canaanite rulers were quite meager. Requests for military assistance from neighbors or Egypt often mention no more than ten to fifty men, while a force of fifty chariots was considered rather extraordinary. Thus, in a letter discovered in the southern part of the country, a prince of Lachish is asked for a consignment, six bows, three daggers and three swords—arms for, say, twelve men, at most.[11] These insignificant numbers reveal the vulnerability of Canaan to even small bodies of invaders who, once having penetrated, could threaten the city-states and sever communications between them.

The Israelites were able to exploit another Canaanite weakness, the heterogeneity of the population, a veritable mosaic of ethnic groups, as is attested, *inter alia*, in the oft-repeated biblical formula listing the seven peoples of Canaan. The Israelites skillfully manipulated local animosities among these groups, who were further differentiated by political and social factors. A prime example is the treaty which Joshua concluded separately with the Gibeonites, themselves of Hivite (non-Semitic) stock, originating in the north, apparently in Anatolia (Jos. 9).

How, however, were the Israelites able to arrive at an accurate appraisal of the land they were about to invade, and to effect the means to assure its conquest? The answer lies in the specific military qualities and skills of the Israelites, aspects which have been treated in part by various experts in both the biblical and military fields.[12] The treatment below, however, attacks the Conquest as a subject in itself, by dealing comprehensively with a number of major fundamentals and the military doctrine of early Israelite warfare.[13]

Intelligence

To assure maximum success, any warlike operation must be preceded by intelligence activities. The Conquest cycle abounds in intelligence and espionage operations, demonstrating a developed awareness

---

[11] For this letter, found at Tell el-Hesi in 1892, see Albright, *BASOR* 87.

[12] See in particular Yadin's thoroughgoing *Art of Warfare*.

[13] For my preliminary study see *Conquest of Palestine in the Time of Joshua*, 1951 (2nd edition, 1954) (Hebrew).

of this prerequisite among the Israelites. There is frequent mention
of reconnaissance units sent out prior to campaigns against the regions
or cities; these missions yielded vital information on Canaan, its
topography, ethnic and demographic make-up, military and political structure, productivity, ecological factors, etc.

These elements receive full expression in the story of the twelve
spies despatched by Moses on first reaching the borders of Canaan.
Their explicit instructions reflect a comprehensive strategic probe,[14]
reading like a modern intelligence brief: ". . . and see what the land
is, and whether the people who dwell in it are strong or weak,
whether they are few or many, and whether the land that they dwell
in is good or bad, and whether the cities that they dwell in are
camps or strongholds, and whether the land is rich or poor, and
whether there is wood in it or not" (Num. 13:18–20). Similarly, the
data gathered on the fertility of the land, the strength of its defenses
and the distribution of the Canaanite peoples (Num. 13:27ff.) have
the true ring of intelligence reports. Further, the opposite stands
taken by the spies testify to divergent attitudes in the evaluation of
intelligence data. Ten of the spies, taking a defeatist stance, rouse
the people against the planned operation, while a minority of two
(Joshua and Caleb) optimistically presses for its implementation (cf.
Num. 13:31–32, as against 13:30 and 14:9).

Admittedly, the story of these spies certainly contains poetic-
legendary embellishment, and has undergone tendentious religious
editing. Nevertheless, it is authentic in its pattern of intelligence activities, which are typical of Israelite warfare. This is observed also in
the Danite campaign to conquer and settle the city of Laish in the
north, during the period of the Judges; this tribal story, of more realistic stamp than the episode under Moses, reveals a similar pattern
of sending out spies and their reporting back (Judg. 18).[15] In other
instances, the Bible merely refers to such matters in passing, in a
single word. The conquest of the land of Jazer in Trans-Jordan
(which fell to the Israelites after the defeat of Sihon, King of Heshbon)
is described in this telescoped manner: "And Moses sent to spy out
Jazer; and they took its villages, and dispossessed the Amorites that
were there" (Num. 21:32). And prior to the conquest of Bethel: "The

---

[14] Cf. Yadin, *Art of Warfare*, 110.
[15] For the typology of the two spy episodes, see Malamat, *Biblica* 51, 2–7 =
chap. 9.

house of Joseph sent to spy out Bethel . . ." (Judg. 1:23). The specific verbal form in the Hebrew[16] indicates that here, too, we are dealing with the despatch of a reconnaissance unit before the operation.

In the hitherto mentioned examples, the Israelites were generally aiming for settlement subsequent to the conquest of the sites, and thus resorted to reconnaissance of a broad, strategic nature, to obtain a comprehensive picture of their objective. In contrast, where destruction *per se* was sought, as at Jericho and Ai, the more limited scope of tactical, field intelligence—yielding purely military information—certainly sufficed.

The spies despatched to Jericho, the first Israelite objective in Canaan according to the "official" tradition, found cover in the house of Rahab the harlot. This particular "contact" was a logical one militarily, for Rahab's house was "built into the city wall, so that she dwelt in the wall" (Josh. 2:15); that is, it was located in a vital spot in the city's defenses. Further, Rahab's profession enabled her to come into contact with much of the city's menfolk, especially suiting her to the spies' needs, providing them not only with details of the city's defenses but also of the fighting forces and the morale prevalent within the town (Josh. 2:15ff.; Josephus, *Antiquities* V, 1, 2, elaborates on the intelligence gathered). This last matter was of particular interest to the Israelite command: "And they said to Joshua, 'Truly the Lord has given all the land into our hands; and moreover all the inhabitants of the land are fainthearted because of us'" (Josh. 2:24).

Failure of Intelligence

A reconnaissance unit was also sent to the next city in the path of the advancing Israelites, Ai at the upper reaches of Wadi Makkuk which leads down toward Jericho. In this instance, however, a mishap in the Israelite intelligence led to the one and only military defeat appearing in the Book of Joshua (though the biblical tradition ascribes this failure to divine wrath). The spies not only reported raw information but also delved into military counsel: "Let not all the people go up, but let about two or three thousand men go up and

---

[16] The Hebrew *wayyātūru*, in the causative *hiph'il* of *tūr*, is properly rendered "they cause a reconnaissance to be made."

attack Ai; do not make the whole people toil up there, for they are but few" (Josh. 7:3). In the initial attack on Ai, this advice was taken, and the small force of 3,000 was routed, with losses. In the second attempt, Joshua threw 30,000 choice troops into battle (Josh. 8:3ff.); though this number appears exaggerated, it indicates that the force in the first operation was but a tenth of the strength necessary to assure success. Thus, the initial intelligence blunder lay in the misestimate of the enemy's strength. We may point to another possible failing of the spies, namely their interference in operational decisions, which most likely in biblical times, as in modern intelligence practice, was prohibited to field agents; such decisions belong exclusively to the level of command.

In accord with its historiographical tendency, the Bible attributes the initial setback at Ai to a sin among the Israelites and regards the subsequent success as feasible only after the expiation of guilt (Josh. 7:11ff.). From a realistic-military viewpoint, the "transgression" was a breakdown in discipline at the time of the conquest of Jericho, that is, Achan's taking of loot which was under divine ban.[17] The glory at Jericho resulted in an over-confidence which infected the Israelite command no less than the ranks; in the sphere of intelligence, this was manifest in the gross underestimation of the enemy. However, the setback at Ai had a sobering effect upon the Israelites. But Joshua seems to have been concerned less by the drop in Israelite morale than by an external factor of extreme significance: The fear of loss of image (note the indicative words attributed to Joshua in 7:8–9) led him to react swiftly with a force sufficiently large to assure an overwhelming victory.[18]

Logistics

The biblical sources can also be gleaned for information on matters of supplies, material and their distribution in the Israelite army, that is, on logistics. The lengthy wanderings with their numerous encampments in the desert, the campaigns in Trans-Jordan, and the later

---

[17] For the imposition of the divine ban (*ḥerem*) as a deterrent to pillaging in early warfare, see Malamat, *Biblical Essays* (*Proceedings, 9th Meeting, Ou-Testam. Werkgemeenskap, Suid-Afrika*; 1966), 43ff.

[18] On the Battle of Ai, see below and Gichon in *Zer Li'gevurot*.

long-range incursions into Cis-Jordan involved complex problems in this field.

Perusal of the Book of Joshua reveals that special attention was paid to organizing equipment and food supplies. Thus, just prior to the crossing of the Jordan, Joshua commanded the people to prepare provisions, setting aside three days for the task (Josh. 1:10–11). In the later episode of the outrage at Gibeah, in the period of the Judges, one in ten of the troops was involved in quartermaster duties, attending to the provisions of the front-line soldiers (Judg. 20:10). The timing for the invasion across the Jordan was apparently determined by logistics considerations, to assure the Israelites of steady supplies. It fell in the early spring, "on the tenth day of the first month" (i.e., Nisan; Josh. 4:19; and cf. "at the return of the year . . . when kings go forth to battle"; II Sam. 11:1), when crops, especially barley, had already begun to ripen in the Jordan valley, but somewhat before harvest in the cooler regions of the land. Indeed, the biblical tradition itself relates that after the Israelites had celebrated the Passover on the plain of Jericho, "they ate of the produce of the land . . . and the people of Israel had manna no more, but ate of the fruit of the land of Canaan that year" (Josh. 5:11–12). Despite the legendary elements in this story, it reflects a real situation of logistics. This raping of the land was double-edged, furnishing the Israelites with provisions and furthering the ruination of Canaan at one and the same time. Another important source for supplies lay in the conquered cities themselves: "And all the spoil of these cities and the cattle, the people of Israel took for their booty" (Josh. 11:14, concerning Galilee; and cf. Josh. 8:27, on Ai).

The "official" tradition ascribes a central role to Gilgal, the initial camp of the Israelites after the crossing of the Jordan. It was from Gilgal, between the Jordan and Jericho (its precise location is unknown), that Israelite task forces would set out into the hill country. Following each operation into southern Canaan, they would retire thence, as after the conquest of Ai, the battle at Gibeon, and even the taking of Canaanite strongholds farther west (Josh. 9:6; 10:15, 43; and cf. 10:6–9). So outstanding a fact has led to various ingenious explanations, for example, the assumption that Gilgal served as a cultic site to which numerous stories became accreted;[19] or that

---

[19] See e.g. Noth, *Josua*, 11f., 31ff.; opposed by Kaufmann, *Conquest of Palestine*, 67ff.

there were several Gilgals; or that the name Gilgal (the Hebrew word conveys a sense of "cairn") was actually a generic term for a fortified campsite surrounded by a circle of stones, the camp being moved with the advance of the invaders.[20]

The central role of Gilgal, however, can be understood readily in terms of logistics and strategy. Firstly, as an operational base, Gilgal was a bridgehead in Canaan, supported by the Israelite hinterland in Trans-Jordan, through which supplies and reinforcements could be channeled as required. Neglect of this vital link would endanger the elongated lines of the invasion and place the Israelite task forces in jeopardy. Secondly, it was the springboard into the mountainous interior, with routes forking out, along which the forces could penetrate. These pathways appear to have stretched through the boundary zone between the territories controlled by the two principal kingdoms in the central hill country, Jerusalem and Shechem. Such a chink offered the Israelites a means of facilitating their various operations into Canaan as described in the Book of Joshua, and, indeed, led toward the propitiating Hivite enclave in the hinterland to the west.

The Indirect Military Approach

After intelligence and logistics, we turn to the very methods which typified Israelite warfare during the period of the Conquest and Settlement. Our focus is upon the tactical plane, the individual engagements—rather than the broad strategic level (though the distinction is often vague in war) which would lead us, irrelevant to our pursuit, toward a fundamentalistic acceptance of the overall scheme of the Conquest as related in the Book of Joshua. The acute military problem facing the Israelites was twofold:

(a) Enemy defense was based upon strongly fortified cities, which appeared to the biblical historiographer as "cities great and fortified up to heaven." These fortresses were a stumbling block even for regular forces such as the mighty Egyptian army, which at times had to resort to long, drawn-out sieges to overcome them. But the very size of the Canaanite cities may well have become a hindrance to

---

[20] This last explanation was put forth orally by Y. Yadin.

their defenders (an average town extended over 10–20 acres, though Hazor sprawled over as much as 200 acres, with a circumvallation of over 3 km). For on the eve of the Israelite invasion, a weakened Canaan (see above) must have had difficulties in mustering the resources necessary for the defense of such extensive fortifications.

(b) The Canaanites deployed well-trained professional forces, the most formidable arm of which was the famed chariotry. This latter was based on a two-wheeled chariot, a light vehicle providing a maximum of maneuverability in battle. Though the tactical role of the chariotry has yet to be elucidated satisfactorily, it may partly resemble that of modern armored forces. Contemporaneous Egyptian reliefs depicting the chariot reveal a dual role: forming a protective screen for advancing infantry, and pursuing a broken enemy in flight.[21] The Canaanite chariot, like its Egyptian counterpart, served as a mobile platform for the longest-range weapon employed in ancient times—the bow whose most sophisticated form, the composite bow, had an effective range of 300–400 meters.[22] The tactical combination of chariotry and archery is inferred, *inter alia*, in the two outwardly conflicting descriptions of the fall of King Saul on Mount Gilboa. In reality these were two views of one and the same circumstance: according to I Samuel 31:3, Saul was surrounded and "the archers found him and he was badly wounded by the archers," while according to II Samuel 1:6, "the chariots and the horsemen were close upon him." Another aspect of the superiority of chariotry over foot-soldiers was its immense psychological impact, especially the terrifying image of galloping horses (cf. Judg. 5:22, and Nah. 3:2).

In the face of a superior enemy, the Israelites achieved success through what is termed in modern military science "the indirect approach"—a concept propounded by Liddell Hart (though he applied it mainly to the strategic plane rather than the tactical, as done here).[23] The notion of the "indirect approach" is one of those novel conceptual frameworks which promises to bring about a new assessment of well-known, ancient battles, at the same time affording deeper insights into the specific manner in which such engagements were

---

[21] Cf. Schulman, *JARCE* 2.

[22] On the "composite bow", see Yadin, *Art of Warfare*, 6ff.; and on the chariot, 4f. and 86ff. there. On the range of the ancient bow in general, cf. W. McLeod, *Phoenix*, 19 (1965), 1–14; 26 (1972), 78–82.

[23] The doyen of British military theorists coined the term "indirect approach" already in the late 1920s; see his classic treatise *Strategy* (last revised edition, 1967).

conducted. Liddell-Hart himself traced the course of the "indirect approach" as far back in history as Classical times, but unfortunately he ignored the Bible. For many of the biblical sources, when stripped of their theological varnish, do present a candid record of military lessons and can still serve as exemplars for Liddell Hart's thesis. Careful analysis of the various battles described—particularly in the Books of Joshua and Judges, and to some extent in Samuel—reveals that the early Israelites gained victory over a technologically and numerically superior enemy through efficient application of what can certainly be regarded as the "indirect approach." Indeed, such a manner of action formed the very pith and fibre of Israelite warfare in this period, and we submit that this artful application of "indirect" means, independent of the technology of the time, was a veritable pinnacle in Military History. But as in their social and political structure, the military practices of the Israelites subsequently underwent a basic change, upon the establishment of a monarchy. With the institutionalization of a regular army, under the kings of Israel, the "indirect" gave way to more direct, conventional modes of warfare, placing greater reliance upon brute force and advanced weaponry.

The indirect approach sought to avoid frontal assault and siege warfare, as well as straightforward encounters with enemy forces, especially chariotry, in the open field. To achieve this the Israelites resorted to tactics based on deception—feints, decoys, ambushes and diversionary maneuvres—any guile to attain surprise in overcoming the enemy. Doctrinal reliance upon such ruses is indicated by a recurring phrase in the Book of Proverbs: "Devices are established by plan; wage wars by stratagems" (20:18); "By stratagems you shall wage war, and victory [comes] through much planning" (24:6); and compare: "For want of stratagems an army falls, but victory [comes] through much planning" (11:14) (transl. A.M., partly based on the new Jewish Publication Society translation). The pairing of the broad Hebrew terms *maḥshavot* and *ʿezah/yoʿez* ("devices" and "plan/planner/planning") with the clearly military terms *taḥbulot* and *milḥamah* ("stratagems" and "war") instills them with a particular tenor here (and compare the analogous usage of this pair in Jer. 49:20 and 30).

The conscious employment of cunning and deception in warfare is noted sporadically in ancient Near Eastern sources already centuries prior to the Israelite Conquest.[24] A piquant instance is King Shamshi-

---

[24] For a treatment of such aspects in modern warfare, see Whaley, *Stratagem: Deception and Surprise in War* (hereafter *Stratagem*), 1969.

Adad's chiding of his son, Yasmah-Adad, in the 18th century B.C.E.: "Devise feints (*shibqu*) to defeat the enemy, and to maneuver against him, but the enemy too will devise feints and maneuver against you, just as wrestlers employ feints (*shibqu*) against each other" (*Archives Royales de Mari*, I, No. 5, lines 4–9).[25] This comparison of warfare to a wrestling match, found also in Classical literature, anticipates Clausewitz' well-known simile by 3,500 years.[26] Throughout the literature of the ancient Near East, however, the Books of Joshua and Judges remain unique in the number and variety of battle schemes gathered. In this regard, we can only ponder on the lost contents of the "Book of the Wars of the Lord" and the "Book of Jashar," both mentioned in the Conquest cycle (Num. 21:14; Josh. 10:13).

Actual collections of stratagems in war have survived, however, only from Classical times (excluding the Far East). Two comprehensive works of this sort, both named *Strategemata*, are extant, each containing several hundred examples, drawn from the Greek and Roman wars. The earlier collection was compiled by Frontinus toward the end of the first century C.E.[27] Of lower military-historical order is the collection of Polyaenus, of the second half of the second century C.E.[28] Whereas the former work was founded upon a methodical, practical classification, the material in the second was arranged according to the generals involved. The partial overlap of examples in the two works reveals that both relied upon earlier compilations. In any event, perusal of these two sources yields quite a few tactical devices resembling various ruses described in the Bible. As these parallels[29] are of considerable importance in bolstering the credibility of the biblical examples, we shall refer to them below, elucidating *inter alia* several instances hitherto overlooked.

---

[25] Cf. Sasson, *Military Establishments at Mari*, 43.

[26] See Clausewitz, *War*, 75.

[27] For an English translation, see the *Loeb Classical Library*; the most recent and accurate edition of the Latin source is by Bendz, *Kriegslisten*.

[28] The standard edition of the Greek text remains that of Teubler, by J. Melber, 1887; the latest translation in a modern language is the antiquated and inaccurate German rendering by Blume and Fuchs, 1833–35. On the textual transmission, see now F. Schindler, Die Überlieferung der Strategemata des Polyainos, *Österreichische Akademie der Wissenschaften, Phil.-Hist. Klasse*, 284, 1973.

[29] Several of these instances have already been noted by Abel, *RB* 56.

Conquest of Fortified Cities

Among the early wars of the Israelites, we find no actual description of an outright, successful assault upon an enemy city. The adoption of an indirect military approach finds expression in two principal categories of tactics employed by the Israelites: covert infiltration—neutralizing the city defenses (like the Trojan horse); and enticement—drawing the city-defenders out into the open.

Neutralization of City Defenses. The fall of Jericho, as described in Joshua 2–6, was a siege culminating in a "miraculous" destruction of the walls (6:20), and a subsequent penetration into the defenseless city. The "official" tradition, however, preserves an early strand, apparently hinting at an actual military conquest of the city. This latter is represented by the episode of Rahab and the spies, an independent literary source, which has been worked into the amalgam of the Jericho cycle (the episode begins in Josh. 2, but continues only in Josh. 6:22ff.). The etiological element of this particular episode (the survival of a Canaanite family "in the midst of Israel"), like Rahab's confession (Josh. 2:9–13), is surely the work of a later redactor. In fact, the story of the spies, of a realistic-secular stamp, is quite out of line with the present tradition, which ascribes the fall of the city to divine providence rather than to human feat (for this historiographical tendentiousness, cf. the introduction, above). Indeed, the factuality of an actual battle at Jericho is indicated in the review of Israel's history in Joshua's valediction (24:11): "And you went over the Jordan and came to Jericho, and the men of Jericho fought against you. . . ." Thus, we conclude that there had once circulated a more realistic account of the capture of Jericho, including an intelligence mission involving a "fifth column" within the city.

We cannot successfully reconstruct that early version of the conquest of Jericho because the suppressed story has been truncated in the extant text, and supplanted by the historiographer's *actus Dei.* Nonetheless some notions can be set forth. Such a version would have Rahab playing a more active role in the Israelite penetration into the city, which was most likely accomplished by stratagem. Thus, when the spies had Rahab tie the scarlet cord *outside* her window in the city-wall (Josh. 2:18), it was not to protect her household from the Israelites rampaging *within* the city after the collapse of the walls, as the later redactor would have us believe. Rather, it would have marked the way for a stealthy entry into the city (analogous to the postern at Bethel; see below), as also intimated in the Septuagint version here.[30]

Could the encircling maneuver around the city, the horn blasts, and the great battlecry preceding the miraculous collapse of the walls (Josh. 6:20) also be survivals from that realistic account of the city's fall? The repeated encircling of Jericho on six successive days,[30a] the Israelites retiring each day to their camp (Josh. 6:3, 14), has sometimes been regarded as a psychological device to lower the enemy's guard, preparing the way for a breach into the city. This stratagem may have been meant to distract the enemy from the specific Israelite design, or it may have been a noted form of surprise, which we may term "conditioning," that is, deceiving the enemy by repeating the same "field exercise" until he has relaxed his vigilance and a decisive blow can suddenly be dealt. Stratagems of this latter sort have been employed throughout history (cf. below, on the conquest of Ai), and Frontinus cites quite a few examples, one of which is particularly similar to our case: A Roman general marched his troops regularly around the walls of a well-fortified city in northern Italy, each time returning them to camp till, when the vigilance of the defenders had waned, he stormed the walls and forced the city's capitulation (*Strategemata* III, 2, 1).[31]

The conquest of Bethel (Josh. 12:16 merely mentions its king in the list of defeated Canaanite rulers) is related only in Judges 1 (22–26), that is, in a deviant tradition of the conquest of Canaan, as we have noted above. Here, the action is ascribed to the Joseph tribes alone, rather than to pan-Israelite initiative under Joshua. Even so, the cursory description reveals several of the patterns typical of the Israelite campaigns of conquest: preliminary reconnaissance (see above) and divine patronage ("and the Lord was with them," 1:22). The latter is indicative of the presence of priests and possibly the Holy Ark at the assault, as at Jericho or in Moses' wars, or of other

---

[30] For similar attempts at reconstruction, see Windisch, *ZAW* 37; and recently Tucker in *The Use of the Old Testament in the New*; cf. also Langlamet, *RB* 78, 321ff. On the battlecry (see immediately below), appearing also in Gideon's stratagem against the Midianites (Judg. 7:21), see P. Humbert, *La "Terou'a"*, Neuchâtel (1941), 16ff., 30f.

[30a] It might be implied here that the city was captured on the Sabbath, as is held in Rabbinic sources; such a timing has a specific purport in the history of military conduct.

[31] Cf. Abel, *RB* 56, 326; Yadin, *Art of Warfare*, 99f.

cultic appurtenances, as on the Danite campaign northward (Judg. 18). Though the text is not explicit, the change of the name of the conquered city from Luz to Bethel (1:23) may well be another feature of the pattern, for the renaming of captured sites is not an infrequent phenomenon in the Conquest traditions.[32]

The actual conquest of Bethel was effected by a ruse well-known in the history of siege warfare, that is, penetration into a fortified city by means of secret ingress. In this instance, the Israelites took advantage of a postern (Hebrew *m'vo ha'ir*, here certainly *not* the city-gate), of the type of secret passage actually discovered on several sites in Palestine and the neighboring lands.[33] The Israelite pickets (Hebrew *shomĕrim*), who kept the city under surveillance, learned of its existence through the treachery of a citizen. As in the Rahab episode at Jericho, the Israelites assured their informant and his family safety in reward: "And he showed them the way into the city . . . but they let the man and all his family go" (Judg. 1:25). Penetration into the city through the hidden passage here, also recalling David's later conquest of Jerusalem, achieved two aims at one blow—maximal surprise, and neutralization of the fortification—leading to the rapid collapse of the city's defense.

Enticement of City Defenders. In the Books of Joshua and Judges, the most satisfactory accounts of city conquests, as far as reconstructing the minutiae of planning and execution of the Israelite operations is concerned, relate to Ai (Josh. 7–8) and Gibeah of Benjamin (the latter destroyed in internecine war; Judg. 20:18–44). In both instances,

---

[32] On the various elements typical of the Conquest campaigns, see Malamat, *Biblica* 51 (= chap. 9). In this story, however, the Luz/Bethel change of name is not explicitly associated with the city's conquest (indeed, cf. Gen. 28:19), though is indirectly indicated by the informer's subsequent emigration to "the land of the Hittites" and his founding there "a city, and he called its name Luz" (Judg. 1:26), certainly in commemoration of his native town. The impression gained is of an early, elusive tradition ultimately linking the biblical toponym Luz (*lwz*) with the well-known Hittite city *Lawazantiya* (note the Anatolian suffix -*ant/diya*). Significant in our context is the fact that the very name of the latter city, situated between the Taurus and the Euphrates, reappears in the late 14th or 13th century B.C.E. (i.e., close to the period of the Israelite Conquest) in Eastern Cilicia, as attested by the city *Lwsnd* in the Ugaritic, and *Lusanda* in the neo-Assyrian texts. See M.C. Astour, *American Journal of Archaeology* 69 (1965), 257; and *idem, Hellenosemitica* (1965), 30ff., where the transfer of city-names is noted as a common phenomenon in Asia Minor, influenced *inter alia* by the invasion of the Sea Peoples—which brings us chronologically to much the same period as the Israelite Conquest.

[33] Cf. Yadin, *Art of Warfare*, 254.

almost identical stratagems are described, in similar terms. This similarity has led many commentators to believe that one or the other of the two accounts served as the literary model, but particularly effective stratagems were undoubtedly re-employed in Israelite tactics. If indeed there was interdependence, the capture of Ai (et-Tell) is more likely the copy of the two,[34] for the archaeological evidence there is quite negative.[35] The latter point, however, has no intrinsic effect upon our military analysis below, which focuses upon the biblical tradition as transmitted.

The stratagem employed in capturing these two cities is clear enough, in spite of the awkward and repetitious presentations in the biblical text, which are generally regarded as coalesced from more than one source. The ruse was based on a diversionary movement intended to decoy the defending forces away from their fortifications (Josh. 8:6, 16; Judg. 20:31, 32), onto open ground, concurrently enabling another Israelite force to seize the now undefended city.[36] The tactical aim was achieved by splitting the Israelite force: the main body was deployed as if to storm the city-walls but, in fact, feigned retreat into the wilderness, with the enemy in hot pursuit. Such simulated, controlled flight, which could be reversed upon order, was a difficult maneuver involving a certain amount of calculated risk. The second body, the "ambush," was concealed behind the city (at Ai, to the west) or around it (at Gibeah; Judg. 20:29). At Ai, it is explicitly stated that the ambush took cover during the night, remaining there "in readiness" (Josh. 8:4–5); this was probably at Gibeah as well.

The fate of the battle pivoted upon precise coordination between the two Israelite wings, a complicated task in any situation. The adversary had to be lured not only to convenient ground but also an optimal distance away from the city before the "flight" could be reversed. This would allow the ambush sufficient time to gain control of the city before the enemy could regroup and counterattack,

---

[34] See the Commentaries, as well as Roth, *ZAW* 75, and most recently Rösel, *ZDPV* 92, 33ff.

[35] For the various (sometimes farfetched) attempts to resolve the inexplicable discrepancy between the excavation results at Ai and the biblical account, see now de Vaux, *Histoire d'Israel*, 563ff.

[36] For the battle of Ai see, in addition to the Commentaries, Gale, *Battles of Biblical History*, 21ff., and especially Gichon, *Zer Li'gevurot*; on Gibeah, see Kaufmann, *Judges*, 289ff. On both battles see Rösel, *ZDPV* 91, 159ff.; 92, 31ff.

yet not so far as to prevent the ambushing force from joining the fracas afield, blocking the enemy's rear. Coordinated timing was assured by predetermined signal. At Ai, it was given to the ambush by Joshua himself (by outstretching his spear toward the city), who was with the "fleeing" force (Josh. 8:15ff.); at Gibeah, the very burning of the city by the ambushing force formed a "smoke signal" initiating the counterattack by the main Israelite body (as explicitly stated in Judg. 20:38). At this point, the tables were turned and disorder and panic reigned in the ranks of the enemy, caught in the enveloping movement as so poignantly depicted in the text: "So when the men of Ai looked back, behold, the smoke of the city went up to heaven; and they had no power to flee this way or that, for the people that fled to the wilderness turned back upon the pursuers. . . . And the others [of the ambush] came forth from the city against them; so they were in the midst of Israel, some on this side, and some on that side; and Israel smote them, until there was left none that survived or escaped" (Josh. 8:20–22). And in the Gibeah episode: ". . . the Benjaminites looked behind them; and behold, the whole of the city went up in smoke to heaven. Then the men of Israel turned, and the men of Benjamin were dismayed, for they saw that disaster was close upon them. . . . Cutting off the Benjaminites, they pursued them and trod them down . . . as far as opposite Gibeah on the east" (Judg. 20:40–43).

In this Israelite stratagem we encounter a factor of as yet unrecognized significance,[37] the fact that in both these cases final success was preceded by abortive attempts upon the fortified cities, each culminating in the actual repulse of the attackers. As noted above, the initial assault upon Ai failed, and in the campaign against Gibeah, there were even two initial setbacks, on successive days (Judg. 20:19–25). The true ingenuity and boldness of the battle-plan put into effect in the final Israelite operations against these cities lies in the seeming repetition of the very tactics which previously led to failure. This, then, is another instance of the "conditioning" we noted at Jericho, in which repetitive moves are designed to lull the enemy into a false sense of security. How well the Israelites foresaw that the people of Ai would fall for the ruse: "[The Israelites] are fleeing

---

[37] See already, in brief, Malamat, *World History of the Jewish People* III, chap. 7 (1971) 163 and n. 92 (note that the last reference there to *Strategemata* should read Book II [not III], 5, 8).

Schematic Plan of the Taking of Ai

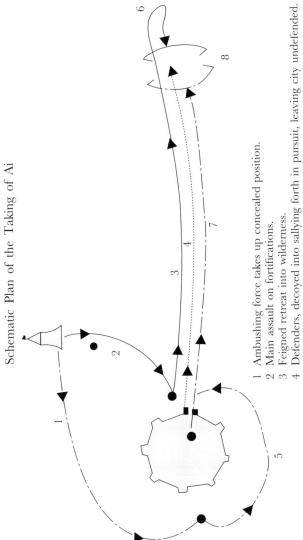

1 Ambushing force takes up concealed position.
2 Main assault on fortifications.
3 Feigned retreat into wilderness.
4 Defenders, decoyed into sallying forth in pursuit, leaving city undefended.
5 Ambushing force emerges to seize city, putting it to the torch.
6 Main force turns to attack pursuing defenders, upon sighting smoke from city.
7 Ambushing force sallies forth to attack defenders from rear.
8 Defenders surrounded and annihilated.

from us, as before" (Josh. 8:6), as would the defenders of Gibeah: "[The Israelites] are routed before us, as at the first" (Judg. 20:32 and cf. 39). In other words, the Israelites had learned the negative lessons of frontal attack, and applied them by shifting to indirect means in attaining their goals. Resorting to deception and subterfuge, they achieved utter surprise and diverted the enemy's attention from the principal objective. Mastering the factors of "time and space," the Israelites retained the initiative and deprived the enemy of the option of seriously influencing the course of the battle, let alone its outcome.

Stratagems of ambush and feigned retreat in capturing fortifications were esteemed practices in antiquity. Two operations of this sort from Palestine proper are attested to in the Greco-Roman period. Interestingly, both were directed against the very same formidable target—fortified settlements on the heights of Mount Tabor. The earlier operation was conducted by Antiochus III, who lured the Ptolemaic garrison down from the summit (218 B.C.E.). Similarly, 285 years later Placidus, one of Vespasian's generals, enticed the Jewish defenders from the mountain top (67 C.E.).[38]

Frontinus devoted an entire chapter to stratagems of this sort (*Strategemata* III, 10); one of his several examples (III, 10, 5), found also in Polyaenus (V, 10, 4) though nowhere else, is particularly relevant to our instances, despite the differences in detail:

> Himilco, the Carthaginian, when campaigning near Agrigentum, placed part of his forces in ambush near the town, and directed them to set fire to some damp wood as soon as the soldiers from the town should come forth. Then, advancing at daybreak with the rest of his army for the purpose of luring forth the enemy he feigned flight and drew the inhabitants after him for a considerable distance by his retirement. The men in ambush near the walls applied the torch to the wood-piles as directed. The Agrigentines, beholding the smoke ascend, thought their city on fire and ran back in alarm to protect it. Being encountered by those lying in wait for them near the walls, and beset in the rear by those whom they had just been pursuing, they were caught between two forces and so cut to pieces.[39]

---

[38] Col. (Ret.) E. Galili has kindly brought these references to my attention; see his paper in *Maarachot* 82, 64–66. The first reference is taken from Polybius V, 70, 6, and the second from Josephus, *Bellum* IV, 1, 8.

[39] Following the *Loeb edition*, 238ff.; on p. 240, n. 1 there, the similarity with Joshua 8 is already noted. The Carthiginian seizure of Agrigentum (in 406 B.C.E.) *per se* is attested to by Diodorus Siculus and most likely by a Punic stela as well; see C. Krahmalkov, *Rivista Studi Fenici* 2 (1974), 171–177.

Frontinus (II, 5, 8) gives a yet closer parallel to the biblical episodes of Ai and Gibeah, as far as the underlying military principle of "conditioning" is concerned, though here even the initial retreats are feigned:

> Fulvius, commander in the Cimbrian war, having pitched his camp near the enemy, ordered his cavalry to approach the fortifications of the barbarians and to withdraw in pretended flight, after making an attack. When he had done this for several days, with the Cimbrians in hot pursuit, he noticed that their camp was regularly left exposed. Accordingly, maintaining his usual practice with part of his force, he himself with light-armed troops, secretly took a position behind the camp of the enemy, and as they poured forth according to their custom, he suddenly attacked and demolished the unguarded rampart and captured their camp.[40]

Surprise Attacks

In the Book of Joshua there are numerous instances which mention no more than the mere fact of the taking of a Canaanite town. We may surmise that many of these strongholds fell not by deceptive methods of the sort treated above, nor by straightforward siege warfare, but corollary to field victories in open battle. Indeed, two examples of such battles—fought against Canaanite leagues at Gibeon (Josh. 10) and at the Waters of Merom (Josh. 11)—were of far-reaching consequence, leading to the capture of entire blocs of towns.

This leads up to our final question: How did the Israelites attain victory in these rare instances of open clash in the field, especially at the Waters of Merom, where the Canaanites employed formidable chariotry (Josh. 11:4, 6, 9)? A glimmer of the Israelite tactics can be found in the brief descriptions of these battles themselves: "So Joshua came upon them *suddenly*, having marched up all night from Gilgal. And the Lord threw them into a panic before Israel, who slew them with a great slaughter at Gibeon, and chased them by the way of the ascent of Beth-Horon, and smote them as far as Azekah and Makkedah" (Josh. 10:9–10); "So Joshua came *suddenly* upon them with all his people of war, by the Waters of Merom, and fell upon them. And the Lord gave them into the hand of Israel, who smote them and chased them as far as Great Sidon . . ." (Josh.

---

[40] *Loeb edition*, 136f.

11:7–8). "Suddenly," the key-word in both passages, evokes the concept of surprise, which the Israelites utilized to the fullest in these attacks.

Surprise has always been one of the most elementary principles of war, an essential in engaging an adversary superior in either technology or numbers.[41] Of its multifarious causes, we have already encountered two which are very typical—the subtle device of "conditioning," and outright deception. In the battles just noted, however, surprise took a more forthright manifestation, that is, it was employed in lieu of stratagem. Its vital components are secrecy and speed—in our two cases the Israelites striking a blow so sudden that the enemy was deprived of the opportunity of assessing his position in order to react effectively. As in any such surprise, the Israelites must have attacked at a time and location quite unexpected by the enemy. Moreover, they exploited the product of surprise—the dislocation of the enemy—pressing him beyond the breaking point and relentlessly hounding him in his headlong flight (Josh. 10:10, 19; 11:8), in classical application of the "principle of pursuit."

In contrast to the vague circumstances surrounding the battle of the Waters of Merom, the historical, geographical and military context of the battle at Gibeon is lucid.[42] The treaty between the Israelites and the Gibeonites exposed the northern flank of the kingdom of Jerusalem, and threatened Canaanite cohesion throughout the southern hill-country, leading to an immediate military reaction against the renegade city of Gibeon. The bold Israelite plan of action, rushing to the aid of their vassals, is unfolded in a single verse: "So Joshua came upon them suddenly, having marched up all night from Gilgal" (Josh. 10:9). Taking advantage of the hours of darkness, the Israelites made a lightning march from Gilgal to Gibeon (el-Jib)—a distance of 25–30 kilometers, involving a climb of over a thousand meters (Gilgal, c. 250 m below sea-level; Gibeon, c. 840 m above sea-level). The attack upon the astonished enemy apparently took place at dawn, when the Canaanites faced the walls of Gibeon with their rear and flanks exposed most dangerously before the assailing Israelites.

---

[41] Cf. Clausewitz, *War*, 198ff.; Erfurth, *Surprise* (see in particular the English translators' introduction); Whaley, *Stratagem*, 86ff.

[42] See Eph'al, in *Military History of the Land of Israel*.

The credibility of the above reconstruction is supported by the renowned verse from the Book of Jashar: "Sun, stand thou still at Gibeon, and thou Moon in the valley of Aijalon . . ." (Josh. 10:12).[43] This wondrous picture well reflects an early morning situation before the setting of the moon in the west, over the Aijalon valley, and after the sun had risen in the east, over Gibeon. The Israelite tactics may have taken into account another factor, the very position of the sun on the horizon, blinding the enemy facing the Israelite troops who were attacking him from the east. That this is not solely a modern military consideration is shown by examples in Frontinus (II, 2, 8) and Polyaenus (VIII, 10, 3). Both relate that the Roman general Marius, fighting barbarian tribes, deployed in such a manner as to cause the sun to blind the enemy facing him. Polyaenus adds: "When the barbarians turned [toward the Romans], the sun was in their faces and they were blinded by its brilliance . . . and when they could not longer bear the rays of the sun, they raised their shields to their faces. Thus they exposed their bodies and were wounded, and were destroyed by the Romans."

Night Operations

Utilization of the veil of darkness in achieving surprise was ingrained in Israelite tactical planning, from the days of the Conquest down to the beginning of the Monarchy. Though much more demanding than daytime operations—in training, courage and leadership—night activities benefit from security of movement, besides providing psychological bonuses.[44] Indeed, their very nature can nearly nullify outward superiority of an antagonist, swinging the balance in favor of a weaker force, if it indeed takes the initiative. Israelite night operations took the form of either outright attacks, or unobserved convergence upon an enemy prior to a dawn or daylight attack—and they are reviewed accordingly below.

---

[43] The present position of the "quotation" from the "Book of Jashar" is peculiar, for its true context would seem to be the battle proper at Gibeon, prior to the pursuit of the enemy by way of the ascent of Beth-horon as far as Makkedah; see Kaufmann, *Judges*, 143f. For a novel explanation of the "miracle" conjured by Joshua by calling upon the heavenly bodies, on the basis of the Mesopotamian "omen" literature, see Holladay, *JBL* 87.

[44] On night operations in general, see Boltze, *Das Nachtgefecht*.

Night movements in anticipation of attack in light occur in the following biblical episodes (the first two have been treated above): (1) in the final attack upon Ai (Josh. 8:3; and cf. vs. 13); (2) at Gibeon (Josh. 10:9); (3) in Abimelech's ambush against Shechem (Judg. 9:34); (4) in Saul's deployment against the Ammonites besieging Jabesh-Gilead (I Sam. 11:11); and possibly (5) in David's raid on the Amalekite camp (I Sam. 30:17).

Bolder still and more exacting in planning and execution were actual night attacks. The classical example—throughout military history—is Gideon's assault upon the Midianites, described in great detail in Judges 7. Despite the theological tendentiousness and several enigmas in the text, analysis of the story reveals characteristics and maxims of night warfare valid still today.[45] Another instance is the sequel to Saul's victory with Jonathan over the Philistines (I Sam. 14:36). We may also note Abraham's night raid to recover his nephew Lot from captivity (Gen. 14:15). Though the historical basis of this latter episode is, admittedly, doubtful, like the other cases it is most indicative of the tried and trusted nature of night operations among the Israelites.

The early Israelites encountered an adversary much their superior in military strength. By preserving a clear view of the objective, and applying means unanticipated by the enemy, a bold and imaginative Israelite leadership was successful in translating what may be regarded today as a specific military doctrine—the "indirect approach"—into spontaneous victory. An overriding factor was the Israelite soldier's basic motivation—his deep sense of national purpose. It was this blend which engendered the momentum of the Israelite Conquest.

Bibliography

Abel, F.M., Les stratagèmes dans le livre de Josué, *Revue Biblique* 56 (1949), 321–339.
Albright, W.F., The Israelite Conquest of Canaan in the Light of Archaeology, *Bulletin of the American Schools of Oriental Research* 74 (1939), 11–23; *idem*, A Case of Lèse-majesté in Pre-Israelite Lachish, with Some Remarks on the Israelite Conquest, *Bulletin of the American Schools of Oriental Research* 87 (1942), 32–38.

---

[45] For a detailed military analysis of Gideon's battle, see Malamat, *PEQ* 85; and cf. *World History of the Jewish People* III, 143ff. For partly different approaches, see Field-Marshal Wavell in *Soldiers and Soldiering*, and Yadin, *Art of Warfare*, 256ff.

Alt, A., Erwägungen über die Landnahme der Israeliten in Palästina; Josua, in *Kleine Schriften zur Geschichte des Volkes Israel* I (1953), 126–175; 176–192.

Boltze, A., *Das Nachtgefecht*[3] (1943).

Bright, J., *A History of Israel*[2] (1972).

von Clausewitz, C., *On War* (ed. and transl. by M. Howard and P. Paret) (1976).

Encyclopaedia Britannica[15], Macropaedia IX (1973), s.v. Intelligence and Counter-intelligence; XIX, Warfare, Conduct of.

Eph'al, I., The Battle of Gibeon and the Problem of Joshua's Southern Campaign, *The Military History of the Land of Israel in Biblical Times* (Heb., 1964), 79–90.

von Erfurth, W., *Surprise* (1942; transl. by S.T. Possony and D. Vilfroy, from the German *Die Überraschung*, 1938).

Frontinus, *Strategemata* (Loeb edition, transl. by C.E. Bennet; 1925); *idem, Kriegslisten* (lat. u. deutsch von G. Bendz; 1963).

Gale, R., *Great Battles of Biblical History* (1968).

Galili, E., The Conquest of Palestine by the Seleucian Army, *Maarachoth* 82 (1954), 52–72 (Heb.).

Garstang, J., *Joshua, Judges* (1931).

Gichon, M., The Conquest of Ai—An Historical Military Examination in *Zer Li'gevurot* (Z. Shazar Jubilee Volume, ed. by B.Z. Lurie; Heb., 1972), 56–72.

Herzog, C., & Gichon, M., *Battles of the Bible* (1978).

Holladay, J.S., The Day(s) the Moon Stood Still, *Journal of Biblical Literature* 87 (1968), 166–178.

Jones, G.H., "Holy War" or "Yahwe War"?, *Vetus Testamentum* 25 (1975), 642–658.

Kaufmann, Y., *The Biblical Account of the Conquest of Palestine* (1953); *idem*, Traditions Concerning Israelite History in Canaan, *Scripta Hierosolymitana* 8 (1961), 303–334; *idem.*, *The Book of Judges* (Heb., 1962); *idem, The Book of Joshua*[2] (Heb., 1963).

Langlamet, F., Josué II—Rahab et les espions, *Revue Biblique* 78 (1971), 321–354.

Liddell Hart, B.H., *Strategy: The Indirect Approach* (1954).

MacVeagh, R., & Costain, T.B., *Joshua, A Biography* (1948).

Malamat, A., The War of Gideon and Midian—A Military Approach, *Palestine Exploration Quarterly* 85 (1953), 61–75; *idem*, The Danite Migration and the Pan-Israelite Exodus-Conquest: A Biblical Narrative Pattern, *Biblica* 51 (1970), 1–16; *idem*, The Period of the Judges, *World History of the Jewish People* III (1971), 129–163, 314–323 (chap. 7); *idem*, Early Israelite Warfare and the Conquest of Canaan, Oxford (1978).

Mazar, B., The Exodus and Conquest, *World History of the Jewish People* III (1971), 69–93.

Miller, P.D., *The Divine Warrior in Early Israel* (1973).

Noth, M., *Das Buch Josua*[2] (1953).

Polyaenus, *Strategemata* (Teubner edition, ed. by J. Melber; 1887); *idem.*, *Kriegslisten* (translated by W.H. Blume & C. Fuchs; 1833–55).

von Rad, G., *Der Heilige Krieg im alten Israel* (1951).

Rösel, H., Studien zur Topographie der Kriege in den Büchern Josua und Richter, *Zeitschrift des deutschen Palästinavereins* 91 (1975), 159–90; 92 (1976), 10–46.

Roth, W.M.W., Hinterhalt und Scheinflucht. *Zeitschrift für die alttestamentliche Wissenschaft* 75 (1963), 296–304.

Sasson, J.M., *The Military Establishments at Mari* (1969).

Schulman, A.R., The Egyptian Chariotry: A Reexamination, *Journal of the American Research Center in Egypt* 2 (1963), 75–98.

Seeligmann, A.L., From Historical Reality to Historiosophical Conception in the Bible, *Praqim* II (Heb., 1969–74), 273–313.

Stolz, F., *Jahwes und Israels Kriege* (1972).

Tucker, G.M., The Rahab Saga (Joshua 2), *The Use of the Old Testament in the New & Other Essays* (ed. by J.M. Efird; 1972), 66–86.

de Vaux, R., *Histoire ancienne d'Israel* (1971).

Wavell, A.P., Night Attacks—Ancient and Modern, *Soldiers and Soldiering* (1953), 159–174.

Weippert, M., "Heiliger Krieg" in Israel und Assyrien, *Zeitschrift für die alttestamentliche Wissenschaft* 84 (1972), 460–495.

Whaley, B., *Stratagem: Deception and Surprise in War* (1969).

Windisch, H., Zur Rahabgeschichte, *Zeitschrift für die alttestamentliche Wissenschaft* 37 (1917/18).

Yadin, Y., *The Art of Warfare in Biblical Lands* I–II (1963).

Yeivin, S., *The Israelite Conquest of Canaan* (1971).

7

THE PERIOD OF THE JUDGES*

A. *Judgeship and the Book of Judges*

The complete lack of extra-biblical sources directly pertaining to the historical events of the period of the judges compels any survey of this period to be based almost exclusively on the collection of narratives contained in the Book of Judges. Assessment of this book as a historical source is determined by the evaluation of its composition, structure and particularly the manner of its recension.[1] A sharp distinction must be drawn between the actual stories of the judges, which are based on ancient, often tribal traditions, and the historiosophical and pragmatic framework into which they were integrated.[2] The pragmatic-theological (the so-called "deuteronomic") editing of these individual stories is based on two doctrines which largely contradict the historical reality of this period: a) the pan-Israelite concept which elevates tribal events and the scope of a judge's actions to a national level; b) the concept of historical periodicity, which views the events of the period as a series of recurring

---

* This article was originally published in: Judges, *WHJP* 3, chap. 7, 1971, 129–163, 314–322.

[1] These question are discussed at great length in the numerous commentaries on the Book of Judges; see the general bibliography for this chapter, below, p. 350; and cf. O. Eissfeldt, *The Old Testament, An Introduction*, Oxford, 1965, pp. 257ff.; E. Sellin – G. Fohrer, *Einleitung in das Alte Testament* (11th edition), Heidelberg, 1969, pp. 223ff. Cf. also E. Jenni, "Zwei Jahrzehnte Forschung an den Büchern Josua bis Könige," *Theologische Rundschau*, (NF), 27 (1961), 1ff.; 97ff.

[2] On this framework cf. the specific discussion by W. Beyerlin, "Gattung und Herkunft des Rahmens im Richterbuch," *Festschrift A. Weiser*, Göttingen, 1963, pp. 1ff. The author diminishes the importance of the deuteronomic editing of the framework; and cf. in particular W. Richter, *Die Bearbeitungen des "Retterbuches" in der deuteronomischen Epoche*, Bonn, 1964. This author distinguishes between several strata in the deuteronomic recension, which in his view was preceded already by a comprehensive work dealing with the deliverer-judges and not by separate tribal accounts. On the contrasting pre-deuteronomic and deuteronomic views of this period, cf. also M. Weinfeld, "The Period of the Conquest and of the Judges as Seen by the Earlier and the Later Sources," *VT*, 17 (1967), 93ff.

cycles, each comprising four successive stages: the people's reverting to idolatry and its subsequent oppression, appeal to God and consequent redeliverance, followed by a period of quiescence.[3]

Current Bible criticism has, however, gone too far in considering the background of the events of the period as entirely tribal and local, and the deliverer-judge as the mere leader of a single tribe or even clan. Yet, the historical reality of the time was that generally several tribes were simultaneously affected by foreign pressure, and that relief from it required a common action, the scope of which was beyond the ability of any individual tribe. The authority of the deliverer-judge undoubtedly extended beyond the confines of a single tribe, and thence the relation of a group, or confederation of tribes, to any particular set of events should not be considered as a later amplification under tendentious pan-Israelite influence.

Admittedly, this is still far from the biblical image of the judge as an actual pan-Israelite ruler. Furthermore, the periodic appearance of the judges cannot be accepted at face value—excluding *a priori* the simultaneous activity of two or more judges—and certainly not the chronological sequence as arranged by the editor of the Book of Judges.

Following Max Weber, the regime of the judges has been defined as a charismatic leadership, distinct from the other types of legitimate rule—both the traditional (i.e. the patriarchal-tribal) authority and the rational-legal (i.e. bureaucratic) authority.[4] This regime was based on the people's belief in the appearance in time of crisis of a divinely appointed deliverer. Thus the long-recognized theological-

---

[3] On the double aspect of the nation's deliverance in the Book of Judges, which ascribes it on the one hand to divine providence, and on the other to human valor—concepts which exist side-by-side in biblical historiography—cf. I.L. Seeligman, "Menschliches Heldentum und göttliche Hilfe," *Theologische Zeitschrift*, 19 (1963), 385ff.

[4] M. Weber, *Aufsätze zur Religionssociologie*, III, Tübingen, 1923, pp. 47f.; pp. 93f.; *idem, Wirtschaft und Gesellschaft* (Grundriss der Sozialökonomik), (2nd edition), Tübingen, 1925, pp. 140ff., pp. 753ff. and cf. pp. 662ff.; W.F. Albright, *From the Stone Age to Christianity* (2nd edition), New York, 1957, pp. 283f. In recent years the previously neglected social aspect of the concept of "charisma" has been stressed (an aspect which is certainly of consequence for Israelite history); see, e.g., W.H. Friedland, "For a Sociological Concept of Charisma," *Social Forces*, 43 (1964), 18ff.; E. Shils, "Charisma, Order and Status," *American Sociological Review*, 30 (1965), 199ff.; cf. now also R.G. Tucker, "The Theory of Charismatic Leadership," *Daedalus*, Summer 1968 (= Proceedings Amer. Acad. Arts and Sciences 97, No. 3), 731ff., who stresses Weber's maxim that charismatic leadership arises "in times of psychic, physical, economic, ethical, religious, political distress" (p. 742) (see chap. 8).

psychological nature of charisma finds its sociological-political manifestation as well. The charismatic personality enjoyed an especially
close relationship with God, expressed in divine revelations and occasionally accompanied by public performances of miracles. This leadership is characteristically spontaneous and personal, the authority
being neither hereditary nor dependent upon social status within the
tribe, and it was certainly not supported by any kind of bureaucratic
apparatus. A national religious awakening would cause the people
to gather around a leader upon whom it became entirely dependent. Hence, government in the period of the judges was characterized by a rather sporadic leadership, stability being achieved only
upon the establishment of a monarchy in Israel (see chap. 8).

The following are the charismatic deliverer-judges: Othniel, Ehud,
Gideon, Deborah, Jephthah and Samson (despite his lack of a popular following), and probably also Shamgar son of Anath. However,
the Book of Judges attests to a different sort of judge, to whom no
acts of deliverance are attributed and consequently does not possess
any charismatic traits. These, today called "minor judges", are five
in number: Tola, Jair, Ibzan, Elon and Abdon (Jud. 10:1–5; 12:8–15).
Following Klostermann and Alt, biblical criticism has generally assumed
that these minor judges were powerful tribal leaders, holding a permanent, pan-Israelite office, and serving as actual jurists and dispensers
of law in the period preceding the monarchy. Their terms of office
were even thought to have been used in chronological reckoning.[5]

The assertion that while the major judges did not achieve national
recognition—notwithstanding their acts of deliverance—it was specifically the minor judges who enjoyed pan-Israelite recognition and
authority, is difficult to accept. No easier to accept is the assumption that the deuteronomic editor made the original stories of the
deliverer-judge conform with the pattern of the minor judges by
attributing to the former pan-Israelite authority, and assuming them
to have simply filled the charge of a *shōfēṭ*, i.e. allegedly a mere

---

[5] Cf. A. Klostermann, *Der Pentateuch*, II, 1907, pp. 418ff.; A. Alt, *Kleine Schriften*,
I, pp. 300ff.; M. Noth, "Das Amt des Richters Israel," *Festschrift A. Bertholet*, Tübingen,
1950, pp. 404ff.; H.W. Herzberg, "Die Kleinen Richter," *Beiträge zur Traditionsgeschichte
und Theologie des AT.*, Göttingen, 1962, pp. 118ff. Smend tried to see in the major
and minor judges the representatives of the two central institutions of that period,
which in his view were the Holy War and the amphictyonic tribal league; R. Smend,
Jahwekrieg und Stämmebund (2nd edition), Göttingen, 1966, pp. 33ff.

dispenser of the law. That this concept of a "judge" replaced that of a supposedly archaic "deliverer" (*mōshīʿa*) in a late editorial stage of the Book of Judges[6] is equally untenable. Indeed, it is proved by the Mari Texts that as early as the 18th century B.C.E. the West Semitic term *šāpiṭum* (as well as its verbal form) indicated a person of prominent rank within the tribal organization, whose authority exceeded that of a mere justice.[7] The Phoenician (and possibly Ugaritic) *šft* and the Punic "*suffetes*" are also used in the sense of a ruler or magistrate. This is certainly also the case in the Book of Judges, where the term *shōfēṭ* and the verb *shāfāṭ* both refer to a leader of the people, whether a major judge or a minor judge, and such activity indeed included the office of arbitrator and judge in the legal sense of the word.

Actually, the modern sharp distinction between minor and major judges in the Bible should probably be toned down to a mere difference in literary sources drawn upon. While the periodic deeds of the deliverer-judges are presented as folk narrative, the data on the minor judges were drawn from strictly factual sources, e.g. family chronicles containing only such details as the tribal affinity of the judge, his seat of office, the exact duration of his charge, his burial-place and notes on his descendants. An intermediate type is found in Jephthah: the end of his story (Jud. 12:7) gives the details generally associated with the minor judges, yet he was certainly a deliverer-judge. His is not a hybrid historical figure, as some would have it,[8] but simply the outcome of the use of several different literary sources.

---

[6] Thus O. Grether, "Die Bezeichung 'Richter' für die charismatischen Helden der vorstaatlichen Zeit," *ZAW*, 57 (1939), 110ff.; M. Noth, *Überlieferungsgeschichtliche Studien*, Halle a/S, 1943, pp. 43ff.; Beyerlin, *op. cit.*, p. 7; and now also I.L. Seeligman, in *Hebräische Wortforschung* (*VT*, Suppl. 16), Leiden, 1967, pp. 273ff. Cf. Kaufmann's justified criticism of these assumptions in his commentary to Judges, pp. 46ff.; and cf. also H.C. Thomson, "Shophet and Mishpat in the Book of Judges," *Transactions of the Glasgow University Oriental Society*, 19 (1961/62), 74ff.; J. Dus, "Die Sufeten Israels," *Archiv Orientalni*, 31 (1963), 444ff. The military aspect of the judge has been stressed in particular by K.D. Schunck, *VT, Suppl.* 15 (1966), 252ff.

[7] On the biblical *shōfēṭ* in the light of Mari and other external evidence, see A. Malamat, *Encyclopaedia Biblica*, 4, s.v. Mari, cols. 576/7 (Hebrew); *idem*, in *Biblical Essays, Die Oud Test. Werkg. Suid Afrika*, (1966), 45; F.C. Fensham, "The Judges and Ancient Israelite Jurisprudence," *ibid.*, 1959, 15ff.; A. van Selms, "The Title Judge," *ibid.*, 41ff.; W. Richter, "Zu den 'Richtern' Israels," *ZAW*, 77 (1965), 40ff.; H. Cazelles, *VT, Suppl.* 15 (1966), 108f.

[8] Cf. Noth, *op. cit.*, pp. 90f.; *idem, Amt und Berufung im AT.*, Bonn, 1958, pp. 21f.

However, the affinity between the two supposed types of judge is best evidenced in the person of Deborah: as a prophetess she was definitely a charismatic figure, able to rouse the people to war; yet even before that war she was renowned as a judge amongst the Israelites in the mountains of Ephraim (Jud. 4:4–5). The same applies to Joshua: along with his wartime leadership he served as an arbitrator among the tribes, as proved by the case of the House of Joseph complaining about their inheritance (Josh. 17:14ff.).[9] It is quite possible, on the other hand, that the minor judges also engaged as leaders in actual battle, but no information of their deeds has come down to us.[10] The mention that the first minor judge, Tola son of Puah, "arose to save [$l^ehōshī‘a$] Israel" (Jud. 10:1) is not necessarily a late editorial interpolation; it might even be the original heading of the entire list of minor judges. The case of Jair the Gileadite may support this assumption for several traditions preserved in books of the Bible other than Judges mention his warlike activities in northern Transjordan (Num. 32:41; I Chr. 2:22). It would thus appear that there was no essential difference between major and minor judges, except for the above mentioned variant manner in which they are portrayed in the Book of Judges. Both types represented the sort of political regime prevailing prior to the monarchy.

While Judges 1, as a chapter, properly belongs to the Conquest cycle, the appendixes to the Book of Judges, dealing with Micah's images and the migration of the tribe of Dan (Jud. 17–18) (chap. 9), and the episode of the outrage at Gibeah (Jud. 19–21), are of quite a different order. In these chapters there are no judges upon the scene; they were later appended to the book and underwent a redaction oriented on the monarchy, as can be seen from the repeated statement: "In those days there was no king in Israel; every man did that which was right in his own eyes" (Jud. 17:6; 18:1; 19:1; 21:25). These facts, however, still leave us in the dark as to the precise dating of the events related. Arguments have been brought forth to place them at the beginning of the period of the judges, and others to support a date much later in this period, which seems preferable. The Gibeah incident and the subsequent inter-tribal war may be ascribed to the span of time somewhat prior to Saul's kingship,

---

[9] Alt, *Kleine Schriften*, II, pp. 190f.
[10] Y. Kaufmann, *The Book of Judges*, Jerusalem, 1962, p. 48 (Hebrew); Kittel, *GVI*, II (6/7th edition), p. 25.

as will be shown below. The dating of the Danite migration, culminating in the conquest of the city of Laish, however, remains
uncertain, as do the precise factors leading up to this uprooting,
whether under Amorite pressure (Jud. 1:34) or because of Philistine
oppression, or both. Without denying the historical substance of this
account, it seems to have been a sort of literary copy of a biblical
narrative pattern evolved for portraying campaigns of inheritance
(which pattern was followed on a much larger, pan-tribal scale, in
the Exodus-Conquest cycle).[11] In any event the occurrence of Jonathan
the son of Gershom the son of Moses (read thus instead of "Manasseh"
in Jud. 18:30), as well as that of Phinehas the son of Elazar the son
of Aaron in the subsequent story of the outrage at Gibeah (both,
interestingly enough *third* generation priests), do not seem to carry
any particular chronological significance, as several scholars have
sought (cf. also below note 87).

It transpires from all the above mentioned that the value of the
Book of Judges as the framework for an historical and chronological survey is problematic, and some scholars go so far as to doubt
the very possibility of exploiting this source for a continuous historical description.[12] Before accepting that the sequence of the stories,
as transmitted in the Book of Judges, reflects the actual historical
process, additional arguments should be adduced. Due to the shortcomings of this book as a historical source, all other biblical references to this period are of special interest, particularly where such
data are independent of the traditions contained in Judges. We shall
first mention the citations in other biblical books of events already
known from Judges which provide a historical perspective of their
evaluation at a later time:

a) Israel's defeat of the Midianites in the days of Gideon, which
became a symbol of God's might, is echoed in Isa. 9:3—"the day
of Midian" and 10:26—"As in the slaughter of Midian at the Rock
of Oreb." (see chap. 6 . . .)

b) Abimelech's death at the "tower of Thebez" is referred to by
Joab while fighting the Ammonites—"Who smote Abimelech the son

---

[11] See A. Malamat, "The Danite Migration and the Pan-Israelite Exodus-Conquest,"
Biblica, 41 (1970), 1ff., and there p. 14 note 1 on the dating of the conquest of Laish
(= chap. 9).
[12] Cf. Kittel, *op. cit.*, 19f. (XI: "Unmöglichkeit einer zusammenhängenden Dar-
stellung").

of Jerubbesheth? did not a woman cast an upper millstone upon him from the wall, that he died at Thebez? why went ye so nigh the wall?" (II Sam. 11:21). Thus, the manner of Abimelech's death served, in later days, as a classical warning against the dangers of siege warfare.[13]

c) Israel's sin at Gibeah is referred to in Hos. 9:9—"They have deeply corrupted themselves. As in the days of Gibeah"; and 10:9—"From the days of Gibeah thou hast sinned, O Israel."

Of particular interest are the data independent of the stories related in Judges which allude to additional details:

d) The prophet Hosea (6:7–9) may allude to the fratricidal war between Gilead and Ephraim in the time of Jephthah. Here, in contrast to the tradition in Judges (which is biased in favor of Gilead), the Ephraimite prophet Hosea takes a clear anti-Gileadite line:[14] "But they at [the city of] Adam [AV: like men] have transgressed the covenant; There they have dealt treacherously against Me. Gilead is a city of them that work iniquity, it is covered with footprints of blood [i.e. the massacre of the Ephraimites]. And as troops of robbers wait for a man, so doth the company of priests; They murder in the way toward Shechem [i.e. the route of flight taken by the Ephraimites], Yea they commit enormity."

e) Samuel in his farewell speech (I Sam. 12:9–11), which is formulated in the same spirit as the pragmatic framework of Judges, lists Israel's oppressors on the one hand and its deliverers on the other, as complementing each other, thus recapitulating the major events of the period of the judges. Unlike the order in Judges, however, the sequence of oppressors is given as: Sisera, the Philistines and Moab; while the deliverers are Jerubbaal (and not Gideon; cf. above, (b), Jerubbesheth), the otherwise unknown Bedan,[15] Jephthah and Samuel himself.

---

[13] Cf. Y. Yadin, *The Art of Warfare in Biblical Lands*, Ramat Gan, 1963, pp. 261f. For the possibility of reading Tirzah instead of Thebez see below, note 61.

[14] See N.H. Tur-Sinai, *Lashon wa-Sefer* (Hebrew), 2, Jerusalem, 1951, pp. 324ff.

[15] Various attempts have been made to explain the name. The Sages interpreted Bedan as *ben-Dan* [the son of Dan] i.e., Samson (Bab. Tal., Rosh Hashanah, 25a); others identified him with the judge 'Abdon (omitting the initial *'ayin*), or with Barak (Septuagint); and cf. the commentaries. All these suggestions are unsatisfactory however; the reference is probably to a judge unknown from any other source. Perhaps he is to be associated with the name Bedan mentioned in the genealogical list of the "sons of Gilead, the son of Machir, the son of Manasseh" (I Chr. 7:17).

f) Ps. 68:8–15 may contain an allusion to the war of Deborah and the episode of Abimelech:[16] first, the theophany parallel to the Song of Deborah, followed by the victory over the Canaanite kings ("kings of armies flee, they flee"), and mentioning the passive stand of a part of the Israelites ("When ye lie among the sheepfolds", etc.; cf. Jud. 5:16), finally, the mention of Zaimon where Abimelech mustered his army for the attack on Shechem (Jud. 9:48).

g) The most comprehensive survey of the period of the judges is contained in Ps. 83, composed probably in the time of the judges or somewhat later.[17] It first gives a list of Israel's oppressors: "Edom and the Ishmaelites; Moab and the Hagrites; Gebal[18] and Ammon, and Amalek; Philistia with the inhabitants of Tyre" (vv. 7–8). The twinning of these peoples suits the historical reality of the period, since on the one hand nomadic tribes joined at times in the incursions of the Transjordanian nations (cf. below, paragraph C), while on the other hand there were special ties between the Phoenician coast and Philistia. It may be that the continuation: "Assyria [Ashur], also is joined with them" alludes to the campaigns of Tiglath-pileser I to the Lebanon and Phoenicia, and to the initial Assyrian appearance on the horizon of Israel (paragraph E). This is followed by mention of the victories over the Canaanites and the Midianites in the days of Deborah and Gideon, adducing additional details about the Midianite defeat at En-dor and Adamah (i.e. the city of Adamah; cf. below).

Despite all the shortcomings of the Book of Judges as a historical source, the narratives therein are of great typological value, as a true

---

[16] Cf. M.D. Cassuto, *Tarbiz*, 12 (1941), 1ff. (Hebrew); and in particular R. Tournay, "Le Psaume LXVIII et le livre des Juges," *RB*, 66 (1959), 358ff.; E. Lipiński, "Juges 5, 4–5 et Psaume 68, 8–11," *Biblica*, 48 (1967), 185ff.

[17] See in particular B. Maisler (Mazar), *Yediot*, 4 (1936), 47ff. (Hebrew); and S.I. Feigin, *Missitrei Heavar*, New York, 1943, pp. 31–33 (Hebrew), who attributes the composition of the psalm to the period immediately preceding Jephthah.

[18] The toponym Gebal, which is doubtlessly the well-known town of Byblos on the Phoenician coast (and not Gebalene in the Arabah) does not fit into the context here neither geographically, nor concerning the structure of the hemistichs. Perhaps the actual name twinned with it (Sidon?) has dropped out and in the original version this pair of names was coupled to the one mentioning Tyre. Another instance of text distortion is apparently that concerning the second hemistich in v. 9: "[Ashur also is joined with them]—they have helped the children of Lot" (namely, Moab and Ammon), which is out of place in the extant text in combination with Assyria, but which would apply to the eastern nomadic tribes (Hagrites and Amalek) and Edom which were mentioned earlier.

portrayal of the mode of life and the historical phenomena distinguishing the period under discussion. The same applies to the Book
of Ruth, which reflects the situation "in the days when the judges
judged" (Ruth 1:1), and throws some light on the relations between
Moab and Judah at that time. The original position of the Book of
Ruth as an appendix to Judges is still upheld by the canon of the
Septuagint, by the writings of Josephus and in the talmudic literature.

Moreover, each episode of the judges describes an encounter with
an enemy of particular type: the war against the Canaanites, the
country's indigenous population (Deborah and Barak), the conflicts
with the nations of Transjordan-Moab and Ammon (Ehud and
Jephthah); the inroads of the nomads from the eastern desert (Gideon);
and finally the ever-increasing Philistine challenge on the west (the
Samson cycle, for which see below the chapter on "The Philistines
and their Wars with Israel"). It is interesting to note the absence of
any reference to a conflict with the Arameans, who were in the
process of settling in Syria and northern Transjordan in the 12th
and 11th centuries B.C.E. It is only at the end of the 11th century,
with their consolidation in states, that they became Israel's sworn
enemy at the time of kings Saul and David.

B. *The War of Deborah and Barak Against the Canaanites*

The consolidation of the Israelites' power, and their numerical growth
at the expense of the indigenous Canaanite population, in increasingly broader areas, led to the greatest and most decisive confrontation
during the period of the judges—the war of Deborah and Barak. In
contrast to the other wars of the judges, it was against the autochthonous element in Canaan they were pitted in this encounter (the Sea-
Peoples may already have participated in it; cf. below), in which the
strongly fortified cities, as well as the chariotry of the enemy, played
a determinant role. This episode serious historical chronological problems, due to the double tradition, prose and poem, preserved in
Chapters 4 and 5 of the Book of Judges and its apparent contradiction with the description of the battle at the waters of Merom,
and the utter destruction of Hazor, as related in Joshua, Chapter 11.

The difficulty in the relationship between the war of Deborah and
the battle at the waters of Merom "in the days of Joshua" is that
both were fought against a wide Canaanite alliance which covered

large areas in Galilee and in the adjacent valleys, both headed by
Jabin, King of Hazor. It is not the name of this king which presents the difficulty, since this might have been a sort of dynastic
name at Hazor.[19] It is inconceivable, however, that Hazor—which
was utterly destroyed at the time of Joshua (Josh. 11:10ff.) as confirmed
by archeological evidence—should have played a primary and decisive role in a Canaanite league several generations later. Moreover,
the archeological finds indicate that the huge lower city at Hazor
was permanently laid waste, and the upper city was not rebuilt until
the time of Solomon. In the period of the judges only a poor, open
settlement, appears to have been established there by the Israelites
(strata XII–XI).[20]

Several suggestions have been made to account for the difficulties
raised by these two contradictory traditions. Of these, two warrant
special attention:

1) The battle at the waters of Merom and Deborah's war are no
more than two closely linked phases of a single armed conflict which
proved decisive in the struggle between the Canaanites and the Israelites in the northern part of the country. Quite opposite to the chronological order in the Bible, the war of Deborah represents the first
stage in this chain of events, when the kingdom of Hazor was still
at the height of its power. The initial defeat of the Canaanite forces
in this war was followed by the second and concluding stage—the
battle at the waters of Merom which finished Hazor off and ended
Canaanite resistance in the north.[21] In this case, Deborah's war must
be considered an integral part of the Conquest cycle and should be
dated as early as the second half of the 13th century, since Hazor
was destroyed at this time according to the archeological evidence.
For the improbability of so high a dating, see below.

---

[19] In this connection it is worth noting the name of the King of Hazor in the
Mari Texts: Ibni-Adad, which is the Akkadian form of a West Semitic name,
Yabni-Addu. Biblical Jabin could easily be a hypocoristic form of the full theophoric
name. Cf. W.F. Albright, *The Biblical Period*, New York, 1963, p. 102 note 83, and
A. Malamat, in *Near Eastern Archaeology in the Twentieth Century* (ed. by J.A. Sanders),
New York, 1970, p. 168, p. 175 note 22.

[20] Cf. Y. Yadin, "Hazor," in *Archaeology and Old Testament Study* (ed. D.W. Thomas),
Oxford, 1967, pp. 245ff.

[21] This solution was first suggested by B. Maisler (Mazar), *HUCA*, 24 (1952/3),
80ff., and followed by Y. Aharoni, "The Battle at the Waters of Merom and the
Battle with Sisera," in *The Military History of the Land of Israel in Biblical Times*, Tel
Aviv, 1964, pp. 91ff. (Hebrew).

2) If the traditional chronological sequence is accepted, we must consider the appearance of Hazor in the story of Deborah, and probably also the name Jabin, as a later interpolation, inspired by the somewhat similar events in the Book of Joshua.[22] Actually, Hazor is only incidentally mentioned together with King Jabin (Jud. 4:2, 17; and cf. I Sam. 12:9; Ps. 83:10, where either one or the other is mentioned but not both together), whose title in this episode is given as "king of Canaan" (Jud. 4:2, 23–24). This title may have been attributed to Jabin either because Hazor was considered "the head of all those kingdoms" (Josh. 11:10) or because a later King Jabin assumed hegemony over the north of the country. Moreover, neither Hazor nor Jabin fit into the topographical or military picture as it emerges from the story of Deborah. Indeed, at that time the enemies of the Israelites were led by Sisera, an army commander (and only he is mentioned in the Song of Deborah) who dwelt in Harosheth-goiim;[23] also the battle-scene differs here completely from that described in Joshua. It might thus be assumed that the introduction of Jabin and Hazor into the Deborah episode was a tendentious scribal move, telescoping the two fateful battles in the north of the country.

It appears that the war of Deborah should be placed in the middle or the second half of the 12th century B.C.E. It has been argued that the words in the Song of Deborah: "Then fought the kings of Canaan, in Taanach by the *waters* of Megiddo" (Jud. 5:19), imply that Megiddo itself lay in ruins at this time and for this reason the less important Taanach was referred to. In this case, the war of Deborah should best be dated within the occupational gap between the destruction of Megiddo stratum VII A and the establishment of stratum VI B, i.e. within the third quarter of the 12th century.[24]

---

[22] Cf. Y. Kaufmann, *Judges*, pp. 116–117; W. Richter, *Bearbeitungen des Retterbuches*, pp. 7f.

[23] Harosheth-goiim is generally identified with el-Ḥarithiyeh or with Tell el-ʿAmr, in the narrow pass between the Jezreel and the coastal plains. Mazar, however, considers it to be the name of a region, viz. the wooded mountainous area of Galilee; cf. his article mentioned above, note 21.

[24] This suggestion goes back to W.F. Albright, "The Song of Deborah in the Light of Archaeology," *BASOR*, 62 (1936), 26ff., while M. Engberg, *BASOR*, 78 (1940), 4ff., would date the war to the gap between Megiddo strata VI A and V in the 11th century (opposing this now is Albright, *The Biblical Period*, p. 102 note 82). It is, however, untenable to accept such a late dating, which most recently was propagated by A.D.H. Mayes, "The Historical Context of the Battle against Sisera,"

Whether this archeological-literary correlation is accepted or not, the date itself is also in accord with the results of the recent excavations at Taanach, which prove that the Canaanite town still existed as late as ca. 1125 B.C.E. (cf. Jud. 1:27), after which date there followed a lengthy occupational gap.[25]

Perhaps such a late dating would also fit in well with certain conclusions arrived at from the Song of Deborah. Thus, the song mentions the tribe of Dan between Gilead and Asher (Jud. 5:17), indicating the previous migration of this tribe to its northern habitat. Secondly, there is a reference in the song to Shamgar son of Anath (v. 6) who defeated a band of 600 Philistine warriors (Jud. 3:31).[26] It is not known for sure whether Shamgar was an Israelite or a foreigner.[27] His name as well as his patronymic, and the fact that he is mentioned in the song together with Jael, who was the wife of Heber the Kenite, would suggest his having been a non-Israelite. Even if he was Canaanite, the Israelites seem to have considered him as a God-sent deliverer, since he averted a Philistine threat to them. Had his deed taken place at an early stage of the Settlement, it could be dated no earlier than the beginning of the 12th century, as the Philistines made their appearance in Canaan only in the days of

---

VT, 19 (1969), 353ff., who holds that Deborah's war was a prelude to the battle with the Philistines at Aphek in the late 11th century B.C.E. For the episodes of Deborah and Shamgar son of Anath in the light of the archeological evidence at Megiddo, cf. also Alt, "Megiddo im Übergang, etc." *Kleine Schriften* I, pp. 256ff.

[25] P.W. Lapp, "Taanach by the Waters of Megiddo," *BA*, 30 (1967), 8ff., who, however, argues that Megiddo VII A was destroyed at the same time as Taanach. The last Canaanite stratum at Taanach produced a tablet in Ugaritic which proves that this script was used in Canaan a considerable time after the destruction of Ugarit itself; for the tablet see D.R. Hillers, *BASOR*, 173 (1964), 45ff.; F.M. Cross, *ibid.*, 190 (1968), 41ff.; A.F. Rainey, *Qadmoniot*, 2 (1969), 89f. (Hebrew).

[26] For a unit of 600 warriors in the Bible representing the force of a "brigade," cf. A. Malamat, *Biblica*, 51 (1970), 9 and note 3 (= chap. 9). Y. Aharoni considers the Philistines here as merely a mercenary force in the employ of the Egyptian garrison at Bethshean; see in *Near Eastern Archaeology in the Twentieth Century*, New York, 1970, pp. 254ff.

[27] For a possible Hurrian etymology of the name Shamgar, cf. B. Maisler (Mazar), *PEQ*, 1934, 192ff.; F.C. Fensham, *JNES*, 20 (1961), 197ff.; and also E. Danelius, *JNES*, 22 (1963), 191ff. There is no doubt that his patronymic ben-'Anath, a name attested in the 13th–11th centuries in Ugaritic, Phoenician and Egyptian documents (also in the forms ben-'Ana, ben-'An) is Canaanite and related to the goddess Anath; cf A. van Selms, "Judge Shamgar," *VT*, 14 (1964), 294ff. It may even have been used as an epithet signifying a professional warrior; cf. O. Eissfeldt, *Festschrift W. Baetke*, Weimar, 1966, pp. 110ff.

Ramses III. Consequently the war of Deborah must be dated later than this.

It would seem that the encounter with the Philistines at that time took place in the northern part of the country, for the Song of Deborah ignores completely the south of the land—including the Philistine area—and because Shamgar's "patronymic" may signify no more than his having originated from Beth-anath, a Canaanite town in Galilee (Jud. 1:33). It has also been suggested that Sisera's name could indicate a relation to the Sea-Peoples.[28] In such a case we would have to assume that already in Deborah's war the Canaanites were led by a new element—the Sea-Peoples, who had penetrated into the north of the country.

As already mentioned, in analyzing the Deborah episode we have two versions before us: the narrative account (Jud. 4) and the Song of Victory (Jud. 5). Such double accounts, prose and poetry, of military victories are found also elsewhere in the Bible (cf. Ex. 14 and 15) and in the Ancient Near East.[29] Deborah's Song is much older than the narrative version and was composed soon after the events related, but the reliability of the prose source cannot be ignored especially since poetic licence plays no part in it, as it does in the song. The prose—despite its present form—still preserves an authentic historical kernel. Though the two sources do not correspond, and seem contradictory at first sight, they may actually complement one another.[30] The outstanding discrepancies between the two—the tribes

---

[28] See W.F. Albright, *JPOS*, 1 (1921), 60f. and now *idem, Yahve and the Gods of Canaan*, London, 1968, p. 218 (for a Luwian origin of the name); see also A. Alt, *Kleine Schriften* I, pp. 266f., who attributes to the name an Illyrian origin. On the other hand, according to S. Yeivin, the name occurs as a component of a place name in the topographical lists of Ramses III (no. 103), and possibly also of Ramses II (no. 8), which he reads as Qaus-Sisera and locates it in Western Galilee; cf. *Atiqot*, 3 (1961), 176ff.

[29] Note in particular the Egyptian prose and poetical versions of the Battle of Kadesh; cf. A.H. Gardiner, *The Kadesh Inscriptions of Ramses II*, Oxford, 1960. On a comparison of Deborah's Song with other ancient Near Eastern victory hymns, see now P.C. Craigie, "The Song of Deborah and the Epic of Tukulti-Ninurta," *JBL*, 88 (1969), 253ff. On the poetical structure of the song, see in addition to the commentaries, W.F. Albright, *Yahve and the Gods of Canaan*, pp. 11ff.

[30] See Kaufmann's attempt to smooth out all the discrepancies between the two chapters, in his *Judges*, pp. 113ff.; and cf. for a detailed analysis of the divergencies W. Richter, *Traditionsgeschichtliche Untersuchungen zum Richterbuch*, Bonn, 1963, pp. 29ff. However, Richter also considers these divergencies as resulting merely from the different literary composition and transmission of these two chapters, but not necessarily as derivations from different historical events.

participating in the battle and the scene of the actual battlefield—
are not indicative of two separate, disconnected battles. On the contrary, they are rather depictions of different stages of one and the
same battle.

The brunt of the Israelite war of liberation was borne by the tribes
of Naphtali and Zebulun, who alone are mentioned in the narrative. They mustered 10,000 warriors, and their commander, Barak
son of Abinoam, was himself of the tribe of Naphtali. Also the Song
of Deborah attributes special military prowess to these two tribes;
"Zebulun is a people that jeoparded their lives unto the death, and
Naphtali, upon the high places of the field" (Jud. 5:18). It is no
mere accident that just the tribes who dwelt in the hilly districts
were particularly disposed toward an uprising. They were less affected
by Canaanite pressure since the latter's chariotry could not take the
offensive in the hill-country. This indeed is the reason why they
attained a certain measure of sovereignty, and tribes such as Zebulun,
Naphtali and Ephraim, respectively the House of Joseph, could even
exact tribute from the Canaanites living in their midst (cf. Josh.
16:10; Jud. 1:30, 33, 35, as against vv. 27, 31, concerning the lowland districts of Manasseh and Asher; while Issachar is conspicuously
absent from the lists).

However, the rather precarious position of the Israelite tribes
dwelling in the lowlands, particularly the Plain of Jezreel—such as
Issachar—obliged them to succumb to the Canaanites (cf. Gen.
49:14–15). These tribes, were, therefore, less able to initiate resistance, though the war was waged in their very territory. (For the
absence of Issachar in Gideon's war see below p. 143). Even if it
were assumed that Deborah was of the tribe of Issachar, which is
doubtful, the initiative of the war was taken at her center of activity in the hill-country of Ephraim, between Ramah and Beth-el (Jud.
4:4–5). Thus, also, Tola son of Puah, "a man of Issachar" actually
lived in Shamir, in the hill-country of Ephraim (Jud. 10:1). The tribe
of Manasseh, as such, is not mentioned in Deborah's war. It appears,
however, that Machir—mentioned in the song as one of the participating tribes—represented those branches of the tribe that still
dwelt in the upland districts west of the Jordan (prior to their migration to the east) thus explaining the emphasis in Deborah's song:
"Out of Machir *came down* governors" (Jud. 5:14).

This difference in disposition between the highland and the lowland tribes may explain the military cooperation evolved in Deborah's

war between the tribes of Galilee and those of the central hill-coun-try mentioned only in the song, i.e. Machir, Ephraim and Benjamin. At any rate, the Song of Deborah reflects the maximal unity achieved by the Israelites in the face of foreign oppression in the period of the judges. This solidarity encompassed tribes from Benjamin in the south to Naphtali in the north, lending support to Deborah's image as "a mother in Israel" (Jud. 5:7). But progress from this situation to actual concerted action of *all* the Israelite tribes was still far off. Indeed, in the song, Deborah censures several of the tribes (Reuben, Gilead [= Gad], Dan and Asher) for having adopted a passive role rather than coming "to the help of the Lord against the mighty." The song mentions only ten tribes, since Judah and Simeon in the south were apparently beyond the poet's horizon. Hence, the Song of Deborah cannot be adduced as evidence for the existence of an Israelite amphictyony, as has been held. The distinctive trait of such an amphictyonic league is a confederation of twelve (or six) tribes focused upon a single religious center; such a situation is lacking in the reality of the period of the judges.[31]

As for the military events as such,[32] the two armies facing each other were ill-matched in strength and organization. The Israelite force, comprising only light infantry, was a poorly armed militia (Jud. 5:8) pitted against a professional, well-trained Canaanite army whose punch lay in its chariotry (see chap. 6). According to the Bible, Sisera had nine-hundred "iron chariots." However exagger-ated the number may be, it still implies a considerable force that was apparently recruited from a number of Canaanite city-states which had leagued up for this war. The main problem facing the

---

[31] For recent doubts concerning the idea of an "Israelite amphictyony," whose chief exponent is M. Noth, see H.M. Orlinsky, "The Tribal System of Israel and Related Groups in the Period of the Judges," *Oriens Antiquus*, 1 (1962), 11ff.; G. Fohrer, "Altes Testament"—"Amphiktyonie" und "Bund"? *Studien zur alttest. Theologie und Geschichte*, Berlin, 1969, pp. 64ff. An intermediate stand is taken by Smend, *Jahwekrieg und Stämmebund*, pp. 10ff.; and now "Gehörte Juda zum vorstaatlichen Israel?" *Fourth World Congress of Jewish Studies*, I, Jerusalem, 1967, pp. 57ff., who rightly criticises the assumption of an amphictyony inferred from the Song of Deborah alone; in any event he attributes to the amphictyonic league a secondary and minor importance in comparison to the institution of the Holy War. For the Israelite tribes in the Song of Deborah as compared to the descriptions thereof in Jacob's and Moses' blessings, see H.J. Zobel, *Stammesspruch und Geschichte*, Berlin, 1965.

[32] For a military and topographical analysis of the war cf. A. Malamat, "Mount Tabor as a Battle Ground in Biblical Times," in *Remnants from the Past*, Tel Aviv, 1951, pp. 64ff. (Hebrew).

Israelite command was, therefore, how to overcome the formidable Canaanite chariotry.

The actual battle, unlike the preparations leading up to it and the depiction of Sisera's murder, is only sketchily related. Moreover, since in accord with the historiographical tendency of the Book of Judges, military leadership and victory were described to the Providence[33] the course of the battle itself is not always clear. An analysis of the biblical text, however, is likely to shed light on the Israelite plan of operations which was based on an "indirect military approach," as usual in the stategy of the wars of the Conquest and of the judges. It seems that the Israelites aimed at neutralizing the Canaanite chariotry by exploiting local topographic and weather conditions. If we consider Chapters 4 and 5 in Judges as two phases of the same war, as we have done above, the chain of events can be reconstructed as follows: Barak summoned 10,000 warriors of the tribes of Naphtali and Zebulun to Kedesh, probably Kedesh-Naphtali, Barak's birthplace in southern Naphtali.[34] Thence he led them to Mount Tabor which possessed several obvious advantages as his operational base: a commanding position overlooking the plain and providing a perfect means of observing even distant enemy movements; further, that position among the wooded mountain slopes—which initially concealed the Israelite force—was beyond the reach of the Canaanite chariotry. This base gave the Israelite command the advantage in timing the attack to suit their needs—certainly a major factor in their operational plan.

The enemy, to whom the Israelite position must have purposely been "leaked" (Jud. 4:12), apparently concentrated forces at the foot of Tabor, in a secondary valley opening into the Jezreel plain (later known as the valley of Chesulloth)—which was far from providing the wide expanse suitable for the deployment of chariotry. Moreover, the Israelites seem to have delayed their uprising till the rainy season which often turns the low lying valleys into quagmires, thus alto-

---

[33] On the Holy War characteristics to be found in the Israelite battles, cf. in particular G. von Rad, *Der Heilige Krieg im Alten Israel* (2nd edition), Zürich, 1952; R. de Vaux, *Ancient Israel*, New York, 1961, pp. 258ff.

[34] For this location at Khirbet Qedesh, where remains of an Early Iron Age settlement were found, see M. Kochavi, *Yediot*, 27 (1963), 165–173 (Hebrew); *idem*, *Doron-Hebraic Studies* (in honor of A.I. Katsh), New York, 1965, pp. 90ff. This city must be distinguished from Kedesh in the northern part of Naphtali which is far from the scene of these events.

gether depriving the Canaanite chariots of their mobility.[35] The Israelite light infantry could then successfully attack the chariotry, a great part of which was certainly bogged down, while others seem to have been able to retreat to their bases in the southwest, i.e. in the vicinity of Megiddo and Taanach. This flight route was, however, blocked by another obstacle—the rain swollen Kishon brook (Jud. 5:21). The final engagement which sealed the enemy's fate must have been fought in the latter locale. Perhaps it was only then that the Israelite tribes dwelling in the central hill-country joined their brother-tribes, similarly to what happened in Gideon's war when the Ephraimites joined in the defeat of the enemy who had already been put to flight (chap. 6).

Even Sisera, the enemy commander, was forced to abandon his chariot and flee on foot to the tent-encampment of Heber the Kenite, who had left his tribe in the Negev and moved to the Plain of Jezreel. Here "Heber" may not be an actual personal name, but rather a personification of a nomadic family unit which had severed itself from its parent tribe.[36] The Kenite clan had cultivated friendly relations with both the Canaanites and the Israelites with whom it concluded later familial ties (Jud. 4:11, 17). Sisera met his death at the hands of Jael, the wife of the head of the clan, who seems to have been a charismatic personality in her own right, similar to Deborah and who—like her—dwelt near a sacred tree, i.e. "Elon [= oak]-bezaanannim which is by Kedesh." The killing of Sisera may have been an obligatory act in accord with a possible covenant concluded between the Kenites and Israel.[37]

---

[35] In addition to the poetical description in the Song of Deborah of the inundation caused by the swollen Kishon brook (Jud. 5:21), allusions to the heavy rains may be found in the description of the theophany at the beginning of the song (vv. 4–5), as well as in a relevant passage in Psalms (68:9: "A bounteous rain"). Josephus already remarked upon the special weather conditions prevailing at the outset of the war of Deborah (*Ant.* V, 4).

[36] Cf. A. Malamat, *JAOS*, 82 (1962), 144ff. Among the Mari documents adduced there on the West Semitic term *ḫibrum* Hebrew *ḥever*, designating a small tribal division, *ARM* VIII, No. 11, is especially illuminating. There reference is made to a *ḫibrum* which constitutes a nomadic unit within the clan of the "sons of Awin" of the Rabbean tribe, paralleling the context of Jud. 4:11, according to which Heber belonged to the clan of the "sons of Hobab" of the Kenite tribe.

[37] On the charismatic character of Jael, see B. Mazar, *JNES*, 24 (1965), 301f.; on the covenant between Israel and the Kenites, cf. F.C. Fensham, *BASOR*, 175 (1964), 51ff.

Following the defeat of the Canaanites in Deborah's war, and despite the fact that their main centers do not seem to have been conquered at that time, the Israelite tribes settled in Galilee were freed of their yoke. In the Plain of Jezreel and its environs in particular, the Israelite position was consolidated, and the tribes of Manasseh, Issachar and Zebulun were able to expand their territories, the latter even to the sea-coast (Gen. 19:13). Further, this victory secured for the first time territorial continuity between the tribes in the northern and central parts of the country—just as this was the first occasion on which these tribes had engaged in a joint military operation of major proportions.

C. *Gideon and the Midianite Incursion*

Deborah's Canaanite victory paradoxically brought about new dangers for the Israelites settled in the north. The weakening of the Canaanite power structure, which came on top of the collapse of Egyptian rule in Canaan in the second half of the 12th century, *World History of the Jewish People* III, 1971, left the eastern frontier open to nomadic incursions. The Israelites had not yet attained a position to insure the country's security through replacing the highly developed Canaanite defence system. The eastern desert tribes exploited this situation by invading the cultivated areas, a phenomenon common in Palestine in times of political instability—such as the period of the Israelite Settlement. This is well reflected in Psalm 83 which mentions the Ishmaelites, Hagrites, Amalekites and Midianites who harassed the Israelite tribes. As late as Saul's time, fierce battles were fought with Amalek (I Sam. 15) and with the Hagrites (I Chr. 5:10). It was only after the establishment of David's stable regime that these incursions were curbed. The proximity of the story of Gideon to that of Deborah in Judges seems, therefore, to follow the actual course of historical events, and not to be due to the arbitrariness of some late editor.

The mass raids into the cultivated areas usually involved several nomadic tribes acting in concert. Thus, the Midianites who invaded Canaan in Gideon's days were joined by the Amalekites and the "Children of the East" (*bᵉnē Qedem*: Jud. 6:3); later, in the days of Saul, the Hagrites who attacked the Israelite tribes in Transjordan acted in concert with the desert tribes of Jetur, Naphish and Nodab

(I Chr. 5.18–19). Fully nomadic tribes would often attach themselves to more settled nations which were setting out on military expeditions (as reflected in Ps. 83; see above, p. 134). Thus, Amalek joined Eglon, the king of Moab, in his war against Israel (Jud. 3:13), Kenite clans joined the tribe of Judah during the campaign of inheritance (Jud. 1:16), and, according to biblical tradition, "a mixed multitude" attached itself to the Israelites during the Exodus from Egypt (Ex. 12:38).

The nomadic wave penetrating into Canaan at the time of Gideon was headed by the Midianites, a loose association of tribes (see below) which appear to have reached their zenith in the 13th–12th centuries.[38] At this time the Midianites concentrated in the fringe regions of southern Transjordan, as is indirectly indicated by their route of flight after their defeat (see below). The Midianites' special ties with southern Transjordan are revealed by their clash with the Israelites in the time of Moses (Num. 25 and 31) and their close contact with the king of Moab (Num. 22:4ff.) and the Amorite King Sihon (Josh. 13:21). However, the Midianite area of movement was enormous, extending as far as Egypt (Gen. 37:25ff.; I Kings 11:17–18) in one direction and the Euphrates in the other (Num. 22:4ff.), while splinter groups reached as far as Sheba in South Arabia (Isa. 60:6). They played a vital part in the spice and incense trade in western Asia, and this may serve to explain Midian's putative relationship to the children of Abraham's concubine Keturah (note that Hebrew *qᵉṭōret* means "incense") in the genealogical tables of Genesis (25:1–2).

The Midianite prosperity in the 12th century; as well as the rise of the desert tribes in general is the direct result of the large scale domestication of the camel.[39] This animal, of little importance previously, had come then into common use as a means of transport

---

[38] On the Midianites, see J. Liver, *Encyclopaedia Biblica* (Hebrew), 4, cols. 686–691, s.v. Midian and the bibliography there; to the latter, add O. Eissfeldt, "Protektorat der Midianiter über ihre Nachbarn" etc., *JBL*, 87 (1968), 383ff.; and W.F. Albright in the next note.

[39] The absence of any evidence for camel caravans before this time has repeatedly been emphasized by Albright; see his most recent statement "Midianite Donkey Caravans" in *Translating and Understanding the Old Testament* (ed. H.T. Frank and W.L. Reed), Nashville-New York, 1970, pp. 197ff., where he points out the shift from the 13th century Midianite donkey nomadism (cf. Num. 31), to camel nomadism a century later. See also W. Dostal, "The Evolution of Bedouin Life," *L'antica società Beduina* (ed. F. Gabrielli), Rome, 1959, pp. 21ff.; J. Henninger, "Zum frühsemitischen Nomadentum," *Viehwirtschaft und Hirten-Kultur* (ed. L. Földes), Budapest, 1969, pp. 38ff.

and even as a vehicle of war, thus becoming a prime factor in the very existence of the tribes of the Arabian desert, in both war and peace.

Gideon's story gives characteristic details of the mode of life and tribal organization of the Midianites which can be supplemented by other biblical sources. It transpires that at the time of the Israelite Settlement, the Midianites comprised five sub-tribes—apparently called *ummōt*, i.e. tribal units (Num. 25:15), ruled by five "kings" or "chieftains" (Num. 31:8; Josh. 13:21), a division indicated also in the genealogical tables of Genesis (25:4).[40] In Gideon's story, only two Midianite kings are mentioned—Zebah and Zalmunna—along with two army commanders—Oreb and Zeeb; these four are also designated as "princes" (Ps. 83:10, 12). It appears that the interchange of the several titles—king (*melek*), chieftain (*nāsī*), prince (*nāsīk*), an appellation also designating heads of the Aramean tribes in southern Babylonia, and commander (*śar*)—merely reflects the various functions of the same tribal heads, i.e. their respective political, administrative, religious and military charges. The Bible mentions also Midianite "elders" (Num. 22:4, 7). Such leadership is characteristic of the tribal associations throughout the Ancient East, particularly the multiplicity of "kings", though their numbers tended to decrease gradually as the result of political consolidation. The restricted number of two Midianite kings in Gideon's account may indicate either an advanced stage of tribal organization or that merely a part of the confederation came into conflict with the Israelites.

The mass incursions of the Midianites and allied desert tribes in Gideon's day apparently took place toward the end of the 12th century B.C.E.[41] Crossing the Jordan into the Beth-shean plain, they

---

[40] Cf. A. Malamat, *JAOS* 82 (1962), 144. The specialized usage of *ummā*, denoting also the sub-tribes of the Ishmaelites (Gen. 25:16), most likely corresponds to the (West Semitic?) Mari term *ummatum*, as employed, e.g. in King Yahdun-lim's Foundation Inscription; see G. Dossin, *Syria*, 32 (1955), 1ff. There it designates first an association of three rebellious sub-tribes of the nomadic Yaminites (col. III: 17, *ummat TUR-mi-im*; and see below notes 44 and 54), and later the tribal organization of Hana (l. 28: *ummat Ḥa-na*).

[41] Such a date seems plausible since the Gideon episode post-dates that of Deborah, as pointed out above, and a similar date can be inferred from a possible, indirect synchronism referred to in Gen. 36:35. According to this passage an Edomite king, Haddad son of Bedad, who flourished five generations before Saul or David, i.e. ca. 1100 B.C.E., "smote Midian in the field of Moab." This clash may have been connected with the general Midianite retreat in Southern Transjordan after their defeat by Gideon. Cf. E. Meyer, *Die Israeliten und ihre Nachbarstämme*, Halle a/S,

aimed at the large and fertile valleys which separated mountainous Galilee from the central hill-country. According to the biblical evidence, they made deep inroads into the south reaching even the area of Gaza (Jud. 6:4), a long-range raid undoubtedly facilitated at that time by the weakness of the Canaanite city-states, and especially the collapse of Egyptian rule along the *Via maris*. As it so often happened, it was during the summer, close to harvest time, that the Midianite hordes broke into the cultivated areas in search of food and pasture. Thus, the Israelite rural population was particularly hardhit, especially in the Jezreel region. Their crops ruined or plundered, and in the absence of proper fortified cities, the Israelites were forced to take to "dens which are in the mountains, and the caves, and the strongholds" (Jud. 7:2). These insecure conditions prevailing in the period of the judges seem to be reflected also in the archeological evidence.[42]

The initiative of effective counter measures was taken by Gideon the son of Joash of the clan of Abiezer, one of the principal branches of the Manasseh tribe. Gideon's family home was at Ophrah, apparently to be located at the present-day village of et̞-Ṭaiyibeh, northeast of the hill of Moreh. This was probably an enclave of the tribe of Manasseh within the territory of Issachar (cf. Josh. 17:11).[43] Thus, Gideon's statement that "my family is the poorest in Manasseh" could be an allusion to the hard-pressed state of his clan as a result of its being cut off from the bulk of the tribe. The Bible describes how Gideon received inspiration for his mission while "beating out wheat in the winepress, to hide it from the Midianites" (Jud. 6:11), that is, while doing his work secretly and personally experiencing the enemy's oppression. As with the other Israelite deliverer-judges, Gideon's military actions were preceded by a national religious

---

1906, p. 381; and W.F. Albright, *Archaeology and the Religion of Israel*, p. 206, note 58 (here however the date is lowered one generation).

[42] Thus, e.g., Tell Beth Mirsim, stratum B of the Early Iron Age, has revealed a particularly large number of granaries within the city limits, indicating that crops stored outside the city boundaries were endangered by marauding groups such as the Midianites; and cf. W.F. Albright, *The Archaeology of Palestine and the Bible*, New York, 1935, pp. 107–8.

[43] Cf. F.M. Abel, *Géographie de la Palestine II*, Paris, 1938, pp. 402ff. Another possible identification for Ophrah with the ancient site at Afula has been suggested by Z. Kallai, *The Tribes of Israel*, Jerusalem, 1967, pp. 356ff. (Hebrew). If so, Gideon's hometown was on Manasseh's borderland and is not to be considered as an enclave within another tribal area.

re-awakening. But only in Gideon's case is the nature of this religious surge explicitly described—that is, the uprooting of Baal and Asherah's worship in Ophrah—similar to Saul's annihilation of the foreign cult on the eve of his decisive battle with the Philistines (I Sam. 28:3ff.).

Besides his fellow tribesmen from Manasseh, Gideon summoned to the war against the Midianites elements from the tribes of Asher, Zebulun and Naphtali who had settled north of Manasseh (Jud. 6:35).[44] Most remarkable, however, is the absence of Issachar, for the events described occurred in the territory of this very tribe which—dwelling in the lowlands—was presumably the most seriously affected. Opinions differ as to the precise location of the battle. Judging by the various topographical data, it would seem that the central Midianite camp which Gideon attacked, was "on the north side of them, by Gibeath-moreh [hill of Moreh] in the valley" (Jud. 7:1) or, more precisely, near En-dor (Ps. 83:11),[45] i.e. in the valley between the hill of Moreh and Mount Tabor. Another intimation for such a northern location is the fact that the Midianite kings slew Gideon's brothers at Tabor (Jud. 8:18–19). Gideon and his men encamped beyond the hill of Moreh, on the north-western slopes of the Gilboa range, above the well of Harod. Similar to Barak's base, this camp was sited beyond the enemy's reach and permitted easy retreat into the mountains of Gilboa if the need arose.

The major military problem facing Gideon was the enemy's numerical superiority and, particularly, his skilful use of camel-warfare; meeting the Midianites openly would have placed the Israelites in a situation which might well have ended in disaster. Thus, Gideon resorted to a night attack that served to neutralize the enemy's superiority and extreme mobility. The meticulous planning and precise execution of this attack constitute a classical example in military history of how a small and poorly armed force can overcome a much

---

[44] This alliance of several tribes seems authentic and should not be considered a later, tendentious enlargement, as held by some critics (see above, p. 99), e.g. W. Beyerlin, *VT*, 13 (1963), 1ff. Such multi-tribal alliances are well documented in the Mari texts, e.g. the joint rebellion of three tribes against King Yahdun-lim, as attested in his Foundation Inscription, see below note 54, and A. Malamat, *JAOS*, 28 (1962), 144.

[45] This place should be identified with Khirbet eṣ-Ṣafsafa, 1 km northeast of the Arab village Indur on the northern slope of the hill of Moreh. See N. Zori, *PEQ*, 84 (1952), 114ff.

larger and stronger one. Though the Book of Judges generally tends to diminish the merit of human genius in military exploits in favor of the Divine, a detailed analysis of the text (Jud. 7) can reveal the still-valid tactics employed in this night-manoeuvre, as summarized below:[46]

The difficulties inherent in night operations caused Gideon to limit the size of his force to three hundred men, selected from among 10,000 warriors who remained with him. So as to compensate for the smallness of his force he selected only highly qualified troops by means of a peculiar test—the crux being the manner in which they drank water from the well of Harod; several explanations have been given of this test. It was the prerequisites of night fighting, however, which must have demanded here such a test, to ensure a well-disciplined force, fully capable of silent action. Without resorting to the usual textual emendations or analysis, it seems that Gideon rejected those warriors who proved their unsuitability by drinking noisily. Thus, "everyone that lappeth of the water with his tongue, as a dog lappeth [i.e. in a noisy manner] him shalt thou set by himself; likewise everyone that boweth down upon his knees to drink" [i.e. those who relaxed their vigilance while drinking] (Jud. 7:5). Gideon rather picked those "that lapped putting their hand to their mouth" [i.e. carefully, so as not to make noise and also to be able to keep watch]—who "were three hundred men" (Jud. 7:6).

Gideon's surprise attack relied upon the cover of darkness and the full effects of psychological warfare. His advance reconnaissance revealed that a defeatist attitude was already prevalent in the enemy camp (cf. the dream in Jud. 7:13–15). Dividing his men into three companies, as usual in Israelite practice (cf. Jud. 8:43; I Sam. 11:11, 13, 17f.), he encircled the Midianite camp; the actual attack came from three sides simultaneously. The action was timed for the "beginning of the middle watch," that is, close to midnight, just after the changing of the guard ("had but newly set the watch," Jud. 7:19), this being the critical moment in the sentry system. The peculiar "weapons" of Gideon's troops—horns and torches, the latter hidden

---

[46] See A. Malamat, "The War of Gideon and Midian—A Military Approach," *PEQ*, 85 (1953), 61ff.; and in greater detail in the parallel chapter in *The Military History of the Land of Israel in Biblical Times*, pp. 110ff. (Hebrew). For other and partly different analyses see Field-Marshall A.P. Wavell, "Night Attacks—Ancient and Modern," in his *The Good Soldier*, London, 1948, pp. 162ff.; Y. Yadin, *The Art of Warfare in Biblical Lands*, pp. 256ff.

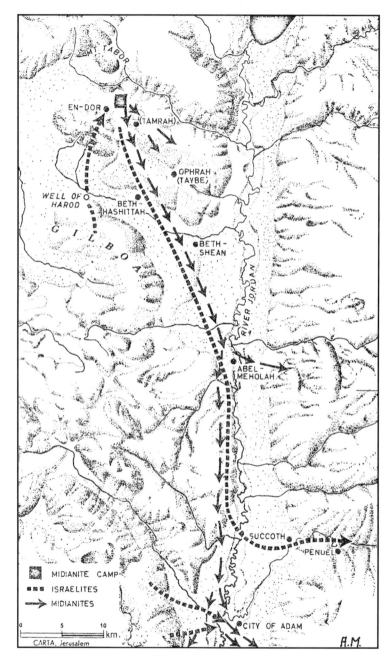

Gideon's Campaign

in jars—proved effective; they were well-suited for signalling the attack and for identification in the dark, and further brought about utter chaos in the enemy camp. The torches were apparently also used to set on fire the tents in the Midianite encampment. The large herds and camels were undoubtedly stampeded by the horn blasts, they being just as unused to night raids as their owners. In the ensuing rout it was impossible to distinguish friend from foe, "and the Lord set every man's sword against his fellow, even throughout all the host" (*ibid.* 22).

Gideon's tactics were a complete success, and his victory lived in the memory of future generations as "the day of Midian" (Isa. 9:4). Gideon's military genius is shown in his following the victory through to the end by pursuing the enemy for some 150 miles beyond the Jordan. The survivors of the Midianite horde fled to the Jordan valley trying to ford the river near Abel-meholah (Jud. 7:22),[47] and apparently also further south at the city of Adamah (Ps. 83:11) (see map p. 145). Using another stratagem, frequently employed in the period of the judges (cf. Jud. 3:28; 12:5), Gideon blocked the enemy's line of retreat by seizing the fords with the aid of the tribe of Ephraim (Jud. 7:20–24). The Ephraimites captured the two Midianite commanders, Oreb and Zeeb, which exploit was also cherished for generations (Isa. 10:26; and cf. below, p. 160) (chap. 6).

Gideon crossed the Jordan and moved up the Jabbok in pursuit of the Midianites who, following nomadic practice, tried to slip away into the open desert. During this lengthy campaign, Gideon requested supplies from the cities of Succoth[48] and Penuel (Tell edh-Dhahab); however, their inhabitants, being unsure of the outcome of the war and fearing Midianite reprisals, refused him (see Appendix, from this article). Gideon surprised the Midianites a second time by taking a short-cut through nomadic territory—the "way of them that dwelt in tents" (Jud. 8:11)—apparently east of Rabbath-Ammon. This time

---

[47] Most likely to be identified with Tell Abu Ṣūṣ; see H.J. Zobel, *ZDVP*, 82, (1966), 83ff.; N. Zori, *Yediot*, 31 (1967), 132ff. (Hebrew).

[48] Succoth has been located by various scholars at Tell Deir 'Älla, which was excavated in recent years by H.J. Franken, see *VT*, 10 (1960), 386ff.; 11 (1961), 361ff.; 12 (1962), 378ff.; however, more recently Franken has given up this identification; *ibid.*, 14 (1964), 422, and cf. now his *Excavations at Tell Deir 'Älla*, Leiden, 1969, pp. 5ff. There is no certainty as to whether the inhabitants of Succoth and Penuel were Israelites, or Canaanites as in Shechem. A foreign population has recently been propagated by H. Reviv, *Tarbiz*, 38 (1969), 309ff. (Hebrew).

he dealt them a fatal blow, catching them entirely off guard and "secure" in their camp at Karkor (in Wadi Sirḥan); in this battle the two Midianite kings fell into his hands. Returning from his distant pursuit, Gideon punished the "princes and elders" of Succoth, razed the citadel at Penuel and killed its inhabitants. At Succoth a *naʿar* (Jud. 8:14) had "written down" for Gideon the names of the 77 town leaders (and cf. below note 82). This person was most probably not a mere "youth", but an official of the town-council to whom the identity of its members was well known and who also knew how to write. Hence, this passage should not be adduced as evidence for wide-spread literacy among the Israelites in this period, as so frequently done.

Gideon's victory put an end to the incursions of the desert raiders into Canaan, though their pressure continued in outlying districts and in the populated areas of Transjordan.

D. *Premature Attempts to Establish a Monarchy and the Episode of Abimelech*

In contrast to the other deliverer-judges, Gideon did not fade subsequently from the historical scene; upon his triumphal return, the Israelites offered him the kingship, similar to the case of Saul who, at least according to one biblical version, was enthroned by the people in the wake of his victory over the Ammonites (I Sam. 11). This was the first attempt to establish a dynastic regime in Israel, prompted by a desire to stabilize the sporadic rule of the charismatic leadership which arose only in times of crisis. According to the biblical source, Gideon rejected the advance of the "men of Israel" to crown him as king and establish a hereditary monarchy on the grounds that this contravened to the concept of divine kingship: "I will not rule over you, neither shall my son rule over you; the Lord shall rule over you" (Jud. 8:23). This ideological anti-monarchism was not necessarily the expression of a later, theocratic editor, as held by biblical criticism, but is true to the mood prevailing in the period of the judges, as derived from the belief in the freedom of the individual.[49]

---

[49] See in particular Kaufmann, *Judges*, pp. 191ff., who strongly rejects the view of the Wellhausen school that Gideon's answer expresses a Second Temple, theocratic concept, and that actually he accepted the people's offer (cf. the commentaries). On

An even sharper expression of this anti-monarchism in the same period is found in Jotham's fable which denounces kingship as a futile and arrogant, absolutist institution. Though parable, it was an excellent reflection of Canaanite monarchy and its decorum, such as the ceremonial anointment of the king ("The trees went forth on a time to anoint a king over them"—Jud. 9:8) and the special protection afforded by the king's shadow (cf. the irony contained in the words of the bramble: "Come and take refuge in my shadow"—Jud. 9:15).[50] At the same time, the very offering of the crown to Gideon as well as Jotham's fable indicate that in certain circles there was already a trend to institutionalise charismatic leadership. This also applies to Jephthah and the elders of Gilead who granted his request to be a "head over all the inhabitants of Gilead", that is, a supreme ruler wielding authority in both war and peace (cf. below).

Notwithstanding his outward refusal, Gideon did *de facto* retain certain important privileges usually belonging to the ruler, relying no doubt on the support of his band of warriors, which represented a sort of private retinue. Such a troop was several times instrumental in seizing the reins of government, as in the case of Abimelech, of David at Hebron and Rezon son of Eliada at Damascus (I Kings 11:23ff.). Indeed, the brief biblical account of Gideon's later days provides several elements characteristic of kingly rule, elements quite foreign to true charismatic authority:[51]

(1) The establishment of an ephod at Ophrah—which may have become a cultic-political center—possibly connected with the religious act of Gideon's official appointment.

---

the other hand, the argument of M. Buber that Gideon's statement represents the one and only authoritative concept prevailing in Israel before the rise of the Monarchy is too extreme, see his *Königtum Gottes*, Berlin, 1932, pp. 1ff.; and cf. now also J.A. Soggin, *Das Königtum in Israel* (*BZAW*, 104), Berlin, 1967, pp. 15ff.; H.J. Boecker, *Die Beurteilung der Anfänge des Königtums in den deuteronomischen Abschnitten des I. Samuelbuches*, Neukirchen, 1969, pp. 20ff.

[50] On Jotham's parable, cf. in addition to the commentaries E.H. Maly, "The Jotham Fable-Antimonarchical?", *CBQ*, 22 (1960), 299ff.; M.C. Astour, "The Amarna Age Forerunners of Biblical Anti-Royalism," *Max Weinreich Festschrift*, Hague, 1964, pp. 6ff.; U. Simon, *Tarbiz*, 34 (1965), 1ff. (Hebrew). The importance of the royal shadow in the Canaanite city-states (in this instance of the King of Byblos) is well reflected in the contemporary tale of Wen-Amon; cf. A.L. Oppenheim, *BASOR*, 107 (1947), 7ff.

[51] Several of the following points have been emphasized in the commentaries; and cf. also E. Nielsen, *Shechem*, Copenhagen, 1955, p. 143, note 1; B. Lindars, "Gideon and Kingship," *JThS* (N.S.), 16 (1965), 315ff.; G. Wallis, "Die Anfänge des Königtums in Israel," *Geschichte und Überlieferung*, Berlin, 1968, pp. 51ff.

(2) The name of Gideon's son, Abimelech, i.e. "the father is king," seems to allude to a royal status.

(3) The double name Gideon-Jerubbaal (not necessarily stemming from two different sources) could be a case of a double royal name, a feature common in the Ancient East and the later Israelite Monarchy.

(4) The setting up of a harem on a royal scale, as indicated by his numerous progeny, and especially his marriage to a woman of the Shechem nobility, a sort of political-royal marriage common in the ancient world.[52]

(5) The allusion to the royal status of Gideon and his brothers by Zebah and Zalmunna, "As thou art, so were they; of one form with the children of a king" (Jud. 8:18).

(6) Even more significant is the demand of Gideon's sons to inherit their father's rule: ". . . that all the sons of Jerubbaal, who are three-score and ten persons, rule over you, or that one rule over you?" (Jud. 9:2).

All these arguments point to the special status and considerable prestige enjoyed by Gideon as a result of his deeds of deliverance. His family and his tribe—Manasseh—grew doubtlessly very influential in the north of the country, even in the Canaanite cities which remained in the hill country of Manasseh, as far as Shechem. The Bible emphasizes that in driving off the Midianites Gideon delivered also Shechem itself (Jud. 9:17), which came under his protection. Untrained in monarchical tradition, Gideon, the originally charismatic leader, did not make proper succession arrangements. Abimelech, the offspring of his marriage into a noble Shechemite family, exploited his maternal connections to rid himself of his brothers and seize power in the foreign city. This city's upper class undoubtedly supported Abimelech, hoping to obtain political and economic advantages under his rule.

The oligarchic "lords of Shechem" (ba^{ca}lē Sh^{e}ḵem) crowned Abimelech king in a public religious ceremony (Jud. 9:6). Not only was Canaanite Shechem a most suitable site for the establishment of a kingship—

---

[52] Since it cannot be presumed that Gideon married into a noble Shechemite family before his act of deliverance, it must be assumed that his rule lasted a long time after, for Abimelech was already grown up when his father died. On the other hand, Gideon must have been middle aged at the time of his war with the Midianites since Jether, his first-born, already bore his own sword at that time (Jud. 8:20). This confirms the biblical statement that Gideon lived to a ripe old age (Jud. 8:32).

it having long harbored monarchist traditions—but it displayed also a remarkable tendency to accept the authority of rulers not native to the town.[53] Thus, it appears that Lab'ayu, Shechem's aggressive ruler in the Amarna period, was an outsider who reigned supported by the Habiru bands in the area; a similar situation is found in Abimelech's time when Gaal the son of Ebed entered Shechem at the head of his kinsmen and seized control for a short while (Jud. 9:26). It seems that the distinctive feature here was that a single authority ruled over both a tribal entity and an urban center. Perhaps such rule is also reflected in the patriarchal tradition in the unique appellation of the eponym Shechem: $n^e\acute{s}\bar{i}^{\,\jmath}$ $h\bar{a}^{\,\jmath}\bar{a}rez$ "prince (actually: chief] of the country" (Gen. 34:2), i.e. personifying both urban and rural elements. Such a political setup is known elsewhere in the ancient Near East, most notably from the Mari documents, which mention kings, each ruling over an urban center and a tribal territory.[54]

The above system of government, based on a covenant between an outsider and the nobility of Shechem, may very well explain the nature of the local deity, "El-berith" or "Baal-berith," i.e. the god of the covenant; that is to say, this deity apparently served as a party to, or rather as the guarantor of, specifically such a treaty. A further allusion to this may be found in the designation of the ruling class of Shechem as the "men of Hamor" (see below), i.e. of a donkey, signifying, as it has been suggested, a party to a covenant, since among the West Semites the donkey was used in the ritual of treaty-making.[55]

Abimelech did not make Shechem his permanent royal residence, but rather appointed Zebul, his minister, as ruler of the city (Jud.

---

[53] See H. Reviv, "The Government in Shechem in the El-Amarna Period and in the Days of Abimelech," *IEJ*, 16 (1966), 252ff.; and cf. M.C. Astour, *op. cit.*, p. 10 note 21. One cannot agree with Kaufmann that Shechem was an Israelite and not a Canaanite city and that the war with Abimelech was an internal Israelite conflict; cf. his commentary on *Judges*, pp. 195–196.

[54] E.g. Yahdun-lim's Foundation Inscription—G. Dossin, *Syria*, 32 (1955), 14 (col. III: 4ff.) "Laum, king of [the city of] Samanum and the country of [the tribe of] the Ubrabeans, Bahlukulim, king of Tuttul and the country of the Amnanum, Ayalum, king of Abattum and the country of the Rabbeans." Cf. also H. Klengel, *Saeculum*, 17 (1966), 211. Our instances would reflect M. Rowton's apt concept of a "dimorphic society" (category IV); see *XVe Rencontre assyriologique internationale*, Liège, 1967, pp. 109ff.

[55] For Baal-berith as a guarantor of a treaty, see recently R.E. Clements, *JSS*, 13 (1968), 21ff.; and for the significance of $h^a m\bar{o}r$, i.e. donkey, in a treaty context, cf. W.F. Albright, *Archaeology and the Religion of Israel*, p. 113.

9:28, 30). Supported by mercenary bands, Abimelech himself began to extend his sway over the Israelite and Canaanite inhabitants in the central hill-country, eventually transferring his residence to Arumah, a secure site southeast of Shechem (Jud. 9:41).[56]

The Shechemites envisaged the increasing connections between Abimelech and other towns as contrary to their own interests; this provided the background for the ensuing strife with their king. Gaal, who incited the Shechemites to rebel, seems to have exploited the social tension prevailing in the town and the ethnic difference between the Hivite element (Gen. 34:2) and the truly Canaanite citizens—by appealing to the rooted nobility, i.e. the "men of Hamor the father of Shechem" (Jud. 9:28). The pretext for the conflict with Abimelech was provided by the Shechemite nobles who had seized control of the roads in the area, thus grossly obstructing the former's mercantile operations (Jud. 9:25). This measure misfired and Gaal, who had made his way in the city—as mentioned above—was ejected from Shechem by Zebul and the elements still loyal to Abimelech.[57] In the end Abimelech himself turned against Shechem and reduced it to rubble.

The archeological evidence from the Late Bronze Period levels unearthed at Tell Balaṭah, the site of ancient Shechem, is particularly illuminating for the story of Abimelech. It transpires that the city was divided into a lower town and, to the north, an acropolis which was built on a 30 foot high foundation of beaten earth. This citadel was apparently the "Beth-millo" mentioned in Jud. 9:6, 20. Here were found massive fortification walls and a large building (ca. 80 × 65 feet) with an entrance flanked by towers. This building complex served as both fortress and temple (such complexes are known as *migdāl* or *migdōl* in Canaanite/Hebrew), evidently the biblical "tower [*migdāl*] of Shechem" to which the "hold [*zᵉrīaḥ*] of the house of El-

---

[56] Arumah has to be located at Khirbet el-'Ormah on the summit of the imposing Jebel el-'Ormah, 10 km. south east of Shechem, an identification confirmed by a recent survey where, *inter alia*, Early Iron pottery was found: cf. E.F. Campbell, *BASOR*, 190 (1968), 38ff. The obscure word *torma* in Jud. 9:31 may perhaps be emended to the place-name Arumah.

[57] On the Gaal incident, cf. also R.G. Boling, "And who is ŠKM?," *VT*, 13 (1963), 479ff. The temporary rule of a band in a city and its expulsion by the local inhabitants is a frequent phenomenon. Cf. for example the episode of David and his band capturing Keilah whence they were expelled by the inhabitants upon pressure by Saul (I Sam. 23:1ff.).

berith" was attached (Jud. 9:46).[58] In this precinct were found an altar and three stelae (*mazzēvōt*), two of which survived from an earlier sanctuary dating from the Middle Bronze Period. The third stele, erected in the courtyard in the Late Bronze Period, could be the one alluded to at Abimelech's coronation (Jud. 9:6), which probably took place here, and not at a sanctuary outside the city as often held.[59] The archeological finds prove that Shechem was a long-standing cultic center and, as such, was adapted into the Israelite traditions of the Patriarchs and Joshua.

There is also archeological support for Abimelech's utter destruction of the "tower of Shechem" (Jud. 9:45ff.), i.e. the fortress-temple, at the end of the 12th century B.C.E., and for the fact that it was never rebuilt. Abimelech performed the symbolic act of sowing the ruins with salt, a ritual known also from other occasions in the Ancient East, and which has been explained in several manners.[60] It appears, however, that it was meant as the penalty for the violation of the covenant (hence the biblical expression "covenant of salt") into which the "lords of Shechem" had entered with Abimelech when accepting his sovereignty.

After the destruction of Shechem, Abimelech continued quelling the rebellion which must have spread to other towns in the central hill-country. He besieged Thebez (a textual corruption of Tirzah?)[61]— apparently also an ancient Canaanite stronghold. The course of the

---

[58] For a general discussion of the archeological finds in Shechem and their bearing upon the story of Abimelech, see G.E. Wright, *Shechem*, New York, 1965, pp. 80ff.; pp. 123ff.; and cf. pp. 126–127 for the term *ẕᵉrīaḥ* ("hold") which *here* means a tower or an upper storey of some structure rather than a crypt, as frequently held. The various attempts to reconcile the complex archeological and biblical data have recently been discussed by J.A. Soggin, "Bemerkungen zur alttest. Topographie Sichems mit besonderem Bezug auf Jdc. 9," *ZDPV*, 83 (1967), 183ff. For the term *migdō/āl* as comprising both temple and fortress, cf. B. Mazar, *Encyclopaedia Biblica*, 4, col. 633ff. (Hebrew), and G.R.H. Wright, *ZAW*, 80 (1968), 16ff.

[59] The location of the temple of El-berith on the slopes of Mount Gerizim is debated in the literature cited in the previous note. Recent archeological evidence refutes this view however, for the sanctuary brought to light there had already been destroyed early in the Late Bronze Period; see R.G. Boling, *BA*, 32 (1969), 81ff.; E.F. Campbell – G.E. Wright, *ibid.*, 104ff.

[60] For the different explanations, cf. S. Gevirtz, "Jericho and Shechem—A Religio-Literary Aspect of City Destruction," *VT*, 13 (1963), 52ff.; and see the note there by J. Greenfield (*ibid.*, p. 61, note 1).

[61] The toponym Thebez is actually a *hapax legomenon* in Jud. 9:50 (this very passage being quoted in II Sam. 11:21; cf. above). Its usual identification with the Arab village Ṭubas, 15 km northeast of Shechem, lacks both archeological and linguistic

siege may have been similar to that of Shechem (Jud. 9:50ff.): first
the lower town was taken and its inhabitants and patrician families
(*ba'ₐlē hā'îr*) fled to the "strong tower" (*migdāl 'ōz*) within the city, i.e.
to the fortress-temple on the acropolis. Just as the Shechemites sought
final refuge in the "hold of the house of El-berith," here the citizens fled to the uppermost part of the fortress (*gag hammigdāl*). In
this attempt, however, while trying to set fire to the fortress, Abimelech
was fatally wounded, following which his army dispersed (see above).

Abimelech's three-year rule—limited in both time and area—may
therefore be considered as an abortive attempt at kingship, particularly as it derived its inspiration from a Canaanite conception of
monarchy. His gaining control was due only to the support of non-
Israelite elements, and this in addition to the wanton slaughter of
his own brothers. The absence of all charismatic flavor in his rule
is stressed by his emphatic reliance upon mercenaries (Jud. 9:4)—
paid from the treasury of the sanctuary of Shechem,—and in Abimelech's indirect rule through Zebul. This is in absolute contrast with
the true charismatic leadership of the judges who relied on voluntary forces and needed no bureaucratic apparatus. Hence, it is not
at all surprising that biblical tradition presents Abimelech in a negative light, regarding him as neither king nor judge: "And Abimelech held sway [*wayyāśar*, i.e. held dominion] over Israel three years"

---

basis (only the letter *b* being held in common; could the modern village-name have
possibly been derived from Tobias?). We assume that Thebez is merely a corrupted
spelling, most likely of the place-name Tirzah; this has been accepted by Y. Aharoni,
The Land of the Bible, London, 1967, p. 242. Such a textual corruption can easily
be explained on the basis of an originally defective spelling of the name Tirzah
(*trz*—without the final *h*), and on account of the similarity of the letters *r* and *b* in
the palaeo-Hebrew script, particularly in cursive script, before the letter *z*.

Indeed, the city of Tirzah fits perfectly into this context, historically, geographically and probably also archeologically. The site has been identified with Tell el-
Far'ah, 10 km northeast of Shechem, and the excavations there have revealed an
important fortified Canaanite town (cf. Josh. 12:24), but the precise dating of the
destruction layer of the Late Bronze Age city is uncertain; see R. de Vaux, "Tirzah,"
Archaeology and Old Testament Study, p. 375, and the bibliography there on p. 383. It
is quite surprising that this important center in the vicinity of Shechem should not
appear in the story of Abimelech. It is further noteworthy that Jeroboam I, founder
of the northern Israelite Kingdom, rebuilt Shechem and Penuel (I Kings 12:25),
both of which were *migdāl*-type cities destroyed in the days of Gideon and Abimelech.
The third town which Jeroboam appears to have rebuilt is Tirzah (I Kings 14:17),
and if the identity with Thebez is accepted, it also had such a Canaanite *migdāl*.

(Jud. 9:22). This was merely an ephemeral episode, since the time was not yet ripe for the establishment of a monarchy in Israel.

E. *Israel and the Transjordanian States*

Israelite fortunes in Canaan in the period of the judges are characterized by the struggle against the country's indigenous, Canaanite population, and later with the Philistines. The story of Abimelech is a good example of the ever-changing relations with the Canaanite elements, as is the Samson cycle regarding the Philistines. At times relations were good, neighborly, at others they deteriorated to the point of open conflict. The tension, increasing with the consolidation of Israelite power, led to hostilities in Transjordan as well. In contrast to Cis-Jordania, the Israelite tribes there were faced by nations somewhat akin to themselves (the Bible links the origin of Edom, Moab and Ammon to the Hebrew Patriarchs) and which had but recently undergone the process of settlement the Israelites were experiencing.[62]

In northern Transjordan, Aramean tribes expanded alongside the Israelites, but no major clashes took place between them in the period of the judges, apparently because of the existence, until then, of vast areas suitable for settlement north of the Jabbok river, such as the sparsely inhabited regions of 'Ajlun and Bashan. Between the Jabbok and Jarmuk rivers numerous settlements were founded in the Early Iron Period, as shown, in a recent survey (see note 63). The relatively stable relations between the Arameans and Israelites in the pre-monarchical times appear to be reflected in the biblical tradition of the covenant concluded by Laban the Aramean and Jacob the Hebrew in northern Gilead (Gen. 31:44ff.).

The situation was different in the region to the south of the Jabbok where the peoples of Ammon, Moab and Edom had achieved political consolidation, establishing kingdoms early in the 13th century B.C.E.

---

[62] On the Israelite settlement in Transjordan and its relationship with the neighboring states, see the series of studies by M. Noth, *PJB*, 37 (1941), 50ff.; *ZAW*, 60 (1944) 11ff.; *ZDPV*, 68 (1946–51), 1ff.; 75 (1959), 14ff.; and R. de Vaux, "Note d'histoire et de topographie transjordaniennes," *Bible et Orient*, Paris, 1967, pp. 115ff. See now also B. Oded, *Israelite Trans-Jordan during the Period of the Monarchy*, (doctoral thesis), Jerusalem, 1968 (Hebrew), unpublished.

More or less stable regimes brought prosperity to these countries and obviously tended to curtail the expansionism of the Israelite tribes. We hear of open clashes between Israel and Moab (the Ehud episode), as well as with the Ammonites (the Jephthah episode), but there is no mention of such a conflict with the Edomites, whose land lay, apparently, beyond the Israelite sphere of interest in this period. It has been suggested that the first oppressor of Israel in the period of the Judges—Cushan-Rishathaim—was a king of Edom, and not of Aram Naharaim (Jud. 3:8ff.); but such an emendation of the biblical text is unconvincing (though the change of *resh* to *dalet* in the word Aram is in itself plausible, the elimination of the second element—Naharaim—is much more difficult). On Cushan-Rishathaim as an oppressor coming from the north.

The lay of the land in southern Transjordan—the fertile valleys and the broad tablelands of the interior—with brooks flowing down to the Jordan river or the Dead Sea, led to intensive cultivation and a proliferation of settlements at the beginning of the Iron Age.[63] Moreover, Transjordan's natural wealth attracted the Israelite tribes of Cis-Jordania the surplus population of which migrated there continually. The Book of Ruth (1:1) provides a good illustration of such migration brought about by economic conditions and periods of drought. On the other hand, Moab and Ammon aspired to extend their dominion over the regions west of the Jordan (see below).

Events in Transjordan, in the period of the judges developed therefore in the shadow of the rapid increase of its population, although the habitable territory there was limited by the desert on the east and the Jordan river on the west. These factors intensified the struggle among the several forces which had crystallized in the area—between the Israelite tribes and the neighboring kingdoms on the one hand, and among these kingdoms themselves on the other. The strengthening of one of these forces necessarily involved the weak-

---

[63] For southern Transjordan in the Early Iron Age, see N. Glueck, "Explorations in Eastern Palestine, I–IV," *AASOR*, 14 (1933–34); 15 (1934–5); 18–19 (1937–9); 25–28 (1945–9); and his recent summary "Transjordan" in *Archaeology and Old Testament Study*, pp. 429ff. On the establishment of about three hundred settlements between the Yarmuk and Arnon rivers in Iron Age I and II, see in particular *AASOR*, 25–28, 228f., 285. Numerous additional settlements of the early Iron Age in the region between the Yarmuk and the Jabbok have been discovered recently by S. Mittmann, see his *Beiträge zur Siedlungs- und Territorial Geschichte des nördlichen Ostjordanlandes*, Wiesbaden, 1970.

ening of the others, as there was no room for two neighboring parties to prosper together in this limited region. Hence, in the 13th–11th centuries B.C.E. the various political factors here entered upon a cycle of alternate ups and downs, each exploiting every opportunity of extending its domain at the expense of the others. This rhythmic process may be sketched as follows:

Moab's ascent under King Eglon meant not only the weakening of its Israelite neighbors but apparently also that of the kingdom of Ammon (see below). And contrariwise, Moab's decline in the 12th–11th centuries, following its defeat by Ehud, restored Israelite strength in Transjordan and paved the way for increased immigration of Israelite elements from the west. These latter entertained neighborly relations with the Moabite population, even intermarrying with them, as evidenced by the Book of Ruth and the genealogical tribal lists of Benjamin and Judah (cf. I Chr. 8:8; also 4:22). At the same time, Moab's decline doubtlessly led to the ascent of Ammon in the north and Edom in the south.

Whereas earlier the Ammonites had been compelled to render military assistance to the Moabites (Jud. 3:13), they now were able to gain ascendancy over them, as can be inferred from the exchange between Jephthah and the king of the Ammonites (cf. below). This posed a new and increasing threat to the Israelites. On the other hand, the remark in the Edomite king-list in Gen. 36:35, according to which a king of Edom—Hadad the son of Bedad—defeated the Midianite tribes in the "field of Moab," points to an Edomite domination in the area. In any case, Moab alone was unable to withstand the inroads of the desert raiders. It is noteworthy that none of the three sources—the story of Jephthah, the passing remark in the list of Edomite kings, and the Book of Ruth—presuppose the existence of a monarchy in Moab. The two latter sources, which may deal with approximately the same period (ca. 1100 B.C.E.)[64] speak only of "the field of Moab." This perhaps infers that Moab had actually ceased to be a monarchy, and could regain its position only after Ammon's defeat by Jephthah, and particularly by Saul.

---

[64] For the time of Edom's war with the Midianites, cf. above, note 41. For the dating of the events related in the Book of Ruth, the lineage of David appended to this book (4:17ff.) may be instructive. According to this list David was the fourth generation after Boaz and Ruth.

This fluctuation of fortunes in Transjordan is particularly conspicuous in the prosperous region between the Arnon brook in the south and the Jabbok in the north, an area which had been for many generations a true bone of contention between Ammon, Moab and the Israelite tribes. Every now and then there was a major change in control. This buffer region, and particularly its western parts—the Plain of Moab (ʿarvōt Mōāb)—was known not only for its economic value but also for its considerable strategic importance. The plains of Moab controlled the Jordan fords and, when dominated by hostile forces, could constitute a dire threat to Cis-Jordania, especially the territories of Benjamin and Ephraim. On the other hand, Israelite domination there prevented the expansion of Ammon and Moab west of the Jordan.

At the beginning of the 13th century B.C.E. this area was apparently divided between Ammon and Moab, though it was soon conquered by Sihon the Amorite king who pushed Ammon eastward beyond the upper course of the Jabbok and Moab to the south of the Arnon (cf. Num. 21:26). At that time Egypt had also become a factor to be reckoned with in the power-struggle prevailing in the region, as shown by a recently published inscription of Ramses II according to which this pharaoh dispatched a military expedition to distant Moab, conquering sites even north of the Arnon.[65] In the wake of the Israelite defeat of Sihon and his Amorite kingdom, the tribes of Gad and Reuben settled extensively there while Moab and Ammon were eager to regain control of their lost territories.

---

[65] For this recently rediscovered and deciphered inscription, see K.A. Kitchen, *JEA* 50 (1964), 47ff., who proposes dating this expedition early in Ramses' reign, before the area was conquered by Sihon. This newly attested Egyptian influence in that region may perhaps explain the discovery of the Baluʿa stele in Moab, north of the Arnon, which bears a relief in distinct Egyptian style and an enigmatic inscription in characters apparently imitating hieroglyphic writing. The relief shows a god and goddess flanking a local ruler of characteristically Bedouin type (could it portray the "first king of Moab" mentioned in Num. 21:26?). For the latest treatment of this stele, see W.A. Ward – M.F. Martin, *Annual of the Department of Antiquities of Jordan*, 8–9 (1964), 5ff., pls. I–VI. In connection with Ramses' campaign to Moab, the recent discovery of an Egyptian mining center at Timna is of interest, the finds there including inscriptions of Ramses II.

1. *Ehud and the Moabites.* Moab's hour struck during the reign of King Eglon, most likely during the 12th century B.C.E. (lack of any chronological data prevents a more precise dating). The Moabites succeeded in expanding northwards beyond the Arnon where they annexed the *mīshōr,* i.e., the northern plateau—and westward to the plains of Moab, becoming due to the domination of these areas a significant political factor.[66] From there the Moabites continued to extend their sway even to the western bank of the Jordan capturing the City of Palms, apparently the site of Jericho (Jud. 3:13).[67] Once in possession of this bridgehead they oppressed the land of Benjamin (for eighteen years) and even threatened the territory of Ephraim.

It was apparently during this period that Moab gained to some extent control over the land of Ammon, as might be inferred from the participation—though only indirectly involved—of Ammonite forces in the Moabite attack on Israel: "And he gathered unto him the children of Ammon and Amalek; and he went and smote Israel" (Jud. 3:13). The Amalekites' joining Moab in this campaign may indicate that the latter also held sway over the desert fringes and the nomadic bands there. The peak of power reached by Moab at that time was matched only in the 9th century during the reign of King Mesha.

There is no information on Edom's political stand at this time, though it was obviously on the defensive against Moab, its flourishing and aggressive neighbor to the north. Moreover, in the first half of the 12th century Edom became involved in a conflict with Egypt when an expedition sent by Ramses III invaded the land of Seir subduing its inhabitants. There may very well have developed closer connections between Edom and Israel during this period of Moab's ascent, since both faced a common danger. This may be indicated by the name of the place to which Ehud fled after killing the king

---

[66] See Glueck, *AASOR*, 18–19, 242ff., who appropriately calls this extended area of Moab "Greater Moab." Cf. also A.H. van Zyl, *The Moabites*, Leiden, 1960, pp. 125ff.

[67] The "city of palm trees" certainly refers to Jericho in Deut. 34:3 and II Chr. 28:15 (but not necessarily in Jud. 1:16). This designation may have referred to the city of Jericho—which lay at that time in ruins—together with the fertile oasis surrounding it. Mention of the city of Gilgal later in the story also points to this area. One cannot accept the view of E. Auerbach, *Wüste und Gelobtes Land*, I, Berlin, 1932, pp. 100f., who identifies the place with Tamar and transfers the geographical scene of Ehud's story to the region south of the Dead Sea.

of Moab (provided the odd name "Seirath" actually does refer to the land of Seir [Jud. 3:26]).[68]

Israel's uprising against Moab was initiated by the Benjaminite leader Ehud, son of Gera, the scion of a noble family (Gen. 46:21; I Chr. 8:3,7), which was still famous generations later (Shimei, who lived in David's day, belonged to the same family). Ehud, who was aided in his struggle by the Ephraimites, seems to have occupied a key position in Benjamin even prior to his heroic exploits for he had headed the delegation which brought tribute to the king of Moab. According to the usual practice, it was precisely the heads of vassal states who appeared before their overlord to do homage.

The biblical account of the actual war between Moab and Israel is very brief and the few geographical data recorded are insufficiently clear,[69] nor is the site of King Eglon's residence specified. Seemingly he dwelt then at his summer residence (in the city of Medeba?) since he received Ehud in the "cool upper chamber" (the early Aramaic version, followed by the AV and RV—Jud. 3:20 has already "in a summer parlour"), i.e. the highest and coolest storey in a building.[70] In accordance with its folkloristic character the Book of Judges does, however, give a detailed and quite realistic description of Ehud's heroic deed and the circumstances of Eglon's assassination, enabling us to comprehend the nature of the stratagem employed by the Israelite deliverer.

---

[68] Since the immediate continuation of the story (v. 27) places Ehud in the hill-country of Ephraim, the location of Seirath has usually been sought along the route from Jericho to the hills of Ephraim; see the discussion, J. Braslavi, "Ha-Seiratha and the Jordan Fords," *Beth-Mikra*, 34 (1968), 37ff. (Hebrew). However, already some of the recensions of the Septuagint add, in v. 27, after the words "[and Ehud] escaped into Seirath. And it came to pass, when he was come" the phrase: "to the land of the children of Israel," before mentioning the mountains of Ephraim. Hence, this version explicitly indicates that Ehud first fled to a place beyond Israel's borders—apparently to the land of Seir—and only thence did he return to Ephraim.

[69] Cf. the commentaries; for an analysis of the story, cf. also E.G. Kraeling, "Difficulties in the Story of Ehud," *JBL*, 54 (1935), 205ff.; W. Richter, *Traditionsgesch. Untersuchungen*, pp. 1ff.

[70] The existence of an *ᶜaliyyā*, "upper chamber", in palaces is attested both in II Kings 1:2 (the palace of Samaria) and in the Egyptian tale of Wen-Amon. Interestingly enough, the latter—as in the story of Ehud—relates that the (Egyptian) emissary was received by the King of Byblos in his upper chamber (the Egyptian text uses here the same word, borrowed from the Canaanite-Hebrew: *ᶜyt*); cf. *ANET*, p. 26b.

Ehud acquired a double edged dagger especially designed for stabbing, a weapon still rare in those days.[71] Because of its small size ("of a cubit length"), and especially as he "girded it under his raiment upon the right thigh" and not upon the left as usual, he was able to approach the king without the weapon being noticed. The manner in which he carried his dagger, and that of his drawing it with an unexpected motion of the left hand to thrust it into the king's flabby belly (Jud. 3:21), prove that Ehud was left-handed or probably ambidextrous, for like the rest of his tribe he was evidently skilled in using both hands to wield weapons (cf. I Chr. 12:2).

After this courageous deed Ehud spread the revolt throughout the mountains of Ephraim where Moabite domination was less strong; from there he began driving the enemy out of western Palestine. The Israelites blocked the crossings of the Jordan to cut off the Moabites' line of retreat (Jud. 3:28; and cf. 7:24; 12:5–7; as well as pp. 146–159). The Bible however does not relate of a pursuit across the river into Moab proper, nor do we learn anything of the tribes of Gad and Reuben who must have been the principal victims of Moab's expansion. This may reflect the fact that the Book of Judges gives only a Benjaminite tradition of the events, or that these two Transjordanian tribes stood aside, as in Deborah's war, because the continuous oppression of the kingdoms of Moab and Ammon had rendered them too weak to join in the struggle.

Ehud scored a decisive victory over Moab resulting—according to the Book of Judges—in the longest period of peace ensured to Israel by an act of deliverance, i.e. some eighty years (Jud. 3:30)—which may simply denote a time span of two generations. Moab did not recover during the period of the judges and even under the early Israelite Monarchy continued to be the weakest of the southern Transjordanian states, Israel's principal enemies on this flank being then Ammon and Edom.

2. *Jephthah and the Ammonites.* As mentioned, Moab's decline and the crushing blow dealt by Gideon to the Midianite tribes allowed Ammon to consolidate and rise to power. The Ammonites had been especially sensitive to the desert raiders because of their front-line position. That kingdom, centered around Rabbath-Ammon (present-day

---

[71] See Y. Yadin, *Art of Warfare*, pp. 254f.

Amman), consisted of a small strip of land on the upper Jabbok which flows to the north. Despite its small size and its location on the fringe of the desert, Ammon was in a strategic and geopolitical position of the first order, due to its command of a section of the "King's highway," i.e. the international artery linking Syria with southern Transjordan, whence it continued to the Gulf of Elath and the Arabian peninsula, while another branch ran across the Jordan river into western Palestine. This domination of an intersection of roads lent Ammon considerable political power and unusual economic prosperity, especially in periods when it could bring under its control the caravan trade of the desert tribes.[72]

On the other hand because of its precarious geographical position, a lack of "strategic depth," and because of the frequent pressure exerted by the marauding desert tribes to the east as well as by the sedentary populations to the west and south, the Ammonites were compelled to fortify their borders far more thoroughly than their neighbors who were able to rely partly on natural defense lines. The great organizational and technical ability of the Ammonites is clearly evidenced in the establishment of the chain of border fortresses surrounding Rabbath-Ammon on the west and south (cf. Num. 21:24), which were discovered during the archeological surveys of the thirties and, again, the fifties and sixties of the present century.[73] These massive forts, some built on a square or rectangular plan, but most of them of a distinct circular type (known as Rujm el-Malfuf), were apparently constructed in the Early Iron Age and continued in use throughout the existence of the Ammonite kingdom. This close network of forts offered an efficient means of communication, vital in foiling attempts of penetration into the heart of the country.

The biblical account of the defeat Jephthah inflicted upon the Ammonites "from Aroer until thou come to Minnith even twenty cities and unto Abel-keramim" (Jud. 11:33) apparently refers to an onslaught against the western line of defence. The twenty "cities"

---

[72] W.F. Albright, "Notes on Ammonite History," *Miscellanea Biblica B. Ubach*, Montserrat, 1953, pp. 131ff.

[73] See Glueck, *AASOR*, 18–19, 151ff. and the later surveys of the Germans who located the continuation of the border line in the south as far as Rujm el-Fehud; H. Gese, *ZDPV*, 74 (1958), 55ff.; R. Hentschke, *ibid.*, 76 (1960), 103ff.; G. Fohrer, *ibid.*, 77 (1961), 56ff.; H. Reventlow; *ibid.*, 79 (1963), 127ff.; and H.J. Stoebe, *ibid.*, 82 (1966), 33ff. and cf. also G.M. Landes, "The Material Civilisation of the Ammonites," *BAr*, 24 (1961), 65ff.

were doubtlessly mere border forts, while Aroer was not the well known city on the Arnon river but "Aroer that is before Rabbah" (Josh. 13:25), located southwest of Amman. South of this Aroer, on the way to Heshbon, are Minnith (ca. 5 km south of Amman) and Abel-keramim which may be located at the village of Naʿur (13 km southwest of Amman).[74] However, unlike David, Jephthah failed to break through to Rabbath-Ammon proper and gain a decisive victory over the Ammonites.

As Ammon grew stronger it expanded far beyond its borders, both in the southwest, into Moab, and northwestwards into the fertile region of el-Buqeiaʿ which is encompassed by the bend of the Jabbok and Waddi Umm ed-Dananir. This western part of "Greater Ammon" may have been referred to in the Bible as "half the land of the children of Ammon" (Josh. 13:25). The Ammonites expanded also further westward into the land of Gilead, then crossed the Jordan attempting to subdue the territories of Ephraim, Benjamin and even Judah. This offensive against the Israelites was contemporaneous with the increased Philistine pressure from the west (Jud. 10:7–9) and may have even been encouraged by the latter. The Israelites retaliated once the Ammonites had gone up against Gilead (Jud. 10:17; the reference here seems to be to the town of Gilead, located at Khirbet Jelʿad 9 km south of the Jabbok, between el-Buqeiaʿ and the plateau of Arḍ el-Arḍa),[75] since their action endangered the densely populated area in the fertile land of Gilead and the lower Jabbok region. This region was settled principally by the tribe of Gad supplemented by immigrants from the tribes of Manasseh and Ephraim.

In this hour of peril the elders of Gilead turned to Jephthah, the outcast whom his brothers had expelled from his father's patrimony since he was the son of a harlot (Jud. 11:1–3).[76] Jephthah had fled

---

[74] S. Mittmann, "Aroer, Minnith und Abel-Keramim," *ZDPV*, 85 (1969), 63ff., proposes, doubtfully, to locate all these sites to the northwest of Amman (nearer to Jephthah's starting-point); and see there for the usual identifications in the southwest.

[75] As with several other toponyms (e.g. Shechem), the name Gilead came to designate both a city and a broader region; a land as well as a mountain range, and even a tribal unit. For the complex problems of the borders of the land of Gilead and the identification of the city of the same name, see M. Noth, *ZDPV*, 75 (1959), 14ff.; and now M. Ottosson, *Gilead-Tradition and History*, Lund, 1969; Z. Kallai, *The Tribes of Israel*, index (p. 435), s.v. Gilead (Hebrew).

[76] Cf. J. Mendelsohn, *IEJ*, 4 (1954), 116ff., who discusses the legal aspect of Jephthah's expulsion, which he thinks could have been effected only by the intervention of the institution of the elders of Gilead.

to the land of Tob, probably in the region of the Jarmuk, where no firm regime was established even in much later times (cf. 2 Sam. 10:6 referring merely to the "men" and not to a king of Tob). There he gathered a band of freebooters which, in the opinion of the elders of Gilead, could enable him to lead successfully in a war against the Ammonites. It was the existence of this band which invested Jephthah with bargaining power concerning his future status (Jud. 11:6ff.). Indeed he declined the initial offer to become the "commander" (*qāzīn*) of Gilead, that is a leadership limited to the duration of the war. He consented only when the elders offered to elect him "head [*rō'sh*] over all the inhabitants of Gilead" i.e. supreme ruler over the entire Israelite region, maintaining his authority in peace time as well (cf. the parallel expression concerning Saul's leadership, I Sam. 15:17). Jephthah's appointment as both "head and commander"[77] was similar to the coronation ceremony of a king—involving the conclusion of a covenant with the people's representatives, namely, the council of elders, and solemnized in a religious act "before the Lord in Mizpah" (Jud. 11:11; cf. the crowning of Abimelech and, in particular, of Saul and David).

The town of Mizpah, apparently called Mizpeh of Gilead later in this story, was the religious and political center of that region, hallowed already in the tradition of the Patriarchs (Gen. 31:49). Opinions differ concerning the site of this town which served as a base for the Israelite army under Jephthah. According to one view it should be located north of the Jabbok, but the biblical context would rather suggest a place south of the Jabbok close to the city of Gilead, for it is stated that the Israelites encamped just opposite the Ammonite army.[78] Before Jephthah decided to attack he took the diplomatic

---

[77] The titles *rō'š* and *qāzīn* (*qāṣīn*) appear in parallel in Mic. 3:1, also as the nation's supreme leaders. For these terms cf. J. van der Ploeg, *RB*, 57 (1950), 52, 58f. For the title *rō'š*, see also J.R. Bartlett, *VT*, 19 (1969), 1ff. These two terms occur also in external documents: *qāzīn* in the Ugarit documents and as a loanword from the Canaanite in Egyptian inscriptions (*ḳḏ/ṯn*), denoting a chariotry commander; and *rō'š* in Assyrian sources from the time of Tiglath-pileser III on, denoting the heads of nomadic tribes (*rēšu, rā'šāni*); cf. e.g. J.A. Brinkman, *A Political History of Post-Kassite Babylonia*, Rome, 1968, p. 265 and note 1705. For an even earlier extra-biblical attestation of *rō'š*, see *Archives Royales de Mari I*, Paris, 1950, No. 10:20— "our lord is our sole chief (*rašani*)".

[78] That is why the suggestion of Noth, *ZDPV*, 75 (1959), 36, to identify it with el-Mishrefe, 2 km north of Khirbet Jel'ad, seems correct, while others would identify it with the latter locality itself (e.g. R. de Vaux) or with Khirbet Umm ed-Danānīr, south of it; Glueck, *AASOR*, 18–19, 100ff.

step of attempting to negotiate with the Ammonite king (Jud. 11:12–28). Though the literary form of the diplomatic negotiations is late and raises various difficulties, it still remains an important historical source reflecting the seemingly authentic claims of both parties to the possession of the contended area between the Jabbok and the Arnon.[79] Jephthah based Israel's claim on the fact that their forebears had conquered this area from Sihon, King of the Amorites, and not from Ammon or Moab. A further argument was that the Israelites had right of possession because of their long residence there. The reference to 300 years in this context is not clear, though it may, similarly to other round figures in the Book of Judges, merely indicate so many generations (reckoning 40 years per generation). By applying to the figure a more realistic reckoning (i.e. on the basis of 25 years per generation) we arrive at a period of slightly under 200 years, which would fit perfectly the time-span between the Israelite conquest of Transjordan (i.e. the first half or middle of the 13th century B.C.E.) and Jephthah's time (i.e. the first half of the 11th century B.C.E.).

The Ammonite counter-claim seems to have been based on the assertion that even prior to Sihon's expansion the Ammonites had occupied the northern part of the area in dispute. Moreover, the Ammonite king appears in the negotiations also as the suzerain of the land of Moab, which entitled him to the territorial claims of that country as well, for Moab once occupied the southern part of the contended region (cf. Num. 21:26). Indeed, Ammon's supposed domination of Moab in Jephthah's days and the consequent assumption of its rights and privileges would account more readily than other alternate explanations for the fact that Jephthah refers to Chemosh—actually the national deity of Moab—as the god of Ammon's king (Jud. 11:24).

Upon failure of the negotiations, Jephthah levied Israelite troops from the tribes of Gad and Manasseh, but his appeal to the Ephraimites went unheeded (Jud. 12:2–3). As already mentioned, Jephthah's was

---

[79] The exegetes generally considered this pericope a later composition, actually reflecting the relationship between the Israelites and *Moab*, which is interpolated into the Jephthah cycle. For recent discussions, see W. Richter, "Die Überlieferungen um Jephthah," *Biblica*, 47 (1966), 522ff.; Ottosson, *op. cit.*, pp. 161ff. The basic authenticity of this episode, however, has rightly been stressed by Kaufmann, *Judges*, pp. 219ff.

not a decisive victory, since it did not take the Ammonites long to recover. However, another event in the aftermath of the war left its mark on Israelite history: the outbreak of the fratricidal strife between the Gileadites and the Ephraimites.

F. *Inter-Tribal Wars*

The initial cause of the bitter and cruel feud between Jephthah and the Ephraimites (Jud. 12:1–6) can be found in the latter tribe's ambition to dominate the Israelite settlement in Transjordan. They were, no doubt, supported in their aspiration by numerous kindred elements which had infiltrated into Gilead from the west. The very name "forest of Ephraim" north of Mahanaim (II Sam. 18:6) points to a considerable settlement of this tribe in Gilead, while the taunting words in the story of Jephthah: "Ye are fugitives of Ephraim, ye Gileadites in the midst of Ephraim and Manasseh" (Jud. 12:4) point, despite their ambiguity, to the same fact.

The Ephraimites went up to the city of Zaphon, which is probably Tell es-Saʿidiyeh[80] near the eastern bank of the Jordan, north of the Jabbok (known from the Amarna Letters and from the list of Gadite towns in Josh. 13:27), with the probable intention to continue on to Jephthah's residence in Mizpah. Being routed and put to flight, they attempted to steal across the Jordan so as to reach their kindred's territory. The heavy Ephraimite losses (42,000 according to the exaggerated biblical account) may indicate that Jephthah exploited this opportunity to clear Gilead of all the Ephraimites who had settled there. In connection with the Ephraimites' flight to the Jordan fords we are told the interesting detail that their pursuers identified them by their pronunciation of the password "Shibboleth": "And he said 'Sibboleth'; for he could not frame to pronounce it right" (Jud. 12:6). Whatever the precise meaning of this, it shows

---

[80] According to Abel and Albright, while Glueck identifies this place with the town of Zarethan. The recent excavations of this site revealed an important cemetery from the 13th–12th centuries B.C.E.; cf. J.B. Pritchard, *BAr*, 28 (1965), 10ff.; *idem*, in *The Role of the Phoenicians in the Interaction of Mediterranean Civilisations* (ed. by W. Ward), Beirut, 1968, pp. 99ff.

that in the 11th century B.C.E. there existed dialectal differences even among the northern Israelite tribes.[81]

The war between Gilead and Ephraim was hardly the only instance of inter-tribal strife in the period of the judges. From the Book of Judges we know of several such conflicts the climax of which was reached in the bitter war described in the story of the outrage at Gibeah (see below). It is worth noting, however, that such feuds were never attributed by the biblical sources to differences over territorial rights or encroachments, but rather to either the refusal of one tribe to come to the aid of other tribes in actions against foreign oppressors or, conversely, to not having been called upon to render such assistance.

Thus, the Ephraimites charged both Gideon and, perhaps unjustifiably, Jephthah of having failed to summon them to war with the enemy (Jud. 8:1; 12:1—both passages explicitly using the term "men ['*īsh*] of Ephraim" in specifically referring to warriors). Their exclusion deprived them of both the glory and, more important probably, their fair share in the spoils. Gideon succeeded in appeasing the Ephraimites by inviting them to join in the pursuit of the Midianites, in which they managed even to win a decisive victory, as we have seen. This latter achievement is well reflected in Gideon's address to the Ephraimites: "Is not the gleaning of Ephraim better than the vintage of Abiezer? [i.e. Gideon's own clan]. God hath delivered into your hand the princes of Midian, Oreb and Zeeb; and what was I able to do in comparison with you?" (Jud. 8:2–3). But the conflict in Jephthah's time led to bloodshed and the slaughter of the Ephraimite warriors.

There were occasions, however, when tribal units or even whole tribes would refuse to participate in a campaign they were requested to render assistance. A case in point is Deborah's war with the Canaanites, when several tribes were denounced for shirking their duty (as we have seen above, p. 138). Here also the inhabitants of Meroz, who could easily have taken part in the battle near Taanach,

---

[81] See E.A. Speiser, "The Shibboleth Incident," *BASOR*, 85 (1942), 10ff.; R. Marcus, *ibid.*, 87 (1942), 39. Cf. D. Leibel, "On the Linguistic Peculiarity of the Ephraimites," *Molad*, 23 (September 1965), 335ff. (Hebrew); and see also the illuminating remarks by the medieval commentator Rabbi David Kimḥi (*ad loc.*). According to him the catchword "Shibboleth" seems to refer here to "the current of the river" rather than to the usual meaning: "ear of corn."

close to their town, were cursed in particular, "because they came not to the help of the Lord" (Jud. 5:23).[82] This reminds of the dire results of the refusal of the people of Succoth and Penuel to provide provisions for Gideon's troops during their pursuit of the Midianites.

Two phenomena stand out in all the above mentioned incidents:

(1) The antagonism or even open rift which frequently appeared between the tribes west of the Jordan and those to the east; there is no extant evidence for a single war of deliverance involving joint action of the tribes on both sides of the river in the period of the judges. This rivalry between the two sections of the Israelites is further manifested in the biblical tradition in Joshua 22, relating the setting up of an aggressive tribal confederacy in the west, with an eye on the Transjordanian tribes who had erected an altar "over against the land of Canaan, in the borders of Jordan" (v. 11).[83]

(2) The principal instigator in the various inter-tribal conflicts, such as the incidents with Gideon and Jephthah, was the tribe of Ephraim; it was also this tribe which was the driving force behind the large-scale operations against Benjamin, the culmination of the episode of Gibeah. Thus, Ephraim became involved with all its neighboring tribes: Manasseh, Gilead (= Gad) and Benjamin. It would appear that the reason for all this strife was the growing power and prestige of these tribes resulting from the victories of Gideon of Manasseh, Jephthah the Gileadite and Ehud of Benjamin and the ever-increasing drive for pre-eminence of Ephraim. The eventual position of superiority of the latter tribe is also reflected in Jacob's blessing of the sons of Joseph, in which the right of primogeniture had been granted to Ephraim instead of Manasseh his elder brother (Gen.

---

[82] Meroz may be identified with Khirbet Mazar on one of the western summits of the Gilboa range, ca. 12 km east of Taanach. See *Encyclopaedia Biblica* 5, col. 451 (Hebrew). As with the people of Succoth and Penuel, it is not clear whether its inhabitants were Israelites (of the tribe of Manasseh) or rather Canaanites in treaty with the Israelites, as assumed by A. Alt, *Kleine Schriften*, I, pp. 274ff. For the significance of the Hebrew verb *'rr* "to curse," see H.C. Brichto, *The Problem of "Curse" in the Hebrew Bible*, Philadelphia, 1963, pp. 77ff. This cursing of a city may resemble the Egyptian Execration Texts, as might the proscription of the leaders of Succoth (R. Grafman's suggestion) mentioned above, p. 146. For the latter practice one may now refer to the recently found Canaanite ostraca from Kamid el-Loz, apparently bearing a malediction formula and personal names; see G. Mansfeld, *Kamid el-Loz-Kumidi*, Saarbrücker Beiträge für Altertumskunde, 7, 1970.

[83] On this episode and its historical setting in the period of the judges, see J. Dus, "Die Lösung des Rätsels von Jos. 22," *ArOr* 32 (1964), 529ff.

48:17ff.; and cf. I Chr. 5:1–2), which most likely anticipates the time after Abimelech's failure and the decline of Manasseh.[84]

The Gilead-Ephraim war which broke out just after Jephthah's victory over the Ammonites seems to have facilitated the recovery of the vanquished nation. About two generations later, on the eve of Saul's kingship, the Ammonites again pressed northward, this time as far as Jabesh-gilead north of the Jabbok. Saul, who was a Benjaminite and as such quite likely a blood relation of the inhabitants of Jabesh-gilead,[85] rushed to their aid. The historical circumstances which led up to this action may be better understood through the episode of the outrage at Gibeah, the most conspicuous and farfamed case of Israelite inter-tribal war in the period of the judges (Jud. 19:21). Though many scholars have doubted the historicity of this episode, and despite all the tendentiousness and literary embellishments, it seems to be based on an early historical kernel still echoing in Hosea's prophecies (Hos. 5:8; 9:9).[86]

As for the historical-chronological background, the episode of the outrage at Gibeah fits well within the interval between Jephthah's days (first half of the 11th century B.C.E.) and Saul's accession (ca. 1025 B.C.E.).[87] On the one hand the story reflects the special bonds

---

[84] See in particular E.C. Kingsbury "He set Ephraim before Manasseh," *HUCA*, 38 (1967), 129ff., who stresses, however, Ephraim's pre-eminence in the cultic rather than in the political sphere, as exemplified by the shift of the cult-center from Shechem to Bethel and Shiloh.

[85] The strong ties between the tribe of Benjamin and Gilead are indicated in several biblical sources, as has been pointed out by E.A. Melamed, *Tarbiz* 5 (1934) 121ff. (Hebrew): (a) the genealogical lists—where the clans of Shuppim and Huppim are affiliated with both Benjamin and Machir the Gileadite (I Chr. 7:12 and 15); (b) the story of Gibeah—attesting to the marriage between the maidens of Jabesh-Gilead and the Benjaminites (cf. below), of which Saul may even have been an offspring, which would in turn more definitely explain both the help he rendered to the besieged city and the conduct of its inhabitants in recovering the bodies of Saul and his sons from Beth-shean; (c) the reference in a much later period to such a connection by the prophet Obadiah (1:19).

[86] For the authenticity and antiquity of the account, cf. Kaufmann, *Judges*, pp. 277ff.; in contrast, see M. Güdemann, *MGWJ*, 18 (1869), 357ff., followed by H. Graetz, who assumed that the story was composed as a piece of political polemics in the rivalry between the House of David and that of Saul (who lived in Gibeah), with the intention of denigrating the latter and his tribe.

[87] The chronology of this story is disputed, as we have noted. At first sight the mention of the priest Phinehas the grandson of Aaron, in Jud. 20:28, may indicate a very early dating within the period of the judges, an opinion held already by Josephus. Yet his appearance is of no particular chronological significance, especially since he tends to figure in biblical tradition in connection with the Ark of

between Benjamin and Jabesh-gilead: this town, alone in all Israel, refused to join in the punitive action against Benjamin and was severely punished by the other tribes for having violated the Israelite confederation's vow. Further, after most of Benjamin had been annihilated, the nubile maidens (i.e. the specific meaning of $b^e t \bar{u} l \bar{o} t$) of Jabesh-gilead were given to the remaining Benjaminites to ensure the survival of the tribe (Jud. 21:8ff.). These facts, namely the weakening of Jabesh-gilead and that city's special relationship with the tribe of Benjamin, link up very well with the above mentioned circumstances on the eve of Saul's reign: the Ammonite offensive against Jabesh-gilead and its subsequent appeal for help addressed specifically to the tribe of Benjamin, and not to the tribe of Ephraim which lived closer.

On the other hand, the story of the events concerning Gibeah may be considered as a continuation of the conflict between Ephraim and Gilead since the days of Jephthah. The tribe of Ephraim was not only the instigator of the pan-Israelite war against Benjamin, as already noted, but was also behind the punitive expedition against Jabesh-gilead. Admittedly, according to the biblical account the immediate cause of the pan-Israelite action was a gruesome sex crime committed at Gibeah in the territory of Benjamin, the victim of which was the concubine of a Levite from Mount Ephraim. But time and again in biblical historiography such seemingly private, individual family incidents actually reflect historio-political events. The actual background to this story was undoubtedly provided by inter-tribal rivalry for hegemony in Israel, especially that between Ephraim and Benjamin.[88]

Whatever the case, the story of the outrage at Gibeah reveals most instructive details on the religious, social, institutional and military facets of the Israelite confederation, as well as its inter and supertribal organization in the period of the judges. Thus we learn of the important role played by Beth-el (but not by it alone) as a religious center and even as the seat of the Ark of the Covenant "in those

---

the Covenant and pan-Israelite undertakings (cf. Num. 31:6; Josh. 22), and may here be the result of later, tendentious recension.

[88] This point has been emphasized by O. Eissfeldt, "Der geschichtliche Hintergrund der Erzählung von Gibeas Schandtat," *Festschrift G. Beer*, Stuttgart, 1935, pp. 19ff. (= *Kleine Schriften*, II, Tübingen, 1963, pp. 64ff.), who considers the part-tribal portrayal as the result of a later recension. And cf. K.D. Schunck, *Benjamin*, Berlin, 1963, pp. 57ff.

days" (Jud. 20:18, 26–27).[89] The story reflects well the Israelite "primitive democracy" in action, and describes the functioning of its central institutions, the "congregation" (ʿēdā) and the "general assembly"
(Jud. 20:1ff.).[90] The tribal representatives were summoned to a general assembly at Mizpah, on the border of Benjamin, (vv. 1–2) to
hear the Levite's accusation (vv. 3–7); they reached a unanimous
decision and passed sentence on the impenitent tribe which had committed the offence (vv. 8ff.). This assembly was also the supreme
authority which declared a general conscription and ordered the
tribes to select a tenth of the potential warriors to furnish provisions
for the army, probably through the clan apparatus (vv. 10–11; and
cf. Jud. 21:10ff.).

This army was summoned by the drastic method of dispatching
parts of the concubine's corpse to each of the tribes (Jud. 19:29)
with the clear intent of spreading horror among the people—similar to the summons to Saul's war against the Ammonites (I Sam.
11:7). Such primitive tribal customs are known also from elsewhere
in the Ancient East, particularly from Mari.[91] The town of Gibeah
or Gibeath-Benjamin was conquered by a stratagem identical to that
of the conquest of Ai (Josh. 7–8): warriors were placed in ambush
behind the city, while another unit of the attackers feigned flight so
as to draw away the defenders of the town thus enabling the ambushing forces to enter without struggle the helpless city.[92] It is of

---

[89] For the significance of Bethel as amphictyonic center as deduced from this
story, see M. Noth, *Geschichte Israels*, (3rd ed.), pp. 91ff.; and cf. also W.F. Albright,
Archaeology and the Religion of Israel, pp. 104f.; J. Dus, *Oriens Antiquus*, 3 (1964), 227ff.

[90] On these institutions and their authority, see A. Malamat, "Organs of Statecraft
in the Israelite Monarchy," *BAr*, 28 (1965), 34ff. (slightly revised in *BAr* Reader, 3,
New York, 1970, pp. 163ff. = here chap. 13); see on the slogan "We will not any
of us go to his tent, neither will we any of us turn unto his house" (Jud. 20:8),
where it is regarded as a formula indicating a positive decision reached by the general assembly. Cf. also R. Gordis, "Democratic Origins in Ancient Israel—The
Biblical 'Edah," *A. Marx Jubilee Volume*, New York, 1950, pp. 369ff.; and H. Tadmor,
in *Cahiers d'Histoire Mondiale*, 11 (1968), 8.

[91] For similar drastic means described in a Mari letter, see "Mari," *Encyclopaedia
Biblica*, 4, col. 575 (Hebrew); G. Wallis, *ZAW*, 64 (1952), 57ff.

[92] The destruction of the city seems to be indicated by the end of stratum I (the
pre-fortress city) at Tell el-Fūl; cf. L.A. Sinclair, "The Archaeological Study of
Gibeah," *AASOR*, 34–35 (1960). For the military strategy, cf. Y. Yadin, *Art of Warfare*,
pp. 262f.; W. Roth, "Hinterhalt und Scheinflucht," *ZAW*, 75 (1963), 20ff. As generally accepted, Roth also considers one of the two descriptions of the city's conquest as a mere literary replica of the other; in his case, the story of Ai was copied
from the episode at Gibeah.

particular interest that in both these instances, at Ai and at Gibeah, the final conquest was preceded by unsuccessful attempts ending in real retreats on the part of the attackers. It may thus be assumed that the stratagem employed in the final attack was based on staging an additional "defeat" to lull the enemy into false confidence (Josh. 8:6–7; Jud. 20:39).

The episode of the outrage at Gibeah is the only instance of a pan-Israelite tribal confederation in the period of the judges acting as a well organized and consolidated body (excluding, of course, the punished tribe) without a judge to lead it, or as yet a king.[93]

Bibliography

Albright, W.F., *Archaeology and the Religion of Israel*, Baltimore 1942 (2nd ed. 1946).
Auerbach, E., *Wüste und Gelobtes Land*, I², Berlin 1938, 95–124.
Bright, J., *A History of Israel*, London 1960, 142–160.
Burney, C.F., *The Book of Judges*, London 1920 (reprinted with *Prolegomenon* by W.F. Albright, New York 1970).
Cundall, A.E., *Judges*, London 1968.
Desnoyers, L., *Histoire du peuple Hebreu*, I: La période des Juges, Paris 1922.
Die Ou Testamentiese Werkgemeenskap in Suid Africa, Papers read at the 2nd Meeting, 1959 (collection of lectures).
Eissfeldt, O., "The Hebrew Kingdom", *CAH* II (rev. ed.) (chap. XXXIV), 1965.
Garstang, J., *Joshua-Judges*, London 1931.
Glueck, N., *The Other Side of the Jordan*, New Haven 1945.
Kaufmann, Y., *The Book of Judges* (Hebrew), Jerusalem 1962.
Kittel, R., *Geschichte des Volkes Israel*, II (sixth and seventh ed.), Stuttgart 1925.
Lagrange, M.J., *Le livre des Juges*, Paris 1903.
Maisler (Mazar), B., *A History of Eretz Israel*, I, (Hebrew), Tel-Aviv 1938.
Malamat, A., "Syrien-Palästina in der 2. Hälfte des 2. Jahrtausends" *Fischer Weltgeschichte*, III, Frankfurt a/M 1966, 177–221, 347–352.
Noth, M., *Geschichte Israels*, (3rd ed.) Göttingen 1956, 131–151.
Olmstead, A.T., *History of Palestine and Syria*, New York-London 1931, 270–293.
Richter, W., *Traditionsgeschichtliche Untersuchungen zum Richterbuch*, Bonn 1963. *Die Bearbeitungen des "Retterbuches"*, etc., Bonn 1964.
Smend, R., *Jahwekrieg und Stämmebund*, (2nd ed.), Göttingen 1966.

Yet it would rather seem that we have here a common stratagem, adopted by the Israelites in several instances. As a matter of fact, this tactic of ambush and deceptive flight is mentioned as a common practice by the Roman tactician Frontinus in his *Strategemata* (see e.g. Book II, 5, 1 and 8; Book III, 10, 1ff.). Moreover, in some instances utter surprise was achieved by repeated feigning of flight (e.g. Book III, 5, 8), which may be compared to the initially real retreats of the Israelites (cf. immediately below).

[93] This English version of the Hebrew original (published in 1967) has been revised and brought up to date in 1970.

Studies in the Book of Judges (Collection of lectures), (Hebrew), Jerusalem 1966.

Täubler, E., *Biblische Studien—Die Epoche der Richter*, Tübingen 1958.

The Military History of the Land of Israel in Biblical Times, (ed. J. Liver) (Hebrew), Jerusalem 1964.

Wright, G.E., *Biblical Archaeology* (2nd ed.), Philadelphia-London 1962, 86ff.

Yadin, Y., *The Art of Warfare in Biblical Lands*, Ramat Gan 1963.

Zapletal, V., *Das Buch der Richter*, Münster 1923.

7A

APPENDIX: THE PUNISHMENT BY GIDEON OF SUCCOTH AND PENUEL IN THE LIGHT OF ANCIENT NEAR EASTERN TREATIES*

After Gideon and his three hundred soldiers defeated the Midianites in Cis-Jordan, they crossed the Jordan and pursued the enemy in the broad expanse of Trans-Jordan into the eastern desert. The Israelites apparently held sway over the northern part of the territory of Trans-Jordan.[1] Clearly, the Israelites were in urgent need of food supplies for their long-range pursuit (Judg. 8:4–9).[2] Gideon approached Succoth (to be identified with Tell Deir 'Alla), and more to the south Penuel (most likely Tullul ed-Dahab) at the mouth of the Jabbok river, both cities being located in northern Trans-Jordan. These cities were requested to supply Gideon's army (here called 'am) with "loaves of bread", the intention most likely being food provisions in general, especially as the text emphasises that the Israelite soldiers were faint with hunger.[3]

Yet, the two cities refused Gideon's demand, claiming: "Are Zebah and Zalmunna (the Midianite kings), already in your hand, that we should give bread to your army?" (Judg. 8:6).[4] The meaning of the above question is: Are the Midianite kings already defeated by Gideon and thus cannot constitute a menace to the aforementioned cities,

---

* This paper is unpublished in English and will appear in the M. Weinfeld FS, being published by Eisenbrauns.

[1] A. Malamat, "The War of Gideon and Midian", ed. J. Liver, *The Military History of the Land of Israel in Biblical Times*, 1964, pp. 118–123 (Hebrew).

[2] See the commentaries on the book of Judges, and especially C.F. Burney, *The Book of Judges*, London 1920, pp. 227–230; J.A. Soggin, *Judges* (OTL), London 1981, pp. 148–151; Y. Kaufmann, *The Book of Judges*, Jerusalem 1963, pp. 184–186 (in Hebrew); Y. Amit, *Judges* (Mikra Leyisra'el), Tel Aviv 1999, pp. 148–152 (in Hebrew).

[3] On the lexeme 'āyēf, "faint" in the sense of "hungry" (ra'eb) see several instances in the Bible; cf., e.g., Gen. 25:29–30 (concerning Esau, coming from the field being 'āyēf and he commands Jacob to feed him).

[4] Cutting off the palm of the hands of the killed enemy is depicted in Egyptian reliefs; see Y. Yadin, *The Art of Warfare in Biblical Lands*, II, Jerusalem—Ramat-Gan 1963, pp. 258–260.

or is Gideon unable to overpower the enemy? Gideon retorted that, after his victory over the Midianite leaders, he would avenge the two obstinate cities and punish their inhabitants (8:7–8). And surely, after the defeat of the Midianites, Gideon returned to Succoth and Penuel, killed the inhabitants and, in addition, destroyed the tower, i.e. the stronghold, of Penuel (8:11–17). At Succoth Gideon captured a young man (na'ar), who may have been a scribe or a member of the city council,[5] since he was able to write down for Gideon the leadership of the city: "the officials and Elders of Succoth, seventy-seven men," the principal citizens of the city (8:14; the ability to write was not a skill acquired by any young man). Thereafter, Gideon slayed Zebah and Zalmunna (8:18ff.).

Already on the basis of the Biblical text it may be assumed that there existed a kind of vassal-treaty between Gideon and the cities of northern Trans-Jordan, obliging to supply his army with food during a military campaign.[6] Indeed, a treaty which encompasses the afore-mentioned stipulation, as well as the punishment for its breach, not unlike the story in the Bible (the killing of the population of Succoth and Penuel), is admittedly rarely found in the treaties of the ancient Near-East, but does exist especially in Hittite treaties.[7]

Let us mention two such treaties, may possibly have formed the basis of the story of Gideon and his war in Trans-Jordan. In the Hittite treaty (and its parallel in the Akkadian version) from the 13th century B.C., made between the Hittite king Murshili II and Tuppi-Teshup, ruler of the land of Amurru, there exist obligations imposed on the vassal (i.e. the land of Amurru), relating to the supply of food, as well as drinks, for the army of the suzerain.[8] The key-sentence for our concern in the treaty is: "The Hittites bring you, Tuppi-Teshup, infantry and chariotry . . . Tuppi-Teshup must regularly

---

[5] See A. Malamat, *Israel in Biblical Times*, Jerusalem 1983, p. 102 and n. 49 (in Hebrew).

[6] As for the Hittite army see R.H. Beal, *The Organization of the Hittite Military*, Heidelberg 1992, p. 132.

[7] On the stipulation of supplying food by the vassal to the suzerain, see the collected essays of Y. Muffs, *Love and Joy*, New York and Jerusalem 1992, pp. 72–76. Muffs deal with tribute and supply for the army in the context of Abraham solely and his journeys (espec. Gen. 14).

[8] See now G. Beckman, *Hittite Diplomatic Texts*, Atlanta, GA, 1996, No. 8, p. 57 (#10). For the original publication of the text and the following discussions on it, see there, p. 172.

provide them with food and drink...". Such stipulations may be found also in another Hittite treaty (again there are three Akkadian versions to this text). The treaty goes back to the middle of the 14th century B.C. and was made between the Hittite king Shupiluliuma and Aziru, the ruler of Amurru, although the stipulations are not as clear as in the former treaty.[9] Finally, we shall cite an example referring to the destruction of the city of a vassal, who infringes the treaty made with the suzerain. It is the treaty of the land of Ishmerika: "If a city within the land sins, you, the men of Ishmerika, enter and destroy the city and kill the male population."[10]

Thus, we may assume that the destruction of Succoth and Penuel at the hands of Gideon was not a matter of mere conquest, but was the expected punishment for the breach of a treaty made with Israel.

---

[9] Idem, No. 5, p. 35 (top). For the original publication of the text and the following discussions on it, see p. 172. For a more convenient translation to us cf. Muffs (*op. cit.*, n. 4), p. 73, who cites A. Goetze, *ANET* 3rd ed., 1969, p. 532 (right column).

[10] On this treaty see in passing Muffs (*op. cit.*, n. 4), p. 74, and for the original publication see A. Kempinski and S. Košak, "Der Išmeriga-Vertrag," *WO* 5 (1969), p. 195.

8

CHARISMATIC LEADERSHIP IN THE
BOOK OF JUDGES*

The History of Israel from the conquest of Canaan in the thirteenth century B.C. to the establishment of the monarchy at the close of the eleventh century was characterized by a unique political system. This regime of judges, which has no extant parallel among the peoples of the ancient Near East, was a response to a chronic state of war imposed upon the Israelites by their neighbors. It is not surprising, therefore, that its main manifestations are in the military sphere. In times of distress, charismatic leaders in the form of deliverer-judges arose sporadically among the Israelites and brought them out from under the hands of their oppressors. The Book of Judges, which is the principal source for observing this historical phenomenon (it is also intimated in the stories concerning Saul, in I Samuel), contains a collection of folk tales on the deliverer-judges, each of which portrays an encounter with an adversary of a particular type, as well as the specific challenge confronting the judge. The Book of Judges also attests to another kind of leader, known in biblical scholarship as the "minor judge" in contradistinction to the deliverers, the "major judges."

Since our discussion is devoted primarily to the historical category of charismatic leadership, we shall not delve into such specific problems of biblical criticism relating to the Book of Judges as the editorial strata, the technical terms *šopeṭ*—which we following convention shall render "judge"—and *mošiaʾ*, "deliverer," or the relation between the "major" and the "minor judges."[1] Nor are we concerned with

---

* This article was originally published in: *G.E. Wright Memorial*, Magnalia Dei, Garden City, NY, 1976; enlarged and revised in German in Max Weber, *Studie über das antike Judentum*, 1982, 152–168.

[1] For a general survey, see A. Malamat, "The Period of the Judges," in *Judges, WHJP*, III, 1971, 129–163, 314–323 (cf. above chap. 7). For the composition of the Book of Judges and its *Redaktionsgeschichte*, see the cited literature, *ibid.*, p. 97, n. 1/2 and p. 146/7 (General Bibliography). Like its West Semitic cognates from the early second millennium B.C. on, the root *špṭ* in the Book of Judges signifies

the "minor judge" per se, for he does not embody the characteristics of a deliverer, at any rate not according to the stereotyped chronicle sources drawn upon in the Book of Judges (10:1–5; 12:8–15). It
should be noted, however, that at least some of the five "minor
judges" may have engaged in military activities and relieved their
people from oppression.[2] Further, the root *yš*, "to deliver, save," is
employed in each of the narratives of the "major judges" with the
exception of Deborah and Barak, either in an epithet, "deliverer"
(applied to Othniel and Ehud—3:9, 15), or in the verbal form *hošia'*
(besides in the account of Othniel, it is found relating to Gideon—
6:14, etc.; 8:22; to Jephthah—12:2–3; to Samson—13:5; and to Tola,
the first of the "minor judges"—10:1; but also to Shamgar the son
of Anath—3:31, for which see below). On the other hand, the root
špt, in the senses "to rule," "to champion," "to judge," occurs in
these stories in relation to Othniel, Deborah, Jephthah, and Samson
(3:10; 4:4; 12:7; 15:20; 16:31) and regularly to all five "minor judges."[3]

I

The first of the deliverer-judges is Othniel, who defeated an invader
who had penetrated deep into southern Palestine, the mysterious
Cushan-Rishathaim, king of Aram-Naharaim. Because of the vague,
schematic formulation of this account, material details of the actual
war are lacking. The episode of Deborah and Barak epitomizes the
confrontation with the autochthonous Canaanite population in the

---

more than merely "judging"; it covers the broad concept of rulership, including the
aspects of judge and champion. Contrary to the generally accepted critical view,
its presence in the deliverer narratives is no less primary than that of *yš*, *mošia'*.

[2] The different representations of the "maior" and the "minor" judges in the
Bible may be merely a carry-over from the literary sources drawn upon by the
compiler—colorful folk narratives on the one hand, and schematic family chronicles on the other hand. Y. Kaufmann, *The Book of Judges* [Hebrew] (Jerusalem,
1962), pp. 47f., entirely assimilated the "minor" to the "major" judges, assuming
that the stories of deliverance once associated with the former had been lost. But
this is an extreme view.

[3] For the literature on *špt*, *šopet*, see *WHJP*, III, 314f., nn. 6–7; and see now also
H. Reviv, 'Types of Leadership in the Period of the Judges," in *Beer-Sheva. Annual,
Studies in Bible* . . . [Hebrew] 1 (1973), 204–221 and T. Ishida, "The Leaders of the
Tribal League 'Israel' in the Pre-Monarchic Period," *RB* 80 (1973), 514–530. On
yš, see now J.F.A. Sawyer, *Semantics in Biblical Research—New Methods of Defining Hebrew
Words for Salvation* (London, 1972), esp. pp. 57f., 94f. And now T. Ishida, *History
and Historical Writing in Ancient Israel*, Leiden 1999, 37–56.

northern part of the country. The chief military challenge in this case was the chariot-force of the Canaanites, confronting the Israelite foot soldiers who, moreover, were poorly equipped (5:8). By reading between the lines of the biblical account, we can reconstruct the Israelite plan of operation in overcoming the situation: exploiting climatic and topographical factors, they rendered the Canaanite chariotry inoperable. The story of Gideon illustrates the conflict with desert marauders headed by the Midianites, who were making incursions into the cultivated region from the eastern fringes of Transjordan. In this instance, the military problem was twofold: the numerical superiority of the enemy and his skilled use of the camel in warfare, which necessitated the adoption of special tactics to which the Israelites were unaccustomed. Gideon found a solution by planning a night attack, enabling him to nullify both these factors. The narratives linked with the names of Ehud and Jephthah describe wars against Moab and Ammon, national states which arose in Transjordan in the thirteenth century B.C. and whose inhabitants, in contrast to the Israelites, were already organized under monarchical regimes at an early stage of their settlement. Finally, the Samson cycle represents the clash with the Philistines in the western part of the country, an enemy which by virtue of its superior technology and its military aristocracy ($s^e r\bar{a}nim$) was destined to jeopardize the very existence of Israel.[4]

We are confronted by the conspicuous fact that in none of the episodes in the Book of Judges is there a recurrence of either the type of enemy fought or the arena of battle, or the ethnic-tribal origin of the "deliverer," who arises in each instance from a different tribe. Concerning the latter aspect, we long ago noted in an unpublished study a point generally overlooked—that the sequence of narratives in the Book of Judges may have been based essentially on a geographical scheme which presents the judges in the order of their tribal-territorial affiliations, from the south of the country to the north: Othniel from Judah, Ehud from Benjamin, Deborah from the hill country of Ephraim (drawing along with her Barak of Naphtali), Gideon from Manasseh (so, too, Abimelech, on whom see the last

---

[4] For an extensive historical survey of the above military encounters, see *WHJP*, III, 135–159. For the possible identification of King Cushan-Rishathaim, see our remarks in *ibid.*, pp. 25–27; on the Philistine threat see B. Mazar, 'The Philistines and Their Wars with Israel," *ibid.*, pp. 164–179.

part of this paper), and Jephthah the Gileadite, which brings us to the area of Gad in Transjordan. Likewise, the two "minor judges" wedged in between the stories of Abimelech and Jephthah—Tola of the tribe of Issachar, and Jair of Gilead, who represents the eastern half of the tribe of Manasseh—are in keeping generally with the tribal-territorial scheme of the book. It is true that Samson, the last of the "major judges," belonged to the tribe of Dan and was active in the southern part of the country, but his cycle of tales constitutes a separate literary pericope within the book. Moreover, from the viewpoint of the later redactor, it was only proper to place the Danite hero at the end of the sequence of judges, for his tribe had long since migrated to the northern extremity of the land. Thus, too, it can hardly be accidental that in Judges 1, where the Israelite tribes are listed also in a principally geographical order from south to north, Dan (in a southern context) appears at the very end of the list.[5] If we posit, however, the tribal-territorial principle as a guideline in the present structure of the Book of Judges, the chronological credibility of the actual sequence of historical events, as presented in the book, is naturally impaired (and see below).

The absence of duplication in the type of enemy and the tribal affinity of the judges raise the possibility that the compiler of the book endeavored to portray only models of oppressors, on the one hand, and of deliverers, on the other hand, emphasizing the features specific to each particular confrontation. In other words, in selecting the stories in the Book of Judges, we deem that the compiler wittingly restricted his choice so as to obtain a paradigmatic scheme of Israel's wars in the premonarchical period. These paradigms would serve a didactic purpose, seemingly alluded to at the beginning of the body proper of the book (3:1–2): "Now these are the nations which the Lord left, to test Israel by them . . . that he might teach war to such at least as had not known it before."[6]

---

[5] The biblical lists of tribes arranged on a geographical principle have been treated most recently by Helga Weippert, "Das geographische System der Stämme Israels," *VT* 23 (1973), 76–89, where, *inter alia*, Dan's ultimate position in the list of Judges 1 is attributed to a late redactor, ascribing the order there to the period of the United Monarchy; for this same dating, see Z. Kallai, *Proceedings of the Fifth World Congress of Jewish Studies* [Hebrew] (Jerusalem, 1969), p. 133, n. 12. By analogy, we can perhaps ascribe the south-to-north sequence of the structure of the Book of Judges as a whole, as outlined above, to the same period.

[6] "To test" (*l'nassot*) in 3:1 is the subject of an exegetical controversy. One view (exemplified by Kaufmann, *Judges* [in Hebrew, 1962], p. 100) holds that a religious

An exception to this scheme, insofar as the identity of the enemy and the military action are concerned, is the heroic exploit of Shamgar the son of Anath: he "smote of the Philistines six hundred men with an ox-goad; and he also delivered Israel" (3:31), an event which recalls Samson's smiting a thousand Philistines with the jawbone of an ass (15:15–16). But it is generally conjectured that this event occurred in the north, and not in the area of Samson's exploit. It may well be that, precisely because of the paradigmatic intent of the Book of Judges, the redactor did not feel the need to give a full account of this event, contenting himself with a mere reference to Shamgar, apparently because his name occurs later, in the Song of Deborah (5:6). At all events, it is reasonable to suppose that not all the deliverers active in the twelfth to eleventh centuries B.C. have found mention in the Book of Judges. This assumption is supported by Samuel's farewell address, in which he counts among Israel's deliverers, alongside Jerubbaal (i.e. Gideon) and Jephthah, the enigmatic Bedan (I Sam. 12:11), a deliverer who is otherwise unknown[7] and whose deed of deliverance is lost to us.

The Book of Judges "compensates" us for its material defects and limitations as a comprehensive, multi-faceted historical source by providing a conceptual schema regarding the unfoldment of the events of the period generally, and the appearance of the deliverer-judge in particular. This schema, unparalleled in the other biblical books for systematic consistency, is founded upon a pragmatic theological interpretation which forms both the general introduction to the events of the period (2:11–19) and the setting into which the narratives of the individual judges were integrated. In this manner, the episodes are concatenated into a single historical chain. It is true that the pragmatic, historiosophic framework is to be ascribed only to an editorial stage of the book—and, according to the prevalent view, to its last redactor, the so-called Deuteronomist. Nevertheless, the content of this framework is not necessarily the expression of a later ideological concept, as most scholars hold. It possibly and even probably,

---

trial of Israel is intended, in the face of heathen temptation. It is preferable, however, and in keeping with the context of vss. 1–2 here, to regard the expression as referring to military experience; cf., for example, C.F. Burney, *The Book of Judges*[2] (London, 1920), p. 54; and esp. M. Greenberg, *JBL* 79 (1960), 276 and n. 5 (where the term is translated as "to give [Israel] experience"). See now also J. Licht, *Testing in the Hebrew Scriptures and in Post-Biblical Judaism* [Hebrew], (Jerusalem, 1973), pp. 15ff.

[7] For the attempts to identify this personage, see *WHJP*, III, 315, n. 15.

contains authentic reflections and preserves elements of ancient historical reality.[8]

The following two doctrines are basic to the pragmatic exposition.

a) The concept of historical periodicity. According to this doctrine
the events of the period of the judges formed a chain of recurring
cycles, each comprising four successive stages: the people sinned by
reverting to idolatry, which brought in its train subjugation by an
adversary; thereupon the people invoked the Lord to deliver them
and ultimately their redemption came about by the hand of a deliverer. The deliverer-judge secured for his people a protracted period
of "rest"; to use biblical terminology—"The land was at rest for
[twenty, forty, eighty] years." But "whenever the judge died, they
turned back and behaved worse than their fathers, going after other
gods, serving them and prostrating themselves to them" (2:19). This
cyclic view imposes a picture of linear development in which the
judges appear in succession, from Othniel to Samson, with gaps
between, when there was no leader. In this manner a historical-
chronological sequence was created, which cannot be accepted *prima
facie* as reflecting actual reality, unless the order of events is corrobo-
rated by additional factors. Furthermore, this approach negates the
possibility—which cannot be excluded *a priori*—of the contemporaneous existence of two or more judges, active in separate parts of
the country.

On the other hand, it seems that the historiosophic framework
expressed an immanent truth in regard to the conditions prevailing
in the premonarchical period, when it emphasizes the frequent vicis-
situdes befalling the people politically and militarily, which to a great
extent were the outcome of the national-religious consciousness; its
decline aggravated the nation's position, while its reinforcement led
to consolidation and prosperity. Moreover, it is a universal phenomenon that in time of danger and crises there is an upsurge of
charismatic sensitivity among the people, which seizes upon a per-

---

[8] This has been stressed in particular by Kaufmann, *Judges*, p. 33, who, however, is too fundamentalistic in his regarding the framework as an early, primary
"historical document," like the deliverer narratives themselves. On the literary complexity of the framework proper, including pre-Deuteronomic strands, cf. W. Beyerlin,
"Gattung und Herkunft des Rahmens im Richterbuch," in *Festschrift A. Weiser*
(Göttingen, 1963), pp. 1–29; for the relationship between the framework and the
Book of Judges as a whole, see esp. W. Richter, *Die Bearbeitungen des "Retterbuches"
in der deuteronomischen Epoche* (Bonn, 1964).

sonality which is able to satisfy, as one sociologist phrases it, "the charismatic hunger"[9] of his contemporaries. This explains the recurring dependence of the Israelites upon deliverer-leaders in times of trouble.

b) The concept of the pan-Israelite dimension. On the basis of this doctrine the tribal events of the period—including the scope of the judge's activity—were elevated to a broad, national level encompassing the entire people and country. Hyperbolic as this may be, the prevalent approach of biblical criticism is likewise unsatisfactory inasmuch as it holds that the judge's action was of only a restricted local and tribal background and confined his authority to a single tribe or even less. It would seem that this radical narrowing of horizon is equally a distortion of the reality of the period.[10] In the actual situation, the individual tribal framework was of little significance to the Israelite judge (see below), and of even less to the external enemy who was not consciously attacking a specific tribe or its territory, but rather Israelites per se. Generally, several tribes were affected simultaneously, and the act of liberation from the foreign pressure, which exceeded the strength of any solitary Israelite tribe, necessitated the cooperation of a confederacy. Thus, any relatively local incident could readily reach a more national plane.

Indeed, the internal evidence within the narratives of the judges clearly reflects these conditions. Thus, for instance, Gideon assembles for his battle against the Midianites not only members of his own clan, Abiezer, and his fellow Manassite tribesmen, but also troops from Asher, Zebulon, and Naphtali (6:35) and, at a later stage, he even seeks the assistance of the Ephraimites (7:24f.). This is also true of other judges, although the scope of their activities was at times more limited. The high point in national solidarity in the period of the judges was achieved at the battle of Deborah and Barak. Here, according to the Song of Deborah, six tribes united in a concerted action—from Benjamin in the south to Naphtali in the north, who came "to the help of the Lord among the fighting men." Thus, the significant epithet "mother in Israel," bestowed upon Deborah (5:7), was quite appropriate.

---

[9] E.H. Erikson, quoted by D.A. Rustow, in *Philosophers and Kings: Studies in Leadership* (New York, 1970), p. 15.

[10] Cf. Kaufmann, *Judges*, pp. 36ff.; *WHJP*, III. 129.

To sum up, the authority of the deliverer-judge transcended the ambit of the individual tribe and was not confined to a restricted locale. It was only natural that his influence should embrace a tribal confederacy, whether broad or limited; and thus his mission and his charismatic attribute also assumed a national dimension, instead of retaining a mere tribal flavor. The judge's action within the inter-tribal and supratribal framework, therefore, justifies historically the use in the Book of Judges of the designation "Israel" for the object of the judge's act of deliverance and rule; hence, this appellation should not be regarded as a later artificial amplification, under ten-dentious, pan-Israelite influence.[11] Although this is still a far cry from pan-Israelite rule, the judges were blazing the path to a new era of leadership—the Israelite monarchy.

II

The best starting point in examining the nature of the judges' regime and the specific characteristics of the deliverer-leader is the theory developed at the beginning of this century by Max Weber concerning the several types of leadership and domination, including charismatic rule. Weber was not the first to resort to the term *charisma* as indi-cating unique qualities—deviating from the common and routine. He expressly states that he borrowed the term from the church his-torian Rudolph Sohm (1841–1917). But he was the first to place the phenomenon of charismatic rule on a broad sociological and polit-ical plane, and to present it as a defined model of one of the types of authority or leadership wielded by extraordinary, singular persons within a society. Thereby he paved the way for the term to become common currency not only in the social and political sciences, but also in daily speech (frequently employed in doubtful usages). Weber

---

[11] As widely held by Bible critics; contrasting this, see the references in the pre-vious note, and now Ishida (note above), p. 520. Attention should be drawn to a similar phenomenon regarding leadership in today's developing nations: the expan-sion of dimensions in tribal leaders and their becoming "nationalized," tribe being "transcended, while the sacred earth [i.e. the optative domain] retains its sacred-ness, its charisma, although it is no longer circumscribed by the area within which one's particular tribe—one's kinship and ethnic group—dwells" (E. Shils, "The Concentration and Dispersion of Charisma, Their Bearing on Economic Policy in Underdeveloped Countries, *World Politics* II [1958–59], 1–19, quotation on p. 4). See also Z. Weismann, "Charismatic Leaders in the Eve of the Judges," *ZAW* 89 (1977), 393–411.

himself used the word charisma primarily in the connotation of the New Testament,[12] namely, as a gift of divine grace. It is particularly his appraisement of the charismatic order as essentially a religious transcendental category—in contradistinction to the majority of his followers, who infused the concept with secular content—that makes Weber's analyses supremely relevant for the biblical phenomenon. Although biblical terminology does not contain the exact semantic equivalent for charisma, it approximates to the expression "spirit [$r\hat{u}^a\dot{h}$] of the Lord," which is bestowed upon the leader and stirs him to action.

In his treatment of charismatic leadership, Weber unfortunately gave only marginal attention to the Israelite judge, for this personality could have served as an exemplar of his *Idealtypus*. In his empirical analyses he was less concerned with the military leaders than with another distinctly charismatic figure which appears in the Bible and in numerous societies, namely, the prophet and the various kinds of diviners. On the other hand, those Bible scholars who in dealing with the period of the judges have adopted Weber's concept of charisma—such as Alt, Buber, Eichrodt, and Albright, to mention only the most outstanding pioneers—have relied mainly on his book *Das antike Judentum*.[13] In the latter, though indeed he did treat the Israelite judge per se, he did little to elucidate his views on charisma. And Bible scholars, on their part, have not generally consulted Weber's brilliant over-all analyses of the phenomenon, to be found in his monumental *Wirtschaft und Gesellschaft*, which presents his most comprehensive and systematic formulation of the types of domination.[14]

---

[12] Almost exclusively in the Pauline epistles (Romans and esp. Corinthians); see most recently H Conzelmann, *Theologisches Wörterbuch zum Neuen Testament*, IX, Lief. 7 (Stuttgart, 1971), 393–397, s.v. *charisma*.

[13] *Gesammelte Aufsätze zur Religionssoziologie* III: *Das antike Judentum* (Tübingen, 1923). English translation by H.H. Gerth and D. Martindale, *Ancient Judaism* (Glencoe, 1952), index, s.v. *charisma, šōpĕṭîm*. For the literature of the Bible scholars, see note 28.

[14] *Grundriss der Sozialökonomik: Wirtschaft und Gesellschaft* (Tübingen, 1925); we use here the 4th edition (henceforth *WuG*), critically revised and with excerpts from Weber's other writings, by J. Winckelmann (Tübingen, 1956), I, 122–176; II, 541–615. English edition by G. Roth and C. Wittich, *Economy and Society, an Outline of Interpretive Sociology* (New York, 1968), I, 212ff.; III, 1111ff. Earlier publications in English of sections on charisma appear in *Max Weber: The Theory of Social and Economic Organization*, ed. T. Parsons, trs. A.M. Henderson and T. Parsons (New York, 1947), pp. 358–392; and *Max Weber: On Charisma and Institution Building*, ed. S.N. Eisenstadt (Chicago-London, 1968).

The concept of charisma has taken on further dimensions, especially in the last decade or so, through the renewed interest in and reappraisal of Weber's *oeuvre*,[15] as well as under the impetus of the emergence of the new states of Asia and Africa. The recent applications in the latter direction are of particular relevance to charismatic leadership in the Bible, despite the considerable differences in time and historical circumstances. The contemporary phenomenon— especially in Africa—has evolved out of tribal society still largely subject to religious-magical motivation and is in that respect closer to the biblical environment than Western civilization, from which most of the analogies hitherto adduced have been drawn.[16]

In order to comprehend the particular quality of the charismatic rule of the judges, we must juxtapose it to the two other basic forms of leadership or authority, included in Weber's classical tripartite typology of legitimate domination.[17] (1) The traditional authority; this was represented in Israel from earliest times by a patriarchaltribal system, in which authority descended through family heads and resided in a gerontocracy. (2) The legal-rational authority; this

---

[15] Of the abundant recent literature on Weber's conception of charisma, we may note the following: the numerous publications of T. Parsons (a recent treatment is his *Politics and Social Structure* [New York-London, 1969], ch. 5, pp. 98–110); the introductions by Parsons and Eisenstadt in the works edited by them [note 14 above]; R. Bendix, *Max Weber—An Intellectual Portrait* (New York, 1962; repr. University Paperbacks, London, 1966), ch. x; P.M. Blau, "Critical Remarks on Weber's Theory of Authority," *American Political Science Review* 57 (1963), 305–316; W.H. Friedland, "For a Sociological Concept of Charisma," *Social Forces* 43 (1964), 18–26; K.J. Ratman, "Charisma and Political Leadership," *Political Studies* 12 (1964), 341–354; K. Loewenstein, *Max Webers staatspolitische Auffassungen in der Sicht unserer Zeit* (Bonn, 1965), pp. 74–88; W.J. Mommsen "Universalgeschichtliches und politisches Denken bei Max Weber," *Historische Zeitschrift* 201 (1965), 557–612, esp. 586ff.; the articles by D.A. Rustow, 'The Study of Leadership," pp. 1–18, and R.C. Tucker, "The Theory of Charismatic Leadership," pp. 69–94 in *Philosophers and Kings: Studies in Leadership*, ed. D.A. Rustow [note 9]; A. Mitzman, *The Iron Cage—An Historical Interpretation of Max Weber* (New York, 1970); J. Séguy, "Max Weber et la sociologie historique des religions," *Archives de Sociologie des Religions* 33 (1972), 71–103, esp. 94ff.; and see the works by E. Shils, cited below [note 21] and by Ann R. Willner [note 24].

[16] Loewenstein [note 15], pp. 78ff., considers genuine charisma as particularly inherent in those political milieus characterized by "magical-ritualistic or mystical-religious elements," as in the pre-Cartesian West and in large parts of Asia and Africa still today.

[17] Cf. *WuG* [note 14], pp. 122ff. Weber's concise formulation of his scheme, included only in the 4th edition of *WuG*, pp. 551–558, did not belong originally to this work and was therefore removed from the subsequent editions (cf. *Studienausgabe*, I [Köln-Berlin, 1964], p. xv, and the English edition of 1968). The development of Weber's concept of charismatic rule is traced in Mitzman [note 15], index, s.v. *charisma*.

approached realization among the Israelites upon the establishment of the monarchy and a budding bureaucratic apparatus (albeit patrimonial) which evolved around it.[18] By their very nature, these two types of rule are mutually antagonistic and are motivated by opposite aims. Traditional authority is inclined toward conservatism and endeavors to maintain the status quo in the life pattern, whereas legal authority is activated by dynamic and rational-utilitarian forces and seeks to adapt the pattern of life to ever-changing circumstances, despite sanctified tradition. But they have a common denominator in their desire for stability and permanence, inasmuch as the leadership is uninterrupted and conventional; and conforms with prevailing interests.

Diametrically opposed is charismatic authority, distinguished primarily by its exclusive, personal character, entirely independent of the hierarchic structure. It is sporadic, unstable, and transient by its very nature and is not subject to the accepted laws of government and the routine social system. In Weber's words, "[this authority] is expressly non-rational in the sense that it conforms to none of the rules." However, the emphatic statement "none of the rules" is undoubtedly exaggerated, as is the apparent rigidity of a threefold typology of authority and leadership.[19] In reality, these types do not appear in their pure and pristine form, but in some measure mix and overlap. In other words, the other two legitimate forms do also contain charismatic traits, a phenomenon which Weber himself clearly acknowledged.[20] But both his followers and his critics have emphasized that the real problem lies in the degree of the charismatic quality—

---

[18] Strictly according to Weber, however, *true* legal rationality was achieved only in modern Western civilization (cf. Bendix, [note 15], pp. 385ff.). My colleague S.N. Eisenstadt has pointed out to me that the Israelite monarchical regime was essentially patrimonial (a traditional rather than legal-rational feature); and besides, all "old bureaucracies were essentially patrimonial in character" (J. Freund, *The Sociology of Max Weber* [New York, 1968], p. 236).

[19] See several of the authors mentioned above in note 15, e.g. Eisenstadt (Introduction, esp. pp. xxiff.); Blau; Ratman (esp. p. 344); Rustow (pp. 14ff.); and further, Shils "Charisma, Order and Status" and his entry on "Charisma" in *International Encyclopedia of the Social Sciences*, II, esp. p. 390; both cited in note 21, below.

[20] Hence Weber's introduction of the concepts *Gentilcharisma* (lineage charisma) and *Amtscharisma* (charisma of office) for the "depersonalization" of the charismatic quality in traditional domination, on the one hand, and the rational-legal domination, on the other hand. See *WuG* [note 14], pp. 681ff., 700ff. and cf. also Bendix [note 15], pp. 308ff.

intense or attenuated—present in the several forms of domination.[21] These qualifications of the Weberian tripartite scheme fully apply to Israelite society in the biblical period.

According to Weber's definition, the charismatic leader was endowed from birth with physical and mental traits that differed from the ordinary and commonplace qualities (his *Ausseralltäglichkeit*). Both the charismatic individual and his following regard these attributes as emanating from a higher force; in this sense, he possesses supernatural gifts and is a leader *Dei gratia*. The charismatic leader arises, in Weber's words, "in times of psychic, physical, economic, ethical, religious, or political distress." This maxim, now regarded as classic, together with the characteristics just mentioned, aptly suits the Israelite judge and the circumstances of his emergence, as revealed in the Book of Judges. The deliverer-judge, distinguished by extraordinary qualities and gifts, appeared in his own estimation and in that of his devotees as a divine agent delivering his people from national crisis, an act which imbued him with supreme authority within his society.

This brings us to the other aspect of the charismatic phenomenon—the prerequisite of a society willing to recognize this type of authority. Without such recognition, charisma lacks all substantiality and remains meaningless. Hence, this phenomenon is to be regarded as a process of interaction between the personality of the leader, on the one hand, and his followers seeking to achieve desired objectives, on the other hand.[22] Viewed in this light the concept of charisma gains a socio-political dimension, which biblical scholarship, with its express theological interest, neglected.[23] Only in a given socio-historical context, the "situation" of the sociologists, could the charistmatic person prevail and his mission come to fulfillment. The specific conditions or situational aspects conducive to the charismatic emergence were not particularly treated by Weber in his comparative analyses, though this facet has drawn great attention in post-Weberian inves-

---

[21] See principally Shils "The Concentration and Dispersion of Charisma" [note 11]; "Charisma, Order and Status," *American Social Review* 30 (1965), 199–213; and "Charisma," in *International Encyclopedia of the Social Sciences*, II (1968), 386–390.

[22] Cf. W.E. Mühlmann, *Max Weber und die rationale Soziologie* (Tübingen, 1966), pp. 18–21; Friedland [note 15], pp. 20f.; Rustow [note 15], pp. 15ff.

[23] This interpretation may serve to mollify recent questioning of the application of "charisma" to the Israelite judge, as notably in G. Fohrer, *Geschichte der israelitischen Religion* (Berlin, 1969), pp. 87f., 138. For the stress on the theological aspect, see the literature cited below toward the end of note 28.

tigation, especially in connection with the nature of leadership in the developing countries.[24]

III

A climate favorable to the emergence of charismatic leadership in Israel's history matured in the era of the judges. The "situation" entailed a dual crisis: externally, enemies made for constant insecurity, with succeeding disasters befalling the Israelites (as seen above); internally, traditional authority was progressively undermined. Increasing sedentation in this period, with its consequent adjustments to the conditions of permanent settlement alongside partial adaptation to the Canaanite urban environment, led the Israelite tribes to a preference for territorial principles over gentilic bonds and consanguinity. Thus, the tribal institutions—indeed the entire inherited societal framework—were on the wane.

Although the routine social system and day-to-day affairs continued under the jurisdiction of the clan heads and the institution of the elders, the traditional elite could no longer maintain its own prestige let alone cope with the task of maintaining Israelite autonomy. A crisis of trust was created, and with it a crisis of authority. The existing leadership which was held responsible for the people's straits was forced aside, to make way for leaders of a new kind who were able to inspire confidence, to steer a course for the people, and to shoulder the task of deliverance. The very weakening of traditional authority within clan and tribe resulted in individuals breaking away from the tight bonds of kinship, freeing them to exercise personal initiative which could eventually lead to attaining a national commission.[25] This polar relationship within Israelite society—the decline of traditional authority and the rise of individuals outside the old order—finds ample expression in the Book of Judges:[26]

---

[24] See notably A.R. Willner and D. Willner, 'The Rise and Role of Charismatic Leadership," *Annals of the American Academy of Political and Social Science* 358 (1965), 77–88; A.R. Willner, *Charismatic Political Leadership: A Theory* (Princeton, 1968), ch. III: "The Charismatic Phenomenon—Convergence and Catalyst"; and e.g. D.A. Rustow, *A World of Nations* (Washington, 1967), pp. 148–169 (Charisma and the Founding of States).

[25] For a similar process in the developing states, see Shils, [note 11], pp. 1, 16.

[26] The relationship between the "establishment" and the charismatic leaders in

Deborah, as a woman, had no standing in the agnatic-patriarchal order; it was she, however, who roused the people to fight for their freedom, who stirred Barak to action and, in short, who was the driving force behind the battle Gideon, "whose clan is the weakest in Manasseh" and who himself was "the least in his family" (6.15), initiated and stood at the head of the forces of liberation—he, not his father or senior brothers, or the representatives of more renowned families. But the most indicative example of the incompetency of the traditional leadership and the rise of a fringe personality is the episode of Jephthah, who stood outside the normal social framework. The elders of Gilead sought in their hour of peril a leader from their own midst, but in vain. Hard-pressed, they turned to Jephthah the outcast, "the son of a harlot"—who had been ousted by his brothers from his patrimony—for he possessed the requisite military qualifications, having gathered around him a band of fighters. The traditional rulers were forced to accede to Jephthah (11:6ff.) and appoint him not only as "commander" (*qāṣîn*), that is, as leader for the duration of the war, but also as "head" (*rôš*), that is, as supreme ruler in peace as well—all of which involved surrendering their authority and the powers vested in them.

In the social and political vacuum created by the crumbling of traditional authority, before the requisite instruments of the legal-rational establishment had been fashioned—such as a standing army and a bureaucratic apparatus—the "floruit" of the Israelite judge was born. The Israelites despaired of deliverance through the existing leadership and languished for a deliverer-leader. This protracted yearning under the harsh conditions of distress, which increased the emotional strain, generated a deep religious national awakening among the people—intensifying the charismatic susceptibility. Yet the "situation" of collective crisis alone is insufficient to trigger a charismatic emergence, as is shown by the lengthy periods of oppression and subjugation preceding the deliverance. In any event, in no instance did a deliverer-judge arise immediately upon the inception of a crisis (see below). Clearly, therefore, a further prerequisite is the appearance of the potential leader, a personage able to alleviate the

---

the period of the judges was insufficiently elaborated upon in Weber's *Antike Judentum* [note 13], pp. 21ff., 92ff.; cf. now Reviv [note 3], who, however, puts too much weight on the role of the elders *vis-à-vis* the judges.

people's frustration and apathy, to define for them their national goals, and to serve as a catalyst for their collective desires.[27] Only the integration of these conditions, in each and every case, could lead to charismatic leadership, personified in Israelite history by the deliverer-judge.

IV

We shall now outline the qualities and principal components inherent in the personality of the Israelite deliverer-judge and his charismatic rule, as can be deduced from Weberian and post-Weberian theories. Apart from and above these, emphasis must be placed, from the outset, on the focal element peculiar to the Israelite phenomenon, namely the politico-military facet of deliverer-leadership integrated with the religious aspect[28] and usually involving personal bravery. The schematic outline below[29] does not intend to minimize the variety and diversity indeed found in the personalities and deeds of the individual judges, just as the absence of one quality or another in a given judge cannot invalidate the basic model of his charismatic leadership. The lack of a particular constituent can be ascribed merely to the manner of presentation by the literary source.

a) A prerequisite for the maturing of the charismatic attribute is a situation of major crisis, above all one induced by an infringement

---

[27] Cf. A.R. Willner, *Charismatic Political Leadership* [note 24], pp. 44ff.

[28] There may well have been a gradual strengthening and emphasis on the religious aspect, due to later tendentious reflections upon the early historical events in the Bible; cf. the conclusions, though extreme, in L. Schmidt, *Menschlicher Erfolg und Jahwes Initiative* (Neukirchen-Vluyn, 1970); F. Stolz, *Jahwes und Israels Kriege* (Zurich, 1972), esp. pp. 100ff., 172ff.; and the more cautious treatment in I.L. Seeligmann, "Menschliches Heldentum und göttliche Hilfe," *Theologische Zeitschrift* 19 (1963), 385–411, esp. 397ff. The primeval nature of "charisma" within Yahwistic faith, already existent in the period of the judges, has long been noted in literature: A. Alt, *Die Staatenbildung der Israeliten in Palästina* (Leipzig, 1930), p. 9; M. Buber, *Königtum Gottes* (Berlin, 1932); W. Eichrodt, *Theologie des Alten Testaments*, I (Leipzig, 1933), 150ff., 237f. (in the seventh edition, 1962, 190ff., 298); and G. von Rad, *Theologie des Alten Testaments*, I (Munich, 1957), 100ff.; and most recently, W. Zimmerli, *Grundriss der alttestamentlichen Theologie* (Stuttgart, 1972), pp. 68–72.

[29] I am indebted to Professor U. Tal for certain features in the outline, which he pointed out during a lecture before a seminar on the regime of the judges, conducted by the author at the Hebrew University in 1959. Of course. Professor Tal could not then utilize the recent abundance of literature on the application of charisma.

upon national and territorial integrity, in other words, subjugation by an enemy.[30] The appearance of each of the deliverer-judges occurred only after oppression by an alien people, which lasted many years—for eight years prior to Othniel (3:8); eighteen before Ehud (3:14); twenty before Deborah (4:3); seven before Gideon (6:1); eighteen before Jephthah (10:8); and forty before and during Samson's time (13:1, and cf. 15:20).

b) The charismatic trait involves direct contact with transcendental powers and identification with the symbols held most sacred by a people.[31] In Israel such experiences were realized in the intimate relationship of the charismatic personage with God, expressed in religious revelations and in the spirit (*rûᵃḥ*) of *YHWH* with which the hero has come to be associated, by himself and by the people. Running through the Book of Judges like a thread are the phrases: "And the spirit of the Lord came upon [Othniel]" (3:10); "But the spirit of the Lord took possession of Gideon" (6:34); "Then the spirit of the Lord came upon Jephthah" (11:29); "And the spirit of the Lord began to stir [Samson]" (13:25); and "And the spirit of the Lord came mightily upon [Samson]" (14:6, 19; 15:14).

c) Sometimes the divine contact required public signs and acknowledgment prior to the act of deliverance, to affirm the authority of the charismatic person both in his own eyes and in the consciousness of the people. The outstanding example is the case of Gideon, who appeals to God, upon being consecrated for his mission, for "a sign that it is Thou who spokest with me" (6:17); and on the eve of his action he twice requests additional signs (the episode of the fleece of wool). There are numerous signs mentioned in the stories of Samson, who was designated for his task even prior to his birth (13:3ff.). The signs in the "call narratives" of these two deliverers were associated with the apparition of an angel of the Lord announcing the mission of the deliverer, a motif intended to enhance the credibility of his mandate.[32]

---

[30] Cf. A.R. Willner, *Charismatic Political Leadership* [note 24], p. 41, noting the ensuing effects of subjugation.

[31] Cf. Shils' "Charisma, Order and Status" and "Charisma" [both in note 21].

[32] Contrasting critical analyses of the literary relationship between the themes of "sign," "call," and "theophanic angel," especially in the Gideon episode, are given by W. Richter, *Die sogenannten vorprophetischen Berufungsberichte* (Göttingen, 1970) and Schmidt [note 28]; earlier literature is noted in both works.

d) The authority bestowed upon the charismatic leader is characteristically spontaneous. The judges were appointed for their task *ad hoc*, and their nomination was specifically personal and consequently non-hereditary or non-transferable. (The sole exception, Abimelech's inheritance of Gideon's authority, is a case of usurpation; see below).

e) The authority of charismatic leadership, by nature, is not dependent on social class or status, nor on age-group or sex. This is attested to by such figures as Jephthah, who was of dubious descent, the "lad" Gideon, who was the youngest of his family, and Deborah, the judges and prophetess. An indication that the deliverer-judges were not of noble lineage is the conspicuous fact that they or their forebears (except Othniel's and Ehud's fathers; see immediately below) do not find mention in the tribal genealogies of the Bible. On the other hand, an inferior social status is not, of course, an essential feature of the rise of a deliverer-judge. Besides Othniel the putative "son of Kenaz, Caleb's younger brother" (3:9), Ehud the son of Gera was a scion of a noble Benjaminite family (Gen. 46:21; I Chron. 8:3, 7), which was still renowned in David's time (II Sam. 16:5). Furthermore, it appears that even prior to his charismatic emergence Ehud held a prominent role within his tribe, for he stood at the head of the delegation bringing tribute to the king of Moab—precisely like a vassal chief would appear before his suzerain. This seems to be a rare instance of a leader who acquired the charismatic quality in the course of his official career, a phenomenon found at times also in other charismatic regimes.[33]

f) The rise and activity of charismatic leaders are not necessarily linked to important religious or civil centers. In this respect it is noteworthy that not even one of the Israelite judges arose in a place of special status in Israel's history, and certainly not at any site of cultic significance such as Shechem, Bethel, or Shiloh. Deborah judges "between Ramah and Bethel in the hill country of Ephraim" (4:5); Gideon's residence, Ophrah, became an Israelite cultic seat only after the act of deliverance; Jephthah found refuge in the land of Tob, a fringe area, and only after his appointment did he move to Mizpah and make it his permanent abode (11:16, 34); while Samson's birthplace was at Zorah, and the beginning of his activity was "in the encampment of Dan, between Zorah and Eshtaol" (13:25).

---

[33] Cf. A.R. Willner, *Charismatic Political Leadership* [note 24], p. 12.

g) Finally, the specific relationship between the charismatic leader and the people, which is not based upon formal rules or administrative organization, and certainly not on coercion; rather, it rests upon emotion, the personal reverence toward the charismatic individual on the part of his devotees. A following gathered around the Israelite judge of its own free will, placing its entire dependence upon him with unshaken faith in his mission (an exception here is Samson the Nazirite). The mustering of warriors took on the form of a voluntary militia—in contrast to a mercenary force—dedicated to the leader with no rational remuneration or predetermined material reward.

In the Book of Judges there is one exceptional figure of a leader who represents the complete antithesis of the above scheme—namely, Abimelech the son of Gideon. His detailed story (Judges 9) was probably included in the book because of its paradigmatic value—in this case, to furnish the model of what I would call an "anti-judge" or "anti-deliverer." Indeed, comparing Abimelech to the typical charismatic leader, following the above outline, we find diametrically opposed traits or no corresponding traits whatsoever:

a) Abimelech's rise was not preceded by a period of foreign subjugation necessitating an act of deliverance, and consequently it did not result in an era of tranquillity.

b–c) Abimelech did not act under divine inspiration, and received no religious revelations. His military engagements, daring as they may have been, hardly constitute acts of deliverance from a foe, but aimed at conquest, oppression, and destruction.

d) Abimelech did not come upon the scene spontaneously, but paved his way to power by political maneuvering, including the slaughter of his brothers. He based his demands for authority on the inheritance of his father's position as ruler (9:2).

e) In his climb to power, Abimelech was aided not only by his paternal pedigree, but also by familial ties on his maternal side since his mother was of the Canaanite nobility of Shechem.

f) In contrast to the other judges, Abimelech became ruler in a key urban center, the city of Shechem, a site long-sanctified even in Israelite tradition.

g) Abimelech's authority was cast in a conventional pattern, that of kingship; the local oligarchy, the "lords of Shechem" (*ba^{ca}lê š^{e}kem*), "made him king" (9:6). He instituted an administration in the city, as is indicated by his appointment of Zebul as "official" (*pāqîd*) or "governor of the city" (*śar haʿîr*; 9:28, 30). Initially, Abimelech utilized a mercenary troop of "idle and reckless men," paid from the temple treasury of Baal-berit, the city's deity (9:4).

Abimelech's rule did not, therefore, emanate from any charismatic quality. His system of government, drawing in great measure upon the Canaanite concept of the city-state, was of a dimorphic structure, a combination of rule over a foreign urban center, on the one hand, and over the Israelite rural, tribal elements, on the other hand.[34] In seizing the reigns of government he acted solely out of personal greed for power—a motive far removed from any legitimate form of domination, most especially charismatic. Indeed, in Israelite tradition, Abimelech's abortive regency was excoriated as a despotic usurpation of power. In summing up his rule, the biblical author avoids calling him king or judge, but employs the unique phrase: "he held sway [*wa-yāśar*] over Israel for three years" (9:22).

The natural desire to stabilize the sporadic leadership of the judges strengthened the tendency among the Israelites to give fixed and permanent form to the charismatic attribute that it might become a stable, organized, and hereditary function—a universal phenomenon known as the "routinization of charisma." Indeed, it is against this background that the kingship offered to Gideon by "the men of Israel" must be viewed: "Rule over us, you and your son and your grandson also; for you have delivered us out of the hand of Midian" (8:22). However, the time was not yet ripe for transmuting the Israelite order. Individual freedom and the egalitarian structure of Israelite society were still major obstructions to change, alongside the

---

[34] For Abimelech's rule and its peculiar nature, see *WHJP*, III, 149ff. Its course of development can also be analyzed in the light of Weber's theorems on modes of domination (though *Antike Judentum* [note 13], p. 16, n. 2, and p. 23, mistakenly we believe, refers to Abimelech as a charismatic leader): Abimelech initially sought support of the "lords of Shechem" and later clashed with them, exemplifying Weber's notion that early kings, originally rural war leaders, had to rely upon the support of cities but, once established, came into conflict with the urban oligarchy. Further, Abimelech attempted to neutralize the influence of the city aristocracy by appointing his own retainers as officials and by mobilizing troops from among the (loyal) Israelites; this conforms with the Weberian king counteracting his dependence upon the local oligarchy by installing personally devoted officials from the ranks of the populace and by recruiting mercenaries from outside. Cf. Bendix [note 15], p. 211, basing on *WuG* [note 14].

deeply rooted belief in the supremacy of the Heavenly Kingdom.[35]

It was only toward the end of the eleventh century B.C. that the requisite internal conditions in Israel matured for the establishment of a new regime, a process accelerated by weighty external factors— principally the Philistine threat. At his stage, charisma ceased to function in its pure, concentrated form and became institutionalized within the framework of the Israelite monarchy.[36]

This paper is based on a lecture given at a symposium on "Types of Leadership in the Biblical Period" held in honor of David Ben-Gurion at the Israel Academy of Sciences and Humanities on 15 December 1971. Throughout this paper, references by chapter and verse alone are to the Book of Judges.

---

[35] See esp. Buber's *Königtum Göttes* [note 28], where he uses Gideon's rejection of the offer of kingship as a point of departure.

[36] Such "routinization" into charismatic kingship is treated in general in Weber's *WuG* [note 14], pp. 678f., 684f.; for the phenomenon in Israel—beyond the scope of the present study—see in particular, recently, J.A. Soggin, *Das Königtum in Israel* (Berlin, 1967), which gives the earlier literature, and now also F.M. Cross, *Canaanite Myth and Hebrew Epic* (Cambridge, Mass., 1973), pp. 219ff.

9

THE DANITE MIGRATION AND THE PAN-ISRAELITE EXODUS-CONQUEST: A BIBLICAL NARRATIVE PATTERN*

The migration of the Danites to northern Canaan, following upon their initial failure to secure an inheritance and culminating in the conquest of Laish, which is related among the appendices to the Book of Judges (i.e., ch. 18, and summed up in Jos. 19,47), is the only explicit account of a campaign of settlement in the Bible on a solely tribal level, and not set against the general national background.[1] We wish to propose here that this tribal episode is a sort of diminutive model of a campaign of inheritance, which pattern appears on the national scale in the Exodus and pan-Israelite Conquest cycles.[2] We shall dwell here upon neither the *Überlieferungsgeschichte* nor the historical aspects of these episodes, such as the factors leading up to the Danite migration (cf. e.g., Jgs. 1,34); whether the entire tribe or merely a part of it was involved; or the exact period of these events;[3] much less the intricacies of the Exodus and the conquest of Canaan. We concern ourselves here only with a structural analysis of the two

---

* This article was originally published in: *Biblica*, 51 (1970), 1–16.

[1] For Judges 18 in general, and for the specific details discussed below, cf. the commentaries of G.F. Moore, *Judges* (ICC; Edinburgh, 1895), 365ff.; C.F. Burney, *The Book of Judges* (London, 1920), 408ff.; V. Zapletal, *Das Buch der Richter* (Exegetisches Handbuch zum AT; Münster, 1923), 261ff.; Y. Kaufmann, *The Book of Judges* (Jerusalem, 1962), 8–9, 267ff. (Hebrew); A.E. Cundall, *Judges* (Tyndale OT Commentaries; London, 1968), 182ff.; cf. also E. Täubler, *Biblische Studien—Die Epoche der Richter* (Tübingen, 1958), 43ff. Of these, Kaufmann especially opposes the generally held hypothesis of the combination of two sources to account for the repetitious style in the story.

[2] This conjecture has already been noted in my contribution to *The History of the Jewish People*, I: *The Ancient Times* (ed. H.H. Ben-Sasson) (Tel Aviv, 1969), 65–66 (Hebrew).

[3] For these and similar problems see, besides the commentaries above, n. 1, the lecture by B.Z. Lurie: "The Settlement of the Tribe of Dan," and the subsequent discussion, in *Studies in the Book of Joshua* (Jerusalem, 1960), 248ff. (Hebrew); as well as Y. Yadin, "And Dan, Why Did He Remain in Ships?," *Australian Journal of Biblical Archaeology* 1 (1968), 9ff., where Yadin sets forth his hypothesis identifying the Danites with the Denen of the "Sea-Peoples."

accounts, distinguishing those elements which are typologically relevant to the narrative pattern under discussion.

The essential themes common to both the Danite migration story and that of the Israelites from Egypt—in spite of differences in historical circumstances—can be outlined as follows:

1. Direct association with Moses or his descendants.[4]
2. Dispatch of spies selected from among the tribal notables, and gathering of intelligence prior to the military campaign.
3. The spies' report and attitude—enthusiastic or pessimistic.
4. The misgivings of the people in reaction to the spies' report.
5. The ethnic character of the campaign, specifically mentioning the non-combatants and cattle accompanying the warriors.
6. The particular number of armed warriors.
7. Oracular consultation, by a Levitic priest, concerning the course of the campaign.
8. Procurement of cult objects while on the move, and their eventual deposition at the final destination of the campaign.
9. Permanence of priesthood secured by a third-generation priest.
10. Renaming of places conquered and resettled by the Israelites.

The Spies

At the point of departure in both accounts, the tribes are in a mobile, unsettled state, in temporary encampments (for *mahᵃnē-dān* "Camp of Dan," cf. also Jgs. 13,25), the common aim being to conquer permanent territories. This initial phase is clearly emphasised in the opening of the Danite story: "... And in those days the tribe of the Danites sought them an inheritance to dwell in; for unto that day all their inheritance had not fallen unto them among the tribes of Israel" (Jgs. 18,1). This introductory statement is immediately followed by the dispatch of the spies, which serves as the overture to the campaign proper, just as the twelve spies were sent to Canaan in the time of Moses only after an extensive period of wandering,

---

[4] See below. Most interestingly, the family of Moses appears in the Bible in an historical capacity *only* in the two episodes which are the subject of this paper; for its appearance in the schematic genealogies in Chronicles, see below.

on the threshold of the Promised Land, again prior to the actual campaign. What distinguishes these two "spy stories"[5] is that the principal objective was conquest so as to realize inheritance, unlike the reconnaissance of, e.g., Jericho and Ai, which was intended to pave the way solely for military attack and destruction. To bring this distinction closer to home, the latter is tactical, the former strategic intelligence, including not only data of a strict military nature, but also economic and demographic-political information.[6]

Several commentators have pointed out the general similarity between our two spy episodes;[7] only a deeper comparison, however, of the specific passages can reveal the manifold typology within this narrative pattern—whether in thetical or antithetical garb—as well as the numerous conclusions stemming from such. To this end we must rely not only upon the basic and detailed account in Nm. 13–14, but also upon the brief summary in Dt. 1.[8]

According to Numbers, the incentive for sending out the spies was divine, whereas in Deuteronomy (1,25) and in Judges (18,2) it was popular. The similarity of the latter two sources, as against Numbers, is further indicated by several other details, such as the ascertaining of their route: "what *way* we must go up" (Dt. 1,22); "that we may know whether our *way* which we go shall be prosperous" (Jgs. 18,5). In contrast to the twelve spies of the pan-Israelite campaign, the Danites sent out only five spies, "from their clan" (though some commentators, preferring the LXX, would point the Hebrew to read

---

[5] To these two we may add the reconnaissance of the land of Jaazer in Transjordan (cf. *l'raggēl*, "to spy out," Nm. 21,32) and that of the city of Bethel (cf. *wayyātīrū*, properly "they caused a reconnaissance to be made" [hiph'il of *tūr*], Jgs. 1,23), though in both cases the extant account is extremely brief. The capture of Bethel displays several other elements of our narrative pattern—i.e. marching under divine auspices ("and the Lord was with them"), and the changing of the name of the conquered site (Luz > Bethel).

[6] This distinction was already noted by Y. Yadin, *The Art of Warfare in Biblical Lands* (Ramat Gan, 1963), 110.

[7] But see also the specific study on the spy stories by S. Wagner, "Die Kundschaftergeschichten im Alten Testament," *ZAW* 76 (1964), 255ff. The weakness in this otherwise instructive article is that Wagner has failed to distinguish between the two types of the numerous spy episodes, as noted above.

[8] For the literary relationship between the spies' description in Numbers and that in Deuteronomy, and for their composition according to the accepted source criticism, see the respective commentaries, and especially N. Lohfink, 'Darstellungskunst und Theologie in Dtn. 1,6–3,25," *Bib* 41 (1960), 105ff.; cf. now also O. Plöger, *Literarkritische, formgeschichtliche und stilkritische Untersuchungen zum Deuteronium* (Bonn, 1967), 44ff.; G.W. Coats, *Rebellion in the Wilderness* (Nashville-New York, 1968), 137ff.

"clans"; cf. Jos. 19,40). The actual intent of this latter number is obscure and no basis can be found for it in the tribal genealogies, only one descendant being ascribed to Dan.[9] However, the common denominator in the two episodes is the rank of the persons selected as spies: in the desert, they were tribal chiefs, "heads of the children of Israel" (Nm. 13,3), and from Dan they were "five men *miqṣōtām*, men of valour" (Jgs. 18,2), *miqṣōtām* signifying the tribal notables.[10]

The macrocosmic nature of the episode in Numbers is recognized in the spies' report on five of the peoples of Canaan occupying the entire land (Nm. 13,29); and in the widespread route of their survey: "from the wilderness of Zin unto Rehob at the entrance to Hamath" (v. 21), which required forty days (v. 25; a typological number denoting a moderate length of time). According to the earlier stratum (source JE) in this story, however, the final destination of the spies was clearly the Hebron region; only the later source (P) extended their mission to include the northernmost limits of Canaan, so as to lend these events an overall, national air.[11] It is interesting to note, in this context, that this northern destination of Rehob also finds mention in the Danite narrative, in the placing of Laish "in the valley which belongs to Beth-Rehob" (Jgs. 18,28).

Detailed instructions on the objectives of the mission are ascribed to Moses (Nm. 13,18–20); the same pattern was undoubtedly followed by the author of the Danite narrative, as is indicated by the findings of the Danite spies. Upon comparing the respective reconnaissance reports, we confront the *schema* and *anti-schema* within the typology of the story. The pessimistic and fear-wrought evidence given by ten of the twelve Israelite spies is, in effect, the very antithesis of the enthusiastic description in the Danite account.

---

[9] Hushim (Gn. 46,23) or the variant Shuham (Nm. 26,42); while 1 Ch. 7,12—where Dan may originally have been listed—is corrupt. In this context, Gn. 47,2 is instructive (as Täubler, *Biblische Studien*, 80, has noted) for Joseph here also "took *miqṣē* his brethren, even *five* men, and presented them unto Pharaoh." For the term *miqṣē*, see immediately below. Here, too, the five were men of rank from a single clan.

[10] For such a meaning of the Hebrew term, already noted by the Sages, cf. A.B. Ehrlich, *Randglossen zur hebräischen Bibel*, I (Leipzig, 1908), 234; III (Leipzig, 1910), 145; S. Talmon, *VT* 8 (1958), 50ff.; and D. Silber, *Leshonenu* 26 (1962), 3–4 (Hebrew).

[11] See H. Holzinger, *Numeri* (KHC; Tübingen-Leipzig, 1903), 55; M. Noth, *Das vierte Buch Mose* (ATD; Göttingen, 1966), 93f. For examples of 40 days as a distinct period in the Bible, see *The New Bible Dictionary* (London, 1962), 898b.

The ten spies, although they, too, told of the fertility of the land, failed to report it in a desirable light: "Nevertheless the people be strong that dwell in the land, and the cities are walled, and very great; and moreover we saw the children of Anak there ... a land that eateth up the inhabitants thereof; and all the people that we saw in it are men of a great stature" (Nm. 13,28.32; and cf. Dt. 1,28), and their report ends with a Gulliver-like flavour to it. Quite the reverse image is to be seen in the Danite narrative: ". . . and (they) came to Laish, and saw the people that were therein, how they dwelt careless, after the manner of the Sidonians, quiet and secure ...[12] and they were far from the Sidonians, and had no business with any man" (Jgs. 18,7).[13] Without going into the somewhat garbled and troublesome Hebrew text, note that: *yōšebet lābeṭaḥ* "dwelt careless" and *šōqēṭ u-bōṭēᵃḥ* "quiet and secure"—which outwardly seem to indicate the peace of mind of the local inhabitants—at times appear in biblical usage to signify the unfortified state of towns (cf. especially Ez. 38,11). Thus, applying Moses' reconnaissance terminology (Nm. 13,19) to Laish, we would consider it one of the *maḥᵃnīm* "open towns," rather than one of the *mibṣārīm* "strongholds" (cf. below, n. 1(b). In accord with their findings, the Danite spies reported that "we have seen the land, and, behold, it is very good. . . . When ye go ye shall come unto a people secure and to a large land: for God hath given it into your hands; a place where there is no want of any thing that is in the earth" (Jgs. 18,9–10)—in vivid contrast to "a land that eateth up the inhabitants thereof."

---

[12] The hiatus left here represents the obscure Hebrew phrase *uᵉ-ᵓēn maklīm dābār bā'āreṣ yōrēš eṣer*, AV: "and there was no magistrate in the land that may put them to shame in any thing"; RSV: "lacking nothing that is in the earth, and possessing wealth"—both rather forced. This may perhaps find a satisfactory explanation, someday, through an antithetical comparison to some point within the account in Numbers. For one treatment of this entire difficult verse, see Täubler, *Biblische Studien*, 81ff., who resorts to glosses here, in addition to a two-source hypothesis for the chapter in general.

[13] The references to "Sidon" in Jgs. 18,7.28 may be of more specific, political significance than seems at first reading Laish, though within the Sidonian sphere, was "far" away, this implying not a mere physical distance, but apparently a particular international relationship. Such a status would have restricted Sidon's obligations as overlord and thus Laish could expect little aid from this or any quarter, for the City "had no business with any man," i.e. had no allies (we prefer the MT reading *ᵓādām*, "man, anyone," in vv. 7 and 28, to the oft-accepted emendation "Aram," already found in ancient versions). More concrete examples of such politically and legalistically "far off" cities and countries may be found in, e.g., Dt. 20,15 and Jos. 9,6; and cf. provisionally A. Malamat, *VT* 5 (1955) 9, 10, n. 1 and now below chap. 26.

But within the antithetical web of denigrating the Land, which typifies the Exodus-Conquest tradition, there is interwoven in Numbers and Deuteronomy the positive thetical theme of praise of the Land whose proponents are Joshua and, particularly, Caleb. Their testimony and attitude thus accord with those of the Danite spies: "And they (Joshua and Caleb) spake unto all the company of the children of Israel, saying, The land, which we passed through to search it, is an exceeding good land. If the Lord delight in us, then he will bring us into this land, and give it us; a land which floweth with milk and honey" (Nm. 14,7–8). It was probably the brevity in Deuteronomy which led to the positive report being ascribed to all the spies, disregarding the negative majority opinion: "And they took of the fruit of the land in their hands, and brought it down unto us, and brought us word again, and said, it is a good land which the Lord our God doth give us" (Dt. 1,25; but see the conflicting, pessimistic report in v. 28). Thus, on the positive facet of this narrative element, the motifs of "a good land" and a land "given by the Lord" are prevalent, the latter notion being an integral part of the Holy War.[14]

The attitude and behaviour of the spies upon their return to the people are the outcome of their positive or negative impressions of the Promised Land—despair and lack of courage on the one hand: "We be not able to go up against the people; for they are stronger than we" (Nm. 13,31; and cf. Dt. 1,28)—and utter confidence and encouragement on the other hand: "And Caleb stilled the people before Moses, and said, Let us go up at once, and possess it; for we are well able to overcome it" (Nm. 13,30; and cf. the words of Joshua and Caleb in Nm. 14,9—"neither fear ye the people of the land; for they are bread for us: their defence is departed from them"). This latter is further parallelled by the Danite spies' call: "Arise, that we may go up against them . . . and are ye still? be not slothful to go, and to enter to possess the land" (Jgs. 18,9). From the expression of doubt concerning their fellow tribesmen: "and are ye still? be not slothful," we learn of the hesitance of the Danite crowd, which, as a theme, is a mere faint echo of the rampant defeatism and even rebelliousness of the Israelites in the days of Moses (cf. Nm. 14,1ff. and Dt. 1,26–27).

---

[14] For the former motif, See Plöger, *Untersuchungen*, 87ff.; on the latter, see G. von Rad, *Der heilige Krieg im alten Israel* (Zürich, 1951), 7ff.

In sum, the typology of the spy story is based on a schema defining the desired objectives and anticipated effects of the mission, the fulfilment of such being a prime factor in the success of the campaign—and on an anti-schema displaying the failings of the spies which, in the case of the Israelites of the desert generation, led to disastrous consequences concerning the conquest of Canaan.[15]

The Campaign

Whereas the typology of the "spy story" is lucid, that of the other themes is less articulate.

It is not surprising that similar phraseology is used in depicting the course of both campaigns, though the action stands out in greater relief in the Danite story, it being much more compact: "And there *journeyed* (*wayyissᵉʿū*) from thence of the family of the Danites, out of Zorah and out of Eshtaol. . . . And they *went up* (*wayyaʿᵃlū*), and *encamped* (*wayyaḥᵃnū*) in Kirjath-jearim. . . . And they *passed* (*wayyaʿabrū*) thence unto mount Ephraim, and *came* (*wayyābōʾū*) unto the house of Micah" (Jgs. 18,11–13). Such parallel expressions of advance, encampment and arrival, of course, occur throughout the Exodus-Conquest cycle as well, though there they are scattered and usually serve to link the successive pericopes: "And the children of Israel *journeyed* (*wayyissᵉʿū*) from Rameses to Succoth" (Ex. 12,37), the continuation of the action appearing many passages later—"And they *journeyed* from Succoth, and *encamped* (*wayyaḥᵃnū*) in Etham" (Ex. 13,20); or "And all the congregation of the children of Israel *journeyed* from the wilderness of Zin, after journeys, according to the commandment of the Lord, and *encamped* in Rephidim" (Ex. 17,1), again to be continued only two chapters later—"For they *journeyed* from Rephidim, and were *come* (*wayyābōʾū*) to the desert of Sinai, and had *encamped* in the wilderness" (Ex. 19,2); etc.

Moreover, just as the Exodus stories are rife with the etiological motif of naming Israelite encampments, such as Marah (Ex. 15,23),

---

[15] The peculiar character of the negative account in Dt. 1–2 was especially dealt with by Lohfink, "Darstellungskunst," 119ff.; and W.L. Moran, "The End of the Unholy War and the Anti-Exodus," *Bib* 44 (1963), 333ff. In connection with the depiction of the sinister events there, where the motifs of the Holy War are inverted, both of the above authors use the well-chosen term "Anti-Exodus"; and cf. now M. Ottosson, *Gilead* (Lund, 1969), 92ff.

Massah and Meribah (Ex. 17,7), Taberah and Kibroth-hattaavah (Nm. 11,3.34), there is an etiological note on an interim station on the Danite march northward: "And they went up, and encamped in Kirjath-jearim, in Judah: wherefore they called that place Mahaneh-dan ("Camp of Dan") unto this day: behold, it is behind Kirjath-jearim" (Jgs. 18,12; and cf. the more universal appellative "camp of Israel" in the corresponding episode in Ex. 14,19).[16]

As for the campaign proper, in both cases the host is not confined to the armed force alone, as in the strictly military expeditions, but comprises an entire ethnic group including women, children and aged, accompanying the warriors.[17] In the Danite campaign, after the incident at Micah's house, specific mention is made of the *ṭaf* and, furthermore, the cattle and chattels, along with the army (Jgs. 18,21). In the Exodus narrative the description is essentially identical: "about six hundred thousand on foot that were men, besides the *ṭaf* . . . and flocks, and herds, even very much cattle" (Ex. 12,37–38). We should point out that in both passages, no special reference is made to the women, who may be implied here within the expression *ṭaf*, usually "children."[18] The mention of "chattels" (the *hapax legomenon* *kᵉbūdā* in the Hebrew; see the commentaries) in the Danite story would indicate that, like the Israelites fleeing Egypt (cf. Ex. 3,21–22; 12,35–36), the Danites did not leave their former habitat empty-handed.

There is, of course, a great difference in scale between the respective armed forces in the two episodes. Closer perusal, however, again leads to an instructive correlation between the small number of "six hundred men appointed with weapons of war" in the Danite van (Jgs. 18,11.16.17) and the enormous army of six hundred thousand

---

[16] On the location of "Mahaneh-dan," see Täubler, *Biblische Studien*, 65ff.; for the etiological motif, see B.O. Long, *The Problem of Etiological Narrative in the Old Testament* (BZAW 108; Berlin, 1968), 15f. The persistence of this name, as stressed by the subjoinder "unto this day," which is lacking in all the Exodus examples (as pointed out to me by Prof. M. Greenberg), lends the Danite story a more "historical" flavour in contrast to the rather lofty tale of the Israelite wanderings in the wilderness.

[17] Women and children are seen riding in wagons drawn by oxen, alongside warriors, in the reliefs of Rameses III at Medinet-Habu, depicting the ethnic invasion of the "Sea Peoples"; see, e.g. Y. Yadin, *Art of Warfare*, 250.

S.E. Loewenstamm, *The Tradition of the Exodus in its Development* (Jerusalem, 1965), 97 (Hebrew) (now, 1998 in English), in passing, has pointed out that in each of our biblical accounts the number of warriors is specified within each ethnic group.

[18] For the term *ṭaf*, at times including women, see U. Cassuto, *A Commentary on the Book of Exodus* (Jerusalem, 1967), 125; D. Daube, *The Exodus Pattern* (London, 1963), 47.

foot which set out from Egypt (Ex. 12,38; Nm. 11,21). I have attempted previously to demonstrate that a unit of 600 warriors in the Bible simply represents a "brigade" in force, adducing various examples of such besides the Danite army.[19] I further inferred that the number of warriors leaving Egypt was expressed, in accord with what was merely biblical convention, in multiples of a "brigade"—i.e. "a thousand brigades." Accepting these assumptions, S.E. Loewenstamm noted[20] the typological connection between the numbers in the two stories, i.e. Dan set out with a single "brigade," whereas the Israelites set out with a thousand, symbolizing an immensely large force. For "a thousand" as a typological number signifying a vast host, note also Moses' address to the Israelites: "The Lord God of your fathers make you a thousand times so many more as ye are, and bless you, as he hath promised you!" (Dt. 1,11). Thus, the numerical element is also clearly indicative of the macro-cosmic nature of the Exodus-Conquest episode, as against the miniature migration of Dan.

The Priesthood and the Cult Objects

Upon approaching the religious aspects, we must note that in military campaigns it was general practice to seek divine instruction concerning the course and outcome of the war, as is often evident in the Bible and the external sources.[21] This is certainly true of the campaigns of settlement, as in the opening to the Book of Judges, on the conquest of Canaan by the various Israelite tribes: "Now after the death of Joshua it came to pass that the children of Israel asked the Lord saying, Who shall go up for us against the Canaanites first, to fight against them? And the Lord said, Judah shall go up: behold, I have delivered the land into his hand" (Jgs. 1,1–2). In contrast to this general description, however, both the Danite and

---

[19] 1 Sm. 13,15; 14,2; 23,13; 27,2; 30,9; 2 Sm. 15,18; cf. *Encyclopaedia Biblica*, II (Jerusalem 1954), cols. 432f. s.v. *g̱dūd* (Hebrew). Add further the band of 600 Philistines in Jgs. 3,31 and the 600 Benjamites in Jgs. 20,47.

[20] *Tradition of the Exodus*, 97 (Hebrew); regarding the Exodus, cf. now also B. Mazar, in *The World History of the Jewish People*, II (Tel Aviv, 1967), 188 and n. 3 (Hebrew). Both these studies refer to earlier suggestions explaining the astounding number of 600,000 warriors leaving Egypt.

[21] In addition to the passages treated below, see Jgs. 20,18ff.; 1 Sm. 14,36–37; 23,2ff.; 30,7–8; 2 Sm. 2,1; 1 Kgs. 22,5ff. In this connection, see the still useful study by F. Schwally, *Semitische Kriegsaltertümer* (Leipzig, 1901).

the pan-Israelite accounts provide specific details concerning the oracular inquiry.

In the Danite account, the spies on the way through Mount Ephraim appeal to the young Levite who was practising as Micah's priest, so as to learn of the fortune of their mission: "Ask counsel, we pray thee, of God, that we may know whether our way which we go shall be prosperous" (Jgs. 18,5). In the other account, while in the desert, it was God himself who guided the Israelites—by means of his angel or a pillar of cloud;[22] upon approaching the Promised Land, however, new provisions were made for determining their future movements. When Joshua is installed as Moses' successor, he is commanded: "And he shall stand before Eleazer the priest, who shall ask counsel for him after the judgment of Urim before the Lord: at his word shall they go out, and at his word they shall come in, both he, and all the children of Israel with him, even all the congregation" (Nm. 27,21). The point in common in the two episodes is the engagement of a Levitic priest for oracular consultation on the future course of the campaign—Eleazar the son of Aaron, by means of Urim, and the young Levite, by similar mantic devices, i.e. the ephod and teraphim.

The presence of a priest and cult objects was thus essential to underwrite the campaign of inheritance, both for the military aspect and for the final settlement. In both episodes it is not only the obtaining of a priest and cultic appurtenances—eventually to be established at their final destination as a permanent cult—which suggests the typology, but also the fact that this was accomplished in one way or another at an intermediate stage of the campaign. When they embarked upon their ventures, neither the Israelites of the Exodus nor the Danites possessed a priest or a cult apparatus. In the desert, such apparatus was specifically fashioned and Aaron was consecrated to serve it as the first priest of Israel (Ex. 25ff.); the Danites, by wantonly despoiling Micah's private shrine in Mount Ephraim, both appropriated the cult objects and impressed Micah's young Levite into their service, he thus becoming "a priest unto a tribe and a family in Israel" (Jgs. 18,13ff.).

As for the cult objects themselves, they exhibit the different shades

---

[22] On these divine manifestations, which ceased upon the termination of the desert wanderings, see J. Dus, "Herabfahrung Jahwes auf die Lade und Entziehung der Feuerwolke," *VT* 19 (1969), 290ff., whose otherwise radical hypothesis cannot be considered here.

of religious practice prevalent among the Israelites. The appurtenances made at the foot of Mount Sinai were hallowed, according to biblical tradition, as the legitimate cultic symbols of pan-Israel: the Tabernacle with the Ark and other equipment, as well as the sacred vestments, among which was the ephod. On the other hand there is Micah's sanctuary, with its "graven image" and "molten image" (*pesel* and *massēkā*—which may merely be a hendiadys for a cast metal image), and the oracular devices, "the ephod, and the teraphim" (Jgs. 18,14.17.18.20). The analogy of the cults in the two episodes[23] can be brought into closer perspective if we adduce the desert heresy of the golden calf image (*ēgel massēkā*; Ex. 32). The relationship would become even clearer if one accepted the hypotheses that Micah's image, which was later installed at Dan, had the form of a bull or calf, and that it was somehow connected with the golden calf set up by Jeroboam I at Dan (see 1 Kgs. 12,28ff.).[24]

Just as the Danites deposited Micah's image in a shrine at Laish, their final destination (Jgs. 18,30–31), so the Israelites placed their cultic apparatus in Shiloh[25] upon the completion of the conquest of Canaan, at least according to biblical tradition: "And the whole congregation of the children of Israel assembled together at Shiloh, and set up the tabernacle of the congregation there. And the land was

---

[23] For the cult in Micah's shrine, see the commentaries to Judges, as well as studies in the next footnote. For the teraphim alone, known now also in Hittite documents, see A.H. Hoffner, *JNES* 27 (1968), 61ff. For the tabernacle and the ark, and their cultic significance, see the recent treatments of S.E. Loewenstamm, *Encyclopaedia Biblica*, V (Jerusalem, 1968), s.v. *miškān* (Hebrew); M. Görg, *Das Zelt der Begegnung* (Bonn, 1967); J. Maier, *Das altisraelitische Ladeheiligtum* (BZAW 99; Berlin, 1965); H. Davies, "The Ark of the Covenant," *Annual of the Swedish Theological Institute* 5 (1967), 30ff.; O Eissfeldt, "Die Lade Jahwes . . .," *Das Altertum* 14 (1968), 131ff. and references in these.

[24] Already in early Rabbinic literature Micah became associated with the making of the golden calf in the desert (see, e.g., *Tanḥuma* 60,19). On the similarity between Micah's image and Aaron's golden calf, see H.M.Y. Gevaryahu, "Micah's Sanctuary in Mount Ephraim and the Danite Campaign," *Studies in the Book of Judges* (Jerusalem, 1966), 547ff. (Hebrew); on its connection with Jeroboam's golden calves, see J. Dus, "Die Stierbilder von Bethel und Dan und das Problem der 'Moseschar'," *Annali Istituto Orientale di Napoli* NS 19 (1968), 105ff. For earlier suggestions on the latter, see O. Eissfeldt, "Lade und Stierbild," *Kleine Schriften*, II (Tübingen, 1963), 294ff., n. 4; and M. Noth, "The Background of Judges 17–18," *Israel's Prophetic Heritage. Essays in Honor of J. Muilenburg* (New York, 1962), 68. Both these authors, however, discount any connection between Micah's image and Jeroboam's calf.

[25] In this context, Dr. S. Abramsky has drawn my attention to the tradition in 1 Sm. 2,27–28, which significantly relates the preordination of Eli's house to the priesthood, which served at Shiloh, while the Israelites were still in Egypt.

subdued before them" (Jos. 18,1; and cf. vv. 9–10; 19,51). Indeed, the typology here is hinted at by the narrator of the Danite episode himself. He brings his story to a close with a note on the ties of destiny between the two cult centres, Dan and Shiloh: "And they set them up Micah's graven image, which he made, all the time that the house of God was in Shiloh" (Jgs. 18,31).

Though not explicitly stated in the text, it is generally surmised that the anonymous Levite youth in Micah's service is to be identified with the head of the priestly line at Dan—Jonathan the son of Gershom the son of Moses (we follow the accepted reading in Jgs. 18,30, eliminating the superlinear *nun*: Moses, instead of Manasseh).[26] In any event, the foundation of the priesthood at the shrine at Dan is ascribed to a scion of the third generation in the Mosaic line, whose descendants served the tribe for centuries to come, "until the day of the captivity of the land" (Jgs. 18,30). In the Exodus-Conquest cycle, too, a third generation priest held a prominent position— Phinehas, the son of Eleazar the son of Aaron (Nm. 25,7ff.; 31,6; Jos. 22,13.[27] It was specifically to Phinehas that God addressed his promise of a perpetual priesthood in the line of Aaron: "Wherefore say, Behold, I give unto him my covenant of peace: And he shall have it, even the covenant of an everlasting priesthood" (Nm. 25,12–13).

---

[26] According to genealogical lists in 1 Ch. 23,15–16; 24,20; 26,24, the line is Moses—Gershom—Shebuel, with no mention of Jonathan. The Sages accounted for this simply by equating Jonathan with Shebuel (*Bab. Tal. Baba Bathra*, 110). S. Talmon has argued that the name was intentionally deleted for the same reason that the name of Moses was modified to Manasseh—i.e. so as to denigrate the shrine at Dan; this, in his opinion, was also behind the association of the fates of the shrines at Dan and Shiloh in Jgs. 18,31, they being rivals to the "official" priestly line of Eleazar the son of Aaron (see *Studies in the Book of Judges* [above, n. 2, p. 12] 574f.).

But it must not be forgotten that many generations are lacking in the genealogies of Moses, for Shebuel in fact flourished in the time of King David.

[27] Our typological approach reduces the chronological significance ascribed by several scholars to the occurrence of Jonathan in the Danite account, and of Phinehas in the subsequent story of the outrage at Gibeah (Jgs. 20,28), for it is thus not imperative to pace both these episodes in the third generation after the Exodus. Indeed, the historical circumstances underlying the above events seem to conflict with such an early dating (for the divergent opinions, see the studies mentioned above, nn. 1 and 3. For an 11th century B.C. dating of the Gibeah episode, see A. Malamat, in "The Period of the Judges," *The World History of the Jewish People*, II (Tel Aviv, 1971), 233 and n. 84 (Hebrew) (= here chap. 7).

Renaming of Conquered Sites

Upon the conquest of Laish[28] and its resettlement by the Danites, the name of the city was changed: "And they called the name of the city Dan, after the name of Dan their father, who was born unto Israel: howbeit the name of the city was Laish at first" (Jgs. 18,29). This is the most explicit and best known instance of the renaming of a site captured by the Israelites, though, of course, not the only such case. The phenomenon is found throughout the Conquest traditions—and indeed four such examples are to be found in Judges 1: Kirjath-arba—Hebron (v. 10; and cf. Jos. 14,15); Kirjath-sepher—Debir (v. 11; and cf. Jos. 15,15); Zephat—Hormah (v. 17; and cf. Nm. 21,3); and Luz—Bethel (v. 23; and cf. Gn. 28,19, where lārîšōnā, "at first," is identical with the expression applied to the earlier name in the Laish/Dan change, as against ľpānîm, "before," in parallel usage in the other passages). However, with the exception of Hormah (which is explained etiologically) in none of the above instances is it explicitly stated that the change was made by the Israelites; and in even greater contrast to "Dan," the new designations are not derived from the patronymic of the conqueror. Furthermore, we may actually have here city-name twinned with their appellations, somewhat like the paired toponyms found here and there in the Bible.[29]

Typologically closest to the Laish/Dan change is the renaming of certain sites in northern Transjordan so as to conform with the tribal units which captured and resettled them: "*Jair* the son of Manasseh took all the region of Argob, that is, Bashan, as far as the border of the Geshurites and the Maacathites, and called the villages after

---

[28] In the recent excavations of the Israel Department of Antiquities at Tel Dan (Tell el-Qaḍi), the Laish taken by the Danites could be represented by either (*a*) a Late Bronze Age II settlement inferred thus far only from ceramic evidence (including a 14th century B.C. tomb with Mycenean wares, found in 1969)—which would support an early dating of the Danite migration; cf. *IsrEJ* 16 (1966) 145; *Hadashot Arkheologiot* 31–32 (1969) 1ff. (Hebrew); or more likely (*b*) the first Early Iron Age settlement (stratum VI), a weak town which could easily have been taken, destroyed evidently at the end of the 12th or at the beginning of the 11th century B.C.—as would suit a later date for the migration; see ibid. 25 (1968) 2; A. Biran, in *All the Land of Naphtali* (Jerusalem 1967) 28–29 (both Hebrew).

[29] Cf., e.g., the paired names in Gn 14; and Y. Aharoni, *The Land of the Bible* (London 1967) 129. As for Hebron, B. Maisler (Mazar), "Hebron," *Dinaburg Jubilee Volume* (Jerusalem 1947) 316ff. (Hebrew) considers Kirjath-arba a mere appellation, though orally he has expressed the possibility that Hebron was named after a Levite family (cf., e.g., Ex. 6,18). For Kirjath-(ha)arba, cf. also n. 31, below.

his own name, *Havvoth-jair*, as it is to this day" (Dt. 3,14 [RSV]); and, in another tradition: "And *Jair* the son of Manasseh went and took Havvoth-ham (thus, emending *havvōtēhem*, "their villages," on the basis of the place-name Ham in Gn. 14,5), and called them *Havvoth-jair*. And *Nobah* went and took Kenath, and its villages, and called it *Nobah*, after his own name" (Nm. 32,41–42; and cf. v. 38 for the general practice of city-name changing).[30]

In passing, we may note that the only renaming of a city in the Bible to which historical credibility is lent by support from external sources is that of Laish/Dan. The name Laish is mentioned both in early Egyptian sources (in the later group of Execration Texts—*ca.* 18th century B.C., and in the topographical list of Thutmes III— first half of the 15th century B.C.) and in an as-yet-unpublished Akkadian document from Mari (18th century B.C.).[31] The variant form "Leshem" in Jos 19,47 finds no support in these external documents and may merely be a scribal error.[32] The town Kenath, too, evidently occurs in the later Execration Texts (E 32), and into the list of Thutmes II (No. 26), as well as in the el-Amarna Letters (No. 204); but its Israelite name, Nobah, which does appear again in Jgs. 8,11, did not gain a foothold. The older name persisted, as seen in 1 Ch. 2,23 and apparently also in the inscriptions of Tiglath-pileser III[33]—as well as in the present-day name of the village—Qanawat. Lacking further relevant external evidence, we possess no means of confirming the historicity of the biblical traditions relating to the renaming of other Canaanite towns.

---

[30] For the emendation Havvoth-ham, see A. Bergman (Biran), *JAOS* 54 (1934) 176. For explanations of Nm. 32,38, and the ambiguous words *mussabōt šēm*, "their names being changed" (AV), see R. de Vaux, *Bible et Orient* (Paris 1967) 116f.; O. Eissfeldt, "Renaming in the Old Testament," *Words and Meanings. Essays Presented to D. Winton Thomas* (Cambridge 1968) 70. Another case is the renaming of Selah to Joktheel following its capture from the Edomites by King Amaziah (2 Kgs. 14,7)— again apparently after the eponym of a Judean family (cf. Jos. 15,38; 1 Ch. 4,18).

[31] See A. Malamat, "Northern Canaan and the Mari Texts," *Near Eastern Archaeology in the Twentieth Century* (ed. by J.A. Sanders; New York 1970, 164–177).

[32] Since P. de Lagarde, it has been accepted that Leshem was an early form of Laish, with mimation; see the Bible dictionaries, s.v. Leshem. It is more likely, however, that Laish was corrupted into Leshem, in one way or another (possibly through fusion of *layiš* and *šēm* which may originally have appeared in the latter part of Jos 19,47).

[33] For the restoration of the name Kenath ([*Qa*]-*ni-te*) in the damaged Akkadian text, see H. Tadmor, in *All the Land of Naphtali* (Jerusalem, 1967), 65 and n. 29 (Hebrew).

The same phenomenon of changing the Canaanite city name to conform with that of the conquering Israelite tribe, so well expressed in the Danite story, undoubtedly held good on the national, pan-israelite level as well. The change in the name of the "land of Canaan" (cf. in our context, e.g., Nm. 13 passim) to the "land of Israel" (1 Sm. 13,19 and cf. Jos. 11,22) is not explicitly stated as such, either in the Conquest cycle or anywhere else, apparently because the new name was brought about through a gradual historical process and not a single, definitive event. Indeed, the macro-cosmic character of the name "land of Israel" can be deduced from the wording of the Laish/Dan change in Jgs. 18,29, emphasising the descent of Dan (the tribal patronymic) "who was born unto *Israel* (the pan-tribal eponym)." Following the conquest of Laish, the new name Dan lent itself to the overall description of the Israelite settlement, denoting its northern extent, as in the stereotyped expression "from Dan to Beersheba."

Far from indicating any direct connection between the two con-generic stories dealt with in this study, our comparative structural analysis points to the conclusion that they are individual models of different scale, following a basic pattern which had evolved for biblical narratives of campaigns of inheritance. The historical reality of the various elements within the pattern is a separate question. In both accounts, certain elements are undoubtedly founded in historical substance, though the concise story in Judges is generally of a more realistic stamp than the broad, national account, which coagulated in a complex literary process bearing dogmatic and legendary overtones.

PART THREE

THE RISE OF THE DAVIDIC DYNASTY

10

A POLITICAL LOOK AT THE KINGDOM OF DAVID AND SOLOMON AND ITS RELATIONS WITH EGYPT*

I

The kingdom of David and Solomon achieved the status of an intermediate power between Mesopotamia and Anatolia on the north, and Egypt on the south, constituting a prime political and economic factor in Hither Asia.[1] It was a "great" or "major power" in its day, to use terms of modern political science, a highly effective analytical tool (and one which I shall often utilize here) in scanning events of the remote past. Neither before nor after were the Israelites capable of consolidating and maintaining a sovereign entity of such significant strength and size. After Solomon's death, the kingdoms of Judah and Israel were merely "small powers" or "weak states" in the hierarchy of the international system, and their combined strength, even when acting in concert as under Ahab and Jehoshaphat, hardly matched that of the United Monarchy.

Unfortunately, the available source material on David and Solomon is entirely lopsided, and in delving into the unique status of their kingdom and its impact on the Near Eastern scene, we are confronted by a serious methodological drawback. The relative abundance of biblical material is left unsustained, by a total lack of contemporaneous external sources. Yet the possibilities for balanced,

---

* This article was originally published in: *Studies in the Period of David and Solomon*, ed. T. Ishida, Tokyo, 1982.

[1] For the author's earlier treatments of the policies of David and Solomon, see "Aspects of the Foreign Policies of David and Solomon," *JNES* 22 (1963), 1–17 (= chap. 11); "The Kingdom of David and Solomon in its Contact with Egypt and Aram Naharaim" (1958) *BAR* 2 (1964), 89–98. On this period in general, see J. Bright, *A History of Israel* (2nd ed.; London, 1972), 190–224; J.A. Soggin, "The Davidic-Solomonic Kingdom," *Israelite and Judaean History* (eds. J.H. Hayes and J.M. Miller; London, 1977), 332–80; B. Mazar, "The Era of David and Solomon," *The Age of the Monarchies: Political History. The World History of the Jewish People* 4/1 (ed. A. Malamat; Jerusalem, 1979), 76–100; D.N. Freedman, "The Age of David and Solomon." *The World History of the Jewish People* 4/1, 101–25; S. Herrmann, *Geschichte Israels* (2nd ed.; München, 1980), 185–233.

controlled research here are thereby drastically curtailed, confined to internal historical evidence. The outstanding and predominant nature of the United Monarchy clearly calls for a broader, far more comprehensive historical perspective than that presented by the biblical canvas. For the Bible is, so to speak, myopic and simply inadequate for a proper grasp of the full significance of David and Solomon's kingdom in its "global" context. Moreover, the reliability of the relevant biblical sources themselves can be questioned: how far do they reflect historical reality and to what extent do they incorporate later literary efforts glorifying David and Solomon.

Nevertheless, the Bible is studded with numerous signposts pointing to the true status of this kingdom on the international scene. Not the least of these is the titulary applied to Solomon, which seems to parallel the Akkadian *šarru rabû*, "imperatore" (to which we shall return later).[2] Typical indicators, besides David's actual extensive military conquests, are scattered throughout the Second Book of Samuel and First Kings (and, of course, the parallel passages in Chronicles), attesting to the contacts maintained by David and especially Solomon with other countries, some of them quite remote. This material would put Israel as an integral factor in the contemporaneous fabric of the ancient Near East, and provide a more adequate picture of this kingdom and its international impact.

Leaving aside the two outstanding points of contact for the moment, Egypt and Syria, what is the evidence of Israel's variegated web of foreign relations?

(1) First of all, the intensive relations between David/Solomon and Hiram, king of Tyre, generated by mutual interests in various spheres.[3]

(2) Solomon's economic ties with the land of Que, in southern Anatolia, from whence he imported horses (1 Kgs. 10:28–29).[4]

(3) The expeditions down the Red Sea to Ophir (1 Kgs. 9:28; 10:11), and the enigmatic "ships of Tarshish" (1 Kgs. 10:22; or, according to the suspect reading in 2 Chr. 9:21, "ships travelling to Tarshish"), in this context apparently not to be associated with the

---

[2] See below, p. 197.

[3] See, in the present volume, H. Donner, "The Interdependence of Internal Affairs and Foreign Policy during the Davidic-Solomonic Period (with Special Regard to the Phoenician Coast)." See also G. Bunnens, "Commerce et diplomatie phéniciens au temps de Hiram 1er de Tyr," *JESHO* 19 (1976) 1–31.

[4] On this obscure passage in 1 Kgs. 10:28–29 see, in the present volume, Y. Ikeda, "Solomon's Trade in Horses and Chariots in its International Setting."

western Mediterranean.[5] The apes and baboons (not peacocks!), the "*almug* wood which has not been seen [in Jerusalem] to this day" (1 Kgs. 10:11–12), the perfumes and spices from Sheba, the precious stones and the huge quantities of gold, all must have aroused intense amazement among the people of Israel.[6] This was clearly a bolstering of Solomon's prestige, with status symbols imitative of the luxuries and exotica wrested from the four corners of the earth by the monarchs of Egypt and Assyria.

(4) Finally, the intriguing tale of the Queen of Sheba, in southwestern Arabia (1 Kgs. 10:1–13).[7] Solomon was impressed by the "gifts" he had received in accord with diplomatic decorum; the Queen for her part was overwhelmed by Solomon's statesmanship and grandeur and largesse. Actually, a strictly political-economic understanding is reflected here, though we can only ponder what Solomon would have had to offer in trade. Logically, it may well have been finished products, in any event, high-value, low-bulk goods of some sort.

These innovative enterprises are clear traits of imperial stature,[8] of a "great power" seeking to expand its political-economic frontiers far beyond its own actual borders. Solomon's role in the international power game was no less potent than that of his predecessor, but it assumed a new dimension. His policies reflect a decided shift of emphasis in foreign affairs from the military sphere to the economic.

---

[5] For the biblical Tarshish as a location in the western Mediterranean (most likely Spain), only from the 8th century B.C. on, see e.g., K. Galling, "Der Weg der Phöniker nach Tarsis in literarischer und archäologischer Sicht," *ZDPV* 88 (1972), 1–18, 140–81. For "Tarshish ships" as a particular type of large, sea-going vessel, see below. For a recent note on Tarshish, cf. S.B. Hoenig, "Tarshish," *JQR* 69 (1979), 181f.

[6] For הכי as "baboon" (supposedly derived from *[t-ʾ] ky[t], rather than the traditional "peacocks", see W.F. Albright, *Archaeology and the Religion of Israel* (Baltimore, 1946), 212, n. 16. For אלמג/אלגמ trees, cf. A. Malamat, "Campaigns to the Mediterranean by Iahdunlim and Other Early Mesopotamian Rulers," *Studies in Honor of B. Landsberger* (AS 16, 1965), 367–69; J.C. Greenfield and M. Mayrhofer, "The ʾalgummīn/ʾalmuggīm-Problem reexamined," *Hebräische Wortforschung. Festschrift W. Baumgartner* (VTSup 16, 1967), 86–89. For luxury commodities coming from Ophir and Sheba, see M. Elat, *Economic Relations in the Lands of the Bible* (Jerusalem, 1977), 192–96 (Hebrew).

[7] For the legendary overtones in the Queen of Sheba episode, see J. Gray, *I & II Kings* (2nd ed.: London, 1970), 257ff.; M. Noth, *Könige 1* (BKAT 9/1, 1968), 223ff.; E. Würthwein, *Das Erste Buch der Könige, Kapitel 1–16* (ATD 11/1, 1977), 119ff. Despite its late literary character, the episode surely reflects the geo-economic reality of a Solomonic context.

[8] Cf. J. Kegler, *Politisches Geschehen und theologisches Verstehen* (Stuttgart, 1977), esp. 212ff.

Entering the realm of long-distance trade, Solomon initiated a north-south political-commercial axis embracing Tyre-Israel-Sheba, with branches across the Mediterranean and Red Seas.

II

Actually, the unprecedented expansion of the United Monarchy, territorial and economic, was a natural outcome of the geo-political situation prevailing at that time. For centuries, the region of Syria and Palestine had been caught between Egyptian ambitions and those of Mitanni and especially, later, the Hittites. In modern political terms, it had been in the clutches of a long-standing "bipolar" power structure. The collapse of this constellation led to a political vacuum in the Syro-Palestinian sphere—till the resurgence of Egypt, toward the end of Solomon's reign, and the rise of Assyria, several decades later. This rare moment of calm, free of all "super-power" interference, provided a unique opportunity for the one nation in this region which would most successfully exploit the interlude, and who would thus gain hegemony over what was normally a buffer region. Of the nations living between the Nile and the Euphrates and now seeking to assert themselves were, foremost, Tyre on the coast, Aram in the north, and Israel to the south. In Machiavellian phraseology, the *occasione* was there, but who was the ruler possessing the *virtu*?

It was David who ultimately fulfilled this destiny. His deep historical perception of current trends was combined with a marked capacity for decision-making—outstanding qualities which enabled him to overcome all rivalry in the fateful intra-regional struggles. In bringing his national goals to realization, David was driven by universal motivations which have steered all great political figures to success: attainment of security, attainment of power, and attainment of glory. Applying what we today would call a "grand strategy,"[9] David built up an empire by a process both gradual and fascinating. David's grand strategy reflects decisive planning and well-defined, specific aims, and a long-range perspective. These dominant traits

---

[9] This concept, elaborated in recent years by political and military analysts, covers economic, and even psychological, aspects no less than military and political facets. See, e.g., B.H. Liddell-Hart, *Strategy* (2nd ed.; New York, 1967), 335f. ("the term 'grand strategy' serves to bring out the sense of 'policy execution'").

enable us to perceive five major phases on his path to empire; they can be likened to five concentric rings in progression: (1) tribal kingdom; (2) national kingdom; (3) consolidated territorial state; (4) multinational state; (5) empire (see figure).

Phase one: Tribal kingdom. Using Hebron as an initial springboard, David was crowned king over the "House of Judah" with the support of his seasoned "troop" (Hebrew *gĕdūd*) and probably with Philistine consent. This early period was exploited intensively in the military sphere—for instance, for the conquest of Jerusalem,[10] as well as for laying diplomatic foundations—such as David's marriage to Maacah, daughter of Talmai, king of Geshur, the future mother of Absalom (2 Sam. 3:3). This alliance with the petty kingdom of Geshur, far to the north in the Gaulan—and possibly the ties with the kings of Ammon (inferred from 2 Sam. 10:2) and Moab (inferred from 1 Sam. 22:34 and, more deviously, 14:47)—enabled David to outflank the northern tribes of Israel, and thus facilitate achievement of his second phase.

Phase two: National kingdom. The most far-reaching political act to take place at Hebron was the alliance between David and the northern tribes of Israel. After the abortive negotiations with Abner, but only following the elimination of Eshbaal, Saul's successor, the elders of the northern tribes came forth to recognize David at Hebron as king over all Israel. The covenant formalizing this recognition sheds light upon the circumstances underlying the split of the United Monarchy after Solomon's death, when the northern tribes once again regarded themselves as free agents to negotiate.[11]

Since Alt's basic study of the formation of the United Monarchy, this union of Israel and Judah has most often been understood as a *Personal-union* under one crown.[12] Yet this term, current as it is, is

---

[10] B. Mazar, "David's Reign in Hebron and the Conquest of Jerusalem," *In the Time of the Harvest. Essays in Honor of A.H. Silver* (ed. D.J. Silver; New York, 1963), 235–44, would place David's capture of Jerusalem at the very beginning of this period, but the shift of the capital of Israel only much later, in David's eighth regnal year. Cf. also N.L. Tidwell, "The Philistine Incursions into the Valley of Rephaim" (ed. J.A. Emerton; VTSup 30 [1979]), 190–212.

[11] Cf. A. Malamat, "Organs of Statecraft in the Israelite Monarchy" (1965) *BAR* 3 (1970), 163–98, esp. 168–70 (see here chap. 13).

[12] A. Alt, "Die Staatenbildung der Israeliten in Palästina" (1925) *Kleine Schriften* 2 (München, 1953), 1–65, esp. 45ff. For the continued use of this concept, cf. the studies noted in n. 1, above. See also G. Buccellati, *Cities and Nations of Ancient Syria* (Studi Semitici 26, 1967), 148ff.

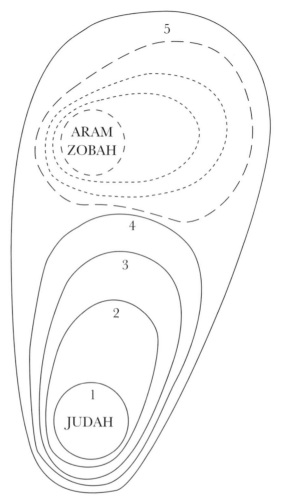

The Growth of the Empire of David and Solomon (schematic).
1. Tribal Kingdom; 2. National Kingdom; 3. Consolidated Territorial State;
4. Multi-National State; 5. Empire.

essentially misleading. Terminology often being more than what meets
the eye, it would be more appropriate to define the relationship as
a *Realunion*.[13] And what is the essential difference? In contrast to a

---

[13] For the *Personalunion* and *Realunion*, respectively, from a political and legalistic
point of view, see G. Jellinek, *Allgemeine Staatslehre* (3rd ed.; Bad Homburg, 1960),
750ff.; L. Oppenheim, *International Law* 1 (ed. H. Lauterpacht; 8th ed.; London,
1955), 171f.; J. Crawford, *The Creation of States in International Law* (Oxford, 1979), 290f.

Personalunion, the *Realunion* is not incidental but results from the reciprocal will of two political entities to join together (as did David and the northern elders). Whereas in a *Personalunion* two or more international legal entities (or "personalities") remain separate in both internal and external affairs, a *Realunion* is internally composite, but a single legal entity in its external aspect. This latter entity finds full expression, *inter alia*, in a united army and a unified foreign policy. Such indeed was the case of the United Monarchy.

Phase three: Consolidated territorial state. The emergence of a Pan-Israelite bloc, upsetting the balance of power in Palestine, inevitably led to military confrontation between David and the Philistines, hitherto uncontested masters of the region. This was well perceived by the biblical historiographer: "When the Philistines heard that David had been anointed king over Israel, all the Philistines went up in search of David . . ." (2 Sam. 5:17).

In the ensuing series of encounters, David eventually grasped the initiative, and though he seems not to have conquered Philistia proper, he did break the Philistine might once and for all. This certainly isolated Philistia and prevented her free access to the Canaanite areas to the north, and to her sources of metal, especially iron, presumably in the Succoth region of Transjordan.[14] Foremost, however, David thus brought about an entirely new political order, for, as Alt has noted, the Philistines had regarded themselves as the legitimate heirs to Egyptian rule in Canaan, and upon their defeat this legacy was to pass to the Israelites, at least nominally.[15] In fact, David had to impose his control over the remaining Canaanite areas (cf. the list of alien enclaves, in Judges 1)—foremost of which were the city-states of the Sharon plain and the Jezreel valley.[16]

The kingdom of Israel at this stage might be characterized in modern international law as a sort of "successor state" to the Philistines.

---

[14] For copper and iron ore slag in that region, see N. Glueck, *The River Jordan* (New York, 1968), 119; and cf. 1 Kgs. 7:45f. Cf. M. Har-El, "The Valley of the Craftsmen (Ge' *Haharašîm*)" *PEQ* 109 (1977), 75–86, esp. 81ff., who assumes that Philistine smithing, which he locates in the Sharon plain, was based on raw materials from the vicinity of Succoth.

[15] A. Alt, "Das Grossreich Davids" (1950), *Kleine Schriften* 2, 68f.; A. Malamat, *BAR* 2, 95.

[16] The destruction layers at such sites as Tell Qasile (level X; see A. Mazar, "Qasile, Tell," *EAEHL* 4 [1977] 966) and Megiddo (level VI A; see Y. Yadin, "Megiddo," *EAEHL* 3 [1977] 851) would seem to reflect David's heavy arm.

This notion of "succession of states"[17] can provide a new perspective in understanding the "special" relations of David and Solomon with the kingdom of Tyre, which seems to have superseded the ties between Philistia and the Phoenician coast. Solomon's commercial enterprises with the land of Que, too, were apparently based on earlier, established ties between the Anatolian coast and the Sea-Peoples, including the Philistines. Furthermore, mercenary troops were drafted into David's ranks from among the Philistines—the Cheretites and Pelethites, and a contingent of Gittites (2 Sam. 15:18). David must have taken over the potent Philistine chariotry too (cf. 1 Sam. 13:5; 2 Sam. 1:6), as well as that of the Canaanite enclaves, for otherwise the later Israelite successes against the "mechanized" Aramean forces would be rather difficult to account for.[18] The Philistine monopoly of metal manufacture (cf. 1 Sam. 13:19–20) must also have fallen into Israelite hands.

In this phase, the kingdom of Israel exceeded the confines of its own national state, having become a consolidated territorial state by incorporating the Canaanite city-states and considerable tracts peopled by remnants of the erstwhile gentile population (e.g., 2 Sam. 24:7; 1 Kgs. 9:20).

Phase four: Multinational state. Having broken through the western flank of the belt of hostility surrounding Israel, David could now turn to the long-standing foes on his eastern and southern perimeter: Edom, Moab and Ammon. The actual order of their conquest and incorporation[19]—whether as a vassal state (Moab; 2 Sam. 8:2), a province (Edom; 2 Sam. 8:14) or annexed outright (Ammon; 2 Sam. 12:30)—is unclear, but a sort of "domino theory" most probably came into play here, that is, the fall of the one led to the fall of

---

[17] On this doctrine see, e.g., L. Oppenheim, *International Law* 1, 156ff.; and recently "Ch. 28: State Succesion" in I. Brownlie, *Principles of Public International Law* (2nd ed.; Oxford, 1973), 631ff.; G. von Glahn, *Law Among Nations* (4th ed.; New York/London, 1981), 119ff.

[18] For the existence of chariotry, however modest, in David's army, see Y. Yadin, *The Art of Warfare in Biblical Lands* 2 (Jerusalem/Ramat Gan, 1963), 285 (where 2 Sam. 8:3–4 is cited as a basis), and cf. now C. Hauer. "The Economics of National Security in Solomonic Israel," *JSOT* 18 (1980), 63ff. Y. Ikeda regards the chariotry of this period primarily as a prestige symbol, its military value having been overrated in modern scholarship (see above, n. 4).

[19] On the varying degree of dependence of these states, see A. Malamat, "The Monarchy of David and Solomon—The Rise of a Power," *Thirty Years of Archaeology in Eretz-Israel, 1948–78. The 35th Archaeological Convention of the Israel Exploration Society* (Jerusalem, 1981), esp. 194–96 (Hebrew).

the next, and so forth. In conducting these campaigns, David had not merely a political aim, but primarily economic-exploitative designs, gaining not only control of the "King's Highway" but also direct access to the Red Sea as a bonus.

This cumulative expansion of Israel dwarfed every previous political entity established in the Palestinian sphere, even exceeding the extent of the Egyptian province in the second millennium B.C.

Phase five: Empire. Coeval with the growth of David's kingdom, a political bloc arose in Syria under the leadership of Hadadezer, king of Aram-Zobah, also attaining "great power" status. Following the principle of "competitive exclusion,"[20] it was inevitable that these two up-and-coming rivals should clash, for they had gobbled up all the independent territories situated between them. The vast power accumulated by Israel and the Arameans on the eve of their final contest predicated that absolute hegemony over the entire region of Syria-Palestine would fall to the winner. David's triple victory thus assured him mastery over the entire kingdom of Hadadezer as far as the Euphrates River (as we have shown elsewhere in detail).[21] This unprecedented territorial expansion of the kingdom of Israel can better be comprehended by assuming that Aram-Zobah already comprised a comprehensive states-system. In the vanquishing of their overlord, these territories passed to David *en bloc*, with all their components more or less intact. It was this legacy which facilitated David's acquisition of empire.

By modern definition, the kingdom of David and Solomon—a highly complex political conglomerate with Judah at its nucleus—was a super-national system of political and economic domination by a center over a periphery, in other words, indeed a true empire.[22]

How does the Bible grasp this new status? David and Solomon are referred to by such obvious phrases as king "over Judah," "over all Israel and Judah," "over all Israel," "over Israel," and twice,

---

[20] This concept has been borrowed by political scientists from the realm of biology; see R.L. Carneiro, "Political Expansion as an Expression of the Principle of Competitive Exclusion," *Origins of the State* (eds. R. Cohen and E.R. Service; Philadelphia, 1978), 205ff., esp. 208f.

[21] *JNES* 22 (1963), 1ff.

[22] For various definitions of "empire," in the context of antiquity, see now "Ch. 1: Introduction" in *Imperialism in the Ancient World* (eds. P.D.A. Garnsey and C.R. Whittaker; Cambridge, 1978); and *Power and Propaganda. A Symposium on Ancient Empires* (ed. M.T. Larsen; Copenhagen, 1979), esp. 21–33 (S.N. Eisenstadt) and 90ff. (M.T. Larsen).

David "King of Israel" (2 Sam. 6:20 and 2 Chr. 8:11). But the Bible goes much further, graphically, at least concerning Solomon: "Solomon ruled over all the kingdoms from the Euphrates, the (sic!) land of the Philistines and to the border of Egypt; they brought tribute and served Solomon all the days of his life.... For he had dominion over all the region west of the Euphrates from Tiphsah to Gaza, over all the kings west of the Euphrates" (1 Kgs. 4:21, 24 [MT 5:1, 4]). Then this passage continues: וְשָׁלוֹם הָיָה לוֹ מִכָּל עֲבָרָיו מִסָּבִיב, "and he had peace on all sides round about him"—a "*pax Salomonica*," so to speak. On a more hyperbolic plane, one of the two Psalms actually dedicated to Solomon poeticizes; "May he have dominion from sea to sea, from the River to the ends of the earth.... May the kings of Tarshish and of the isles render him tribute, may the kings of Sheba and Seba bring gifts. May all kings fall down before him, all nations serve him" (Ps. 72:1, 8, 10–11).[23]

Is such magnitude ever channeled into a specific, grandiose titulary? There appears to be a particular biblical expression befitting this majesty—*melek rab*—associated with Solomon in both of its two occurrences: one possibly relates to the builder of Jerusalem in all its splendour, while the other definitely refers to the builder of the Temple. Ps. 48:2 (MT 48:3), glorifies: קִרְיַת מֶלֶךְ רָב, "the city of the great king." Now, regardless of whether this king is heavenly (as is usually held) or earthly, the imagery here is of a mortal ruler. In the second instance, an Aramaic passage in Ezra (5:11) retrospectively refers to וּמֶלֶךְ לְיִשְׂרָאֵל רַב בְּנָהִי וְשַׁכְלְלֵהּ, "a great king of Israel built it and completed it." This latter instance certainly reflects the parallel Akkadian title *šarru rabû*, "great king," "emperor." Elsewhere in the Bible the expression *melek gādōl*, also translating into English as "great king," is applied either to God or to the king of Assyria,[24] and the *melek yareb* in Hosea (5:13; 10:6) refers to the Assyrian king

---

[23] B. Mazar relates this psalm to the days of an assumed coregency of David and Solomon, on the basis of its superscription (and final verse); B. Mazar, "The Phoenicians and Eastern Shore of the Mediterranean Sea," (1965) *Cities and Districts in Eretz-Israel* (Jerusalem, 1975) 262 (Hebrew). For such a coregency, cf. recently T. Ishida, *The Royal Dynasties in Ancient Israel* (BZAW 142, 1977), 153f., 170; E. Ball, "The Co-Regency of David and Solomon," *VT* 27 (1977), 268–79 (who suggests that this institution was introduced into Israel under Egyptian influence).

[24] It is also applied to Sihon, king of the Amorites, and Og, king of Bashan (in Ps. 136:17–19; and cf. Ps. 135:10–11), but only poetically, as is obvious from the context.

alone. But, interestingly, both Ugaritic and Early Aramaic (e.g., the Sefire inscriptions) use the term *mlk rb*. We can thus assume that the usage *melek rab* in the Bible represents a stylistic stratum different from that of *melek gadol*, which latter is strictly a Hebrew loan-translation of *šarru rabû* (and note *melek gadol* in Hebrew script upon a Nimrud ivory of the late eighth century B.C.).[25]

In other words, a title applied (albeit retrospectively) to Solomon, alone of all the Israelite kings, evokes a particular category of major potentate, the "overlord," which later history was to call "emperor." That this title was no empty shell is shown by Solomon's marriage to Pharaoh's daughter, further confirmation of the image of Israel as an empire. With this happy event we enter into a discussion of Solomon's relations with Egypt, and his activities within the traditional Egyptian sphere of influence.

III

Royal diplomatic marriages, as a means of cementing international relations and a practical alternative to warfare, were a cornerstone of Solomon's foreign policy. Solomon thus long anticipated the apt Habsburg witticism: *Bella gerant alii! tu, felix Austria, nube!* "Let others fight wars! Thou, O happy Austria, marry!" The full significance of Solomon's marriage with Pharaoh's daughter eluded the biblical historiographer, who failed even to mention the name of the Pharaoh, let alone that of the bride. Indeed, the event was entirely unique in both Israelite and Egyptian annals. Solomon's various other political marriages were with states of the second rank (Moab, Ammon, Edom, or the Phoenician coastal cities and the Neo-Hittite kingdoms). From ancient Near Eastern records in general—and especially those from the Amarna Letters down to Herodotus—it is now clear that Egyptian kings rarely, if ever, married off their daughters to foreign potentates,

---

[25] On *šarru rabû*, see M.J. Seux, *Épithètes royales akkadiennes et sumériennes* (Paris, 1967) 298ff. For its West-Semitic and biblical equivalents, cf. J.C. Greenfield, "Some Aspects of Treaty Terminology in the Bible," *Fourth World Congress of Jewish Studies* 1 (Jerusalem, 1967) 118f., who already pointed out that מלך גדול is "a sure calque on *š. r.*" For the Nimrud inscription, see A. Millard, "Alphabetic Inscriptions on Ivories from Nimrud," *Iraq* 24 (1962), 45ff. On the Great King in the ancient Near East and the Bible see: P. Artzi – A. Malamat, "The Great King—A Preeminent Royal Title in Cuneiform Sources and in the Bible", chap. 20 in *A. Malamat 1998*, 192–215.

whom they apparently regarded as inferior.[26] Of this fact, too, the biblical historiographer appeared to be ignorant.

In the book of Kings (with parallels in Chronicles), Pharaoh's daughter is mentioned in no less than five unrelated contexts, most of them likely of a pre-deuteronomic layer. Though this would lend historical credibility to the marriage, the Bible has neglected to disclose the motivations underlying this unusual event. Since the extant Egyptian records contain no trace of it whatsoever, we must construct a rational scenario if we are to arrive at a plausible historical assessment. The Israelite kingdom at this time was of a magnitude never before seen upon Egypt's eastern doorstep. Moreover, until midway through Solomon's reign, Egypt was split into two political units, the kings of the relatively weak twenty-first dynasty (1070–945 B.C.), with their capital at Tanis, ruling the north, and the theocracy at Thebes, firmly entrenched in the south. The outline which follows is a restatement, up-dated and revised, of a hypothesis which I put forth some years ago.[27]

1) The data in the Bible would place the marriage with Pharaoh's daughter early in Solomon's reign. Thus, the campaign to Gezer by Solomon's future father-in-law—most likely Siamun, penultimate king of the twenty-first dynasty (ca. 978–960 B.C.)—must have taken place at the very beginning of (or just prior to?) Solomon's reign as sole ruler (ca. 967/66 B.C.).[28]

2) The conquest of Gezer (now attested also by archaeological evidence)[29] on the northern border of Philistia was part of an Egyptian attempt to recover the southern coast of Palestine and part of the

---

[26] Cf. A. Malamat, *BAR* 2, 91f.; and see most recently A.R. Schulman, "Diplomatic Marriage in the Egyptian New Kingdom," *JNES* 38 (1979) 177–93; "Königstochter," *LÄ* 3/21 (1979), 659–61.

[27] *JNES* 22 (1963), 10ff. (= chap. 11); and see there for further details and bibliographical references.

[28] For a most recent review, see A.R. Green, "Solomon and Siamun: A Synchronism between Dynastic Israel and the Twenty-First Dynasty of Egypt," *JBL* 97 (1978), 353–67.

[29] W.G. Dever, ("Further Excavations at Gezer, 1967–71," *BA* 34 [1971] 110) assumes "Post-Philistine/Pre-Solomonic . . . Stratum 7 was brought to a violent end in the mid-10th century B.C." (at least in area 1 there); cf. also *ibid.*, 130; Dever et al., *Gezer* 1 (Jerusalem, 1970), 60–63. The relevance of Siamun's relief from Tanis as evidence for a campaign to Philistia has recently been negated by H.D. Lance, "Solomon, Siamun and the Double Ax," *Magnalia Dei: The Mighty Acts of God. Essays on the Bible and Archaeology in Memory of G.E. Wright* (eds. F.M. Cross et al.; Garden City, New York, 1976), 209–23.

Shephelah, lost to Egypt some two centuries before. Pharaoh surely did not undertake an entire campaign against Gezer solely in order to hand this fortress over to Solomon (1 Kgs. 9:16), as a token of friendship. Historically, such an act would hardly be comprehensible.

3) This conquest of Gezer, lying on the main road to Jerusalem, presented a direct threat to Israel. Pharaoh's ultimate goal may well have been the very capital of the kingdom of Israel (as it was in Shishak's campaign, some forty years later), in an attempt to topple the Israelite dynasty in the opportune moment following David's demise. It would have thus restored Egyptian hegemony over the Land of Canaan.

4) This Pharaoh, however, certainly underestimated Israelite potential. Since Solomon had secured his kingdom internally, having eliminated all domestic opposition, he could have concentrated his strength against the invader, and thus no doubt turned Pharaoh from his aggressive intentions in favour of rapprochement. In other words, a diplomatic course proved a more desirable alternative than stark confrontation.

5) A treaty, to which Solomon was at least an equal party, encompassed territorial concessions to Israel. This treaty, ratified (so to speak) by the marriage to Pharaoh's daughter, involved the transfer of Gezer, under the guise of a dowry, probably only part of Solomon's gains in Philistia at this time. Much later, after the rise of Shishak, Solomon may well have extended his control even further into Philistia, strengthening his position in the face of a new Egyptian threat.

And, finally (6), the previous assumption leads us to a true understanding of the borders of the Kingdom of Israel. Returning to the passage in 1 Kgs. 4:21 and 24 (MT 5:1, 4), we read that "Solomon ruled over all the kingdoms from the Euphrates, the (sic!) land of the Philistines and unto the border of Egypt. . . . For he had dominion over all the region west of the Euphrates (MT *'eber hannahar*) from Tiphsah unto Gaza." Philistia is mentioned here as a separate, distinct unit *under* Israelite control—if we follow the Massoretic text as it stands (the standard English translations insert "to" or "unto" the land of the Philistines, following the parallel passage in 2 Chr. 9:26). With this expansion to the southwest, the United Monarchy arrived at its fullest extent—not under David but as a result of Solomon's own political achievements.

This picture leaves many secondary questions unanswered, some of them quite intriguing. For example, why does the Bible make no mention of a Philistine amongst Solomon's numerous foreign wives? Could Pharaoh's daughter—daughter of the traditional suzerain over the southern coastal plain—have also "represented" Philistia, so to speak?

In any event, the above scenario has met with varying degrees of approval. Most recently, Manfred Görg has adopted its general aspect in his forthcoming book *Die Tochter Pharaos*, where he holds that the episode of Solomon and Pharaoh nurtured the story in the book of Exodus, on the Israelites in Egypt. Both stories involve an unnamed Pharaoh and a daughter. To paraphrase Görg, in Exodus is there not a Pharaoh who prevents the Israelites from leaving Egypt but then allows them to go, only to relent again and pursue them? Is this not like Siamun in the days of Solomon, who threatens Israel— only later to make peace, who takes Gezer and then presents it to Solomon? Furthermore, in both stories the role of Pharaoh's daughter is a positive one, beneficial to Israel.[30]

Many scholars, however, assume that Siamun was favorably disposed toward Israel in the first place, that his campaign to Philistia, (still under Egyptian hegemony) was merely a police action, or was limited to punishing a rebellious Gezer alone. It may also have been intended to eliminate Philistia from trade with Tyre.[31] Handing Gezer over to Solomon was a small price to pay for maintaining friendly ties with Israel. But whether Siamun's initial intentions were hostile or friendly, the fact remains that the marriage inaugurated an Egyptian-Israelite *détente* which lasted some twenty years—until the twenty-first dynasty was superseded by Shishak (*ca.* 945 B.C.).

What impact did these new relations have upon either party? What did Egypt receive in tangible exchange for her concessions? And what mutual interests evolved, if any? On these points we can only speculate, for even the circumstantial evidence is rather motley.[32]

---

[30] Pending publication of M. Görg's book, cf. his article "Ausweisung oder Befreiung," *Kairos* NF 20 (1978), 272–80.

[31] Thus recently A. Green, *JBL* 97, 365; for a similar view, see K.A. Kitchen, *The Third Intermediate Period in Egypt* (Warminster, 1973), 281f. On the other hand, S. Yeivin, "Did the Kingdoms of Israel Have a Maritime Policy?" *JQR* 50 (1960), 193ff., supposes that Siamun's campaign sought to counter an Israelite-Phoenician threat to the Egyptian monopoly over trade to the South.

[32] For Egyptian influence of Israel in the administrative and literary spheres, outside our present scope, see now T.N.D. Mettinger, *Solomonic State Officials* (CB OTS 5, 1971); D.B. Redford, "The Taxation System of Solomon," *Studies in Relations*

One service Solomon could have rendered Siamun was political support for his dynasty. Libyan elements—settled in Egypt some two centuries, much in the manner of the "Sea-Peoples"—gradually had come to the fore within the Egyptian army, occupying even top command positions. Foremost amongst their leaders were the grandfather and the father of Shishak, the future Pharaoh, as well as Shishak himself, and all three bore the title "Great Chief of the Me" (or "Meshwesh"), the latter being the name of a major Libyan people.[33] This faction, which was already seeking to topple the twenty-first dynasty, may well have held more than mere ties of tradition with the Philistines, harking back to the days of Ramesses III when their forefathers shared a common cause against Egypt.[34] Siamun may have sought in Solomon a means of neutralizing this potential threat in Philistia.

Another advantage undoubtedly sought by Siamun was a share in Solomon's international trade, or at least a "right-of-way" for his own agents and goods into Asia. This was apparently vital to him, for access to and from Nubia was currently controlled by the rival authorities in Thebes and was thus denied to him. Concerning possible trade with Israel, a clouded passage in I Kgs. 10:28–29 (and the parallels in 2 Chr. 1:16–17 and 9:28) may indicate that Solomon imported Egyptian chariots and teams. In general, however, Siamun's expectations were thwarted. Not only did Solomon exclude Egypt from his commercial ventures, but he even set up a rival cartel, bypassing the traditional Egyptian monopoly over raw materials precious metals, and exotica coming from Africa.

The major motive for Solomon's entry into the Red Sea trade—like his direct horse-trading with Que—was to obtain luxury goods

---

between Palestine and Egypt during the First Millennium B.C. (eds. J.W. Wevers and D.B. Redford; Toronto, 1972), 141–56; and E.W. Heaton, *Solomon's New Men* (London, 1974). A.R. Green, "Israelite Influence at Shishak's Court?" *BASOR* 233 (1979), 59–62, speculates on Israelite influence on Shishak's administration.

[33] On the Libyans in general and the Meshwesh in particular, see W. Hölscher, *Libyer und Ägypter* (Glückstadt, 1937); "Libyen, Libyer," *LÄ* 3/23 (1979), 1015–33. For the forbears of Shishak, to five or six generations, bearing the title "Great Chief of the Me(shwesh)," see Kitchen, *The Third Intermediate Period*, 285, and n. 244.

[34] See W.F. Edgerton and J.A. Wilson, *Historical Records of Ramses* III (Chicago, 1936), 20ff., 35, 44–47, 146f.; A. Gardiner, *Ancient Egyptian Onomastica* (Oxford, 1947), 119ff.; Cf. *LÄ* 3/23 (1979), 1022. For similarities in weapons (long sword) between the Meshwesh and the Philistines, cf. K. Zibelius, *Afrikanische Orts-und Völkernamen . . .* (Wiesbaden, 1972), 131.

straight from their source, eliminating the middleman, but such activities called for a maritime lore not available amongst the Israelites themselves, and hence Solomon sought the cooperation of Hiram of Tyre. Their Red Sea enterprises, based on Ezion-Geber,[35] must have been highly lucrative, despite adverse conditions of navigation in those waters. The Red Sea is known proverbially for its ever-changing winds and currents, "uncharted" islets and hidden reefs— dangers vividly illustrated by the ancient Egyptian *Tale of the Shipwrecked Sailor* (and cf. 1 Kgs. 22:49). In the first book of Kings, Solomon's Red Sea ventures are noted in three instances (I Kgs. 9:26–29; 10:11–12, 22, with significant variants in the parallel passages in 2 Chr. 8:17–18, 9:10–11, 21); two of these mention Ophir as the destination, while the third merely notes the use of "ships of Tarshish," presumably large "freighters" (like the "Byblos" and "Coptos" ships used by the early Egyptian voyagers to the Land of Punt). The goods brought back by Solomon's agents were gold, silver, ivory, "*'algum*" or (preferably) "*'almug*" wood, precious stones, monkeys, and baboons.[36]

This entire enterprise indeed recalls the Egyptian expeditions to Punt, from the time of Sahure (*ca.* 25th century B.C.) down to Ramesses III (12th century B.C.).[37] The products brought back by the expedition of Queen Hatshepsut in the fifteenth century B.C. included virtually all those sought by Solomon, and many more— incense and incense trees, and such exotic animals as giraffes. Hatshepsut's reliefs at Deir el-Bahri are also indicative of the sort of

---

[35] Solomon's hold over this port would indicate that an Edomite attempt to regain independence after the return of Hadad the Edomite from Egyptian exile, was abortive; see I Kgs. 11:14–22. For a recent study of this episode, see J.R. Bartlett, "An Adversary against Solomon, Hadad the Edomite," *ZAW* 88 (1976), 205–26.

[36] On Tarshish, see above, n. 5 and on "Tarshish" and "Byblos" ships see T. Säve-Söderbergh, *The Navy of the Eighteenth Egyptian Dynasty* (Uppsala, 1946) 47ff.; on baboons and אלמג/אלנם, see above, n. 6.

[37] For the more recent literature on Punt, see R. Herzog, *Punt* (Glückstadt, 1968), and the important review article by K.A. Kitchen, "Punt and How to Get There," *Or* 40 (1971), 184–207; A. Théodoridès, "Les escales de la route égyptienne de la côte de Somalie," *Recueils de la Société Jean Bodin* 32 (1974), 51–64; and W.W. Müller's brief summary, "Das Puntproblem," Pauly-Wissowa, *Realenzyklopädie der classischen Altertumswissenschaft, Supp.* 15 (Stuttgart, 1978), 739ff. For the occurrences of Punt in the Egyptian texts, see now Zibelius, *Afrikanische Orts-und Völkernamen*, 114ff. For a Red Sea port of departure for voyages to Punt, at Wadi Gawasis east of Coptos, as indicated by inscriptions found there, see A.M.A.H. Sayed, "Discovery of the Site of the Twelfth Dynasty Port at Wadi Gawasis on the Red Sea Shore," *Revue d'égyptologie* 29 (1977), 139–78; "The Recently Discovered Port on the Red Sea Shore," *JEA* 64 (1978), 69–71.

goods probably offered by Solomon in Ophir: bead necklaces, weapons, jewelry and the like—the usual trinkets palmed off on primitive peoples in trade throughout history.[38]

Where are these lands to be located? The animals, trees, and products of Punt would all point to the northern coast of Somalia, between Djibouti and Cape Guardafui, and though opinions are divided widely, it is here that the "emporium" of Ophir is preferably to be sought.[39] The fascinating *Periplus of the Erythrean* (or Red) *Sea*, from the first century A.D. describes this coast, as well as the Arabian coast opposite and the Red Sea in general. This seaman's manual lists in detail the many ports of call and their imports and exports, on the Somali coast, often the very sort of goods as at Punt and Ophir.[40] The latter name is noteworthy among the sons of Joktan in the Table of Nations in Gen. 10:26–30, which reads almost like a periplus of Arabia for ships and "ships of the desert." In this same Table, the two names Sheba and Havilah, "brothers" of Ophir, also occur amongst the sons of Cush; in other words, geographically they lay across the Red Sea as well, in Africa. In any event, the Joktan list in the Table of Nations may well stem from Solomonic times, when the South Arabian sphere, including the Horn of Africa, was just coming into the Israelite scope of awareness.[41]

The advent of the twenty-second dynasty in Egypt, in the person of Shishak, brought Israel's brief "flirt" with Egypt to an abrupt end. Shishak's aggressive policy soon reunited Egypt and apparently even regained Nubia.[42] We can arrive at a date for this turning-point by reference to an event much later in Shishak's reign, his campaign

---

[38] For Queen Hatshepsut's Punt expedition, see E. Naville, *The Temple of Deir el Bahari III* (London, 1894), pls. 64–76; for the Egyptian goods offered at Punt, see p. 14 there. The most recent summary concerning this expedition is S. Ratié, *La Reine Hatchepsout. Sources et problèmes* (Leiden, 1981), 141–61.

[39] For the various hypotheses of the location of Ophir (the three main locations being South Arabia, India, and Somalia), see recently G. Ryckmans, "Ophir," *DBSup* 6 (1960), 744–51; R. Hanslik, "Ophir," Pauly-Wissowa, *Realenzyklopädie der classischen Altertumswissenschaft, Supp.* 12 (1970), 969–80.

[40] See, still, W.H. Schoff, *The Periplus of the Erythraean Sea* (New York, 1912; reprinted New Delhi, 1974), esp. 24ff. and 75ff.

[41] Cf. C. Westermann, *Genesis 1–11* (*BKAT* 1/1, 1974) 704.

[42] On Shishak's foreign policy, see now Kitchen, *The Third Intermediate Period*, 292ff. On his possible domination of Nubia, which would have opened trade southward, cf. *ibid.*, 293 and n. 284 (as well as below). Mention of Cushites (i.e., Nubians) in 2 Chr. 12:3, alongside Libyans and Sukki, among Shishak's troops invading Palestine, may also be relevant.

to Palestine, singularly documented not only in the Bible but also in his monumental inscription at Karnak and by a fragmentary Egyptian stele found at Megiddo. On the basis of other evidence from Egypt, it can be inferred that the campaign took place around Shishak's 21st year, shortly before his death. According to 1 Kgs. 14:25 (2 Chr. 12:2), the invasion occurred in the fifth year of Rehoboam, Solomon's successor. Reckoning backward, Shishak must have reigned for about sixteen years coeval with Solomon, placing his accession in Solomon's 24th year or thereabouts (*ca.* 945 B.C.).[43]

We can note here only a few repercussions of this new Egyptian policy, concerning the second half of Solomon's reign. Shortly after Solomon's 24th year (cf. 1 Kgs. 6:1, 37–38; 7:1; 9:10, 24), Jeroboam led a rebellion against him and upon its failure was forced to flee to Shishak (cf. 1 Kgs. 11:26–28, 40). One wonders what connection the new Pharaoh Shishak may have had with these events. Either Jeroboam, an Ephraimite, deemed that a new dynasty in Egypt antagonistic to Solomon bettered his chances of success, or Shishak himself was inciting anti-Davidic elements, especially in the embittered northern Israel.[44]

Solomon also built a network of strategic fortresses after his 24th year—at Hazor and Megiddo in the north, and at Gezer, Beth-horon, Baalath, and Tamar in the south (1 Kgs. 9:15–18), and perhaps also at Ashdod, where recently a "Solomonic" gate has apparently been uncovered.[45] This new measure was certainly in response to internal unrest, as well as in anticipation of external threats, foremost from Egypt. But, these activities forced Solomon to increase the burden of taxation and the corvée, especially in the north—the major factor ultimately leading to the schism of the United Monarchy after his death. Solomon thus also fell deeper into debt with Tyre,

---

[43] See, in short, Malamat, *BAReader* 2, 94; and now a résumé of the chronological problematics, by A. Green, *JBL* 97 (1978), 353–67, with detailed bibliographical references.

[44] Cf. A. Malamat, *BAReader* 3, 192f. For a different explanation of Jeroboam's rebellion, relating it to the sale of Cabul (i.e., of "northern" lands by Solomon), see B. Halpern, "Sectionalism and the Schism," *JBL* 93 (1974), 524ff.

[45] For Hazor, Megiddo, and Gezer, see Y. Yadin, "The Archaeological Sources for the Period of the Monarchy," *The Age of the Monarchies: Culture and Society. The World History of the Jewish People* 4/2 (ed. A. Malamat; Jerusalem, 1979) 190, 195f., 208f. For the gate at Ashdod, see M. Dothan, "Ashdod," *EAEHL* 1 (1975), 114; and *idem*, "*Ashdod IV*," *'Atiqot* 15; for a post-Solomonic ascription of the Ashdod gate, see Y. Yadin, *The World History of the Jewish People* 4/2, 217f., 229.

which he placated with territorial concessions in the Cabul region of western Galilee (also around his 24th year; 1 Kgs. 9:10ff.).

The visit of the Queen of Sheba, too, must have taken place after Solomon's 24th year—a fact generally overlooked—for Solomon feted the queen in his already-completed palace (cf. 1 Kgs. 10:4ff.). She came not only to conclude commercial ties and thus secure her hold over trade with South Arabia, which Solomon has long been circumventing, for both she and Solomon, we can assume, foresaw the restoration of Egyptian trade in the Red Sea under the forceful Shishak and would have sought to counter this threat. That Shishak did have his eye on Israelite Red Sea connection is quite apparent from his side-thrust through the southern Negev, possibly toward Ezion-Geber, during his campaign, years later.[46]

In conclusion, the age of David and Solomon was indeed a unique chapter in Israelite history, and especially concerning relations with Egypt. It was the only point in history that the Holy Land ever attained primary status in international politics.

---

[46] For the inclusion of Ezion-Geber amongst the sites in the Negev listed by Shishak, see B. Mazar, "The Campaign of Pharaoh Shishak to Palestine," *Volume du Congrès, Strasbourg, 1956* (VTSup 4, 1957), 57–66; Y. Aharoni, *The Land of the Bible* (London, 1967), 283–90. The reading of this toponym is questioned, however, by Kitchen, *The Third Intermediate Period*, 439 and n. 87.

11

ASPECTS OF THE FOREIGN POLICIES
OF DAVID AND SOLOMON*

A. *David and the Kingdom of Hadadezer*

The point of view which rejects the biblical evidence for the expansion of the kingdom of David and Solomon deep into Syria up to the Euphrates (I Kings MT 5:1, 4; English Version 4:21, 24) as having no value has once again been vigorously defended, holding that "'the great empire' of David is merely a figment of the historical imagination."[1] The partisans of this position maintain that the United Israelite Kingdom did not extend very far beyond the borders of Palestine, and included at the very most the region around Damascus and Coelesyria. They have not, however, offered any convincing explanation of how the so-called "legend" of the far-flung empire of David and Solomon came into being.[2] In actual fact, the vast terri-

---

* This article was originally published in: *JNES* 22 (1963), 1–17.

[1] Cf. A. Biram, The Northern Limit of David's Kingdom, *Yehezkel Kaufmann Jubilee Volume* (1960), (Hebrew), pp. סה–פב (the quotation is taken from p. פב), and the literature cited there concerning the various arguments against an Israelite empire.

[2] Cf. e.g. E. Meyer, *Geschichte des Altertums*, II, 2³ (1953), pp. 253–54, n. 3: "Späte Phantasie ist die Ausdehnung des Reichs Salomon über die ganze persische Provinz Abarnahara von Tapsakos bis Gaza, (Reg. I. 5, 4)." It may be true that the biblical description of the extent of Solomon's kingdom bears the stamp of late terminology, especially in the use of the expression *'ebær hannāhār* (I Kings 5:4, MT), referring to the area west of the Euphrates, which is found outside the Old Testament only in late Assyrian and especially Persian sources. Cf. O. Leuze, Die Satrapieneinteilung in Syrien und im Zweistromlande von 520–320, *Schriften der Königsberger Gelehrten Gesellschaft*, XI, Heft 4 (1935), pp. 183ff. (For the use of *ebirtim* for "Transeuphratia" [i.e. the west bank of the Euphrates], which is attested already in the Mari documents, cf. now J.J. Finkelstein, *JNES*, XXI [1962], pp. 83f.) Nevertheless, this fact in itself is not sufficient to negate the actual historical tradition about this extent. Nor can we accept the argument that the biblical historiographer deliberately falsified the boundaries of the Davidic-Solomonic empire in order to bring them into accord with those of the Promised Land. The discrepancy between these two sets of borders has been tellingly pointed out by Y. Kaufmann, cf. his *Commentary on the Book of Joshua* (1959), p. 20 (Hebrew). David's empire extended over territories of Edom, Moab, Ammon, and the Aramean states which were outside of the Promised Land; while, conversely, it did not include the Phoenician seacost.

torial expansion of this kingdom appears to have been a corollary of the outcome of David's struggle for power with Hadadezer, the king of Aram Zobah.[3] From the enormous accumulation of power which the two contestants had attained on the eve of their clash[4] it was inevitable that the victor would gain political hegemony over the area between the Euphrates and Egypt. Consequently David's threefold victory over the Arameans gave him undisputed control of the full extent of Hadadezer's kingdom.

What was the political structure of the kingdom of Aram Zobah and how was it incorporated into the framework of Israelite rule? The present writer believes that David took over Hadadezer's realm not only territorially, but also structurally. That is to say, the diverse political entities of Aram Zobah were absorbed by Israel with no change in the status which they previously held—a practice which seems to have been not uncommon in the international relations of the ancient Near East.

The biblical evidence relating to Hadadezer and his followers is so scanty that it is difficult to form a clear conception of the structure of the political bloc which he dominated; but still it suffices to give us an insight into the complexity of this bloc. It is an over-simplification to assume that the kingdom of Zobah was merely the head of a confederacy of Aramean (and also non-Aramean)[5] states in Syria and northern Transjordan; on the contrary, the political organization established under the vigorous leadership of Hadadezer probably had a very complex structure similar to that of David's kingdom at the height of its power. Just as the latter comprised various disparate components—regions associated with it by *Personalunion*, conquered territories, vassal states and satellites[6]—so too Hadadezer's

---

[3] On the general geo-political position of the United Israelite Kingdom between Egypt and Aram Zobah, cf. the present writer's paper, "The Kingdom of David and Solomon in Its Contact with Egypt and Aram Naharaim," *BA*, XXI (1958), 96–102.

[4] For the extent of Aram Zobah at its zenith cf. A. Malamat, *Encyclopaedia Biblica*, Vol. I (1950), s.v. Aram Zobah (col. 582–83) (Hebrew); M.F. Unger, *Israel and the Aramaeans of Damascus* (1957), pp. 43ff.

[5] In his paper, "Geshur and Maacah," *JBL*, LXXX (1961), p. 27, B. Mazar has pointed out the non-Aramean population of the kingdom of Maacah and the land of Tob in the time of David.

[6] Cf. the thorough discussion by A. Alt, "Die Staatenbildung der Israeliten in Palästina," *Kleine Schriften* (henceforth *KS*), II (1953), 33ff.; "Das Grossreich Davids," *ibid.*, pp. 66ff.

kingdom, although it was still somewhat nomadic in character, was composed of states which varied in the degree of their dependence on him and with different types of political regimes.

Eduard Meyer long ago inferred, from the reference to Hadadezer as the son of Rehob (II Sam. 8:3), that there was a close affinity between Aram Beth Rehob and Aram Zobah. However, this does not mean, as Meyer at first conjectured, that these two states were identical, but merely that Beth Rehob was the homeland of Hadadezer.[7] Apparently, in the first phase of his career, Hadadezer was the ruler only of Aram Beth Rehob and then subsequently made himself master of Aram Zobah as well, amalgamating the two kingdoms in a *Personalunion*. Proof of this may be found in the fact that, in the list of the allies who hastened to the aid of Ammon in the latter's war against Israel, the armies of Aram Beth Rehob and Aram Zobah are mentioned as a single contingent, in contrast to those of Maacah and of Tob (II Sam. 10:6).[8] An analogy to this type of political association is provided by David's unification of his native land of Judah with the northern kingdom of Israel under his own personal rule. In each of these unions the native country of the ruler was the smaller of the two confederate states. Just as, in the Old Testament, David is known as the "King of Israel" (and not King of Judah), so Hadadezer's title, "King of Zobah" (II Sam. 8:3), is taken from the major political unit in his kingdom.

We may surmise that Aram Damascus was annexed to the confederation of Beth Rehob-Zobah as an occupied territory (see below), while other states became Hadadezer's satellites and kept their own rulers. Of the latter the Old Testament specifically mentions Maacah and the Land of Tob, which bordered on the kingdom of Israel and, as already stated, possessed autonomous armies. Since the king of

---

[7] Meyer, *Geschichte des Altertums*, I (1884), 364, first supposed that Beth Rehob was simply the name of the ruling dynasty in Aram Zobah, but in the later edition of his history (see n. 2), p. 252, n. 1, he regards the two as distinct entities. At the same time, he considers the reading *ben rᵉḥōḇ*, "the son of Rehob," as a corruption for the name of the country Beth Rehob. Cf. also E.G. Kraeling, *Aram and Israel* (1918), p. 42.

[8] In the parallel passage in I Chron. 19:6, Aram Beth Rehob is not mentioned. It may have been included in Zobah; or perhaps substituted by Aram-Naharaim or Aram Maacah (whose king is again referred to in the next verse). In connection with the close relation of Beth Rehob and Zobah, the LXX version of I Sam. 14:47 is also worthy of note; there not only Zobah, but also Beth Rehob is specifically listed among the enemies of Saul.

Geshur, however, is not mentioned in the struggle between Israel and Aram, it appears that he had succeeded in maintaining his neutrality between the two blocks.

The first repulsion[9] of the Arameans, which took place in the plain of Medeba (I Chron. 19:7) when they sent a relief force to the Ammonites, left Hadadezer's kingdom still intact. However, the defeat of Hadadezer in the subsequent battle of Helam, where the Arameans had been reinforced by troops from the east bank of the Euphrates (II Sam. 10:16),[10] greatly weakened his kingdom. Its more loosely attached portions, the vassal states, now threw off their allegiance completely: "And when all the kings that were servants to Hadadezer saw that they had been defeated by Israel, they made peace with Israel, and became subject to them" (II Sam. 10:19). From this it is clear that Hadadezer's satellites kept their former political regime and merely exchanged Israelite for Aramean suzerainty. This is certainly what happened on the southern periphery of Aram Zobah, when the kingdom of Maacah and the Land of Tob passed under David's rule.[11] That the border states in the north also threw off Hadadezer's yoke at this time may be inferred from the campaign which he was compelled to undertake to the Euphrates region, in order "to restore [I Chron. 18:3: to set up] his power at the river Euphrates" (II Sam. 8:3).[12] Taking advantage of Hadadezer's absence from central Syria, David launched an attack against the heart of Aram Zobah and inflicted a crushing defeat on it.

It was in this third campaign, where David took the offensive, that he succeeded in striking a really damaging blow at the core of

---

[9] The two battles described in II Samuel, chapter 10, certainly preceded that mentioned in chapter 8, which contains a resumé of David's campaigns. The war against the Arameans referred to in the latter chapter was simply the final campaign that sealed the doom of Hadadezer's kingdom. For a discussion of the chronological order of David's wars with the Arameans cf. K. Elliger, "Die Nordgrenze des Reiches Davids," *PJb*, XXXII (1936), 91ff.; A. Malamat, *The Aramaeans in Aram Naharaim and the Rise of Their States* (1952), pp. 61–62 (Hebrew).

[10] In this passage the phrase *'ebær hannāhār* is used descriptively for the area east of the river (cf. also Josh. 24:2) and not as a geographical term as mentioned above in footnote 2.

[11] David in all likelihood lopped off from the kingdom of Maacah the district to the west of the Jordan with its centre at Abel-Beth Maacah. The designation of this latter place as "a city which is a mother in Israel" (II Sam. 20:19) may indicate that a change had occurred in its political status. Cf. Mazar, *JBL*, LXXX, 28.

[12] The subject of בלכתו and ידו in II Sam. 8:3 and I Chron. 18:3 must be Hadadezer and not David as suggested by several commentators.

Hadadezer's kingdom, which thenceforth disappears from the stage of history. This core, which consisted of Aram Zobah proper and Aram Beth Rehob, embraced Coelesyria (up to the border of the land of Hamath) and the Anti-Lebanon, and bypassing the territory of Damascus extended east and north towards the Syro-Arabian desert. In the first of these regions, namely Coelesyria, lay the cities of Tibhath (II Sam. 8:8 wrongly: Betah, Egyptian: *Ṭbḥ* and cuneiform: *Tubiḫi*), Berothai and Cun, which are expressly called in the Old Testament "cities of Hadadezer" (II Sam. 8:8; I Chron. 18:8); and on the northeastern frontier was the important desert city of Tadmor (Palmyra) which commanded the caravan routes to the Euphrates.[13]

In line with our initial assumption about the manner in which the various components of Hadadezer's realm were incorporated into Israel, we must suppose that Beth Rehob and Zobah proper, which had been directly subject to Hadadezer, now passed under Israelite control as fully occupied territories and did not—as is generally held—merely become vassal states.[14] These districts henceforth formed an integral part of the empire of David and Solomon, and were consequently treated by these kings as their rightful property; David took possession of the stores of metal in the cities of Hadadezer in Coelesyria (II Sam. 8:8); and Solomon rebuilt the desert city of Tadmor, as he had done with other cities entirely subject to him (II Chron. 8:4, I Kings 9:18, according to the *qᵉri*). Moreover, the repeated biblical reference to Lebo-Hamath,[15] as a fixed point on the northern boundary of the kingdom of Israel undoubtedly indicates that Coelesyria was thought of as purely Israelite territory. It even may be conjectured that during David and Solomon's reigns there was also a spread of Israelite settlement into this region. It is

---

[13] Attempts to localize Zobah proper have been based on the data about the later Assyrian province of *Ṣubatu*. While E. Forrer, *Die Provinzeinteilung des assyrischen Reiches* (1921), p. 62, placed Zobah in Coelesyria, as well as to the east of the Anti-Lebanon range, north of Damascus, Elliger and Noth located it only in the latter area, cf. M. Noth, "Das Reich von Hamath als Grenznachbar des Reiches Israel," *PJb*, XXXIII (1937), 40ff. On the proximity of Zobah to the edge of the desert cf. W.F. Albright, *Archaeology and the Religion of Israel* (henceforth *ARI*) (1942), p. 211, n. 7. Leaving aside the precise location of Zobah—it appears certain that the combined territories of Beth Rehob—Zobah occupied both sides of the Anti-Lebanon.

[14] Cf. e.g., Alt, *KS*, II, 72.

[15] For the understanding of לבוא חמת as a distinct locality and not as the general "entrance to Hamath" cf. Noth, *ZDPV*, LVIII (1935), 242f.; *PJb*, XXXIII, 50; Elliger, *PJb*, XXXII, 40ff.; Maisler, *BJPES*, XII (1945–1946), pp. 91ff.

noteworthy in this respect that the biblical historiographers specified Lebo-Hamath as the extreme limit of the area occupied by the Israelites whose representatives gathered in Jerusalem for David's installation of the Ark (I Chron. 13:5) and again for Solomon's inaugural festivities for the Temple (I Kings 8:65; II Chron. 7:8).

In connection with David's final war against the Arameans, mention is made of a clash between his forces and those of Aram Damascus which were hurrying to Hadadezer's aid. The absence of any reference to Aram Damascus in the two previous wars cannot be used to support the assumption that II Sam. 8:5–6 is a later addition entirely devoid of historical foundation;[16] on the contrary, the appearance of the Damascene army at this late stage of the conflict shows that the Israelite invasion of Syria had created such a critical situation that Hadadezer had to mobilize all of his military resources. Quite possibly the intervention of the auxiliary contingents from Damascus had a specific strategic objective. The Israelite forces were at the time in hot pursuit of Hadadezer's army which, as stated above, had been campaigning in the direction of the Euphrates. They may actually have caught up with it somewhere in the vicinity of Hamath, as indicated in I Chron. 18:3. Clearly, then, David had advanced deep into Syria, far beyond Damascus, whose army may have planned to attack him in the rear, thus cutting the Israelite forces' extended lines of communication. A similar maneuver had been employed by the Arameans in the first engagement with Israel, when their forces had been deployed in the plain of Medeba behind Joab's army, so that "the battle was set against him both in front and in the rear" (II Sam. 10:9; I Chron. 19:7–10). But now, as then, the Israelites forestalled their enemies' stratagem and slew the Arameans' reinforcements.

It is particularly noteworthy that, in contrast to Maacah and Tob, the Old Testament makes no mention of a king or other kind of ruler of Aram Damascus. The reason for this is undoubtedly that

---

[16] Thus E. Meyer (cf. above, n. 2), p. 253 (continuation of footnote from p. 252) followed by Biram (cf. above, n. 1), pp. 79ff. They come to the surprising conclusion that Aram Damascus did not yet exist in David's time and accordingly deny the presence of an Israelite governorship there. Equally unacceptable is Biram's view, based on I Kings 11:23–25, that Hadadezer was still ruling over the kingdom of Aram Zobah in the reign of Solomon. For a historical analysis of this passage see below.

Damascus did not enjoy the status of a vassal state, but was actually a conquered territory. Hadadezer probably deposed the local dynasty and replaced it by governors appointed by himself, in much the same way as David reorganized the political regime of Edom after he had conquered it (II Sam. 8:14). If so, after Israel's victory over Aram Damascus no change was made in its existing political status, as attested by the Old Testament: "Then David put governors in Aram of Damascus" (II Sam. 8:6). It should be stressed that Damascus alone of all the districts of Syria and northern Transjordan was placed under Israelite governors. There is no basis for the commonly expressed opinion that David instituted a governorship throughout the whole of Syria, with Damascus as its administrative seat.[17]

Further proof that Aram Damascus was not an autonomous state in the time of Hadadezer may be found in the story of Rezon the son of Eliada. The Old Testament describes briefly how Rezon assumed kingship in Damascus in the reign of Solomon and how hostile relations between the two kingdoms resulted from this: "God also raised up an adversary to him, Rezon the son of Eliada, who had fled from *his master* Hadadezer king of Zobah. And he gathered men about him and become leader of a marauding band, after the slaughter by David; and they went to Damascus and dwelt there, and made him king in Damascus. He was an adversary of Israel all the days of Solomon" (I Kings 11:23–25). In all likelihood, Rezon was a native of the region of Damascus of which he was subsequently to make himself king. His direct subordination to his overlord Hadadezer implies that there was no local ruler, even of vassal status, in Damascus. The train of events that led to the establishment of the independent kingdom of Damascus has its exact analogy in David's rise to power: he too first served in Saul's army, then fled from his master, assembled a military following with whose help he finally gained the throne first in Hebron and later in Jerusalem (cf. I Chron. 11:10). Both David and Rezon took advantage of the political and military crises in their respective countries to defy their central governments; both may have been helped by their former masters' adversaries. David was welcomed by the Philistines, Saul's inveterate foes; and Rezon was perhaps at first encouraged in his separatist designs by Israel.

---

[17] Cf. e.g., Elliger, *PJb*, XXXII, 62; J. Bright, *A History of Israel* (1959), p. 182.

Two other regions must be considered in connection with David's domination of the kingdom of Hadadezer: the districts beyond the Euphrates, and the Land of Hamath. It would seem possible to find Hadadezer's conquests in the first of these two regions in later Assyrian sources.[18] These conquests took place in the reign of the Assyrian king Ashurrabi, to be more precise, in the period between his ascension to the throne (in *ca.* 1012 B.C.) and the outbreak of open hostilities between Hadadezer and David in the first decade of the tenth century B.C. Hadadezer's rule in the Trans-Euphratean region could have lasted only a few years, being brought to an end by his defeat by Israel at the battle of Helam. His subsequent attempt to re-establish his authority in this region (II Sam. 8:3) was thwarted, as already noted, by the advance of the Israelite army into Syria. In fact the biblical attribution of the border of the Israelite kingdom on the very line of the Euphrates properly reflects the complete independence of the Trans-Euphrates at the time when Hadadezer's realm disintegrated and passed under the control of David. As no information about the ultimate fate of this rebellious territory has come down to us, we cannot decide whether it became a sovereign Aramaic kingdom or was annexed to one of its neighboring states on the Euphrates, such as Beth Eden (the Bīt Adini of the cuneiform sources).[19]

B. *Israel and Hamath*

Of particular interest are the relations between Israel and Hamath, which are reflected by the embassy sent by Toi, king of Hamath, to David, following the latter's victory over Hadadezer, their common Aramean enemy (II Sam. 8:9–10; and, with slight variants, I Chron. 18:9–10). This event is usually interpreted as the conclusion of a treaty of parity between two sovereign states, which resulted incidentally in blocking any further Israelite expansion into central Syria.[20] The present writer has already suggested elsewhere[21] that the dispatch of this embassy should in actual fact not be regarded as a mere gesture of friendship but rather as an indication of Hamath's

---

[18] For further details cf. the present writer's paper, *BA*, XXI, pp. 101–102.
[19] On this state cf. Malamat, *Encyclopaedia Biblica*, Vol. II (1954), s.v. Beth Eden (cols. 94–95) (Hebrew).
[20] Cf. Alt, *KS*, II, 72–73.
[21] Cf. above, n. 3.

dependence on Israel. Among the arguments in favor of this view, stress should be laid on the great value of the gifts presented to David by the king of Hamath, the more so since they are mentioned alongside of the tribute from conquered territories and the booty taken from Hadadezer, as well as on the unusual fact that the son of the king of Hamath headed the deputation, an extraordinary measure for a routine diplomatic mission.

Further support for Israelite domination may be found in the name of the king of Hamath's son. The original name is undoubtedly preserved in the Book of Chronicles as *Hadoram* (I Chron. 18:10), a shortened form of the typically West-Semitic name Hadadram. In contrast to his father's Anatolian or Hurrian name, To'i, or To'u,[22] which is appropriate for the ruler of a neo-Hittite kingdom like Hamath, that of the son testifies to the spread of Aramaic influence in Hamath, perhaps as a result of the rise of Aram Zobah. The parallel verse in II Sam. 8:10, on the other hand, gives the son's name as *Joram*, an abbreviated form of Jehoram, replacing Hadad by a distinctly Israelite theophoric element. This should not be regarded as a textual corruption[23] but simply as a second name which the prince adopted, a practice which is well attested in royal circles throughout the Near East.[24] We do not know when Hadoram received his second name: during the embassy's stay in Jerusalem or on his accession to the throne in Hamath—or was it in some way connected with Solomon's activities in Hamath (cf. below)? At any rate the change of his name should be regarded in the light of the case where the two Judean kings Eliakim-Jehoiakim and Mattaniah-Zedekiah had their names changed at the instigation of their respective Egyptian and Babylonian overlords (II Kings 23:34; 24:17).

However that may be, the new name Joram obviously points to the existence of considerable Israelite influence in the internal affairs

---

[22] For the cuneiform equivalents of the name cf. Koehler and Baumgartner, *Lexicon in Vet. Test. Libros* (1953), p. 1035; M. Liverani, *RSO*, xxxvii (1962), 70.

[23] In contrast to the general opinion held in the commentaries on the book of Samuel (e.g. S.R. Driver, *Notes on the Hebrew Text of Samuel*[2] [1913], p. 282), which derive their support for such a corruption from the Septuagint where the name is given as Ἰεδδουράμ. However, this name apparently reflects a mixed form of the two Hebrew names, cf. *Encyclopaedia Biblica*, III (1958), col. 537.

[24] For a recent discussion cf. R. de Vaux, *Les Institutions de l'Ancient Testament*, I (1958), 165–67 (and bibliography, p. 330). For the Hittites in particular, where double royal names were a common phenomenon, cf. I.J. Gelb, "The Double Names of the Hittite Kings," *Rocznik Orientalistyczny*, XVII (1953), 146–54.

of Hamath and probably to the spread of Jahwe's worship there.[25] A similar historical situation apparently took place in the last years of the kingdom of Hamath. It seems that the last king of Hamath also bore a double name since he is called in Assyrian documents (from *ca.* 720 B.C.) either *Ilu*bidi, or *Jau*bidi, i.e., Jeho-bidi.[26] Here too the theophoric Israelite element in the name is, in our opinion, the result of respectively Israelite or Judean influence in, or even domination of, Hamath under Jeroboam II (cf. II Kings 14:28) and Uzziah.[27]

In view of all this it would seem reasonable to assume that Hamath—whose independence had already been curtailed by Hadadezer—became a satellite of David as a result of the latter's victory.[28] Israel's domination of this region at that time is also implied by what is related in the biblical source about the later conquests of Jeroboam II: "And now *he recovered* for Israel Damascus and Hamath" (II Kings 14:28). The references in Chronicles to Solomon's activities in the region of Hamath also do not appear, as has been widely accepted, to be completely devoid of historical foundation: "And Solomon went to Hamath-Zobah, and took it.[29] He built

---

[25] It must be admitted, however, that we possess no explicit evidence for the spread of the cult of Jahweh amongst other nations; but cf. n. 28. Mazar (Maisler) has already remarked on the replacement of foreign theophoric elements by the Jahwe-element in the names of David's ministers, cf. B. Maisler, "The Scribe of King David and the Problem of the High Officials in the Ancient Kingdom of Israel," *BJPES*, XIII (1946–1947), 105–14. Cf. also A. Murtonen, "The Appearance of the name *YHWH* outside Israel," *Studia Orientalia*, XVI, 3 (1951), 3ff.

[26] For the various spellings of this name cf. M. El-Amin, "Die Reliefs mit Beischriften von Sargon II," *Sumer*, X (1954), 27, who, however, wrongly supposes that they go back to an original compound form Ilujaubidi. The theophoric change in our case has its exact parallel in the change of the royal Judean name *Eli*akim-*Jeho*iakim.

[27] For Uzziah's influence in Hamath cf. now H. Tadmor, "Azriyau of Yaudi," *Scripta Hierosolymitana*, VIII (1961), 232ff. There is no justification for going as far as Eduard Meyer (*Geschichte des Altertums*, II, 2³, 433) and Albright (*Encyclopaedia Biblica*, III [1958], col. 200), who concluded from the name Jau-bi'di that the king of Hamath was of actual Israelite origin.

[28] This possibility is also hinted at, but without any supporting evidence, by A. Dupont-Sommer, *Les araméens* (1949), pp. 27–28. O. Eissfeldt sees a reference to the subject status of Hamath in David's reign in Ps. 76:11 (English Versions 76:10), which he renders: "*Hamath Aram*" (for חֲמַת אָדָם i.e. "the wrath of men") bekennt dich, der Rest von *Hamat* (for חמה, "wrath") "feiert dich";—meaning that both, the part of Hamath which was previously under Aramean rule, and the rest of Hamath, now acknowledge of Jahweh. See *ThLZ*, LXXXII (1957), 801ff.

[29] Unger (*Aramaeans*, p. 54) infers from these words that Solomon made a punitive expedition against Hamath after it had revolted. The compound name Hamath-Zobah

Tadmor in the wilderness and all the store-cities which he built in Hamath" (II Chron. 8:3–4). If we accept this statement it would mean that David's successor tightened his hold on Hamath, carrying out extensive building projects in its territory. Perhaps the beginning of stratum E in the excavations of the city of Hamath may be assigned to this activity.[30] It may be noted in this connection that one of the buildings in this stratum, which the excavators conjectured to be a sanctuary, had an entrance which was, apparently, flanked by two pillars. This feature may have been influenced by Solomon's temple (which had two pillars called "Yachin" and "Boaz")[31] even though the architectural origin appears to go back to a Phoenician source.

Solomon presumably intensified Israel's control over Hamath in pursuance of his policy of developing trade relations with the neo-Hittite states, and particularly with the land of Kue in southern Anatolia (I Kings 10:28–29), whose products were transshiped to Israel via Hamath. In this connection it is instructive to note that the verse from II Chronicles quoted above attributes to Solomon the building of *store-cities*[32] which were specifically intended for the warehousing of goods.

C. *David's and Solomon's Foreign Marriages*

Marriage alliances between royal houses, as a means of concluding treaties and cementing the relations between the two states concerned, were a common occurrence in the ancient Near East, the more so since in antiquity diplomatic contacts were primarily intended

---

would appear to indicate that the territory of Hamath was subject to Zobah. However, the generally accepted view is that the Chronicler here made use of a purely geographical designation current at a later period, when Zobah no longer existed as a sovereign state. Cf., Elliger, *PJb*, XXXII, 56ff.; Noth, *PJb*, XXXIII, 46ff. For another explanation of the name cf. J. Lewy, *HUCA*, XVIII (1944), 443–54.

[30] Though the exact date of the beginning of this stratum is still uncertain, it cannot be brought down any later than the tenth century B.C. Albright favors an early date for stratum E and even considers assigning the reign of Toi to it (*Encyclopaedia Biblica*, Vol. III, col. 196). The excavators of the site, on the other hand, lower its beginning to the end of the tenth century. This would make Solomon's reign correspond to stratum F I (*ca.* 1075–925 B.C.). Cf. E. Fugmann, *Hama, L'architecture des périodes préhelléniques* (1958), pp. 149, 275, 278.

[31] Cf. Fugmann, *ibid.*, p. 190.

[32] For another explanation of the Hebrew phrase *'ārey misk'nōt*, "cities [built] by forced labor," cf. E.A. Speiser, *Orientalia*, XXVII 1958), 27.

to serve the interests of the ruling dynasties. The imperialistic nature of Israelite foreign policy in the reigns of David and Solomon is strikingly demonstrated by the wholesale adoption of this practice.

Almost at the very start of his reign, David resorted to this expedient in his marriage to the daughter of Talmai, King of Geshur (II Sam. 3:3; I Chron. 3:2). This step, taken by David while he was still king of the House of Judah at Hebron, was no doubt aimed against the northern tribes loyal to Ishbaal, for the bond of marriage gained for David an ally to the north of Ishbaal's kingdom and placed the latter in a precarious strategic position between Geshur and Judah. A further result of this alliance was the neutralization of Geshur during the later conflict between Israel and Aram (see above, p. 3). David used the political institution of foreign marriage for his sons as well as for himself. Thus he married Solomon to Naamah, an Ammonite princess, from whose union Rehoboam, the heir to the throne, was born (I Kings 14:21,[33] 31). Since Rehoboam was forty-one when he ascended the throne, he must have been born a short time before the beginning of Solomon's forty years' reign. This means that Solomon's marriage to Naamah took place in the last years of David's reign, apparently at the time when open rivalry between his sons for the succession broke out. By such a marriage David may have intended to strengthen Solomon's claim to the throne since Solomon, who was not the firstborn, would not automatically become king on David's death. See now chap. 12.

Of all the kings of Israel and Judah Solomon is outstanding for the widespread scale of international marriages in which he engaged, making them a corner-stone of his foreign policy. The Old Testament mentions his marriages with Moabite, Ammonite, Edomite, Sidonian, and Hittite princesses, and—most important of all—with the daughter of Pharaoh (I Kings 11:1). However, apart from the last, only one of these foreign wives, Naamah the Ammonite, is specifically mentioned. The Hellenistic sources also speak of Solomon's marriage to a daughter of Hiram, king of Tyre, i.e., a "Sidonian" princess;[34]

---

[33] According to the addition in the LXX, Naamah was the daughter of the Ammonite king Hanun, the son of Nahash. Cf. chap. 13.

[34] See the references in L. Desnoyers, *Histoire du peuple hébreu*, III (1930), 40, n. 1 (add the evidence of Eupolemos, in Eusebius *Preap. Evang.*, IX, 34). Perhaps an allusion to this marriage may also be found in Psalm 45, where the nuptials of the king of Israel and a Tyrian princess are referred to. Although this Psalm is usually

but the historical validity of this tradition is doubtful. It may be just another of the later legends that grew up around the relations between Solomon and Hiram.

It was only natural for a shrewd politician like Solomon, who regarded diplomatic marriage as fundamental for his foreign relations, to make use of this political device in the case of his heir. He therefore caused Rehoboam to marry, in addition to his wives from the house of David, a princess from one of the neighboring countries, namely Maacah, the daughter of Ab(i)shalom, who became the mother of the crown prince Abijah-Abijam (I Kings 15:2; II Chron. 11:20–22).[35] That this marriage was brought about during the reign of Solomon and most likely at his instigation can be determined from the length of reign of Rehoboam (17 years) and of Abijah (3 years) and from the fact that Abijah's son, Asa, had already reached the age of manhood when he ascended the throne. This would make Abijah over thirty when he died, which means that he was born, at the latest, in the twenties of Solomon's reign. Maacah's non-Israelite origin is evident not only from her name[36] but even more so from her introduction of the *asherah*-cult into Jerusalem (I Kings 15:13). The *asherah* was worshipped in Phoenicia, from where its cult spread into the adjoining regions. Presumably, then, Maacah was a native of one of the countries to the north of Israel, and "the abominable *asherah*-image" which she set up in Jerusalem should be looked upon as one in the series of foreign deities whose worship took root in the Israelite capital as a result of Solomon's own marriages (I Kings 11:4–8).

It is noteworthy that the first three successors of David on the throne in Jerusalem were apparently all the offsprings of foreign wives: it stands to reason that Solomon's mother, Bathsheba, once

---

assigned to Ahab or one of his successors, there is no valid reason why it cannot be dated to Solomon's time. For such an early date cf. Desnoyers, *op. cit.*, p. 40, n. 1 and 2, also N.H. Tur-Sinai, *Halashon We-Hassefer*, II (1950), 19–20 (Hebrew).

[35] Because of the contradictory evidence in the Bible, the identity of Abijah's mother is disputed; but the majority of the biblical sources give her name as Maacah. Cf. S. Yeivin, "Abijam, Asa and Maacah the Daughter of Abishalom," *BJPES*, X (1942–1943), 116–19 (reprinted in his book, *Studies in the History of Israel and Its Land* [1959], pp. 236–39 [Hebrew]).

[36] On the foreign character of the name cf. Abright, *ARI*, pp. 158, 219, n. 104. The name of her father, Abshalom, as well as those of her children, Abijam (which was, apparently, later changed to Abijah), Ziza, and Shelomith, also have a non-Israelite ring (cf. chap. 12).

the wife of Uriah the Hittite, would have been herself a foreigner, probably stemming from the local aristocracy of Jerusalem;[37] Naamah was an Ammonite princess, and Maacah as noted above was a foreigner. This was certainly no mere coincidence but rather the result of a policy deliberately followed by the Davidic dynasty in its early days (chap. 13).

Of all of Solomon's wives, pride of place at the royal court was accorded to the daughter of Pharaoh. She is mentioned no fewer than five times in the chapters dealing with Solomon's reign: (1) At the opening of the records of Solomon: "Solomon made a marriage alliance with Pharaoh king of Egypt; he took Pharaoh's daughter and brought her into the city of David, until he had finished building his own house and the house of the Lord and the wall around Jerusalem" (I Kings 3:1). This is the only explicit reference to the actual marriage. (2) In the description of the construction of the royal palace: "He also made a house like this hall for Pharaoh's daughter whom he had taken" (I Kings 7:8). (3) In the passage about the Egyptian conquest of Gezer: "Pharaoh king of Egypt had gone up and captured Gezer and burnt it with fire, and had slain the Canaanites who dwelt in the city, and had given it as dowry to his daughter, Solomon's wife" (I Kings 9:16). (4) In the description of the building activities in Jerusalem: "But Pharaoh's daughter went up from the city of David to her own house which Solomon had built for her; then he built the Millo" (I Kings 9:24; cf. II Chron. 8:11). (5) In the list of Solomon's foreign wives: "Now king Solomon loved many foreign women: the daughter of Pharaoh, and Moabite, Ammonite, Edomite, Sidonian, and Hittite women" (I Kings 11:1).

This fivefold repetition indicates the importance of Solomon's marriage to the daughter of Pharaoh in Israelite historiography. Furthermore, the mention of this event in five quite different contexts, all of them of apparent archival nature, places its veracity beyond doubt. It is therefore remarkable that scholars have thus far paid little attention to the politically significant consequences of this absolutely unique event in the annals of not only Israel but Egypt as well.[38] In every

---

[37] For the Jebusite-Hurrian origin of Uriah and Bathsheba, and the implications of David's marriage to the latter, cf. Yeivin, *Zion*, IX (1944), 63–67; Maisler, *BJPES*, XIII (1947–48), 111–14 (Hebrew).

[38] Some scholars actually minimize the importance of this event, e.g. R. Kittel, *Geschichte des Volkes Israel*, II⁶⁻⁷ (1925), 147; M. Noth, *Geschichte Israels*³ (1956), 198.

other instance of a diplomatic marriage made by one of the kings of Israel, the wife was taken from a second-rank state; and while Egypt, in the heyday of its greatness, conducted an intensive policy of marriage alliances, it did so only with the leading contemporary powers (e.g. Mitanni, Babylonia, Hatti). But for our purpose, the supremely significant fact is that, whereas the kings of Egypt frequently took the daughters of foreign potentates as wives, there is no other attested instance apart from that of Solomon, of a *daughter* of Pharaoh being given in marriage to a foreign ruler.[39] Indeed, there is explicit evidence, from the Amarna age[40] down to the time of Herodotus,[41] that an actual daughter of Pharaoh was never married to a foreigner.

D. *The Historical Implications of Solomon's Marriage with the Daughter of Pharaoh*

It follows from the foregoing facts that Solomon's marriage with Pharaoh's daughter was an act of exceptional political significance which testifies, in our opinion, to Egypt's inferior status as a political power vis-à-vis Israel at that time. This view is confirmed by Pharaoh's handing over to Solomon the important fortress city of Gezer, obviously a territorial concession made in the guise of a dowry for his daughter. Israel's military and political superiority over Egypt

---

For a contrasting view cf. Thieberger, *King Solomon* (1947), p. 136, where the significance of the event is stressed but no conclusions are drawn from it.

[39] On specious instances of the daughters of Egyptian kings being given in marriage to foreign dignitaries cf. the present writer's article in *BA*, XXI, 97f. None of the proposed examples has any validity.

[40] The request of the king of Babylon for the hand of the daughter of Amenhotep III was rebuffed in the following words: "From of old a daughter of the king of Egypt has not been given to anyone," (EA, 4, ll. 6–7). Cf. S.A.B. Mercer, *The Tell El-Amarnah Tablets*, I (1939), 12–13. Found at Boghazkeui was a badly preserved Akkadian copy of a communication between the Egyptian and Hittite courts in which the latter suggests that a daughter of Ramesses II—born to him presumably by his Hittite wife—be sent to Hatti "for queenship in another country." (KBo, I, 23; cf. B. Meissner, *ZDMG*, LXXII [1918], 62f.) What is implied is an eventual marriage with an Anatolian ruler. No text containing the Egyptian reply to this suggestion is extant, but, in all probability, as in the EA letter referred to above, it would comprise a denial. And this appears to be anticipated in that it was found necessary to lay claim to an approval by the Egyptian gods of the Hittite request (cf. ll. 5ff.).

[41] Herodotus iii.1.

at this juncture is not very surprising, when the following two facts are borne in mind: (a) The political weakness of Egypt in the Twenty-first Dynasty (*ca.* 1085–945 B.C.),[42] resulting from the split of the country into the kingdom of Tanis in the north and the Theban theocracy in the south. We would expect that only the former came into contact with Israel. (b) The great strength of the Israelite kingdom in the early years of Solomon's reign, when the new monarch skillfully took full advantage of his father's military and political achievements.

We shall now examine the historical circumstances which led to Solomon's marriage, as well as its political implications. The biblical source specifies neither the date of this event nor that of the Egyptian attack on Gezer which preceded it. However, the vague chronological reference in I Kings 3:1 implies that both occurred in the first years of Solomon's reign, before the completion of the temple and certainly before the construction of the royal palace had been finished. The work on the temple was ended in the eleventh year of Solomon's reign (I Kings 6:38), i.e., 959 B.C., according to the widely accepted chronology, thus providing the *terminus post quem* for the date of the marriage. Moreover, there is good reason to suppose that the Egyptian attack on Gezer took place shortly after the death of David, which occurred in the second or third year of Solomon's reign.[43] As in other cases after the long reign of a monarch whose death offered his enemies a good opportunity for attack, so Pharaoh presumably regarded David's death as the favorable moment for launching an Egyptian invasion of Palestine, all the more so since Solomon was at this time occupied with liquidating his domestic rivals. This assumption finds support in the action of the Edomite prince Hadad, who had found asylum in Egypt after David's conquest of Edom. As soon as the news of the deaths of David and Joab, his commander-in-chief, reached Egypt, Hadad hurriedly returned to his native land, in order to liberate it from Solomon's rule (I Kings 11:21). The dating of the marriage with the daughter of Pharaoh to the beginning of Solomon's reign as sole ruler is in keeping with the position occupied by the event in the sequence of the biblical

---

[42] On this dynasty, see the recent discussions in E. Drioton and J. Vandier, *L'Egypte*[3] (1952), 511–22; A. Gardiner, *Egypt of the Pharaohs* (1961), pp. 316ff.

[43] Solomon apparently reigned for two or three years as coregent with his father; cf. Yeivin, *Encyclopaedia Biblica*, Vol. II, col. 640.

narrative. The report of the marriage (I Kings 3:1) follows immediately on the story about Shimei, who was put to death in, of shortly
after, the third year of Solomon's reign (I Kings 2:39)—that is to
say soon after David's death—and before the account of the building of the temple, which began in the fourth year of the reign (I
Kings 6:1).

Who was the Egyptian king who invaded Palestine and formed a
marriage alliance with the house of David? Although no definite
answer can, in the present state of our knowledge, be given to this
question, the choice, on chronological grounds, rests between Siamun
and Psusennes II, the last two kings of the Twenty-first Dynasty,
who ruled in the first half of Solomon's reign. On the basis of the
chronological data provided by the contemporary Egyptian sources—
as in contrast to Eusebius' recension of Manetho according to which
Psusennes ruled 35 years—the Pharaoh in question can only be
Siamun, who came to the throne several years before Solomon and
reigned for about seventeen years (ca. 976–958 B.C.).[44] Further
confirmation for this identification may be found in a relief from
Tanis, on which Siamun is shown smiting an enemy armed with a
weapon characteristic of the Sea Peoples. From this Montet, the
excavator of the site, has conjectured that Gezer was captured by
Siamun in the course of a campaign against the Philistines.[45] However,
Montet has recently modified his view in that it was only Siamun's
successor. Psusennes II, who was compelled to cede the city to
Solomon and enter into a marriage alliance with him.[46] This latter
theory is not only without foundation, but actually runs counter to
the biblical evidence, according to which Solomon's father-in-law
was identical with the Pharaoh who conquered Gezer.

The possibility of a campaign of Siamun into Philistia is also suggested by various archeological finds unearthed in Palestine. An illuminating discovery is that of a scarab bearing the name of Siamun,
which was found in the excavations of Tell el-Farʿah in the western

---

[44] Cf. J. Goldwasser, *BJPES*, XIV (1949), 82–84 (Hebrew). Goldwasser rightly
rules out any possibility of identifying the father-in-law of Solomon with Shishak
(Sheshonk), as was done by scholars of the previous generation. On the various versions of Manetho for the length of the reigns of the Egyptian kings cf. W. Helck,
Untersuchungen zu Manetho und den ägyptischen Königslisten (1956), p. 72.

[45] P. Montet, *Le drame d'Avaris* (1940), pp. 195ff.; Fig. 58.

[46] *Idem, L'Égypte et la bible* (1959), p. 42.

Negeb.[47] This site, which is apparently to be identified with ancient Sharuhen, was one of the keypoints on the road running northwards from Egypt to the Philistine cities. From the very beginning of the Eighteenth Dynasty, when it was captured by Ahmose I, until the breakdown of Egypt's domination of Canaan, Sharuhen was an Egyptian stronghold. Accordingly, it would appear that Siamun may have re-established Egyptian control there at the time of his attack on Gezer. At any rate, the scarab certainly is evidence of some sort of connection between Egypt and this site during the reign of Siamun. The strategic importance of Tell el-Far'ah in the tenth century is evident from the discovery there of the remains of a fortress which excavators have attributed to Shishak, who campaigned in Palestine in the fifth year of Rehoboam. Nevertheless, there are indications that the construction of the fortress should be dated earlier and might therefore be ascribed to Siamun.[48]

Another indication that Siamun overran Philistia is provided by the archeological evidence from Tel Mor, 6 km. to the northwest of ancient Ashdod. M. Dothan, who excvated the site in 1959–1960, has shown that the settlement there (i.e. stratum III) was completely destroyed in the first half of the tenth century.[49] It would be difficult to date this destruction as late as the reign of Shishak because of the complete absence of the Cypro-Phoenician pottery which is found in abundance in all the other coastal sites from at least the middle of the tenth century onwards. Nor can the place have been destroyed by David, since there is no reason to suppose, as we shall see below, that he ever penetrated so deep into Philistia. The only possible historical candidate who was capable of capturing the site would have been the same Egyptian ruler who attacked Gezer; just as he destroyed this latter place without re-building it himself, so he razed Tel Mor so completely that no new settlement arose on the site till the eighth century. Possibly other Philistine cities also felt the military might of

---

[47] Cf. F. Petrie, *Beth Pelet*, I (1930), Pl. 29:259.

[48] On the fortress cf. Petrie, *ibid.*, Pl. LIX. For its possible dating to Solomon's time cf. M. Dothan, *BJPES*, XVIII (1953–54), 287. It could of course have been Solomon himself who built it, as he did in the case of another site in Philistia (see below, p. 16).

[49] See the report on the first season's dig: "The Excavations at Tel Mor in 1959," *BJPES*, XXIV (1960), 120ff. Dr. Dothan has informed me that the results of the second season's work confirm the above conclusions. (In contrast to the remarks of S. Yeivin [cf. below, n. 52], *JQR*, L, 208f., n. 69).

the Pharaoh in the course of his march on Gezer and were similarly laid waste.[50] In the light of this assumption, a re-evaluation of the archeological finds unearthed in various sites in the Philistine region would seem to be called for.

Even if the archeological evidence from this area is not yet as clear as might be wished, it can be confidently asserted that an Egyptian campaign against Gezer, on the northeast border of Philistia, was fully in accord with Egypt's traditional policy from the time of the New Kingdom of regarding Philistia as an appendage. Gezer had been one of the last strongholds in Canaan which remained under the rule of the kings of the Twentieth Dynasty, as is evident from the discovery there of a faience inlay bearing the name of Ramesses IX (end of the twelfth century B.C.).[51] It is, therefore, not at all surprising that Siamun should have tried to regain the control of Philistia which it had lost about a century and a half earlier. Moreover, we may wonder whether the ultimate objective of Siamun's campaign was anything less than the conquest of the kingdom of Israel itself.[52] Such an assumption would explain the advance of the Egyptian forces as far as Gezer, which stood right on the Israelite frontier. As in the days of the Egyptian empire, when Philistia had been the bridgehead for the conquest of all Canaan, so now it could have been expected that, with the fall of Gezer, the way would be paved for the victorious Egyptian army to penetrate into the heart of the kingdom of Israel. Any such expectation was thwarted, however, by the military strength of Israel at the time.

The scholars who hold that the whole of Philistia ws subject to David, with Gezer remaining a foreign enclave within his domain, might ponder how Pharaoh could have had access to Gezer without

---

[50] It may be that Beth-Shemesh (level II b) was also destroyed by Siamun, a possibility suggested by Professor G.E. Wright to me in the course of a lecture which I delivered at Harvard in April 1962. Professor Wright formerly attributed the destruction of the city to Pharaoh Shishak (*JBL*, LXXV [1956], 216; cf. also *BASOR*, No. 155 [1959], pp. 28–29). However Shishak does not include this town in the list of his Palestine conquests at Karnak.

[51] R.A.S. Macalister, *The Excavation of Gezer*, III (1912), 195:74. The author has misread the name as Ramesses X, as Mr. M. Broshi has pointed out to me.

[52] S. Yeivin has suggested this campaign and especially the later one of Shishak had the primary economic objective of forestalling the threat from an Israelite-Tyrian alliance to the trade monopoly, which he alleges was in Egyptian hands, in southern Palestine. Cf. S. Yeivin, "Did the Kingdom of Israel Have a Maritime Policy?" *JQR*, L (1960), 203.

violating Israel's territorial integrity, thereby provoking an open war. It is also hardly credible that both David and Solomon, who ruled over an empire, were not strong enough themselves to wipe out this foreign enclave but had to depend upon Egypt's magnanimity for its acquisition. Albright, who believes that the Philistines were subject to David, attempts to overcome the difficulties by emending the pertinent biblical text.[53] He takes exception to the threefold mention of Gezer in I Kings 9:15–16 and for the first two occurrences substitutes the graphically close name *Gerar*, a city in the northern Negeb. However, the general structure of the passage shows that such an emendation is unnecessary. The reference to the rebuilding of Gezer by Solomon is in fact accompanied by a gloss on the city's recent history, as is the case with other cities;[54] this is why the name Gezer is repeatedly mentioned (see below). Nor can we rely on the statement of Macalister, the excavator of Gezer, that there are no certain traces indicating the destruction of the city in the tenth century. On the contrary, in a recent re-examination of the data given in the archeological report on Gezer, Yadin has found evidence for assuming that the city wall had been breached at that time by, in his opinion, the Pharaoh mentioned in the Bible.[55] In view of this, no objections appear to be forthcoming which might invalidate the foregoing assumptions that Gezer seems to have been the northeasternmost outpost of a solid area of Philistine-ruled territory.

A close examination of the biblical sources actually shows that, although David broke the military power of the Philistines, he did not, for some reason, conquer their country.[56] The only support that can be found for the opposite view—apart from the description of the extent of Solomon's kingdom (see below)—is a single passage and that of uncertain meaning: "After this David defeated the Philistines and subdued them, and David took *mæṭæg hāammā(h)* out

---

[53] Cf. *JPOS*, IV (1924), 143–44; *ARI*, pp. 137; 213, n. 29.

[54] For further examples cf. the present writer's paper, Hazor, "The Head of All Those Kingdoms," *JBL*, LXXIX (1960), 12.

[55] Cf. Y. Yadin, "Hazor, Gezer and Megiddo in Solomon's Times," in *The Kingdoms of Israel and Judah* (ed. A. Malamat, 1961), p. 77 (Hebrew).

[56] For this widely held opinion for which several explanations have been proposed, cf. e.g., R. Kittel, *Geschichte des Volkes Israel*, II[6-7] (1925), 115; T.H. Robinson, *A History of Israel*, I (1932), 224; E. Auerbach, *Wüste und Gelobtes Land*, I[2] (1938), 223; M. Noth, *Geschichte Israels*[3] (1956), 178. An intermediate approach is adopted by Alt, *KS*, II, 49, 69, who holds that David established only his own personal authority over Philistia without really occupying it.

of the hand of the Philistines" (II Sam. 8:1). Unfortunately, no satis-factory explanation of the obscure expression *mœtæg hāammā(h)* has been hitherto found.[57] In the parallel verse I Chron. 18:1, it is replaced by "*Gaṯh u-ḇ'nōṯœ(y)hā*"—"and he took *Gath and its villages* out of the hand of the Philistines." Even though this statement in itself may have a historical basis it is merely to be regarded as an ancient attempt to interpret the obscure wording in Samuel. In any case whether *mœtæg hāammā(h)* is a place-name or a designation of an object (real or symbolic), its usage in the sentence presumably has a restrictive force, i.e. though David actually did subdue the Philistines, it was only *mœtæg hāammā(h)* which he took from them. Nothing is said here about the occupation of Philistia, the imposi-tion of tribute on it, or the establishment of an Israelite governing authority within its borders. The silence on these details is particu-larly significant in the light of the documentary nature of the chap-ter from which the passage under discussion comes. Indeed, in the case of Moab, Aram, and Edom—the other countries defeated by David—the form of their subjection to Israel is explicitly specified: "And the Moabites became servants to David and brought tribute" (II Sam. 8:2); "then David put governors in Aram Damascus; and the Arameans became servants to David, and brought tribute" (II Sam. 8:6); "and he put governors in Edom, and all the Edomites became servants to David" (II Sam. 8:14). The absence of any such details about the Philistines, therefore, speaks for itself.[58]

It is true that the Old Testament extols the great deliverance wrought by David for his people in freeing them from the Philistine yoke (II Sam. 3:18; 19:10) and even lists the Philistines among the defeated nations from whom David carried off spoils (II Sam. 8:12). However, these verses, couched as they are in the most general terms, undoubtedly refer to David's victories over the enemy outside the

---

[57] The many far-fetched explanations of this phrase—supposing indeed that the text is not corrupt—are due to the fact that the word אמה is capable of several different interpretations ("arm," "cubit," or "water-channel"). See the commentaries on the Book of Samuel and the literature listed there, to which may be added the special discussion of S. Tolkowsky, "Metheg ha-Ammah," *JPOS*, I (1921), 195–201; A. Alt, *ZAW*, LIV (1936), 149–52; W.F. Albright, "Dwarf Craftsmen," etc., *IEJ*, IV (1954), 3ff.

[58] This point was stressed by O. Eissfeldt, Israelitische-Grenzverschiebungen, etc., *ZDPV* LXVI (1943) 118, a study which was not available to us before the com-pletion of this article. I thank Dr. J.E. Kiew, librarian at the Hebrew Union College-Jewish Institute of Religion, for supplying a photostat of Eissfeldt's paper.

confines of Philistia or—at the very most—in its border regions. This is also the picture that emerges from all the passages in which the theater of operations against the Philistines is explicitly stated.

After the expulsion of the enemy from Judah proper, the battle-front shifted to the northern borderlands of Philistia: "And David . . . smote the Philistines from Geba [I Chron. 14:16: from Gibeon] to Gezer" (II Sam. 5:25). Gezer itself did not fall to David but remained under Philistine rule, even though its population must have been predominantly Canaanite (cf. I Chron. 20:4). The same holds true for the engagements with the Philistines described in the tales of the heroic feats performed by David's champions (II Sam. 21:15–22; cf. the parallel passage in I Chron. 20:4–8, which has many variants). The text mentions three battlefields: Nob, Gob, and Gath. The first of these is, no doubt, a corruption of Gob which occurs twice further on. There are good grounds for the conjecture that Gob, a name found only here, is simply an abbreviated form of Gibbethon, a city close to Gezer;[59] while Gath, whose capture is apparently also referred to in I Chron. 18:1, is not the well-known Philistine city-state (see below) but a place in northern Philistia the location of which should also be sought in the vicinity of Gezer.[60] The battles in question were therefore fought in the vicinity of Gezer, on the edge of the territory of Ekron (Khirbat al-Muqanna?). David may have actually lopped off one of the northern border districts of this latter kingdom but he did not penetrate deep into Philistia, nor did he conquer its principal cities.

The correctness of this conclusion is confirmed by the case of the city-state of Gath, in southern Philistia, which still retained its independence in the third year of Solomon's reign, as is evident from the incident of the flight of Shimei's slaves to Achish king of Gath (I Kings 2:39–40). The remission of these fugitives to their master

---

[59] For this identification cf. O. Eissfeldt, *op. cit.*, 120–22. On the location of Gibbethon at Tel el-Melat, 5 km., west of Gezer, cf. G. von Rad, "Das Reich Israel und die Philister," *PJb*, XXIX (1933), 30ff.

[60] Alt in *PJb*, XXXV (1939), 100–104, and particularly Mazar, *IEJ*, IV (1954), 227–35 (cf. also "Gittaim" in the *Encyclopaedia Biblica*, Vol. II) have shown that a distinction must be made between the city of the Philistine Pentapolis and that of a northern Gath. The latter which may be identical with Gittaim, Mazar would locate at Tell Ras Abu Hamid near Ramlah, about 7 km., northwest of Gezer. In the present writer's opinion, the passage under discussion here should be added to the list of references for a northern Gath.

does not necessarily imply, as usually held, that Gath was a dependency of Israel.[61] The extradition of refugees of all kinds (whether nobles or men of lower class) was not only one of the legal obligations imposed on a vassal state, but even an article of a "parity treaty," i.e. one between equally sovereign states.[62] However, by Rehoboam's reign Gath had become an Israelite city, as is shown by its inclusion in the list of the cities which he fortified (II Chron. 11:8). In other words, Gath's independence came to an end at some time between the third year of Solomon's reign and the time when Rehoboam began to fortify the Judean border. This change of status was most likely related to the events which took place during the course of Solomon's marriage with the daughter of Pharaoh and the subsequent handing over of Gezer to him.[63]

It would seem that not only Gezer but the whole kingdom of Ekron, of which Gezer was apparently a part,[64] also came under Israelite rule. This likelihood is suggested by Mazar's study of the list of cities in the territory of Dan in Josh. 19:40–46, the compilation of which he assigns to the time of the United Kingdom.[65] On various grounds, Mazar concludes that those regions of the territory of Dan which stretched to the east and north of Gezer had already been included within the kingdom of David, while those to the west and south of Gezer (Timnah, Ekron, Gibbethon, and Baalath), which are in fact coterminous with the area occupied by the kingdom of Ekron, were not annexed to Israel until Solomon's time.

In this respect it is instructive that, in the list of the fortified cities built by Solomon, Gezer is mentioned together with Baalath (I Kings 9:18; II Chron. 8:6). There is nothing to prevent us from identifying the latter with the Baalath in the territory of Dan (Josh. 19:44),

---

[61] Cf. e.g. J.A. Montgomery, *The Books of Kings*, "Int. Crit. Com." (1951), p. 96.

[62] As clearly exemplified by the clauses of the treaty between Ramesses II and Hattushili III, cf. *ANET* (1950), pp. 200–201.

[63] Cf. Eissfeldt, *op. cit.*, p. 123.

[64] For Ekron as a metropolis with other cities dependent on it cf. Josh. 15:45.

[65] Cf. his paper, "The Cities of the Territory of Dan," *IEJ*, X (1960), 65–77. Mazar is of the opinion that the second of Solomon's nomes (I Kings 4:9), like the whole administrative division of his kingdom, goes back to David's reign; whereas the list of the Levitical cities (including Gezer and the Danite cities of Eltekeh, Gibbethon, Ayalon and Gath-rimmon) dates, in the main, from Solomon's time. For a different view see Y. Aharoni, "The Districts of Israel and Judah," in *The Kingdoms of Israel and Judah* (ed. A. Malamat, 1961), pp. 112ff.

which lies about 10 km. to the west of Ekron.[66] This would mean that Solomon fortified a second city in Philistine territory, which like its neighbor Gezer may also have been destroyed at the time of Siamun's campaign.

The implication of the preceding is that Gezer's annexation to Israel should be regarded as only one incident of a large scale transfer of Philistine areas to Solomon's rule. It is quite possible that, in addition to the states of Ekron and Gath, other regions stretching towards the territories of Gaza also came under Israelite control.[67] On this assumption, the statement of the extent of Solomon's empire in the south takes on new significance: "Solomon ruled over all the kingdoms from the River (Euphrates), *the land of the Philistines*,[68] and unto the border of Egypt. . . . For he had dominion over all *'eḇær hannāhār* from Tiphsah *unto Gaza*" (I Kings, MT 5:1, 4; English Versions 4:21, 24). Taken together, these two passages amount to an explicit statement that all Philistia as far as (but excluding) Gaza was within the boundaries of the Israelite empire. This expansion to the south is not, as generally taken, a retrospective reflection of the territorial expansion of Israel in David's reign but rather a result of Solomon's own political achievements.

If the assumption that considerable areas of Philistia had been transferred to Solomon's control is correct, the question then arises

---

[66] The identification of the two places is seemingly already implied by Josephus (*Antiq.* viii. 6,1). Cf. also Z. Kallai, *The Northern Boundaries of Judah* (1960), pp. 31–32 (Hebrew), where Baalath is identified with El-Mughar. Aharoni, "The Northern Boundary of Judah," *PEQ*, XC (1958), 30, has located it at Qatra, a little to the south.

[67] E.g. the kingdom of Ashdod. On the other hand, it is most improbable, in the present writer's opinion, that Ashkelon and its dependencies came under Israelite rule. This seems to be indicated by the absence of Jaffo—which the Assyrian sources show to have been part of the kingdom of Ashkelon—from the list of Danite cities, which, as was stated above, reflects the political situation prevailing at the time of the United Kingdom. Equally characteristics is the absence of Ashkelon and its dependencies—in contrast to Ekron, Ashdod, and Gaza—from the list of cities in the tribal territory of Judah (Josh. 15:45–47), though we cannot be certain of the exact period reflected by this document.

[68] This wording is to be preferred, as a *lectio difficilior*, to the parallel passage in II Chron. 9:26, "*unto* the land of the Philistines" (עד ארץ פלשתים), which is an attempt to explain the reading in Kings. At the same time, the passage in Kings may well be "defective and may have included originally a brief list of the principal subject countries (of Israel)" of which only the mention of Philistia has survived; cf. Albright, *ARI*, p. 213, n. 29. In any case, the phrase "the land of the Philistines" is certainly not to be regarded as a later gloss as proposed by some commentators (cf. Montgomery, *Kings*, pp. 127, 131).

why the Old Testament mentions only Gezer in this connection. The answer is to be found in the nature of the context. It has already been suggested above that the report given in I Kings 9:16 of Pharaoh's campaign against Gezer and the subsequent ceding of the city of Solomon is only a parenthetical remark, whose insertion was brought about by the listing of the cities fortified by Solomon.[69] In other words, the main subject of the passage is not Solomon's marriage and the dowry that went with his Egyptian bride but the city of Gezer and what had happened to it immediately before it was rebuilt by Solomon.

It is difficult to regard the ceding of Gezer as no more than the Egyptian demonstration of friendship for Israel; nor is it really credible that the Egyptian army would have undertaken a military operation involving a march of hundreds of miles, just to capture a city for the king of Israel. Is it not much more reasonable to suppose that the annexation of Gezer and all the other Philistine regions was in fact a clear territorial and political concession by Egypt to Israel? Not only must the Egyptian advance into Philistia have upset the delicate political balance in Palestine, but the capture of Gezer undoubtedly constituted a direct Egyptian threat to the kingdom of Israel. Therefore, it is only natural that this move would have been vigorously opposed by Solomon, who had at his disposal the vast resources which he had inherited from David. The Pharaoh would have been compelled to accept an arrangement whereby he had to hand over to Israel at least part of his conquests in Philistia. The treaty between the two rulers was confirmed by a marriage alliance, a practice not infrequently used in the diplomatic relations of the time, while the territorial concession took the form of a dowry given by the Pharaoh to his daughter.

This analysis leads us to evaluate the personality of Solomon in a manner somewhat different from the generally stereotyped image of a static ruler who developed a purely defensive foreign policy. Solomon was not merely the son of a dynamic conqueror, content

---

[69] The LXX transposes this verse, attaching it to the report on Solomon's marriage in I Kings 3:1 and presenting both of them after I Kings 5:14 (English Versions 4:34, at the end of the passage about Solomon's wisdom). Though this sequence has been accepted by various commentators (cf. Montgomery, *Kings*, p. 102), it should be regarded as a purely arbitrary re-arrangement which ignores the parenthetical character of the self-evident gloss in I Kings 9:16.

to retain what he had inherited and gradually frittering away his father's far-flung conquests. Such neat labels do not agree with the historical situation. We have seen that Solomon not only extended Israelite rule in the south but also strengthened it in the north, in the region of central Syria (see above, pp. 217f.).[70] The Israelite empire evidently reached the apogee of its power in the first years of Solomon's reign, particularly after the treaty with Egypt; it was only in the second half of his reign, i.e., with the rise of the ambitious Twenty-second Dynasty in Egypt, that the process of deterioration began.

---

[70] Solomon's consolidation of his rule in these two decisive sectors gives a more realistic meaning to the passage which deals with his position as a middleman in the trade between Egypt and the Hittite and Aramean kings (I Kings 10:28–29).

12

NAAMAH, THE AMMONITE PRINCESS, KING SOLOMON'S WIFE*

Summary

The only wife of King Solomon known by her personal name was Naamah, the Ammonite princess, mother of Rehoboam, heir to the throne. According to Biblical chronology, Naamah was married to young Solomon by King David and thus this international marriage has to be viewed as the result of the latter's policy and not that of Solomon. The possible motives for David's initiative are considered. We may speculate that much later, Ishmael son of Nethaniah "of the seed of the royal family", who entertained special ties with Ammon and was sent by its king to eliminate Gedaliah son of Ahikam, may have been a distant descendant of Rehoboam and Naamah, the Ammonites.

Sommaire

La seule épouse de Salomon qui ait été connue par son nom est Naamah, la princesse ammonite, mère de Roboam, héritier du trône. Selon la chronologie biblique, Naamah a été mariée au jeune Salomon par le roi David. Ce mariage international résulte de la politique de David, et non de celle de Salomon. Les raisons de l'initiative de David sont examinées. On peut supposer que, bien plus tard, Yishmaël, fils de Netanya, «de souche royale», a pu être un lointain descendant de Roboam et de Naamah, l'Ammonite; il entretint des rapports privilégiés avec Ammon, et fut envoyé par son roi pour éliminer Godolias, fils d'Ahiqam.

From among the thousand wifes (of them, three hundred concubines) which the biblical narrative ascribes to Solomon, only one wife is known in the Bible by her personal name. Even his wife is not mentioned in the story of Solomon, itself, neither in Kings nor in Chronicles, but she is registered as the king's mother at the conclusion of

---

* This article was originally published in: *RB* 106 (1999/1), 35–41.

the account of King Rehoboam: "And his mother's name was Naamah the Ammonitess" (1 Kings 14:21, 23; 2 Chron. 12:13).[1] This means that she was the wife of Solomon, of whom it is told that he married many foreign wives, including an Ammonite princess, or several princesses from Ammon (cf. 1 Kings 10:1). According to the addition preserved in the Septuagint to 1 Kings 12:24a, Naamah was the daughter of Hanon, son of Nahash, the king who ascended the throne of the Ammonite kingdom during the days of David (2 Sam. 10:2).[2] The name of *Na'amah* seems also to indicate foreign origin, as names derived from the same root (such as Elna'aman) are, as a rule, frequent in the West-Semitic onomasticon.[3]

If we adopt the set of dates for Solomon and Rehoboam as provided in the Book of Kings it turns out that Rehoboam was forty one years old when he ascended the royal throne, which is to say that he was born about a year before Solomon's reign commenced, a reign which lasted forty years. David arranged the marriage of Naamah the Ammonite woman to Solomon when the latter was still young in years, apparently a teenager, which is to say, some years before he began to rule as king. We ought not, therefore, to attribute the step taken in this international marriage to Solomon's initiative, as is the prevailing view,[4] but rather to the strategic and political calculations of his father, David.[5]

It is to be assumed that Naamah bore Solomon sons in addition to the first-born son Rehoboam and that these, together with other brothers who were born out of Solomon's numerous marriages are, in my view, the sons being referred to in the statement about Rehoboam that "he took counsel with the young men (*hayyĕlādîm*) who grew up with him" (1 Kings 12:8).[6] In other words, Rehoboam turned to the counsel of the princelings of the royal court, after having been disappointed over "the counsel of the elders" in matters of

---

[1] See the commentaries on 1 Kings, as, for example, Šanda 1911:371; De Vries 1985:184; and monographs on the Ammonites: Oded 1971:254–271, s.v. Ammon; Hübner 1992:179ff.

[2] Šanda 191:371; Hübner 1992:181ff.

[3] A seal bearing the name *Na'amah* is thought to be a forgery. Cf. the seal *Na'am'el*. Avigad 1997:603. In languages akin to Hebrew see: Benz 1972:362, s.v. N'M; Aufrecht 1989:370, s.v. n'm.

[4] Cf. by way of example: Gray 1970:342; Schearing 1992 IV:967, s.v. Naamah 2.

[5] See Malamat 1963a:8.

[6] See Malamat 1963b:248ff.

policy. This would apply especially to the economic policy which he had decided upon with respect to the northern tribes, namely, their suppression by an iron hand.

Rehoboam's brothers and step brothers, who were most probably numerous, were of the family of the House of David, and their descendants apparently survived in Judah for generations. Possibly, the biblical idiom "of the seed of the royal family" (mizzera' hammĕlūkâh) pertains primarily to royal descendants of this kind who never actually sat on the throne. At times they were distributed by the reigning king in various places throughout the kingdom of Judah (cf. the rather obscure passage in 2 Chron. 11:23 concerning Rehoboam and his sons). We may speculate that one of these very descendants, who had a strong relationship with the Ammonites, was Ishmael son of Nethaniah "of the seed of the royal family" (Jer. 41:1)[7] who was sent by the king of Ammon to Mizpeh in the land of Benjamin to eliminate Gedaliah son of Ahikam (Jer. 40:14–41:15). The political assassination of the governor of Judah, who had been appointed by King Nebuchadnezzar, was surely intended to pave Ishmael's way in seizing the reins of government in Judah in place of the immediate House of David, itself, which had been eliminated by the Babylonians.

Admittedly, the gap in time between the days of Solomon and Rehoboam and the end of the kingdom of Judah is great. And yet, just as the pagan cults which Solomon introduced into Jerusalem persisted until the days of Josiah (2 Kings 23:13) it is not impossible that Ishmael "of the seed of the royal family in Judah," who was active soon after the destruction of the First Temple, could trace his ancestry back to Naamah, the Ammonite woman. Even then, after hundreds of years, he may have sought to become heir to the House of David, and to do so with the encouragement and support of Ammon.

In any event, Rehoboam gained great influence through his mother, and through the cult of the deity she worshipped, "Milkom, the abomination of the Ammonites" (1 Kings 11:5).[8] Rehoboam's chief wife, Maachah, daughter of Abisalom, known as haggĕbîrâh "the First Lady," who had been married off to him by Solomon, was the mother of his heir, king Abiah (1 Kings 15:2, 7; 2 Chron. 13:2).[9]

---

[7] See MacKane 1996 II:1013ff.
[8] On the character of this Ammonite deity see Šanda 1911:303; Noth 1968:248.
[9] Cf. Schearing 1992 IV:429ff.

Even Maachah was, from all indications, of foreign origin, and she introduced into the kingdom of Judah the despised cult of the Asherah. But Asa, the son of Abiah, and the grandson of Rehoboam (1 Kings 15:10 lists Asa as Rehoboam's brother and son of Maachah, not as her grandson)[10] brought an end to the pagan deterioration in the kingdom of Judah, and removed both Maachah and "the Asherah abomination (*mipleṣet hā'ašērâh*)" from Judah (1 Kings 15:13).

Furthermore, the princess' name, *Ma'akah*, was, it seems, unusual in Israel, and may be a Phoenician or Aramean name, or even the name used by one of the Transjordanian peoples.[11] A few of the names of Maachah's sons may also provide evidence of her foreign origin (see 2 Chron. 11:20). Moreover, the blood of Rehoboam and of Abiah was considerably diluted. They were Judeans by halves and quarters, and this is even more the case if we assume that Solomon, himself, was born to a foreign mother. His mother, Bathsheba (another version cited in the Bible is *Batšū'a*) was probably related to the pre-Israelite aristocracy of Jerusalem, and had initially been the wife of Uriah, the Hittite, a foreigner as his gentilic ethnonym indicates. The "blue blood" that ran in the veins of the first kings of the House of David was intended to solidify the dynasty, and it was preferred over an exclusively Judean Derivation.[12]

Finally, we should inquire as to the possible motives which lay behind David's initiative in arranging the marriage of an Ammonite princess to his son and heir, one who would become the mother of the subsequent heir to the throne, Rehoboam. The series of wars between David and the Ammonites is depicted relatively extensively in 2 Samuel, chapters 10–12.[13] A central focus of the biblical account are the words of condemnation hurled at King David by the prophet Nathan. The king is held responsible for the death of Uriah: "You had him killed by the sword of the Ammonites" (2 Sam. 12:9). In contrast, David's relations with the Ammonites during the insurrection

---

[10] The genealogy of Asa is entangled in biblical sources. As has been noted, one version lists Maachah as Abiah's mother and Rechoboam's wife, while another states that she was Asa's mother and Abiah's wife. A third version in 2 Chron. 13:2, lists as Abiah's mother a certain Michaiah, daughter of Uriel from Gibeah. See the commentaries to Kings, and the summary in Schearing IV:423ff.

[11] On the name Maachah see Schearing IV:429ff.

[12] See Malamat 1967:165–167.

[13] Cf. in the commentaries on 2 Samuel: McCarter 1984:266–313; Stoebe 1994: 266–318.

of Absalom were friendly. Shobi, son of Nahash, from Rabbat Ammon (the new king in Ammon, according to 2 Sam. 17:27) was among David's supporters when he was pursuing his son in Transjordanian territory, and the king of Ammon at that time provided material assistance to David when the King of Israel was staying in Mahanaim.

David's choice of an Ammonite princess for his son may have been motivated by the following factors: His action was intended to express gratitude to the Ammonite king for the attitude the latter took during Absalom's rebellion. Viewed from a different perspective, this step was aimed at symbolizing David's hegemony of Israel over Ammon. Indeed, this latter view is in accord with the unique manner described in the Bible of confirming the conquest of Ammon by Israel: "The crown was taken from the head of their king (Hebrew *malkām'* perhaps read *Milkôm*, the Ammonite deity) . . . and it was placed on David's head . . ." (2 Sam. 12:30).[14] The royal marriage was thus intended to cement relations between the two kingdoms.[15]

Bibliography

Aufrecht, W.A. 1989. *A Corpus of Ammonite Inscriptions*, Lewiston: Mellen Press.
Avigad, N. 1997. *Corpus of West Semitic Stamp Seals* (revised by B. Sass), Jerusalem: Israel Academy.
Benz, F.L. 1972. *Personal Names in the Phoenician and Punic Inscriptions*, Rome: Biblical Institute Press.
Berridge, J.M. 1992. *ABD* II, p. 512, s.v. "Ishmael 2", New York, Garden City: Doubleday.
De Vries, S.J. 1985. *Kings* (Word Biblical Commentary), Waco, Texas: Word Books.
Gray, J. 1970. *I & II Kings*, London: SCM Press.
Horn, S. 1973. "The Crown for the King of the Ammonites", *Andrews University Sem. Studies* 11, pp. 173–180.
Hübner, U. 1992. *Die Ammoniter*, Wiesbaden: Harrassowitz (ADPV 16).
McCarter, P.K. 1984. *II Samuel* (Anchor Bible), Garden City, NY: Doubleday.
McKane, W. 1996. *Jeremiah II* (ICC), Edinburgh: T & T Clark.
Malamat, A. 1963a. "Aspects of the Foreign Policies of David and Solomon," *JNES* 22, 1–17.
——, 1963b. "Kingship and Council in Israel and Sumer: A Parallel," *JNES* 22, 247–253.
——, 1967. "Comments on E. Leach: The Legitimacy of Solomon . . .," *Archives Européennes Sociologie* 8, 165–171.

---

[14] On 2 Sam. 12:30 cf. McCarter 1984:310–311; Stoebe 1994:117; Horn 1973.

[15] A Hebrew version of this paper is published in the *Festschrift* G. Sauer ("Theologie, Archäologie und Philology", ed. J.A. Loader), Vienna 1998.

——, 1983. *Das davidische und salomonische Königreich . . .*, Wien: Österreichische Akademie der Wissensch. (Phil.-Hist. Klasse, Sitzungsberichte, Band 407).

Noth, M. 1968. *Könige* (BK), Neukirchen: Neukirchner Verlag.

Oded, B. 1971. "Ammon" in *Encyclopaedia Biblica* VI (Hebrew), Jerusalem: Bialik Institute, 254–271.

Šanda, A. 1911. *Die Bücher der Könige I* (Exeget. Hb zum A.T. 9), Münster, Aschendorffsche Verlagsbuchhandlung.

Schearing, L.S. 1992. *ABD*, s.v. Maacah; Naamah; New York: Doubleday.

Stoebe, H.J. 1994. *Das zweite Buch Samuelis* (Komm. zum A.T.), Gütersloh: Güterslohe Verlagshaus.

Wiseman, D.J. 1993. *1 and 2 Kings* (Tyndale OT Comm.), Leicester: Inter-Varsity Press.

13

ORGANS OF STATECRAFT IN THE
ISRAELITE MONARCHY*

The following lecture was presented on August 22, 1963, before a Bible study group at the home of the former Prime Minister of Israel, Mr. David Ben-Gurion, and with the participation of the President of Israel, Mr. Zalman Shazar. The meeting was presided over by Justice of the Supreme Court, Prof. Moshe Silberg. The lecture and discussion were subsequently published with notes and a few minor changes in English translation, in the series El Ha‘Ayin, *by the World Jewish Bible Society and the Israel Society for Biblical Research. We have decided to reprint it here both because we feel that this address is of such interest that it deserves a wider audience and because we think our readers will be interested to learn, as evidenced by the discussion, of the keen interest taken in biblical studies by laymen as well as scholars in Israel.*

Rehoboam and the Schism Within the Kingdom

The main burden of my remarks will concern the specific aspects of the political apparatus and organs of statecraft as they emerge from the first half of I Kings 12.[1] This section deals with king Rehoboam and the circumstances surrounding the split within the United Monarchy, i.e. the kingdoms of David and Solomon.

The reference here is twofold: 1) the demand of the northern tribes to alleviate the burden of taxes and corvée imposed upon them by Solomon, Rehoboam's father, this being a prior condition to their acquiescence in Rehoboam's election; 2) Rehoboam's consultation with the "elders" and "young men" before replying to the tribes' ultimatum. The uncompromising attitude adopted by Rehoboam on this matter brought about the end of the United Kingdom of Israel

---

* This article was originally published in: *BA Reader* 3, 1964, 163–198.
[1] See commentaries: A. Šanda, *Die Bücher der Könige*, I (1911), 334ff.; J.A. Montgomery, *The Books of Kings* (1951), pp. 248ff.; J. Gray, *I and II Kings* (1964), pp. 278ff.; also E. Nielsen, *Shechem* (1955), pp. 171ff.; and D.W. Gooding, *VT*, XVII (1967), 173–89; for the discussion of textual problems which are not dealt with here.

and determined the course of Jewish history for generations to come.

As a starting point, I should like to dwell upon the question of Rehoboam's enthronement or rather lack of enthronement, at Shechem which, in fact, serves as the framework for the events described in the chapter under discussion. The opening phrase refers to Rehoboam's arrival in Shechem, "For all Israel were come to Shechem to make him king." I accept the assumption of some scholars that we are confronted here with a second enthronement or, put somewhat differently, that Rehoboam had been automatically acclaimed king previously in Judah, where the Davidide house had taken root. This was not the case, however, as regards the northern Israelite tribes, who by no means took it for granted that Solomon's offspring ought to rule over them. For it must be borne in mind that those tribes had attached themselves to the house of David by a covenantal act (II Sam. 5:1–3).

Covenant Between King and People[2]

As prelude to the covenant we read in II Samuel 3 of the negotiations between David and Abner, intended to bring the northern tribes under David's sway. In verse 12, it is stated: "Make thy league with me and my hand shall be with thee to bring over all Israel unto thee." Verse 17 then relates that Abner has urged the elders (sic!) of Israel to enter into a treaty with David. Note how the institution of the elders is still playing an authoritative role in covenant-making and the election of kings. Abner then goes to meet David in Hebron, taking along twenty men to conduct the negotiations. David greets them with a feast, a ceremony which has, at times, been associated with the covenantal act, according to the Bible and ancient Near Eastern sources.

Further on in the same chapter (v. 21) we hear Abner saying to David: "I will arise and will gather all Israel unto my lord the king, that they may make a covenant with thee, and that thou mayest

---

[2] For the problem in general see the studies by G. Widengren, *JSS*, II (1957), 1–32, and by G. Fohrer, *ZAW*, LXXI (1959), 1–22. Important extra-biblical material on the general problem of covenant between king and people is to be found in the recent work of D.J. McCarthy, *Treaty and Covenant* (1963).

reign over all that thy soul desireth." In other words, preparations are afoot to conclude a treaty in Hebron with the northern tribes. Typologically speaking, we are confronted with an exact parallel to the Rehoboam incident. Rehoboam has come to Shechem where the northern tribes have convened for the coronation ceremony. We are justified in inferring that here, too, preparations are being laid for a covenant betwixt king and populace.

As it turned out Abner was murdered, but the Bible is most explicit in stating that all of Israel came under David's rule as a result of the pact between him and the elders (again!) of the north: "So all the elders of Israel came to the king to Hebron; and King David did make a covenant with them in Hebron before the Lord and they anointed David king over Israel" (II Sam. 5:3).

The Shechem Event in the Light of David's Enthronement over Israel

The enthronement of David may offer some concept as to what might have happened at Shechem. True, there are important circumstantial differences, pointing to Rehoboam's weakness as against David's position of strength at the time of the coronation. The delegation from the north came to David at *his* capital in Hebron for the conclusion of the treaty. Rehoboam, on the other hand goes, or is compelled to go to Shechem, center of the northern tribal confederation, in order to have them make their pact with him. Yet both incidents are basically one: the rule of the Judean kings over the northern tribes is conditional upon a covenantal agreement between the king and his future subjects.

David Ben-Gurion: Why by-pass Solomon when discussing the covenant?

Lecturer: I shall come back to this intriguing question in my reply. In any event, it is not feasible to include in our discussion the broader problem as to whether, in the course of time, a new covenant was required with each royal accession. It seems reasonable, however, to assume that such a covenant renewal was required procedure only with the advent of a new dynasty or when the royal succession was interrupted. In Israel there were ten such change-overs during a period of two hundred years, and one is justified in assuming that a royalty-pact was customary in such cases, even though the Bible makes no specific mention of such a detail.

As for Judah, there is one definite instance of covenant-making within the context of the coronation-ritual. A crisis had been brought about by the rule of queen Athalia, regarded in Judah as an alien from the north whose rule had, in fact, severed the Davidic line. Consequently, at her dethronement and assassination, the need was felt for a covenant-renewal between the new king, Jehoash, one of the progeny of the house of David, and his subjects. Thus we read in II Kings 11:17: "And Jehoiada made a covenant between the Lord and the king and the people . . . and between the king also and the people." The verse seems a bit cumbersome and has led Bible critics to propose alternate emendations:

1) The latter part of the verse "between the king also and the people" is to be deleted. In other words, a covenant was concluded only between the Lord and the people, whose representative was the king.

2) In contrast with this Martin Noth, in a recent study, does away with the first part of the verse. Yet there is no real difficulty in accepting the complete phrase which presents us with a two-fold covenant: between God and the king on the one hand, betwixt king and people on the other.[3] Since the Davidic line had been sundered it was necessary to renew the treaty between the people of Judah and the lineal descendant of the house of David. Incidentally, we have here a most interesting type of covenant between two parties effected by an intermediary, in this case Jehoiada, the High Priest.[4]

Dr. Haim Gevaryahu: Perhaps Jehoiada was acting as guardian of the under-age king (Jehoash was only seven when he was officially acclaimed).

Lecturer: He was certainly acting both as High Priest and as the supreme authority in Judah during the period of royal crisis.

The People's Representative Body

The covenantal act, in the cases of David and Rehoboam, is preceded by negotiations with the representative body of the people. It

---

[3] M. Noth, *Gesammelte Studien zum Alten Testament* (1957), pp. 151f., and K. Baltzer, *Das Bundesformular* (1960), pp. 85ff.; Gray, *I and II Kings*, pp. 523f., even sees here a threefold covenant.

[4] For this type of treaty see for the present H.W. Wolff, *VT*, VI (1956), 316–20.

is this body which participates in the covenant ceremony if the negotiations are successfully concluded. The elders served in this capacity in David's case, whereas, regarding Rehoboam, I Kings 12:3
relates: "and Jeroboam and all the congregation (*qāhāl*) of Israel
came and spoke unto Rehoboam saying. . . ." A problem of no immediate moment to us is whether Jeroboam actually participated in the
delegation or whether he was still in Egyptian exile, appearing only
later when called to the northern assemblage (*ibid.*, v. 20). If so, the
mention of Jeroboam in verse 3 (as well as in v. 12), would be a
later addition, as maintained by some authorities.

The Hebrew term for the aforementioned representative body is
qāhāl (usually translated "congregation" but it refers more precisely
to an assembly). It is noteworthy that the same term is used in a
case where covenant-making with royalty is specifically mentioned,
namely, in the previously mentioned coronation ritual of Jehoash:
"And all the congregation (*qāhāl*) made a covenant with the king in
the house of God" (II Chron. 23:3; the parallel account in II Kings
is completely lacking in these details). The word *qāhāl* is virtually
synonymous with the term *'ēdā* ("assembly"), also frequently used,
both terms at times serving interchangeably or even in combination.
It would appear that the biblical source known as the Priestly Code
tends toward the usage *'ēdā*, in contrast to the other sources which
employ *qāhāl* overwhelmingly.[5]

The question of terminology is especially apropos here, as in a
later passage of our chapter (I Kings 12:20) this very *'ēdā* (referred
to only once in the book of Kings) elects Jeroboam, following the
unsuccessful negotiations with Rehoboam. While no covenant is
explicitly mentioned, it is certainly implied in this instance of the
founding of the first Israelite dynasty. It is not entirely impossible,
however, that one may assume a slight difference in connotation
here, with *qāhāl* referring to the group (in vs. 12–16 called simply
'am, "people") conducting the negotiations with Rehoboam and, in
effect, acting as the representative of the broader gathering, the *'ēdā*.

---

[5] On the significance of these two terms see L. Rost, *Die Vorstufen von Kirche und
Synagoge im Alten Testament* (1938); R. Gordis in *Alexander Marx Jubilee Volume* (1950),
pp. 171ff. For the term *'ēdā* and *mō'ēd*, "assembly", see also C.U. Wolf, *JNES*, VI
(1947), 100ff. A parallel institution designated by the same term is attested for the
kingdom of Byblos in the 11th century B.C.; see J.A. Wilson, *JNES*, IV (1945), 245.

The assembly, comprised of the people's representatives, was the supreme authoritative body especially during the pre-monarchic period. It was empowered both to elect kings as in the case of Jeroboam) and to reject would-be rulers (as was done with Rehoboam). To cite yet another example from Shechem some 200 years earlier, there is the enthronement of Abimelech by the leading people of that town (*ba⁽ᵃ⁾lê š⁽ᵉ⁾kæm*) as stated in Judges 9:6. Most enlightening in this respect is the reference in Deuteronomy 33:5: "And there was a king in Jeshurun, when the heads of the people were gathered, all the tribes of Israel together." Here is additional testimony that the accession ceremony required an assembly of leaders, regardless whether the interpretation of our verse refers to the enthronement of the Lord or of a king of flesh and blood.[6]

Dissolution of Covenant and Assembly

The comparison between the Shechem event and David's coronation over Israel may tend to clarify the closing episode in the Rehoboam affair. On the one hand, we have the case of David, whose negotiations with the northern representatives are brought to a successful close with the conclusion of the treaty. In accordance with the theological orientation of the redactor of the book of Samuel, the depiction of the covenantal act is preceded by the following insertion: "And the Lord said to thee: thou shalt feed my people Israel, and thou shalt be prince over Israel" (II Sam. 5:2).

The very antithesis of this is the Rehoboam affair, with the latter's failure to negotiate economic concessions to the northern tribes. Thus we hear of Rehoboam in I Kings 12:15: "So the king hearkened not unto the people", followed by the redactor's parenthetical remark: "For it was a thing brought about of the Lord, that He might establish His word which the Lord spoke by the hand of Ahijah the Shilonite." The biblical historiographer attributes Rehoboam's adamant refusal, in the last analysis, to divine causality. The

---

[6] On this problem see now I.L. Seeligmann, *VT*, XIV (1964), 75ff. For a similar function of the assembly (Sumerian: *unkin*; Akkadian: *pukhrum*) in Mesopotamia, see the bibliographical references in notes 16, 17, and 26. For the assembly (*pankus*) in the Hittite kingdom which, according to some authorities, was originally an elective monarchy, see O.R. Gurney, *The Hittites* (1952), pp. 63ff.; A. Goetze, *Kleinasien* (2nd ed., 1957), pp. 86ff.

net result is that instead of a covenant we have the people's negative reaction (v. 16): "What portion have we in David? neither have we inheritance in the son of Jesse; to your tents, O Israel; now see to thine own house, David."

This last verse has been the subject of a great deal of debate. The usual suggestion has been that it intimates the actual slogan of rebellion. Yet the immediate reaction to this call shows the opposite to be the case, namely, the people dispersed and returned to their homes. It seems to me that this matter should be viewed within the context outlined here: the convening of the Shechem assembly to conclude a covenant as a prerequisite to Rehoboam's coronation. The striking slogan "To your tents, O Israel" then becomes no more than a formula signifying assembly disbandment, with the emphatic addition "what portion have we in David," etc., an outright nullification of the treaty with the Davidide house.[7] This general formula, employing the characteristic terms "tents" and "portion and inheritance" may well date back to the days of Israelite settlement, the formula having its roots in the tribal organization and assembly (cf. Gen. 31:14; Deut. 10:9; etc.).

The very same connotation of covenant nullification would appear to be intended in the second instance where the formula is mentioned, namely, in Sheba, the son of Bichri's stand against David. We note, in passing, that here "Every man to his tents, O Israel," (II Sam. 20:1), is secondary to the direct and perhaps original exclamation, "To your tents, O Israel" in the Rehoboam affair. Understandably, the dissolution of the covenant tends to act as precursor of the revolt. The fact of revolt is specially indicated in II Samuel 20:2: "So all the men of Israel went up from following David and followed Sheba, the son of Bichri," as well as in I Kings 12:19: "So Israel rebelled against the house of David unto this day" (referring to the Rehoboam incident). The actual slogan for military alignment, on the other hand, must be in reverse form: "We will not any of us go to his tent, neither will we any of us turn unto his house" (Judges 20:8). This, in fact, is the well-versed outcry of the confederation of Israelite tribes, as they prepare for war against Benjamin to avenge the disgrace of Gibeah. It is noteworthy that here, too, it is the assembly (ʿēdā), convening at Mizpah (Judges 20:1) which serves

---

[7] See Fohrer, *ZAW*, LXXI (1959), 8.

as the organ for major policy decisions, in this case the matter of joint military action. In conclusion, therefore, we find that the negative usage "We will not any of us go to his tent" etc. indicates that a common decision has been reached by the assembly, in contrast to the opposite slogan which signifies a severing of mutual ties and dissolution of assembly and covenant.

In this connection, one may revert briefly to David's enthronement. There we find a positive conclusion to the royal covenant expressed in the remark: "We are of thy bone and thy flesh" (II Sam. 5:11; cf. also 19:12–13), which is antithetical to our formula "What portion have we in David, neither have we inheritance in the son of Jesse." Similar phraseology (although in this instance based partially on genealogical ties) is employed by Abimelech in his attempt to induce the people of Shechem to crown him king: "Remember also that I am your bone and your flesh" (Judges 9:2).

As regards the covenant, we revert to our original contention that this same act of treaty bound the northern tribes to the Davidide monarchy. Consequently, they felt it their prerogative to stipulate the conditions for the covenant's renewal leading to the enthronement itself. Should their conditions be rejected, they would have no hesitation in undoing the bond of union. We note in the coronation ceremony two basic elements that have already been pointed out by various scholars, especially by Alt in his penetrating analysis of kingship in Israel: the anointing, or divine aspect of the covenant, and the acclamation, expressing approval of the king by the populace.[8] This approval was indicated by the joyous shout ($t^er\bar{u}^c\bar{a}$) of the assemblage, as in the case of Saul and Jehoash: "and all the people shouted and said: 'Long live the king!'" (I Sam. 10:24); "And they clapped their hands and said: 'Long live the king!'" (II Kings 11:12). This ancient procedure of publicly acknowledging a legal act contrasts with the written signature in modern pact-making.

---

[8] A. Alt, *VT*, 1 (1951), 2–22, reprinted in *Kleine Schriften*, II (1953), pp. 116–34. For the coronation rites see R. de Vaux, *Ancient Israel* (1961), pp. 102–7. There see also pp. 70–72 and 524 on the institution of the "people of the land," whose investigation lies outside the scope of this lecture; but for their role in the accession of the Judean kings see, for the present, my remarks in *IEJ*, XVIII (1968), 140 and note 6.

"Elders" and "Young Men"—In Advisory or Decisive Capacity?[9]

It is significant that during the negotiation with Rehoboam on alleviating the tax burden of the northern tribes, the king did not exercise his prerogative of immediate decision. Instead, he asked for a three-day delay in order to take counsel with both the elders (*z^{e}qēnīm*) and "young men" (*y^{e}lādīm*) whom the Bible describes as advisory bodies to royalty.

Here we are confronted with several hypothetical questions, the solution of which may help clarify both the political situation and the machinery upon which Rehoboam depended in the hour of his decision.

1) Why did Rehoboam have recourse to these two bodies? Was he empowered to take an independent course of action? Would David or Solomon have reacted in the same fashion under similar circumstances?

2) Was it incumbent upon him to turn to the "young men" after having consulted with the elders? Or did he rather consult them because the elders' conciliatory counsel did not suit his disposition?

3) What actual competence did these two bodies possess? Were they acting in advisory capacity, their word not being binding on the king? Or was it possibly the counsel of the "young men" that was solely binding?

Before we pursue these questions further, we shall endeavor to establish the elders and "young men" as actual bodies or institutions that participated in policy making, and not mere biological groupings, as commonly held.

It would be superfluous to go into any lengthy discussion of the elders.[10] It is common knowledge that they served as a central institution

---

[9] For a somewhat fuller treatment of several points in the following part of the lecture, see my paper, *JNES*, XXII (1963), 247ff. (chap. 11). This paper has in the meantime led to some criticism. I still regard I Kings 12 as having a historical-institutional background, though it is of undeniable literary character (*contra*, e.g., J. Debus, *Die Sünde Jerobeams* [1967], pp. 30ff.). In pointing out the occasionally more-than-advisory capacity of the elders and young men, it was of course not my intention to give them legislative status in the modern sense, but rather to regard them as an active force in the *Realpolitik* of the day (see further below), in modern terms a powerful "lobby" (in answer to, e.g., D.G. Evans, *JNES*, XXV [1966], 273–79, and recently M. Noth, *Könige* [1968], pp. 265ff., esp. p. 274).

[10] For the institution of the "elders" in the biblical sources, see especially J.L. McKenzie, *Analecta Biblica*, X (Vol. I, 1959), 388–406, and J. van der Ploeg, *Festschrift Hubert Junker* (1961), pp. 175ff.

in the patriarchal-tribal society throughout the Near East, including pre-monarchic Israel. As is well known, this institution persisted far into the days of the monarchy, especially in the more conservative northern kingdom, where we find the elders much more active than in Judah. Their powers, nevertheless, waned with the passing years. We will confine ourselves here to the appearance of this institution in decisions of state under royalty.

Ahab, like Rehoboam, stood in need of the elders' counsel. To be more precise, he may have been virtually dependent upon the decision of the elders in his fateful dilemma, namely, the Aramean siege of his capital Samaria and his response to the degrading terms of surrender imposed on the Israelite king by Ben-Hadad (I Kings 20:1ff.). Two Aramean delegations present an ultimatum to Ahab. While accepting the terms of the first, Ahab is defiant to the harsher demands of the second and decides to convene an emergency council. In vs. 7–8 of chapter 20 we read: "Then the king of Israel called all the elders of the land and said, 'Mark, I pray you, and see how this man seeketh mischief; for he sent unto me for my wives, and for my children, and for my silver, and for my gold and I denied him not,' and all the elders and all the people said unto him: 'Hearken thou not, neither consent.'" Whereupon Ahab accepts the elders' advice and rejects the surrender terms.

Yet another instance of political counselling is that of Amaziah, king of Judah, faced with the decision of launching a war against Jehoash of the sister-kingdom of Israel. In the Chronicler's version (II Chron. 25:17) we read: "Then Amaziah . . . took advice and sent to Joash, the son of Jehoahaz, the son of Jehu, king of Israel, saying: 'Come, let us look one another in the face!'" (The parallel passage in II Kings 14:8, omits the phrase "took advice"). There can be no doubt that this refers to a political body which the king was wont to consult in an emergency, as did Rehoboam and Ahab. It is not inconceivable that here, too, it is the elders that are implied. In any event the words "took advice," when appearing in the context of a peace-or-war decision, are ones to ponder.

During the days of David, the elders were equally well known as a body wielding great political influence. We have already noted their decisive role in concluding the treaty with David by which he assumed the crown over the North, as well as during his preliminary negotiations with Abner. The institution of the elders of both North and South is remembered particularly for its activity during

Absalom's revolt. When Ahithophel offered his counsel, it was directed to Absalom and the elders of Israel (II Sam. 17:4 *et al.*). This is the forum accredited to act upon his advice. On liquidation of the revolt, David turns to Zadok and Abiathar saying (II Sam. 19:12) ". . . 'Speak unto the elders of Judah saying: Why are ye the last to bring the king back to his house?'" Once again, we note the importance of this body—here the "elders of Judah."

The Various Branches of Government

As far as the Solomonic kingdom is concerned, no real mention is made of the elders, save for one passage, product of a late redactor (I Kings 8:1–3), on the installation of the Ark in Solomon's temple. But the existence of the elders as a special council during this period clearly emerges from the chapter under review (I Kings 12:6), reading: "And king Rehoboam took counsel with the elders, that had stood before Solomon his father while he yet lived." Various commentators here identify the elders with the ministers (*śārīm*) of Solomon in precisely the same way that "the young men" are identified with the ministers of Rehoboam. There is no valid foundation in this case, either, for such a hypothesis. On the contrary, several passages offer proof that ministers and elders are distinctly separate entities of government, on the town as well as on the national level. In fact the two appellations appear side by side, in Judges 8:14, portraying the city government of Succoth in the Gideon story, and in I Kings 21:8, which depicts the royal administration in the time of Ahab and Jezebel.

Of special interest is a third passage which mentions the elders separately from the ministers of the northern kingdom. This concerns the negotiations between Jehu and the leadership in Samaria to transfer rule into his hands (II Kings 10:5). Here the capital authorities are comprised of two ministers, the royal chamberlain (*ᵃśær ᶜal habbayit*) and the city governor (*ᵃśær ᶜal hāᶜīr*), the elders, and the guardians (*ōmᵉnīm*). The same leaders are mentioned in verse 1 of this chapter, although in comparison with the Masoretic text greater clarity is evinced by the Greek and Latin versions (Septuagint and Vulgate), which read: "Jehu wrote a letter and sent: it to Samaria: to the governors of the city (!) and to the elders and to the guardians."

Despite the lack of sufficient grounds for a clear distinction between the various divisions of government (today's executive, legislative, and judiciary), it may nevertheless be assumed that the ministers, as under David and Solomon, are the equivalent of today's executive authority, while the elders may have served in an advisory capacity.

Among all the lists of officialdom during the reigns of David and Solomon, as recorded in II Samuel and I Kings, there is no mention of the title "counsellor." Ahithophel, even though acting as "David's counsellor," is not included in the list of ministers since these comprise the executive branch which is the only one recorded.

On the other hand, Adoram, who is "over the levy," is included as befits a member of the executive arm, having been sent to mobilize the corvée in Ephraim (I Kings 12:18). Only in I Chronicles 27:32–33, do we read: "also Jonathan, David's uncle, was a counsellor and Ahithophel was the king's counsellor." This verse, however, is not to be taken as evidence of an official ministerial listing, but rather as a record of the king's personal entourage. True, Adoram was considerably advanced in years during the time of Rehoboam, having served under David (II Sam. 20:24) and Solomon (I Kings 4:6), i.e. over a period of 40 years. This would place him at least in his sixties at the outset of Rehoboam's reign. All this notwithstanding, he is still not entitled "elder," but comes under the category of ministers or senior officials.

J. Braslavi: In other words, not the Latin "senex" but "senator." In Arabic, too, the word "sheikh" denotes both an old man and one holding an important position, young though he be.

Lecturer: These are illustrative parallels. Various other languages distinguish between the biological and the functional concepts embodied within the one term. The Mari documents of the early second millennium B.C., with their striking portrayals of tribal society, serve as a fine example of this.[11] In conclusion one must nevertheless be mindful of the fact that the elders, as patriarchal notables, were frequently elderly individuals.

---

[11] See H. Klengel, *Orientalia*, XXIX (1960), 357ff.; for the role of the elders in Asia Minor in the Hittite period, see idem, *Zeitschrift für Assyriologie*, XXIII (1965), 223ff.

"Elders" and "Young Men—Two Political Outlooks

While the general topic of the "elders" has been sufficiently dealt with in the past, this is not the case with the "young men," whose clarification is the task at hand.

In contrast with the elders, the "young men" whom Rehoboam consulted are unknown as a distinct entity or institution elsewhere in the Bible. It is therefore difficult to determine the nature of this group. The designation "young men" (*y^{e}lādīm*—actually, "boys," "children"), is in-appropriate to a political institution of any sort. Nevertheless, the term is not to be taken in its literal sense. The Bible explicitly states that they *grew up together* with Rehoboam, who was 41 years of age when he ascended the throne (I Kings 14:21). This is a rather high accession age when compared with Solomon, who may well have been under twenty when he assumed the crown, and with other rulers who were still in their teens.[12] As a matter of fact it is the highest accession age of any Judean king. The *y^{e}lādīm*, consequently, must have been middle-aged, and as such could easily constitute a political body.

It is more likely that the informal usage "young men" is one of the flowery epic embellishments, not without its pejorative note, to which the narrator resorted in order to emphasize the psychological and biological differentiations between both groups. The elders, wise in the ways of the world and in statecraft (Job 12:12), preach a policy of moderacy. As for the "young men," force is their refuge and impatience their lot; and if results are to be the measuring rod, their political vision, too, was on the short side. Yet above and beyond the disparity in maturity and temperament, still another factor is at work here: the elders are the "old guard" brought up in David's generation on the ideal of the twelve-tribe confederation. The "young men," on the other hand, represent the "new wave" rising to eminent position along with Rehoboam, and growing up in the later, oppressive years of Solomon's administration. We have here a decisive gap of one generation between the time of David, visionary of the greater Israelite empire, and the generation of Solomon, which

---

[12] S. Gevirtz, *Patterns in the Early Poetry of Israel* (1963), pp. 30ff., stressed the point that persons of an extremely young age became kings and military leaders in the ancient Near East.

witnessed the firm establishment of a powerful, heavy-handed regime especially as it affected the northern tribes.

It is difficult to ascertain what grouping the "young men" comprised. Nor should it be assumed that they were Rehoboam's newly-appointed ministers. There is no evidence for the opinion expressed at times that Rehoboam, upon his accession, embarked on an administrative reform of sorts, replacing his father's ministers with people from his own circle. On the contrary, the example of the sole minister mentioned during his reign, Adoram, chief of the corvée, testifies to a continuity of royal administration. Certainly the veteran Adoram could not have been one of the "young men" who grew up together with Rehoboam.

The "Young Men"—Princes of the Court

I am of the opinion that the "young men" were primarily princes, the offspring of Solomon, reared together with their half-brother, Rehoboam. While the 1,000 wives of Solomon appear exaggerated in number, it is clear that the sovereign had embarked on ramified marriage alliances, with the international aspect of his manifold ties of wedlock becoming a mainstay of his foreign policy. I have discussed this subject elsewhere.[13] But what seems most apparent is that these royal scions must have attained high status at the court and most probably also held high rank in the military. Their opinions conceivably carried great weight, upon the death of Solomon, in domestic and foreign affairs.

One should draw attention in this respect to a noteworthy passage previously referred to concerning Jehu's negotiations with the Samaria leadership, upon the deaths of Ahab and Jehoram. Listed among the central authorities we find, in addition to ministers and elders, the guardians who brought up Ahab's seventy sons (II Kings 10:1–6). It would appear that these three bodies had been functioning during Rehoboam's reign, with the exception that at the time, the "young men" or princes appear as such in their own right.

Concerning the identification of the "young men" with the king's offspring, one should note the especially instructive Rehoboam family chronicle as preserved in II Chronicles 11:18–23. Here Rehoboam,

---

[13] *JNES*, XXII (1963), 8ff.

continuing in his father's footsteps, is described as having a considerable harem and fathering 28 sons and 60 daughters. Abijah, moreover, who was crown-prince and heir-apparent, was appointed at the head of his brothers and made ruler (*nāgīd*) over them. This portrayal bears eloquent testimony to the internal organization of the royal household, the princes serving as a political entity under the heir-apparent, Abijah. It is a fair assumption that the crown-prince Rehoboam was himself appointed over his brothers during his father's lifetime and that they acted as a kind of "young men's" council. Abijah has been similarly credited with a considerable progeny—22 sons and 16 daughters (II Chron. 13:21) and one may anticipate court-organization comparable to that of Rehoboam. Abijah's short-lived reign of three years, however, may have precluded the routine functioning of just such a princely council.

As a further example we may refer to the various sons of king Jehoshaphat, mentioned in the Bible by their names and the noteworthy remark of the Chronicler: "And their father gave them great gifts, of silver, and of gold, and of precious things, with fortified cities in Judah (!); but the kingdom gave he to Jehoram, because he was the first-born" (II Chron. 21:3).

Participation and Voting in the Assembly

It is evident from the foregoing that the assemblages of elders and "young men" of Rehoboam's reign were not spontaneous gatherings but official bodies within the framework of the kingdom. This is implied further in the very terminology which describes each grouping: "that had stood before Solomon" and "that stood before him," that is, before Rehoboam (I Kings 12:6, 8).

The expression "to stand (*ʿōmed*) before" denotes, as is well known, attendance upon a high-ranking personage. More significantly, however, it may bear the occasional reference of membership or participation in assembly or council. Several instances of this usage are to be found throughout the Bible, depicting a heavenly assembly or "council of the Lord," which, in effect, is a reflection of its earthly counterpart. It would be impossible to enumerate these passages fully within the framework of this lecture.[14]

---

[14] *JNES*, XXII (1963), 250, note 11, and there further bibliographical references.

An intriguing problem posed by the assemblies of the elders and "young men," is the manner in which decisions were reached at these gatherings, which were convened from time to time to advise and even decide on matters of vital importance. Owing to the regrettable lack of evidence on the overall procedure at such meetings, this question remains unresolved, Even the more abundant material on the ancient Near Eastern assemblies provides but scattered hints on this score. Ephraim A. Speiser has pointed out that there were times when the assembly did not succeed in reaching a final decision.[15] This attests to the fact that discussions took place among different members of the assembly with the possibility of divergent views among them. However, the vote, as a means of reaching a decision, is not to be accepted with assurance. Thorkild Jacobsen, in his fundamental work on ancient Mesopotamian institutions, found no evidence for the voting technique as being in use there, this system apparently first coming into common practice in post-Homeric Greece. Basing himself on Sumerian myths, Jacobsen could demonstrate that the assembly's assent was voiced by the shouts of individual members, "let it be!"[16] The foregoing surmises open possible avenues of approach for a fuller comprehension of the workings of Israelite assemblies. In any event, the voting technique hardly enters the historical picture.

The Rehoboam Event in Light of the Sumerian Epic

It might be highly revealing to produce external parallels to our subject matter, which treat historical situations wherein the ruler is compelled to turn to various political bodies for vital decisions. I will restrict myself here to citing but one example which, from the typological point of view, bears a unique resemblance to the Rehoboam episode. I refer to the Sumerian epic known as "Gilgamesh and Agga" which reflects political conduct in the city-states of Sumer

---

In addition see now H.P. Müller, *Zeitschrift für die neutestamentliche Wissenschaft*, LIV (1963), 254ff.

[15] E.A. Speiser, *The Idea of History in the Ancient Near East* (1955), p. 53.

[16] See Th. Jacobsen's basic study, *JNES*, 11 (1943), 159–72, and, on the point in question, p. 171, note 68; *Zeitschrift für Assyriologie*, XVIII (1957), 101 and note 12. For the introduction of voting as a parliamentary device in Greece, see J.A.O. Larsen, *Classical Philology*, XLIV (1949), 164ff.

during the first half of the 3rd millennium B.C. For the publication and detailed treatment of this epic, thanks are due to Samuel Noah Kramer, as well as to other Sumerologists such as Jacobsen, Evans and Falkenstein, who have devoted special studies to the subjects.[17]

Briefly put, the plot is as follows: Gilgamesh, lord of Uruk, biblical Erech, listed in the "table of nations" (Gen. 10:10) and Agga, ruler of Kish, are engaged in a power struggle for hegemony in Sumer. The king of Kish issues an ultimatum to Gilgamesh that he and his subjects submit themselves as corvée to Kish, otherwise Agga will wage war against them. Gilgamesh, like Rehoboam, does not reply to the emissaries on his own. Instead, he approaches two bodies in his kingdom for their resolution on the matter. Like Rehoboam he first appeals to the "assembly of the elders" or, more precisely, to the "town fathers." These pursue a path of moderacy and suggest that Gilgamesh submit to the enemy, that he avoid war at all costs. Gilgamesh rejects this proposal and turns to the council of "men," the young armsbearers of the realm who favor rejecting the terms even at the price of war. Gilgamesh, like Rehoboam, acquiesces in their urging but, unlike Rehoboam, goes off to war.

In addition to the "bicameral" nature of the institutions and their respective policies regarding peace and war, one may even find parallel terminology employed in the biblical account and the Sumerian epic where these institutions are dealt with. The "council of men" in the Sumerian city-state is composed of various sectors: "those who stand," "those who sit," "those who were raised with the sons of the king," etc.; the first group immediately calls to mind "those who stood" before Solomon and Rehoboam. Aside from this, the biblical and Sumerian narratives present a striking similarity in literary features, such as the recurring use of metaphor describing the onerous corvée.

The focal point, however, is that notwithstanding all differences in historical circumstances and literary character of the two accounts, the similarity lies in the ruler's lack of freedom in independently exercising his prerogative of decision. It would appear that as far as

---

[17] For the scientific edition see S.N. Kramer, *AJA*, LIII (1949), 1–18; translated also in *ANET*, pp. 45f., and with slight improvements in Kramer, *The Sumerians* (1963), pp. 187ff. For a discussion of the epic, see the articles of Jacobsen cited in the preceding note, as well as G. Evans, *JAOS*, LXXVIII (1958), 1ff. Cf. now also Kramer, *RA*, LVIII (1964), 149ff.; and A. Falkenstein, *AfO*, XXI (1966), 47ff.

the two councils are concerned, it is their advice and, perhaps even more, their backing and consent which ought to be underlined. It is interesting that in both instances, the elders' counsel is rejected (thereby placing them, *ipso factor*, in an advisory capacity), reflecting as it does the philosophy of the older generation. Preference is given to the stand of the "young men," these being representative of the social strata and political forces to which Gilgamesh and Rehoboam belong.

The issue we have raised on the degree of competence of the two bodies in the Rehoboam affair, has been debated by scholars in connection with the Sumerian epic: were these merely advisory entities, or was the council of "men" at least, sovereign and possessor of ultimate authority?[18] On this latter point, there is no clue in the sources themselves and any inference to be drawn must remain hypothetical. Considering, however, the relatively primitive character of the societies in question, it would seem that concrete forces rather than abstract legalities determined the course of events. Put somewhat differently, the king was obliged to rely on the active support of those bodies which, in fact, or at least in his opinion, had the power to aid him in implementing his decisions and without whose assistance no decision could be of any real consequence. One may conclude, then, that these bodies consisted of the council of "men" under Gilgamesh and the assembly of "young men" during Rehoboam's reign.

In any event, the very fact of reliance in crucial matters of state on these councils representing various social levels of the populace is symptomatic of the relative weakness of the crown and testifies to a severe political crisis. It is not entirely unexpected, therefore, to find that in grave moments such as these, both Gilgamesh and Rehoboam had recourse to such bodies for moral and physical support. In the last analysis, conduct of this sort on the part of the ruler points up the restriction of his absolute powers and the democratization of the political process.

It has been my main purpose to present various ideas in connection with Rehoboam's kingship and I trust that my discourse may serve to clarify the political apparatus and organs of statecraft during the biblical period.

---

[18] For the former opinion, see A. Falkenstein, *Cahiers d'histoire mondiale*, I (1954), 801; for the latter, Jacobsen's articles cited in note 16, and cf. my remarks in *JNES*, XXII (1963), 252f.

Discussion

"Elders" and "Young Men"—the Moral to be Drawn

Amos Hacham: I should like to pose several questions. Firstly, the matter of Rehoboam's age. It is difficult to accept 41 as his accession age at face value for, according to this, he would have been born before Solomon's enthronement. Rehoboam was the son of Naama of Ammonite origin, whom Solomon married presumably after becoming king, since we know that marriage with foreign princesses was part of his royal policy.

Another question concerns the covenant renewal upon a king's accession to the throne. Now David was certainly a new king over Judah as well as Israel. Yet we have no information that the house of David existed before the kingdom of David, or that it held any sort of authority within Judah. Therefore, he should have been required to conclude a covenant with Judah similar to that with Israel, Why is no mention made of this?

On the matter of elders and "young men" there are indeed many instances to show that elders were a specific institution. But the very type of story in question places it in the category of wisdom literature. It were best, therefore, to accept the words *z^eqēnīm* and *y^elādīm* as biological terms per se. We could then draw the proper moral, namely, that the counsel of the experienced in life's ways is preferable to the advice of the young. The counsel of the elders is not overly moral, but it does contain a type of political wisdom used by tyrannical rulers throughout the ages. The despot can hold sway to his heart's desire but he must give the outward appearance of ruling on behalf of the people and with their interest at heart. Is it not the story's intent to prove the king's folly in having given ear to the flattery of the young men, rather than to the wise counsel of the elders, thereby bringing down disaster upon himself?

Whence the Opposition to Solomon?

David Ben-Gurion: First of all, concerning David's covenant: David was not the first king over Israel—Saul had preceded him. He was in need of some special act that would make his rule acceptable to the northern tribes. This is where Abner came in. This case, however, cannot serve as proof that the covenant between king and people was an established institution. Moreover, during all of Solomon's reign we hear of no covenant with the people. He had simply inherited David's kingdom, as the latter had already been ruler over all Israel.

Another point which should be stressed: The split in the kingdom actually began in the days of Solomon. It must have been discussed quite openly during Solomon's reign. What indeed brought about the contracting attitudes between elders and "young men" regarding concessions to the north? I should like to defend Rehoboam somewhat. The split, after all, was the result of Solomon's errors. He paved the way for the split while Rehoboam merely reaped the fruit of his father's act.

I see the matter as follows: Solomon, during his latter years, adopted an increasingly oppressive policy. True, he introduced foreign trade and increased the national income to a very great extent. But his wisdom seemed to have failed him in his last days when his hand grew heavy upon the people. After all, 1400 chariots, 12,000 horsemen, and considerable infantry were a burdensome yoke in those days. He built his foreign policy around international marriages, not necessarily through love of foreign women as much as from a desire to keep the peace. But all this engendered hatred toward the regime and full-scale opposition against Solomon.

There are two references to this: a) Jeroboam's "lifting a hand against the king" (I Kings 11:27). It is possible that the redactor (who was either of the house of David or in any case not antagonistic toward it) drastically cut the story. There can be no doubt that an attempt at rebellion was made during Solomon's reign.

b) In close proximity to the intended rebellion we have the incident of Ahijah the Shilonite (I Kings 11:29ff.). Discontent had been brewing increasingly during Solomon's last days. There had also been divisive attempts. It is against this backdrop that one may comprehend the counsel of both the elders and the "young men." The elders, who had experienced both Solomon's efforts on behalf of his people and his oppressive rule in his declining years, realized that he had erred toward the last, hence their advice to Rehoboam that he ease the people's burden. The "young men," however, knew Solomon only from his last years—years of heavy taxation, and large-scale chariotry. To them this was royalty's prerogative and they suggested a similar path for Rehoboam. The latter thus became the victim of his father's misdoings and of the wrong counsel of people who had lost sight of the beginnings of the monarchy.

Pres. Zalman Shazar: Stimulating material and ideas have been presented for our cogitation. No doubt one of the most enlightening points is the Gilgamesh–Rehoboam parallel of elders and "young men." Yet it is precisely this aspect of things which is problematic. If memory serves me correctly, the time gap between Gilgamesh and Rehoboam is a thousand years. I would be much more convinced if we had other comparisons to go by from the Rehoboam period itself.

Was There a Revolt against Rehoboam?

Dr. Menahem Naor: The lecturer has nicely interwoven the passage dealing with the negotiations between Abner and David and the Shechem affair. One verse, however, has not entered the discussion but is important for a proper understanding of the continuity of the story. During those very negotiations it is said of Abner (II Sam. 3:19): "And Abner went also to speak in the ears of David in Hebron all that seemed good to Israel, and to the whole house of Benjamin." If a Judean king wishes to rule over Israel, he must hearken to Abner's advice to do "what is good in the eyes of Israel and Benjamin."

A point on which I disagree with the lecturer concerns the significance of the call, "what portion have we in David? neither have we inheritance in the son of Jesse; to your tents, O Israel." One ought to differentiate between two aspects: revolt which is a passive matter and war-preparedness which is a positive act. In II Kings 8:20, it is written: "In his days Edom revolted from under the hand of Judah and made a king over themselves." The people of Edom do not wage war against the people of Judah. All they desire is that the people of Judah should not do battle against them.

D. Ben-Gurion: In II Chronicles 10:19, we read: "So Israel rebelled against the house of David unto this day" (cf. parallel verse in I Kings 12:19).

Dr. M. Naor: That was a revolt but it did not necessitate a war on Israel's part as long as Judah did not attack her. Judah, for her part, was constrained from so doing by the prophet. As far as Israel was concerned, however, it was undoubtedly a revolt.

Now as regards the elders and "young men," I have no idea as to whether we are dealing with two institutions or not. The Bible certainly has no intention here of appraising us of two bodies. Despite the nice difference between "senex" and "senator," the reference in our case is undoubtedly to old men. Those who "stood before" Solomon were, understandably, old people, while those before Rehoboam were younger men. There would simply be a change of personnel within the group at the side of the king. It is these younger men against whom Isaiah inveighs (3:4) "and I will give young men (*n⁽ᵉ⁾ārīm*) to be their ministers and babes shall rule over them." It is this grouping of "young men" who were to reign together with the king. But the attempt to identify them with the king's sons seems improbable as the latter did not grow up together with Rehoboam. The first born does not grow up with his younger brothers. The words "that were grown up with him" refer to those who were of the same age as the king.

D. Ben-Gurion: His father had many wives and his brothers could conceivably have been the same age as he.

Dr. M. Naor: But this is not what the biblical story-teller had in mind. When we hear of the king's sons, as in the case of Adonijah, aspiring to the throne, there is the explicit statement (I Kings 1:9): ". . . and he called all his brethren the king's sons . . ." It is noteworthy that when the king's sons are considered a special grouping, they are expressly referred to as "his brethren" and not "those who stand before him." The latter should rather be interpreted as ministers and outsiders.

Dr. Benjamin Uffenheimer: I have no doubt the lecturer was correct in his assumption that the *y⁽ᵉ⁾lādīm*, the "young men," were actually sons of the king, and that they were versed in the ways of the kingdom. I do not know whether they can be conceived of as a permanent institution. The illuminating verse in II Chronicles 11:22 which concerns the appointment of crown-prince Abijah over his brethren is indubitable proof that we are dealing here with a politically influential group.

As additional testimony to the lecturer's opinion and in refutation of Dr. Naor's attitude, I wish to quote Isaiah 9:5: "For a child (*yæled*) is born unto us, a son is given unto us, and the government is upon his shoulder." The sages of the Talmudic period interpreted this phrase as referring to king Hezekiah. Alt, moreover, has made the interesting point that this phrase indicates Hezekiah's accession to the throne and not the time of his birth. It would seem as though Isaiah has employed a folk term of endearment, *yæled*, used for the regent and the plural *yᵉlādīm*, for the young princes. In the case of Rehoboam the narrator was using a popular term most artistically in presenting the two extremes: elders and "young men."

"Young Men" as Expert Body

Dr. H. Gevaryahu: The lecturer's interpretation of the "young men" as princes of the court may find additional substantiation elsewhere in the Bible. The finest equivalent of such a reading is in Daniel 1:3–4: "And the king spoke unto Ashpenaz his chief officer, that he should bring in certain of the children of Israel, and of the seed royal, and of the nobles, youths (*yᵉlādīm*) in whom was no blemish, but fair to look on and skillful in all wisdom, and in knowledge, and discerning in thought, and such as had ability to stand in the king's palace; and that he should teach them the learning and the tongue of the Chaldeans."

These "youths" then are endowed at the time of their selection with special physical and mental characteristics. But we see that though they possess all manner of wisdom, they can neither read nor write the language of the Chaldeans. Their "curriculum" therefore, is confined to this aspect of learning. After their three-year period of study, they are considered capable of filling administrative posts and of being included amongst the "wise men of Babylon."

As to the "young men" being a group of boys, the *ōmᵉnīm* (guardians) in the Jehu episode are a case in point. The word *ōmᵉnīm* stems from a root connected with the concept of wisdom as well as with the rearing and educating of the young. Thus the "young men" were a corporate group of young wise men, fully versed in the various branches of the wisdom of their time and consulted by the king.

Yet another instructive instance of the *yᵉlādīm* is found in Ecclesiastes 4:13–16. We are told here of two such individuals—to my notion referring to Rehoboam and Jeroboam—who ascended the ladder of fame and eventually became a byword for wisdom: "Better is a poor and wise child (*yæled*) than an old and foolish king ... For out of prison he came forth to be king, although in his kingdom he was born poor (*ibid.*, 13 and 14)." This child or "young man" is identifiable with Jeroboam, whose family antecedents were lowly and who had apparently been released from prison. Verse 15 continues: "I saw all the living . . . that they were with the child ($y\alpha l\alpha d$), the second, that was to stand up in his stead." This "second child" refers simply to Rehoboam as following the first child, without any implication of a second generation.

Finally, I should like to pose a question concerning the northern tribes' demand to alleviate their overall burden. Can one find any relationship between this request and the so-called *misharum*-procedure of Mesopotamian kings? This refers to the custom whereby a new king would introduce various facilitations, cancel debts, release slaves and the like. Dr. Malamat, who is conversant with the external sources relating to the Bible, can well give his opinion on the matter.

David Zakkai: It was truly pleasant having this systematic presentation, lacking as it did any tone of finality. The various hypotheses on the problem of the "young men" have left us with somewhat of a feeling of an even score. We are still unable to say with absolute certainty whether the "young men" constituted a specific body. I do feel, however, that in rendering the word $y^e l\bar{a}d\bar{\imath}m$ "children," "young men," the narrator or redactor has expressed his bitterness at Rehoboam. He is definitely set against the king and employs the word $y^e l\bar{a}d\bar{\imath}m$ with contempt and irony.

Prof. Yehuda Elizur: I should like to make a few minor comments. On the subject of the organization of the royal progeny, I would add II Samuel 13:23ff. I refer to the scene between Absalom and David concerning the feast of the sheepshearers. We learn from this episode that the king is the one to grant permission to join the celebrants. When, however, he himself refuses to go, Amnon, in his capacity as head of the princes, is to go in his stead.

As to the question of Solomon's covenant-renewal, I should like to refer you to I Chronicles 28. In this chapter we read of David's assembling the leadership of Israel, while in 28:22 we are told: "And they made Solomon the son of David king the second time, and anointed him unto the Lord to be prince." I feel that in discussing the entire question, these verses are not to be overlooked.

One must also take issue with the lecturer on his conclusion, namely that the king turned to the groups that were in a position to implement his proposals. The advice of the elders certainly required no power of execution. Rehoboam, however, chose the difficult and burdensome road. Had he given ear to the elders, there would have been no need for any sort of executive power.

Joseph Braslavi: On the matter of the "young men" who grew up with Rehoboam, the lecturer has cited one Mesopotamian parallel, and Dr. Gevaryahu, one from the book of Daniel. An additional example could be supplied from I Kings 11:17ff., namely, the story of Hadad, the Edomite prince and adversary of Israel, who fled to Egypt. He was well received by Pharaoh, and the son born to him by Pharaoh's sister-in-law, was raised at Egypt's court with the undoubted intent of having him serve Egyptian interests later on.

The distinguished lecturer has properly stressed the character of the covenant with David. This did not represent submission to David but was an actual pad, somewhat loose instructure, and subject to renewal or cancellation. What I wish to point out is that the Bible does not emphasize David's domination over all of Israel, but rather his sovereignty in the covenant between Israel and Judah. This is instanced, for example, in David's return from Trans-Jordan after the Absalom revolt. (II Sam. 19:44): "And the men of Israel answered the men of Judah and said: 'We have ten parts in the king, and also more right in David.'" Before us is the covenantal emphasis: "ten parts" in king David. Again when David appoints Solomon as his successor, he says (I Kings 1:35): "... 'and I have appointed him to be prince (*nāgīd*) over Israel and over Judah,'" stress being laid on the covenant between Israel and Judah, with Israel as the first-mentioned.

Moshe Weinfeld: Dr. Malamat's point on the literary-epic expressions embodied in our story is well taken. But these literary motifs and expressions seem to me to be the Achilles heel of our story, revealing the tendentiousness of the whole chapter. Dr. Gevaryahu has already dwelt upon the parallel in the book of Daniel. There we encounter "children" being "nourished" for three years in the king's palace that they might stand "before the king," the selfsame expressions employed in our story. A like thought is to be found in I Kings 10:8 dealing with Solomon's wisdom: "Happy are these thy servants which stand continually before thee that hear thy wisdom." In the book of Ecclesiastes the problem of the old and the young in connection with the act of ruling appears again, although in paradoxical fashion: "Better is a poor and a wise child than an old and foolish king who will no more be admonished" (4:13).

This brings me to my next question: Are we not to view the Gilgamesh-Agga story as a literary parallel more than a historical one? The enigmatic sayings and proverbs both in that epic and in our chapter which Dr. Malamat referred to are a matter of literary genre rather than historical reality. Dr. Gevaryahu has raised the query whether the request for relief from the yoke has any connection with the *misharum*-act which was implemented by the Babylonian and Assyrian kings upon ascension to the throne. Indeed it seems that this motif was invoked in our story by the author who was acquainted with the habit of *misharum* in monarchial courts, an act consisting of cancellation of debts, release from corvée, etc.

I am of Dr. Malamat's opinion that the kernel of the story is to be found in an authentic historical background. I believe, however, that the historical base of the story was blurred by the literary embellishments woven into it. We may conjecture that the old men advising the abatement of the heavy burdens were actually the elders of northern Israel, who came to make covenant with Rehoboam on condition that he fulfills their demands. Rehoboam, being influenced by his ministers, rejected their proposal, and this brought about the division of the state. In other words, the "old men" and the "children" belong to the wisdom theme, while the authentic story told about elders as the representatives of the northern tribes, and ministers representing the court. Support for our conjecture may be found in some of the Greek versions to our chapter. According to these, the "old men" are the elders of Israel and not the king's council.

Dr. Israel Mehlman: We have been given some well-presented arguments about institutions during the days of the monarchy, which certainly may be regarded as adaptations and developments of those in existence during tribal times. The "elders of the people" serve as one such example. Still another is mentioned in connection with Absalom's revolt (II Sam. 19:10): "And all the people were at strife throughout all the tribes of Israel"—a reminder of the national or tribal assembly. Later we hear of the dispute between the "men of Judah" and "men of Israel," which afford the impression of soldier combatants. The question then arises whether the national assembly, "elders of the people," "men" of Judah and Israel were temporary or permanent institutions? Secondly, can one define their authority or, at the least, their area of activity during the period of the monarchy?

Concerning the "young men," it appears that Amos Hacham struck home with his remarks. The question actually is, whether one may seek a real institution such as a "young men's council" in this wisdom-type story. It may well be that both the "young men" and the elders participated in the national council despite the age disparity, with the expression "young men" aimed at mocking their political immaturity.

Chairman, Justice M. Silberg: The lecturer has correctly noted the act of anointment in the enthronement ceremony. The Bible contains five such cases: the anointments of Saul, David, Solomon, Jehu and Jehoash.

Pres. Shazar: There is also the anointment of Hazael.

Chairman: I was referring solely to the kings of Israel and Judah. The Talmud also bears this out. The act of anointment is without doubt a folk act and entails agreement en masse.

D. Ben-Gurion: Yet David's anointment was accomplished in secluded fashion.

Chairman: I should like to pose the following question: What, in the lecturer's opinion is the connection between the covenant and the anointing?

LECTURER'S REPLY

Fiction or Political Reality?

First I should like to thank the participants for their noteworthy remarks and questions, and I shall try to cover as much ground as possible.

My first remark will be directed to Mr. Hacham, one of whose queries has been echoed by other participants, namely, the basic problem of the nature and function of the elders and "young men." Is our chapter no more than mere fiction? I grant that it falls into the category of wisdom literature, when taken in the broadest sense of the term. However, it was not my intention to analyse the chapter from its literary or textual aspects. My basic contention premises a clear and concrete historico-political background to our story. On the other hand, I have pointed out that there are literary features in the narration, witness the term *yᵉlādīm*, "boys," "young men." Mr. Zakkai is certainly correct in regarding this word as a touch of contempt and irony on the redactor's part, who may have substituted it for original institutional terminology, possibly "king's sons," "princelings," or the like.

Mr. Hacham maintains that it is unreasonable to accept Rehoboam's accession age as 41, as this would presuppose his having been born before Solomon became king. It is possible that Solomon was enthroned at an age when royal offspring could already have sprung from his loins. From the infamous Uriah and Bathsheba episode, we learn that Solomon's birth took place after David's Ammonite war. I accept Prof. S. Yeivin's chronology that this war occurred during the first decade of the 10th century B.C.[19] It is thus entirely possible for Solomon, who reigned 40 years, to have been 18–20 years old at his accession (about 970 B.C.) and for Rehoboam to have been born a year earlier.

I have pointed out elsewhere the historical significance of Solomon's marriage with the Ammonite princess, Naama (Rehoboam's mother), in close proximity to his accession.[20] The act of wedlock took place at the time that the struggle for royal succession flared up among David's sons, specifically between Adonijah and Solomon. By virtue of this royal match, David would secure Solomon's place in the line of succession as the latter was not the firstborn and could not automatically claim the throne.

Mr. Ben-Gurion and others have raised the problem of Solomon's enthronement. Why, they ask, is there no mention in his case of a covenant with the northern tribes? One may attempt to answer this by surmising that the question of a covenant with Israel was not nearly as acute for Solomon as for David or Rehoboam. Solomon's position at the time of his accession was most secure. There was no reason for the northern tribes to challenge the glorious Davidide dynasty. Moreover, Solomon acted as co-regent with David and required no new recognition of his authority. Had there been such a covenant-renewal with the Israelite tribes, it would have been a mere formality, undeserving of special notice.

One should pay due note to the oblique reference in the book of Chronicles to a second coronation of Solomon, as mentioned by Prof. Elizur. Before kingship became well institutionalized, kings were apparently crowned several times. I am inclined to interpret in this manner the various biblical traditions concerning Saul's coronation (I Samuel 9–11). I would not regard these as mere literary treatment of one factual instance as commonly held, but rather as reflections of historical nuclei. Thus Saul could conceivably have been crowned twice or even three times.[21]

---

[19] See his article on David in *Encyclopaedia Biblica* (Hebrew), II (1954), cols. 640ff.
[20] *JNES*, XXII (1963), 8.
[21] See now G. Wallis, *Wissenschaftliche Zeitschrift der M. Luther Universität Halle-Wittenberg, Gesellschafts- und sprachwissenchaftliche Reihe*, XII (1963), 24ff.

The Egyptian Factor in Solomon's Policy

Now I come to Mr. Ben-Gurion's main theme which defends Rehoboam and casts all blame upon Solomon. I, for one, would like to put in a plea on the latter's behalf. One should view the deeds of the second half of his reign not as the product of sheer malicious intent, but as the result of the emerging and highly involved political constellation. I should like to point out one factor in particular, which has been overlooked too often, namely, the advent of the Pharaoh Shishak to the Egyptian throne, roughly during Solomon's 24th year. It is at this time that the turning point in Solomon's reign comes about.

The chronological picture is as follows: Solomon commenced temple construction during the fourth year of his reign. This lasted seven years. When it was completed, palace construction began, lasting for an additional 13 years, making a total of 23–24 years. Upon completion of the palace, he began to build the *millo* (possibly the rampart linking the upper and lower town of Jerusalem). It was while engaged in this work that Jeroboam's revolt against Solomon broke out, during the king's 24th year or slightly thereafter. Jeroboam then fled to Egypt, as the Bible explicitly states, to Pharaoh Shishak (I Kings 11:30), who had ascended the throne about this time and founded the 22nd dynasty.[22]

There would appear to be an inter-relationship between the dynastic changes in Egypt and Jeroboam's revolt: Shishak, who had replaced weak precursors, embarked upon an aggressive foreign policy directed against Palestine among others. His ambitions of conquest were not realized during Solomon's lifetime, but they came to fruition during Rehoboam's fifth year when he carried out an extensive military campaign throughout Palestine.[23] During Solomon's reign, nevertheless, Shishak undoubtedly began to stir up trouble between Judah and Israel and to support Jeroboam's revolt, with the intent of weakening Solomon's throne. Jeroboam's flight to Shishak upon failure of the revolt stands out in bolder relief when viewed in this light.

---

[22] A. Malamat, *BA*, XXI (1958), 96ff., reprinted with slight additions in *The Biblical Archaeologist Reader*, II (1964), esp. p. 94.

[23] The actual route of this campaign has been reconstructed by B. Mazar, *VTS*, IV (1957), 57ff., Cf. also S. Hermann, *ZDPV*, LXXX (1964), 55ff.

Another point of information connected with Solomon's 24th year is the renewed treaty concluded with Hiram of Tyre (I Kings 9:10ff.) which stipulated appreciable concessions by Solomon. The Israelite king was forced to hand over the area of Cabul in western Galilee to the king of Tyre in return for various supplies and services.

This matter may also be related to the new tough Egyptian policy and its after-effects in northern Israel. Owing to the potential unrest in this area, Solomon finds it necessary to fortify its three strongholds: Megiddo, Hazor and Gezer.[24] This defense-policy lies at the root of the heavy tax burden and corvée placed upon Israel, and explains the increased aid from his Phoenician ally. This it was that compelled him to make territorial concessions to his northern neighbor.

A Problem of Methodology

His Excellency, the President, has raised a methodological problem in questioning the validity of the comparison between the Rehoboam affair and the Gilgamesh-Agga epic. He noted the time gap between the two as one thousand years, but in point of fact the disparity is almost two millenia.

Pres. Shazar: The editing of the epic took place a thousand years later.

Lecturer: The extant fragments of the epic refer to the Old Babylonian period, the first centuries of the 2nd millennium. But it reflects the historical situation of some 1,000 years earlier. Such a historical inter-relationship of widely-spaced periods is quite conceivable at times and is precisely what occurred in the case we have been discussing. This problem has occupied my mind, as well. Consequently, I stressed the fact that we have before us nothing more than a typological parallelism, not a direct relationship. Were I to agree that we are confronted here with a literary parallel, as apparently posited by Mr. Weinfeld, I should encounter a serious methodological complication of the kind propounded by President Shazar. The distance between the two works is so great in time and place that one would then

---

[24] See I Kings 9:15, and for the new archaeological evidence Y. Yadin, BA, XXIII (1960), 62–68, with references to the discoveries at Hazor and Gezer.

have to seek out interim links in order to establish a firmer basis for our parallel. It is true that a fragment of the Gilgamesh epic was found several years ago at Megiddo, dating from the middle of the second millennium.[25] This, however, is a relic of the famous and widespread Gilgamesh composition, written in the Akkadian language, whereas we have been dealing with a lesser-known creation composed in the Sumerian tongue, whose central figure again is Gilgamesh. The relationship, therefore, is to be grasped from a typological aspect—similar political and social circumstances brought about similar problems and ultimately similar reactions.

The question, of course, is why we had to go back some two millennia before meeting an extra-biblical parallel to the Rehoboam event. Since the regimes an Mesopotamia and the rest of the ancient Near East were so completely absolutistic even by the end of the 3rd millennium B.C., at the latest, I am inclined to think that there was little real scope left for political groupings. This, of course, is the situation where literate, as distinct from illiterate, societies are concerned, whose records have provided us with whatever information we possess on their political systems.[26] To be sure, royal advisors are a common phenomenon of the ancient Near East. As for an active "bicameral" assembly, however, as in our instances, that is another matter. Yet it is precisely the social and political systems of the Sumerian city-states in the 3rd millennium, aptly named "primitive democracy"[27] by Prof. Jacobsen, that show resemblance to Israel in its pre-monarchic and early-monarchic periods. Both Gilgamesh and Rehoboam appeared in their respective countries at the stage before monarchy had become fully institutionalized and when central authority rested to an appreciable extent on representative government.

Actually, Rehoboam's is a recurring historical phenomenon where a ruler, in moments of dire national stress, is confronted with his

---

[25] A. Goetze and S. Levy, *Atiqot*, II (1959), 121–28.

[26] See the enlightening symposium *Authority and Law in the Ancient Orient*, *JAOS*, Supplement XVII (1954); for the limited authority of advisory bodies in Egypt and in the Hittite kingdom see pp. 4, 18ff. See also W.F. Albright, *History, Archaeology and Christian Humanism* (1964), pp. 180ff.

[27] However, some reservations concerning the appropriateness of this term for the Sumerian situation have been voiced, reservations now shared by Jacobsen himself. See Larsen, *IXᵉ Congrès international des sciences historiques*, II (1951), 225f. See also Albright, *History, Archaeology and Christian Humanism*, p. 183, and note 8. Cf. the doubts raised concerning a comparison with ancient Israel in J.A. Soggin, *Das Königtum in Israel* (1967), pp. 136–48.

people's ultimatum. He must choose between losing face or showing an iron hand, with the wrong choice, as so often in history,
bringing disaster in its wake.

Additional Aspects of the Covenant and Covenant Terminology
(the Hebrew Term ṭōbā)

I am gratified by the illuminating material from the Bible as presented by Drs. Uffenheimer and Gevaryahu concerning the "young
men," in support of my thesis which sees this group as a princely
council. As to Dr. Gevaryahu's inquiry on the *misharum*-procedure
in Mesopotamia, it may positively fit into the framework of the
Rehoboam story and has, in fact, recently been mentioned in this
context.[28] The people of Israel could rightly expect alleviation of
their economic burden, in connection with the impending coronation. Knowledge of actual royal decrees of the ancient Mesopotamian
kings (especially of the Old Babylonian period), lends greater
clarification and concreteness to the concept behind the "heavy yoke"
and the alleviation which the people demanded of Rehoboam. Thus
one king from the beginning of the 2nd millennium (one of the successors of Lipit-Ishtar of the Isin dynasty), explicitly states that he
has reduced taxes and greatly restricted the period of corvée service,
etc., which had been imposed by his forefathers.[29]

As to Dr. Braslavi's remarks on Hadad's flight to Egypt, may I
say that I have in fact discussed this very matter elsewhere.[30] The
rearing of Hadad's son "among the sons of Pharaoh" (I Kings 11:20),
was in accordance with widely-practiced Pharaonic policy of the New
Empire, whereby progeny of foreign vassals were brought up at
Egypt's court. The very presence of royal offspring in goodly number in the courts of the Near East is yet another point which prevents my sharing Dr. Naor's objections against identifying the "young
men" with royal princelings.

On the other hand, Dr. Naor has drawn attention to an interesting detail in connection with Abner's negotiations with David. As

---

[28] See D.J. Wiseman, *JSS*, VII (1962), 168.
[29] See F.R. Kraus, *JCS*, III (1949), 35. On the general problem of the *misharum*-
act, see Kraus, *Ein Edikt des Königs Ammi-Ṣaduqa von Babylon* (1958) and J.J. Finkelstein,
JCS, XV (1961), 91ff.
[30] *BA*, XXI (1958), 97; *BA Reader*, II, 90ff.

prerequisite to concluding the covenant with the northern tribes, the latter (David) is urged to do "all that is *good* in the eyes of Israel" (II Sam. 3:19). As a matter of fact, this instance also finds a fine parallel in the Rehoboam story. In I Kings 12:7, we hear the elders advising Rehoboam to accept the terms of the northern tribes, saying among other things: "If thou wilt . . . speak *good words* to them, then they will be thy servants for ever." While working on the subject of covenants in the ancient Near East, I noticed that the expression "good words" or "good things" recurs repeatedly in reference to the act of treaty-making, to the extent that this expression, at times, becomes synonymous with "covenant." Thus, in the Aramaic treaty of the 8th century B.C., discovered at Sefire near Aleppo, a term used for covenant is *ṭābtā* (pl. *ṭābātā*), the equivalent of Hebrew *ṭōbā*, *ṭōbōt*, i.e. "good (things)." This has been recently emphasized by W.L. Moran, who has assembled citations from the Akkadian on this point.[31]

This usage, however, may also be detected in various biblical passages other than the two mentioned before, e.g. David's prayer before God (II Sam. 7:28): ". . . and thy words are truth and thou has promised this *good thing* (*ṭōbā*) unto thy servant." The reference is to the Lord's covenant with David's dynasty, and finds its sole terminological indication here in the word *ṭōbā* (but cf. Ps. 89:4 and *passim*; 132:12, where the term *bʿrīt*, "covenant," is expressly mentioned). Another example, this time in connection with the High Priest Jehoiada, may be found in II Chronicles 24:16: "And they buried him in the city of David among the kings, because he had done good (*ṭōbā*) in Israel, and toward God and His house." In my opinion, the reference here is once again to a covenant, in this instance the one mentioned earlier which Jehoiada, the High Priest, effected between God and the people of Israel. Lastly, may one not find food for thought in the "good words" (*ṭōbōt*) spoken by Evil-Merodach, Nebuchadnezzar's successor, to Jehoiachin (II Kings 25:27ff.), during the former's accession year? Perhaps here too there was a type of legal arrangement whereby Jehoiachin's throne was "set above the throne" of the other kings that were with him in Babylonian

---

[31] *JNES*, XXII (1963), 173ff. Cf. D.R. Hillers, *BASOR*, No. 176 (Dec. 1964), 46f. Add further to the biblical examples adduced by Hillers and by us, the expression *ṭōbā* (followed by *šalōm*) in Jer. 33:9. Note that in the Akkadian, Aramaic, and Hebrew usage the feminine forms of the respective terms are preferred.

captivity. I hope to treat this subject more fully at some future date.

On the dispute relating to Israel's revolt under Rehoboam, I feel that the question is largely one of semantics. My aim was to stress that the slogan "to your tents, O Israel" was merely a formula for the dispersal of the assembly rather than a signal for active rebellion.

D. Zakkai: But if one says "Now see to thine own house, David," is this not an actual threat?

Lecturer: This phrase simply means: We do not agree to conclude a treaty with the Davidide dynasty.

Dr. M. Naor: Which means rebellion!

Lecturer: Of course the nullification of the covenant is at times rebellion, but it should not be regarded as identical with warlike preparations. The latter act would entail a completely reversed formula, as I have tried to show.

Pres. Shazar: In other words, the northern tribes came to crown the king and decided against this.

Lecturer: Finally, the question posed by Justice Silberg: Can one see a relationship between the covenant with the king and his anointment? Most definitely. The act of anointing expresses the divine aspect of the covenant, the king-God relationship mentioned before.[32] The question brings us back to the problem raised at the outset of our lecture: were these acts of covenant-making and anointing permanent or sporadic practices? This is an age-old argument, already raised in Talmudic literature.[33] I return to my contention that the covenantal act (and, for that matter, the act of anointing) can be regarded as a customary affair, at least where a new dynasty was concerned or during a crisis on matters of succession.

In reference to the anointment, attention should be paid to still another detail. Not only are there five or six sole instances of the anointing of kings but, to the best of my knowledge, only two Israelite sovereigns are specifically referred to as messiah ("the anointed")—Saul and David. The term may have been employed also in the cases of Solomon (II Chron. 6:42) and Zedekiah, if the latter is indeed the one referred to in "the breath of our nostrils, the anointed of the Lord" (Lam. 4:20).

---

[32] See now E. Kutsch, *Salbung als Rechtsakt im Alien Testament und im alten Orient* (1963), pp. 52ff., 59.

[33] See for example *Jerusalem Talmud*, Horayoth, Chap. 3, p. 47; *Babylonian Talmud*, Horayoth, 11b.

PART FOUR

TWILIGHT OF JUDAH AND THE DESTRUCTION
OF THE FIRST TEMPLE

14

THE HISTORICAL BACKGROUND OF THE
ASSASSINATION OF AMON, KING OF JUDAH*

The sanguinary events described in 2 Kings xxi, 19–26, and in 2 Chron. xxxiii, 21–25, the slaying of Amon, son of Manasseh, King of Judah, by his courtiers and the subsequent retaliation upon the conspirators by 'Am ha-'Areṣ—the 'people of the land'—have remained an enigma. The undercurrents of these court intrigues are overlooked in the Biblical account, and, so far, no suitable explanation has been discovered in the general historical development of the Ancient Near East. The theory, currently accepted among historians, attributes to these events merely a religious background: according to this theory the King of Judah was assassinated by the Religious Reform Party, but, as a reaction, the "people of the land" restored the status quo.[1] There is, however, no undisputed evidence supporting this hypothesis, nor do the social classes involved in these events ("the servants of the King" and "the people of the land") display dominantly religious characteristics. We shall endeavour to show that the regicide and the subsequent retaliation were enacted against a political and military background. We shall also endeavour to link these Judaean fluctuations of power with other events in the contemporary history of the Near East.

The murder of Amon was doubtless an anti-Assyrian repercussion of his foreign policy, since the Bible unequivocally presents him as a loyal satellite of the Assyrian regime. In these respect, the Chronicler is most outspoken in describing Amon's devotion to Assyrian customs as being more extreme than that of his sire, Manasseh: "But he did that which was evil in the sight of the Lord, as did Manasseh his father: for Amon sacrificed unto all the carved images which Manasseh his father had made, and served them. And humbled not

---

* This article was first published in: *IEJ* 3 (1953), 26–29.
[1] Cf. E. Sellin: *Geschichte des israel.-jüd. Volkes*, I, 1924, p. 282; R. Kittel: *Geschichte des Volkes Israel*, II, 6 & 7th ed., p. 402. On the other hand compare *Encyclop. Biblica*, I, 1950 (Hebrew) s.v. Amon.

himself before the Lord, as Manasseh his father had humbled himself; but Amon trespassed more and more." (2 Chron. xxxiii, 22–23). According to the most reasonable chronological calculation Amon's death occurred in the year 640–639.[2] Indeed from Assyrian sources we learn that in this very same period a rebellion was organized in 'Eber ha-Nahar, i.e. the region between the Euphrates and the Mediterranean Sea; the Arabians, including the tribes of Qedar and the Nebaioth, revolted against the rule of Ashurbanipal. This uprising seems to have been quite extensive, since we hear of it also in connection with the defection of Acre and Ushu (Tyre on the mainland). The Assyrians, however, were as yet strong enough to conduct a successful military campaign westward, and to defeat the Arabian tribes on the Syrian border (in the vicinity of Damascus and the Bashan region) decisively. The revolt was suppressed with all the usual severity, as we learn from the fate of Acre and Ushu. These cities fell at the end of Ashurbanipal's campaign and their inhabitants were killed or exiled to Assyria.[3]

It seems most likely that this was some connection between these events and the progress of matters in Judah. We may assume that the coup d'etat in Jerusalem was aimed against the pro-Assyrian policy of Amon and that the conspirators wanted to join the general uprising against Ashurbanipal. However, upon the approach of the Assyrian army to Syria and Palestine and its initial successes against the rebels, those forces in Judah who wished to prevent a military encounter with Assyria gained the upper hand. Thus a counter-revolution was achieved and the nobles, who had wished to throw off the yoke of Assyrian rule, were exterminated. It was a stitch in time, and it seems to have placated the Arabian, for we hear of no punitive action being taken against Judah by their army. A similar development took place among the Arabian tribes. The rebel chieftain, Uaite II, son of Bir-Dadda, was finally deposed by his subjects, in order that his tribe might escape the reprisals of the Assyrian army.

It is possible that during these same period other events occurred in Palestine, which were also connected with the general uprising

---

[2] Cf. E.R. Thiele, *JNES*, 3, 1994, p. 180.

[3] Unfortunately we have no exact date for this campaign of Ashurbanipal; it was apparently the second one against the tribes in revolt. We may however assume that these events took place during the great revolt of Elam between the years 641–639 B.C.; cf. M. Streck: *Assurbanipal I*, 1916, p. ccclxi; *Cambridge Ancient History*, III, p. 125. But cf. Addenda.

against the Assyrian suzerainity: perhaps the Assyrian province of Samaria also joined the mutiny. The note in Ezra iv, 9–10; concerning the settlement of foreign peoples in Samaria by Asenappar (usually identified with Ashurbanipal), may indicate an extreme measure against an uprising in that country. Evidence for deferring the date of this event to the period under consideration may be found in the list of nations exiled to Samaria, which includes exiles from Elam and its capital, Susa. The last campaign of Ashurbanipal against Elam took place at the beginning of the year 642 and the complete destruction of Susa was accomplished by 641–640. Thus there is a connection between at least part of the nations that in the reign of Ashurbanipal were exiled to Samaria, beyond the Euphrates and 'Eber ha-Nahar in general, and his campaign to Syria and Palestine mentioned above.[4]

The list of exiles in Ezra, which is indeed somewhat questionable in its present form, also mentions settlers from Erech (Archevites) and Babylon. This information, if authentic, would tend to advance the date of the part of the list's contents by several years, i.e. until after the fall of Babylon (648). In that case the settling of these nations in 'Eber ha-Nahar would be linked with the first campaign of Ashurbanipal against the Arabian tribes. However, with regard to the settlers from Erech, it is worth noting that this city did not join the Babylonian revolt in the years 652–648: on the contrary, its governor fought at the side of the Assyrian King against Shamash-shum-ukin, the insurgent monarch of Babylon.[5] It is, therefore, improbable that the inhabitants of Erech, if it is they who are actually referred to by the term "Archevites,"[6] were exiled at that time. For this event too we must seek the background in a later period.

Along with the Babylonians and Elamites mentioned in the list of exiles there are also Persians (Apharsites): this fact seems to indicate that the list should be assigned to a later date. In two new passages from documents of Ashurbanipal, one published by Thompson[7] and

---

[4] Cf. Streck, *op. cit.* (supra, n. 3), p. ccclxiv ff. and also *Encycl. Biblica* I, s.v. Asenappar.

[5] Cf. Streck, *op. cit.* (supra, n. 3), pp. cxvi–cxxiii, ccxciv; *Cambridge Ancient History*, III, p. 122.

[6] Against this identification cf. P. Jensen, *Zeitschr. f. alttest. Wiss.*, N.F., 11, 1934, p. 121f., and N.H. Torczyner, *BJPES*, 14, 1945, p. 6.

[7] R.C. Thompson & M.E.L. Mallowan, *AAA*, 20, 1933, p. 95.

the other by Weidner,[8] there is mention of Cyrus, King of Parsemash (whose inhabitants were Persians), and rulers from other lands; "Kings whose home is distant and who dwell on the far-off border of Elam." The date of these documents and especially of the second passage, which tells that Cyrus I capitulated to the Assyrians after the final destruction of Elam, was justly fixed by the publishers in the year 640–639.[9] In any case, the mention of the Persians in connection with the abortive revolt of Elam is an interesting fact *per se*. To the writer's knowledge, its parallelism with the list of exiled nations in the time of Asenappar has yet to be pointed out.

It is not improbable that at the same time occurred Egypt's first actual attempts to annex Assyrian territories in Southern Palestine and especially those in the Philistine area. According to Herodotus (II, 157) the Egyptians besieged for 29 years the city of Ashdod, the capital of the Assyrian province in Philistia, until it fell at the hands of the Pharaoh Psamtik I. If we take us trustworthy the word of Herodotus, who is generally reliable where the history of the Near East during that period is concerned,[10] then 639 is the latest possible date we can give for the beginning of the siege, as Psamtik I died in 610–609. A later date for this event, as has been suggested,[11] is out of the question. On the other hand, the date 640–639 serves well to link the event with the period of his reign (664–663 to 610–609), since several years previously (about 650) he had begun to throw off the Assyrian yoke.[12] Evidence of the control of Philistia by Psamtik I is provided by an Egyptian fortress of the same type as was erected by him in Daphne and Naukratis. This fortress was discovered by Petrie at Tell Jemmeh (13 km. south of Gaza), which he identified with Gerar.[13] Herodotus' description (I, 105) of Psamtik's

---

[8] E. Weidner, *Archiv. f. Orientf.*, 7, 1931, pp. 1ff.

[9] But compare also A.T. Olmstead: *A History of the Persian Empire*, 1948, p. 31, who connects the above event with the first revolt of Elam beginning in the year 651.

[10] Cf. H. de Meulenaere: *Herodotos over de 26ste Dynastie*. Louvaine, 1951, p. 32, in which he relegates Herodotus' account of the siege of Ashdod to the status of a mere folk tradition.

[11] Cf. Streck, *op. cit.* (supra, n. 3), p. ccclxii, who dates the beginning of the siege in 634.

[12] There has already been one suggestion that this Pharaoh may have invaded Philistia in 640, but there has been no proof that he did so, nor has any attempt been made to integrate the extended siege of Ashdod in the reign of Psamtik. Cf. J.H. Breasted: *A History of Egypt*, 1945, p. 580.

[13] Cf. F. Petrie: *Gerar*, 1928, p. 4. The same phenomenon is apparent from the results of Petrie's excavations at Tell ez-Zuweid, 15 km. south of Raphia, within

encounter with the Scythians, south of Ascalon, indicates a similar situation.[14]

If the above hypothesis agrees with the historical facts, we have, therefore, a new synchronism between Assyria, Judah, and Egypt, and so additional proof of the extensive political and military activity in Palestine in the year 640–639.

the Sinai region, which was reconstructed "rather late in the reign of Psamtik I" Cf. F. Petrie: *Anthedon*, 1937, p. 7.

[14] For the details of this event and its chronology, cf. A. Malamat, *IEJ*, 1, 1950–51, esp. p. 156.

15

JOSIAH'S BID FOR ARMAGEDDON:
THE BACKGROUND OF THE JUDEAN-EGYPTIAN ENCOUNTER IN 609 B.C.*

In attempting to clarify the historical background of the clash between Judah and Egypt at Megiddo in the summer of 609 B.C., we are faced with a double dilemma: historically and militarily, we must ask who held Megiddo at this time. Did Josiah, king of Judah, seek here to block the Egyptian advance to the north? Or did Megiddo already serve as an Egyptian base? And then, there is the archaeological quandary concerning Stratum II at Megiddo, generally ascribed to the second half of the seventh century B.C. Was the massive building discovered in this stratum an Israelite fortress built by Josiah, as often thought, or should it be regarded as Egyptian, whether actually built by Egyptians or merely appropriated?

In my recent studies on this period, I have noted the latter possibility, and have assumed that Josiah's move was intended, *inter alia*, against the center of the former Assyrian province of *Magiddu* which, in the meantime, had most likely been taken over by the Egyptians, recently acquired allies of Assyria.[1] The lack of clear-cut data, however, leaves any preference between the above alternatives in the realm of conjecture.

---

* This article was originally published in: T.H. Gaster FS, *JANES* 5 (1973/4), 267–279.
[1] See A. Malamat, "The Last Kings of Judah and the Fall of Jerusalem," *IEJ* 18 (1968), 137f., n. 1, and the passing remarks in my lecture on "Jeremiah according to the Bible and the External Sources," delivered in the autumn of 1969 at the Jerusalem Bible Circle, subsequently published in the anthology, *Studies in the Book of Jeremiah*, vol. 1, ed. B.-Z. Luria (Jerusalem, n.d.), and see pp. 14 and 30 there [in Hebrew]. Prof. Y. Milgrom, who was present at my lecture, followed this point up in a paper in *Beth Mikra* 44 (1970), 23–27, claiming that the already declining Assyrians had little choice but to turn Megiddo over to the Egyptians, in return for military assistance.

I. *Megiddo Stratum II—Israelite or Egyptian?*

Let us first review the archaeological evidence from Megiddo Strata III–II (see plan).[2] It is almost unanimously agreed today that Megiddo Stratum III represents the seat of the Assyrian province founded after the annexation of the northern parts of the kingdom of Israel by Tiglath-pileser III in 732 B.C. or, in any case, after the fall of Israel in 720 B.C. This settlement—which underwent slight repairs during its existence—was well fortified and well planned, with a regular street network and blocks of houses. Near the city gate, two structures were discovered (Buildings 1052 and 1369), of the "Assyrian open court" type, in best Assyrian architectural style.[3] In their report on Megiddo, the excavators ascribe this stratum to 780–650 B.C. W.F. Albright raised the final date of this stratum to as early as 732 B.C., that is, until the conquests of Tiglath-pileser III in Palestine. This chronology was adopted by Ruth Amiran and I. Dunayevsky in their study on the buildings of the Assyrian court type.[4] Such a high dating, however, seems unlikely and several other archaeologists have shown that the end of Stratum IV A at Megiddo is to be placed in the second half of the eighth century B.C., and, consequently, ascribe Stratum III to the period of Assyrian rule there.[5] It is noteworthy that the excavations revealed no traces of the destruction of Stratum III, and the transition to Stratum II seems to have been rather smooth.

The duration of Stratum II has been fixed by the excavators, "arbitrarily," as 650–600 B.C. This settlement came to a close, on

---

[2] See the excavation report of R.S. Lamon and G.M. Shipton, *Megiddo* (Chicago, 1939), 1:62–87. I am much obliged to Dan Bahat, of the Israel Department of Antiquities and Museums, for preparing the plan of Megiddo Strata III–II as presented here, and for an informative discussion with me on the archaeological material. The fortress of Stratum II at Megiddo is shown in our plan with full restorations, whereas in the excavation report (p. 84, fig. 95), the extant ruins as found are marked, with restorations dotted.

[3] See Ruth B.K. Amiran and I. Dunayevsky, *BASOR* 149 (1958), 25–32, and figs. 1–2 on p. 27.

[4] *Ibid.*, 31f., after W.F. Albright, *AASOR* 21–23 (1943), 2, n. 1.

[5] Cf. K. Kenyon, *Archaeology in the Holy Land* (London, 1960), 286; Y. Yadin, in *The Kingdoms of Israel and Judah*, ed. A. Malamat (Jerusalem, 1961), 104 and n. 86 [in Hebrew]; Y. Aharoni, *Encyclopaedia Biblica* (Jerusalem, 1962), 4:629, s.v. *Megiddo* [in Hebrew]. Similar, too, was Albright's earlier opinion, in his review of *Megiddo*, vol. 1, in *AJA* 44 (1940), 549, where he suggested the dates 733–*ca.* 670 and 670 (?)–609 (?) for Strata III and II, respectively.

the basis of the findings, in what would appear to be a partial destruction. While many of the earlier private dwellings continued in use in Stratum II, the city wall and Assyrian buildings of Stratum III were abandoned, and the city was left unfortified. The large structure built in Stratum II partly overlies the "offset and inset" wall of the earlier city and was seemingly the sole fortification on the site in this period (see plan). This massive structure was built at the eastern edge of the mound (area C), providing a clear view of the Plain of Megiddo and the pass from Wadi Ara. The building is of unusually large dimensions, as seen from the plan: 68 meters (average) length and 48 meters (average) width; the walls are up to 2.5 meters thick. It differs from the Assyrian court buildings of the previous stratum not only in its size but also in its plan. The spacious court is not surrounded on every side by rows of chambers, but is bordered on the east by the outer wall of the entire structure. The suggestion of the excavators that there were rooms on the eastern flank as well, which "had collapsed and been washed down the steep slope," is most unlikely because of the proximity of the edge of the mound. Indeed, extensive erosion here is precluded by the fact that parts of the Stratum III city wall were found *in situ* at the very edge (see plan). In any case, this is certainly a fortress, with storage facilities for a considerable amount of equipment and provisions, as well as space for a large garrison. The paucity of finds from within the building (none even warranting mention in the report) does not enable a more precise dating, or even an identification of its occupants.

The excavators somewhat hesitatingly ascribed Stratum II, including the fortress, to Josiah, actually only on the basis of historical considerations—that is, because of the expansionist tendencies of this Judean king within the territories of the former kingdom of Israel. This ascription has been accepted by other archaeologists, who thus regard the destruction of Stratum II as the outcome of Josiah's defeat here at the hands of the Egyptians in 609 B.C.[6] Theoretically, however, there are three other possibilities with regard to the construction and control of Megiddo Stratum II: (1) a continuation of Assyrian occupation; (2) a fortress built by the Babylonians following Nebuchadnezzar's conquests in the West, beginning in 605 B.C.; and (3)

---

[6] Cf. Lamon and Shipton, *Megiddo*, 87, followed by Aharoni, *loc. cit.* (above, n. 5), and Y. Yadin, *Encyclopaedia of Archaeological Excavations in the Holy Land* (Jerusalem, 1970), 315 [in Hebrew].

a site under Egyptian control with a fortress built by Psamtik I or at least passed into his hands.

The first possibility is untenable. By the second half of the seventh century B.C., not only had Assyrian rule in Palestine disintegrated, but it is inconceivable that the Assyrians themselves would disregard the plan of their own earlier city—with its fortifications—in favor of an isolated fort, built in a style varying from theirs. The second possibility would force us to lower the date of the end of Stratum III to at least 605/604 B.C., that is, we would have to ascribe to this stratum a duration of a century or more; though this is not an impossibility, Stratum II would have been of very short duration—indeed, only a few years—a most unlikely proposition. This chronological conclusion derives from the fact that the pottery of Stratum I still included typical Iron II forms, signifying that the beginning of this stratum was around 600 B.C. (according to the excavators) and, in any event, not much later than this.[7]

Moreover, there is another possible factor negating both of the above two possibilities—the measurements of the fortress in relation to the standard employed. The measurements do not seem to suit the standard Assyrian or Babylonian cubits; that is, the short cubit of 49.5 centimeters commonly found in the Assyrian and Babylonian building projects. In contrast, they do suit the short cubit of 44.5 centimeters used by both the Israelites and the Egyptians (alongside the "royal" Egyptian cubit of 52.2–52.7 centimeters).[8] Employing this shorter cubit, the outer dimensions of the fortress measure 150 × 108 cubits (67 × 48 meters); the courtyard, 60 × 60 cubits (27 × 27 meters); and the basic square of the structure (without the rooms on the south), 108 × 108 cubits (48 meters square). If the "reed" (*qāneh*) measure of six cubits, known to have been current in Palestine,[9] was

---

[7] See Lamon and Shipton, *Megiddo*, 87; cf. also Albright, *AJA* 44, 549. For the same reasons we cannot accept the variant proposed by Milgrom, *Beth Mikra* 44, 24, according to which the Assyrian Stratum III itself later passed into Egyptian hands. He completely ignores Megiddo Stratum II.

[8] For the linear measurements in the ancient Near East, and in the Bible, see E. Stern, *Encyclopaedia Biblica* (Jerusalem, 1962), 4:848–52 [in Hebrew]. For the standard Assyrian and Babylonian cubit, cf. now also D.J. Wiseman, *Anatolian Studies* 22 (1972), 143; for the Israelite and Egyptian cubits, see especially R.B.Y. Scott, *JBL* 77 (1958), 205–14.

[9] See the previous note. I must thank R. Grafman who brought to my attention the possibility of employing standards of measure as a criterion in attributing structures; and to the field architect Y. Mintsker who, at my request, calculated the measurements of the fortress according to the plan published in the excavation

employed here, then these all are whole numbers, as would suit such a monumental building. With all due reservation in reaching any definite conclusions based on measurements, the results of such an investigation would appear to be of aid in identifying the fortress as being of Israelite or Egyptian foundation, rather than Assyrian or Babylonian. Any actual or supposed resemblance of the plan of the fortress to the Assyrian open court plan, even if regarded as a degenerate version of the Assyrian prototype,[10] can be of little historical significance.

Generally speaking, the archaeological findings in Megiddo Stratum II leave us with the alternative which we raised initially—to regard this stratum as an Israelite or Egyptian settlement. This latter suggestion may seem surprising, for, at least according to the meager remains recovered, Stratum II is not of an Egyptian character.[11] Thus, we must seek a solution based on strictly historical considerations.

II. *Psamtik I and Josiah*

The gradual disintegration of Assyrian rule in Palestine in the second half of the seventh century B.C. is obscured by a paucity of data. The latest datable evidence for Assyrian control in the various

---

report. He was able to confirm the assumption that this fortress was built according to a reed based on the cubit of 44.5 centimeters. He further suggested emending the reconstruction so as to eliminate the southeastern corner room (broken line in our plan), which he regards as impossibly close to the edge of the mound there; this would make the eastern wall conform to the curved edge of the mound.

[10] As proposed by Amiran and Dunayevsky (*BASOR* 149, 25f.) in their second category (Series II) of buildings. These buildings, however, in contrast to the true Assyrian open court type (their Series I), hardly seem to form a coherent group (see figs. on p. 30 there). The above suggestion of a derivative, local version has been followed by some scholars, who claim that the fortress was erected by Josiah in imitation of the Assyrian prototype. See most recently E. Stern, *Qadmoniot* 6 (1973), table 1; and *idem, The Material Culture of the Land of the Bible in the Persian Period* (Jerusalem, 1973), 57–59 [in Hebrew]. There, he drew attention, inter alia, to the palace of Pharaoh Hophra at Memphis (see W.M.F. Petrie, *The Palace of Apries, Memphis* II, [London, 1909], pl. 1), whose plan is of the open court type. But rather than regarding this as a parallel to a derivative version of the Assyrian type, as does Stern, we can see in it a parallel to the Megiddo building insofar as it was surrounded, too, by rooms on only three sides (Stern accepts the Megiddo excavators' hypothetical row of rooms on the fourth side; see above).

[11] But we should note that in two loci of Megiddo Stratum II, Egyptian faience figurines were found, one of them identical with figurines of the 26th dynasty in Egypt; see *Megiddo*, vol. 1, pl. 76: 2, 3.

regions of this country is as follows: Assyrian deeds of sale found at
Gezer, dating to 651 and 649 B.C., pointing to an Assyrian administration at this site; the mention of an Assyrian governor at Samaria
in 646 B.C.; and the punitive expedition undertaken by Ashurbanipal
to Akko and Usu (mainland Tyre), now to be dated 644/643 B.C.,
or a year or two earlier.[12] If our longstanding assumption that the
bloody events at the Judean court in the days of King Amon (2
Kings 21:19–26) reflect hostility toward Assyria is basically correct,
then the Assyrians were still of some weight in the West in 640/639
B.C.[13] This assumption loses much of its substance, however, with
the discovery of a new prism of Ashurbanipal, which necessitates
dating the above Assyrian punitive expedition several years prior to
the events of King Amon's reign. In this light, we might venture to
attribute the murder of Amon to Egyptian instigation; Egypt was
possibly already seeking to bring a sympathetic faction to power in
Judah. This finds support in the fact that it was the ʿam haʾ āręṣ who
undertook the counter-coup in Jerusalem, eliminating "them that had
conspired against King Amon," and placing his son Josiah on the
throne. For the ʿam haʾ āręṣ appears to have been a steadfastly anti-
Egyptian faction, as is indicated by its support of both Josiah and
Jehoahaz, two kings of clear anti-Egyptian sentiment—whereas the
pro-Egyptian Jehoiakim, Josiah's first-born, natural heir to the throne,
was purposefully rejected by this body.

In any event, we may assume that Assyrian rule in Palestine had
already come to an effective end by the early thirties of the seventh
century B.C.—that is, a decade prior to the death of Ashurbanipal
in 627 B.C. The political vacuum and the "no-man's land" left in
the Assyrian districts in this country were the objects of rivalry primarily between Egypt and Judah. From the description of Josiah's

---

[12] For the Assyrian deeds at Gezer, cf. K. Galling, *PJb* 31 (1935), 81f.; for the
Assyrian governor (*šaknu*) at Samaria, cf. R.A. Henshaw, *JAOS* 88 (1968), 478; and
for the date of Ashurbanipal's campaign to the Phoenician coast in 644/643 B.C.,
cf. H. Tadmor, *Encyclopaedia Biblica* (Jerusalem, 1968), 5:109f. [in Hebrew]. For a
645/644 B.C. dating of this latter campaign, calculated on the basis of Ashurbanipal's
prism F (published by J.M. Aynard, *Le prisme du Louvre AO 19.939*, [Paris, 1957]),
see I. Ephʿal, *The Nomads on the Border of Palestine* . . . (Doctoral Dissertation, Jerusalem,
1971), 114 and n. 315 [in Hebrew].

[13] See *IEJ* 3 (1953), 26–29, (= here chap. 14); however, according to Ashurbanipal's
prism F (see preceding note), Susa had been destroyed by 646 B.C. and not *ca.*
640, as previously held; and its inhabitants were most likely exiled to Samaria several years earlier than we proposed there.

reform in the Book of Kings, it would appear that in the twenties of this same century the Judean king extended his rule over territories which coincided, more or less, with the former Assyrian province of *Samerina*. Besides the cult at Bethel, Josiah systematically destroyed "all the houses also of the high places that were in the cities of Samaria" (2 Kings 23:15, 19). In contrast, the Book of Chronicles—according to which the cultic reform in the north reached "as far as Naphtali" and spread "throughout all the land of Israel" and "all the territory that belonged to the people of Israel" (2 Chronicles 34:6, 7, 33)—is little more than a late, tendentious expansion of the geographical extent of the reform.[14] Thus, this source is hardly proof of Josiah's political control reaching into Galilee, though he may well have sought to annex parts of the former province of *Magiddu* which encompassed the Jezreel valley and Galilee.

A minimalistic approach would limit Josiah's annexations in the north to the area of Mount Ephraim alone. Thus, B. Mazar, followed by Z. Kallai, contends that the actual borders of the kingdom of Judah at that time are reflected in the delimitation of the reform: "from Geba to Beersheba" (2 Kings 23:8); Geba here, according to Mazar, is the Geba of Ephraim, which he identifies with et-Tell, some five kilometers southwest of Shiloh.[15] This approach leaves open the matter of the spread of Josiah's political influence towards Megiddo—in contrast to actual control. On the western flank, Josiah did extend his territorial rule, apparently obtaining a sort of corridor in the northern Sephela, and reaching the sea. This is indicated by the Hebrew epigraphic finds at Gezer, on the one hand, and at Meṣad Ḥashavyahu, a small fortress on the coast, one and a half kilometers south of Yabne-yam (Minet Rubin, which also may have been a Judean Settlement at this time), on the other hand.[16]

---

[14] For such a tendency on the part of the Chronicler, cf., e.g., M. Noth, *Überlieferungs-geschichtliche Studien* (Halle, 1942), 1:178 (= p. 200); for the exclusion of Galilee from Josiah's rule, but not the sphere of his reform, cf. Milgrom, *Beth Mikra* 44, 26.

[15] See *Bulletin of the Jewish Palestine Exploration Society* 8 (1940), 35–37; Z. Kallai, *The Northern Boundaries of Judah* (Jerusalem, 1960), 75f. [in Hebrew]. For an even more minimalistic view, see the early study of A. Alt, *PJb* 21 (1925), 100–16, and recently P. Welten, *Die Königs-Stempel* (Wiesbaden, 1969), 163f.—both of whom have Josiah's territories in the north reaching only as far as Bethel. H.D. Lance, *HTR* 64 (1971), 332, excludes even the latter city from the Josianic kingdom, on the basis of the complete absence of the *lamęlęk* royal jar stamps at this site.

[16] Josiah's rule over Gezer is evidenced by the number of *lamelek* jar stamps found there; see most recently, Welten, *Die Königs-Stempel*, 65f., 180; and Lance, *HTR* 64,

In the scramble over inheritance of the former Assyrian territories, a decided advantage in time was held by Psamtik I, who reigned in 664–610 B.C.—for Joshia's expansion apparently began only in 628 B.C., upon the institution of his reform in his twelfth regnal year (cf. 2 Chronicles 34:3; he came to the throne as a minor in 639 B.C.). Psamtik's variegated relations with the Assyrians can be divided into four phases:[17] (1) Initially, with the reconquest of Egypt by Ashurbanipal in 663 B.C., he was an Assyrian vassal; (2) Between 656 and 652 B.C. he threw off the Assyrian yoke, with the support of Gyges king of Lydia, who died in 652 B.C.; (3) Shortly after, he undoubtedly began undermining Assyrian rule in Palestine. This is reflected in Herodotus (II, 157), concerning Psamtik's conquest of Azotus, that is, Ashdod, after a siege of supposedly twenty-nine years.[18] The excavators of Ashdod tend to relate this conquest to the destruction of Stratum VII there, the city of Stratum VI (which presumably endured till Nebuchadnezzar's conquest) now undoubtedly having come under the Egyptian aegis.[19] The extension of Egyptian hegemony over Phoenicia, as well, at least towards the end of Psamtik's reign, is indicated by an Egyptian stele from his fifty-second year, that is, 612 B.C. This inscription shows the princes of Lebanon to

330. For the Hebrew ostraca from Meṣad Ḥashavyahu, see J. Naveh, *IEJ* 10 (1960), 129–39; *idem*, *IEJ* 12 (1962), 27–32, and cf. 89–99. For a seal weight found at Minet Rubin (and not *Nebi* Rubin, further inland, as often erroneously stated), bearing unit marks and a Hebrew (?) name, see N. Glueck, *BASOR* 153 (1959), 35–38.

[17] For recent studies on Psamtik I vis-à-vis Assyria, see the following books: H. de Meulenaire, *Herodotos over de 26ste Dynastie* (Louvain, 1951), 22–43; Mary F. Gyles, *Pharaonic Policies and Administration, 663 to 323 B.C.* (Chapel Hill, 1959), 16–25; E. Drioton and J. Vandier, *L'Égypte*, 4th ed. (Paris, 1962), 574–92; F.K. Kienitz, in *Fischer Weltgeschichte* (Frankfurt a/M, 1967), 4:256–62; K.A. Kitchen, *The Third Intermediate Period in Egypt* (Warminster, 1973), 399–406.

[18] For an attempt to correlate the beginning of this Egyptian siege with the assassination of King Amon of Judah, in 640/639 B.C., see Malamat, *JNES* 9 (1950), 218; *IEJ* 3 (1953) (= here chap. 14), 29, followed by H. Cazelles, *RB* 74 (1967), 25f., 42. For *ca.* 655 B.C. as the beginning of this siege, see F.K. Kienitz, *Die politische Geschichte Ägyptens vom 7. bis zum 4. Jahrh.* (Berlin, 1953), 17. Interpreting Herodotus's statement as implying the twenty-ninth year (!) of Psamtik's reign (instead of a twenty-nine year duration), Tadmor (*BA* 29 [1966], 102) arrives at a date of 635 B.C. for the siege.

[19] See M. Dothan, "*Ashdod* II–III," *'Atiqot* 9–10 (1971), 21, 115. The discovery of fragments of Egyptian faience "New Year bottles," two of them bearing Egyptian inscriptions (37, 170f.; figs. 3:15 and 96:17), in Stratum VI is significant of more than ordinary relations with Egypt. On the other hand, the assumption of the excavators, that later the same stratum was incorporated within Josiah's kingdom (assumed on the basis of finds such as a single *lamelek* jar stamp and inscribed Hebrew weights; cf. p. 22 there), is stretching the evidence.

have been vassals placed under an Egyptian commissioner and paying tribute to Pharoah;[20] (4) The weakening of home-rule in Assyria
proper, following the rise of Babylonia (and later also the Medes),
led finally to a community of interests with Egypt, and thus to a
league between the erstwhile rivals.

This Egyptian-Assyrian alliance came into existence, apparently,
between 622 and 617 B.C., as can be inferred from the data in
Nabopolassar's Babylonian Chronicle ("Gadd's Chronicle").[21] Such a
dating is based on the fact that, in the first tablet of the Chronicle
(BM 25127), reporting on Nabopolassar's first years, 626–623/622
B.C., there is no mention of Egypt in the struggle between Assyria
and Babylonia; however, in line ten of the following tablet (BM
21901), which opens with the events of 616 B.C.—after a gap of six
years—mention is already made of the military assistance rendered
to the Assyrians by Egypt. Similar Egyptian aid was rushed to the
Euphrates in 610 and 609 B.C. But in 606 and twice in 605 B.C.—
the last instance being the renowned battle with Nebuchadnezzar at
Carchemish (cf. Jeremiah 46:2)—the Egyptians alone were left to
face the Babylonians, as is revealed by the Neo-Babylonian Chronicle
published by Wiseman (end of BM 22047 and beginning of BM
21946). By analogy, we may assume that in previous cases, too,
Carchemish served as the central Egyptian base on the Euphrates;
this is supported by the Egyptian finds uncovered in the excavations
there, which include a bronze ring bearing the name of Psamtik I,
and four clay sealings of Pharaoh Necho.[22] Carchemish is also specifically mentioned in 2 Chronicles 35:21 as the destination of Necho's
campaign in 609 B.C., which passed through Megiddo. Based on

---

[20] See recently K.S. Freedy and D.B. Redford, *JAOS* 90 (1970), 477. For an
early translation of this stela see Breasted, *ARE* IV, §959f.; the following inscription
there, "Statue Inscription of Hor", §967f., also indicates Egyptian control over the
forests of Lebanon, but its attribution to the time of Psamtik I remains conjectural.

[21] Published by C.J. Gadd, *The Fall of Nineveh* (London, 1923), and with minor
revisions, together with the publication of additional Neo-Babylonian chronicles, in
D.J. Wiseman, *Chronicles of Chaldaean Kings (626–556 B.C.)* (London, 1956). A similar
dating for the alliance has been suggested by J. Yoyotte, *Supplément au Dictionnaire
de la Bible*, 6:374, s.v. *Néchao*. The alliance may have been initiated under Sinsharishkun,
whose actual rule over Assyria began in 623 B.C.; for the chronology of this king,
cf. recently J. Reade, *JCS* 23 (1970), 1–9.

[22] These, as well as other Egyptian finds, were uncovered in House D in the
lower city of Carchemish, which may have served the Egyptian garrison; see C.L.
Woolley, *Carchemish* (London, 1921), 2:123–29, pl. 26:1–4.

this latter campaign, in turn, we may assume that the other campaigns had also been conducted via Megiddo, which undoubtedly was an essential staging base for the Egyptians in their lengthy route to the Euphrates.[23] An additional base on this military route was surely at Riblah in Syria—as is to be inferred from 2 Kings 23:33, as well as from the flight of the Egyptian army from Carchemish to the land of Hamath (in which Riblah was situated), where it was finally annihilated by Nebuchadnezzar, in 605 B.C. (BM 21946, lines 1–7).

We can thus conclude that Megiddo became an Egyptian base certainly *prior* to 616 B.C., and at some time *after* 646 B.C. As noted, in this latter year an Assyrian governor is mentioned at Samaria, implying Assyrian presence still in the province of *Magiddu* (an Assyrian governor at Megiddo proper is mentioned last in 679 B.C.). This, then, is the range for dating the end of Stratum II at Megiddo, and for the construction of the Stratum II fortress there. But, whether the fortress was built by Psamtik or by Josiah, we can safely assume that Megiddo was already a logistic base, or at least a vital way-station, for the Egyptian army in campaigns to Syria no later than 616 B.C., and probably even several years earlier. Megiddo Stratum II remained under Egyptian control till Nebuchadnezzar's campaign to the West in 605 B.C., or at the latest, the autumn of 604 B.C., when the Babylonian Chronicle has the king of Babylonia leading his army into southern Palestine and to the conquest of Ascalon.

III. *The Battle at Megiddo*

The political and strategic factors which may have governed Josiah in deciding to attack Necho's army at Megiddo have been treated by us previously.[24] One of the possible additional factors behind this bold step—I believe not yet noted—was the Egyptian military failure on the Euphrates in 610 B.C., half a year or so before the battle at Megiddo. The Egyptian intervention in the north in 610 B.C.

---

[23] There are no grounds for assuming that the Egyptians reached Syria by sea in previous campaigns, bypassing Palestine, as is sometimes held; cf., e.g., Yoyotte, *Supplément*, 6: 375.

[24] See my article in *JNES* 9 (1950), 219f.; and cf. M. Noth, *Geschichte Israels*, 3rd ed. (Göttingen, 1956), 251f. (who maintains that Megiddo was in Josiah's possession).

seems to have been passed over generally, for in the Babylonian
Chronicle the name of Egypt in the relevant passage is damaged,
and must be restored: ^{māt} mi-[sir] (BM 21901, line 61).[25] In Marheshvan
of the same year (November 610), the Babylonians and their allies,
the Umman-Manda tribes, attacked the city of Harran where Ashur-
uballit, the last king of Assyria, had based himself after his capitals
at Ashur and Nineveh had already fallen. The document continues
(lines 61–62); "As for Ashur-uballit and the army of Eg[ypt] which
had come [to his help], fear of the enemy fell upon them; they abandoned the city and . . . crossed [the river Euphrates]." That is, they
fell back, most probably, upon Carchemish. And so, the defenseless
Harran—the last Assyrian capital—was plucked by the king of
Babylonia.

The failure of the Egyptian army—whether merely garrison troops
brought up from Carchemish to the battlefield or, even more so, an
expeditionary force dispatched especially from Egypt—undoubtedly
left its impression in both Egypt and Judah (unlike the moderately
successful operations of 616 B.C.). Chronologically, it has recently
been ascertained that Necho already reigned at this time, for Psamtik
died between the end of July and the end of September, 610 B.C.[26]
But we cannot know whether Necho personally took part in the
unsuccessful military operation, in other words, whether he himself
passed through Palestine less than a year prior to the battle at
Megiddo. His not being mentioned in the Babylonian Chronicle is
of no significance, for in 609 B.C., too—when Necho stood at the
head of a military expedition, as witnessed by the Bible—the fact
was overlooked in this Babylonian source. In any event, in the spring
or early summer of 609 B.C., Necho made intensive efforts to field
a new expedition, for the Chronicle emphasizes that in Tammuz "a
great Egyptian army" crossed the Euphrates (lines 66–67). But still
Egypt and her Assyrian allies were unable to retake Harran. The

---

[25] Gadd read ^{māt} gul-[ ], but the initial sign of the country's name is certainly mi,
as first suggested by J. Lewy, MVAG 29 (1923), 85, followed by Wiseman, Chronicles,
62 and cf. pl. xii, line 61. Since then, several scholars have noticed the allusion to
Egypt in 610 B.C.—e.g. E. Vogt, VTS 4 (1957), 69; Yoyotte, Supplément, 6: 375;
Cazelles, RB 74, 26; Freedy and Redford, JAOS 90, 474f.—but without drawing
any conclusions for the battle at Megiddo.
[26] Cf. E. Hornung, ZÄS 92 (1965), 38f.; Freedy and Redford, JAOS 90, 474 and
n. 48.

Egyptian military defeat the year before was undoubtedly an encouraging factor in Josiah's decision to stand up to Necho at Megiddo—which battle unluckily ended in an Israelite fiasco.

Actually, the details of the conflict between Egypt and Judah in 609 B.C. are still quite muddled. The Book of Kings, which merely outlines the events (2 Kings 23:29–30), does not even relate the opening of a battle; this has sometimes led scholars, unjustifiably, to doubt the military background of the episode.[27] But in this instance we may prefer the fuller version in Chronicles, according to which matters did not go beyond a mere skirmish because of Josiah's fatal wound at the very outset (2 Chronicles 35:20–24). It is this version on which the tradition in 1 Esdras (1:23–31) and Josephus (Ant. X, 1, 5) is based. The latter, besides his embellishments, drew additional data from reliable sources independent of the biblical account, for he appears to be acquainted with the geopolitical situation revealed in "Gadd's Chronicle" relating, as he does, that Necho went up to the Euphrates in order to fight the Babylonians and Medes. The version in Chronicles has Pharaoh declaring to Josiah that his campaign is not intended against Judah: "But he sent envoys to him [Josiah], saying 'What have we to do with each other, king of Judah? I am not coming against you this day, but to *bêt milḥamtî* [see below]; and God has commanded me to make haste. Cease opposing God, who is with me, lest he destroy you'" (2 Chronicles 35:21). It has been suggested[28] that Necho's words were of little point if actually stated near Megiddo, and more sensible if delivered in southern Palestine, before Josiah could guess Necho's intentions and true destination; we shall return to this below.

Many scholars have connected the battle at Megiddo with Herodotus II, 159, relating Pharaoh Necho's defeat of the Syrians at Magdolos, that is, Migdol, and the subsequent capture of Kadytis, "a large city

---

[27] See now—in addition to the references already given in *JNES* 9 (1950), 220, n. 13—S.B. Frost, *JBL* 87 (1968), 369–83; and G. Pfeiffer, *MIO* 15 (1969), 297–307. Hence, these scholars, and many others, consider the account of the military encounter in Chronicles as a mere midrashic exposition of the version in Kings; cf. most recently T. Willi, *Die Chronik als Auslegung* (Göttingen, 1972), 159. On the other hand, a plethora of exegetes as well as historians have strongly defended the reliability of the Chronicler in this case; see, e.g., W. Rudolph, *Chronikbücher* (Tübingen, 1955), 332f.; and recently J. Bright, *A History of Israel*, 2nd ed., (London, 1972), 324.

[28] Orally by Y. Yadin in a private conversation; and see his treatment of Josiah's battle in his *The Art of Warfare in Biblical Lands* (Jerusalem-Ramat Gan, 1963), 2:311f.

in Syria," undoubtedly Gaza.[29] They generally assume that "Megiddo" was corrupted by Herodotus to read "Migdol," but sometimes the opposite, emending the biblical text to read "Migdol." Among the latter scholars, some have suggested locating Migdol in the vicinity of Ascalon, for instance at Majdal, or at some fortress (Hebrew *migdā/ōl*) erected by Josiah along the coast, in the border area between Judah and Philistia.[30] Thus, they hold that the battle took place in the south, rather than at Megiddo, and Pharaoh's message would thereby become more intelligible.

But the supposed corruption of the name of the city, whether in this text or that, is entirely superfluous, and we ought clearly to distinguish between the biblical Megiddo and Herodotus's Magdolos. The latter was most probably the well-known Egyptian border fortress of Migdol, west of Pelusium (some identify it with Tell el-Ḥer, northeast of Qantara), and mentioned by Jeremiah together with Tahpanes (Jeremiah 44:1; 46:14), the Daphne of the Greek sources, west of Qantara. Only in this case can sense be made of the course of Necho's campaign according to Herodotus, for Gaza lies on the *via maris* east of Migdol, whereas the emendation reading "Megiddo" would create difficulties in the geographical order. Moreover, the invasion of an enemy into Egypt is more likely if subsequent to Necho's defeat at Carchemish in 605 B.C., and assuming that it took place at the instigation of the Babylonians. Could this penetration have indeed been associated with Nebuchadnezzar's campaign to the border of Egypt in the winter of 601–600 B.C., of which we are now informed by the Babylonian Chronicle, in spite of the fact that Herodotus identified the invaders as Syrians rather than Babylonians?[31] This Babylonian campaign to Egypt may well

---

[29] For an abundant bibliography, which could easily be expanded, cf. E. Lipiński, *Annali Istituto Orientale di Napoli* 32 (1972), 19f., n. 3, who, however, justly denies any connection between the two events.

[30] For the last opinion see Yadin, *Art of Warfare*, 311. For a location of Josiah's battle at a supposed Migdol near Ascalon, see already L.E. Binns, "The Syrian Campaign of Necho II," *JThS* 18 (1917), 40, and the earlier literature cited there; cf. now also Yoyotte, *Supplément*, 6: 390 (who, himself, however, opposes the equation of Megiddo with Magdolos).

[31] See Freedy and Redford, *JAOS* 90, 475, n. 57, and especially Lipiński, *Ann. Ist. Or. di Napoli* 32, 235–41. The latter (p. 239) disregards our assumption in *IEJ* 18 (1968), 142f. that the Aramaic letter found at Saqqarah, requesting Egyptian aid against the approaching Babylonians, was sent within this context; moreover, he identifies the vassal with a ruler of Tyre or Sidon (following J.T. Milik) rather than the king of Gaza, Ekron or, less likely, Ashdod. But this letter, sent by king

find echo in Jeremiah's prophecies concerning the nations, for his second prophecy on Egypt, after the oracle on the defeat at Carchemish, is superscribed: "The word which the Lord spoke to Jeremiah the prophet about the coming of Nebuchadnezzar king of Babylon to smite the land of Egypt" (Jeremiah 46:13).[32] The invective does not, however, reflect the actual circumstances in which the Babylonian forces were repelled at the border of Egypt, suffering heavy casualties, as frankly related in the Babylonian Chronicle itself. Coming back to the passage in Herodotus, we should note that the first spot in Jeremiah's prophecy to be smitten is significantly Migdol (Jeremiah 46:14), and that at the end of the prophecy (verse 26, possibly an editorial addition), mention is made of "Nebuchadnezzar, King of Babylon, and his servants," the latter very likely his Syrian and Palestinian = Transjordanian vassals.[33] Cf. 2 Kings 24:2 for (his?) use of such auxiliaries.

In fact, without resorting to Herodotus and to emendations of the biblical text, we can suggest here a reasonable interpretation of Necho's seemingly peculiar message, and of the historical-military course of events. We may assume that Pharaoh was still in southern Palestine when he became aware of Josiah's military preparations,

---

Adon (or Adonimelek, as preferably to be read) must be predated by some two or three years if either of these latter cities had been conquered earlier (for Gaza, see n. 33 below).

[32] On this prophecy, see recently J.G. Snaith, *JSS* 16 (1971), 15–32, who, however, is very vague about its chronological context. Our prophecy has usually been ascribed (see the commentaries on Jeremiah 46) either to the aftermath of the Egyptian debacle in 605 B.C. or to Nebuchadnezzar's supposed invasion of Egypt in 568 B.C. (an entirely obscure event due to the broken state of the relevant cuneiform tablet; cf. Wiseman, *Chronicles*, 94f.; and Addendum below)—but both assumptions are unsatisfactory.

[33] If our above dating of Jeremiah's second oracle is correct, then the superscriptions of all three successive prophecies in Jeremiah (MT) concerning Egypt represent the actual chronological chain of events: (a) 46:2—battle of Carchemish in 605 B.C.; (b) 46:13—Babylonian invasion of Egypt, 601/600 B.C.; (c) 47:1, "against the Philistines before whom Pharaoh smote Gaza"—alluding to the Egyptian capture of Gaza sometime later in 600 B.C., subsequent to the repulse of the Babylonians (and not in 609 B.C., my previous view, in keeping with the general trend—*JNES* 9 [1950], 221; *IEJ* 1 [1950/51], 154–59), in accord with Herodotus II, 159; cf. Lipiński, *Ann. Ist. Or. di Napoli* 32, 240. It follows that Egypt's control over Gaza must have been lost to the Babylonians in the meantime, most likely in the campaign of Nebuchadnezzar's second year (after the conquest of Ascalon in the previous year). Indeed, A. Rainey has suggested restoring "Gaza" in the lacuna in Wiseman's Chronicle (BM 21946; beginning of line 22; *Chronicles*, 70), thus placing its conquest by the Babylonians in the summer of 603 B.C. (cf. Rainey's chapter in the forthcoming report by Y. Aharoni on the Tel Aviv University's excavations at Lachish).

and he attempted to forestall any attack on the Egyptian army by explaining his intentions to the Judean king. But it was this very message which told Josiah of his route, passing through the Egyptian base at Megiddo. It might even be that the enigmatic term *bêt milḥamtî* (literally "house of my war") refers to a "fortified base" or "garrison city."[34] Then this *hapax legomenon* would refer to the Egyptian base at Carchemish or Riblah, as already suggested—though it could equally be the fortress in Stratum II at Megiddo.

Josiah's chances of blocking the passage of the Egyptian army in the south, in the Judean corridor between Gezer and Meṣad Ḥashav-yahu, were hardly favorable, for this fairly level region would have necessitated a pitched battle with Pharaoh's forces. The topograph-ical conditions farther south especially in the Ascalon region (or near Raphia between the sand-dunes and the sea-coast), are much better suited for such an attack. But Josiah was certainly denied access to this region by the cities of Ashdod, Ascalon and Gaza. Under the circumstances, he preferred to spring an ambush on his enemy in the Plain of Megiddo, more precisely at the strategic pass leading out of Wadi Ara, before the Egyptian army could deploy on the plain or find protection within Megiddo. Admittedly, initiating such an attack at this spot, 1.5–2 kilometers from Megiddo, necessitated considerable daring on Josiah's part—especially if Megiddo itself were in Egyptian hands; but even so, the risk was no unreasonably cal-culated. Josiah thus hastened, at the head of his army, through Samaria to the Megiddo region in order to intercept the Egyptian column winding its way up Wadi Ara. Such a reconstruction quite suits the chain of events as described in Chronicles, following Necho's appeal: "Nevertheless, Josiah would not turn away from him but *girded himself*[35] in order to fight with him. He did not listen to the

---

[34] For this obscure technical term in 2 Chronicles 35:21, numerous unsatisfac-tory explanations have been put forward; see, e.g., Rudolph, *Chronikbücher*, 330, and bibliographical references there; he suggests, inter alia, emending *byt* to *bbl*. The most likely interpretation seems to me to be B. Alfrink's translation in *Biblica* 15 (1934), 176: "Kriegsstadt, Festungstadt, Garnisonstadt"; he takes the term as refer-ring to Pharaoh's headquarters at Riblah in Syria.

[35] This would appear to approach the meaning of the Hebrew verb here, *hithappēś*, which has never been explained satisfactorily; for the various interpretations, ancient and modern, see, e.g., Rudolph, *Chronikbücher*, 330; and Pfeiffer, *MIO* 15, 300. The usual translation, "he disguised himself," based on the other occurrences of this word in the Bible (cf. W. Baumgartner, *Hebräisches und Aramäisches Lexikon* [Leiden, 1967], 328a), is certainly wrong—seemingly in all the instances. The verb appears

words of Necho from the mouth of God, but joined battle in the plain of Megiddo" (2 Chronicles 35:22). Thus, Josiah put his military plan into operation in spite of Pharaoh's attempt to dissuade him; in fact, it was Necho's very message which prompted him to march toward Armageddon as he so fatefully did.

Addendum to note 32:
It has now been demonstrated that this broken tablet is merely a list of foreign mercenary contingents in Babylonian service, rather than areas conquered by Nebuchadnezzar in his supposed campaign to Egypt in 568 B.C. (with which the prophecy in Ezekiel 29:17–21 has sometimes been associated). Cf. P.-R. Berger, *Die neubabylonischen Königsinschriften, AOAT* 4/1 (Neukirchen-Vluyn, 1973), 6. See also: A. Malamat, Megiddo 609 B.C.: The Conflict Reexamined, *Acta Antiqua* 22 (1974), 445–449.

---

in 1 Kings 22:30 = 2 Chronicles 18:29, in a similar military context and thus appears simply to mean 'gird oneself'. Furthermore, in this latter instance, as well as in 1 Sam. 28:8, it is in opposition to *lābaš bęgęd* 'to put on a garment'; this might indicate a more specific meaning of 'covering the head', that is, putting on a helmet. This interpretation would suit 1 Kings 20:38 as well (also in a military context): "So the prophet departed and waited for the king by the way, *girding himself* with an *ᵃpēr* ('bandage', 'helmet'?) over his eyes." (On *ᵃpēr* and its Akkadian equivalent, cf. the biblical dictionaries and J.C. Greenfield, *JCS* 21 [1967], 91a). Such a headdress may, of course, have made the wearer unrecognizable—and thus became, in effect, a disguise; still, a new investigation of the original meaning of *hithappēś* is surely warranted.

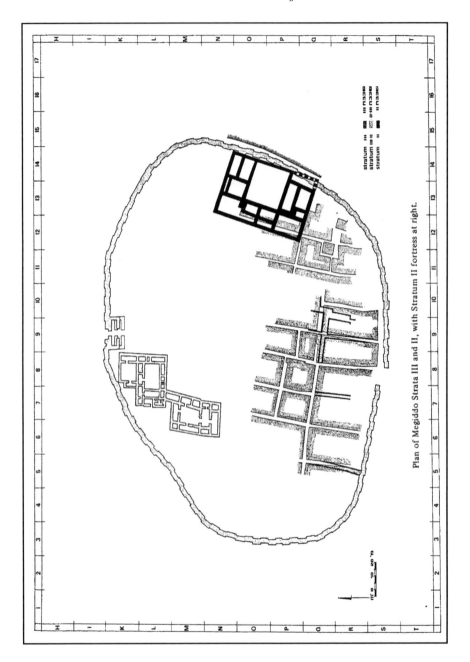

Plan of Megiddo Strata III and II, with Stratum II fortress at right.

16

THE TWILIGHT OF JUDAH:
IN THE EGYPTIAN-BABYLONIAN MAELSTROM*

The late seventh century B.C., noted for its reshufflings in the international political sphere, saw the collapse of the Assyrian empire and the subsequent power-struggle between the up-and-coming Babylonia and Egypt over inheritance of the now-orphaned territories spreading from the Euphrates to Sinai. The geopolitical plight of this buffer region swept a most reluctant Kingdom of Judah—like many of her neighbours—into the alternating open conflict and "cold war" which ensued. Indeed, if outside factors were most influential throughout Judah's history, they became overbearing in the two decades following the Battle of Megiddo, in 609 B.C.,—until, in 586 B.C., the little kingdom finally succumbed to international machinations.[1]

A wide range of sources for this tense period provides a particularly detailed insight into much of the political development and internal activities in Judah: besides the Books of Kings and Chronicles, these decades are illuminated by the Book of Jeremiah, and their final years by the Book of Ezekiel. The contemporaneous epigraphical material in Hebrew is plentiful and varied, more so than in earlier periods, and the effects of the political-military events have been revealed in the archaeological excavations on numerous Judean sites. But a proper perspective for evaluating the historical factors underlying the final fate of Judah—factors which determined the policies of its rulers—is to be obtained only from sources beyond Palestine— primarily the Neo-Babylonian Chronicles and, to a lesser degree, Egyptian documentation. The twining of biblical data with external sources—especially the detailed framework of dates they contain— enables a sort of micro-analytic study of this period. Thus, we can

---

* This article was originally published in: *SVT* 28, 1975, 123–145.
[1] For a complementary study of this period, as treated particularly in the first two sections of the present lecture, see A. Malamat, "The Last Kings of Judah and the Fall of Jerusalem," *IEJ* XVIII 1968, pp. 137–156, and the bibliographical references there.

trace the historical process in time units much more minute than is generally feasible for the Israelite period—in terms of a specific year, month or even day.

The chronological method applied here has more than once influenced our reconstruction of the chain of events. Though there is a general consensus that the post-dating system, involving accession years, was employed in Judah at this time, another point is still particularly controversial—the month of the Judean regnal new year. Our reckoning is based on an autumnal calendar beginning on 1 Tishri, and not on the spring calendar accepted by many scholars and which was in general use in Babylonia. On previous occasions I have sought to demonstrate the preference of this Tishri reckoning in Judah, and its propensity for reconciling a majority of the variegated data, at least for our period.[2] To facilitate the tracing of the chain of events, a Chronological Table is appended. The months of the year, it must be remembered, were counted from Nisan, in keeping with the Judean civil calendar.

I

The loss of Josiah at Megiddo in 609 B.C. put an effective end to the prosperity of the Judean kingdom and dispelled all hopes for restored grandeur. Indeed, this tragedy was so deeply felt that a day

---

[2] See especially *ibid.*, pp. 146ff.; and cf. n. 19 there, for studies adopting a spring calendar, to which now add: K.T. Andersen, *Stud. Theol.* XXIII 1969, pp. 109–114; D.J.A. Clines, *Austral. Jour. Bibl. Arch.* (= *AJBA*) II 1972, pp. 9–34; *idem, JBL* XCIII 1974, pp. 22–40. In support of the autumnal calendar see the references in *IEJ* XVIII 1968, p. 146, n. 20; and now, with conclusions partly similar to ours: K.S. Freedy and D.B. Redford, "The Dates in Ezekiel . . .," *JAOS* XC 1970, pp. 462–485 (= *Freedy & Redford*); M. Weippert, *Edom*, Tübingen 1971, pp. 351–372, 649–660. Weippert (*ibid.*, pp. 356–357), like E.R. Thiele (*The Mysterious Numbers of the Hebrew Kings*, Grand Rapids 1965, pp. 161–172) and S.H. Horn (*Andrews Univ. Seminary Stud.* V 1967, pp. 12–27) but contrary to our view, assumes that the regnal years of Nebuchadnezzar himself were reckoned in the Book of Kings according to the Tishri calendar, in contrast to official Babylonian practice. He thus seeks to reconcile the discrepancy—illusory in our opinion—between the date of Jehoiachin's exiling as given in II Kings xxiv 12b and as indicated in the Babylonian Chronicle; see below, in section II.

For the conversion of the ancient dates into "absolute" dates, cf. the tables in R.A. Parker & W.H. Dubberstein, *Babylonian Chronology 626 B.C.–A.D. 75*, Providence (R.I.) 1956.

of remembrance was commemorated for generations (II Chron. xxxv 25; and cf. Josephus, *Ant.* X, 5, 1). The background of Josiah's (639–609 B.C.) clash with Necho II (610–595 B.C.) lies in the geopolitical developments which we noted in opening. In the rivalry between Judah and Egypt over the formerly Assyrian territories in Palestine, Psamtik I (664–610 B.C.), Necho's father, had held a clear advantage in time. It would seem that Psamtik gained sway over the cities of Philistia, in the south, and the province of *Magiddu*, which spread over the Jezreel Plain and Galilee, in the north, and thus came into possession of the city of Megiddo.[3] At least as early as 616 B.C., Megiddo must have become a logistics base for the Egyptian forces on the march to the Euphrates in support of their newly-made allies, the Assyrians; it was undoubtedly such a base in 610 and, again, in 609 B.C.[4] Josiah was able to launch his annexation policy only after initiating his reform (around 628 B.C.; cf. II Chron. xxxiv 6), and he seems to have gained control solely over the former Assyrian province of *Samerina* and to have established a corridor reaching the coast in the northern Shephelah, as possibly witnessed by the Hebrew epigraphic finds at Meṣad Ḥashavyahu.

The woeful results of the battle of Megiddo (apparently in Sivan of 609 B.C.)[5] led to rapid political fluctuations in Judah,—and from then till the Destruction of the First Temple,—a mere score years,— the rulers of Judah changed loyalties—to either Egypt or Babylonia— no less than six times. The international scene at this time demanded extreme skill in manoeuvring, and the kings of Judah were repeatedly

---

[3] For a detailed discussion of the historical circumstances which preceded the Battle of Megiddo, and an analysis of the battle itself, see A. Malamat, *The Gaster Festschrift* (*JANES* V 1973), pp. 267–279 (= chap. 15). For similar general conclusions concerning the rule of Psamtik I over considerable territories in Palestine and Syria, see B. Otzen, *Studien über Deuterosacharja*, Copenhagen 1964, pp. 78ff.

[4] For the Egyptian expedition to the north, noted in Nabopolassar's Chronicle, see C.J. Gadd, *The Fall of Nineveh*, London 1923, pp. 31ff., B.M. 21901, lines 10, 61, 66; D.J. Wiseman, *Chronicles of Chaldaean Kings 626–556 B.C.*, London 1956 (= *CCK*), pp. 55ff.

[5] Cf. *IEJ* XVIII 1968, p. 139. But note now that the Egyptians required almost a month, rather than two weeks, to cover the distance to the river (which they crossed in Tammuz 609 B.C.), for the actual distance between Megiddo and Carchemish is about 650 km, and the advance of the rushing Egyptian army should be estimated at about 25–30 km *per diem*. See similarly Clines, *AJBA* II 1972, pp. 30ff.; and also M. Vogelstein, *Biblical Chronology*, Cincinnati 1944, pp. 27f., who, however, considered the march from Megiddo to Carchemish to have taken at least six weeks.

forced to come to terms with kaleidoscopic situations and astonishingly frequent political dilemmas of a most fateful order. The first exigency was the selection of a successor to Josiah, who apparently had not seen a need to designate his heir. Some thirty years earlier, Josiah himself had been enthroned by the ʿam ha-ʾareṣ, that body of landed aristocracy in Judah which is found to be involved wherever the natural succession of the Davidic line was brought in jeopardy. The assassination of Josiah's father, Amon, was undoubtedly of Egyptian instigation, and already then Egypt seems to have been intriguing to install a sympathetic regime in Judah. The ʿam ha-ʾareṣ managed to suppress the revolt at court (II Kings xxi 19–26), enthrone the young Josiah and surely also set the deeply anti-Egyptian tone of his policy.

The successor to emerge was Josiah's son Jehoahaz (Shallum), in opposition to the principle of primogeniture—Jehoiakim (Eliakim) being the older of the brothers by two years. This irregular enthronement, a sort of *coup d'état*, was again effected by the ʿam ha-ʾareṣ (II Kings xxiii 30; II Chron. xxxvi 1).[6] The political significance of this step comes into focus when we consider the decidedly anti-Egyptian stand generally taken by the ʿam ha-ʾareṣ in this period. The choice of Jehoahaz was apparently based on his maternal lineage, for his mother Hamutal "daughter of Jeremiah of Libnah" (II Kings xxiii 31; who is depicted allegorically as a "lioness . . . among lions" in Ezek. xix) was of the Judean rural nobility which comprised the ʿam ha-ʾareṣ. Eleven years later, Nebuchadnezzar's selection of a ruler seems to have been governed by similar considerations, for Zedekiah was of the same mother and thus also represented the anti-Egyptian faction of the Davidic line. In contrast, Jehoiakim's maternal lineage seems to have been odious to the Judean nobility, for his mother was Zebidah "daughter of Pedaiah of Rumah" (II Kings xxiii 36), the latter a Galilean town in the valley of Beth Netopha, most probably in territory under Egyptian control since the days of Psamtik (as noted above). Thus, in spite of the defeat at Megiddo, the Judean leadership is seen to have continued its anti-Egyptian line, a policy rather premature under the circumstances.

---

[6] For the irregularity surrounding the enthronement, see *IEJ* XVIII 1968, pp. 139f. and nn. 6–7 and the bibliography on the ʿam hā-ʾāreṣ there. For the latter see now also T. Ishida, *Annual of the Japanese Biblical Institute* I 1975, pp. 23–38.

After reigning for only three months, Jehoahaz's fate was put in the balance by Necho's intervention. Jeremiah, for one, was already confident that "he shall return no more to see his native land" (Jer. xxii 10–12; and cf. Ezek. xix 1–4). The king was indeed deposed and exiled to Egypt, probably at the urging of his brother, Jehoiakim, who sought recognition of his rights of primogeniture.[7] Jehoiakim's subsequent enthronement by Necho seems to have been based on mutual interests: Pharaoh assisted him in realizing his legitimate claim to the throne (note the specific wording in II Kings xxiii 34: "Necho made Eliakim . . . king in the place of *Josiah his father* . . ."—which entirely bypasses his brother's reign); in turn, Pharaoh gained a loyal vassal and ally. The punishment meted out to Judah by Necho, apparently hand-in-hand with Jehoiakim, fell poignantly upon the *'am ha-'areṣ*; with the tables turned, it was the anti-Egyptian faction which had to bear the burden, rather than the palace or Temple treasury in Jerusalem (II Kings xxiii 35).[8] Jehoiakim apparently came to the throne only in Tishri 609 B.C. (though he may have imposed the reckoning of his reign as if he had succeeded his father directly).[9] The summer and autumn of 609 B.C. were thus days of turmoil in Judah, typified by a rapidly changing political situation and the successive reigns of three kings, in rather unusual circumstances.

---

[7] In I Esdras (i 36) there is a specific tradition that Jehoiakim was behind his brother's arrest, along with other Judean leaders; see J.M. Myers, *I & II Esdras* (*Anchor Bible*), Garden City 1974, pp. 30, 32. Jehoiakim's possible intervention in the overthrow of Jehoahaz has been alluded to in J. Scharbert, *Die Prophetie Israels um 600 v. Chr.*, Köln 1967, p. 128.

[8] Professor B. Mazar has brought to my attention the relatively low sum of the tribute imposed here by the Egyptians (II Kings xxiii 33), in comparison with that exacted from Menahem king of Israel (II Kings xv 19), or Hezekiah, who had to draw upon the royal and Temple treasuries in Jerusalem (II Kings xviii 14). This would seem to confirm that Necho's tribute was to be borne by a particular class rather than by the populace in general, as held in the Commentaries; see J.A. Montgomery, *The Books of Kings* (*ICC*), Edinburgh 1951, p. 551; J. Gray, *I & II Kings*[2], London 1970, pp. 750ff. In any event, the royal palace was hardly affected and Jehoiakim was able to erect splendid royal buildings (cf. Jer. xxii 13ff.).

[9] (a) If Jehoiakim came to the throne only subsequent to 1 Tishri 609 B.C. (as we uphold in *IEJ* XVIII 1968, p. 141, and in the Chronological Table below), a conclusion reasonable in itself, then the period up till Tishri 608 B.C. should be considered his accession year (Akkadian *rēš šarrūti*); this would have been Jehoahaz's first regnal year, in purely chronological terms. (b) On the other hand, if the contemporaneous reckoning of Jehoiakim's years, during his reign, was from Josiah's death—1 Tishri 609 B.C. would have ushered in his first regnal year. This would reconcile the chronological difficulty in Jer. xlvi 2 (see n. 11, below), though it raises an outward conflict with II Kings xxiii 36, where the length of Jehoiakim's reign is given as eleven years.

Necho now controlled the entire area "from the Brook of Egypt to the river Euphrates, all that belonged to the king of Egypt," to use the contemporaneous biblical phrase (II Kings xxiv 7).[10] But this period of Egyptian glory was to be short lived. Already in the summer of 605 B.C., Nebuchadnezzar, still Crown Prince, dealt the Egyptians a stunning blow, in the Battle of Carchemish, and subsequently defeated the remnant Egyptian force in the land of Hamath.[11] This, then, truly sealed the fate of Syria and Palestine. But neither then—nor, fatally, even later—did the Judean leaders grasp the full significance of events in the international arena. The traumatic experience of the Battle of Megiddo, and the mutuality of interests between Necho and Jehoiakim may well have shackled the leadership in Jerusalem with the image of a mighty Egypt which would rush to the aid of its allies in time of need. Other states held Egypt in

---

[10] The Egyptian control of the Lebanon already in the days of Psamtik I is evidenced by an Egyptian stele of 612 B.C.; see *Freedy & Redford*, p. 477; and possibly also by a second inscription, cf. Malamat, *Gaster Festschrift*, p. 273, n. 20 (= chap. 15). Egyptian influence in the Phoenician coastal cities is witnessed by a statue of Psamtik I from the port-city of Arvad; a fragment, possibly also from his reign, discovered at Tyre; and a stele of Necho II at Sidon—for which see J.J. Katzenstein, *The History of Tyre*, Jerusalem 1973, pp. 299, n. 24; 313, n. 100. Katzenstein also associates the passage in Nebuchadnezzar's Wadi Brisa inscription (col. IX, lines 23–24)—relating of an enemy who had subdued and plundered the Lebanon region—with Egypt. But he assumes that all the above evidence points only to commercial ties between Egypt and Syria, rather than actual Egyptian control; see *ibid.*, pp. 298–304. In contrast, see Otzen, *Deuterosacharja*, pp. 90ff., who regards the above as proving Egyptian rule in Asia, finding additional support for this in the prophecy in Zech. ix 1–8.

[11] On the Babylonian source, see D.J. Wiseman, *Chronicles of Chaldean Kings*, 1956 (= *CCK*), pp. 66ff. (BM 21946). Jer. xlvi 2 places the Battle of Carchemish in Jehoiakim's fourth regnal year, the only substantial instance of a date conflicting with our Tishri reckoning, which would put this battle in his third year (cf. the Chronological Table). See *IEJ* XVIII 1968, p. 147, n. 21, where we have also cited Horn's suggestion to reconcile the difficulty here by attributing this date to the time of the oracular utterance rather than to the battle itself. Although problematic, this might find support in Jer. xxxvi 1–2, where the date of the Prophet's first scroll, which recorded *inter alia* Oracles on the Nations, is fixed in Jehoiakim's fourth regnal year. The chronological notation at the head of the Oracles on the Nations in Jer. xlvi 2 thus may well have been harmonized with this. Weippert (*Edom*, p. 653, n. 1238) assumes that the Battle of Carchemish and the subsequent Babylonian campaign, which latter took place in the winter of 605/604 B.C., after the enthronement of Nebuchadnezzar, were regarded in Judah as one continuous military episode, which thus would have fallen already in Jehoiakim's fourth regnal year; but Jeremiah's prophecy specifically deals with the defeat of "the army of Pharaoh Necho" which no longer took part in events half a year after the Battle of Carchemish. But for a possible corroboration of the date as given in Jer., see n. 9(b).

similar regard, as revealed in an Aramaic letter discovered at Saqqara:[12] The ruler of some city, apparently in Philistia, urgently appeals to Pharaoh for military assistance to repell the approaching Babylonians, reminding his suzerain of his treaty obligations.

Thus, we can appreciate all the more such level-headed persons as Jeremiah, possessing deep foresight and historical perspective. A mere few months after the Battle of Carchemish, Jeremiah already proclaimed his steadfast belief in Nebuchadnezzar's impending rule over Judah and Hither Asia in general (Jer. xxv 1–14; and see the Chronological Table).[13] Like Isaiah in his day, or Ezekiel his younger contemporary, Jeremiah strove to smash the popular image of Egypt, which had led to a false sense of security among the Judean leadership and spread a spurious hope of military support (cf., e.g., Egypt as "a staff of reed to the house of Israel . . . and when they leaned upon thee thou didst break," in Ezek. xxix 7–8). In Jeremiah's mind, the only way to save the nation was to surrender voluntarily to Babylonia, to which cause he remained loyal to the bitter end (Jer. xxi 8–9; xxxviii 2, etc.). Thus, political orientation became an acute issue among the people of Judah, gradually intensifying the polarity between the pro-Egyptian and pro-Babylonian factions.

The Babylonian subjugation of Judah was not long in coming. The exact date is still a matter of controversy, and even Nebuchadnezzar's Chronicle is indefinite. Military campaigns to the West are recorded for each of the years between 605 and 601 B.C., but no specific names of subjected states are mentioned (except Ashkelon).[14] Briefly, there are several possibilities:

---

[12] Cf. Donner-Röllig, *KAI*, No. 266; and *IEJ* XVIII 1968, p. 143, n. 11, for additional bibliography. The treaty relations between the vassal king and Pharaoh are inferred in line 8 in the letter: *wṭbth* (i.e. a treaty) *ʿbdk nṣr*.

[13] The oracle took place "in the fourth year of Jehoiakim . . . the first (*riʾšōnīt*) year of Nebuchadrezzar" (Jer. xxv 1); if the unusual term for "first" year here refers to Nebuchadnezzar's accession year (*rēš šarrūti*), the prophecy would have been uttered between Tishri 605 and Nisan 604 B.C.; but if it refers to his first actual regnal year, the synchronism covers the period between Nisan and Tishri 604 B.C. (see the Chronological Table at the end of this chap.). C.F. Whitley (*ZAW* LXXX 1968, pp. 38–49) holds that Jer. xxv was the Prophet's earliest oracle and that Jeremiah began his activity only in 605 B.C. (rather than two decades earlier, as recorded in Jer.), but this seems untenable. In support of the traditional dating of Jeremiah's call, see recently T.W. Overholt, *CBQ* XXXIII 1971, pp. 165–184.

[14] See *CCK*, pp. 66–71. The relevant passage is BM 21946, lines 1–23 and verso lines 1–7, from which the following citations are taken.

a) Judah was conquered immediately after the Egyptian defeat at the Battle of Carchemish. This is supported by the opening of the Book of Daniel (i 1–4) relating the siege of Jerusalem by Nebuchadnezzar in the third year of Jehoiakim (see Chronological Table at the end of this chap.), the looting of "vessels of the house of God," and the exiling of certain Judeans. Further the last datum is in accord with a tradition related by Josephus (*Ant.* X, 11, 1; *Contra Apionem* I, 19), that Judean captives, amongst others, were carried off to Babylon after the victory at Carchemish. In another passage (*Ant.* X, 6, 1), Josephus even specifies that at this same time Nebuchadnezzar conquered all the lands of the West as far as Pelusium on the border of Egypt—but he explicitly adds: "except the land of Judah." It is difficult, however, to rely upon the chronological accuracy of these traditions (which apparently refer to events occurring several years later).[15] Though Josephus's data largely agree with those of the Babylonian Chronicle, the Chronicle itself does not bear out any widespread conquests in the West while Nebuchadnezzar was still Crown Prince. Immediately after the victory at Carchemish, as we now know, Nebuchadnezzar conquered only the "entire land of Ha[ma]th,"[16] and not the "entire land of Hatti" (that is, Syria-Palestine), as formerly read.

b) Judah submitted a year later, when Nebuchadnezzar devastated Ashkelon, in Kislev of his first regnal year (December 604 B.C.). This date corresponds exactly with the ninth month of the fifth regnal year of Jehoiakim, when a general day of fasting was proclaimed in Jerusalem (Jer. xxxvi 9ff.; see the Chronological Table). Jeremiah's foreboding words, brought before an emergency council of ministers

---

[15] See *IEJ* XVIII 1968, p. 142, n. 10, where we emend in Dan. i 1 "third" year of Jehoiakim to "sixth" year, a minor difference in the Hebrew text, and a suitable date for the subjugation of Judah (see below). For the implausibility of the round date of "third year" here, see most recently Clines, *AJBA* II 1972, pp. 20ff.; and M. Delcor, *Le Livre de Daniel*, Paris 1971, pp. 59f. The latter assumes that this date was erroneously derived from II Kings xxiv 1, on Jehoiakim's rebellion against Babylonia after three years. Josephus's reference to Judean captives after the Battle of Carchemish may indicate that Judah, like other vassals, had supplied troops in support of the Egyptian army. A list of Egyptian prisoners (?) from Sippar in Babylonia, from the third year of Nebuchadnezzar, may also be noted in this context; see D.J. Wiseman, *Iraq* XXVIII 1966, pp. 156ff. On the other hand, Josephus may have been telescoping two originally distinct events when he describes Nebuchadnezzar's campaign as far as Pelusium, which would appear, actually, to refer to the Babylonian invasion to the border of Egypt in the winter of 601/600 B.C. (see below).

[16] This restoration was proposed by A.K. Grayson, *Bibbia e Oriente* VI 1964, p. 205; B. Oded, *Tarbiz* XXXV 1965, p. 104 (Hebrew).

on the fastday, warned of the impending national calamity—the full drama of which we can trace today by means of the Babylonian Chronicle.[17] But Jehoiakim, belittling Jeremiah's warning "that the king of Babylon will certainly come and destroy this land" (Jer. xxxvi 29), burned the Prophet's scroll of doom, which leads to the conclusion that Judah at this time was still not subdued.

c) The submission of Judah may have occurred only in the autumn or winter of 603 B.C., during Nebuchadnezzar's campaign in his second regnal year. Unfortunately, the broken state of the Babylonian tablet here does not enable us to confirm this. In this campaign, which was certainly to the West, the Babylonian king set out in the month of Iyyar with a "mighty army" supported by siege machines, indicating that strong opposition was anticipated. Nebuchadnezzar was most probably seeking to subdue all Philistia and gain control of Judah—all as a prelude to his ultimate goal—the conquest of Egypt, his arch-rival. If this be the case, the lacuna here is to be restored with the conquest of a specific city in Philistia, such as Ashdod, Ekron or more probably Gaza[18] (cf. Jer. xxv 20; xlvii 5; Zeph. ii 4); the subsequent missing section of the tablet might then relate to the submission of Jehoiakim (cf. II Chron. xxxvi 6–7; Dan. i 1–2—both apparently relating to this event).[19]

The latter proposal for dating the subjugation of Judah is in good accord with the circumstances which led to Jehoiakim's rebellion against Babylonia. According to II Kings xxiv 1, Jehoiakim submitted to Babylonia for three years; in other words, he submitted to

---

[17] See A. Malamat, *IEJ* VI 1956, pp. 251f. But A. Baumann (*ZAW* LXXX 1968, pp. 350–373) now opposes any connexion between Jeremiah's oracles read on the fastday and the Babylonian campaign.

[18] A.F. Rainey now proposes to restore the name "Gaza" in the lacuna in the Chronicle (BM 21946) at the start of line 22; see his chapter in the forthcoming report by Y. Aharoni on the excavations of the Tel Aviv University at Lachish. The restoration "Ashdod" there is equally possible. This city is signally denoted "the *remnant* of Ashdod" in Jer. xxv 20, among the Philistine cities condemned to fall before the Babylonians. This would suit its reduced status (represented by stratum VI on the site) on the eve of Nebuchadnezzar's conquest, undoubtedly the result of the lengthy siege by Psamtik I; cf. Malamat, *Gaster Festschrift*, p. 272 and n. 19 there (= chap. 15, a.m.).

[19] See *IEJ* XVIII 1968, p. 142 and n. 9 there. For a similar dating of the subjugation of Judah, cf. already E. Vogt, *Biblica* XLV 1964, pp. 354f.; and, even prior to the publication of the Babylonian Chronicle, J.T. Nellis, *RB* LXI 1954, pp. 387–391; while W.F. Albright, *JBL* LI 1932, pp. 89ff., brought the surrender of Judah down to 603/602 B.C.

the annual tribute three times. If this tribute was yielded the first time in the autumn or winter of 603 B.C., the third payment would have been made in the autumn or winter of 601 B.C., during the Babylonian campaign in Nebuchadnezzar's fourth regnal year. In Kislev (December) 601 B.C., the King of Babylonia took command of his armies, already mustered in the land of "Hatti" and poised to attack Egypt proper. The ensuing war, in the winter of 601/600 B.C.—an international event of outstanding significance—was first revealed to us by the Babylonian Chronicle, which makes no effort to hide the shortcomings of the Babylonian army in its most ambitious campaign to date. Heavy casualties on both sides are reported, and the Babylonians were forced to withdraw. It was this failure, before their very eyes, which most probably encouraged the Judeans and several neighbouring kingdoms to shake off Babylonian hegemony (see the Chronological Table).[20]

II

This blow forestalled the Babylonian reaction to Jehoiakim's revolt. Nebuchadnezzar spend his fifth regnal year (600/599 B.C.) rebuilding his chariot force. The next year he raided among the Arabs (winter of 599/98 B.C.), taking much spoil, as finds reflection in Jeremiah's oracle on "Kedar and the kingdoms of Hazor which Nebuchadrezzar ... smote" (Jer. xlix 28–33; and see the Chronological Table).[21] In his seventh year (598/597 B.C.), however, Nebuchadnezzar's full wrath fell upon Judah, the force of which surely was not lost upon Egypt and her other camp-followers, as well. Indeed, the Chronicle entry for this year deals entirely with the conquest of Jerusalem, the deposing of Jehoiachin and the installing of Zedekiah. This entry fully substantiates the biblical version, and as *baksheesh*

---

[20] See Malamat, *IEJ* VI (1956), p. 251; XVIII 1968, p. 142; Vogt, *VTS* IV 1957, p. 90. On the Babylonian-Egyptian encounter in 601/600 B.C., and further possible evidence for it, see E. Lipiński, *AION* XXXII 1972, pp. 235–241; and Malamat, *Gaster Festschrift*, pp. 276f.

[21] See *CCK*, pp. 31f.; and cf. *IEJ* VI 1956, pp. 254f.; Vogt, *VTS* IV 1957, p. 92. On the various motives which may have been behind the Babylonian raids on the Arab tribes, see I. Ephal, *The Nomads on the Border of Palestine* ... (Doctoral Dissertation, Jerusalem 1971), pp. 125–129 (Hebrew); and W.J. Dumbrell, *AJBA* II 1972, pp. 99–108.

gives the precise day of the surrender of Jerusalem—2 Adar, 16 March, 597 B.C.—a dating unique in the extra-biblical sources touching upon Israelite history. This date, and the almost simultaneous replacement of the Judean ruler, provides a fixed point of reference for the chronology of this period, as well as a keystone in the matter of the regnal new year in Judah, a problem extensively treated by scholars.[22] Moreover, it can guide us toward a fuller understanding of the actual course of the siege and of the resultant exile.

We now know that Nebuchadnezzar mustered his troops and set out for Jerusalem in Kislev (18 December 598–15 January 597 B.C.), and since the march required at least two months, he could have arrived with the bulk of his army only shortly before the city's surrender. But Jerusalem was already under full siege by his "servants" (II Kings xxiv 10–11), probably Babylonian occupation troops and possibly also auxiliary forces (cf. *vs.* 2) stationed in the West. The Chronicle might be supporting this in the entry for the previous year, noting only that the king returned to Babylonia, and thus apparently implying that heavy reinforcements were left in the West.[23]

The biblical sources on the exile of Jehoiachin are in outward contradiction, in both the extent of the exile and its exact date. According to II Kings xxiv, the exile encompassed 10,000 (*vs.* 14) or 7,000 (*vs.* 16) persons, mostly military, to either of which we must add a thousand armourers and sappers.[24] This mass exile, headed by Jehoiachin and his entourage, occurred according to this source in the *eight* year of Nebuchadnezzar's reign (*vs.* 12), the year beginning on 1 Nisan 597 B.C.—at least a month after the surrender of

---

[22] The Babylonian source is BM 21946, verso lines 11–13; *CCK*, pp. 70f. For the complex Chronological problems it raises, see *IEJ* XVIII 1968, pp. 144ff., and the bibliography there.

[23] The specific formulation of the Chronicle entry for the sixth year has already been pointed out by Wiseman, *CCK*, p. 32. On the timing of Nebuchadnezzar's appearance before Jerusalem, see in particular M. Noth, *ZDPV* LXXIV 1958, pp. 136ff.; and Malamat, *IEJ* XVIII 1968, p. 144.

[24] The term *masgēr* (paired with *ḥārāš*), usually translated "smith," refers rather to some occupation involved with fortications, as do several other usages of the same root, such as *misgæræt* and the verb *sgr* (cf., e.g., II Sam. xxii 46 ‖ Ps. xviii 46; I Kings xi 27; Micah vii 17). For an Akkadian cognate and a possibly related loanword in Egyptian, cf. W. Helck, *Die Beziehungen Ägyptens zu Vorderasien im 3. und 2. Jahrtausend v. Chr.*[2], Wiesbaden 1971, p. 525, No. 297. In the exiling of the "armourers and sappers," Nebuchadnezzar achieved a double purpose, depriving Judah of elements essential for its defence and, on the other hand, gained a skilled labour force for his own military designs at home.

Jerusalem. Moreover, II Chronicles xxxvi 10 also implies that Jehoiachin was exiled around the time of the civil new year, and that
Nebuchadnezzar had already returned to his capital, surely for the
annual festivities. But according to the list of exiles in Jeremiah lii
(based undoubtedly on some official source), a mere 3,023 "Jews"
were exiled—in the *seventh* year of Nebuchadnezzar's reign (*vs.* 28).
These have generally been regarded as contradicting traditions on
one and the same matter, or it has been thought that different
chronological systems were employed in the Book of Kings and in
Jeremiah lii, respectively[25]—though even then the numbers for the
deportees disagree. The discrepancies between the two sources can
be reconciled, however, by proposing that the exile evolved in two
successive deportations:[26]

a) The first phase (already intimated in Jer. xiii 18–19) was a limited deportation prior to or upon the surrender of Jerusalem—still
in Nebuchadnezzar's seventh year (Jer. lii 28). The particular appellative here, "Jews"—implying the provincial element of Judah—is
brought into perspective by the designation "from Jerusalem," applied
to the exiles deported during the final siege, in Nebuchadnezzar's
18th year (*vs.* 29; and see the Chronological Table). Several years
after the destruction of Jerusalem, in Nebuchadnezzar's 23rd year,
the deportees are once again, and quite appropriately, called "Jews"
(*vs.* 30).

b) The second, principal phase of the exile, described in the Book
of Kings, comprised the cream of Jerusalem and thousands of her
defenders, including the armourers and sappers specifically mentioned
as exiled from the capital (Jer. xxiv 1; xxix 2). The organization of

---

[25] See, e.g., W.F. Albright, *BASOR* CXLIII 1956, pp. 28–33; D.N. Freedman,
BA XIX 1956, pp. 50–60; both of whom hold that the dates in Jer. lii 28–29 are
the only biblical instance of official Babylonian figures, thus identifying the exiles
of Nebuchadnezzar's seventh and eighteenth years with those of his eighth and
nineteenth years, respectively, W. Rudolph, *Jeremia*[3], Tübingen 1968, p. 324, following earlier commentators, emends the "seventh" year of Nebuchadnezzar to "sev-
enteenth," taking the figure (as in the next verse) for the final siege—an emendation
which seems unwarranted.

[26] For the following solution, see briefly *IEJ* VI 1956, pp. 253f.; XVIII 1968,
p. 154, and n. 32 there. E. Thiele, *BASOR* CXLIII 1956, pp. 22–27, proposed a
similar solution which, however, he subsequently abandoned. The 832 deportees of
Nebuchadnezzar's eighteenth year (Jer. lii 29), like the 3,023 in his seventh year,
represent a minor deportation preceding the major waves in his eighth (see below)
and nineteenth years (for which the actual number is missing in the Bible); cf. *IEJ*
XVIII 1968, p. 154.

this mass exile surely necessitated several weeks from the time of the surrender of the city, on 2 Adar, and thus it would have fallen only in Nebuchadnezzar's eighth regnal year, by which time he had already left the country.

The assumption of two separate deportations can also serve to reconcile the discrepancies in the numbers of deportees, as given within II Kings xxiv—10,000 and 7,000 (besides the armourers and sappers, in both cases). There is no need to see here two parallel but conflicting sources, as often presumed. The number 7,000 may well be intended for the main deportation, at the later stage; while the number 10,000 would represent the total of the two deportations, including the 3,000 captives from the initial phase.[27]

III

In the last decade of the kingdom of Judah, from the first Babylonian conquest of Jerusalem till its final fall, the Bible relates only one incident of international relevance—the anti-Babylonian "conference" summoned by Zedekiah. From Jeremiah xxvii we learn that this conspirational meeting in Jerusalem was attended by envoys from the trans-Jordanian states—Edom, Moab and Ammon (who in 599/98 B.C. were still harassing Judah, alongside the Babylonians; II Kings xxiv 2), and the Phoenician coastal cities—Tyre and Sidon (Jer. xxvii 3). But besides the states participating in this plot (which conspicuously omit the Philistine cities, already for some time Babylonian provinces), we know little of the particular circumstances leading to the convening of the conference, of the consequences thereof, or even its precise date. The chronological heading to Jeremiah xxvii is, of course, faulty. But the smooth continuity of the events described in Jeremiah xxvii–xxviii (which latter chapter opens with the notation:

---

[27] A similar calculation was already made by the early Jewish authors; see *Seder Olam Rabba*, ch. 25; and cf. Rashi on II Kings xxiv 16 and David Kimchi on vs. 14 there. For a modern approach, close to ours though by a different reconstruction, see Vogelstein, *Chronology*, p. 15; and cf. S. Herrmann, *Geschichte Israels*, München 1973, p. 342. The usual assumption today, however, is of duplicate sources in II Kings xxiv; see e.g. J.A. Montgomery, *Books of Kings*, pp. 554ff.; J. Gray, *I & II Kings*, pp. 760ff.; and the early treatment of B. Stade, *ZAW* IV 1884, pp. 271ff., who arbitrarily ascribed all the numbers of deportees to 586 B.C. On the number of exiles, see also E. Janssen, *Judah in der Exilszeit*, Göttingen 1956, pp. 28ff.

"In that same year"), would point to Zedekiah's fourth regnal year, that is, between Tishri 594 and Tishri 593 B.C. (see the Chronological Table).[28] Moreover, the date can probably be pinpointed even more accurately—to only slightly prior to the clash between Jeremiah and the false prophet Hananiah, which occurred in the fifth month of that year, that is, in Ab 593 B.C.—and indeed Jeremiah appears at this confrontation just as he had before the envoys to the conference, with a wooden yoke still about his neck.

The time seemed opportune for the nations of the West to rebel against Babylonia, for the empire had been in straits, at both home and abroad, in the two years prior to the plot, as is apparent from the Babylonian Chronicle.[29] In 596/95 B.C., the King of El[am] marched upon Babylonia, but was repelled—an event which probably inspired Jeremiah's invective against "Elam, in the beginning of the reign of Zedekiah king of Judah" (Jer. xlix 34ff.; and see the Chronological Table). In the winter of 595/94 B.C., revolt broke out even in Babylonia proper, but Nebuchadnezzar was able to suppress it, and immediately after even made a brief campaign to the West. Less than a year later, in Kislev of his eleventh regnal year (December 594 B.C.), Nebuchadnezzar set out once again to the West—the last event mentioned in the Chronicle prior to its breaking off. If our above assumption is correct—that the plot was hatched in Jerusalem several month later—then this Babylonian campaign, of which we have no detailed information, was indecisive and may

---

[28] For the textual difficulties of the chronological superscriptions in Jer. xxvii and xxviii, see the Commentaries; for the LXX versions of xxviii 1 (which omit either the phrase "at the beginning of the reign of Zedekiah" or the phrase "in the fourth year"), see now J.G. Janzen, *Studies in the Text of Jeremiah*, Cambridge (Mass.) 1973, pp. 14f.

For the various chronological attempts to place the anti-Babylonian conference, see Weippert, *Edom*, pp. 327ff. Dating it as late as Zedekiah's seventh year, 591 B.C., is untenable; cf. H. Schmidt, *ZAW* XXXIX 1921, pp. 138–144. On the other hand, equally unsatisfactory is a date as early as the very beginning of Zedekiah's reign, as proposed by H.G. May, *JNES* IV 1945, pp. 217f.; Vogelstein, *Chronology*, p. 32f.; G.R. Driver, *Textus* IV 1964, p. 86; and now N.M. Sarna, in *Hagut Ivrit be Amerika*, Tel Aviv 1972, pp. 121–130 (Hebrew). In Jer. xxviii 1, Sarna (*ibid.*) regards the "fourth year" as referring to the Sabbatical cycle, and thus equates it with "the beginning of Zedekiah's reign." But H. Seebass (*ZAW* LXXXIII 1970, pp. 449–452) distinguishes between the two notations, relating the "beginning" (597 B.C., in his opinion) only to the prophecy in Jer. xxvii 16–22 (following the LXX version here), on the looting of the Temple vessels at the time of Jehoiachin's exile, whereas the confrontation with Hananiah occurred in Zedekiah's fourth year.

[29] For the following citations from the Babylonian Chronicle, see *CCK*, pp. 72ff.

well have even encouraged the ferment in the West. During his fourth regnal year, Zedekiah went to Babylon, or at least sent his "quartermaster" (Jer. li 59), but we do not know the precise date. It may have occurred prior to or in conjunction with Nebuchadnezzar's campaign to the West, or it may have been a corollary to the Babylonian reaction to the conspiracy, and therefore took place in the late summer of 593 B.C.[30]

The anti-Babylonian conference in Jerusalem provoked the sharp encounter between Jeremiah and the faction of false prophets who preached open revolt against Nebuchadnezzar, not only in Judah (Jer. xxvii 9–5; xxviii) but also among the Judean exiles in Babylonia (Jer. xxix 8–9). In Jeremiah's epistle to the exiles he even mentions the names of two prophets executed by Nebuchadnezzar, and a third who had made libellous accusations against him (Jer. xxix 21–32). These increased prophetic activities, we maintain, were the context for Ezekiel's call: his inaugural vision occurred on the fifth day of the fourth month in the fifth year of Jehoiachin's exile, that is, on 31 July 593 B.C. (see the Chronological Table).[31] If this is converted to the calendric system then used in Judah, according to Zedekiah's regnal years (from 1 Tishri 597 B.C.), it took place on the fifth day of the fourth month of Zedekiah's fourth year—a mere few weeks before Jeremiah's confrontation with Hananiah. Thus, it must have occurred at about the time of, or possibly even during, the anti-Babylonian meeting being held at Jerusalem. Could it have been this parley—portentous for the Babylonian exiles no less than for Judah—which aroused Ezekiel to his mission?

The ideological platform of the false prophetic faction was aptly conveyed by Hananiah, proclaimed in Yahwe's name, during his encounter with Jeremiah at the Temple in Jerusalem: "I have broken

---

[30] *Freedy & Redford*, p. 475, assume that Zedekiah was obliged to accompany Nebuchadnezzar upon his return to Babylon, but that in Ab he had already come back to Jerusalem and found the time ripe to rebel. According to the LXX version, Zedekiah himself did not go to Babylon, but merely sent a deputation; see Rudolph, *Jeremiah*, p. 317.

[31] For the date, combining data in Ezek. i 1–2, see the commentaries, and recently W. Zimmerli, *Ezechiel* I, Neukirchen-Vluyn 1969, pp. 40ff. Cf. also C.G. Howie, *The Date and Composition of Ezekiel*, Philadelphia 1960, pp. 27ff. Of all the commentators of Ezekiel, as far as is known to me, only G. Hölscher (*Hesekiel*, BZAW XXXIX 1924, pp. 12ff.) noted the proximity in dates between Ezekiel's call and the superscription in Jer. xxviii 1, and the significance of this correspondance.

the yoke of the king of Babylon. In another $(b^{e'}\bar{o}d)^{32}$ two years I will bring back to this place all the vessels of the Lord's house, which Nebuchadnezzar king of Babylon took away from this place and carried to Babylon. I will also bring back to this place Jeconiah the son of Jehoiakim, king of Judah, and all the exiles from Judah who went to Babylon . . ., for I will break the yoke of the king of Babylon" (Jer. xxviii 1–4). In his slighting response to this prophecy, Jeremiah entirely bypasses the specific notion of the return of King Jehoiachin (Jer. xxviii 6). This may well have been a deliberate cut, reflecting a bone of contention between the "true" and "false" prophetic circles in the political-ideological controversy over relations with Babylonia—the legitimacy of the royal succession in Judah.[33] This controversy derived from the co-existence of two kings of the Davidic line in the last decade of the First Temple period—the exiled Jehoiachin and his uncle Zedekiah, appointed in his stead; both had supporters in Judah, further splitting the people. This duality, of course, tarnished the standing of the last of the kings of Judah, undermined his authority and restricted his manoeuvrability. On the other hand, it might throw light on Zedekiah's paradoxical behaviour in rebelling—contrary to his own interests—against the very power which installed him.[34] Jeremiah countenanced Zedekiah, despite his drawbacks, and

---

[32] The word $b^{e'}\bar{o}d$ is generally translated "*within* (two years)"; however, in biblical usage it often connotes "after," and hence our translation "*in another* (two years)." Cf., e.g., Gen. xxx 13, 19; Josh. i 11. Whereas Hananiah set a specific time for the return of the sacred vessels, etc., the other false prophets used the more general phraseology "now shortly" (Jer. xxvii 16). This latter phrase is omitted here in the LXX, as in the second instance of "*in another* two years" Jer. xxviii 11. These two instances may have been inserted into the MT on the basis of Jer. xxviii 3.

[33] See A. Malamat, *PEQ* LXXXIII 1951, pp. 81–87 (= chap. 23); and cf. also K. Baltzer, in *Studien zur Theologie der alttest. Überlieferungen* (G. von Rad Festschrift, ed. R. Rendtorff and K. Koch), Neukirchen 1961, pp. 33–43.

[34] See *PEQ* LXXXIII 1951, pp. 86f., where we further assume that the change of Mattaniah's name to Zedekiah, upon his appointment by Nebuchadnezzar, occurred under the inspiration of Jeremiah's prophecy on the Messianic King (Jer. xxiii 5–6; xxxiii 14–16)—in direct reversal of the usual interpretation, regarding this prophecy as based on accomplished fact. Recognition of the legitimacy of Zedekiah's rule is intimated even after the destruction of Jerusalem in Lam. iv 20. The theory of Albright (*JBL* LI 1932, pp. 77–106) and his followers (e.g. H.G. May, *AJSL* LVI 1939, pp. 146–148), that even after his deportation Jehoiachin in effect remained king *de jure* of Judah, and that Zedekiah was only regent or *locum tenens*, is not sufficiently supported in the sources. The seal-impression "(Belonging) to Eliakim servant (*na'ar*) *of* Yaukin" lends no support, for the seals of the *na'ar* class are not indicative necessarily of royal officials; see now N. Avigad, "New Light on the *Na'ar* Seals," *G.E. Wright Volume*. Palaeographically, too, it would seem that the above seal

thoroughly rejected the legitimacy of Jehoiachin (or for that matter any of Jehoiakim's seed; cf. Jer. xxxvi 30), as advocated by the false prophets, with Hananiah at their head.

In Hananiah's prophecy, he boldly sets the fulfillment date for the release of the exiles and the return of Jehoiachin, even repeating it after symbolically breaking the wooden yoke on Jeremiah's neck: "Even so will I break the yoke of Nebuchadnezzar king of Babylon from the neck of all the nations in yet ($b^{e\varsigma}\bar{o}d$) two years" (Jer. xxviii 11). Since this prophecy was uttered in the fifth month of the fourth regnal year of Zedekiah (see above), the fulfillment date fell in the fifth month of Zedekiah's sixth regnal year, that is, in Ab 591 B.C. In the chronological terms employed among the exiles, as manifest in the Book of Ezekiel, this was in the fifth month of the seventh year of Jehoiachin's exile (reckoned from 1 Nisan 597 B.C.). How surprising, then, that so similar a date should appear in the superscription to Ezekiel xx: "In the seventh year, in the fifth month, on the tenth day of the month [that is, on 10 Ab, 14 August 591 B.C.], certain of the elders of Israel came to enquire of the Lord . . ." (Ezek. xx 1; and see the Chronological Table).

Is this correspondence in dates, hitherto unnoticed, merely coincidental, or—as in Ezekiel's other chronological notations—is there some underlying significance? Though the object of the enquiry of the elders of Israel is not specified here,—as in other cases where the leadership sought divine tidings, it certainly concerned some pertinent national issue. In contrast to the prevailing interpretations of Ezekiel xx, Zimmerli has recently suggested that the enquiry might have concerned the release of the exiles of Jehoiachin, but he made no connection with Hananiah's prophecy. Freedy and Redford have connected it with the hopes for redemption raised among the exiles by the campaign of Psamtik II to Asia, which they date in 591 B.C.[35] But this latter dating is spurious, as we shall see below.

---

should be dated long before Jehoiachin's reign (F.M. Cross, Jr.—orally). Further, the designation of Jehoiachin as "King of the land of Judah" in the Weidner Tablets, like that of other deposed kings in exile, is not decisive in this matter; see the several documents in *ANET*, p. 308a and b.

[35] For these views, see Zimmerli, *Ezechiel*, I, p. 441; *Freedy & Redford*, pp. 469f., 480. Anticipating these was the medieval commentator David Kimchi, who regarded the elders in Ezek. xx 1 as seeking knowledge of the return to Judah. M. Greenberg—in *Oz leDavid* (*D. Ben-Gurion Festschrift*), Jerusalem 1964, pp. 433–442 (Hebrew)—in contrast, regards the rebuke in Ezek. xx as the prophet's reaction to the exiles'

Would it not be much more reasonable to assume that the enquiry was related specifically to Hananiah's prophecy of redemption "in yet two years"? The acute question at that time—at exactly the term of the prophecy—would have been whether, indeed, redemption was to come. The absolute refusal of the Lord ("Is it to enquire of me that you come? As I live . . ., I will not be enquired of you"; Ezek. xx 3, 31), and the prophet's chastisement of the elders, instead of the expected words of salvation, both show that Ezekiel in exile, like Jeremiah in Judah, was totally opposed to the oracles of early redemption uttered by Hananiah and those like him.

The elders turned to Ezekiel, probably on this same matter, on another occasion as well, and were then, too, rejected by the Lord (Ezek. xiv 1–3: "Should I let myself be enquired of—at all by them?"). Moreover, on that occasion they were clearly warned that if a "prophet be deceived and speak a word, I, the Lord, have deceived that prophet . . ., and will destroy him from the midst of my people Israel" (Ezek. xiv 9). Indeed, this was the very fate which soon befell Hananiah (cf. Jer. xxviii 16–17).[36]

One last chronological notation remains in the Book of Ezekiel prior to the final siege of Jerusalem (Ezek. xxiv 1), for which no historical circumstance has been found—the heading of Ezekiel viii: the fifth day, in the sixth month (LXX: fifth month) of the sixth year of Jehoiachin (that is, 17 September 592 B.C.). This is also the third and only other notice of the leaders of the community in exile coming to Ezekiel (in contrast to the two other instances, here they are specifically denoted the elders of *Judah*, not Israel; in Ezek. xxxiii 30ff., no mention is made of leaders *per se*). Again we may assume that the elders came to the prophet on some particular occasion which was considered fateful for the nation. In his trance, Ezekiel was transported to Jerusalem and he luridly depicts the abomination of the Temple cult. In the syncretistic cult described, Egyptian elements are prominent, alongside other foreign features (e.g. Tammuz

---

acceptance of their fate. In his opinion, the visit of the elders to Ezekiel occurred a year after (!) Hananiah's prophecy had proved false (*ibid.*, p. 439), but we cannot accept this dating.

[36] The conceptual bond between the type of prophet mentioned in Ezek. xiv 9 and the prophetic faction which Hananiah represented has been alluded to by J.W. Miller, *Das Verhältnis Jeremias und Hesekiels Sprachlich und Theologisch Untersucht*, Assen 1955, p. 164.

worship), as has been noted often.[37] These elements seem to include typical animal symbolism—"And there, portrayed upon the wall round about, were all kinds of creeping things, and loathsome beasts . . ." (Ezek. viii 10); the mysteries performed by "the elders of the house of Israel . . . in the dark, every man in his room of pictures" (*vs.* 12); and the worship of the sun (*vs.* 16), in which "they put the branch (*zᵉmōrāh*) to my nose" (*vs.* 17; the last word of the phrase here in MT, *appam*, "their nose," is a *tiqqun soferim* for *appi*, "my nose," that is, presenting the branch to the deity, similar to the presentation of flowers or papyrus garlands to Egyptian gods; and see below).[38]

In a previous study we have already noted that the dates in Ezekiel, besides being of intrinsic value, are "Judah-centric," that is, they are oriented upon events which took place at home, in Palestine. Thus, we sought to show that the chronological notations heading oracles of doom on Egypt correspond with the despatch and subsequent failure of the Egyptian expedition to Judah during the final Babylonian siege of Jerusalem, in the spring of 587 B.C. (see the Chronological Table).[39] Might not the above-mentioned date heading Ezekiel viii be ascribed to another stirring development which befell Palestine— the campaign of Psamtik II to Kharu (that is, Palestine and the Phoenician coast) in his fourth regnal year, and its political and religious implications? Psamtik II's fourth year essentially corresponds

[37] See especially G. Fohrer, *Ezechiel*, Tübingen 1955, pp. 51f.; and for the numerous earlier commentators who emphasized the Egyptian cultic elements in this chapter, see G. Fohrer, *Die Hauptprobleme des Buches Ezechiel*, Berlin 1952, p. 175, n. 48. To them we might add H. Schmidt, *Die grossen Propheten* (*Die Schriften des Alten Testaments* II, 2), Göttingen 1915, pp. 39ff.; idem, *ZAW* XXXIX 1921, pp. 140f., who distinguishes between the overtness of the Babylonian worship here and the clandestine nature of the Egyptian; and, in part, W. Eichrodt, *Der Prophet Hesekiel*, Göttingen 1966, pp. 59f. And cf. also: W.F. Albright, *Archaeology and the Religion of Israel²*, Baltimore 1946, pp. 165ff.
[38] For the various explanations of the word *zᵉmōrāh*, and the foreign cult described in this context, see—besides the commentaries on Ezekiel—the studies devoted specifically to this matter, e.g.: R. Gordis, *JThS* XXXVII 1936, pp. 284–288; H.W.F. Saggs, *ibid.*, NS XI 1960, pp. 318–329; N.M. Sarna, *HThR* LVII 1964, pp. 347–352, all of which appear to fall wide of the mark. More convincing than Saggs' attempt— to explain the passage on the basis of a Mesopotamian rite—is Fohrer's view (*loc. cit.*), which regards the *zᵉmōrāh* (a vine-branch) as a local Palestinian manifestation of the Egyptian ritual of presenting plants to gods, especially the sun-god; such would explain the close connections of this verse with the preceding *vs.* 16, specifically mentioning sun worship.
[39] See *IEJ* XVIII 1968, p. 152.

with 592 B.C., rather than 591 (or even 590) B.C., as generally still held (see the Chronological Table).[40] From the Egyptian source, it is apparent that this was more of a cultic "showing of the flag," than a military campaign, a sort of tour or pilgrimage to holy sites in the land of Kharu.[41]

Accompanying Pharaoh on this tour were priests bearing garlands (specific mention is made of a priest of Amun and of garlands of this deity), probably for the cult of the local or Egyptian gods in the temples of Kharu. Psamtik's destination has been regarded as the city of Byblos and the cult of Osiris there, but shrines in Palestine may well have been visited too. In the autumn of the same year, Ezekiel had his vision on the defiled Temple of Yahwe (see the Chronological Table). Could the touring Pharaoh, or at least his priests, have come to the Temple in Jerusalem? Could the abominous ritual blasted by Ezekiel—the proffering of the $z^e m \bar{o} r \bar{a} h$ within the Temple—be a reflection of the rite involving such cultic garlands as those brought by the Egyptian priests?[42]

---

[40] For the revised Egyptian chronology of the Twenty-sixth Dynasty, retarding the initial year of each reign by a year, see: R.A. Parker, *MDAIK* XV 1957, pp. 208–212 (and cf. E. Hornung, *ZÄS* XCII 1965, pp. 38f.). These dates have been accepted in such histories as A. Gardiner, *Egypt of the Pharaohs*, Oxford 1961, p. 451; W. Helck, *Geschichte des alten Ägypten*, Leiden-Köln 1968, pp. 253ff.; and now also F.K. Kienitz, *Fischer Weltgeschichte* IV, Frankfurt 1967, pp. 269f.—in contrast to his previous *Die politische Geschichte Ägyptens von 7. bis zum 4. Jahrhundert vor der Zeitwende*, Berlin 1953, pp. 25ff., 158.

Thus, Psamtik II ruled from 595 to 589 B.C.—rather than in 594–588 B.C., and Hophra began his reign already in February 589 B.C. Psamtik II's fourth year would have fallen between 18 January 592 and 17 January 591 B.C., as Prof. Hornung has kindly informed me. The obsolete figures for the dates of Psamtik II's reign have unfortunately been retained by, e.g., *Freedy & Redford*, p. 476. In any event, it is now clear that Psamtik II came to the throne more than two years prior to the anti-Babylonian conference in Jerusalem, and thus we can no longer accept a direct connection between these two events, as has been assumed by various scholars.

[41] See now the inscription, published by F.L. Griffith in 1909, in *ibid.*, pp. 479f. (and the bibliography there). In contrast to the oft-held assumption that Psamtik II carried out a basically military campaign to Kharu, *Freedy & Redford* justly stress the peaceful character of this Egyptian undertaking (cf. similarly the two works of F.K. Kienitz, mentioned in n. 40, above; and Weippert, *Edom*, p. 376), and further assume that political contacts were then made with Zedekiah. M. Greenberg (*JBL* LXXVI 1957, pp. 304–309) even assumed that Zedekiah was stirred into open rebellion against Babylon already by Psamtik II's appearance in Kharu.

[42] For the Egyptian ritual of presenting garlands of flowers or papyri to the gods (including by Pharaoh), see G. Roeder, *ZÄS* XLVIII 1910, pp. 115–123; A. de Buck, *OTS* IX 1951, pp. 18–29; H. Bonnet, *Reallexikon der ägypt. Religiongeschichte*, Berlin 1952, pp. 120f., s.v. *Blumen*; D.B. Redford, *Orientalia* XXXIX 1970, p. 36,

Ezekiel's harsh oracle of doom on Jerusalem and its Temple (Ezek. viii–xi) should have served to preclude as vain any illusions among the Judean leadership—whether in Jerusalem or in exile—which may have been raised by Pharaoh's campaign. The appearance of Psamtik II in Kharu certainly had diplomatic overtones and undoubtedly fanned the anti-Babylonian sentiments already held by many local rulers, including the King of Judah. But it was only after the ambitious Hophra had acceded to the Egyptian throne (in early 589 B.C., and not 588 B.C.) that Judah openly rebelled, thus goading Babylon to war.

At this juncture Judah's plight was extreme: politically, her diplomatic efforts to achieve an anti-Babylonian front had collapsed, and the frailty of Egyptian support left her virtually isolated. Militarily, the Babylonian subjugation a decade earlier had deprived her of the cream of her fighting potential. Internally, the nation was divided over the dilemma of facing Babylon or giving in to fate. But the stand of the political leadership, which had inevitably drawn Nebuchadnezzar to the gates of Jerusalem once again, now spurred the remarkable resistance which enabled the city to withstand the two and a half years of siege prior to its fall (see the Chronological Table).[43]

In final analysis, the policy advocated by the "true" Prophets — Jeremiah and Ezekiel—could have steered Judah clear of the maelstrom which, as we know, did engulf her.

Postscriptum

I was unable to refer to the article of E. Kutsch, "Das Jahr der Katastrophe: 587 v. Chr.," *Biblica* LV 1974, pp. 520–543, which reached me while the present paper was in proofs. The article is a careful and comprehensive defense of the alternative dating of the fall of Jerusalem, but I have not found its arguments of sufficient weight to alter my stand as set forth in this paper.

---

n. 1 and, most recently, E. Brunner-Traut, *Lexikon der Ägyptologie* I, Wiesbaden, 1974, pp. 836–9, s.v. *Blume; Blumenstrauss.*

From the many Egyptian depictions of the presentation of plants to the face of the god, we may call attention to an example from Palestine—on a stele from Beth Shean, showing a lotus being presented to the nose of a goddess; see *ANEP*, No. 475.

[43] On the final siege of Jerusalem and its duration, basing on a Tishri calendar, see *IEJ* XVIII 1968, pp. 150ff.

Chronological Table of the Last Decades of the Kingdom of Judah

Events mentioned in the Babylonian Chronicles	Julian year B.C. beginning in January	Regnal years in Babylonia beginning in Nisan (1st mo.)	Regnal years in Judah beginning in Tishri (VIIth mo.)	Events mentioned in the Bible
Egyptian army crosses Euphrates	609	Nabopolassar 17—IV—	Josiah 31 → *Jehoahaz (1)	Battle of Megiddo (2 Kings 23:29; 2 Chron. 35:20–23)
	608	18	*Jehoiakim	
	607	19	1	
	606	20	2	
Battle of Carchemish / Conquest of "entire land of Ha[ma]th"	605	21—*Nebuchadrezzar	3	Oracle on Battle of Carchemish (Jer. 46:1–2; date in vs. 2 problematic)** [Subjugation of Judah according to Dan. 1:1ff]
Sack of Ashkelon	604	1	4 (or)	Oracle on Nebuchadrezzar's rule over Hither Asia (Jer. 25:1ff.)
Campaign to West (?) [text broken]	603	IX / 2	5 — IX	Fast and emergency council (Jer. 36:9)
	602	3	6	Subjugation of Judah?
	601	4	7	
Babylonian invasion of Egypt fails	600	5	8	Oracle "about the coming of Nebuchadrezzar . . . to smite the land of Egypt" (Jer. 46:13ff); Revolt of Jehoiakim (2 Kings 24:1)?

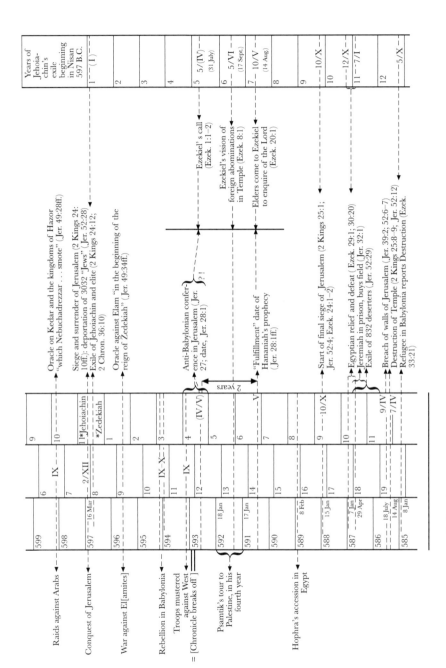

			Years of Jehoia-chin's exile beginning in Nisan 597 B.C.
599	9		1 — (I)
598	10 — IX	Raids against Arabs	2
	6 —		
	7 —	Oracle on Kedar and the kingdoms of Hazor "which Nebuchadrezzar . . . smote" (Jer. 49:28ff.)	3
597 — 16 Mar — 2/XII — 8 — 11*Jehoiachin	Conquest of Jerusalem	Siege and surrender of Jerusalem (2 Kings 24: 10ff.); deportation of 3032 "Jews" (Jer. 52:28). Exile of Jehoiachin and elite (2 Kings 24:12; 2 Chron. 36:10)	4
*Zedekiah — 1			5 — 5/IV) (31 July) Ezekiel's call (Ezek. 1:1–2)
596 — 9	War against El[amites]	Oracle against Elam "in the beginning of the reign of Zedekiah". (Jer. 49:34ff.)	6 — 5/VI (17 Sept.) Ezekiel's vision of foreign abominations in Temple (Ezek. 8:1)
2			7 — 10/V (14 Aug) Elders come to Ezekiel to enquire of the Lord (Ezek. 20:1)
595 — 10			8
594 — IX–X — 3	Rebellion in Babylonia		9 — 10/X
11 — 4 — (IV/V)	Troops mustered against West = [Chronicle breaks off]	Anti-Babylonian conference in Jerusalem (Jer. 27; date, Jer. 28:1) ?!	10
593 — IX — 5 — (V)			11 — 7/I
592 — 18 Jan — 12 — 6	Psamtik's tour to Palestine, in his fourth year	"Fulfillment" date of Hananiah's prophecy (Jer. 28:1ff.)	12
591 — 17 Jan — 13 — 7			5/X
590 — 14 — 8			
589 — 8 Feb — 15 — 9 — 10/X	Hophra's accession in Egypt	Start of final siege of Jerusalem (2 Kings 25:1; Jer. 52:4; Ezek. 24:1–2)	
588 — 15 Jan — 16 — 10			
587 — 7 Jan / 29 Apr — 17 — 11		Egyptian relief and defeat (Ezek. 29:1; 30:20) Jeremiah in prison, buys field (Jer. 32:1) Exile of 832 deserters (Jer. 52:29)	
586 — 18 July / 14 Aug — 18 — 9/IV		Breach of walls of Jerusalem (Jer. 39:2; 52:6–7) Destruction of Temple (2 Kings 25:8–9; Jer. 52:12)	
585 — 8 Jan — 19 — 7/IV		Refugee in Babylonia reports Destruction (Ezek. 33:21)	

2 years

* Accession year.

** For date, see notes 9 and 11.

17

THE KINGDOM OF JUDAH BETWEEN
EGYPT AND BABYLON:
A SMALL STATE WITHIN A GREAT POWER
CONFRONTATION* **

First, let me thank you for inviting me to deliver the Mowinckel Lecture in memory of that great Scandinavian Bible scholar to whom all of us are so greatly indebted. Our lecture is based on several of my studies on the final years of the kingdom of Judah,[1] though now from a specific geopolitical or geostrategic point of view. Attention to this particular facet, that finds expression in the "power game" of the day, can sharpen our observation, especially since we resort here to Political Science and International Relations.[2] Admittedly, we must be wary of the pitfalls in submitting to anachronistic concepts. To mention but one example, the concept of a "State" of Judah is an obvious anachronism, yet one certainly would not forego this terminology. Nevertheless, our distinct awareness of anachronistic perceptions is bound to curb the methodological difficulty in using categories of modern disciplines. Indeed, such contemporary categories prove efficient analytical tools when applied to ancient phenomena as well.

---

* This article was originally published in: *Stud. Theol.* 44 (1990), 65–55.

** The Mowinckel Lecture, University of Oslo, delivered 28th September 1989.

The present text is a slightly different and expanded version of my contribution to *Text and Context* (Studies for F.C. Fensham, ed. W. Claassen), *JSOT* Suppl. 48, Sheffield (1988), pp. 117–129. Here also a detailed, updated apparatus has been appended which can be completed by the footnotes in my previous articles.

[1] See in particular A. Malamat, "Josiah's Bid for Armaggedon," *JANES* 5 (= the Gaster Festschrift), (1973), pp. 267–79 (Chap. 15); *idem*, "The Twilight in Judah: In the Egyptian-Babylonian Maelstrom," *SVT* 28 (1975), pp. 123–45; (Chap. 16) idem, "The Last Years of the Kingdom of Judah," *The Age of the Monarchies: Political History* (World History of the Jewish People IV, 1), (ed. A. Malamat), Massada; Jerusalem (1979), ch. 10, pp. 205–21, 349–53.

[2] On the theoretical framework used here, see e.g., R.L. Rothstein, *Alliances and Small Powers*, Columbia University Press: New York, (1968); J.N. Rosenau (ed.), *International Politics and Foreign Policy*, Free Press: New York, 2nd ed. (1969); I.M. Handel, *Weak States in the International System*, Cass: London (1981).

A word on the source material is in order, considering its rami-
fications on the historical method to be applied to this period. A
wide range of sources for this tense period provides a particularly
detailed insight into much of the political situation and development
in Judah. Besides the Book of Kings and Chronicles, these decades
are illuminated by the Book of Jeremiah, and their final years by
the Book of Ezekiel.

The contemporaneous epigraphical material in Hebrew is plentiful and varied, more so than in any earlier period. One need only
refer to the Lachish[3] and now the Arad ostraca, the over fifty inscribed
bullae, just prior to Nebuchadnezzar's conquest, from a Jerusalem
archive published only recently,[4] and the further hoard of the two
hundred bullae from this period, published now by Professor Avigad,
the most thrilling one referring to "Berachyahu ben Neriyahu ha-
sofer"—the scribe of Jeremiah mentioned in the Bible.[5] The effect
of the political-military events have revealed utter destruction in the
archaeological excavations throughout Judah,[6] from Tell Batash
(Timnah)[7] in the west to Ein Gedi in the east, from Jerusalem in
the north to Lachish in the south.

Yet, a proper perspective for evaluating the historical factors underlying the final fate of Judah—factors which determined the policies
of its rulers, is to be obtained *only* from sources beyond Palestine—
primarily the Neo-Babylonian Chronicles[8] and, to a lesser degree,

---

[3] For a new approach to the Lachish ostraca as local *copies* of letters despatched
from the place rather than letters sent there, see now Y. Yadin, "The Lachish
Letters—Originals or Copies and Drafts?," *Recent Archaeology in the Holy Land of Israel*
(ed. H. Shanks) Biblical Archaeology Society and Israel Exploration Society: Washington
and Jerusalem, (1981), pp. 179–186.

[4] Y. Shiloh, "A Group of Hebrew Bullae from the city of David," *IEJ* 36 (1986),
pp. 16–38.

[5] N. Avigad, *Hebrew Bullae from the Time of Jeremiah*, Israel Exploration Society:
Jerusalem 1986.

[6] See in general E. Stern, "Israel at the Close of the Period of the Monarchy:
An Archaeological Survey," *BA* 38 (1975), pp. 26–34. For the settlement in the Negev
see the discussion by N. Na'aman, A.P. Rainey, A. Biran, Y. Beth-Aryeh, *Cathedra*
42 (1987), pp. 3–38 (Hebrew), and specifically for the destruction of the towns of
Irah and Aroer see A. Biran, *IEJ* 29 (1979), pp. 124/5 and 31 (1981), p. 132.

[7] See G.L. Kelm and A. Mazar, Tel Batash (Timnah) Excavations, *BASOR* Supp.
23 (1985), pp. 111f. As a border town Timnah may have belonged according to
some opinions to the Philistine realm, especially to the kingdom of Ekron.

[8] See D.J. Wiseman, *Chronicles of Chaldaean Kings*, British Museum: London (1956);
A.K. Grayson, *Assyrian and Babylonian Chronicles*, Augustin: Locust Valley, N.Y. (1975),
pp. 99–102.

Egyptian documentation. The combining of biblical data with external sources, especially the detailed framework of dates they contain,
enables a sort of micro-analytical study of this period. Thus, when
we can trace the historical process in time units much more minute
than is generally feasible for the Israelite period—in terms of a specific
year, month, or even day—we gain the fascinating immediacy that
is microhistory.[9] Here, as well as in the likewise fascinating macro-
historical analysis, new issues can sometimes be detected and raised
by the astute historian from sources long considered over-exploited.
The originality of the historian often lies in his ability to make these
sources talk and reveal new insights.

Finally, a note on chronology. The chronological method applied
here has more than once influenced our reconstruction of the chain
of events. Though there is an almost general consensus that the post-
dating system, involving accession years, was employed in Judah at
this time, the month of the Judean regnal new year is still open to
controversy. Our reckoning is based on an autumnal calendar beginning on 1 Tishri, and not on the spring calendar accepted by a
majority of scholars and which was in general use in Babylonia. On
previous occasions I have sought to demonstrate the preference of
this Tishri reckoning in Judah, and its propensity for reconciling a
majority of the variegated data, at least for our period.[10] So I shall
not enter here into a discussion of that matter (but cf. below n. 33).
Rather, it is international politics and grand strategy, involving the
various actors, with which we are concerned here.

With the decline of the mighty empire of Assyria toward the end
of the seventh century B.C., and the striking victories of the young
Nebuchadnezzar in the summer of 605 B.C., a most reluctant Judah
was swept into the ensuing confrontation that erupted between the
Neo-Babylonian empire and Egypt.

These two powers were a keen and novel political phenomenon
in the Near East. North of Judah, the up-and-coming Neo-Babylonian
or rather, Chaldean empire, had become a decisive military and

---

[9] See our chart in *SVT* 28, pp. 144–45 (= chap. 16, p. 320–21).

[10] Especially in "The Last Kings of Judah and the Fall of Jerusalem," *IEJ* 18
(1968), pp. 137–156 and in *Israel in Biblical Times* (Hebrew), Bialik Institute: Jerusalem
(1983), pp. 243–247 ("A Chronological Note"). According to this chronological system Jerusalem lasted until 586 B.C. and not 587 B.C. as accepted by the majority of scholars (see below n. 33).

political factor in Mesopotamia, while to the south, whereas previously Egypt had long abandoned its *"Ostpolitik,"* the Pharaohs of the twenty-sixth dynasty in Egypt (Psammetich I, Necho II, Psammetich II, Hophra) were now renewing intervention in Asia, as the occasion arose.[11] The struggle between the two powers alternated from open military conflict to "cold war." The small state of Judah, located at the particularly sensitive crossroads linking Asia and Africa, was influenced more than ever before by the international power system, now that the kingdom's actual existence was at stake.

In Political Science terms, Judah was now poignantly caught up in a bi-polar system, meaning that the exclusive control of international politics was concentrated in two powers, solely responsible for preserving peace or making war.[12] Though the ancients clearly lacked such a modern concept of bi-polarity, they were nevertheless empirically aware of this power sytem category; thus, for example, Thucydides' approach to the struggle between the two centers— Athens and Sparta.[13] Similarly, the prophet Jeremiah expresses the idea metaphorically: "And now what do you gain by going to Egypt, to drink the waters of the Nile? Or what do you gain by going to Assyria to drink the waters of the Euphrates?" (Jer. 2:18); and later in the same chapter: "How lightly you gad about, changing your way! You shall be put to shame by Egypt as you were put to shame by Assyria" (*ibid.*, v. 36).[14] Hence, bi-polarization of power had entered biblical consciousness.

Apparently, a multi-polar system accommodates small or secondary states, insofar as it is more capable of maintaining the fragile balance of power, thus deterring violation of the states within the region. However, the bi-polar system, whose stability as such is still debated by political scientists,[15] also entails tranquility for secondary states, granting that the big states adopt policies of peaceful coexistence. Once the equilibrium is disturbed or upset by one of the partners

---

[11] See A. Spalinger, "Egypt and Babylonia: A Survey c. 620 B.C.–550 B.C.," *SAK* 5 (1977), pp. 221–44.

[12] J.N. Rosenau (ed.), *op. cit.* (n. 2), ch. 27 by M.A. Kaplan (especially pp. 296ff.) and ch. 30 by R.N. Rosecrance (pp. 325ff.).

[13] See P.J. Fliess, *Thucydides and the Politics of Bipolarity*, Louisiana State University Press: Louisiana (1966).

[14] The political circumstances reflected in these passages are occasionally dated to the years 623–617 B.C., a time when both Assyria and Egypt could have been considered potential allies of Judah. Cf. J. Milgrom, *JNES* 14 (1955), pp. 66–9.

[15] See in Rosenau, *op. cit.* (n. 12).

seeking hegemony, the secondary power, lacking sufficient economic and military potential, turns to inexpensive diplomatic means to alleviate its plight.

Such was the fate of Judah. In the last two decades of its existence, the rapid pace of the international scene demanded of the Judean rulers exceedingly skilful manoeuvring in order to cope with kaleidoscopic situations. Within these twenty years a series of no less than six critical turning points in Judah's foreign policy can be discerned, marking drastic shifts in loyalty from one major camp to the other. In other words, the political orientation of Judah alternated radically at an average intensity of every three years. In reacting to external temptations, the little kingdom eventually succumbed not only to international intrigues, but to her own risky policies as well. What were these six crucial stages, alternating between loyalty and rebellion?

I

The chain of events in Judah's fate began with the Battle of Megiddo in the summer of 609 B.C., though this incident occurred several years prior to Judah's direct involvement in the Egyptian-Babylonian conflict. Possibly, the budding bi-polar system already influenced Josiah's decision to halt Pharaoh Necho, who was rushing northward in support of his previous rival, the Assyrians, in their deteriorating struggle against the newly rising Babylonians. It is difficult to ascertain, but possibly Judah was somehow acting in concert with Babylonia to hinder this Egyptian aid.

There were several factors in Judah's favor: the newly enthroned Pharaoh Necho II was as yet inexperienced; the Egyptian army was far from its base when the Judeans chose to launch their surprise attack near Meggido; above all, a fact generally overlooked, only half a year before, the Egyptians had sustained a setback in the Euphrates region by the up-and-coming Babylonians. At any rate, this is a rare example of bold military initiative taken by a relatively small state, Judah, against the army of the biggest power of the day, Egypt, of the twenty-sixth dynasty.

At this point, I shall take the opportunity of drawing attention to a possible additional source for the battle of Megiddo, namely a fragmentary ostracon from Arad. The "curious case of ostracon" no. 88,

whose left half is missing, has received two different interpretations
and restorations, one by the late Professor Aharoni and another by
the late Professor Yadin, the only attempts as far as I am aware
and both are, in my opinion, rather dubious. The Hebrew text reads:

I have come to reign in all . . .	אני. מלכתי, בכ
Take strength and . . .	אמץ. זרע. ו.
King of Egypt to . . .	מלר. מצרים. ל.

Aharoni[16] assumed that it refers to the enthronement of Jehoahaz,
as successor of Josiah, while Yadin[17] ventured it to be a declaration
of Asshur-uballit, the last king of Assyria. Since neither version seems
acceptable, I risk an alternative proposal and restore:

אני מלכתי בכ [ל הגויים] :בכ [ל הרי יהודה] (or)
I reign over all the nations (or: all the mountains of Judah)

אמץ זרוע ו [צא לקראת] :ו [התחזק נגד] (or)
Take strength and go up against (or: muster your forces against)

מלר מצרים ל [הלחם בו] :ל [בקעת מגידו] (or)
The King of Egypt to make war against him (or: to the Valley of
Megiddo)

This daring military initiative at Meggido was rooted in ideology, as
it finds expression in the Book of Deuteronomy, Josiah's guiding
light. Furthermore, we can confidently conjecture that this initiative
received the support and encouragement of the prophetic circles.
Judging primarily by the style of the inscription, we seem to have
here a prophetic-political text, where God speaks through his prophets,
apparently encouraging Josiah to go war against Egypt. This is no
king of flesh and blood, as both Aharoni and Yadin had assumed,
but God speaking: אני מלכתי. The very style of the wording infers
that the verb "מלכתי" is inscribed in the past tense, but to be understood here in the present, as is frequently found in the Biblical tense
system.[18] Our restoration is supported by such verses as Psalm 47:9:
"God reigns over the nations; God sits on his holy throne"—"מָלַךְ אֱלֹהִים
עַל גּוֹיִם אֱלֹהִים יָשַׁב עַל כִּסֵּא קָדְשׁוֹ", or I Ch. 16:31: "Let the heavens

---

[16] Y. Aharoni, *Arad Inscriptions*, Israel Exploration Society: Jerusalem (1981), pp.
103f.

[17] Y. Yadin, *IEJ* 26 (1976), pp. 9–14; similarly now A. Green, *ZAW* 100 (1988),
pp. 277–280; and see the forthcoming paper by M. Luijken ("Inscription 88 from
Arad Reconsidered").

[18] F.R. Blake, *A Resurvey of Hebrew Tenses*, Pontifical Biblical Institute: Rome (1951),
pp. 16f.

be glad, and let the earth rejoice, and let them say among the na-
tions, The Lord reigns"—"יִשְׂמְחוּ הַשָּׁמַיִם וְתָגֵל הָאָרֶץ וְיֹאמְרוּ בַגּוֹיִם ה' מָלָךְ".

In the second line, note the word "זְרוֹעַ"—*arm*. This type of exhor-
tation is repeated time again, especially in the political prophecy of
Ezek. 30:22–26: "Therefore thus says the Lord God: Behold, I am
against Pharaoh king of Egypt, and will break his *arms*, both the
strong *arm* and the one that is broken; and I will make the sword
fall from his hand. I will scatter the Egyptians among the nations,
and disperse them throughout the lands. And I will strengthen the
arms of the king of Babylon, and put my sword in his hand; but I
will break the *arms* of Pharaoh, and he will groan before him like
a man mortally wounded. I will strengthen the *arms* of the king of
Babylon, but the *arms* of Pharaoh shall fall; and they shall know that
I am the Lord . . ." The completions in lines 2 and 3 are based on
what we know of the Battle of Megiddo in II Chr. 36. If this restoration (as well as the dating of the ostracon—I do agree with Yadin
on this point) is, in fact correct, then it seems that this is a prophetic
proclamation in the name of the Lord, dispatched to the cities of
Judah for the purpose of recruiting military aid in the campaign
against Egypt. Finally, underlining my belief that this may be the
true reconstruction is the harmonious spacing and outline of the
Hebrew letters, obviously written by a mature, professional scribe
and characteristic of its prophetic origin. None of the numerous other
ostraca found at Arad can compare with this very unique one in
elegance and beauty of script.

Now, returning to the first of our six stages: Despite the failure
at Megiddo, this should not, *a priori*, be considered a suicidal undertaking, as is so often done, but rather a carefully calculated political move within the international power game, as I have pointed
out elsewhere.[19] However, the chance death of Josiah in the Plain
of Megiddo, put an effective end to the renewed prosperity of the
Judean kingdom. Yet, Judah persisted in an anti-Egyptian policy, as
witnessed by the enthronement of Jehoahaz, the younger son of Josiah

---

[19] See in particular Malamat, "Josiah's Bid" (above, n. 1). For recent different
views on the Megiddo affair see H.G.M. Williamson, *VT* 32 (1982), pp. 242–7;
C.T. Begg, *VT* 37 (1987), pp. 1–8; and N. Na'aman, "The Town Lists of Judah . . .,"
Zion 54 (1989), pp. 17–71 (Hebrew). The last author reviews the entire Josianic
rule, taking a minimal stand on it.

(contrary to the principle of primogeniture) due to the intervention of the anti-Egyptian ʿam haāreṣ. This policy was unfortunately premature at that particular stage, and indeed Necho deposed the new king installing Jehoiakim, a loyal scion of the pro-Egyptian faction of the Davidic dynasty, on the throne as an Egyptian vassal. Necho's appointment of Jehoiakim as king served their mutual interest: Jehoiakim's claims as legitimate heir to the throne were realized at the same time that he became Necho's vassal and loyal ally. Judah's territory was once again "cut down to size," reduced to its minimal dimensions. Egypt now controlled the entire region west of the Euphrates, or, in biblical phraseology, "from the Brook of Egypt unto the river Euphrates, all that pertained to the king of Egypt" (II Kings 24:7). But its hegemony was shortlived.

II

The second fateful turning point occurred four years later, in the summer of 605 B.C. when Egypt was utterly defeated by King Nebuchadnezzar, the rising star of Babylon, in the Battle of Carchemish on the Euphrates, at the present Turkish-Syrian border. This renowned battle was a superb demonstration of sheer Babylonian military superiority, and in fact, by determining the power set-up in the Near East for years to come, sealed the fate of Syria and Palestine.

Nonetheless, the Judean leadership failed to grasp the shift in balance of power, and continued to cling to the dubious image of a strong Egypt which would rush to the aid of its allies in time of need. The other states in Palestine sought Egyptian aid against Babylonia is recorded in an Aramaic letter from Saqqara (Memphis in Egypt). In this letter, a ruler, most likely from Ekron in Philistia,[20] approaches Pharaoh for urgent military assistance against the impending Babylonian onslaught, reminding his suzerain of his treaty obligation. This document possibly concerns one of the Babylonian expeditions against Philistia either in the summer of 603 or the winter of 601/600 B.C. Further proof may be found in the recent

---

[20] On the reverse of the papyrus has recently been detected in Demotic script the placename of the sender perhaps to be read as Ekron, see B. Porten, *BA* 44 (1981), pp. 36–52.

excavations of Tel-Miqneh—Ekron, where a total destruction level
was discovered from the end of the seventh century B.C. (Stratum
IB).[21] Thus, in antiquity, probably more so than in modern times,
a small state had difficulty in correctly assessing early warning sig-
nals of a shift in the "global" power structure. There is a common
assumption in International Relations that small states conduct pru-
dent relations in foreign affairs. Judah's behavior during this period
contradicts this model and demonstrates that small states may in
their ineptness, coupled with the inherent lack of a developed intelligence system, adopt high-risk policies, often with fatal consequences.[22]

In this light, we can appreciate, all the more, the deep foresight
and realistic historical perspective of the prophetic circles in Judah,
who had a genuine understanding of the international scene at the
time. The great prophets of the day, Jeremiah and Ezekiel (or Uriah,
the son of Shemaiah from Kiriath-jearim, who prophesied "in words
like those of Jeremiah," Jer. 26:20), unlike the false prophets, were
entirely free of the "establishment" line of thought[23] and were thus
able to grasp the situation in more realistic terms. Therefore, their's
was a sober and unbiased appreciation of the long-range welfare of
the nation as opposed to the concerns of the establishment and its
supporters—the false prophets, such as Hananyah, so focused on
immediate and feasible interests. In Ezekiel's words Egypt resembled
"a staff of reed to the house of Israel . . . when they leaned upon
you, you broke" (Ez. 29:6–7), and in her threats against Babylonia,
but a "paper tiger": "Pharaoh with his mighty army and great company" will be of no avail in battle (*ibid.*, 17:17). Ezekiel was dis-
tressed by Egypt's enticement of Judah, likening Judah to a harlot,
whereas its lover, Egypt, could only tempt but could not sustain
(*ibid.*, 16:26, 23:8,21,27). Foreign policy, indeed International Relations
as such, were likened in prophetic imagery, especially that of Ezekiel,

---

[21] On Tel Miqneh in the seventh century and its destruction by the Babylonians
see now S. Gitin in *Recent Excavations in Israel: Studies in Iron Age Archaeology* (eds.
S. Gitin and W.G. Dever), Eisenbrauns: Winona Lake, In. (1984), pp. 24–58, esp.
pp. 27, 46.

[22] For this contrasting model of the current opinion concerning the phenomenon in modern times see: M.A. East, "Size and Foreign Policy Behaviour," *World
Politics* 25 (1972/3), pp. 556–76.

[23] On the attitude of the "true" prophets and the prophetic books see now also
C.R. Seitz, *Theology in Conflict: Reactions to the Exile in the Book of Jeremiah*, BZAW 176,
de Gruyter: Berlin (1989); C. Hardmeier, *Prophetie im Streit vor dem Untergang Judas*,
BZAW 187 (1990).

to prostitution.[24] On the other hand, Jeremiah, who regarded Nebuchadnezzar as "God's chosen rod" (of chastisement) realized that the opportune moment had passed: now only voluntary submission to the Babylonian could save Judah; it was the choice between "the way of life and the way of death" (Jer. 21:8–9). We do reject the widely accepted assumption that the prophets' outspoken stands were merely the machinations of later redactors, to make them conform with the outcome of events. On the contratry, we believe their orientation as expressed in the biblical sources, reflects the reality of their views.

In modern terms, these prophets served—*with due recognition of their far more profound motives*—as analysts and commentators, quite independent of official policy and general concensus. In doing so, they played an active role in the acute issue of foreign political orientation, which had gradually intensified the polarity between the pro-Egyptian and pro-Babylonian factions. Thus polarity crossed lines—from the royal court, onward through state officials and priestly circles, and finally down to the masses. Likewise, political orientation and ideology proved the main bone of contention between the true and false prophets. Indeed, small states in general are more preoccupied with external than domestic affairs, a phenomenon known as "*das Primat der Aussenpolitik.*"

The Babylonian subjugation of Judah was not long in coming, although its exact date is still disputed. Judah seems to have held out for another two years after the Battle of Carchemish, surrendering only in the winter of 603 B.C. even though Nebuchadnezzar had already reached as far as Ashkelon and utterly destroyed it a year earlier.[25] In view of this Babylonian threat, Egypt earnestly sought to bring Judah back into its fold, which introduces us to the third turning point, again entailing direct military confrontation between Egypt and Babylonia.

---

[24] See in this context also the prophetic visions in Jer. 2:3 and Hos. 2. For Ezek. 16 see M. Greenberg, *Ezekiel 1–20*, Doubleday: Garden City, N.Y. (1983), pp. 270ff. and T. Krüger, *Geschichtskonzepte im Ezechielbuch, BZAW* 120 (1989), pp. 139ff.; for this chapter as well as Ezek. 23 see now R.W. Klein, *Ezekiel—The Prophet and his Message*, University of South Carolina Press: Columbia, SC (1988), pp. 81–96.

[25] Of this destruction, we now have archaeological proof from the first seasons of excavations at the site. See personal communication of the excavator L. Stager.

III

Some two and a half years after submitting to Babylonia, King Jehoiakim found an opportune moment to throw off its yoke. In the winter of 601/600 the Babylonian king waged his most ambitious campaign—an attack on Egypt proper, a major historical event revealed only relatively recently through publication of the Babylonian Chronicle from the time of Nebuchadnezzar (known as the Wiseman Chronicle). This official historical record conceals neither the Babylonian shortcomings during this campaign, which led to heavy losses on both sides, nor the subsequent, empty-handed Babylonian retreat. It was this Babylonian failure which, assumably exploited by Egyptian propaganda, encouraged the Judean leadership to rebel and defect to the Egyptian camp. For the next two years the Babylonians were unable to retaliate against Judah, and they concentrated on recouping their strength, and above all re-equipping the chariot force.

IV

Only in the winter of 598/97 B.C. did Nebuchadnezzar strike at Judah, in a show of strength which, no doubt, werved as a warning to Egypt and her other allies. The first Babylonian siege of Jerusalem, well documented in the Bible, was the fourth turning point. The biblical account is now fully borne out by the Babylonian Chronicle, which even specifies the precise day of the city's surrender by Jehoiachin (the son of Jehoiakim who died under obscure circumstances) on 2 Adar or March 16, 597 B.C.

This precise date now enables us to reappraise the actual course of the siege and the ensuing exile from Judah.[26] Jerusalen had apparently been under siege for several weeks prior to the arrival of Nebuchadnezzar and his choice troops, an event which broke the spirit of the defenders, who were already demoralized by the lack of any sign of Egyptian aid forthcoming. Albeit, the Judean king's surrender saved Jerusalem from physical destruction, and Judah from the status of a conquered country within the Babylonian empire. Nevertheless, its human resources were seriously depleted—ten thousand

---

[26] See in detail Malamat, "Twilight," pp. 133f. (chap. 16), "Last Years," pp. 210ff.

of its inhabitants having been exiled to Babylonia, including the elite of the nation, the "good figs" in Jeremiah's prophecy (chap. 24), and the higher military echelons.[27]

Nebuchadnezzar's policy of deportation and "heavy tribute" ultimately proved shortsighted. The very foundations of the kingdom were undermined. Social and economic chaos, as well as psychic and spiritual distress prevailed, as can be discerned in the prophets' words. This was the *mise-en-scène* for the appearance of irresponsible elements in Judean leadership. Such was the fate, time and again, of vanquished states who had been burdened with such harsh conditions of surrender.

V

Bereft of experienced leadership and saddled with a puppet king, Judah soon became entangled again in international intrigue, leading up to the fifth turning point. The new king and last monarch of Judah, Zedekiah summoned, or was forced to summon, to Jerusalem an anti-Babylonian conference of delegates of petty kingdoms in the year 594/93 B.C., thus rebelling against the power which had enthroned him, a step paradoxical to his own personal interest. The motivation for this plot is not clear, but it was assumed to be connected with the enthronement of the new Egyptian king Psammetich II. Yet according to a relatively recent chronology for this period (that has been widely overlooked) Psammetich II had already ascended the throne in 595 B.C., *not* 594 as was previously held.[28] It seems more likely that the intrigue (accompanied by the intensive activity of the "false" prophets, predicting the prompt return of the exiles from Babylonia) was inspired by the severe revolt which had broken out the previous winter in Babylonia proper. Though immediately crushed by Nebuchadnezzar, we still hear a year later (i.e. close to the Jerusalem conference) that an important functionary of the

---

[27] It seems possible that the Babylonian army, which was weakened two years earlier, now incorporated within its rows Judah's military personnel which had been deported. In this case the latter may well have served in Nebuchadnezzar's further campaigns to the West.

[28] For the initial of the revised Egyptian chronology of the 26th Dynasty, see R.A. Parker, *MDAIK* 15 (1957), pp. 208–212, and cf. E. Hornung, *ZÄS* 92 (1965), pp. 38f.

king is on trial, accused of "high treason."[29] Thus the time may have
seemed opportune for the nations of the west to rebel against Babylonia
and for Judah to nourish illusory hopes for an immediate ingather-
ing of the Judean exiles. The states represented in the Jerusalem
conference—this "mini-summit" of petty states—were Edom, Moab
and Ammon in Trans-Jordan, and the cities of the Phoenician coast.
Thus, Judah was attempting to set up a league against Babylonia,
encompassing the area of modern Jordan, Israel, and the coastal
plain of Lebanon.

As so often occurs in military history, this alliance of several small
and rather weak states was of little avail against the big power.[30]
Such a coalition of six states also suffered from a serious lack of
political and military cohesion, for each component state still sought
to promote its own narrow interests and priorities. Thus it actually
comprised no real threat to Nebuchadnezzar. Here again it would
seem that Egypt subverted Judah against Babylonia, though we have
no clear evidence. We do know however, that the new Pharaoh,
Psammetich II staged an expedition to Palestine and Phoenicia in
592 B.C. (and *not* 591 B.C.), undoubtedly arousing anti-Babylonian
sentiments within Judean leadership.[31] Nevertheless, it wasn't until
the succession of the aggressive Pharaoh Hophra (Apries) to the
throne in Egypt, that open rebellion erupted against Babylonia, and
with this we arrive at the sixth and final turning point.

VI

When Nebuchadnezzar finally reacted in the winter of 589/88 B.C.,
Judah found herself in a highly vulnerable position.[32] From both a
diplomatic and military point of view, Judah was left in the lurch
and had to face the Babylonian might alone—"all her friends have

---

[29] On the document see E. Weidner, "Hochverrat gegen Nebukadnezar II," *AfO*
17 (1954–56), pp. 1–9.
[30] Cf. Rothstein, *op. cit.* (n. 2), pp. 169ff. and M. Handel, *op. cit.* (n. 2), pp. 153ff.
for the political military phenomenon in general.
[31] See in detail Malamat, "Twilight" (above n. 1), pp. 141–42 and there further
bibliographical references, cf. chap. 16.
[32] On the fall of Jerusalem mainly from a theological point of view see H. Migsch,
Gottes Wort über das Ende Jerusalems, Katholisches Österreichisches Bibelwerk: Kloster-
neuburg (1981). See now also Seitz, *op. cit.* (above, n. 23), ch. 4 (pp. 203ff.).

dealt treacherously with her" (Lam. 1:2). In addition, the nation was internally divided between the "hawks," determined on total war and the "doves," advocating appeasement and surrender. Under the circumstances, Jerusalem's resistance for as long as a year and a half was quite remarkable, the more so, if we adopt the variant, more likely Tishri chronological calculation, according to which, the siege lasted for two and a half years.[33] The rest of the kingdom had quickly been overrun, a few royal fortresses such as Lachish having taken somewhat longer to subdue. At one point, prospects brightened and the siege of Jerusalem was even temporarily lifted when the Babylonians moved to counter a rumored Egyptian relief force; but this in the end proved abortive as the prophets Jeremiah and Ezekiel correctly foresaw.

The Babylonian army now proved its flexibility as well as superiority in military strategy. Initially deployed to quell a rebellious city, they were now obliged to change from siege warfare to open field battle (and back again), a difficult task, indeed![34] The conquest of the capital city was a serious challenge for Nebuchadnezzar and so, reorganizing again, he employed his finest military commanders and the most advanced siegecraft of the day: dikes and ramps, upon which were stationed weapons such as the battering rams. It was, however, that veteran of siege warfare, famine, that ultimately turned the tide for the population of Jerusalem, which had constantly to accept the flow of refugees from provincial towns.

Scholars have often been perplexed by the time lapse between the breaching of the walls of Jerusalem on 9 Tammuz (July 18, 586 B.C. according to one of the chronological systems) and the beginning of the total destruction of the city, not until a month later on 7 or 10 Ab (August 14 or 17, 586 B.C.). Once the enemy penetrated its walls, why wasn't the vulnerable city razed immediately? This delay can hardly be attributed to the fighting spirit of the city's

---

[33] For the preference of the Tishre over the Nisan chronology at this period, see the series of my articles since 1956 (the latter devoted to the publication of Nebuchadnezzar's Babylonian Chronicle). The most detailed statement see in *Israel in Biblical Times* (above, n. 10). For an opposite view see recently H. Cazelles, "587" ou "586'?" in *The Word of the Lord Shall Go Forth* (Essays in Honor of D.N. Freedman, eds. C.L. Meyers and M. O'Connor), Eisenbrauns: Winona Lake (1983), pp. 427–35, and M. Cogan & H. Tadmor, *II Kings*, Anchor Bible (1988), pp. 315ff.

[34] Cf. I. Eph'al in *History, Historiography and Interpretation* (eds. H. Tadmor and M. Weinfeld), Magnes Press: Jerusalem (1983), pp. 97f.

defenders, so characteristic of the last siege of Jerusalem in the Second
Temple Period. Rather, the destruction of the city seems to have
been postponed by the Babylonians, pending a final verdict by
Nebuchadnezzar.[35]

At that time, Nebuchadnezzar's headquarters were stationed at
Riblah, in the land of Hamat, in central Syria (to the south of
Kadesh on the Orontes); a distance of 350–400 km from Jerusalem,
or a ten to twelve day march, bearing in mind the long summer
days. Zedekiah and his entourage stole away from the city upon the
breaching of its walls, only to be captured later near Jericho and
dragged to Riblah. It was there that the Judean leadership was tried
for treason and evidently then that the fate of Jerusalem was decided
by the king of Babylon. Nebuzaradan, the commander-in-chief of
the Babylonian army, was dispatched to the Judean capital to carry
out his master's orders. Following the exacting biblical sources, the
date 7 or 10 Ab refers to Nebuzaradan's arrival in Jerusalem (II K.
25:8) rather than the city's destruction. This chain of events accords
well with the lapse of time between the breaching of the walls of
Jerusalem and Nebuzaradan's appearance before its gates, which
sealed the fate of the city. With the fall of Jerusalem and the total
destruction of the palace and the holy temple, the Davidic dynasty
came to an end, and Judah was divested of its polity for generations to come.[36]

In conclusion, the case study of Judah in its final years may serve
as a universally valid paradigm for the conduct and function of a
small or secondary state in a bi-polar power system. Unable to remain
detached in a major confrontation between the great powers, the
small or weak state must side with either of the big actors. In time
of conflict, the precarious status of neutrality for a small state, particularly when it is located in the center of the system, is practically
impossible or at least not advantageous, a fact already stressed by
Machiavelli. By remaining neutral, it would invariably and eventually arouse the enmity of each of the big competitors. Genuine neutrality, resting on independent strength, contains a prerequisite: the
peaceful coexistence of the two big powers or the existence of a

---

[35] Cf. E.J. Bickerman, "Nebuchadnezzar and Jerusalem," *Proceedings of the American Academy for Jewish Research*, 46–47 (1979–80), pp. 69–85, esp. p. 84.

[36] On the history and archaeology of Judah during the exilic period see the recent study by H.M. Barstad, *OLP* 19 (1988), pp. 25–36.

multiplicity of political entities of roughly equal power—namely, a multi-power system.

The decision, with which antagonist to side, is a crucial factor for the small state and poses a serious dilemma. In order to survive, this choice must be based on sober calculations and long range interests. At best, Egypt was able to offer her camp-followers only short-range advantages, and proved powerless in the hour of peril. Instead of turning to powerful Babylonia, the Judeans toyed with false hopes created by the misleading image of Egypt, and hazardously gambled on her protection. On the international scene—as in Judah's case—both major powers watch the small state carefully and are ready to intervene to prevent defection to the rival camp, eventually leading to complete control and ultimate conquest.

PART FIVE

HISTORICAL EPISODES IN THE FORMER PROPHETS AND IN THE PROPHETICAL BOOKS

18

DOCTRINES OF CAUSALITY IN HITTITE AND BIBLICAL HISTORIOGRAPHY: A PARALLEL* **

The increasing number of Hittite texts has furnished some important comparative material for the study of the Bible. This is especially true of the field of historiography, which was a literary genre in the Ancient Near East, apparently introduced by the Hittites and brought to artistic perfection by the Israelites. Hittite historiography[1] was the prototype of the later Assyrian annalistic literature and possibly influenced the historical writing of the Bible as well, in spite of the latter's uniqueness.[2]

The present paper attempts to point out a parallel between Hittite and Biblical historiography involving similar methods, based on the doctrine of causality,[3] which explain national catastrophy. We shall deal first with the chronological earlier example, taken from the Hittite sources.

Murshili, the Hittite king (c. 1340–1310), composes a prayer to the Hattian Storm-god and other Hattian gods concerning a catastrophic plague[4] which had broken out in the Hittite Empire during

---

* This article was originally published in: *VT* 5 (1955), 1–12.

** A paper presented at the XXIII International Congress of Orientalists, Cambridge, 1954.

[1] For Hittite historiography in general cf. Götze, *Hethiter, Churriter und Assyrer* (Oslo, 936), pp. 73f., and especially Güterbock, "Die historische Tradition bei Babyloniern und Hethitern," *ZA* XLIV (1938), pp. 94ff.

[2] If so, the extent of this influence and the manner in which it was transmitted remain to be studied. One possible way of absorbing features of Hittite civilization would have been the ancient population of Jerusalem, which was, according to Biblical tradition, partly Hittite. After the conquest of Jerusalem by David its prominent citizenry would certainly have been incorporated into the Israelite administration; cf. Yeivin, "Jerusalem under the Davidic Dynasty," *VT* III (1953), pp. 149ff.; also Maisler, *BJPES* XIII (1947), pp. 105ff. (Hebrew).

[3] For the Hittite sources, especially the annals of Murshili, this doctrine was clearly recognized by Furlani, *Saggi sulla civilta degli Hittite* (Udine, 1939). It seems that Murshili, whose Plague Prayers are discussed in our paper, advanced the historiographical character of the annalistic literature more than anybody else. As to Biblical historiography, the principle of causality would appear to be one of its most basic features; cf. the remarks of Cassuto, "The Rise of Historiography in Israel," *Eretz-Israel (Archeol. Histor., and Geogr. Stud.)*, vol. I (Jerusalem, 1951), pp. 85ff. (Hebrew).

[4] The Hittite word translated by "plague" is *ḫinkan*, literally, "dying," cf. Friedrich,

the reign of his father, Shuppiluliuma I (c. 1375–1340), and had already lasted for twenty years. Murshili asserts his innocence in connection with the deadly disease and is eager to expose the causes of the national disaster by means of an omen, a dream, or prophecy. The king finally consults an oracle whereby he learns of the existence of two ancient tablets providing a clue for the outbreak of the epidemic. For our problem, we are interested only in the second tablet, concerning which we quote the relevant passage:[5] "The second tablet concerned Kurushtama. When the Hattian Storm-god had brought people of Kurushtama to the country of Egypt and had made an agreement concerning them with the Hattians so that they were under oath to the Hattian Storm-god—although the Hattians as well as the Egyptians were under oath to the Hattian Storm-god, the Hattians ignored their obligations; the Hattians promptly broke the oath of the gods. My father sent foot-soldiers and charioteers who attacked the country of Amqa, Egyptian territory. Again he sent troops and again they attacked it."

At this point Murshili tells of the Egyptians murdering one of Shuppiluliuma's sons which led to another war against Egypt whereby many prisoners were taken. The plague first broke out among these prisoners and was carried by them into Hatti.

This is the factual record of the origin of the plague. Yet to the King's mind there is a deeper reason for the misfortune. He finds it in the violation of the peace treaty made between the Hittites and the Egyptians, as follows: "Now, when I found that tablet dealing with the country of Egypt, I made the matter the subject of an oracle of the god (and asked): 'Those arrangements which were made by the Hattian Storm-god,—namely that the Egyptians and the Hattians as well were put under oath by the Hattian Storm-god, that the Damnashsharas deities[6] were present in the temple of the

---

ZA XXXV (1924), pp. 19f. Cf. also the Akkadian *mutānu* "pest, epidemic," literally "deaths," plural from singular *mutū*, "death."

[5] The translation of the Plague Prayer followed here is that of Goetze, *apud* Pritchard, *Ancient Near Eastern Texts* (Princeton, 1950) (hereafter abbreviated *ANET*), p. 395, § 4f. Cf. also the same scholar's edition of these prayers in *Kleinas. Forsch. I* (1929), pp. 209ff.

[6] The exact character of these deities, apparently witnesses to the treaty, remains doubtful. Cf. the suggestion of Forrer, *PEFQSt* 1937, pp. 108ff. and Gaster, *The Oldest Stories in the World* (New York, 1952), p. 153. We only know for certain that they were female and that Hittite goddesses figure quite commonly beside gods as witnesses in treaties.

Hattian Storm-god, and that the Hattians promptly broke their word—has this perhaps become the cause of the anger of the Hattian Storm-god, my Lord?' And (so) it was established." Murshili then relates how he tried to appease the gods by humbling himself and by presenting them with offerings, and how he was prepared to make restitution for his father's sin.[7]

The circumstances surrounding the treaty between Hatti and Egypt and its violation furnish important historical data. The conclusion of the treaty is connected with the somewhat obscure emigration of the people of the city of Kurushtama, located in the country of the Kashkeans, in northern Anatolia.[8] The reason for the departure of this people remains unknown and thus we are unable to determine whether it occured voluntarily or as the result of compulsion. The movement of individuals, as well as of entire cities,[9] must have been a well known phenomenon in the 14th and 13th century, as demonstrated by some treaties which have been recovered, although in these treaties only fugitives, political or otherwise, are referred to. In general the policy of the Hittites with regard to such refugees, as

---

[7] In this connection it is interesting to note the statement by Murshili that "it is only true, however, that the father's sin falls upon the son. So, my father's sin has fallen upon me" (cf. *ANET, op. cit.*, § 9). This doctrine is in accord with the Biblical idea expressed in the third of the Ten Commandments (Ex. xx. 5; Deut. v 9) and in the popular proverb "The fathers have eaten sour grapes and the children's teeth are set on edge" (Ez. xviii 2). See also the tragic fate of the sons of King Saul who suffered death for their father's crime, discussed *infra* p. 8. The prophets, however, emphasizing individual responsibility, sharply opposed this principle (Ez. *ib*; Mi. vi 7 and cf. also Deut. xxiv 16).

Dr. W.F. Geers (Oriental Institute, Chicago) informs me that in a Babylonian prayer the god Marduk is entreated to remove not only the sin of the suppliant himself but, also, that of his ancestors, from his father's side as well as his mother's (Cf. King, *Babylonian Magic and Sorcery* [London, 1896], No. 11: 22ff.).

[8] For the geographical location of Kurushtama see the Great Speech of Hattushili III, col. ii: 8, 54, and a parallel text *KBo* VI 29 i: 28 (cf. Götze, "Hattušiliš," *MVAG* XXIX [1924], pp. 14, 20, 46).

[9] An express reference to a city or district is made in the famous treaty between Ramses II and Hattushili III, Hittite version, rev. 11. 10ff. (cf. Goetze, *ANET*, p. 203); Egyptian version, ll. 23ff. (Wilson, ib. p. 200); in the treaty between Murshili II and Duppi-Teshup, col. iii: 12ff. (cf. Friedrich, "Staatsverträge des Hatti-Reiches," *MVAG* XXXI [1926], p. 20), and in the treaty between Shuppiluliuma and Shunashshura, col. i: 14ff. (cf. Weidner, *Boghazköi-Studien* [Leipzig, 1923], p. 90, who erroneously took the Hittite king to be Muwatalli, but see Bilabel, *Gesch. Vorderasiens*, etc. [Heidelberg, (1926)], pp. 294ff. and Meyer, *Geschichte* II/I² [Stuttgart & Berlin, (1928)], p. 372 n. 2). For an earlier allusion to the movement of an entire settlement, probably from the second half of the fifteenth century, cf. the treaty of a Hittite king and the country of Kizzuwatna published recently by G. Meyer, "Zwei neue Kizzuwatna Verträge," *Mitt. Instit. Orientfor.* (1953), pp. 108ff.

evidenced by the treaties, was to insist on their extradition to Hatti.[10] In contrast to that in our case it is not stated that the people of Kurushtama must return to Hatti. Indeed the very agreement with Egypt came into existence on behalf of the Kurushtameans and as a result of their settlement in Egyptian territory, by which is meant, most probably, the Egyptian dependencies in Asia.[11] That the move of the Kurushtameans took place with the full consent of the Hittites is also suggested by the part ascribed to the Hattian Storm-god.

New light is shed on this, as well as on other points, by a fragment of a new version of the annals of Shuppiluliuma I, compiled by Murshili, dealing with the request of an Egyptian queen, the widow of Tutankhamon, to marry one of the sons of the Hittite king. The text of the annals known hitherto already exhibited certain links with the Plague Prayer, describing as it did how an attack on Amqa apparently led to the famous bid of the Egyptian queen, and how this request was granted, one of Shuppiluliuma's sons being sent to Egypt.[12] The further course of events, as we have already seen, is recorded in the Plague Prayer, which relates the murder of the son by the Egyptians, and the consequences it brought about.[13]

Turning now to the new version, published by Güterbock,[14] we find that it includes an important additional passage about a tablet

---

[10] In the case of a so-called *Paritätsvertrag*, i.e. treaty between equal partners, such as the one discussed in our paper, the one between Ramses II and Hattushili III, and the one with Kizzuwatna published by Meyer (cf. foregoing note), extradition was reciprocal. In treaties made with subordinate partners, however, the agreement was unilateral, i.e., only the vassal was obligated to return refugees, whereas the Hittites had to extradite solely peasants and craftsmen but not regular fugitives. For the time of Shuppiluliuma cf. that king's treaty with Mattiwaza, king of Mitanni, rev. ll. 9ff. (cf. Weidner, *op. cit.*, p. 22). For other similar treaties cf. Korošec, *Hettitische Staatsverträge* (Leipzig, 1931), pp. 80f.

[11] I.e. Palestine and Southern Syria. This fact led Forrer to his theory regarding the origin of the Hittites in the hill country of Palestine, cf. his study "The Hittites in Palestine," *PEQSt* 1936, pp. 190ff.; 1937, pp. 100ff., and also Gurney, *The Hittites* (Penguin ed., 1952), pp. 60ff.

[12] *KBo* V 6 iii: 1ff. Cf. the recent translation by Goetze, *ANET*, p. 319.

[13] Other documents probably deal with the same events. Forrer, *Forschungen*, II, pp. 28ff., published a badly damaged copy of a letter sent by Shuppiluliuma to an Egyptian king (now *KUB* XIX 20), holding the latter responsible for the murder of the Hittite king's son and declaring war on Egypt as a result of it.

The name of the murdered son himself is possibly revealed as Zannanza in the fragment *KUB* XIX 4 (cf. Güterbock, *Zeit. Indog. For.* LX [1950], pp. 208ff.).

[14] "Neue Texte zur Geschichte Šuppiluliumas," ib., pp. 199ff. I am obliged to Prof. H.G. Güterbock, Chicago, for discussing with me various problems concerning the Hittite sources.

which, in view of its contents, is without any doubt the one referred to by Murshili in his Plague Prayer. Shuppiluliuma, who was encamped before Carchemish, had a certain tablet brought before him at his special request in order to emphasize the traditional friendship between Hatti and Egypt. This was on the occasion of the king's acceding to the Egyptian queen's request. The tablet, which was read before the Egyptian delegation,[15] designated the people of Kurushtama as "sons of Hatti," i.e. Hittite subjects, and added explicitly that they had become Egyptians.

Another problem is the dating of the treaty, as no specific time is recorded in connection with it. The explicit reference to Shuppiluliuma concerns only the violation of the agreement. Its instigation, however, must similarly be attributed to this king, since a Hittite-Egyptian pact before his period seems highly improbable. Furthermore, the famous later treaty between Hattushili III and Ramses II specifically mentions an earlier compact between the two countries from the time of Shuppiluliuma,[16] which most probably represents our treaty. Nevertheless we cannot accept Forrer's assumption that the treaty dates from a rather late period in Shuppiluliuma's reign, just before the siege of Carchemish or even contemporary with it.[17] For the tablet which recorded a Hittite-Egyptian peace treaty already enjoyed a certain antiquity when brought to Carchemish, as is shown by the new version of Shuppiluliuma's annals. It is true such a peace treaty certainly could have been concluded only subsequent to a contact between Hittites and Kashkeans, because this document is connected with the emigration of the Kurushtameans, who originated in the country of the Kashkeans. Forrer accordingly links this treaty with the conquest of the Kashkeans a year or so before the siege of Carchemish.[18] There was, however, another war with the Kashkeans

---

[15] The repeated public recital of previously concluded treaties was a common practice. One of its main purposes was undoubtedly to remind parties of the various obligations binding them. Cf. Korošec, *op. cit.*, pp. 101f.

Note also the Biblical injunction to read "the words of the book of the covenant" to the people which was carried out, for instance, by King Josiah in his new covenant with God (2 Kings xxiii 1ff.).

[16] The name of the Hittite king is expressly mentioned only in the Egyptian version of the treaty, l. 14.

[17] Cf. *PEQSt* 1937, pp. 111f.

[18] Cf. *ib.*, pp. 110f. The relevant documents are *KBo* V 6 and the previously mentioned letter of Shuppiluliuma to an Egyptian king, *KUB XIX 20*.

at the beginning of Shuppiluliuma's reign, or, more, precisely, when the king still served as a commander under his father. It seems likely therefore that the peace treaty was associated with this earlier war.[19]

So early a date for a treaty of peace between Hittites and Egyptians is favored also by the evidence of a letter from Shuppiluliuma to Amenophis IV (EA 41) demonstrating their friendship and pointing to the friendly relations which existed between that Hittite king and Pharaoh's father. It may be, therefore, that the Hittite-Egyptian treaty under discussion represents an alliance between Shuppiluliuma and Amenophis III (c. 1398–1361).[20] Even if it represents a pact between Shuppiluliuma and Amenophis IV (c. 1369–1353), it must have been concluded many years before the siege of Carchemish, since there is no longer any doubt that this latter event synchronizes roughly with the death of Tutankhamon (c. 1344).[21]

Another argument in favor of the same conclusion can be drawn from letter No. 170 of the El Amarna archive. This much debated letter already bears witness to an ignoring on the part of the Hittites of the peace agreement between them and Egypt, as it mentions a Hittite rain on Amqa, the disputed border zone between the two powers.[22] Now this raid on Amqa cannot be identical with the one begun just prior to and continuing during the time of the siege of Carchemish by Shuppiluliuma, a nearly axiomatic identification accepted by scholars.[23] For besides certain discrepancies inherent in

---

[19] For this war cf. 2 *BoTU* 33 ii: 12; 34 i: 6 (*KUB* XIX 11) and Cavaignac, *Subbiluliuma et son temps* (Paris, 1932), pp. 15f. In this connection it may be worth recalling the demand of Pharaoh Amenophis III that the king of Arzawa dispatch Kashkean people to him (EA 31: 25; cf. the new translation by Cavaignac, *Le problème hittite* [Paris, 1936], p. 28; also Forrer, *Forschungen*, II, pp. 21f.). If this is actually a reference to the matter of the Kurushtameans, their resettlement must be dated in a rather early period.

[20] In the matter of Egyptian chronology we follow Wilson's most recent attempt, although this, in his own words, remains rather tentative; cf. *JNES* XIII (1954), p. 128.

[21] The name of the deceased husband of the Egyptian queen sending ambassadors to Carchemish is rendered in the new version of Shuppiluliuma's annals as Niphururiya (a preferable form to the name Piphururiya, known hitherto, cf. *KBo* V 6 iii: 7). This is one of the throne names of Tutankhamon, not of Amenophis IV, and the identification with the former is now accordingly definite, cf. Edel, *JNES* VII (1948), pp. 14f.

[22] For the precise location of this region in the Liṭâni Valley, i.e. the southern part of the so-called Biqʿah, cf. now Aharoni, *Israel Explor. Jour.* III (1953), pp. 153ff.

[23] Cf. most recently Smith, "Amarna Letter 170 and Chronology," *Halil Edhem Volume*, I (1947), pp. 33ff., and references to earlier studies there.

the sources dealing with the two attacks, the Amarna letter must go back to the time of Amenophis IV, the city of El Amarna having been deserted soon after that Pharaoh died. The other attack, however, as stated before, occurred about the time of Tutankhamon's death which is at least ten years later.[24] In my opinion, therefore, EA 170 and other letters from the archive of El Amarna dealing with a Hittite attack on Amqa (EA 140, 174, 175, 176, AO 7097)[25] coincide with the first raid on Amqa mentioned in the Plague Prayer, which constituted the original violation of the Hittite-Egyptian peace treaty. The second campaign to the same region recorded in the Plague Prayer ("again he sent troops and again they attacked it") could easily be identical with the later attack on Amqa which occurred just before the siege of Carchemish.

To sum up, we shall try to provide a tentative chronological arrangement of Hittite-Egyptian relations in the time of Shuppiluliuma as illustrated respectively by the conclusion and each successive violation of the treaty between them:

1) emigration of the Kurushtameans and Hittite-Egyptian alliance—earlier period of Shuppiluliuma, after first war against the Kashkeans.

2) original violation to treaty: 1st campaign to Amqa—time of Amenophis IV, identical with campaign of EA 170 and other EA letters cited above.

3) 2nd campaign to Amqa—time of siege of Carchemish and death of Tutankhamon.

4) final attack on Egyptian territory in Asia-period after murder of Shuppiluliuma's son, time of Pharaoh Eye, pestilence carried into Hatti.

We cannot here enter into a discussion of how the foregoing arrangement affects the more general question of Shuppiluliuma's campaigns to Syria. This problem should be dealt with only after a renewed investigation of all the material about this Hittite king, available today, together with the EA correspondence.[26]

---

[24] Cf. the excellent analysis by Sturm, "Wer ist Piphururiaš?," *RHA* II (No. 13 [1933]), pp. 161ff.

[25] Cf. Thureau-Dangin, *RA* XIX (1922), pp. 94f.

[26] Cf. tentatively Götze, "Šuppiluliumas syrische Feldzüge," *Klio* XIX (1925), pp. 347ff. Goetze adduces evidence for some five separate campaigns of the Hittite King in Syria; cf. also Cavaignac, *Subbiluliuma et son temps, passim*. New light on this problem, as well as on Hittite relations with Egypt, will udoubtedly be shed by the new tables from Ugarit—among them a letter from Shuppiluliuma—recently unearthed

Having examined the events which, according to Hittite historiography, resulted in the national misfortune, we may turn to the Bible, which yields a surprisingly similar picture in connection with the outbreak of the famine in the days of King David (c. 1005–965): "Now there was a famine in the days of David for three years, year after year: and David sought the face of the Lord. And the Lord said, 'There is blood guilt on Saul and on his house, because he put the Gibeonites to death.' So the king called the Gibeonites and said to them—Now the Gibeonites were not of the people of Israel, but of the remnant of the Amorites; although the people of Israel, had sworn to spare them, Saul had sought to slay them in his zeal for the people of Israel and Judah.—And David said to the Gibeonites: 'What shall I do for you? And how shall I make expiation, that you may bless the heritage of the Lord?'" (2 Sam. xxi 1–3). The Gibeonites asked David, from vengeful motives and, apparently, also for some symbolic reasons, to deliver to them seven sons of Saul (c. 1020–1005) in order that they might kill them.[27] The king was eager to fulfill their request. The narrative goes on to describe the exposure of Saul's descendants and their subsequent burial, together with the bones of Saul himself and Jonathan, and concludes: "After that God heeded supplications for the land" (ib. vs. 14).

Even at first glance the parallel features with the Plague Prayer are striking. Similar external circumstances gave rise to corresponding interpretations: in both sources the national disaster is understood to be the consequence of the violation of a treaty. It did not matter whether the catastrophy consisted of a plague as among the Hittites, or of a famine as inflicted upon the Israelites. Both calamities were considered corresponding punishments for a national offense.[28]

---

at Ras-Shamra, and as yet unpublished; cf. *The Manchester Guardian*, February 11, 1954.

[27] The blood-thirsty demand of the Gibeonites is in accord with the retribution clauses in the Hittite treaties, which state explicitly that in case of neglect of the treaty provisions the whole family is liable. For examples cf. the references in Korošec, *op. cit.*, pp. 102ff.

[28] For the threat of a famine in the Hittite sources for ignoring an oath cf. The Soldiers Oath, col. ii: 31ff.; iii: 39ff.; 5ff. (Goetze, *ANET*, pp. 353ff.). On the other hand a plague as well as a famine are listed among the sore judgements of God in the Bible (Ez. xiv 21; 1 Kings viii 37ff.) and are offered as alternatives to David for expiating his sin of compiling a census (2 Sam. xxiv 13).

Such punishments were not only typical of Hittite or Biblical treaties (cf. the curses and the covenant with God in Deut., chaps. xxviiif.) but seem to have had a universal prevalence in the Ancient Near East. For the Assyrians see especially

David, like Murshili, asked the oracle for an explanation of the famine,[29] and in both cases the answer is that not the living king himself but his predecessor is responsible. Yet Saul's guilt cannot consist merely in the slaying of the Gibeonites, as he had killed other people as well. The actual sin is, in my opinion, explained clearly enough by the statement that the Gibeonites had been slain "although the people of Israel had sworn to spare them." 2 Sam. xxi 2, therefore, is in keeping with the historiographical doctrine, stated more explicitly in the Hittite sources, and need not be a later gloss as maintained by the commentators.[30]

Fortunately for our purpose, the events surrounding the conclusion of the treaty with the Gibeonites are recorded elsewhere in the Bible. The episode is narrated in the Book of Joshua (chap. ix 3ff.) according to which the Gibeonites alarmed by the decisive victories of the conquering Israelites, secured an alliance with them rather than meet them on the battlefield. This alliance was established by means of a trick, the Gibeonites, emissaries succeeding in obtaining a peace treaty from Joshua by pretending to have come from a far-away country, outside the Israelite sphere of interest. The people of Israel discovered the deception and became enraged with their leaders for concluding the treaty, but, once executed, it could not be repudiated:[31] "We have sworn to them by the Lord, the God of Israel, and now we may not touch them. This we will do to them and let them live, lest wrath be upon us, because of the oath which we swore to them" (Josh. ix 19–21). The Gibeonites were, however, condemned to the *corvée*, in accordance with Biblical law, and the tradition has it that they became "hewers of wood and drawers of water to all the congregation."[32]

---

the treaty between Shamshi-Adad V and Marduk-zâkir-shumi I, l. 19 (Weidner, *AfO* VIII [1932], pp. 27ff.) and for the Aramean states in Syria cf. Bauer, "Ein aramäischer Staatsvertrag aus dem 8. Jahrhundert," *ib.*, pp. 1ff.

[29] The Biblical text has "sought the face of the Lord," clearly referring to an oracle (see Vulgate), the exact nature of which, however, remains uncertain. The later Talmudic literature interprets the expression as an appeal to the obscure Urim and Tummim, cf. *Babyl. Tal., Jeb.*, 78b f.; *Bam. rabbah*, chap. 8.

[30] Cf. H.P. Smith, *The Books of Samuel* (New York, 1899), p. 374; Nowack, *Bücher Samuelis* (Göttingen, 1902), pp. 237f.; Caird, *Interpreters Bible*, vol. II (New York, 1953), p. 1158; and others. For the genuineness of this passage cf. Kroner, "Die Misshandlung der Volksfremden eine Entweihung Gottes," *Festschrift A. Schwarz* (Berlin & Wien, 1917), p. 68 n. 2.

[31] Cf. Kraetschmar, *Die Bundesvorstellung im Alten Testament* (Marburg, 1896), pp. 10f., 28, *et passim*; Begrich, "Berit," *etc.*, *ZAW* LX (1944), p. 3.

[32] Cf. Deut. xx 10–18, where for the conduct of the holy war an express distinction

The ethnic origin of the Gibeonites remains obscure. In the passage in Samuel discussed above they are presented under the name of Amorites, which of course has there the mere meaning of the autochthonous population of Palestine. In the Book of Joshua, however, the Gibeonites are designated as Hivites (chap. ix 7; cf. also xi 19), a term which may refer to a non Semitic element and possibly to Hittites or Hurrians, as the reading of the Septuagint gives it.[33] In any case, in the Book of Joshua (ix 17) the term Gibeonites is a collective name referring to a confederacy of four cities: Gibeon, Chephirah, Beeroth and Kiriath-Jearim, named after the most important of these places.[34]

Mindful of this fact, we may try to clarify the historical circumstances which led to the violation of the treaty with the Gibeonites by Saul. Indeed, we have no direct information in the Bible concerning any annihilation of the Gibeonites by Saul. However, it seems rather likely that this occurred, since the Gibeonite confederacy, consisting of a chain of foreign "pockets" on the Western border of the territory of Benjamin, constituted an obvious security risk, especially during Saul's wars with the Philistines. Gibeon proper occupied an important strategic position (cf. also Josh. x 2), controlling the roads to the Western lowland and in the South the road to Jerusalem. This is clearly shown by the immediate action taken against Gibeon by a coalition of Canaanite principalities, headed by the king of Jerusalem, in response to the peace treaty with Joshua. Furthermore, Joshua's subsequent victory over the Canaanites at Gibeon had far reaching military results, rendering helpless before his troops the whole Western border of the Judaean mountain slopes.[35]

---

is made between a distant enemy and a hostile city in the midst of the Israelite territory. Only the former was privileged to enter a peace treaty which, however, subjected the foreign population to menial service.

Many scholars believe the enslavement of the Gibeonites to reflect the situation of a later period when they supposedly served in the temple of King Solomon. The authenticity of all the details of Josh., chap. ix, is, however, irrelevant for an analysis of the historiographical method of the Bible, as undertaken here; cf. also Balscheit, *Gottesbund und Staat* (Zürich, 1940), pp. 38f.

[33] In our place (Josh. ix 13 in the Greek version) and in Gen. xxxiv 2 the Septuagint has χορραῖος, whereas in Josh. xi 3 Hittites and Hivites are translated interchangeably by Cod. Vat.; cf. Speiser, *AASOR* XIII (1933), pp. 29f. and Paterson, *Present. Vol. to W.B. Stevenson* (Glasgow, 1945), pp. 100ff.

[34] For the precise location of the four cities and their modern identifications cf. Abel, *Géographie de la Palestine*, II (Paris, 1938), ad. loc.

[35] Cf. Malamat, *The Conquest of Palestine in the Time of Joshua²* (Jerusalem, 1954), p. 26 (Hebrew), (also chap. 6).

Indeed, we have some indirect evidence that such a policy was pursued by Saul with respect to the Hivite cities. In connection with the murder of Ishbaal (Ishbosheth), Saul's son and successor, by two army officers who were from Beeroth, the historian notes that "Beeroth also is reckoned to Benjamin" and that "the Beerothites fled to Gittaim and have been sojourners there to this day" (2 Sam. iv 2–3). These remarks indicate that the aforementioned city was incorporated into the Israelite tribal system, whereby, in all probability, its former inhabitants had to take refuge elsewhere. Obviously these events took place in the time of Saul and could easily be understood as the result of that king's action against Beeroth.[36] The express accusation by the surviving Gibeonites in their discussion with David that Saul "planned to destroy us so that we should have no place in all the territory of Israel" (ib. xxi 5) seems to support our inference.

The animosity between Saul and the Hivite confederacy may be illustrated by a further incident. One of David's most important military adherents, joining him on his escape from Saul, was a Gibeonite. This person, Ishmaiah of Gibeon, "a mighty man among the thirty (נִבּוֹר בַּשְּׁלֹשִׁים) and a leader of the thirty" i.e. a former commander of David's military band, joined the future king, who "could not move about freely because of Saul of the son of Kish," at Ziklag (1 Chron. xii 1–4).

The Bible sees Saul's conduct toward the Gibeonites as originating not from personal hatred but from political motives for the benefit of his people ("in his zeal for the people of Israel and Judah"). However, according to the Biblical historiography, this was no excuse for ignoring the terms of a treaty once concluded, as in the case of the Hittites, where Shuppiluliuma's campaign against Egypt was undoubtedly in itself a patriotic step. It does not seem to have mattered how much time elapsed between the conclusion of a treaty and its violation; nor that the effect of the sin may have occurred a considerable time later, even after the death of the king who violated the treaty. In any case the transgression was not absolved with the death of the guilty king. In both sources, the Hittite and the

---

[36] Cf. Kittel, *Geschichte des Volkes Israel*, II[6,7] (Gotha, 1925), p. 131; Maisler, *Toledoth Eretz-Israel* (Tel-Aviv, 1938), p. 267; and specially Auerbach, *Wüste und gelobtes Land*, I[2] (Berlin, 1938), pp. 179ff. The last scholar argues among other things that Kiriath-Jearim was likewise incorporated into the Israelite tribes by Saul, but his evidence is insufficient; cf. Kaufmann, *Toledoth ha'emunah hay-Yiśre'elith*, 1/3 (Tel Aviv, 1938), p. 647.

Biblical, the guilt was laid to a king, who, as the representative of the entire people, seems to have been held responsible for a disaster of national proportions.[37]

But the most notable parallel between the two sources lies in the phenomenological structure of cause and effect, as revealed in the sequence: conclusion of treaty, violation of treaty and consequent national catastrophy.[38]

---

[37] Cf. Pedersen, *Israel, its Life and Culture*, III–IV (London & Copenhagen, 1940), pp. 81f.

[38] Our case seems not to be an isolated phenomenon as there is at least one other Hittite-Biblical parallel touching upon the period of David, and likewise concerning the violation of an oath. In this instance the oath was sworn by the army to its king. Cf. Y. Sukenik [Yadin], "The Lame and the Blind and the Conquest of Jerusalem by David," *World Congress of Jew. Studies*, I (Jerusalem, 1952), pp. 222ff. (Hebrew).

19

MILITARY RATIONING IN PAPYRUS ANASTASI I AND THE BIBLE*

Papyrus Anastasi I is a satirical letter, dating apparently from the reign of Ramses II (1290–1224 B.C.), and composed by an Egyptian scribe in reply to a letter from a colleague.[1] Hori, the author of the epistle, who was a high Egyptian official, proves in a sarcastic vein to his "friend" Amenemope how utterly ignorant the latter is in the role of a military scribe in the service of His Majesty, Pharaoh of Egypt. The documents contains a detailed description of Palestine and Southern Syria at the beginning of the period of the Israelite settlement and therefore may claim the title of the most ancient "guide-book" of the Holy Land.

Despite the fact that the document stresses the geographical aspect, its contents are not restricted merely to topographical matters. Some light is cast upon the characteristics and customs of the population of Palestine, as well as upon the relationship of the people to their Egyptian overlords. Hori's letter contains *inter alia* an interesting passage on the mission of an Egyptian expeditionary force to Palestine, pointing out the various problems that such a mission entailed. These problems were not only strategical, but also of a logistical nature, such as the furnishing of provisions for the military forces and the distribution of the single "field-rations." The passage is included in the fourth of the "tests" which Hori, attempting to deprecate Amenemope, places before him for solution. It is worthy of note that matters of administration and supply in ancient armies were part of the duties of an army scribe, who thus resembles the modern executive officer.[2] We shall present the translation of the above passage,

---

* This article was originally published in: *Mélanges biblique a la mémoire d'A. Robert*, Paris 1957, 114–121.

[1] The standard edition was published by Gardiner, in *Egyptian Hieratic Texts, Series I. Part I. The Papyrus Anastasi I*, etc., 1911; cf. also the recent translation by Wilson, apud Pritchard, *ANET*, 1950, p. 475f.

[2] The Egyptian text known as "*The Onomasticon of Amenope*," which dates from the end of the 12th century, enumerates various types of military scribes, e.g. the Scribe

which immediately precedes the last and major test, containing the problem of the Geography of Palestine.[3]

O alert scribe, understanding of heart, who is not ignorant at all, torch in the darkness at the head of the troops—and it gives light to them! Thou art sent on a mission to *Djahan*[4] at the head of the victorious army, to crash those rebels called *Nearin*.[5] The bowmen of the army which is before thee amount to 1.900, the *Sherden* 520, the *Qeheq* 1.600, the *Meshwesh* (100),[6] and the Negroes 880—Total 5.000 in all, not counting their officers. There is brought thee a peace offering[7] before thee: bread, cattle and wine. The number of men is too great for thee, whereas the provisions are too small for them.[8] Loaves of . . . flour[9]— 300; cakes[10]—1.800; goats (small cattle) of various sorts—120; wine— 30. The soldiers are too numerous, the provisions are underrated as compared with (?) that which thou takest of them. Thou receivest them, placed in the camp.

The troops are ready and prepared. Make them quickly into portions, that of each man at his hand. The Bedouin[11] look on furtively, (saying): "*Sopher yodea!*"[12] Midday is come, the camp is hot. "Time to start! Don't let the troop commander be angry! Much marching is

---

of the infantry, the Scribe of distribution and the Scribe of the assemblage; cf. Gardiner, *Ancient Egyptian Onomastica*, 1947, nos. 88, 107, 108. In the Bible, the Scribe of the commanding general is mentioned in 2 *Rg.*, 25:19; cf. *Jer.*, 52:25; see also 2 *Chr.*, 26:11.

[3] *Papyrus Anastasi I*, XVII 2ff. The translation is Wilson's version, *op. cit.*, p. 476, which diverges slightly from that of Gardiner.

[4] The name of the country is to be emended to *Djahi* (*D'hj*), as remarked by Wilson and Gardiner. The latter regards the name as referring to the whole of Palestine, cf. A. Gardiner, *Anc. Egyp. Onom.*, pp. 145ff. According to another opinion, the area designated is limited to the Phoenician coastal area, cf. Yeivin, *JEA*, 36, 1950, p. 57.

[5] Hebrew-Canaanite *n^{e}ārīm*, literally "young men," but used here as *terminus technicus* for warriors.

[6] This number should be restored in the original text, whereas in our version it apparently was omitted and added to the number of the *Sherden*; cf. Gardiner, *ad loc.*

[7] The text reads here *šrm.tí*, which is the Hebrew-Canaanite word *šālōm*, meaning peace, and serving as well as the conventional salutation.

[8] Wilson omits the following section of the food list, which is supplied here from Gardiner's edition.

[9] The text employs a Canaanite loan word, *kmḥ* = *qemaḥ* modified by an adjective *nḏm* "sweet"—which would seem to imply some specific sort of sweetbread.

[10] The text here uses a foreign word *'pt*, derived from the Semitic *'py* "bake."

[11] The word is defective, but obviously we must restore *š3sw*, which occurs several times in the papyrus and corresponds to the root *šsh* "spoil, plunder" in Biblical Hebrew.

[12] The Egyptian text transcribes a Hebrew-Canaanite phrase meaning "wise scribe."

ahead of us.[13] What bread have we at all? Our night quarters are far away. O, who-is-it, what does it mean, this beating of us?"

So thou art an experienced scribe, if thou (canst) approach to give the provisions, (but) an hour comes into a day for lack of a scribe from the Ruler—life, prosperity, health? This (business of) bringing thee to beat us—it's no good, my boy! He (the king) will hear and will send to destroy thee.

The author draws a vivid picture of the supplying of victuals to the Egyptian expeditionary force, consisting of 5,000 men, i.e. a single division at the time of the New Kingdom.[14] First the composition of the division, which included foreign units of unequal size, is described. Foreign elements comprised a considerable portion of the Egyptian army at the time of the New Kingdom, since the Egyptian made a frequent practice of conscripting conquered nations into the ranks of their combat units. Negro, or to be more precise, Nubian troops were included among Pharaoh's units from the earliest times and as early as the Amarna Age, the *Sherden*, one of the Sea-Peoples, appear as a mercenary corps. However, special contingents of *Qeheq* and *Meshwesh* soldiers are mentioned for the first time in these document, and it would seem that the mobilisation of this Libyan peoples was one of Ramses II's innovations.[15]

The list of the various units is headed by the archers, whose nationality is not designated, yet they obviously were of native Egyptian extraction. This fact would seem to indicate that the ethnic classification of the troops had an underlying tactical significance. The various nations were differentiated not only by character and customs, but also by weapons and methods of warfare in which they were wont to specialize. Numerous reliefs, dating from the Eighteenth to the Twentieth Dynasties represent these ethnic groups in various military situations in which each one of them has its peculiar uniforms and weapons.[16] However, the nature of the numerical data contributed

---

[13] In Gardiner's opinion, this marks the end of the soldiers' conversation and the remainder consists of Hori's remarks.

[14] Cf. Faulkner, *Egyptian Military Organization, JEA*, 39, 1953, p. 42.

[15] "*The Onomasticon of Amenope*," composed approximately one hundred years after *Papyrus Anastasi I*, mentions in the list of foreign nations *inter alia: Meshwesh* (no. 240), *Qeheq* (no. 242) and *Sherden* (no. 268); cf. Gardiner's book (*supra*, n. 2) on these numbers. The *Sherden* and *Qeheq* are also mentioned together as warriors in the service of Ramses III, cf. *Harris Papyrus*, pl. 76, 5, pl. 78, 10.

[16] See, for example, the depiction of Ramses III's first war against the Libyans, from Medinet Habu; Wreszinski, *Atlas zur altägypt. Kulturgeschichte*, II, 1935, pl. 127–128;

by our document is far from clear, nor we have any idea whether the size of the single units affected the distribution of food. Nonetheless, it is self-evident that Hori realistically described an Egyptian formation in accordance with the military standards current at that time, thereby displaying his up-to-date knowledge of all matters concerning the Egyptian army.

The test involving the food supply for the warriors, which Hori set before his "friend," is no less realistic than the description of the army proper. The problem is both mathematical and administrative, involving both the computation of the personal field ration out of the total supply available, and the technical problem of distribution. From the contents, we may deduce that the scribe began his task in the morning, but because of his incompetence the work was yet unfinished at high noon. Such a superfluous delay caused a serious obstruction in the operational planning and it is indeed small wonder that the scribe was called to account for his inefficiency.

The geographical background, which forms the basis of Hori's hypothetical situation is of paramount interest. The Egyptian army is described conducting a punitive expedition to Palestine against its rebellious population. Incidentally, the latter is referred to in the papyrus as "*Nearin*," the Hebrew-Canaanite term for the local infantry, which is frequently used in the Bible (below). The document gives a live description of another stratum of the Palestinian population, i.e. the Bedouin (*Shasu*), who composed the nomad segment of the population.[17] An exclamation in Canaanite, which expresses admiration for the skill of the Egyptian executive, is attributed to them. From the foregoing, we may conclude that the supplies were distributed in Palestine itself and were obviously derived from local produce. The types of foodstuffs, which are characteristically Palestinian, and the Hebrew-Canaanite terms used to describe some of them bear witness to the accuracy of the above conclusion. The provisions themselves are referred to by a typical Canaanite lingual usage

---

Nelson and Hölscher, *Medinet Habu, 1924–28, Or. Inst. Com.*, 5, 1929, p. 5, in which Pharaoh's army is depicted marching with full combat gear. The army, arrayed in parade order, four ranks abreast, is arranged according to the nationality of each contingent: first the native Egyptians; after them the *Sherden*, mingled with warriors identifiable, probably, as *Qeheq*; the third rank consisted of Canaanite soldiers and the rearguard was made up of Nubian units.

[17] Compare, for example, *Jud.*, 2:14, to mention one example involving approximately the same period as *Papyrus Anastasi I*.

šālōm, meaning not merely "peace," but inferring here a concrete offering, as appears in various instances in Biblical language and in other sources.[18]

In conclusion, it may be stated that the author of the letter actually visualised the provisioning of a conquering Egyptian army by the indigenous residents of Palestine. It is a certainty that the Canaanites were called upon more than once, in Hori's time, to supply the needs of the armies of occupation and that more than one Egyptian scribe must have performed the duty attributed to Amenemope in our document. Hence, Hori's problem was far from being abstract, but had a definite *Sitz im Leben*.

Therefore, it is not surprising that a similar situation arises in the Bible, such as in I *Sm.*, 25, which deals with the narrative of Nabal, the Carmelite, and the encounter between David and Abigail. In spite of the vast differences in the historical circumstances and the type and scope of the armies involved, the basic military situation is identical in both cases, in that both the Egyptians and David faced the same logistical problem. David also was obliged to secure provisions for his military forces from the local landholders and he eventually obtained a limited supply of food, which he was required to distribute among his warriors.

However, David's functions were much less complex than those of the Egyptian commander, since his forces consisted merely of his private army, numbering 600 men. The "battalion" was composed of a force of shock troops numbering 400 men and of 200 men "who abode by the stuff"—i.e. one-third of the battalion functioned as a reserve and as guards (I *Sm.*, 25:13).[19] The more primitive organizational set-up of the Israelite forces in comparison with that of the Egyptians makes it quite questionable whether the former possessed a special functionary, who served as executive officer. It is more likely that David himself, as commander, performed this administrative duty as well as others. He sent a squad of ten "young

---

[18] Compare below our remarks to *I Sm.*, 25:5. Also compare *Jud.*, 19:20; *I Sm.*, 10:4; 17:18. A rather enlightening passage appears in one of the Taanach letters from the fifteenth century: "Further, why dost thou not send thy greetings (*šu-lum-ka*) to me?" Taanach, no. 1, 13–14; cf. W.F. Albright, *BASOR*, 94, 1944, p. 17. Here we have an apparent Canaanism in an Accadian letter.

[19] The same structure of David's troop appears also in his raid on Ziklag described in *I Sm.* 30:9–10, and cf. A. Malamat, *Encyclopaedia Biblica* (Hebrew), vol. II, 1954, col. 432f. (s.v. *gᵉdūd*—troop).

men"—the term applied here (*Ib.*, v. 5) and used frequently throughout the narratives of David's troops is *Nᵉˤārīm*—to Nabal the Carmelite
to greet him; "And thus shall ye say, to him that liveth in prosperity, Peace be both to thee, and peace be to thine house, and peace
be unto all that thou hast." (*Ib.*, v. 6) It is clear that David's over-
tures were not meant to be mere courtesies. David's messengers asked
for no less than a *peace offering*, to use the terminology of *Papyrus
Anastasi I.*

The story of Nabal the Carmelite indicates that the "great men"
did not always give in to the demands of the scavenging bands and
that the warriors were occasionally obliged to resort to force.[20] Nabal's
wife, Abigail, however, wisely avoided an open clash with David by
furnishing him with considerable quantities of food: "And then Abigail
made haste and took two hundred loaves, and two bottles of wine,
and five sheep[21] ready dressed, and five measures of parched corn,
and a hundred clusters of raisins, and two hundred cakes of figs,
and laid them upon asses." (*Ib.*, v. 18). The Bible itemises the types
of food and their quantities, as does *Papyrus Anastasi I.* It is not surprising that the *menu* was similar in both cases, since each time the
very same country supplied the food. However, neither the Bible nor
the papyrus inform us of the length of time the victuals were intended
to last. Yet, it would seem that the provisions were destined to suffice
for a short time only, since some of the products, such as meat and
baked bread, were highly perishable.

The quantities of food obtained by David were only a fraction of
those enumerated in the Egyptian document, as was his army much
smaller than its Egyptian counterpart. In order to comprehend the
exact provisioning of the two armies it is necessary to calculate the
personal "field-ration," issued to each soldier of the Egyptian division or of the Israelite battalion. Actually, we shall repeat the com-
putations performed by the ancient military executives in dividing
the totals of the supplies by the number of men, in one case 5,000,
and in David's case by his 600 warriors. If the reader should assert
that Abigail's donation was apportioned only to the 400 men who
accompanied David on his projected foray against Nabal, the clinch-

---

[20] Compare, for example, the attitude of the rulers of Succoth and Penuel to
Gideon's troop, during the pursuit of the Midianites, *Jud.* 8:4f. and cf. chap. 7a
above.
[21] Actually the Hebrew text reads *ṣōʾn*, which is a collective noun including both
sheep and goats.

ing answer to such an argument is given by the military ordinance exacted by David himself: ". . . but as his part is that goeth down to the battle, so shall his part be that tarrieth by the stuff: they shall part alike." (I *Sm.*, 30:24).

An exact comparison of the two ration lists is feasible only in the case of the quantities of meat, given in both lists in heads of small cattle. Calculation of a single portion shows that the soldier in the Egyptian army received three times the quantity of mutton or goat's flesh supplied to David's warriors. However, in neither case can any inference be made as to the frequency of a meat ration issue. Unfortunately, a comparison of the remaining items is hampered by the lack of clarity regarding the exact nature of the foodstuffs involved or the magnitude of the measures mentioned in our source.[22]

In each source figure two items derived from cereals, which vary in quality of the grain and in the methods of preparation. While the papyrus mentions "loaves of flour" and "cakes," the Bible has *lehem* "bread" and *qālī* "parched grain." It may well be that the Biblical "bread" corresponds to the "cakes" of the papyrus, since the latter refers to the "cakes" by the standard Hebrew-Canaanite term for baking (see p. 115 n. 8), thus indicating that the author had a peculiarly Palestinian kind of bread in mind. The original meaning of "cake" in English, given by the *Shorter Oxford English Dictionary* as "a smallish flattened sort of bread, regularly shaped, and usually turned in baking," most likely does justice to the bread mentioned herein.

---

[22] Therefore, there is no sure basis of comparing the quantities of foodstuffs mentioned on various occasions even in the Davidic narratives themselves:

A) David brings to his three brethren provisions consisting of an *ēphāh* of parched corn and ten loaves of bread (I *Sm.* 17:17).

B) During the war against the Amalekites, an Egyptian prisoner was taken and issued rations consisting, *inter alia*, of "a piece of a cake of figs and two clusters of raisins" (I *Sm.* 30:11–12).

C) At the time of Absalom's rebellion, Ziba supplied David and his troops with ". . . a couple of asses saddled, and upon them two hundred loaves of bread, and a hundred bunches of raisins, and a hundred of summer fruits, and a bottle of wine" (2 *Sm.* 16:1). This food supply is similar to that in 1 *Sm.* 25:18 and implies, perhaps, that there too provision was made for the needs of all the troops that accompanied David when he fled from Absalom, as Ziba himself says: ". . . the bread and summer-fruit for the young men (*Ne'ārīm!*) to eat . . ." (2 *Sm.* 16:2). The reference to the pair of asses, which were required to transport the above mentioned supplies, is of special interest. It should be remembered that a pair of asses harnessed together could transport a heavier load than the same two animals loaded separately.

If the foregoing assumption should prove correct, there would be practically no difference between the bread rations issued to the Egyptians and the Israelites respectively, totalling in each instance one-third of a loaf. On the other hand, despite the similarity apparent at first glance, it does not seem feasible to equate the "bread" of the Biblical source with the "loaves of flour" in the papyrus. The latter employs here the Canaanite loanword *qemah* whose use seems to have been restricted in the Egyptian language to the flour of the highest quality, i.e. wheat flour, which was not generally used for baking bread.[23] It is noteworthy that another document of the New Kingdom explicitly specifies *kmh*-loaves, together with "assorted loaves of Asiatics," as food of the Egyptian army.[24]

As far as beverages were concerned, both military forces were supplied with wine, which is not at all surprising in a grape raising country *par excellence* such as Palestine. The Egyptian soldier seems to have enjoyed a double amount of wine, compared to his Israelite counterpart, assuming that the papyrus refers to wine skins of vessels of approximately the same volume as those mentioned in the Bible, which is indeed possible.[25] David's soldiers could hardly have had more than a single cup apiece, since 300 men had to content themselves with a single wine-skin. However, in addition, David issued his troops a ration of fruits, namely 100 clusters—or perhaps cakes— of raisins, and 200 cakes of pressed dried figs.[26]

In conclusion we shall present the Egyptian and Israelite ration scales. In spite of all the unelucidated material in these scales, their analysis and mutual comparison prove illuminating, for although they reflect specific circumstances, they give us and idea of the diet of an ancient army encamped in Palestine and living off the country. Also the size of the single rations, issued to the individual soldier, is quite enlightening, for from the dawn of history "armies have marched

---

[23] Cf. Kees, *Ägypten*, 1933, p. 68.

[24] *Papyrus Anastasi IV*, XVII, 6; see now Caminos, *Late Egyptian Miscellanies*, 1954, p. 201.

[25] The Egyptian text does not indicate the measure referred to given in connection with the quantity of wine. However, one must presume that it refers, as in the Biblical source, to a *nēbel*, i.e. either a skin-bottle or a large earthen jar. For the application of this term cf. Kelso, *The Ceramic Vocabulary of the Old Testament*, *BASOR, Supplement no.* 5–6, 1948, p. 25f.

[26] The use of dried fruits by David's soldiers is also mentioned in 1 *Chr.* 12:40 as well as in the passages mentioned above.

on their stomachs." Yet, one must bear in mind the reiterated statement of *Papyrus Anastasi I* that the provisions were inadequate, as well as the fact that the supplies furnished to the Israelite troops were not dictated by David's calculations, but consisted of a donation made by Abigail. In any case, the detailed data given in the Bible and in the papyrus enable us to reconstruct a ration table similar to the supply tables of modern armies.

Military Ration Scales[27]

Number of soldiers	Item	Total Quantity	Field Ration
Egypt (according to *Papyrus Anastasi I*)			
5,000	Small cattle	120	1/42 head[28]
	Cakes	1,800	1/3 loaf
	Loaves of flour	300	1/16 loaf
	Wine	30	1/166 wineskin?
Israel (according to *I Sm.*, 25:18)			
500	Small cattle	5	1/120 head
	Bread	200	1/3 loaf
	Parched corn	5.5 *s^eāh*	1/120 *s^eāh*[29]
	Wine	2 *nebel*	1/300 wineskin
	Raisins	100	1/6 cluster
	Figs	200	1/3 cake

---

[27] Modern ration scales differ from our tables in that they list most food items by weight; more recently their nutritional value is given also in calories. Provision tables in modern armies also deal with the computation of the lading and transportation of foodstuffs. Ancient armies must also have been confronted by the same problems, as is indicated from the above Biblical example. Abigail is said to have loaded the provisions which she presented to David on asses. The maximum carrying capacity of the single beast of burden must have been known in order to compute the number of animals required to transport a given quantity of supplies.

[28] The fact that none of the above numbers can be divided exactly into a simple fraction might well have been the point of the trick question which Hori posed to Amenemope.

[29] The Bible quotes, as a unit of grain measure, the *s^eāh*, which was a unit of volume, apparently, one third of an *ēphāh*. According to one opinion, it equalled 13.12 *liters* and by another estimate it came to one half of this volume; cf. Barrois, *Manuel d'archéologie biblique*, II, 1953, pp. 250–252. Accordingly each warrior received *ca.* 0,1 liter, or half of this amount.

20

FOOT-RUNNERS IN ISRAEL AND EGYPT IN THE THIRD INTERMEDIATE PERIOD*

Among the ten instances listed in the Midrashic literature of *a minori ad maijus* (*qāl wā-ḥomer*) arguments (i.e. Bereshit Rabba 92,7) appears a rather curious passage in Jer. 12:5: "If you race with the foot-runners and they exhaust you, how then can you compete with horses? If you *bōṭēḥ* in a tranquil land, how will you fare in the jungle of the Jordan?"[1] This verse, perhaps a popular metaphor, which comes as somewhat of a surprise as the divine answer to the prophet's charges, demonstrates the feeling of helplessness and gloomy reality in which Jeremiah found himself. God's response is basically that the prophet isn't even capable of coping with relatively simple tasks, let alone (*qal wā-ḥomer*) with heavy and difficult burdens. It is not our intention to discuss, in this short paper, the theological aspect of God's words, but rather to elucidate only the realistic background reflected in these passages.

The beginning of the verse alludes to a competition between foot-runners, racers in modern jargon, in which the competitors easily overtake the prophet, tiring him out and completely exhausting him. Perhaps a slightly different explanation can be suggested, which to my knowledge has not yet been considered, namely that the "foot-runners" (Hebrew *raglim*) here are foot-soldiers or infantry as elsewhere in the Bible (i.e. Ex. 12:16). In this case, the race was intended to train the soldiers for attack, an explanation which coincides not only with the subsequent mention of the "horses," but also with the Egyptian document we shall present below. The difference, however, between the generally accepted exegesis and that suggested here, is insignificant, as far as our subject is concerned: in both cases the

---

* This article was originally published in: Hommages à J. Leclant, Cairo 1994 (vol. 4), 199–201.

[1] Jewish Publication Society, New Translation. See commentaries on this passage in the Book of Jeremiah, especially the latest and most detailed exegesis: W. McKane, *Jeremiah* I, *ICC*, Edinburgh, 1986, pp. 263–266.

verse deals with a race between foot-runners or a competition between footmen and horses.

In view of the fact that the Bible rarely mentions runners, the five examples of long-distance races (albeit not for competitive purposes) are impressive: the Benjaminite refugee from the battle at Eben-ezer—Aphek, who after Israel was routed by the Philistines, ran to Shiloh (a distance of approximately 30 kilometers) to inform Eli of the defeat (I Sam. 4:12). This race is reminiscent of the "original" Marathon race in ancient Greece, except that the tidings brought by the runners were opposite in content. The two runners, Ahima'az and the Cushite who brought David tidings of Absalom's death (II Sam. 18:19–26); Gehazi, who purported to act as Elisha's servant, chased the chariot carrying Na'aman the commander, outstripping it (II Kgs. 5:20–22), in other words a sort of contest between a foot-runner and a chariot, as in Jeremiah's metaphor. The other instance is that of the prophet Elijah's outrunning Ahab's royal chariot from Mount Carmel to the city of Jezreel in the valley (a distance of approximately 25 kilometers; I Kgs. 18:46).

Races in the ancient world, especially long distance as well as horse-racing, received frequent mention in Greek literature; to this we might add the illustrations on pottery.[2] However, with regard to the ancient near East, material of this kind is very rare, particularly when dealing with competitions between runners.

Nonetheless, several rather interesting details have recently been revealed in an Egyptian stela from the reign of Pharaoh Taharqa of the twenty-fifth (the Nubian-Cushite) dynasty, published in 1981. The stela, dated to 685 B.C.E., a mere seven or eight decades prior to Jeremiah, is characteristically designated in both the inscription itself and by modern scholars "The Race Stela of Taharqa."[3] The monument stood, like those of other pharaohs, on the Desert Road, near the site of *Dahshur*, on the way from the capital of Egypt,

---

[2] For surveys of sports in the ancient world, see: I. Weiler, *Der Sport bei den Völkern der alten Welt*, Darmstadt, 1988, 2nd edition, 146ff.; J. Jüthner, *Die athletischen Leibes-übungen der Griechen* II, Wien, 1968, pp. 15–156 (Wettlauf).

[3] The Egyptian text was published by A.M. Moussa, "A Stela of Taharqa from the Desert Road at Dahshur," *MDAIK* 37, 1981, pp. 331–337; H. Altenmüller-Moussa, "Die Inschriften auf der Taharkastele von der Dahschurstrasse," *SAK* 9, 1981, pp. 57–84. For an analysis of the sportive aspect of this document, cf. W. Decker, *Sport und Spiel im alten Ägypten*, München, 1987, pp. 68–74; and also: *id.*, "Die Lauf-Stele des Königs Taharqa," *Kölner Beiträge zur Sportwissenschaft* 13, 1984, pp. 7–37.

Memphis, to the Fayyum oasis. It's contents, of relevance to us, describe soldiers in the Pharaoh's army training by running daily back and forth along this route, a distances of 100 kilometers in both directions.[4] A record is made of the time the runners needed to cover this distance, namely nine hours, which is an average of 11 kilometers per hour. The stela commemorates the soldiers' race which Pharaoh personally supervised and even participated for a part of the way, and the exemplary runners were rewarded.

Here we have a unique example of a long-distance race, the type with which the author of the Book of Jeremiah was unfamiliar. Contrary to foot-races, we have no clear information with regard to competitions between footmen and horses or horse-back riders, and possibly Jeremiah alludes to chariots (represented by the word "horses"). Indeed, several Egyptian reliefs on the walls of temples and tombs depict soldiers running in front of or behind the pharaoh's chariot. Regardless of whether they served as the chariot's entourage or for its protection, they had to keep up with the rhythm of galloping horses.[5]

Occasionally it was the Egyptian method of warfare, whereby one of the chariot's crew would descend from it in the heat of battle and continue on foot next to the horses, up against the enemy.[6] We may venture to speculate that various peoples held races between foot-runners and horses (or rather chariots) and it is highly likely that Jeremiah's words are based on such reality.

In the second half of Jeremiah's passage, we ostensibly enter into a new subject, also a *qal wā-ḥomer* instance, although it appears that topic is directly associated with the previous one; for it may be assumed that the words "in a tranquil land you fall" still refer to the race track. The meaning is that this is a peaceful territory, suited for racing as opposed to the continuation "the jungle of the Jordan," which is a dense jungle-like thicket, where wild beasts have their habitat (cf. Jer. 49:9; 50:44), an area obviously unsuitable for run-

---

[4] For technical terms regarding the race see Decker, *Sport und Spiel*, p. 71f., and articles in the Egyptian Lexicon of the same author: "Sport," *LÄ* V, 1984, cols. 1161ff.; "Wettkampf," *LÄ* VI, 1986, cols. 1238ff.; "Lauf," *LÄ* III, 1980, cols. 939f.

[5] Cf. Decker, *Kölner Beiträge*, p. 20, and pl. 6, from the tomb of Mahu at El-Amarna.

[6] Cf. R. Schulman, "The Egyptian Chariotry: A Reexamination," *JARCE* 2, 1963, p. 89 sq.

ning.[7] The connection between the two parts of this passage is asserted on the basis of the proper understanding of the verb *bṭḥ* as in "if you feel secure in a safe country."

Contrary to the generally accepted interpretation of the root *bṭḥ* as tranquility and safety, it appears in several biblical passages, and apparently here as well, in a different meaning, one parallel to the Arabic lexeme: "to fall to the ground," "to fall flat on your belly/face," in other words, to fall prostrate. This rendering was suggested already by the mediaeval lexicographer Al-Fasi and has been adopted by several modern commentators.[8] In fact, it appears in as early as the Aramaic Targum of Jeremiah.[9]

If we accept, therefore, the rare and unconventional exegis of *bṭḥ*, it follows then that even the second half of our passages depicts a race and its failure due to the collapses of the runner. In other words, not only is the prophet incapable of keeping up with the pace of the other runners, but even on a convenient race track ("safe land") he collapse and doesn't reach his destination.

In short, it may be concluded from this discussion that in Israel, as in Egypt and Greece,[10] though to a lesser extent, there existed a spirit of competitive sports, at least with regard to racing.

---

[7] See Rashi on the passage: "In a safe land . . . they exhaust you," i.e. the words refer back to the beginning of the verse and are interconnected.

[8] See: S.L. Skoss, *The Hebrew-Arabic Dictionary of the Bible known as Kitāb al-Jāmi ʿal-ʿalfāz* (Agron) of David ben Abraham al-Fasi I–II, New York, London, 1936–1945, I 215. See also Rashi on Prov. 14:16. Among the modern commentators, Skoss adopted this meaning in *Jewish Studies in Memory of G.A. Kohut*, 1935, pp. 549–553.

[9] Targum explicitly adds ונפיל to את מחבטה (perhaps already indicating our sense).

[10] Cf. Decker, "Das sogenannte Agonale und der alt-ägyptische Sport" *Festschrift Elmar Edel*, Bamberg, 1974, pp. 90ff.

21

AMOS 1:5 IN THE LIGHT OF THE
TIL BARSIP INSCRIPTIONS*

There are various unelucidated passages in Amos's prophecy against the nations, and among them is his threat against the Aramaeans. Without entering into an extensive discussion of the prophet's statements on Aram and their historical background (Amos 1:3–5), we shall deal here with a single detail: "And him that holds the scepter from Beth-Eden" (v. 5). It is quite difficult to establish the time to which the prophet refers in his oracle on Damascus, and it seems that the subject hinges on events which occurred before Amos's prophetic ministry. At any rate, it seems that the prophet, in speaking of Beth-Eden, refers to contemporary historical events. Recent epigraphical material discovered in Syria, tends to support this view.

It has now become apparent that the accepted theories which consider Beth-Eden as a city in Syria, west of the Euphrates, are baseless[1] and that, instead, it should be identified with Bît-Adini, the Aramaean state which lay on the banks of the Middle Euphrates near the great bend of the river, and which was often mentioned in Assyrian documents from the ninth century on down.[2] Only a state of such importance would be worthy of mention in the same breath as Damascus, while other Scriptural passages bear witness to this identification (in a shortened form: Eden). II Kings 19:12 (Is. 37:12) refers to the "children of Eden who were in Thelasar," in juxtaposition to Gozan, Haran and Rezeph, while in Ez. 27:23 Eden is

---

* This article was originally published in: *BASOR* 129 (1953), 25–26.

[1] Cf. the commentaries on Amos 1:5, e.g. W.R. Harper, *Amos and Hosea* (ICC), p. 19. Even the early translators had difficulty with the name *Beth-Eden*. The Vulgate translates *Domus Voluptatis*, "house of delight," from the Hebrew root, *DN*, and following the Vulgate's lead, Haupt, OLZ X (1907), p. 306, explained the name as an appellation for Damascus.

[2] This view is expressed, for example, in Sellin's, *Das Zwölfprophetenbuch* (1922), p. 167. On the Aramaean kingdom of Beth-Eden, cf. Kraeling, *Aram and Israel* (1918), pp. 54ff., *Reallexikon der Assyriologie* II (1938), s.v. "Bît-Adini," and O'Callaghan, *Aram Naharaim* (1948), p. 104. Cf. also my thesis, *The Aramaeans in Aram Naharaim and the Rise of Their States* (Hebrew) (1952), Chap. VIII.

mentioned with Haran and Canneh. All these sites are in Aram-naharaim, i.e. in Eastern Syria.

The state of Beth-Eden was founded in the 10th century, and during the first half of the 9th century it rose to the rank of the supreme Aramaean state in Aram-naharaim. It was conquered in 855 by Shalmaneser III and became an Assyrian province. Thus Amos, preaching in the middle of the eighth century, knew only the Assyrian province, which had replaced the ancient Aramaean principality of Beth-Eden. At the time of Amos Beth-Eden was administered by an Assyrian governor, to whom the title, "Who holdeth a sceptre," may aptly be applied, as the Hebrew idiom does not exclude a subroyal status.[3]

Who was this Assyrian governor of whom Amos prophesies? The solution of this problem may be found in the Assyrian documents excavated at the end of the 1920's at Tell Aḥmar, on the eastern bank of the Euphrates across from the mouth of the Sajur river. This site, 16 miles south of Carchemish, was ancient Til Barsip, capital of Beth-Eden.[4] The documents are dominated by the brilliant personality of an Assyrian noble, Shamshi-ilu, who was the ruler of the western regions of Aram-naharaim, including Beth-Eden. Shamshi-ilu was not an ordinary Assyrian governor, but rather an aggressive ruler, who concentrated the highest offices of the Assyrian Empire in his own hands.

This last is shown by the Assyrian inscription engraved on the statues of the lions, which were erected in the northeastern portal of Til Barsip.[5] In this inscription, Shamshi-ilu is embellished with lavish titles such as *turtân* (second to the king), *nâgiru rabû* (supreme governor), Administrator of the Temples and Commander-in-Chief of the Army (lines 9 and 14). In addition, he governed the "Land of Ḥatti, the Land of Guti and all the Land of Namar," and subjugated several other countries, including Urarṭu, Biblical Ararat (line

---

[3] Cf. Nowack, *Die kleinen Propheten*[3] (1922), p. 122. This appellation is repeated in the same chapter, verse 8, in relation to Ashkelon. However, the repetition is a problem for itself, as the verse involved was influenced by the style of v. 5.

[4] The details of the excavation of this site were published in the archaeological report by Thureau-Dangin and Dunand, *Til-Barsib* I–II (1936). After the conquest of Beth-Eden, the Assyrians changed the name of the city to Kar-Shulmanashared, "Shalmaneser's Quay" in honor of the conquering king.

[5] Cf. the inscription in the report mentioned in the preceding note, pp. 145ff. The inscription was first published by Thureau-Dangin, "L'Inscription des Lions," etc. RA XXVII (1930), pp. 11–21.

10, etc.). Of special interest is the fact that nowhere in the inscription is the name of the reigning Assyrian monarch mentioned, a unique fact in Assyrian historiography and decisive evidence for the weakness of Shamshi-ilu's royal master.

The era of Shamshi-ilu's ascendancy may be easily established from the list of the eponyms, in which he is mentioned in the year 780, during the reign of Shalmaneser IV, in 770, under Asshurdân III and in 752, under Asshurnârâri V. We find, therefore, that Shamshi-ilu held sway for at least 29 years, and his influence in the Assyrian Empire was enhanced by the impotence of the Assyrian kings of that epoch, from Shalmaneser IV (782–773) until the rise of Tiglath-pileser III (746).

The time of Shamshi-ilu's grandeur coincides with the era of the prophet Amos, who lived in the days of Jeroboam II, king of Israel (784–744), and Uzziah, king of Judah (784–743). It is logical to assume that the prophet would refer to an aggressive personality of Shamshi-ilu's stature. The mighty Assyrian autocrat, who attained a high degree of autonomy, was undoubtedly famous throughout the Near East, and his name must have been familiar, even in Palestine. The title, "He who holds the scepter," is a fitting appellation for him, and he is indeed worthy to appear with Ḥazael and Ben-Hadad, Kings of Damascus.

It may well be that Amos's prophecy of the imminent doom awaiting the sceptre-holder from Beth-Eden has an historical basis. Although we have no information of the final fate of Shamshi-ilu, it is known that the triumph of the aggressive Tiglath-pileser III in 746 brought far-reaching changes in the organization of the Assyrian colonial administration. In his efforts to secure centralized domination of the entire empire, which had been feeble in the days of his predecessors, Tiglath-pileser divided the Assyrian provinces into smaller prefectures. Clear indications of this policy come from the excavations at Tell-Aḥmar (Til-Barsip) and the neighboring Arslan-Tash, the ancient city of Ḥadattu. From the archaeological discoveries here, it is apparent that Tiglath-pileser III renewed royal authority and administration in these cities.[6] Thus Til-Barsip was severed from the city of Harran and became a petty Assyrian prefecture, while local autonomy became extinct in the entire western region. This must have

---

[6] Thureau-Dangin, Barrois, Dossin, Dunand, *Arslan-Tash* I (1931), pp. 7ff.

been effected during the first years of his reign as a means of consolidating his political position in the region of the Euphrates, prior
to his Syrian campaigns, which began in 743. If Shamshi-ilu was
still alive in the first years of Tiglath-pileser's reign, his fate must
have been similar to that of his province. If so, Amos based his
prophecy of Shamshi-ilu's doom on the policy of the Assyrian monarch,
who appears as the rod of God's wrath, raining down destruction
on Beth-Eden and its ruler, who was probably of Assyrian extraction himself, as well as upon Damascus and its kings. This view is
in full accord with the chronological situation, as Amos prophesied
until at least 738.[7]

The Greek Bible (LXX) comes to the aid of our identification of
the "Scepter-holder from Beth-Eden" with Shamshi-ilu. All recensions of the LXX have Harran instead of Beth-Eden.[8] This interpretation was drawn from a reliable source and is not a graphical
error as some commentators have assumed.[9] It is known that the
center of Shamshi-ilu's province was actually in Harran, on the banks
of the upper Baliḫ, and that from this seat of power Shamshi-ilu
held sway over Beth-Eden. The Massoretic text refers to Beth-Eden,
because this area was the westernmost part of Shamshi-ilu's domain
and thus closer to the Israelite horizon.

---

[7] Cf. Albright, "The Biblical Period," in *The Jews* I (1949), ed. Finkelstein, p. 38.
[8] However, the LXX reads "tribe" instead of "scepter."
[9] The assumption being that the letters *D* and *R* were interchanged. Cf. Harper,
op. cit., p. 22.

22

THE HISTORICAL BACKGROUND OF TWO
PROPHECIES OF THE NATIONS*

Most Biblical prophecies which are concerned with "the Nations," despite their cloaking in flowery style, contain much material of historical value, which has yet to be studied and clarified. There are those, however, that defy further explanation, because of a lack of sufficient external data confirming and supplementing them. Of the prophecies on Philistia, for instance, some, Isaiah xiv, 28–32, Ezekiel xxv, 15–17, Joel iv, 4–8, Amos i, 6–8, Zephaniah ii, 4–7, can hardly be further elucidated; but two of them, the prophecy in Zechariah ix, 1–8 (10), on the cities of Philistia (and on several other cities and nations) and the one of Jeremiah xlvii, can probably be placed in their proper historical context.

1. *Zechariah IX, 1–6*

The prophecy in Zechariah ix, 1–6, is part of a sermon which deals with the cities of Philistia, with Tyre, and with other Syrian and Palestinian towns and countries. By piecing together all available details we are able to reconstruct the real sequence of events with which this prophecy is concerned. The antiquity of the prophecy itself seems already proven by some scholars and especially by Kraeling,[1] though the generally accepted view dates this sermon, together with all the chapters of the "second Zechariah," much later, even as late as the Hasmonean era. As to the events referred to in the prophecy, Kraeling has tried to draw a rough historical outline, which, in regard to the cities of Philistia, is apparently correct, although doubt is cast upon his theory in respect to the first part of

---

* This article was originally published in: *IEJ* 1 (1951), 149–159.
[1] Kraeling, E.G.H.: The Historical Situation in Zech. 9:1–10, *Amer. Jour. Sem. Lang.*, 41, 1924, pp. 24–33. Compare also Olmstead, A.T.: *History of Palestine and Syria*, 1931, pp. 457–458.

the sermon. The more recent publications on this subject which ignore or attempt to refute him, are, apparently, mistaken.[2]

The prophecies on the towns of Gaza and Ashdod (vs. 5–7), according to information in Assyrian sources, tie up with the campaigns against them of the Assyrian king, Sargon II (722–705). In 720 Sargon subdued Gaza, exiling its king Hanun to Assyria.[3] It would seem that the words in the prophecy "And the king shall perish from Gaza" (vs. 5), refer to these events. The verse about Ashdod is an obvious reference to the events which preceded and caused Sargon's campaign against this city in 711. A political coup d'état, the beginning of a revolt against the Assyrian yoke, overthrew Ahimiti, the Assyrian vassal in the local dynasty of Ashdod: "The Hittites, plotters of iniquity, hated his rule and elevated (to reign) over them Iamanî without claim to the throne."[4] Since this name Iamanî means "Greek" (i.e. Ionian) he was, of course, a foreigner. It was of him that the prophet was speaking: "And a *bastard* shall dwell in Ashdod; and I will cut off the pride of the Philistines" (vs. 6).

---

[2] After this article was written, two papers were published each putting forward independently a new theory to the effect that our prophecy is connected with Alexander the Great's campaign to Syria and Palestine in 332 after the battle of Issus. Cf. Elliger, K.: Ein Zeugnis aus der jüdischen Gemeinde, etc., 332 v. Chr., *Zeitschr. Alttest. Wiss.*, N.F. 21, 1949–1950, pp. 63ff.; Delcor, M.: Les allusions à Alexandre le Grand dans Zach. ix, 1–8, *Vetus Testamentum*, 1, 1951, pp. 100ff. For the more usual opinion cf. Sellin, E.: *Das Zwölfprophetenbuch* II, 2nd edit., 1930, p. 547. He opposes Kraeling's view, postdating the prophecy to the Hellenistic period.— On the other hand the opinion has been advanced that the prophecy is of an early date but of a late redaction. The scholars agreeing with this opinion, erroneously antedate the prophecy to the reign of Tiglath Pileser III., cf. for instance Steuernagel, C.: *Lehrbuch der Einleitung in das Alte Testament*, 1912, p. 465; and cf. also Horst, F.: *Die zwölf kleinen Propheten*, 1938, p. 238. Horst claims correctly that the substance of the early prophecy ends with line 6. Jepsen, A.: Israel und Damaskus, *Archiv f. Orientf.*, 14, 1941–1942, p. 171 (and *Zeitschr. Alttest. Wiss.*, N.F. 14, 1939, p. 242f.) dates the prophecy even earlier, about the middle of the 8th century, and sees in it a reference to the wide conquests of Jerobeam II in Syria.

[3] The Annals of Sargon, line 30; cf. Luckenbill, D.D.: *Ancient Records of Assyria* (ARA) II, 1926 § 5; Display Inscription, line 25ff. (ARA II, § 55); Cylinder Inscription, line 19 (ARA II, § 118).

[4] Display Inscription, line 90ff., especially lines 95–96 (ARA II § 62). The corresponding lines in the Annals, line 215ff. (ARA II § 30), read Iatna instead of Iamani. For the etymology of the name Iatna cf. Albright, W.F.: Some Oriental Glosses on the Homeric Problem, *Amer. Journ. Archaeol.*, 54, 1950, pp. 162–176, ref. pp. 171ff. Both names refer to a man whose origin is Greek or Cyprian. Cf. also the Broken Prism from Nineveh, fragment D (ARA II § 194), and the new Assyrian parallel, published by Weidner, E.F.: *Archiv f. Orientf.*, 14, 1941, p. 50.

Zechariah's words pertaining to the other places mentioned in the prophecy (vs. 1–4) are clarified by other sources. The first part of the prophecy on Tyre, "And Tyrus did build herself a stronghold" (vs. 3), can be explained, as already pointed out by Kraeling, by the testimony of Menander, cited by Josephus (*Antiquities* ix, ch. xiv, 2), on the siege of the city by Shalmaneser V (727–722).[5] The prophecy refers (apart from the paronomasia in the Hebrew text: צוֹר-מָצוֹר) to this siege of the city by Shalmaneser. The second part of the prophecy regarding the destruction of the city, cannot, however, be reconciled with the rest of Menander's testimony concerning Shalmaneser, for even his two successive sieges of Tyre failed, nor did he ever succeed in dealing the Tyrian fleet a decisive blow. On the contrary, according to Menander, the small Tyrian fleet defeated the combined naval powers of the various Phoenician cities which fought for the Assyrian king. This hardly fits in with the prophecy "(The Lord) . . . will smite her power in the sea; and she shall be devoured with fire" (vs. 4).

An historical situation appropriate to this prophecy of destruction should, therefore, be sought at another time, and, in our opinion, is to be associated with the slightly later activities against Tyre, of Sargon, Shalmaneser's successor. Sargon explicitly mentions the surrender of Tyre in a passage that has hitherto not been fully appreciated by scholars.[6] From this evidence, and from the fact that Sargon boasted of his naval victory over the fleet of the Greeks (meaning Cypriots),[7] it is probable that he fought a naval battle against Tyre as well. It may even be conjectured that there is some connection between the naval battle with the Cypriots and the surrender of Tyre. Supporting this conjecture is the proximity of these events in the Assyrian source,[8] and Menander's testimony that the king of

[5] This evidence is contradicted by certain chronological difficulties, and the identification of the Greek form Σελάμψας with the name Shalmaneser is doubted as well. Cf. Eiselen, F.C.: *Sidon*, 1907, p. 47; Honor, L.: *Sennacherib's Invasion of Palestine*, 1926, p. 102; but contrast with Wiener, H.M.: *The Prophets of Israel in History and Criticism*, 1923, pp. 67ff.

[6] Cylinder Inscription, line 21 (ARA II § 118). This reference was overlooked by Kraeling (and likewise by Elliger, *op. cit.* [*supra* n. 2], p. 86); hence his search for extraneous explanations; cf. Kraeling, *op. cit.* (*supra*, n. 1), pp. 27–28.

[7] Cylinder Inscription, *op. cit.* (*supra*, n. 6); The Pavement Inscriptions from Khorsabad, line 34 (ARA II § 99); etc.

[8] Cylinder Inscription, line 21 (ARA II § 118). Between those two events, there is mentioned only the surrender of Que in Asia Minor.

Tyre expanded his authority to include the Kittians who are none other than the Cypriots. In any case, the siege of Tyre lasted five years, according to Menander, and apparently the final stage of the battle for the city took place in the reign of Sargon. If we accept the supposition that the beginning of this Assyrian campaign against Tyre under Shalmaneser was simultaneous with the siege of Samaria in 725–724, then the Assyrian siege of Tyre lasted till 720–719 when the city was finally captured by Sargon. It would seem, therefore, accepting the above evidence, that the prophecy of Zechariah is referring to Sargon's military activities against Tyre.[9]

It is our opinion that the prophecy concerning the other places with which Zechariah opens his sermon, may be attributed to approximately the same time: Hadrach, Damascus, Israel (he emphasizes "*all* the tribes of Israel," thus including the district of Samaria too) and Hamath (vs. 1–2). This opinion is in opposition to that of those who attribute the historical situation to the earlier reign of Tiglath-Pileser III (cf. note 2), and to that of Kraeling who sees in this prophecy a reference to the sequence of events from the year 739 (the conquest of Hadrach), 732 (conquest of Damascus), 721 (conquest of Samaria), to 720 (conquest of Hamath). This passage then would seem to refer to a single event that took place in the reign of Sargon, i.e., the western punitive campaign of the Assyrian king in 720 which was intended to suppress the revolt of the league of Syrian and Palestinian cities.

It is known from several inscriptions of Sargon, that Yaubidi, king of Hamath, led the revolt, and that both Damascus and Samaria participated in it.[10] As for Hadrach, a new Assyrian source, discovered in North Syria, which has not received adequate attention, seems to shed new light on the question. This, a stela erected by Sargon after his victory at Karkar over the combined Syro-Palestinian forces in 720,[11] mentions Hadrach besides Hamath in a rather obscure

---

[9] The military history of Samaria is clearly parallel to that of Tyre. The sieges of both were begun at the same time during the reign of Shalmaneser; both reached their end during that of his successor. The Assyrian source gives no information on the date of Tyre's fall, nor is it of any help for the determination of its chronology that this event is mentioned in close proximity to the naval war against Cyprus. The general opinion dates this naval war in 713 or 709, and if this were the case, it would throw doubt upon its connection with the fall of Tyre.

[10] Annals, line 23ff. (ARA II 5); Display Inscription, line 33ff. (ARA II 55), and other inscriptions.

[11] Thureau-Dangin, F.: La Stèle d'Asharné, *Rev. d'Assyr.*, 30, 1933, pp. 53–56.

passage, which seems to indicate the victory of the Assyrian king over both cities. Thus all four countries mentioned by the prophet in the beginning on his sermon were involved in the events of 720.[12]

The above discussion of Zechariah ix, 1–6, leads us to the conclusion that the sermon was written following the military exploits of Sargon II of Assyria, who about 720, served as a "rod of God's anger" against Hadrach, Damascus, Israel, Hamath and subdued Gaza and Tyre as well. The coup d'état in Ashdod cannot be dated as exactly, but it probably preceded the Assyrian campaign of 711 by some years, and may have taken place shortly after the above mentioned events of 720.[13] External evidence on the fate of Ashkelon and Ekron, mentioned in this prophecy, is lacking.

This inscription was discovered in 1924 at Asharné on the Orontes near Apamaea, which is within the area conquered by the Assyrians in 720. (I wish to extend my thanks to the Pontificum Institutum Biblicum and its Jerusalem director, Father L. Semkowski, S.J., for their help in obtaining a photostatic copy of this article.)

[12] It should be noted that the suggested emendation of the text (vs. 1) to: ′וכלו ′שפטי שמאל, i.e., "and there vanished the judges of Sam'al" (an Aramaic kingdom in North Syria), from: ′וכל שבטי ישראל′, i.e., "and all the tribes of Israel," is unnecessary and lacks an historical basis. Compare the text in Kittel's *Biblia Hebraica*, 3rd edit., and Procksch, *Die kleinen prophetischen Schriften nach dem Exil*, 1916, p. 101.

This emendation is made in order to adapt this verse to the contents of the verse that follows: "And Hamath also shall border thereby" (vs. 2), so that Hamath would have bordered on the kingdom of Sam'al and not on the territory of the tribes of Israel. Cf. Elliger: Sam'al und Hamath in ihrem Verhältnis zu Hattina und Arpad, *Festschrift O. Eissfeldt*, 1947, pp. 69ff. In this detailed study of the emendation, Elliger shows that there never was a common boundary between Sam'al and Hamath. If, therefore, the two verses quoted above have a connection with one another, it is more logical, and fitting to the historical reality of the period, that the territory of the tribes of Israel, or rather the Assyrian provinces established in that territory, which did border on Hamath (Cf. Noth, *Paläst. Jahrb.*, 33, 1937, p. 47) is being referred to.

No more acceptable is Elliger's own emendation of the ext to, ′נבהלו שפטי צמר′ i.e., "the judges of Ṣemer (one of the primary Phoenician cities) were frightened," on which he bases some of the main points for his dating of the prophecy to the time of Alexander (cf. *supra*, n. 2).

It is more likely that the text has been distorted in vs. 1 in the words: ′עין אדם′ i.e., "(To the Lord belongs) the eye of man" and should be emended, with Klostermann, *Theol. Lit. Zeit.*, 4, 1879, p. 566, to: ′ערי ארם′, i.e., "The cities of Aram" or, as in my opinion, to ′עיר ארם′, i.e., "The city of Aram," meaning Damascus; cf. Malamat, A.: *Tarbiz*, 22, 1950, p. 64 (Hebrew).

[13] Cf. now Alt, A.: *Zeitschr. Deutsch. Paläst. Ver.*, 67, 1945, pp. 138ff.

2. Jeremiah XLVII

The historical circumstances surrounding the prophecy of Jeremiah xlvii, a sermon devoted entirely to Philistia, have, so far, not been adequately explained. The scholars who have associated it with the campaign of the Babylonian army, have done so solely on conjecture.[14] There is no doubt that Nebuchadnezzar's army did invade Philistia during its campaigns in Palestine, and probably more than once,[15] but it is difficult to reconcile the contradiction between the dates of these campaigns and the chronological indication at the beginning of the prophecy: "before that Pharaoh smote Gaza" (vs. 1).

Scholars have long admitted the connection between these words and the testimony of Herodotus on the conquest of Gaza by the Pharaoh Necho after the battle at Megiddo.[16] Obviously, the fall of Gaza took place a short time after the battle between Necho and Josiah at Megiddo in 609. Its conquest can perhaps be understood as consistent with Necho's firm policy of settling the troublesome political questions in Palestine (such as the exile of Jehoachaz and the coronation of Jehoiakim in Judah), and may be related to the return home of the Egyptian army after its campaign in Syria. At any rate, the event took place a fair time before the first Babylonian invasion of Syria and Palestine in 605.[17]

---

[14] Recently the opinion has been expressed that the prophecy was composed in the years 617–615, and refers to the conquests of Josiah in Philistia. Cf. Bardke, H.: Jeremia der Fremdvölkerprophet, *Zeitschr. Alttest. Wiss.*, N.F. 12, 1935, pp. 235–239.

[15] Compare with the Aramaic papyrus recently discovered at Saqqarah, Egypt, testifying to the preparations of the Babylonian army for the storming of the Philistine cities, and also the discussion of the campaigns of Nebuchadnezzar in Philistia in *Bull. Jew. Palest. Explor. Soc.*, 15, 1950, pp. 34ff., and in *Journ. Near East. Stud.*, 9, 1950, pp. 221ff.

[16] Compare Hitzig, *De Cadyti urbe Herodotea*, 1829, and his commentary on the book of Jeremiah, 2nd edit., 1866. The name of Megiddo in Herodotus, ii, 159, is corrupted to Μάγδολον, while the Greek form of Gaza used by Herodotus is Κάδυτις. That the latter name does not refer to Kadesh on the Orontes, an opinion which is still occasionally held, may be proved from archaeological evidence which apparently indicates that the city was abandoned after the Late Bronze Age until the Hellenistic period; cf. Noth, *Welt des Orients*, 1948, p. 233, n. 57.

[17] It is unthinkable that Gaza was conquered by the Egyptians after the battle of Carchemish in 605, as maintained by several scholars; for at that time the Egyptian army was in disorderly retreat, pursued by the Babylonian army. On the historical situation of this period, cf. Malamat, A.: The Last Wars of the Kingdom of Judah, *Journ. Near East. Stud.*, 9, 1950, pp. 218ff.

The scholars who have attributed the deeds described in this prophecy to the Babylonian armies, assumed that the words "before that Pharaoh smote Gaza" were erroneously interpolated by a later editor.[18] It seems, however, that, on the contrary, we have before us a chronological marker purposely introduced to separate the event concerned in our prophecy from similar events which occurred a few years later. The historical situation appropriate to this prophecy of destruction must be sought in the sequence of events which occurred before 609–608. Therefore, the Babylonian campaigns are irrelevant here.

The key in our opinion is to be found in Herodotus (i, 105), who records that the Scythians overran Philistia during the rule of Pharaoh Psamtik I. The appearance of the Scythians in the Near East cannot be gone into in detail here, but on the evidence brought to light by the publication of a Babylonian chronicle describing the years 616–609,[19] it may be assumed that this appearance took place towards the end of the reign of Psamtik I. This chronicle mentions certain nomadic tribes called "Umman Manda," fighting about 612 as the allies of Babylonia and Media against the coalition of Egypt and Assyria. The identification of these Umman Manda with the Scythians seems very probable.[20] They, together with the Babylonian army, conquered the city of Harran in 610, thereby casting their shadow over the territories west of the Euphrates. Afterwards the Babylonian army returned home. The course of the wanderings of the hordes of Umman Manda, however, is unknown to us, there being unfortunately a lacuna in the Babylonian chronicle (line 65).[21]

There can be little doubt that the subsequent events are those described by Herodotus: these Scythians, after the fall of Harran,

---

[18] So do most of the commentaries on Jeremiah, as those by Cornill, Giesebrecht, Condamin, Volz, etc. On the other hand, Kaufman, J.: *Toledoth ha-Emunah ha-Yisraelith*, VII, 1948, p. 410, dates this chapter to 609, which in our opinion is correct, but he brings no argument to support his view.

[19] Cf. Gadd, C.J.: *The Fall of Nineveh*, 1923; cf. also the latest translation of the Babylonian Chronicle by Oppenheim, A.L., apud *Ancient Near Eastern Texts* (ed. Pritchard), 1950, pp. 303ff.

[20] Compare especially Lewy, J.: Forschungen zur alten Geschichte Vorderasiens, *Mitt. Vorderas. Gesell.*, 1924, and with recent histories, as Kittel, R.: *Geschichte des Volkes Israel* II, 6 & 7th edit., 1925, p. 416, n. 1. Various arguments have been put forward against this identification by Schnabel, *Zeitschr. f. Assyr.*, N.F. 2, 1924, pp. 82ff. and a few other scholars.

[21] The completion of the line in *Ancient Near Eastern Texts*, p. 305, remains doubtful.

crossed the Euphrates to invade Syria and Palestine.[22] Herodotus tells us that Psamtik, having met the invaders, succeeded, by means of gifts and entreaties, in persuading them not to invade Egypt. In their retreat the Scythians stopped at Ashkelon at least long enough to destroy the famous temple of the "Celestial Aphrodite."[23] From this information, it is certain that the Scythians were south of Ashkelon, and almost certainly reached as far as Gaza. Near there, or perhaps even further south, they met Psamtik.

The various sources at hand are adequate to determine the exact dates of these happenings, and to intercalate them into the general sequence of events. If there has been no error in the above discussion, and if we accept the position of those scholars who see a connection between the last action of the Egyptian army in 609, reported in the new Babylonian chronicle, and the campaign of Necho in Palestine, as described in the Bible, then the following chronological sequence can be outlined:

Marcheshwan (November) 610: (The sixteenth year of the reign of Nabopolassar): The Umman Manda (Scythians), with the Babylonian army, besiege the city of Harran (Bab. Chronicle, lines 59–60).

Adar (March) 609: The Babylonian army returns home; the Scythians penetrate quickly into Syria and Palestine (*ibid.*, lines 64–65). They do not tarry to loot these countries (note that the prophecy on Judah reflects a threat of the "Scythian danger" only), and even the Philistine coast is looted only during their retreat. These facts seem to demonstrate that the Scythians in their military alliance with the Babylonians and Medes, took upon themselves the role of destroying the Egyptian army in particular. They pursued the Egyptians from the Euphrates to the Egyptian border, without delays or diversions.

[Nisan-Siwan] (April-June) 609: The Scythians are halted by Psamtik; they suddenly retrace their steps and disappear, partially devastating Philistia on the way. The echo of their sudden burst into the Philistine cities can be heard in the prophecy with which we are dealing

---

[22] These events are not to be ante-dated by 20 years as currently held. Cf. the detailed research of Lewy, J., *op. cit.* (*supra*, n. 20), pp. 51ff., who dates the Scythians' first appearance in Mesopotamia in 612, but post-dates their invasion of Palestine to 593–590, that is to the reign of Psamtik II.

[23] This temple of Ashkelon is described by Herodotus as very ancient. It should be noted that some years later, when Nebuchadnezzar exiled the inhabitants of this city to Babylon, the temple singers were specifically mentioned. Cf. Weidner, E.F.: *Mélanges Syriens offerts à M.R. Dussaud*, II, 1939, p. 928.

(Jeremiah xlvii, 2–3). Afterwards, the Scythians are no longer mentioned in the Babylonian Chronicle. They undoubtedly withdrew from further military intervention, persuaded by gifts from Psamtik.

In the meantime Psamtik died (is his death connected with his surrender to the Scythians?). The new Pharaoh, Necho, dispatched urgent military aid to the remnants of the Assyrian army in the vicinity of the Euphrates. The Egyptian army passed through Palestine on its way to Syria in the early months of spring ("the time when kings go forth"), and was stopped by Josiah near Megiddo (2 Kings xxiii, 29–30; 2 Chronicles xxxv, 20–24). Perhaps the Egyptian humiliation at the hands of the Scythians a few weeks before is one of the reasons for the Judaean king's audacity in making a stand against the Egyptian army.[24] At any rate, the Egyptian troops did not hesitate long in Palestine, but hastened on to Syria—"And God has said to me to make haste" (2 Chronicles xxxv, 21).

Tammuz (July) 609: The Egyptian army joined the army of Ashurubalit, the last Assyrian king, and with united forces they attack Harran (Bab. Chronicle, line 66).

[Tammuz-Elul] (July-September) 609: Their combined siege being at first successful (*ibid.*, line 68), Necho from his political headquarters in Riblah, seized the opportunity to settle the political situation in Judah. He exiled Jehoachaz three months after the latter had succeeded Josiah to the throne, setting up Jehoiakim in his stead and exacting, as well, a heavy fine from the inhabitants of Judah (2 Kings xxiii, 31ff.).

Elul (September) 609: The indecisive siege of Harran was lifted and Necho returned to Egypt (Bab. Chronicle, line 69).[25] The Egyptian army, on its way home, conquered Gaza, which apparently had revolted at the same time as Judah (Jeremiah xlvii, 1; Herodotus ii, 159).

From the above it is clear that the Scythian attack on Philistia took place between the months of Adar and Tammuz of 609, when the Egyptian army was renewing its campaign in Syria, whether this

---

[24] For other factors which motivated Josiah to make a stand at Megiddo, *cf. Journ. Near East. Stud.*, 9, 1950, p. 219f.

[25] The translation of Oppenheim for the end of line 69 [*op. cit. (supra*, n. 19), p. 305], following the interpretation of Albright (*Jour. Bibl. Lit.*, 1932, p. 87, n. 33), "and they (the Egypto-Assyrians) returned" is preferable to the translation of Gadd and Ebeling, apud Gressmann, *Altorientalische Texte zum Alten Test.*, 2nd edit., 1926, p. 365.

campaign was led by Psamtik or by Necho. This period of time coincides with the historical setting of the prophecy of the destruction of Philistia in Jeremiah xlvii. It is likewise clear that half a year elapsed from the time that the Scythians stormed Philistia to the time that Pharaoh conquered Gaza in the autumn.[26] This half year is precisely the interval between the subject of our prophecy and the chronological marker at the beginning of the prophecy. Even if it is demonstrated that the action of the Egyptian army mentioned in the Babylonian chronicle is not the campaign of Necho known to us from the Bible, a campaign which in any case could hardly have taken place later than 608,[27] it is still impossible to separate the Scythian attack from the fall of Gaza by more than a year and a half; the latter would then have occurred in the autumn of 608.

It should be noted that the prophet mentions only Gaza and Ashkelon, the cities which the Scythians really passed through on their retreat through Palestine (the former very probably, the latter certainly), as we have seen above. The attempts of some scholars to emend the text to include Ashdod or some other city are thus historically unfounded.[28] There is even a parallel between Herodotus' account of the fate of Ashkelon and the special emphasis in our prophecy on its destruction.—"Ruined is Ashkelon . . . the sword of the Lord . . .; but how can it be at peace, since the Lord has given it a charge, has made it an appointment against Ashkelon and the seashore" (vs. 5–7).

In our opinion, the special style of this chapter gives further proof to the above arguments. This style is the one that Jeremiah usually uses to describe the "nation from the north," which has been generally interpreted as referring to the Scythian invasion of the Palestine. Of

---

[26] That the fall of Gaza did not take place immediately after the battle of Megiddo is also deducible from the fact that Necho had already reached the Euphrates in the month of Tammuz, probably an impossibility if he had returned to Philistia to reduce Gaza.

[27] This date is preferred by some scholars and most recently by Rowton, M.B.: Jeremiah and the Death of Josiah, *Journ. Near East. Stud.*, 10, 1951, pp. 128–130. Gadd, *op. cit. (supra,* n. 19), p. 24, considers for the date of the battle of Megiddo even the year 607, which is obviously too late. On the other hand see Alfrink, B.J.: Die Schlacht bei Megiddo und der Tod des Josiah (609), *Biblica*, 15, 1934, pp. 173ff. For the problem of chronology, cf. Thiele, E.R.: *Journ. Near East. Stud.*, 3, 1944, pp. 180ff.

[28] Cf. commentaries of Cornill, Condamin and Rudolph, and the 3rd edition of Kittel's *Biblia Hebraica*. Perhaps Ashdod was already laid waste in those days as the result of the long Egyptian siege (Herodotus, ii, 157).

course this evidence is inconclusive in itself, for descriptions in a similar style may be found in the prophecies on Babylonia[29] and even on Assyria, though not on Egypt.[30] When added to the other arguments, however, this detail strengthens our conclusions concerning the historical setting of this chapter.

---

[29] Cf. especially Wilke, F.: Das Skythenproblem im Jeremiabuche, *Beitr. Wiss.d.Alt.Test.*, 9, 1913.

[30] And for this reason alone it is impossible to accept the opinion that our prophecy refers to the conquest of Philistia by the Egyptian army, as held by a few scholars. Cf. commentary of Giesebrecht on Jeremiah.

23

JEREMIAH AND THE LAST TWO KINGS OF JUDAH*

In the spring of 598 B.C., the young king of Judah, Jehoiachin, was exiled to Babylonia, together with his court, after having reigned for only three months. In his place Nebuchadnezzar enthroned his uncle Mattaniah, called thenceforth Zedekiah. The duties thrown upon the new king were not slight; for a whole decade Zedekiah struggled for the existence of his kingdom since peace and order were continually disturbed. The exile of thousands of its foremost citizens caused the social economic anarchy which prevailed then, and prepared the ground for the ascent of various political adventurers.

In the Bible we have insufficient information on the fate of Jehoiachin in his exile. The Biblical historiographer tells us only that in the thirty-seventh year of his exile Jehoiachin was freed from his confinement by Evil-Merodach, the successor to Nebuchadnezzar's throne, and was even awarded great honours.

The theory advanced recently that Jehoiachin in reality retained the status of king of Judah even after his exile and that he was perhaps held by the Babylonians as a threat against Zedekiah, has been surprisingly verified by additional epigraphic material, lately discovered in the Palace of Nebuchadnezzar in Babylonia. The material was published by Weidner on the eve of the outbreak of the second World War.[1] These tablets not only reveal to us a very interesting portrayal of the honourable status of Jehoiachin and his household in Nebuchadnezzar's Court, which was similar to the status of other exile-kings, but Jehoiachin is expressedly termed in these tablets by the formal title "King of the Land of Judah."

Additional evidence for defining the status of Jehoiachin in his exile might also be drawn from the seal imprints on jar handles found in Tell-Beit-Mirsim and Beth-Shemesh. These imprints read: "To Eliakim, steward of Yaukin" (the name Yaukin is surely the

---

* This article was originally published in: *PEQ* 83 (1951), 81–87.
[1] E.F. Weidner, *Jojachin-König von Juda in babylonischen Keilschrifttexten, Mélanges Syriens offerts a M. René Dussaud*, Vol. II, 1939, pp. 923–935.

abridged form of Jehoiachin) from which we may learn, as was
assumed by Albright, that Jehoiachin kept an administration in Judah
to take care of his royal property during his stay in Babylonia.[2] It
is also possible that we may have grounds for the special status of
Jehoiachin even after the period of Zedekiah, on two more seals
which were discussed by H.G. May.[3] If these seals or seal impressions, the first: "To Ya-azaniah, servant of the king" (found in Tell-
en-Nasbeh) and the second: "Gedaliah, who was over the house"
(assuming of course that this reading of the seal impression from
Tell-ed-Duweir is correct) really belong to the time of Gedaliah,[4] son
of Ahikam, then the same Gedaliah was certainly the Regent of
Jehoiachin.[5]

Evidently, this duality in the status of the monarchy (Zedekiah in
Jerusalem and Jehoiachin in exile) made itself strongly felt in Judah
itself, dividing the Judeans into two opposite camps: one of which
continued to see in Jehoiachin the king "de jure" even after he was
exiled; these undoubtedly strongly desired his return. The others were
ready to submit to and to accept as lawful the rule of Zedekiah, the
adherent of the Chaldean king. The first group apparently identified
itself with that part of the nation which strove for national deliverance from the yoke of Babylonia and tended therefore to a positive
orientation towards Egypt, while the followers of Zedekiah who indeed
gradually diminished in numbers sought support for the nation in
Babylonian rule.

The stand of Jeremiah in this internal controversy was unques-
tionably clear: he was the sworn enemy of Egypt. It is of interest,
however, to scrutinize the Prophet's view on the question of legiti-

---

[2] W.F. Albright, *The Seal of Eliakim and the Latest Preexilic History of Judah, etc.,* JBL
51, (1932), pp. 77–106; *King Joiachin in Exile* (BA V, No. 4), 1942.

[3] H.G. May, *Three Hebrew Seals and the Status of Exiled Jehoiakin* AJSL, 1939, pp.
146–148.

[4] See now: McCown, *Tell en-Nasbeh,* Vol. I, p. 163.

[5] We know besides of other similar circumstances in the time of Nebuchadnezzar
of enthroning a vassal in place of an exiled king who nevertheless continues to be
the legal ruler. So when Tyre was captured in 574 B.C. a regent named Baal was
appointed instead of the exiled Itobaal. (cf. R. Pietschmann, *Geschichte der Phoenizier,*
1889, p. 306).

Perhaps that was the situation also in the case of the kingdoms of Sidon, Arwad,
Ashdod and Gaza cf. Unger (ThLZ), 1925, pp. 481ff.; 44 (ZAW), 1926, pp.
314ff.), and possibly even in the case of Ashkelon (cf. the Aramaic Saqqarah Papyrus
published by Dupont-Sommer, *Semitica* I, 1948; and also the writer's remarks on
the above Papyrus in *BJPES,* XV, 1–2, 1949, pp. 33–39).

macy in the Judean monarchy. This angle of the problem has hitherto not been particularly investigated.

Jeremiah's viewpoint on the above dispute was given expression
in his ideological discussion with the false prophets during the fourth
year of Zedekiah's reign. The outline of opinion of the false prophets
is revealed to us on this occasion by one of their prominent spokes-
men Hananiah, son of Azur, the prophet from Gibeon, in the following words: "Thus speaketh the Lord of hosts, the God of Israel,
saying, I have broken the yoke of the king of Babylon. Within two
full years will I bring again into this place all the vessels of the
Lord's house that Nebuchadnezzar king of Babylon took away from
this place, and carried them to Babylon. And I will bring again to
this place Jechoniah the son of Jehoiakim king of Judah, with all
the captives of Judah, that went into Babylon," etc. (Jer. XXVIII,
2–4).

Jeremiah's opinion of this prophetic declaration is clearly understood from his reaction in response to it. "Amen the Lord do so,
the Lord perform thy words which thou hast prophesied to bring
again the vessels of the Lord's house and all that is carried away
captive, from Babylon into this place," etc. (ib., vs. 6). It might be
assumed from this that Jeremiah was inclined to consent to this
assertion by his disputant, although it completely opposes his own
prophetic tradition, as is clearly understood from what follows in the
discussion.

However, it is clear that Jeremiah disagrees with the political pro-
gramme of his opponents on one point, and that is, on the question of the royal succession. While the false prophet is hostile to the
rule of Zedekiah and categorically demands the return of Jehoiachin
to the throne, as an integral part of his party's political platform,
Jeremiah intentionally skips over this problem.

The prophet's silence on this detail is more significant than appears
at first. That *this* is not a mere coincidence is proved by the prophecy
that Jeremiah devotes to Jehoiachin. The sacred oath at the opening of Jeremiah's word on the forlorn king leaves no room for mis-
understanding. "As I live saith the Lord, though Coniah (Jehoiachin)
the son of Jehoiakim, king of Judah were the signet upon my right
hand, yet would I pluck thee thence" (Jer. XXII, 24). His disincli-
nation to leave the rulership of the country in Jehoiachin's power is
defined most distinctly, for it is the prophet's opinion that the legal-
ity of this power expired with the exile. The consequence of this

prophetic thought requires, however, a more general far reaching conclusion, by which the prophet winds up the above matter: "Thus saith the Lord, write ye this man childless, a man that shall not prosper in his days; for no man of his seed shall prosper, sitting upon the throne of David, and ruling any more in Judah" (ib., vs. 30).

Entirely baseless is the opinion of those commentators, ancient as well as modern, who attempt to conclude from the above sentences that at the time of his exile Jehoiachin was childless and that his sons were born at the time of his release from prison thirty-seven years later. One of Weidner's above mentioned tablets of the year 592 B.C., mentions distinctly five sons of Jehoiachin and there is no logical necessity to fix the date of their birth after the exile.

The above cited prophetic assertion was apparently intended not only to disqualify Jehoiachin himself from kingship, but to exclude his entire posterity.

When, after some decades, one of his descendants was chosen nevertheless as the nation's ruler, this ancient prophecy was intentionally referred to again, just to annul it. Thus were the words of Haggai to Zerubbabel: "In that day, saith the Lord of hosts, will I take thee, O Zerubbabel, my servant, the son of Shealtiel, saith the Lord, and will make thee as a signet: for I have chosen thee, saith the Lord of hosts." (Haggai II, 23).

Moreover, Jeremiah set the illegitimacy of Jehoiachin as king on a more secure foundation by denying the right of succession to all the descendants of Jehoiakim, his father: "Therefore thus saith the Lord of Jehoiakim king of Judah, He shall have none to sit upon the throne of David," etc. (Jer. XXXVI, 30). The conclusion of Jeremiah as to the illegitimacy of the rule between the two exiles is unambiguous.

It remains for as then to clarify the other side of the problem, to prove the authorization of Zedekiah's rule by this prophet. There is no need of much argument here as the attitude of Jeremiah toward Zedekiah is well known to have been constantly sympathetic though he often reproved from the king severely. Even during the bitter critical days, when the Babylonian was besieging the capital and only Lachish and Azekah were holding their own against the enemy, he remained faithful to Zedekiah, revealing to him the path to salvation if only he would repent: "Yet hear the word of the Lord, O Zedekiah king of Judah. Thus saith the Lord of thee, Thou shalt not die by the sword; but thou shall die in peace: and with the burnings of thy fathers, the former kings which were before thee, so shall they burn odours for thee, and they will lament thee saying Ah Lord," etc. (Jer. XXXIV, 4–5). These words are of greater importance if we consider that in the prophet's vision of a king's final fate is expressed the essence of his opinion on the king's character. Thus Jehoiakim was condemned by him to an "Ass's Burial" and was not to be lamented honourably with exclamations: "הוֹי" "אָדוֹן (Ah Lord') as Zedekiah deserved. Indeed, the tragic personality of this last king of David's House was never forsaken by the prophet even at the most crucial moments.

For further clarification of this point let us once more reflect upon the words dedicated by the prophet to the vision of the Messianic King in Chapter XXIII:

"Behold, the days came, saith the Lord that I will raise unto David a righteous Branch and a King shall reign and prosper and shall execute judgement and justice in the earth. In his days Judah shall be saved and Israel shall dwell safely: and this is the name whereby he shall be called, The Lord our Righteousness." (Jer. XXIII, 5–6.)[6] Justly have some scholars pointed out the fact that the historical connection between this delineation of the Messiah and the personality of King Zedekiah cannot be overlooked.[7]

The problem arises here of how to explain this fact. It seems to me that we are bound to search for a solution differing from the one proposed by various scholars. Jeremiah probably does not refer in the above cited phrase to Zedekiah, connecting his name (as assumed by some) with a Messianic aspiration. Such a view is in distinct contrast to the idealistic outlook of prophets, which makes it irrelevant to connect an aspiration with a materially living object or person. On the contrary, it is more logical to suppose that the process was reversed, that the change of the name Mattaniah to Zedekiah upon his ascent to the throne, was a subsequent result of Jeremiah's prophecy on King Messiah, and, what is more probable, the new name was imposed with obvious intent. As might be logically deduced from this supposition we detect in Zedekiah from his very first appearance on the arena of history, a true and loyal disciple of Jeremiah and his group of true prophets. And not of least

---

[6] Compare the difference in the version of the Messiah's name and the addition in the LXX: Ἰωσέδεκ ἐν τοῖς προφήταις.

[7] Cf. J. Klausner, הרעיון המשיחי, 2nd ed., 1927, pp. 64–65.

significance is the fact that the very interpretation of the new name given to him צִדְקִיָּהוּ. Zedekiah points at devotion to one of the basic ideas of the great prophet: צֶדֶק—Justice. This close intimacy between the new name acquired by the king and the prophetic primary idea establishes their mutual spiritual kinship from the very outset.

In conclusion we may add some observations on the political conduct of Zedekiah. Our above analysis of the internal dispute over the legitimacy of the king during the last decade of the monarchy in Judah requires also a more thorough comprehension of Zedekiah's ways and methods. Probably, the reaction of Zedekiah to this quarrel and his endeavour to pacify his personal opponents, who, as mentioned above, included the most virulent enemies of Babylonia, give us the clue to the paradoxical behaviour of the king which eventually placed him as leader of his own antagonists. This may possibly be the most acceptable explanation of the paradox as to why Zedekiah finally took over the leadership of the rebellion against Babylonia, the very power that had placed him on the throne and thanks to whom he succeeded in maintaining his rule for a comparatively long period of time. Seeing the order of events in this light, enables us more easily to defend Zedekiah's unwise steps which brought disaster upon him and his people. It may also help us to discard the traditionally accepted doctrine of the lack of courage and fickleness of character in the last king of the House of David, by affording a clearer appreciation of the psychological background to his behaviour.

EXCURSUS

24

LONGEVITY: BIBLICAL CONCEPTS AND SOME
ANCIENT NEAR EASTERN PARALLELS*

This paper will consider two aspects of the concept of longevity in the Bible, with occasional comparisons to ancient Near Eastern literature: (1) the Biblical assessment of what constitutes a full life-span; and (2) longevity as a human ideal, and as a function of religious and moral behavior.[1]

The Bible displays a varied vocabulary for describing longevity. Aside from *zāqēn* ("old") and *ziqnāh* ("old age"), the following idioms occur: *'ōrek yāmîm* (lit. "length of days"); *yāmîm rabbîm* (lit. "many days"); *śᵉba' yāmîm* (lit. "sated with days"); *mᵉlē' yāmîm* (lit. "full of days"); and as opposed to these, *qᵉṣar yāmîm* (lit. "short of days"). Also, *bā' bayyāmîm* ("advanced in years"); and *śēbāh ṭôbāh* ("a ripe old age"). Verbal forms include *haᵃ'rēk yāmîm* ("to endure long"; lit. "to lengthen days"); *harbôt yāmîm* (lit. "to increase days"); and *hôsēp yāmîm* (lit. "to add days"). A few years ago, the expression *'rk. ymm.* (*'ōrek yāmîm?*) turned up in one of the Hebrew inscriptions from Kuntillet 'Ajrud, from the late 9th or early 8th century B.C.E.[2]

Several of the phrases above have exact counterparts both in other West Semitic languages, and in Akkadian.[3] To mention one recent

---

* This article was originally published in: *AfO*, Beiheft 19 (1982), 215–224.

[1] The question of longevity in the Bible and ancient Near Eastern literature still awaits a comprehensive study, but on life-span in general, cf. the still useful L. Dürr, *Die Wertung des Lebens im Alten Testament und im antiken Orient* (Münster, 1926). For the Bible, see provisionally the recent, valuable contributions of J. Scharbert, "Das Alter und die Alten in der Bibel," *Saeculum*, 30 (1979), 338–354; J. Maier, *ibid.*, 355–364. The present study will exclude the life spans of mythical proportions attributed to primordial generations in the Bible.

Biblical quotations (except for those noted as "lit.") follow the new Jewish Publication Society translation.

[2] See Z. Meshel, *Kuntillet 'Ajrud*, Israel Museum Catalogue, no. 175 (Jerusalem, 1978), "The Inscriptions," section D. For *brk* Meshel now reads *'rk*. Thus the words preserved in the line in question are:] . . . *'rk. ymm. wyśb 'w* . . . [. *For the last* word, read rather *wyśb'w*, as in the Biblical expression *'ōrek yāmîm 'aśbîᵉēhû* (Ps. 91:16).

[3] Apart from the dictionaries of Hebrew and other Semitic languages, see also H. Tawil, *Orientalia*, 43 (1974), 48–50, who cites various examples from Hebrew, Ugaritic, Phoenician, Aramaic, and Akkadian.

discovery, the expressions *lm'rk ywmwh wlkbr šnwh* ("to lengthen his days and increase his years"; cf. Job 15:10); *lm'rk ḥywh* ("to lengthen his life") appear in a 10th(?) century B.C.E. Aramaic inscription from Tell Faḥariyya.[4] As for the Akkadian vocabulary, a tablet from Sultantepe categorizes the stages of life from age 40 through age 90: 40—*lalûtu* ("prime of life"); 50—*ūmū kurûtu* ("short life"); ˹60˺—*meṭlûtu* ("maturity"); 70—*ūmū arkûtu* ("long life"); [80]—*šībūtu* ("old age"); 90—*littūtu* ("extreme old age").[5] As already recognized, a division of life into stages in a similar manner occurs in Pirqe Aboth 5:21ff.

Interestingly, another such delineation of the "ages of man" is found in an Egyptian source of the Ptolemaic period:

(17,21)	The life that approaches the peak, two-thirds of it are lost.	
(22)	He (man) spends ten years as a child before he understands death and life.	[*i.e.*, age 10]
(23)	He spends another ten years acquiring the work of instruction by which he will be able to live.	[*i.e.*, age 20]
(18,1)	He spends another ten years gaining and earning possessions by which to live.	[*i.e.*, age 30]
(2)	He spends another ten years up to old age before his heart takes counsel.	[*i.e.*, age 40]
(3)	There remain sixty years of the whole life which Thoth has assigned to the man of god.	[*i.e.*, age 100][6]

---

[4] Lines 7–8 and 14. The Aramaic of this bilingual inscription is to be published by P. Bordreuil. The Akkadian equivalents to the above are *urruk ūmīšu, šum' ud šanātīšu* (lines 10–11) and *urruk palûšu* (line 21).*)

[5] STT 400, rev., lines 45–47; see CAD L, 220. *s.v. littūtu*; and cf. J. Nougayrol, RA, 62 (1986), 96; A.W. Sjöberg, ZA, 64 (1974), 164. See now M. Weinfeld, *B. Ben Yehuda Festschrift* (ed. B.Z. Lurie, Tel Aviv, 1981), 312–317 (Hebrew). Weinfeld, following Nougayrol, still reads the Akkadian text as "60—*belûtu* ('lordship')," instead of *meṭlûtu*, as correctly read by Sjöberg. On the latter term, see CAD M/II, 45. The reading *mētellûtu* ('excellence'; *ibid.*, 43) is also possible for this broken word, as kindly pointed out to me by R. Borger.

[6] My thanks to Prof. H. Polotsky, who drew my attention to this text, Papyrus Insinger. It is cited here in the translation of M. Lichtheim, *Ancient Egyptian Literature, III* (Berkeley, 1980), 199. Lichtheim points out that if the 40 years described in detail are understood as equal to the lost two-thirds of life (line 21), the peak of life comes at age 60. This would conform roughly to the outlook of the Akkadian text cited above (60—*meṭlûtu* ["maturity"]), but not to that of Pirqe Aboth (60—*ziqnāh* "old age").

I

Only five individuals in the Bible are depicted, at their deaths, as having attained extreme old age, as specified by one or more of the above expressions: (1) Abraham: "You shall be buried at a ripe old age" (Gen. 15:15); "And Abraham breathed his last, dying at a good, ripe age, old and contented" (Gen. 25:8). (2) Isaac: "he breathed his last and died . . . in ripe old age" (lit.: "old and contented"; Gen. 35:29). In contrast to Abraham, who died at the age of 175, and Isaac, who died at 180, Jacob complains, in his dialogue with the Pharaoh, about the shortness of his life—he was then 130 years old, and he died at 147 (Gen. 47:8–9). (3) Gideon: "Gideon died . . . at a ripe old age. . . ." (Jud. 8:32);[7] (4) David: "He died at a ripe old age, having enjoyed long life . . ." (I Chron. 29:28; cf. 23:1, and I Kings 1:1); (5) Job: "So Job died old and contented" (Job 42:17).

Apart from these characters, of whom three (Abraham, Isaac, and Job) belong to the realm of legend, it is said also of Joshua, of Samuel, and of the high priest Jehoiada that they lived exceptionally long lives (Josh. 13:1; 23:1–2; I Sam. 8:1; 12:2; II Chron. 24:15). The advanced age is not surprising in the case of Joshua, who appears among the heroic figures of Israel's photo-history. (He died at 110 [Josh. 24:29; Jud. 2:8], like Joseph—the ideal age in Egyptian tradition.) But it is astonishing in the case of Jehoiada who, living in the 9th century B.C.E., attained, we are told (though only by the Chronicler; see above), the remarkable age of 130.

Moreover, the Bible may register an individual's extreme longevity by recording the generations of his descendants who are born in his own lifetime. One such example among the figures above is Job, of

---

The maximal age according to this papyrus (as well as other Egyptian sources) is 100 years, while the ideal lifetime in the Egyptian view was 110 years. For this latter figure as the sum of 100 + 10 years—that is, a century plus a serene bonus granted to the worthy—see E. Hornung, "Zeitliches Jenseits," *Eranosjahrbuch*, 47 (1978).

[7] The following circumstances point in fact to Gideon's advanced age at the time of his death: During his war with the Midianites, he was middle aged, judging by the fact that Jether, his first-born, at that time already bore arms (Jud. 8:20). Secondly, Gideon married into an aristocratic Shechemite family, certainly only *after* his victory over the Midianites, which brought him renown, and also saved Shechem (Jud. 9:17). His subsequent rule must have lasted a considerable time, for Abimelech, the offspring of this union, was already a grown man at the time of his father's death. The same is true of David, who was about 70 when he died (II Sam. 5:4).

whom it is said, "Afterward, Job lived one hundred and forty years, to see four generations of sons and grandsons" (Job 42:16). In this, as in several other respects, the portrayal of Job in the narrative framework of his story (prologue, epilogue) resembles that of the Israelite Patriarchs.[8] Similarly, "Joseph lived to see children of the third generation of Ephraim; the children of Machir son of Manasseh were likewise born upon Joseph's knees (Gen. 50:23). Thus within his own lifetime Joseph saw his own fourth generation descendants, through both Ephraim and Manasseh.

Indeed, the idea of the fourth generation as a maximum life span is grounded in reality, as two examples from extra-Biblical sources attest. In an Aramaic inscription from Nerab in northern Syria (7th century B.C.E.), the priest Si'-gabbari states: "Because of my right-eousness before him, he [the god] afforded me a good name, and prolonged my days . . . On the day I died, my mouth was not closed to words, and with my eyes I was beholding children of the fourth generation (*bny rbʿ*)."[9] That is to say, at the end of his life he saw (Aramaic *ḥzy*; note the Hebrew synonym *rʾy* in the Biblical exam-ples cited above) children belonging to his fourth generation, griev-ing at their impending loss (of him). Another example is found in a neo-Babylonian inscription from Harran, attributed to Adad-guppi', the aged mother of Nabonidus (mid-6th century B.C.E.). Adad-guppi', who died at the extreme age of 104, eulogizes herself "I saw my [great-] great-grandchildren, up to the fourth generation, in good health, and (thus) had my fill extreme old age."[10] The point is, then, that in these cases, persons blessed with long life could see their great-grandchildren with their own eyes.

---

[8] For other similarities between Job and the Patriarchs of Israel, see B. Mazar, *Zion*, 11 (1946), 1–16 (Hebrew); S. Spiegel, *Louis Ginzberg Jubilee Volume* (New York, 1945), 305–355. The latter stresses Job's righteousness, through which his descen-dants were saved from destruction.

[9] See J.C.L. Gibson, *Textbook of Syrian Semitic Inscriptions*, II (Oxford, 1975), 97f. H. Tawil, in his remarks on this inscription (see above, n. 3, pp. 63–64) points out the various references regarding the fourth generation. However, he is concerned with a different aspect, namely the usage of the verbs *rʾy* and *ḥzy* ("to see") in these instances.

[10] For the publication of this inscription, see C.J. Gadd, *AnSt*, 8 (1958), 50f., lines 33/4. The editor still translates *littūtu* as "offspring," but in the meantime the true meaning has been established as "extreme old age"; cf. CAD L, 220; Oppenheim *apud* ANET[3], 561. On the Aramaic character of the Harran Inscriptions and their relation to the Nerab stela, cf. B. Landsberger, *Halil Edhem Volume* (Ankara, 1947), 140ff.

It seems that the idea of the fourth generation as the maximum
life span is the basis for the divine admonition to the sinner that he
will not escape retribution even into his descendants' lifetimes. This
warning is repeated verbatim three times in the Bible: ". . . visiting
the guilt of the fathers upon the children, upon the third (*šillēšîm*)
and fourth generations (*ribbēʿîm*) . . ." (Ex. 20:5; Num. 14:18; Deut. 5:9)
and, with a slight expansion, it occurs a fourth time: "visits the iniquity of fathers upon children and children's children, upon the third
and fourth generations" (Ex. 34:7). Presumably, the text's intention
is not that justice should be exacted upon succeeding generations as
such, à la "The fathers have eaten sour grapes, and the children's
teeth are set on edge," but rather, specifically upon those generations whom the sinner could conceivably expect to live to see. If he
meets no other retribution, he may yet be punished by witnessing
the affliction of his dear ones.[11] By contrast, Job, the "righteous man"
(Ezek. 14:14), Si'-gabbari, Adad-guppi', and others like them derive
enjoyment from seeing their great-grandchildren flourish.

The notion that punishment may be manifest as late as the fourth
generation certainly illuminates the enigmatic statement, in the
covenant between Abraham and God: "And they [Abraham's descen-
dants] shall return here in the fourth generation, for the iniquity of
the Amorites will not be fulfilled until then" (Gen. 15:16). This passage has been interpreted in various ways. It may be assumed that
we have here a vestige of a divergent tradition concerning the return
of Abraham's fourth generation from Egypt to Canaan. At that stage,
which evidently corresponds to the fourth generation of Amorites,
the latter will be destroyed (= punished) (cf. Amos 2:9–10), since
their sin is as yet incomplete in Abraham's time.[12] Such a tradition
may be intimated in Jacob's valediction to Joseph: "I give you one
portion (*šᵉkem*) . . . which I wrested from the Amorites with my sword
and bow" (Gen. 48:21–22).[13] Joseph, Abraham's fourth generation,

---

[11] See, e.g., D.Z. Hoffmann, *Deuteronomium*, I (Tel Aviv, 1959), 87–88 (Hebrew).

[12] See esp. B. Jacob, *Genesis* (Berlin, 1934), 400f. He follows Naḥmanides in posit-
ing that the "fourth generation" in v. 16 refers to the Amorites rather than to the
Israelites. Naḥmanides had already suggested a connection between the fourth
generation here and the stipulations of Mosaic law. Some scholars equate the four
generations with the "400 years" of v. 13, suggesting that a generation here was
calculated as 100 years (which seems unlikely). See, e.g., W.F. Albright, BASOR,
163 (1961), 50f.

[13] Regarding a remnant of a divergent tradition (contradicting Genesis 34) according to which Jacob himself conquered Shechem, and furthermore from the Amorites,

will be accorded a special portion in his ancestral land, at the expense of the Amorites, by dint of his father's conquest.

The assessment of longevity by a standard of four generations matches the Bible's realistic appraisal of maximal life expectancy: "The span of our life is seventy years, or, given the strength, eighty years" (Ps. 90:10). A figure of 70 years (and even more so, 80 years), would reasonably allow for the birth and even the coming to maturity of the fourth generation in a man's lifetime.[14] In the light of what has been said above, the specification of 70 years may therefore evoke the Mosaic scheme of divine retribution.

This argument offers a rationale for the stipulation of 70 years for the duration of national catastrophe, in two separate instances in the Bible: (a) Seventy years is the term of the Babylonian exile and of Jerusalem's desolation in Jeremiah's prophecies (Jer. 25:11–12; 29:10; referred to in II Ch. 36:21 and Dan. 9:2; cf. Zech. 1:12; 7:5). (b) Isaiah states: ". . . Tyre shall remain forgotten for seventy years, equaling the lifetime of one king," until God restores Tyre to His favor (Is. 23:15–18).[15] Some scholars, in light of the verse from Psalms cited above, already dismiss a literal interpretation of 70 years in Jeremiah, and take it as a round figure, signifying a complete life-cycle.[16] Obviously, no member of the sinning generation can then survive the catastrophe to see the next generation's redemption. Thus, "70 years" may equal "the fixed term of divine punishment," which according to the Pentateuch extends into the fourth generation.

In any event, it is of significance that the formulaic "70 years of catastrophe" finds a precise counterpart in an Assyrian source, as several scholars long ago pointed out.[17] Some of Esarhaddon's inscrip-

---

see, inter alia: E. Meyer, *Die Israeliten und ihre Nachbarstämme* (Halle, 1906), 227f.; cf. G. von Rad, ATD, 4 (Göttingen, 1953), 366.

[14] L. Köhler, *Der hebräische Mensch* (Tübingen, 1953), 48ff., calculates that in ancient times, a father would be 19 years old at the birth of his first child, and consequently 57 at the birth of his first great-grandchild, a rather low figure in comparison to modern averages.

[15] The oracle regarding Tyre remains opaque, and may go back to an ancient source now lost. On emendation of the obscure כימי מלך אחד to בימי מלך אחר, see O. Kaiser, ATD, 18 (Göttingen, 1973), 137, n. 1, and H. Wildberger, *Jesaja* 13–27 (BK X/2; Neukirchen-Vluyn, 1978), 879ff.

[16] On the significance of 70 years of the Babylonian exile, see commentaries on Jeremiah, *ad loc.*; and in addition, P.R. Ackroyd, JNES, 17 (1958), 23–27; and R. Borger, *ibid.*, 18 (1959), 74. For the re-interpretation of the passages from Jeremiah in the Books of Daniel and Chronicles, see O. Plöger, *Festschrift F. Baumgärtel* (Erlangen, 1959), 124–130; M. Fishbane, JBL, 99 (1980), 356ff.

tions describe the destruction of Babylon and the exile of its inhabitants, which according to the god Marduk's original sentence, was supposed to have lasted 70 years (but the god relented and lightened the punishment).

II

We have seen that the Bible presents a factual assessment of biological age, mentions exceptionally long-lived individuals; it also offers stock descriptions of the hardships and infirmities of old age (see especially Ecc. 12:1–7; cf. II Sam. 19:36, and Ps. 71, among others). But, as is to be expected, Biblical literature (and ancient Near Eastern literature generally) treats life span as an expression of moral and religious evaluation, long life a divine reward, and short life a punishment. Insofar as it is possible to generalize, the Bible's view is not deterministic, as if the length of a person's life were predestined.[18] On the contrary, longevity is explicitly the outcome of love of God and observance of His laws," . . . for thereby you shall have life and shall long endure . . ." (Deut. 30:20; cf. 32:47). In contradistinction to the notion among other nations and religious groups, that "he whom the gods love, dies young,"[19] the Bible considers longevity desirable, as witness the Psalmist's words regarding a man facing death: "I will let him live to a ripe old age . . ." (Ps. 91:16).[20]

The very fact that longevity is conceptualized in the Bible as contingent upon proper religious and moral behaviour serves as an effective educational device, promoting compliance with divine commandments. Several Mosaic laws, accompanied by the promise of

---

[17] The first to recognize this parallel was D.D. Luckenbill, AJSL, 41 (1924–25), 167, and cf. R. Borger (previous note). For the Assyrian sources see the latter's *Die Inschriften Asarhaddons* (Graz, 1956), 15 and *BiOr*, 21 (1964), 144.

[18] For a refutation of such a deterministic view of life span, based in part on Biblical sources, see *Maimonides über die Lebensdauer—Ein unediertes Responsum* (herausgegeben . . ., G. Weil; Basel, 1953); and now the Hebrew edition annotated by M. Schwartz (Tel Aviv, 1979).

[19] See, e.g., the general comment of A. Bertholet, *Deuteronomium* (KHC; Freiburg i. B., 1899), 18, on Deut. 4:26. For this well known saying of the Greek poet Menander (latter half of the 4th century B.C.E.), see Plutarch, *Consolatio ad Apollonium*, ch. 34; and Latin translation in Plautus, *Bacchides*, IV, 7, 18.

[20] For Heb. *'ōrek yāmîm aśbî'ēhû*, note the parallel phrase in Akkadian: *littūta (balāṭa, etc.) šebû/ šubbû*; CAD L, 220b.

long life, are addressed to the individual; others, to the nation as a
whole. Some are highly specific (see below); most are general exhor-
tations to observe the Law (so always in Deuteronomy; cf. 4:40; 5:30;
6:2; 11:9; 11:21; 32:47). By contrast, lack of fear of God, and transgression of His laws, bring about shortened life, for the nation:
". . . you shall soon perish from the land . . . you shall not long endure
in it . . ." (Deut. 4:26; cf. 30:18), or for the individual, as in the
proverb, "The fear of the Lord prolongs life, while the years of the
wicked will be shortened" (Pr. 10:27). The latter motif is also well-
known in ancient Near Eastern literature. A concrete, historical
instance is to be found in the divine sentence pronounced on the
priestly house of Eli, after his sons' affront to the cult: ". . . I will
break your power and that of your father's house, and there shall
be no elder in your house . . . there will never be an elder in your
house" (I Sam. 2:31–32), and the two culprits will die in the prime
of life.

Four specific commandments in the Torah carry the explicit promise
of long life upon their fulfillment: (1) The best known is the fifth of
the Ten Commandments, "Honor your father and your mother, that
you may long endure . . ." (Ex. 20:12; cf. the parallel version in Deut.
5:16, with its slight, but significant addition, "that you may fare
well").[21] Conversely, in Akkadian wisdom literature: "A man who
does not fear his father will perish quickly." (2) Less clear is the reasoning behind the commandment concerning sparing the mother
bird: ". . . do not take the mother together with her young. Let the
mother go and take only the young, in order that you may fare well
and have a long life" (Deut. 22:6–7). Is this commandment, whose
motives seem to involve humane sentiments, somehow connected with
that to honor one's parents, as commmentators generally suggest?[22]

(3) Another commandment concerns honesty in trade: "You must
have completely honest weights and completely honest measures, if
you are to endure long on the soil that the Lord your God is giving you" (Deut. 25:15). In a similar vein, Proverbs enjoins: ". . . he

---

[21] On this commandment, see recently R. Albertz, ZAW, 90 (1978), 348–374.
For the Akkadian source quoted subsequently, see p. 363. On the characteristic
Deuteronomistic addition, see M. Weinfeld, *Deuteronomy and the Deuteronomic School*
(Oxford, 1972), 308f. (The commandment was regarded by some medieval exegetes
as being addressed to the nation as a whole; and see Dürr [above, n. 1], 21ff.)

[22] Already proposed by medieval exegetes; among modern commentators cf.
Hoffmann (above, n. 11), II (1961), p. 429; also, Bertholet (above, n. 19), 68.

who spurns ill-gotten gains will live long" (Pr. 28:16). Likewise, in Babylonian wisdom literature, "the honest merchant . . . . is pleasing to Šamaš, and the latter will prolong his life."[23]

(4) Finally, the Law of the King, in Deuteronomy 17, ends with the advice: "Thus he will not act haughtily toward his fellows or deviate from the Instruction to the right or to the left, to the end that he and his descendants may reign long in the midst of Israel" (Deut. 17:20). As befits the political context, the emphasis here is on a long reign, rather than a long life, for the humble and observant monarch.

III

Length of reign, as against length of life, becomes an issue in the case of Solomon; God promises him just after his accession: "And I will . . . grant you long life, if you will walk in My ways and observe My laws and commandments . . ." (I Kings 3:14). The pursuit of longevity for the monarch is a widespread motif in the ancient Near East and frequently appears in royal petitions to patron deities. Particularly close in time and location to Solomon, kings of Byblos entreat their gods to grant them long life.[24] An inscription of King Yeḥimilk (mid-10th century B.C.E.) states:

> May Baalšamem and the Lady of Byblos and the Assembly of the Holy Gods of Byblos prolong the days and years of Yeḥimilk over Byblos, for [he is] a righteous and upright king before the Holy Gods of Byblos!

The king emphasizes his righteous and upright behavior as justification for his plea for long life—a motif we noted above in the Aramaic inscription of Si'-gabbari, from Nerab. In the following inscriptions from Byblos (from the second half of the 10th century B.C.E.), this statement of justification is absent; "May the Lady of Byblos prolong the days and years of Elibaal over Byblos"; "May the Lady of Byblos prolong the days and years of Šiptibaal over Byblos."

---

[23] See W.G. Lambert, *Babylonian Wisdom Literature* (Oxford, 1960), 133, lines 107ff. (Šamaš Hymn). The preceding lines speak of a dishonest merchant and deceptive scales.

[24] See KAI, nos. 4–7.

Similar petitions for long life are found elsewhere in the ancient Near East, and they are especially common in Akkadian literature.[25] We can present here only a few examples at random from among the multitude of inscriptions in Akkadian, from the early 2nd millennium to the middle of the 1st millennium B.C.E.—though of course this literary/religious tradition extended over a considerably longer span of time. Thus Yaḫdun-lim, king of Mari (ca. 1800 B.C.E.), in his Foundation Inscription for the temple of Šamaš, asks "May Šamaš . . . grant . . . to Yaḫdun-lim . . . a long and happy rule and everlasting years of abundance and happiness."[26] Over a century later, the goddess Ištar promises King Ammiditana of Babylon, who brings offerings to her and her consort, "an enduring, long life."[27] Skipping to the Neo-Babylonian period, we find many illustrations in inscriptions of Nebuchadnezzar II. One such petition, addressed to the god Marduk, reads: "May I attain old age within (the temple), and may I be fulfilled with extreme old age!" Another, addressed to Šamaš, states: "Under your just command, may I be fulfilled with extreme old age, life into far-off days . . . may my dynasty last long and flourish forever."[28]

---

[25] See the references cited by Tawil (above, n. 3), notes, pp. 49–50. For Akkadian in particular, see CAD L, 220, and H. Ringgren, ThWAT, II (1977), 878f.

For Hittite petitions concerning the longevity of a king see, e.g., Puduḫepa's entreaties for life and health for her husband Ḫattušili III; in H. Otten, *Puduḫepa— Eine hethitische Königin in ihren Textzeugnissen* (Wiesbaden, 1975), 22ff. For Egyptian hymnic literature (a subject beyond the present paper) on the longevity of kings, see, e.g., the following bibliographical references (courtesy I. Shirun-Grumach): H. Bonnet, *Reallexikon der ägyptischen Religionsgeschichte* (Berlin, 1952), 397f.; S. Morenz, *Ägyptische Religion* (Stuttgart, 1960), 74ff., and esp. the hyperbolic phrases concerning length of the pharaonic-divine reign collected in B. Birkstam, "Given Life Like Re Eternally—A Royal Epitheton," *Boreas* (*Uppsala Studies in Ancient Mediterranean and Near Eastern Civilizations*), 6 (1974), 15–35 (and there further literature).

[26] G. Dossin, *Syria*, 32 (1995), 16, col. IV:14–23: *Šamaš . . . ana Yaḫdunlim . . . palâm arkam ša ṭūb libbim u šanāt ḫegallim rīšātim ana ūmī dārûtim lišrukšum.*

[27] F. Thureau-Dangin, RA, 22 (1925), 173, lines 46/8: *dārâm balāṭam arkam, mādâtim šanāt balāṭim ana RN tušatlim.*

[28] On these documents, see: S. Langdon, VAB IV, no. 15, col. X:6–8 (p. 140): *ina qerbiša šībūti lukšud, lušbâ littūti;* no. 12, col. III:5–10 (p. 102): *ina qibītika kitti lušbâ littūti, balāṭam ana ūmī rūqūti . . . līriku lištēlipû palûa ana dārâti.* (For the last phrase, cf. CAD E, 87b, *s.v. elēpu*). For a German translation, see A. Falkenstein – W. von Soden, *Sumerische und Akkadische Hymnen und Gebete* (Zürich/Stuttgart, 1953), 283–285, 391 (nos. 27a, 28a). Von Soden there still translated *littūtu* as "Nachkommenschaft." See also the newer, French translation, M.J. Seux, *Hymnes et prières aux dieux de Babylonie et d'Assyrie* (Paris, 1976), 506f., 509f.

For additional pleas by Nebuchadnezzar to grant him long life, see: VAB IV, no. 1, col. III:43f.; no. 2, col. III:33ff., no. 3, col. II:23ff.; no. 4, col. II:19ff., no. 5, col. II:21ff.; *et passim.*

Clearly, Solomon's request of God in his dream at Gibeon[29] differs sharply from these stereotypical petitions. Omitting the standard "shopping list" of royal petitioners, Solomon asks *only* for an "understanding mind" that he may judge the people righteously—the latter, another motif which is well-known in Israel, and throughout the ancient Near East.

A negative rehearsal of stock royal petitions emerges from God's response to Solomon: ". . . you did not ask for long life, you did not ask for riches, you did not ask for the life of your enemies . . ." (I Kings 3:11).[30] The formulaic language of this text suggests that the Biblical historiographer was familiar with the conventional model (apparently in use also in Israel) for rulers' petitions of their deities. Evidence that in Israel the king did indeed request longevity is provided *inter alia* by a royal psalm: "He asked You for life; You granted it; a long life, everlasting" (Ps. 21:5; cf. 61:7). Note also Hezekiah's plea for his own life during his grave illness, and God's response: ". . . I have heard your prayer, I have seen your tears. . . . I will add fifteen years to your life" (II Kings 20:5–6; cf. Is. 38:5).[31]

The episode involving Solomon concludes on a note of divine benevolence. In addition to granting Solomon's specific request for an "understanding mind," God takes the initiative and promises, "And I also grant you what you did not ask for—both riches (*'ošer*) and glory (*kābôd*) all your life" (I Kings 3:13). Significantly, the defeat of Solomon's enemies is omitted here. The conditional promise of long life (*w^eha'^araktî 'et yāmêkā*, I Kings 3:14) noted above follows as a sort of climax, but Solomon later sinned, so although he reigned for forty years, he did not achieve longevity.[32]

---

[29] On Solomon's dream and God's answer, see commentaries on Kings, and esp. S. Zalevsky, "The Revelation of God to Solomon in Gibeon," *Tarbiz*, 42 (1973), 215–258 (Hebrew), and M. Garsiel, *B. Ben Yehuda Festschrift*, 1981 (191–217) (Hebrew). Both authors consider the Gibeon episode authentic, dating the composition to Solomon's own time, including the conditional promise of longevity for the king in the last verse (I Kings 3:14). This verse is usually taken as a late, Deuteronomic addition. See Zalevsky, pp. 232ff.; Garsiel, pp. 201ff.

[30] Contrast the Nebuchadnezzar inscriptions cited in note 28 above, all of which call, apart from longevity, for the defeat of enemies as well (as pointed out to me by my colleague Prof. M. Greenberg).

[31] See commentaries on the Books of Kings and Isaiah, *ad loc*. For a parallel case in Sumerian of a king pleading for recovery from illness and for long life, see W.W. Hallo, "The Royal Correspondence of Larsa: A Sumerian Prototype for the Prayer of Hezekiah?," *Kramer Anniversary Volume* (ed. B.L. Eichler, Neukirchen-Vluyn, 1976), 209–224.

[32] It is generally assumed that Solomon succeeded to the throne before age 20

The dialogue between Solomon and God appears to be cast in the mold of wisdom literature, as witness its close similarity to Proverbs 3, which deals with the praise of law and wisdom. The chapter opens: "My son, do not forget My teaching, but let your mind retain My commandments; for they will bestow on you length of days, years of life, and well-being" (Pr. 3:1–2). It then describes the intrinsic value of wisdom: "In her right hand is length of days (*'ōrek yāmîm*), in her left riches (*'ošer*) and honor (*kābôd*)" (Pr. 3:16). Wisdom, thus, offers precisely the same threefold promise—longevity, riches, and honor—which God held out to Solomon, "wisest of men," and which his father, David, had actually attained: "He died at a ripe old age, having enjoyed long life, riches and honor . . ." (I Chron. 29:28). Elsewhere, Proverbs places the highest emphasis on the connection between wisdom and life (Pr. 4:13; and cf. 3:18; 8:35; 13:14),[33] and significantly, on the direct correlation to longevity (Wisdom is speaking): "For through me your days will increase, and years be added to your life" (Pr. 9:11).

But lest we conclude that wisdom in turn increases with days, the Bible admits a certain skepticism: "Is wisdom in the aged and understanding in the long-lived?" (Job 12:12; cf. 32:7–9).

---

and thus died before age 60. See, e.g., S. Yeivin, *Encyclopedia Biblica*, VII (Jerusalem, 1976), 693 (Hebrew), who holds that Solomon was 16 years old at his accession. Solomon's relatively short life is in Zalevsky's opinion (above, n. 29, pp. 257ff.) the reason for the elimination of the divine promise of longevity from the parallel version in II Chron. 1:7ff. Indeed, Chronicles in general avoids portraying Solomon in any unfavorable light.

[33] On the casual relationship between wisdom and consequent life, and correspondingly, between foolish and evil behavior and consequent death, cf. the remarks in passing of J. Fichtner, *Die altorientalische Weisheit in ihrer israelitischen—jüdischen Ausprägung* (Giessen, 1933), 64f. and cf. Dürr (above, n. 1), 7ff.

*) [The inscriptions have in the meantime been published; for a preliminary fashion by A. Abou Assaf, see MDOG 113 (1981), p. 3–22.]

25

"YOU SHALL LOVE YOUR NEIGHBOR AS YOURSELF": A CASE OF MISINTERPRETATION?*

One of the fundamental commandments of the Pentateuch, about which Rabbi Akiva declared "This is a great principle in the Torah" (Genesis Rabbah 24,7), is the verse "(You shall not take vengeance or bear any grudge against the sons of your people), but you shall love your neighbor as yourself (וְאָהַבְתָּ לְרֵעֲךָ כָּמוֹךָ): I am the Lord" (Lev. 19:18). This dictum has been exemplary of Jewish morality and eventually characterized Christian faith as well (see Matthew 24:39 etc.; Luke 10:27 etc.), becoming over the course of history a watchword of these two great religions. It comes therefore as no surprise that this verse has been widely discussed by exegetes of both persuasions—Jew and Gentile alike. Recently it has even been the subject of a special monograph.[1]

Most of the exegetical debate about this commandment, consisting in Hebrew of only three words, has concentrated on the exact meaning of the two latter vocables רע and כמוך. רע has been understood variously as an upright person, a friend, a fellow Israelite or simply a fellow human-being regardless of nationality.[2] כמוך too, has been explained in several different ways such as "who resembles you," since the רע is a man who, like yourself, has also been created in the image of God.[3] In contrast to these two words, the verb ואהבת has been taken simply and unquestioningly at face value to mean "you shall love." This brief note aims at elucidating this latter concept, and will suggest a meaning differing from the accepted

---

* This article was originally published in: FS R. Rendtorff, Neukirchner Verlag, 1990, 111–115.

[1] H.P. Mathys, Liebe Deinen Nächsten wie Dich selbst. Untersuchungen zum alttestamentlichen Gebot der Nächstenliebe (Lev. 19,18), OBO 71 (1986). This book lists most of the previous studies of the subject. We refer the reader to it for the full scope of the problem and all the details.

[2] The New Testament expanded the concept of רע to include both foe and friend; see Matthew 5:43 etc.

[3] See Mathys, *op. cit.* (note 1), 6ff. with literature, especially M. Buber and E. Ullendorf.

interpretation, which dates back centuries at least to the time of Hillel in the Jewish traditions and of Jesus and Paul in the Christian.[4]

The first matter to be noticed, as several interpreters have indeed done, is that the verb אהב in this verse takes an indirect object לרעך, rather than the accusative את רעך as usually found in the Hebrew Bible.[5] The combination אהב ל appears in the Hebrew Bible in three other places: (1) In the present chapter, in a verse dependent on the one under discussion וְאָהַבְתָּ לוֹ כָּמוֹךָ, "and you shall love him as your-self" (Lev. 19:34); (2) In the account of Solomon's correspondence with Hiram King of Tyre כִּי אֹהֵב הָיָה חִירָם לְדָוִד כָּל־הַיָּמִים, "for Hiram always loved David" (1 Kgs. 5:15; English 5:1); (3) In a prophetic rebuke of King Jehoshaphat וּלְשֹׂנְאֵי יהוה תֶּאֱהָב, "Should you . . . love those who hate the Lord?" (2 Chr. 19:2). The use of אהב ל in the two latter passages has usually been ignored by scholars, at least when discussing the commandment in Leviticus. The question may be asked, however, whether the peculiar turn of expression typical of all these verses has any significance for determining the semantic range of the verb אהב, or whether the exceptional usage derives from some other factor.

Adhering to the literal meaning of the text (and ignoring the pecu-liar employment of the rare אהב ל), it has been customary to explain the commandment as meaning "You shall love your neighbor just as much as you love yourself." This understanding has been adopted consistently by ancient as well as modern Bible translations, yield-ing such English renditions as "But you shall love your neighbor as yourself" (RSV); "Love your fellow as yourself" (NJPS) or German renderings as "Du sollst deinen Nächsten lieben wie dich selbst" (ZB). Although this has been the most popular translation throughout the ages, there have been, nonetheless, certain ancient authorities and an even greater number of modern scholars who felt uneasy about the resultant adoration of self love (narcissism in Freudian termi-

---

[4] S.G. Quell/E. Stauffer, Art. ἀγαπάω, ThWNT I 20–55. 24, 43; O. Procksch/K.G. Kuhn, Art. ἅγιος, ThWNT I 87–116. 115; H. von Soden, Art. ἀδελφός, ThWNT I 144–146.

[5] Mathys, *op. cit.* (note 1), 5, does not attribute any significance to this linguistic distinction and regards the combination with lamed as a sign of late Biblical Hebrew and an Aramaism. On the other hand, D.Z. Hoffmann, Das Buch Leviticus II (1906), 43 (= Hebr. Transl. ³1954, 36), differentiates between the two usages: אהב ל is a love expressed by deeds, in particular deeds of loving kindness, which are within the capability of all people, while ואהבת את יהוה demands knowledge of God.

nology) or who saw this idea as an aberration of biblical thought.[6] Thus these interpreters tend to understand the verse as meaning "You shall treat kindly, lovingly, your neighbor, *for he is a human being like yourself*."

When attempting to clarify the meaning of the verb אהב in the verse under discussion, it is irrelevant which of the two interpretations mentioned above is adopted. For my part, I tend towards the first, literal meaning, which, as has been pointed out, is accepted by most ancient renderings (e.g. Onqelos *ad loc.* ותרחמיה לחברך כותך) as well as modern translations despite the considerations brought against it. The malaise which this interpretation is liable to engender is in any case eliminated by the interpretation to be proposed here. First of all, it should be noticed that the verb אהב only in frequently describes relationships between a man and his fellow,[7] while in the majority of cases it designates a person's relationship with God, a mans relationship with a woman, parents' relationships with their children, etc. We assume that in our verse and some additional ones as well the verb אהב has a nuance different than its usual one.

Indication of an alternative meaning may come from the passage in 2 Chr. 19:2 mentioned above. In this verse Jehoshaphat is rebuked by the prophet Jehu ben Hanani who asks scornfully "Should you help the wicked and *love* those who hate the Lord?" The two synonymous stichoi contain the parallelism of עזר and אהב and permit us to take "love" here (where אהב takes the indirect object ל) to mean "providing assistance" and "being useful."

It seems that the verse in Leviticus is also hospitable to a verb meaning "to be of use to," "to be beneficial to," "to assist," "to serve" or the like.[8] If so, a proper English translation would be something like "Be useful to your neighbor as to yourself." In German we

---

[6] See E. Ullendorf, Is Biblical Hebrew a Language? (1977), from which the English translation cited below is borrowed (*ibid.* 56). And see already M. Buber, Zwei Glaubensweisen (1950), 68ff. For criticism of Buber's approach see Th.C. Vriezen, Bubers Auslegung des Liebesgebots, Lev. 19,18b, ThZ 22 (1966), 1–11.

[7] See H. Rücker, Warum wird 'ahab (lieben) im Alten Testament selten zur Bezeichnung für Nächstenliebe gebraucht?, in: G. Hentschel u.a. (ed.), Dein Wort beachten—Alttestamentliche Aufsätze (1981) 9–15.

[8] Our verse was interpreted in this vein already by Malbim in his Hebrew commentary to Leviticus התורה והמצוה (1860): "... That he should try in all circumstances to be of utility to his fellow, both as regards his physical well-being and his material success just as he is of utility to himself, and he should not cause anything to befall him which he would want to avoid himself...." A like interpretation was

would suggest "Sei hilfreich/behilflich deinem Nächsten wie dir selbst." Such an interpretation will remove from the verb אהב the abstract flavor commonly attributed to it and will render to it a more concrete and pragmatic sense. To be sure, such a concrete meaning better suits the biblical conceptual world, as is the case with certain other supposedly "abstract" terms.

The understanding of אהב proposed here would seem at first glance to be precluded by the previous verse (Lev. 19:17) where we find "You shall not hate (לא תשנא) your brother in your heart, but you shall reason with your neighbor...." Taking the two as a pair presents us with apparent antithetic parallelism between the pair of words תשנא and ואהבת, which would then effectively guarantee that ואהבת is to be interpreted in the usual manner. But this conclusion is by no means obligatory, especially if we accept the assumption of several exegetes that Lev. 19:18 occupies a special position in the pericope, disassociating it from its immediate context.[9] Some see the commandment "Love your neighbor" as isolated from the rest of the pericope, while others consider the verse to contain a summary or explanation for the rest of the injunctions and prohibitions listed in Lev. 19:11ff. Still others view "Love your neighbor" to be the result of fulfilling the conditions stipulated in vss. 17–18, and the like.

If we have properly understood אהב in our verse, the question may be asked whether the other verses containing the exceptional combination אהב ל may also be explained anew as referring to being useful and providing services to the opposite party. Let us reexamine the verses mentioned above in light of the new proposal: (1) כמוך ואהבת לו (Lev. 19:34)—As mentioned above, this verse is derived from and dependent upon the one under consideration. As a consequence it is to be interpreted in a like manner, and its meaning will be "You shall be useful to him (your neighbor) as you are to yourself." (2) The observation that Hiram was "David's lover"

---

presented in modern times by Y. Kaufmann, The Religion of Israel, transl. and abridged by M. Greenberg (1960) 320: "... What is meant by this is not a mere state of mind, but its actualization in deeds of generosity and kindness." In the original Hebrew version of the book 'History of the Israelite Religion' II/2 (1945) 568, Kaufmann also refers to the love of the גר (sojourner) in Deut. 10:17–19, which includes providing him with bread and garment. On the other hand, even the most recent dictionary of biblical Hebrew adopts the accepted meaning; see W. Gesenius, Hebräisches und Aramäisches Handwörterbuch über das Alte Testament (18., völlig neubearb. Aufl. 1987, hrsg. von R. Meyer/H. Donner) s.v. אהב.

[9] Cf. Mathys, op. cit. (note 1) 3.

(1 Kgs. 5:15; English 5:1) has been made retrospectively from the vantage point of Solomon's reign. Hiram had certainly been useful to David and had helped him steadily and faithfully (cf. 2 Sam. 5:11),[10] so he can be said here to have been "helpful/useful/beneficial to David all the years." (3) 2 Chr. 19:2, concerning Jehoshaphat has already been discussed previously.

It is likely that the meaning of אהב proposed above, or a similar meaning is found at least once, but probably even more often, without the dative particle ל, namely where אהב takes the regular accusative particle. In the description of King Uzziah's works which included agricultural reforms throughout the Land we read "And he built watchtowers in the desert . . . farmers and vineyard keepers in the mountains and the Carmel, for he was an אֹהֵב אֲדָמָה (2 Chr. 26:10). Exegetes have usually passed over this surprising expression or have taken it simply to convey the "romantic" meaning "lover of the soil." In this spirit it is translated variously "for he loved husbandry" (RSV); ". . . for he was a lover of agriculture" (Moffatt);[11] ". . . for he loved the soil" (NJPS); ". . . er liebte nämlich den Landbau" (ZB). In contrast to this "anachronistic" understanding of the verse, it is more reasonable to view Uzziah as having invested his efforts in cultivating and fertilizing the land. It is these activities which are referred to by the expression אהב אדמה היה,[12] and this cannot be described merely as "love." It is certainly possible to find additional instances of the verb אהב (for instance Hos. 10:11 "Ephraim is a trained calf, אֹהַבְתִּי [י] לָדוּשׁ . . . you are *used* to threshing") with the tangible, concrete meaning proposed here rather than the usual meaning of Platonic love.

---

[10] The "love" in this passage is usually taken to refer to the political, diplomatic connection and the fostering of treaty relations between David and Solomon on the one side and Hiram, King of Tyre, on the other. For this usage see in particular W.L. Moran, The Ancient Near Eastern Background of the Love of God in Deuteronomy, CBQ 25 (1963) 77–87, esp. 78–81.

[11] J. Moffatt, The Old Testament. A New Translation (1924).

[12] A similar understanding was indicated already by the late Prof. Benno Landsberger in a lecture he gave in Chicago in 1965.

26

DISTANT LANDS AND CITIES AS A SPECIFIC CATEGORY
IN INTERNATIONAL RELATIONS IN THE BIBLE
AND IN THE ANCIENT NEAR EAST*

In the past I have touched upon the issue of the international status of a remotely situated city or country. I dealt, however, with the subject merely in passing,[1] now I intend to investigate it more thoroughly and adduce further examples.

In the Bible occur expressions such as distant land, distant city (or distant cities), a long way of, far-off place, distance. On the whole, these expressions refer to ordinary words in the sense of geographical, physical distance, occasionally even to distance in time,[2] but in some rare cases these expressions hint at a distinct diplomatic, political meaning. The classic case in the Bible where a distinction is made between near and distant cities in political or strategic relations, and which may serve as a kind of paradigm in international affairs, is to be found in the episode concerning the Conquest of Canaan, namely in the religious rules and the accompanying military laws of Deuteronomy 20: 15–18.[3] To the invading Israelites of Canaan, the remotely located foreign cities are less menacing than those nearby and are thus treated in a more restrained manner, i.e. by making a peace treaty with them, in contrast to the harsher treatment meted out to the other cities.

On the other hand it may occur that the expression "near-by way" does hint to a military menace, such as the description of the Exodus

---

* Now is being published in Hebrew in the FS S. Ahitub, eds. Sivan *et alii*, Beersheba.

[1] Many years ago in an article: A. Malamat, *VT* 5 (1955), pp. 10f.; and more recently A. Malamat, *Eretz Israel* 23 (A. Biran Volume), 1992, pp. 194/5 (Hebrew; English Abstract 153).

[2] See the root "דרך" in the dictionaries and espec. *THAT* 2 (1976), pp. 767ff.; *ThWAT* 7 (1993), pp. 490ff.; cf. now the word in a legal sense: F.M. Cross in ed. M. Fox *et alii*, *Texts, Temples and Traditions—A Tribute to M. Haran*, Winona Lake 1996, pp. 318ff.

[3] See, e.g., A Rofé, "The Laws of Warfare in the Book of Deuteronomy," *JSOT* 32 (1985), espec. pp. 28ff.; and see on Deut. 20:15ff. J.M. Tigay, *Deuteronomy (The JSP Torah)*, Philadelphia 1996, pp. 188–190.

of the Israelites in Ex. 13:17. The passage cautions the Israelites not to wander: "by the way of the land of the Philistines, although that was near, for God said: 'Lest the people repent when they see war and return to Egypt.'" The "way of the Philistines" signifies the northern route in Sinai, which runs parallel to the Mediterranien sea-shore. This route was fortified with a tight network of strong-holds by the Pharaohs of the 13th century B.C., the possible time of the Exodus.[4] Thus this route may easily have become a trap to the wandering Israelites. Yet the Biblical historiographer does not mention this argument, but only claims that God alone warns the Israelites to move on the near-by way and this expression, as stated above, hints at military danger.

The story of the Gibeonites in Joshua 9 is based on the above Deuteronomistic conception.[5] The Gibeonites according to their own testimony given to Joshua, came from a "distant-land" or even "from a very (מֵאֹד) distant land" (Jos. 9:6–9), a testimony which might be based on fact and not, like the present story, on sheer deception. It is possible that the origins of the Gibeonites, who at the 'time' of Joshua had already settled in central Palestine, lay in far-off Anatolia or in its vicinity. The Gibeonites considered themselves to be of Hiwwite stock (Jos. 9:7), which went back most likely to a northern ethnic element, advancing southwards into Syria and Palestine at the period of the destruction of the Hittite kingdom around 1200 B.C.[6] Yet, the author or the editor of the story in Joshua maintained a line of deception conforming to the Gibeonites' new area of settlement.

---

[4] See A. Malamat, "Exodus: The Egyptian Analogies," in eds. E.S. Frerichs, and L.H. Lesko, *Exodus: The Egyptian Evidence*, Winona Lake, IN, 1997, pp. 15–26 (= above chap. 5). See there (n. 8) references to A. Gardiner, "The Ancient Military Road between Egypt and Palestine," *JEA* 6 (1920), pp. 99–116; E.D. Oren, "Ways of Horos in North Sinai," *Egypt, Israel, Sinai*, Tel-Aviv 1987, pp. 69–119.

[5] On the connection between the military laws in Deuteronomy and the story of the Gibeonites see: Malamat, *VT* 5 (1955), p. 10 and n. 1; E. Kaufmann, *The Book of Joshua*, 2nd ed., Jerusalem 1958, p. 134; also the treatment of J. Blenkinsopp, "Are there Traces of the Gibeonites' Covenant in Deuteronomy?," *CBQ* 28 (1966), pp. 207–213; B. Halpern, "Gibeon: Israelite Diplomacy in the Conquest Era," *CBQ* 37 (1975), pp. 303–316; Ch. Schäfer-Lichtenberger, "Das gibeonitische Bündnis im Lichte deuteronomischer Kriegsgebote," *BN* 34 (1986), pp. 58–81.

[6] Some scholars assume that the Hiwwites grafted themselves on the Hurrians (the Septuagint reads here *Hori* instead of *Hiwwi*); cf. E.A. Speiser, *AASOR* 13 (1933), pp. 39f.; H.A. Hoffner in D.J. Wiseman (ed.), *Peoples of Old Testament Times*, Oxford 1973, p. 225; F.M. Bush, *IDB Supp.* (1976), pp. 423/4, s.v. Hurrians. The terms *Hori* and *Hiwwi* also interchange in the Bible. Apparently some of the "seven peoples of Canaan" came from the north (Anatolia) to Palestine in the 13th–12th centuries.

Nevertheless, the Israelites were forced, according to the storyteller, to make a peace treaty with the Gibeonites as if they were a people living in a country far from Palestine, instead of binding them by a treaty of submission as was usual with a place nearby. "Joshua established friendship with them; he made a pact with them to spare their lives . . ." (Jos. 9:15).

Close in time to the above event, according to the Biblical source, was the migration of part of the tribe of Dan from the central sector of Palestine (the inheritance of Dan) to its northeastern border and the conquest of the Canaanite city of Laish by the Danites (Judg. 18). From an historical-chronological point of view we may date this conquest to the twelfth century B.C., possibly to its first half. The recent excavations at Tel Dan prove that control of this site changed hands at that period.[7] The biblical historiographer explains the relatively easy fall of Laish to the Danites as follows: "There was none to come to rescue (i.e. of Laish) for it was distant from Sidon . . ." (Judg. 18:28; cf. v. 7: ". . . Moreover, they were distant from the Sidonians . . ."). That is, Laish "which dwelt carefree after the manner of the Sidonians" (Judg. 18:7) was far from the city of Sidon, which was located on the Phoenician coast. Thus the inhabitants of the city did not consider themselves obliged to rush to the help of Laish, even though there may have been from the outset mutual legal obligations between the two cities.

A last case dawn from the Bible, which is based on the political category of a "distant country," may have some historical reality to it. It concerns the behaviour of Hezekiah, king of Judah, upon the arrival of a Babylonian delegation in Jerusalem sent by King Merodach-Baladan (2 Kings 20:12–14 = Isa. 39:1–8).[8] Diplomatic contact between Judah and Babylonia at that time (between 705–703 B.C. or rather during the latter year) is possible, since they were both vassal states under the sway of Sennacherib, king of Assyria and both would attempt to enter alliances to rid themselves of the foreign yoke.[9]

---

[7] See A. Biran, *Biblical Dan*, Jerusalem 1994, pp. 134f.

[8] On the story of Merodach-Baladan in the Book of 2 Kings 20 see the commentaries: B. Würthwein, *Die Bücher der Könige (ATD)*, Göttingen 1984, pp. 435–37; M. Cogan & Tadmor, *II Kings (AnBi)*, Garden City, N.Y., 1988, pp. 258ff. For the Book of Isaiah 39 see the commentary: O. Kaiser, *Der Prophet Jesaja (Kap. 13–39) (ATD)*, Göttingen 1973, pp. 323–27; cf. the Biblical story and the veracity of the prophecy in Isaiah B. Oded, "The Babylonian Embassy Narrative . . .," *Shnaton—An Annual for Biblical and Anc. Near-Eastern Studies* 9 (1985), pp. 115–126 (Hebrew).

[9] On the historical background in Mesopotamia and on the date of the Babylonian

Hezekiah, therefore, welcomed the Babylonian messengers, especially since they were purportedly visiting him on his sick bed, and he opened (פתח) his palace in Jerusalem to them, with all its treasures and weaponry.[10] This incident is similar to the tale of Solomon and the Queen of Sheba who also came to Jerusalem from a distant land (i.e. from southern Arabia). Solomon, too, displaced before her the enormous treasures assembled at his place (1 Kings 10:1ff.). King Hezekiah was sharply rebuked by the Prophet Isaiah for his deeds (Isa. 39:1ff.). But Hezekiah justifies himself thus: "From a distant land they came to me from Babylon" (2 Kings 20:14 = Isa 39:3), i.e. because Babylon is so remote, there is no danger for Judah.

The assumption of a specific diplomatic usage of the expression "distant land" in the Bible may be supported by ancient Near Eastern sources, although the examples found so far are few and may be increased in the course of time. A convenient source for our subject is the El-Amarna archive (of the 14th century B.C.) including correspondence with distant rulers.[11] Thus in Letter 7 of this archive Burnaburiash II, king of Babylonia, expresses his annoyance to Amenhotep IV (?), i.e. Echnaton, king of Egypt, that despite the illness which has befallen the king of Babylonia, the ruler of Egypt has not asked after his well-being as is customary between allies (ll. 8–18)[12] and as Merodach-Baladan enquired after Hezekiah. The envoy of the king of Egypt justifies himself by pleading that the lack of attention was caused by the very lengthy journey, between the two countries (ll. 19–22: *mātu rūqatu*; 1.32: *girru rūqatu*). Countering this, Babylonia's king expresses his astonishment: "Is (my brother's) land far or near?" (l. 27: *mātu rūqtu u qerubtum*). In the further exchange

---

delegation to Jerusalem see in addition to the bibliography in 7: P. Artzi, Merodach-Baladan, *Enc. Biblica* 5 (1968), cols. 446–449 (Hebrew) and cf. R.H. Sack, Merodach-Baladan, *ABD* 4 (1992), pp. 714/5 and there references to the articles of J.A. Brinkman.

[10] Among the magazines and treasures in his palace, Hezekiah showed the Babylonians his House of *Nekotoh* (2 Kings 20:13). The latter term is identical with the Akkadian word *bit nakkamti* (cf. *CAD N*, 182), "treasury."

[11] The most recent edition of the El-Amarna archive is W.L. Moran, *Les lettres d'El Amarna* (English edition *The Amarna Letters*, Baltimore 1992). For Akkadian, "*rūqu*" etc. "distance, far off," see *AHw* pp. 995 and now *CAD R*, cols. 401–425.

[12] See J.A. Knudtzon, *Die El-Amarna Tafeln*, Leipzig 1915 pp. 78ff. 85; Moran (*op. cit.*) n. 10, pp. 73ff. (and the relevant notes on pp. 76–78) (English edition, pp. 12–14 and notes on p. 15). On this document and on visiting the sick ruler cf. also D. Elgavish, *The Diplomatic Service in the Bible and Ancient Near Eastern Sources*, Jerusalem 1998, pp. 82f., 104 (Hebrew).

between the kings of Babylonia and Egypt, the latter suggests enquiring of the Babylonian messenger concerning the above issue. The messenger confirms that the road is lengthy (ll. 28–32). In any case, this incident contrasts with that of Merodach-Baladan, whose envoys came to the distant country of the king of Judah for a visit, although possibly in the guise of visiting the sick.

In El-Amarna, Letter 16, sent by Ashur-uballiṭ, king of Assyria, the Great King, to Amenhotep III or IV, the Great King of Egypt, the former emphasizes the fact that "We are in a distant country" (ll. 35/6). This is in connection with the complicated and lengthy journeys between these distant countries, where envoys had to ship great quantities of gold from Egypt to Assyria.[13] The king of Assyria apparently advises that the Assyrians too, and not only the Egyptians, should be responsible for the Egyptian envoys, possibly to ensure that the Egyptian investment (i.e. in gold) in a "distant country" is more profitable.

Indeed, from a Mesopotamian point of view, one can conceive in fact of Judah as located far-away, as attested in the Nimrud Inscription of Sargon II, king of Assyria, which precedes by several years the Merodach-Baladan and Hezekiah affair (see above). In the inscription King Sargon is described as "the pursuer of the land of Judah whose place is far (rūqu)." (14) Babylonia, as we have seen, in the history of the dispatch of its delegation to Jerusalem, is called a "distant country" while, vice versa, in the Sargon inscription, it is Judah which is termed a place far-away from Assyria.

---

[13] See Moran (op. cit.) n. 10, pp. 106ff.; P. Artzi, EA 16, AoF 24 (1997; FS H. Klengel), pp. 320–336, espec. pp. 322, ll. 35/6, 333, note 9 and n. 24.
[14] H. Winckler, Die Keilschrifttexte Sargons, I, Leipzig 1889, p. 118, l. 8; D.D. Luckenbill, Ancient Records of Assyria and Babylonia, Chicago 1927, p. 72.

Chap. 1: In recent years a fierce debate has been taking place in the Biblical field between the so-called "maximalists," who, on the whole, accept the Biblical text, and between the "minimalists," who are suspicious and disregard the text and its testimony (cf. B. Halpern, "Erasing History: The Minimalist Assault on Ancient Israel," *Bib Rev* 11 [Dec. 1995], 26–35, 40; ed. H. Shanks, "The Biblical Minimalists Face to Face Meet their Challengers," *BAR* 23/4 (1997), 26–42,66); Ph. Davies, "What Separates a Minimalist from a Maximalist? Not Much," *BAR* 26/2 (2000), 24–27, 72–73. Our stand in this chapter is closer to the "maximalists" than to the "minimalists." See, e.g., N.P. Lemche, "On the Problem of Studying Israelite History—A Propos Abraham Malamat's View of Historical Research," *BN* 24 (1984), 94–124, for some misgivings with regard to my approach; for a "minimalist" approach see further Lemche's most recent work *Prelude to Israel's Past*, Peabody, MA, 1998. See now also the general survey of Th.L. Thompson, *The Bible in History*, London 1999. For an opposite trend see, e.g., the collection of papers eds. A.R. Millard et alii, *Faith, Tradition & History*, Winona Lake, IN, 1994. It should be pointed out that the "minimalists," not unexpectedly, conceive of a late date for Israel's origins and place them in the Iron Age (after c. 1200 B.C.), and in extreme cases date them after the first half of the first millenium B.C. See, e.g., Th.L. Thompson, *The Historicity of the Patriarchal Narratives*, Berlin 1975; J. van Seters, *Abraham in History and Tradition*, New Haven 1975; *idem, Prologue to History*, Louisville, KY, 1992. On the other hand, the "maximalists" would date the origins of Israel to the Bronze Age, especially to the Middle Bronze Age (c. 1800–1600 B.C.), or even earlier. For this view see the gist of my paper in Chap. 1 and now, e.g., J.-M. Durand, "Réalités amorrites et traditions biblique." *RA* 92 (1998), 3–39; D. Fleming, "Mari and the Possibilities of Biblical Memory," ib., 41–78; D. Charpin, "Toponymie amorrite et toponymie biblique: La ville de Ṣibat/Sobah," ib., 79–92 (see below, Addenda end of Chaps. 2 and 3).

Chaps. 2 and 3: For a more extended picture on Mari and the Bible or early Israel, see now the books: A. Malamat, *Mari and the Early*

Israelite Experience (the Schweich Lectures for 1984), London and Oxford 1989 (paper 1992), and the more recent *idem, Mari and the Bible,* Leiden 1998 (the former abbreviated henceforth A. Malamat 1989, the latter A. Malamat 1998). See now also the Colloquy of Mari and the Bible arranged by J.-M. Durand and B. Lafont (Paris)— Actes de la Table Ronde: "Les traditions amorrites et la Bible," *RA* 92/1–2 (1998), 1–181, and *RA* 93/1 (1999), 1–77.

Chap. 2: See especially A. Malamat 1998, Introductory Essay, 1–10.

Chap. 3: For a further, more recently discovered gentilic term in Mari and the Bible, namely *lim = lĕom,* originally "clan," see A. Malamat: "A Recently Discovered Word for 'Clan' in Mari and Its Hebrew Cognates," in Zevit Z. et alii, *Solving Riddles and Untying Knots (FS J.C. Greenfield),* Winona Lake, IN, 1995, 175–179. See now J.M. Sasson, "About Mari and the Bible," *RA* 92/2 (1998), 97–123.

Chap. 4: On Biblical genealogies and history see now the following works: R.R. Wilson, *Genealogy and History in the Biblical World (Yale Near Eastern Researchers),* New Haven 1977; M.D. Johnson, *The Purpose of the Biblical Genealogies* (2nd ed.), Cambridge 1988; G.A. Rendsburg, "The Internal Consistency and Historical Reliability of the Biblical Genealogies," *VT* 11 (1990), 185–206; M. Chavalas, "Genealogical History as 'Charter': A Study of Old Babylonian Period Historiography and the Old Testament," in eds A.R. Millard et alii, *Faith* etc., Winona Lake, IN, 1994, 103–128; A. Malamat 1998, chap. 22: "Kinglists of the Old Babylonian Period and Biblical Genealogies," 219–236; originally published in *Essays in Memory of E.A. Speiser, JAOS* 88 (1968), 163–171.

Chap. 5: For recent investigations into the Book of Exodus, with which we did not deal specifically in our study, see ed. M. Vervenne, *Studies in the Book of Exodus,* Leuven 1996; see also the recent commentaries: B. Jacob, Exodus (original in German) Hobuken, NJ, 1992; J.H. Durham, *Exodus (WBC),* Waco 1997; W.H.C. Propp, *Exodus 1–18 (AnBi),* New York 1998; C. Houton, *Exodus,* vol. 3, Leuven 2000. Cf. also recent commentaries of the Book of Numbers: J. Milgrom, *Numbers (The JPS Torah),* Philadelphia 1990; B.A. Levine, *Numbers 21–36 (AnBi),* New York 2000. Similar conclusions at times to our study have been reached recently by J.C. de Moor, *The Rise of Yahwism,* Leuven 1997, 131ff., 221ff., 234ff.; eds S. Ahituv and E.D. Oren, *The Origin of Early Israel—Current Debate,* Beer-Sheva 1998, espec. chapters K.A. Kitchen and S. Ahituv; J.A. Soggin, *An Introduction to the History of Israel and Judah* (3rd ed.), London 1999, 118–151.

Chap. 6: See also A. Malamat, *Early Israelite Warfare and the Conquest of Canaan*, Oxford 1978; *idem*, "How Inferior Israelite Forces Conquered Fortified Canaanite Cities," *BAR* 8/2 (1982), 24–35. For the opponents to my essay on the Conquest of Canaan, it may be useful to repeat some words from the introduction of my paper; "we shall avoid a factual reconstruction of the course of the Conquest, as so often sought by those who presuppose its actual military nature . . . our analysis of real historical situations [of the Israelite Conquest] is complemented by schematizied, hypothetical projections. Such an approach, it is hoped, will prove a point of departure for reaffirming the tenability of much of the biblical traditions. . . ." For the conflicting source material see, e.g., the remarks of M. Weinfeld, *The Promise of the Land*, Berkeley 1983, espec. chaps 5 & 6 on the Conquest, and see the commentaries of R.S. Hess, *Josua (Tyndale OTC)*, Leicester 1996; and recently the treatment of E. Noort, *Das Buch Josua*, Darmstadt 1998 and A.G. Auld, *Joshua Retold (OTSt)*, Edinburgh 1998.

Chap. 7: Recent commentaries of the Book of Judges, not mentioned in this chapter, but which are of concern to our study, see: R.G. Boling, *Judges (AnBi)*, Garden City, NY 1975; J.A. Soggin, *Judges (OTL)*, London 1981; Y. Amit, *Judges (Mikra Leyisrael*; Hebrew), Tel Aviv 1999; T.J. Schneider, *Judges (Berit Olam)*, Collegeville, Minnesota 2000.

Chap. 8: In this chapter on "Charisma," I deal *inter alia* with two methodological questions: First, what is the issue for those who deal with Max Weber? To which degree may Weberian concepts, such as charisma, be applied to ancient events? Can the past in general be discerned by modern means or can ancient conceptions throw light on it? In the face of the inadequacy and the considerable subjectivity of our empathy, I tend to utilize modern concepts as analytical tools also for events in the remote past, being aware of the danger of such an approach. But why should the application of modern concepts of Sociology or Politology for antiquity be more anachronistic than the application of modern linguistic concepts for the ancient Oriental languages.

The second question is: What is the most suitable definition of our topic? Should it be "Charismatic Leadership in the Book of

Judges" or ". . . in the Period of the Judges"? The former titles implies
that the issue has been removed from the realm of history to the
realm of literature. Thus, it may be supposed that the description
of the charismatic leader in the Book of Judges is nothing more than
a theological invention without any historical basis, reconstructed by
an editor or, more probably, by a school of editors, especially the
so-called Deuteronomist. However, we do not analyze political and
social situations. I am of the opinion, like Max Weber, that the
Biblical text forms a supportable, legitimate basis for a reconstruction of a historical event, not least because of a deep rooted historical consciousness peculiar to ancient Israel. On the Weberian concept
of charisma see also Ch. Schäfer-Lichtenberger, *Stadt und Eidgenossenschaft
im Alten Testament*, Berlin 1983 (*BZAW* 156), 1–150.

Chap. 10: See also A. Malamat, *Das davidische und salomonische Königreich
und seine Beziehungen zu Ägypten und Syrien. Zur Entstehung eines Grossreichs,*
Oster. Akademie der Wissenschaften, 407, Wien 1983; G.W. Ahlström,
The History of Ancient Palestine . . ., Sheffield 1993, 421–542. For a
different approach see A. Lemaire, "The United Monarchy: Saul,
David and Solomon" *Ancient Israel* (revised edition) Washington, D.C.,
1999. Recently, some archaeologists argue that the archaeological
levels at the various sites in Palestine are to be attributed to the 9th
rather than to the 10th century B.C. (See I. Finkelstein, *Levant* 30
[1988], 167–174, as against A. Mazar, *Levant* 29 [1997], 157–167).
If so, there is no basis to the Davidic—Solomonic kingdom. But the
majority of archaeologists adhere to the previously held view, indicating the factuality of the kingdom of David and Solomon. The
name of king David, as well as of king Solomon, had not been found
in extra—Biblical sources, but David is now attested in the toponym
bytdwd (House of David, i.e. the name of the kingdom of Judah) in
an Aramaean inscription from the 9th century B.C., found at Dan.
For the new inscription see A. Biran and J. Naweh, *IEJ* 43 (1993),
81–98; 45 (1995), 1–18.

Chap. 11: For the international policies and the treaties of David and
Solomon see: A. Malamat, "The Kingdom of David and Solomon
in its Contact with Egypt and Aram Naharaim," *BA Reader* II, New
York, 1964, 89–98; D.J. McCarthy, *Treaty and Covenant* (new edition),
Rome 1978; P. Kalluveeutil, *Declaration and Covenant*, Rome 1982. For
the relations with Egypt see now B.U. Schipper, *Israel und Ägypten in
der Königszeit*, Freiburg 1999; and P.S. Ash, *David, Solomon and Egypt*

(*JSOTSS* 297), Sheffield 1999. For various facets of King Solomon see now L.K. Handy (ed.), *The Age of Solomon* (espec. chapters by W.G. Dever, K.A. Kitchen, A. Millard and N. Na'aman), Leiden 1997; M.I. Mulder, *1 King 1–11*, Leuven 1998. On kingship generally in the ancient Near East with references to King David, see now the remarks of W.W. Hallo, *Origins*, Leiden 1996, 188–195.

Chap. 13: 1 Kings 12 (espec. the passage on the "elders" and the "young men," see the following articles (not mentioned in my paper): E. Lipiński, "Le récit the 1 Rois XII 1–19" *VT* 24 (1974), 430–437; B. Halpern, "Sectionalism and the Schism," *JBL* 93 (1974), 519–532; R.P. Gordon, "The Second Septuagint Account of Jeroboam," *VT* 25 (1975), 368–393. And see the commentaries: E. Würthwein, *Das erste Buch der Könige (ATD)*, Göttingen 1977, 150–160; S. de Vries, *1 Kings (WBC)*, Waco 1985. For a different view on the "young men," see M.S. Fox, "Royal Officials . . . A New Look at the *yeladim* 1 Kings 12," *BA* 59 (1996), 225–32.

Chap. 14: According to newer Assyrian sources the great revolt of Elam and the defeat of its king by Ashurbanipal took place somewhat earlier than the date adhered to before, i.e. c. 645–643. See e.g., P.D. Gerardi, *Assurbanipal's Elamite Campaigns . . .* 1987 (unpublished dissertation, Ann Arbor, MI), 14.

Chap. 16–17: See also A. Malamat, "The Last Years of the Kingdom of Judah," *WHJP* 4/1 Jerusalem 1979, 205–221, 349–353; N. Na'aman, *Tel-Aviv* 18 (1991), "The Kingdom of Judah Under Josiah," 3–71; G.W. Ahlström, *The History of Ancient Palestine . . .*, Sheffield 1993, 754–803; J.A. Soggin, *An Introduction . . .* (see above chap. 5), London 1999, 276–282. For recent relevant Biblical commentaries see: M. Cogan and H. Tadmor, *II Kings (AnBi)*, Garden City, NY, 1988; W. McKane, *Jeremiah* I (*ICC*), Edinburgh; *idem, Jeremiah* II (*ICC*), Edinburgh 1996; G.R. Lundbom, *Jeremiah 1–20 (AnBi)*, New York 1999; G.L. Keown et alii, *Jeremiah 26–52 (WBC)*, Dallas 1995; M. Greenberg, *Ezekiel, 1–20 (AnBi)*, New York 1983; *idem, Ezekiel 21–37*, New York 1997; D.J. Block, *The Book of Ezekiel, chaps. 1–24*, Grand Rapids 1993; *idem, Ezekiel, chaps. 25–48*, Grand Rapids 1998.

A Chronological Note: My reckoning of dates in these chapters is based on an autumnal calendar beginning on 1 Tishri; the spring calendar (beginning on 1 Nisan) accepted by a majority of scholars was in general use in Babylonia, but not in my view, in Judah. See my position in "The Last Kings of Judah and the Fall of Jerusalem," *IEJ* 18 (1968), 137–156. According to the chronological system which I use, Jerusalem survived until 586 B.C. rather than the more frequently accepted date of 587 B.C. Thus, according to the chronology used here, the siege of Jerusalem lasted not, as is widely held, one-and-a half years, but two-and-a half years.

A Note in the Territory of Benjamin: The territory of Benjamin seems not to have joined the struggle of Judah against Babylonia. It succumbed peacefully to Babylonia and its towns were not destroyed according to the evidence of various archaeological excavations. The time of this event is, however, not clear. It may have already occurred in 597 B.C. in connection with the first conquest of Jerusalem or it may have occurred only in 589/588 B.C. at the beginning of the final conquest of the capital city. Other territories may also have succumbed, such as the Beth-Lehem area (see A. Malamat, "The Last Wars of the Kingdom of Judah," *JNES* 9 [1950], 226–227, latest reference in *idem*, "Caught Between the Great Powers," *BAR* 25/4 [1999], 37b, 41a). See now O. Lipschits, "The History of the Benjamin Region Under Babylonian Rule" *Tel Aviv* 26 (1999), 155–190. The author adopted my assumption regarding the Babylonian occupation of Benjamin (as stated by him in his earlier articles in Hebrew).

Chap. 18: On causality in historiography in general see A.O. Lovejoy in ed. H. Meyerhoff, *The Philosophy of History*, New York 1959, 173–188; E.H. Carr, *What is History?*, London 1961, espec. Chap. 4: "Causation in History." On our subject in particular see B. Albrekston, *History and the Gods*, Lund 1967 (espec. pp. 107f.); H. Cancik, *Grundzüge der hethitischen und alttest, Geschichtschreibung*. Wiesbaden 1976.

Chap. 19: See the relevant passages in recent commentaries of the First Book of Samuel: H.W. Hertzberg, *Die Samuel Bücher (ATD)*, Göttingen 1960; P.K. McCarter, *1 Samuel (AnBi)*, New York 1980; R. Klein, *1 Samuel (WBC)*, Waco 1983.

Chap. 21: See the recent commentaries on Amos I: 5 F.I. Andersen and D.N. Freedman, *Amos (AnBi)*, New York 1989 (pp. 255f.); S.M. Paul, *Amos (Hermeneia)*, Mineapolis 1991 (pp. 32ff.). For partly revisions of my paper see now the suggestions by P. Bordreuil, "Amos 1:5. La Beqa' septentrional d'l'Eden au Paradis" *Syria* 75 (1998), 55–59.

Chap. 22: See the recent commentaries on Zechariah, chap. 9: C.L. Meyers and E.M. Meyers, *Zechariah 9–14 (AnBi)*, New York 1993; E.H. Merrill, *Haggai, Zechariah, Malachi (Exegetical Com)*, Chicago 1994, 239–248. See also on Jeremiah, chap. 46 the commentaries, above Addenda, chap. 16–17.

Chap. 23: See the commentaries on Jeremiah (above chap. 16–17), espec. on chaps. 22, 28, 34, 36, as well as the entries of Jehoiachin in *ABD*, vol. 3, New York 1992, 661–663; and Zedekiah, *ABD*, vol. 6, New York 1992, 1068–1071.

INDEX OF THE SOURCES

SUBJECT INDEX

CULTURE AND HISTORY
OF THE ANCIENT NEAR EAST

ISSN 1566-2055

1. Grootkerk, S.E. *Ancient Sites in Galilee*. A Toponymic Gazetteer. 2000. ISBN 90 04 11535 8
2. Higginbotham, C.R. *Egyptianization and Elite Emulation in Ramesside Palestine*. Governance and Accommodation on the Imperial Periphery. 2000. ISBN 90 04 11768 7
3. Yamada, S. *The Construction of the Assyrian Empire*. A Historical Study of the Inscriptions of Shalmanesar III Relating to His Campaigns in the West. 2000. ISBN 90 04 11772 5
4. Yener, K.A. *The Domestication of Metals*. The Rise of Complex Metal Industries in Anatolia. 2000. ISBN 90 04 11864 0
5. Taracha, P. *Ersetzen und Entsühnen*. Das mittelhethitische Ersatzritual für den Großkönig Tuthalija (CTH *448.4) und verwandte Texte. 2000. ISBN 90 04 11910 8
6. Littauer, M.A. & Crouwel, J.H.and P. Raulwing (ed.) *Selected Writings on Chariots and other Early Vehicles, Riding and Harness*. 2001. ISBN 90 04 11799 7
7. Malamat, A. *History of Biblical Israel*. Major Problems and Minor Issues. 2001. ISBN 90 04 12009 2
8. Snell, D.C. *Flight and Freedom in the Ancient Near East*. 2001. ISBN 90 04 12010 6